1999

Beneath the United States

Beneath the United States

A HISTORY OF U.S. POLICY
TOWARD LATIN AMERICA

Lars Schoultz

HARVARD UNIVERSITY PRESS
Cambridge, Massachusetts
London, England   1998

Library of Congress Cataloging-in-Publication Data

Schoultz, Lars.
    Beneath the United States : a history of U.S. policy toward Latin America /
Lars Schoultz.
        p.   cm.
    Includes bibliographical references (p.   ) and index.
    ISBN 0-674-92275-1 (cloth : alk. paper).
    ISBN 0-674-92276-X (pbk. : alk. paper).
    1. Latin America—Foreign relations—Latin America.
    2. United States—Foreign relations—Latin America.
    3. United States—Foreign relations—Moral and ethical aspects.
    4. Politicians—United States—Attitudes.
    5. United States—Foreign relations—Philosophy.
    I. Title.
    F1418.S388   1998
    327.7308—dc21   97-35338

To Karina

Contents

Maps

Preface

In late 1989 President George Bush traveled to Costa Rica to participate in a Central American summit meeting, which came near the end of the most difficult decade in the history of U.S.–Latin American relations. The United States was standing toe-to-toe with the Panamanian government of Manuel Noriega, openly threatening the military invasion that was to come two months later. In just two weeks, the rebel Farabundo Martí National Liberation Front would launch daring attacks on cities throughout El Salvador, prompting the retaliatory murder of six Jesuits by the Salvadoran military and revealing how little progress had been made in pacifying that country despite a full decade of U.S. effort. Worst of all, Nicaragua's Sandinistas were continuing to thumb their nose at the United States, four years after Mr. Bush's predecessor had warned that he would stop attempting to overthrow them only "if they'd say 'Uncle.'" When the surrender was not forthcoming, President Reagan had gone before a prime-time television audience and declared the Sandinistas an outlaw regime.[1]

As Air Force One was carrying President Bush from Washington, Nicaraguan President Daniel Ortega was also flying to the meeting. Arriving in San José dressed in military fatigues and the black-and-red Sandinista bandanna that so annoyed U.S. officials, Mr. Ortega promptly announced that his government might end its cease-fire with the U.S.-supported rebel Contras. That announcement was enough for President Bush, who took advantage of a news conference to call President Ortega "that unwanted animal at a garden party." He also twice referred to the Nicaraguan chief of state as a "little man," giving such obvious emphasis to the term that it prompted a reporter to ask at the very end of the press conference, "Why do you keep calling him a little man?" The President's final words were "Because he is—that's why."[2]

Today these belittling statements and the policies that triggered them may seem only a reminder of a prior generation's Cold War conflicts, but they also reflect a historical attitude toward Latin Americans. Eighty years earlier, in 1909, Secretary of State Philander Knox had made similar comments about one of President Ortega's predecessors, José Santos Zelaya, declaring his government "a blot upon the history of Nicaragua," and Knox's assistant secretary had called Zelaya "an unspeakable carrion." These views, in turn, were a continuation of the already established U.S. opinion of Nicaragua, which one mid-nineteenth-century envoy summarized as "small in Extent, its Govt feeble and its population inconsiderable in number, though turbulent & disorderly." And this observation was similar to an even earlier description by the U.S. consul in León, who reported in 1848 that "the revolutions here, are of so terrible a character, that no good is expected from any change of men, as all such changes have proved for the worse, and it is a positive belief, that were it not for the proximity of the civilizing influence of the United States, this country would by degrees *revert* to the aboriginal state in which Alvarado the Spaniard found it."[3]

This book is an explanation of the logic that underlies these statements. It is not about Nicaragua, nor is it about the other countries that lie beneath the United States, in a region called Latin America. It is about the policies the United States has used to protect its interests in Latin America. It is about the way a powerful nation treats its weaker neighbors.

A realist would explain the U.S.–Latin American relationship with Thucydides' aphorism that "large nations do what they wish, while small nations accept what they must." This is the best way to begin—but only begin—any explanation of U.S. policy, with a frank recognition of the enormous disparities between the United States and Latin America. The United States is the world's commanding power—not omnipotent, perhaps, but significantly more powerful than any rival force that the world will see in our lifetime and, barring a cataclysm, almost infinitely more powerful than any Latin American nation can ever hope to be. This power is deeply rooted in the nation's wealth. The typical U.S. citizen generates a per capita gross national product ten times that of the average Latin American, and this absolute difference in wealth underlies a nearly infinite range of derivative disparities, in everything from mortality measures to fast food franchises.

Perhaps the most obvious indicator of these asymmetries is that the United States continues to spend hundreds of millions of tax dollars each year to alter the behavior of its neighbors, while Latin Americans do not. Today, for example, the U.S. Agency for International Development is pay-ing to install U.S.-style adversarial criminal procedures in four different Latin American countries, while no Latin American country is attempting to change the procedures used by the U.S. judicial system. Similarly, the government-funded National Endowment for Democracy is prepared to assist any Latin American country to hold a clean election, while no Latin American country has ever offered to help the United States boost its low voter turnout, nor advised the United States on the reform of its campaign financing laws. Today, U.S. law requires the President to report each year on the efforts that Latin American governments are making to stem the supply of narcotics (and to "decertify" those that fail to meet our standards, making them ineligible for aid), while no Latin American government reports on U.S. efforts to reduce the demand for drugs. Even the Cuban challenge is gone, symbolized by the fact that Washington's archrival can no longer afford to blanket the shortwave bands with Radio Cuba, while the U.S. Information Agency's Radio Martí continues to provide Cubans with all the news that's fit to broadcast. And, of course, U.S. armed forces are still found throughout Latin America—at bases in Cuba and Panama, and as mobile training teams in nearly every other country in the region—while no U.S. citizen believes that we have anything useful to learn from the Latin American military.

"Hegemony" is the term social scientists use to capture the essence of these one-way relationships. Depending on their personal preferences about specific programs, U.S. citizens praise Washington's hegemonic behavior, criticize it, or, like Thucydides, treat it as a fact of life. We do some good things, some bad things, and some things that great powers have always done (and presumably will always do) to their weaker neighbors. The question is *why*. What determines United States policy toward Latin America?

Self-interest would be a realist's answer. Throughout history, hegemons have sought to protect their interests by controlling the behavior of weaker neighbors. This hegemonic oversight is costly, of course, but the expense of a Marine detachment or an AID mission is usually justified with the common-sense logic that it is better to prevent something unpleasant from happening rather than to reverse it once it has happened. For more than a century the United States has rarely waited to let a problem develop. Instead, it has tried to prevent the emergence of the threat.

Driven by self-interest, this hegemonic oversight has reached unprecedented levels in the late twentieth century. Today it seems unexceptional for

Washington to be nudging and nurturing Latin Americans not simply to reform their economies (something we have long encouraged), but to revamp their judicial systems and reconstitute their democracies. Woodrow Wilson, whom many consider the most patronizing of all U.S. Presidents, would not believe his eyes; he would marvel at the mere fact that the United States has created and maintained not only an Agency for International Development to assist Latin America's economic improvement but also a National Endowment for Democracy to help with the region's political development. President Wilson may have wanted to teach Latin Americans to elect good leaders, but he would never have recommended that U.S. taxpayers pick up the tab for other peoples' economic and political development.

The slowly growing belief that self-interest requires ever-increasing efforts to influence the behavior of a weaker people—"hegemony creep"—is common among great powers, but its full significance in U.S.–Latin American relations was masked until recently by the Cold War imperative of excluding the Soviet Union from the Western Hemisphere. But when the Soviet Union disappeared and U.S. security interests no longer required the same level of dominance, Washington identified new problems—everything from drug trafficking to dictatorship to financial mismanagement—and moved to *increase* its control over Latin America.

Recent U.S. administrations have justified this preventive hegemony with the argument that today's problems are every bit as threatening as yesterday's Soviet adventurism. Reflecting general public opinion, these administrations argue, for example, that illicit drug use underlies a broad array of U.S. social problems, making our schools unsafe and converting our urban neighborhoods into free-fire zones. It is not difficult to see why many U.S. officials believe that it is just as important to prevent drug production as it was to stop communism. Equally threatening, say many, is the repression by authoritarian Latin American governments, which sends refugees streaming toward the United States, where they overwhelm state and local governments. California's 1994 Proposition 187, which denies government services to illegal immigrants, may seem mean-spirited and shortsighted to many of us, but not to the local officials who are struggling to provide legal residents with public education and indigent health care. It is easy to see how these officials (and their constituents) believe that it is as much in their self-interest to put an end to refugee-generating dictatorships as it was to stop communism. Similarly, if Latin American governments are so incapable of managing their finances that they require bail-outs by the U.S. Treasury, it is understandable why U.S. officials insist on Latin America's structural adjustment.

Overall, the dominant post–Cold War opinion in Washington is that revolutions in transportation and communication have facilitated closer ties with Latin America, one aspect of which is the export of Latin Americans' problems. In response, U.S. officials have claimed the right to respond with ever-increasing attempts to control Latin Americans' undesirable behavior. What is consistent over two centuries in Washington's policies toward Latin America is not the behavior of the United States, but the motivation. For nearly two centuries, U.S. policy has invariably intended to serve the interests of the United States—interests variously related to our nation's security, to our domestic politics, or to our economic development. As the challenges to these interests ebb and flow, U.S. policy adjusts to meet them. What remains unchanged are the interests.

Although these three interests are central to any explanation of United States policy toward Latin America, there is more to a full explanation. Underlying these three interests is a pervasive belief that Latin Americans constitute an inferior branch of the human species.

The precise definition of Latin American inferiority has shifted many times over two hundred years, but for the past half-century it has been summarized by the omnibus term "underdeveloped." As we begin the twenty-first century, corruption is the political indicator of underdevelopment, seen particularly in the bribes that Latin America's public officials are said to accept from drug traffickers. A few years ago, the indicators were authoritarianism and human rights violations; a few years before that, the indicator was unreasonable radicalism. Some of these indicators of underdevelopment are vague and unqualified, whereas others—especially the economic indicator of persistent poverty—are more obvious to the eye, but they all underscore what one U.S. envoy reported from Brazil in 1839: "there is a sad defect somewhere either in the institutions of the country, or the temper and habits of the People."[4]

A belief in Latin American inferiority is the essential core of United States policy toward Latin America because it determines the precise steps the United States takes to protect its interests in the region. Since this belief has existed from the beginning, one way to understand today's policy and its underlying assumptions is to return to the eighteenth century and examine how today's hegemonic thinking began to evolve as the logical corollary of beliefs about the character of Latin Americans. Other beliefs would not have changed U.S. interests, but they would have led to different policies for protecting these interests and, in general, to a different relationship with the neighbors who lie beneath us. These eighteenth-century beliefs set us off on the path that we still follow. Along the way, a hegemonic attitude developed gradually, so slowly that it went unnoticed until, by the end of the nineteenth century, the notion of controlling the behavior of Latin Americans seemed as natural to U.S. officials as it did to Thucydides. Then Theodore Roosevelt's Big Stick generation began to institutionalize this control by creating formal organizations to channel the U.S.–Latin American relationship, a process that continued through the Depression, World War II, and the Cold War, when a panoply of permanent bureaucracies was created to promote U.S. economic interests and to protect U.S. security. It is true, as a realist would argue, that today's hegemony is the natural product of efforts to protect these interests, but it is also the product of solicitude for neighbors who, we have kept telling ourselves, will probably remain underdeveloped unless we provide them with our assistance.

To understand contemporary United States policy toward Latin America, then, either we can accept Thucydides' rendering of the law of the jungle and let it go at that, or we can sift through the peculiar evolution of the U.S.–Latin American relationship, searching for evidence of a subtle but powerful mindset that has precluded a policy based on mutual respect. There, in the minds of U.S. officials, we will find the explanation of U.S. policy in a process that blends self-interest with what the Victorian British called their White Man's Burden and the French their *mission civilisatrice,* a process by which a superior people help a weaker civilization overcome the pernicious effects of its sad defect.

The sifting process requires us to analyze how U.S. officials process the information that they receive about Latin America. Stripped of nuance, the actual process is fairly simple. For example, when a State Department official begins a meeting with the comment "we have a problem with the government of Peru," in less than a second the other participants instinctively turn to a mental picture of a foreign state that is quite different from the one that would have been evoked if the convening official had said, in contrast, "we have a problem with the government of France."

What exactly *is* the difference? To begin, Peru is in Latin America, the "other" America; France is in northwestern Europe, the cradle of the dominant North American culture. Peru is poor; France is rich. Peru is weak; France has nuclear weapons. Peru has Incan ruins, which many consider the peak of cultural development in that part of the world; France has ancient ruins, too, but it also has the Louvre. Peru makes pisco; France makes claret. Peru is not so firmly democratic; France is. Peru is a Rio Treaty ally, which, as alliances go, is something of a charade; France is a NATO ally, which is a very serious alliance. In most of our history, Peru hasn't mattered much in international relations; France has mattered a lot. These differences can be listed almost forever, and each policy maker will have a slightly (but only slightly) different list. The list may or may not be accurate; it may or may not be fair. But the point is that such a list exists in the mind of virtually every U.S. official, and that it explains why U.S. policy toward Peru is *fundamentally* unlike U.S. policy toward France, despite the fact that both policies are driven by self-interest.

Today's public opinion polls indicate that the rough outlines of this "Latin American" mind-set are shared by a broad spectrum of the U.S. public. The initiation of new officials into the policy-making environment is largely a process of refining this unpolished collection of beliefs by incorporating additional information about the region and, at the same time, by organizing, weighing, and interpreting this information so that it fits with the pursuit of U.S. interests. The result is a distinctive mental orientation that officials use to interpret the bewildering array of incidents and problems that constitute the raw data of international relations. This is the mind-set that led President Monroe to announce his Doctrine, that pushed President Polk to declare war against Mexico, that inspired President Roosevelt to wield a Big Stick, that induced President Taft to implement Dollar Diplomacy, that encouraged President Wilson to teach the Latin Americans to elect good leaders, that prompted President Kennedy to establish the Agency for International Development, that influenced President Reagan to create the National Endowment for Democracy, and that led President Bush to call Nicaragua's President an unwelcome dog at a garden party.

Beneath the United States

Chapter 1 ～

Encountering Latin America

They are lazy, dirty, nasty and in short I can compare them to nothing but a parcel of hogs.

～ *John Quincy Adams, age 12*

It took a direct order from President Monroe to make Secretary of State John Quincy Adams recognize the newly independent countries of Latin America. In 1820, when Henry Clay had urged recognition, Adams had scoffed at the idea of developing a cooperative relationship with the people of the region, writing in his diary that "there is no community of interests or of principles between North and South America."[1] But Adams and his generation were acutely aware that the United States and Latin America shared, at a minimum, an interest in evicting Europe from the Western Hemisphere. When the Latin American wars of independence had erupted a decade earlier, this interest had prompted President Madison to treat the rebels with what he called a spirit of "enlarged philanthropy," meaning that he would permit U.S. merchants to sell them arms. Always less oblique, Congress simply blurted out its "friendly interest" in Latin American independence, and soon Secretary of State James Monroe notified the European powers that the United States had "an interest in the independence of the Spanish provinces."[2]

Since it made little sense to suggest that the United States shared no interests with its neighbors, John Quincy Adams's comment probably reflected the belief, common among his contemporaries, that any relationship with Latin Americans would be difficult, because differing principles governed their behavior. He meant them no insult; he simply was pointing out that Latin Americans were Hispanics, and that his people were Anglos. To Adams and his generation, that made all the difference in the world.

Anglo-America was expanding rapidly at the beginning of the nineteenth century, when Adams embarked upon a half century of public service. The united states now numbered sixteen, and their five million citizens were pushing vigorously into land claimed by others. To the south and southwest, they shared a border with the colonies of Spain, one that only moved further west after Spain's transfer of the continent's midsection to France and Napoleon's quick resale to the United States in 1803. The Louisiana Purchase was but the first of several major nineteenth-century land transactions in North America, virtually all of them favorable to the United States, and by mid-century the nation spanned the continent, thirty-one states with over twenty-three million citizens.

Eighteen new nations were created in Latin America during this same half century. In much of the region the bloody struggle for independence was significantly more disruptive than that of the United States, and, once free of colonial control, Latin American republicans were clearly unable to weave effective states from the war-weakened threads of fragmented civil societies. Visitors to these new republics, including an early U.S. chargé in Colombia, were dismayed by the challenge of forging nations out of "twenty millions of people spread over a pathless continent, separated from each other by immense tracts of uninhabited region, without concert, without resources, and totally ignorant of civil government." Many agreed with Bolívar's deathbed lament when, looking back at his life's labor, the Liberator concluded that republican Latin America had reverted to "primeval chaos."[3]

It was during this half century that officials in Washington began to create the mind-set that continues to influence U.S. policy toward Latin America. Initially it was shaped by an urgent security interest: as the War of 1812 approached, officials in Washington worried that England might take possession of Spanish Florida, an ideal base for harassing U.S. commerce and for launching military attacks.[4] Since 1808 the British had been fighting alongside the Spanish to oust Napoleon from Iberia in the vicious Peninsular War—the conflict in which Spanish irregulars perfected a new form of combat and, in the process, added the term *guerrilla warfare* to our vocabulary. As the struggle dragged on, the Spanish became increasingly reliant upon British aid, and the English probably could have obtained Florida for the asking. In mid-1810 Secretary of State Robert Smith warned the British to stay out of Florida; then, in September, Congress passed its first formal statement of U.S. policy toward Latin America, the No-Transfer Resolution: "the United States, under the peculiar circumstances of the existing crisis, cannot, without serious inquietude, see any part of [East Florida] pass into the hands of any foreign power; and that a due regard to their own safety compels them to provide, under certain contingencies, for the temporary occupation of the said territory."[5]

Officials in Washington continued to worry about Spanish Florida when U.S. expansion resumed after the War of 1812. "East Florida in itself is comparatively nothing," argued Secretary of State Monroe in 1815, "but as a post, in the hands of Great-Britain, it is of the highest importance. Commanding the Gulph of Mexico, and all its waters, including the Mississippi with its branches, and the streams emptying into the Mobile, a vast proportion of the most fertile and productive parts of this Union, on which the navigation and commerce so essentially depend, would be subject to its annoyance."[6] Florida was seen by Monroe exactly as many of his successors would see other parts of Latin America—as pieces of unattractive land that nonhemispheric adversaries might use as a base to attack the United States.

A policy of excluding these adversaries seemed increasingly appropriate as the third decade of the nineteenth century unfolded. Under the leadership of Austrian Prince Metternich, in 1821 the Holy Alliance approved the principle of counterrevolutionary intervention to stifle republicanism: "States which have undergone a change in Government due to revolution, the results of which threaten other states, ipso facto cease to be members of the European Alliance," reads the Troppau Protocol. "If, owing to such alteration, immediate danger threatens other states, the Powers bind themselves, by peaceful means, or if need be by arms, to bring back the guilty state into the bosom of the Great Alliance." Shortly thereafter, the Austrian army was used to squelch republican revolutions in Naples and the Italian Piedmont, and at Verona in 1822 the Alliance authorized France to destroy Spanish constitutionalism and restore Ferdinand's absolute monarchy. With Secretary of State John Quincy Adams and his colleagues worried that Spain's rebellious New World colonies were next in line to be brought back into the bosom of the Great Alliance, in late 1823 President Monroe announced his seminal doctrine in a message to Congress; and for nearly two centuries that doctrine has remained the bedrock principle of U.S. foreign policy.

But national security was not the only Latin American interest of John Quincy Adams's generation, for the region also contained products for U.S. consumers and markets for U.S. producers. Despite restrictive Spanish mercantile policies, trade between colonial Latin America and the United

States had blossomed in the second half of the eighteenth century, and in 1781 the Continental Congress had appointed Robert Smith as its first special agent in Latin America "to reside at Havanna, to manage the occasional concerns of Congress, to assist the American traders with his advice, and to solicit their affairs with the Spanish Government."[7] At the same time, New England and mid-Atlantic merchants were developing markets at the farthest reaches of the hemisphere, especially after the Napoleonic wars swept European traders out of Latin American markets. By the turn of the nineteenth century, nearly one-third of all U.S. exports went to Europe's colonies in Latin America and the Caribbean; then, when the wars of Latin American independence erupted, this trade mushroomed. It did not take long for Yankee merchants from politically powerful port cities to become accustomed to serving markets that had often been closed by Spain's restrictive trade policies, and they turned to their government for help in keeping the markets open. "The situation of these Countries has thrown them open to commercial intercourse with other nations, and among the rest with these United-States," wrote John Quincy Adams in 1818; shortly thereafter, he informed the counterrevolutionary Holy Alliance that "we can neither accede to nor approve of any interference to restore any part of the Spanish supremacy, in any of the South-American Provinces."[8]

Seeking, then, to protect the nation's security *and* to promote its economic interests, officials in Washington set out to establish relations with newly independent Latin America. They knew (or thought they knew) much about the basic character of the people who inhabited the region, and no one was more confident of his knowledge than the most influential U.S. foreign policy official of the era of Latin American independence, John Quincy Adams, Secretary of State from 1817 to 1825 and President from 1825 to 1829. Just before initiating the process of diplomatic recognition, Adams told Henry Clay that Latin Americans "have not the first elements of good or free government. Arbitrary power, military and ecclesiastical, was stamped upon their education, upon their habits, and upon all their institutions. Civil dissension was infused into all their seminal principles. War and mutual destruction was in every member of their organization, moral, political, and physical."[9]

Adams's opinions had their origin in his eighteenth-century New England upbringing and, in particular, in the views of his father, who felt nothing but disdain for all Hispanics. At almost the exact time that his son was talking with Clay, the senior Adams, now eighty-five years old, wrote Jefferson that "a free government and the Roman Catholick religion can never exist together in any nation or Country, and consequently that all projects for reconciling them in old Spain or new are Eutopian, Platonick, and Chimerical. I have seen such a prostration and prostitution of Human Nature to the Priesthood in old Spain as settled my judgment long ago, and I understand that in new Spain it is still worse, if that is possible."[10] Adams's reference to "long ago" was a midwinter trip across northern Spain in 1779–1780—a trip so trying that, upon crossing the border into France, he wrote, "never was a Captive escaped from Prison more delighted than I was, for every Thing here was clean, sweet and comfortable in Comparison of any Thing We had found in any part of Spain." In combination with his anti-Catholic upbringing, John Adams's singularly unpleasant experience in Spain clearly influenced his attitude toward Latin America. Thereafter he met few Hispanics and virtually no residents of Latin America, but the die was cast: three decades after his unfortunate trip, the senior Adams wrote that "the people of South America are the most ignorant, the most bigoted, the most superstitious of all the Roman Catholics in Christendom"; as a result, attempts to establish democratic governments in the newly independent region were "as absurd as similar plans would be to establish democracies among the birds, beasts, and fishes."[11]

Young John Quincy Adams accompanied his father on the ill-starred trip across northern Spain. The twelve-year-old John Quincy's diary emphasizes that country's brutish population ("they are lazy, dirty, nasty and in short I can compare them to nothing but a parcel of hogs"); its grinding poverty; its filthy lodgings ("they never wash nor sweep their floors"); and especially its repressive Catholicism. "Poor creatures, they are eat up by their priests. Near three quarters of what they earn goes to the Priests and with the other quarter they must live as they can. Thus is the whole of this kingdom deceived and deluded by their religion. I thank Almighty God that I was born in a country where anybody may get a good living if they please."[12]

John Quincy was also influenced by another towering figure of his father's generation, Thomas Jefferson, with whom he developed a friendship in Paris in 1784 and 1785. One day's diary entry notes, "spent the evening with Mr. Jefferson whom I love to be with, because he is a man of very extensive learning, and pleasing manners."[13] Jefferson's exceptionally inquisitive mind regularly included the exploration of subjects related to

Latin America—he told the younger Adams that he had learned Spanish during a nineteen-day sea voyage; he met with revolutionaries from Brazil and Mexico while in Europe during the 1780s; and in 1787 he commissioned the U.S. chargé in Madrid to purchase books for his library, indicating his interest in Spanish volumes about the New World and, if possible, information about the idea of a canal across Panama. These early contacts led Jefferson to a pessimistic evaluation in the late 1780s: "The glimmerings which reach us from South America enable us only to see that its inhabitants are held under the accumulated pressure of slavery, superstition, and ignorance."[14]

Jefferson's knowledge about Latin America was subsequently enlarged by contact with others who had firsthand knowledge of the region. The American Philosophical Society (of which Jefferson was the presiding officer from 1797 to 1814) established relations with intellectuals in Mexico and Cuba, and Jefferson was on familiar terms with the Abbé José Francisco Correia da Serra, a Portuguese naturalist who was named the Portuguese-Brazilian minister to Washington in 1816. The Abbé was such a regular visitor to Monticello that Jefferson's granddaughter referred to one first-floor bedroom as "the Abbé Correa's room"; and although Jefferson did not meet Francisco de Miranda when the Venezuelan patriot spent nineteen months in the United States from mid-1783 until late 1784, the two men did talk when Miranda stopped in Washington on his way home from Europe in late 1805. Perhaps the acquaintance who most influenced Jefferson's view of Latin America was the German naturalist Alexander von Humboldt, who passed through the United States on his return to Europe after five years of exploring Spanish America. The two men quickly formed an easy friendship, and in mid-1808 von Humboldt sent Jefferson a copy of his *Essai politique sur le royaume de la Nouvelle Espagne.*[15]

The information gained from these acquaintances led Jefferson to conclude that partial independence would be best for Latin America—"an accord with Spain, under the guarantee of France, Russia, Holland, and the United States, allowing to Spain a nominal supremacy, with authority only to keep the peace among them, leaving them otherwise all the powers of self-government until their experience in them, their emancipation from their priests, and advancement in information, shall prepare them for complete independence."[16]

In addition to Jefferson's views of Latin America, John Quincy Adams was influenced by reports from early U.S. agents in Latin America, the most interesting of whom was Joel Roberts Poinsett, a remarkably cosmopolitan Southerner who is best remembered for bringing the Mexican Christmas flower, *nochebuena,* to the United States, where he renamed it the *poinsettia.* In early 1811, a decade before his assignment to Mexico, Poinsett was sent by President Madison to Buenos Aires and then to Chile, where his deep involvement in revolutionary politics led local authorities to declare him persona non grata. Six years later, when Secretary of State Adams asked Poinsett to write up his observations about the Southern Cone, he seemed optimistic about the distant future but skeptical about the immediate prospects: "The spirit of litigation pervades all classes," he reported; "the lawyers are a numerous body; and the practice is not, as in the United States, an open appeal to impartial justice, but the art of multiplying acts and of procrastinating decisions until the favor of the judge is secured by influence and bribery." Poinsett found the Creole political leaders of Buenos Aires to be especially unprincipled ("nothing but low cunning, trick, and artifice"), and so revolutions were frequent.[17]

Another observer of Latin America was Alexander Scott, the first U.S. foreign aid official, who was sent to Venezuela in 1812 with six boatloads of flour to relieve the suffering caused by one of history's most devastating earthquakes, in which thirty thousand people perished. At the time, the Venezuelans were in open rebellion against Spain, but Scott quickly concluded that neither the revolutionary war nor the natural calamity was responsible for the conditions he observed. The problem, he reported, was that the residents of Venezuela were "timid, indolent, ignorant, superstitious, and incapable of enterprise or exertion. From the present moral and intellectual habits of all classes, I fear they have not arrived at that point of human dignity which fits man for the enjoyment of free and rational government."[18]

Sensing the need for fresh information, in 1817 President Monroe appointed John Graham and Caesar Augustus Rodney as commissioners to visit Latin America. Secretary of State Adams added a third member, Theodorick Bland, a Baltimore judge, and together with their secretary they set out for Argentina. The commission arrived in Buenos Aires in early 1818, observed conditions for two months, then returned to the United States and filed three separate reports. Rodney held the most positive view. He noted that Argentines "appear to be an amiable and interesting people. They are considered brave and humane; possessing intelligence, capable of great exertions and perseverance, and manifesting a cheerful devotion to the cause of freedom and independence." The revolution against Spain had "awakened the genius of the country which had so long slumbered," and "the spirit of improvement may be seen in every thing." Graham was somewhat less favorable, observing a "character of indolence" among the Argentine lower classes, but finding the middle and upper classes "more industrious and active. Their manners are social, friendly, and polite. In native talents, they are said to be inferior to no people; and they have given proofs that they are capable of great and persevering efforts, that they are ardently attached to their country, and warmly enlisted in the cause of its independence." Bland (who had also traveled to Chile) was highly critical. He complained about almost everything, especially "the hebetating political and ecclesiastical institutions" of Buenos Aires.[19]

John Quincy Adams read all three reports with great care, dismissed Rodney's positive views ("an enthusiastic partisan of the South American cause, but communicating scarcely any information additional to that which was already known") and accepted Bland's critical report ("more solid information, and more deep and comprehensive reflection, than all the rest put together").[20] Adams's choice was not based solely upon predisposition, however, for at the time Bland's analysis of Buenos Aires was being reinforced by despatches from other U.S. agents. A U.S. commercial agent, Thomas Lloyd Halsey, who for several years had been sending overwhelmingly negative assessments to Washington, was particularly critical of Argentine leaders, noting the absence of "those able and disinterested patriots who led and pushed on the people of the United States to the happy Independence they acquired."[21] Equally negative reports came from Chile, where Consul John Prevost characterized the nation's constitution as a "crude, complicated and indefinite instrument"; and where the U.S. commercial agent in Valparaiso noted that "Integrity, Honor, truth, or Justice, is as little understood as the word Patriotism which is hacknied only to cover acts of Despotism and injustice."[22]

Occasional positive evaluations crossed Adams's desk, such as those from William G. D. Worthington in Buenos Aires and Santiago, but just as he ignored Rodney, the Secretary of State summarily dismissed Worthington,[23] accepting instead the opinions of envoys such as Consul Robert Lowry, who wrote from Venezuela that "this people is ill prepared for the rights of civil liberty, and the leaven of Spanish Despotism, has infected their present rulers, as much as it ever did their former masters." Even the Portuguese monarchy in Brazil had "degenerated to complete effeminacy and voluptuousness," reported the U.S. consul in Rio. "Hardly a worse state of society can be supposed to exist any where, than in this Country; where the climate also excites to every sort of depravation and delinquency."[24]

Self-described as "a man of reserved, cold, austere, and forbidding manners," John Quincy Adams was not one to be hurried into association with either the depraved or the delinquent.[25] Until 1821 he had a perfect excuse to keep his distance: recognition of Latin America's independence, he argued, would jeopardize Spanish ratification of the pivotal boundary treaty of the nineteenth century, which ceded East Florida to the United States, accepted U.S. claims to West Florida, and defined not only the southwestern boundary of the Louisiana Purchase but also its northwesterly course to the forty-second parallel and then to the Pacific Ocean. The Senate ratified the Adams–de Onís treaty unanimously in early 1819, but the Spanish, convulsed by domestic and European intrigues, delayed ratification until February 1821. Once that occurred, Adams had no good argument to counter President Monroe and others who considered it unwise to ignore the fact of Latin America's independence, and in mid-1822 the recognition process began when a reluctant secretary of state presented the aging Colombian patriot, Manuel Torres, to President Monroe. In December the United States established diplomatic relations with Mexico, then Chile, the United Provinces of the Río de la Plata, and the Brazilian empire. By the end of Adams's tenure as secretary of state in early 1825, five of the thirteen U.S. legations were in Latin America.

Each of the new envoys needed instructions, and that undertaking provided Monroe and Adams with the first formal opportunity to outline U.S. policy toward independent Latin America. The diplomats were told to encourage republicanism, discourage piracy, and obtain freedom of religious expression for U.S. citizens. Although they were instructed to obtain commercial equality with other trading states, a task that eventually consumed most of their time, the envoys were not expected to develop new markets. Adams told Caesar Augustus Rodney, the first minister to Argentina, that "our commercial intercourse itself with Buenos Ayres cannot for ages, if ever, be very considerable," and so he could "perceive no necessity and have no desire for the negotiation of a treaty of commerce." Similarly, he instructed Richard Anderson, the first minister to Gran Colombia (today's Colombia, Venezuela, and Ecuador), that "as producing and navigating nations, the United States and Colombia will be rather competitors and rivals than customers to each other." Both envoys were warned about the unsettled political situation. Rodney was cautioned that Argentines had "a hankering after Monarchy" which "produced its natural harvest of unappeasable dissentions, sanguinary civil Wars, and loathsome executions, with the appropriate attendance of arbitrary imprisonments, a subdued and perverted press, and a total annihilation of all civil liberty and personal security." Seeking to reacquaint Rodney with events in Buenos Aires since his South American commission five years earlier, Monroe and Adams emphasized that Argentina "has undergone many changes of Government, violent usurpations of authority, and forcible dispossessions from it; without having so far as we know to this day settled down into any lawful establishment of power by the only mode in which it could be effected—a constitution formed and sanctioned by the voice of the people."[26]

Nested between the lines of these instructions were clear statements of the foreign policy beliefs of John Quincy Adams and his generation. One statement focused on the desirability of geographic isolation, especially once the War of 1812 had convinced U.S. officials of their vulnerability. In the years immediately ahead, everyone expected the British to protect and, if possible, to expand their colonial possessions that surrounded so much of the United States. At the same time, U.S. officials were acutely aware that the war-weakened states of Latin America offered the Holy Alliance a tempting target—an awareness made all the more worrisome by the corollary belief that Latin Americans were unable to defend themselves, and that many of them, monarchists at heart, did not recognize the need to do so. As a result, each new minister was instructed to guard against European chicanery.[27]

Alongside these beliefs about European intentions and Latin Americans' inability or unwillingness to defend themselves was the belief that a deep gulf separated Anglo and Hispanic American character—the absence of shared principles that John Quincy Adams had mentioned to Henry Clay in 1820. In Adams's case, the basic raw material for this belief came from several sources: from his early socialization in Protestant New England, from his brief travels as a child in northern Spain, from his contact with the nation's principal intellectual and political leaders, and from the reports of initial U.S. envoys. Together, these influences led Adams to conclude that the United States should have as little as possible to do with the people of Latin America; he ridiculed the Abbé Correia's suggestion that the United States and Portugal create an "American system" to halt privateering: "As to an American system, we have it; we constitute the whole of it." On another occasion Adams wrote that he "had little expectation of any beneficial result to this country from any future connection with them, political or commercial. We should derive no improvement to our own institutions by any communion with theirs."[28]

With little hope for Latin America's future, with recognition complete, and with the Monroe Doctrine announced and (for the moment) unchallenged, in 1824 Adams shifted his focus to U.S. politics and his candidacy for the presidency. It was a contest among four aspirants, none of whom could muster an absolute majority in the electoral college. With responsibility for selecting the President thereby transferred to the House of Representatives, one of the four, Henry Clay, threw his support to Adams in order to stymie the ambitions of Andrew Jackson, who held a plurality of both the popular and the electoral college vote. In turn, Adams named Clay his secretary of state, which, at the time, was the position of heir-apparent to the presidency.

Eight years earlier, Clay had sought the position as secretary of state while he was serving as Speaker of the House, and his disappointment over Monroe's choice of Adams was reflected in a general bitterness toward the administration.[29] A principal bone of contention was Clay's insistence on prompt recognition of the new Latin American republics, a dispute which came to a head in 1818, shortly after Monroe asked Congress to pay the expenses of the three-member commission to South America. Clay countered with a motion to appropriate funds for the establishment of a legation in Buenos Aires, which would be the equivalent of recognition, of course, and in Adams's view, a damaging blow to his delicate negotiations with Spain. The four-day speech that Clay offered in support of this appropriation ranged far beyond U.S.–Argentine relations. He demanded that the administration act not only to seize East Florida but also to recognize immediately the independence of all Spain's rebellious colonies, calling neutrality "an act for the benefit of his majesty the king of Spain." After bitter debate, the Speaker's proposal was rejected by a humiliating margin of 45 to 115.[30]

Clay's term as Adams's secretary of state was not conspicuously more successful; indeed, the Jacksonians' outrage over what they considered a corrupt bargain was sufficient to hamstring Adams's presidency. When the nineteenth Congress that was elected in 1824 along with Adams finally convened on December 5, 1825, the opposition was lying in wait for any issue that would give them an opportunity to attack their two enemies simultaneously. The chance came in early 1826 when, in its first foreign policy initiative of the session, the administration asked Congress for authority to participate in Bolívar's inter-American conference at Panama. The House began considering the request on February 1 and continued its deliberations until April 25, devoting nineteen days to the issue. The Senate began in mid-February with four days of executive proceedings, followed by four days of public debate, with the final day's discussion occupying an extraordinary 195 pages of the *Congressional Globe*.[31] The proceedings were anything but civil, and at one point Virginia Senator John Randolph overstepped the bounds of propriety by characterizing President Adams and his secretary of state as "the Puritan and the blackleg." Incensed by this allegation that he had cheated by exchanging his electoral votes for the secretary's job, Clay challenged Randolph to a duel. Tempers had cooled when the moment came on April 8, 1826, and Randolph fired into the air. Clay also fired over his adversary's head, and then, still peeved, he reloaded and shot a hole in Randolph's overcoat.

Boys will be boys, of course, and everyone recognized that neither this Yankee machismo nor the heated Congressional debate had much to do with the wisdom of attending an international conference. Rather, the debate was an early example of a now-common aspect of United States policy toward Latin America: the tendency of unconnected U.S. domestic political disputes to spill over into inter-American relations. This had already been seen in the Clay-Adams dispute over recognition, which was in large measure a struggle for leadership of the Whigs, and which featured both Clay's May 1821 prorecognition speech in Lexington, Kentucky, and Adams's scorching 4th of July response. In the case of the Panama conference, the disputes were over two domestic issues: slavery (the Panama agenda included consideration of the recognition of Haiti) and the Adams-Clay "theft" of the White House. In the end, neither the advocates of slavery nor the angry Jacksonians could prevent U.S. participation, but they made Adams and Clay regret ever proposing to send a delegation.[32]

The Panama Congress convened less than two months after Congress granted its approval. One of the two U.S. delegates, Richard Anderson (the U.S. minister to Colombia), became ill on the Magdalena River and died in Cartagena; fearing the same tropical fever, the other never left the United States. That was probably a wise decision, for at the time Panama was a public health horror, with delegates succumbing to the black vomit, which was both fatal to the victim and disagreeable to behold. The Congress met only briefly, then adjourned to resume deliberations in early 1827 in Tacu-baya, outside Mexico City.[33] Two U.S. envoys were present, but unstable political conditions in other participant nations kept the Congress from assembling.

By this time, Secretary of State Clay exhibited little of his early enthusi-asm for Latin America, his ardor tempered by the reports he received from the region. Typical were the despatches of Heman Allen, the first U.S. minister to Chile, all of which stressed a single theme: "in her advance towards civilization, she is thought by many, to have actually retrograded in her march."[34] Other descriptions were equally bleak. Beaufort Watts lik-ened the typical Colombian to "an obedient animal that fawns when chas-tised"; and from Lima, Consul William Tudor evaluated the Liberator, Simón Bolívar, as "ardent, vehement, arrogant; his passions uncontrollable & restrained by no principle public or private: & with frequent sallies of frankness or rather indiscretion, he is capable of the most profound, sol-emn hypocrisy. He considers words as conveying no obligation, but wholly subordinate in whatever shape or profession to promoting his designs." One 1827 despatch from Heman Allen's successor in Chile captured per-fectly the general picture reaching Washington: "the situation of the new States is much less promising than it was some years back . . . freedom will, I fear, be, for a season, merged in anarchy, despotism and military rules."[35]

Confronted by these assessments from every corner of the region, Henry Clay's early enthusiasm for Latin American independence did more than decline; it vanished. The Spanish had been expelled, the threatened en-croachment by other European powers had subsided, and U.S. commercial interests were as secure as could be expected. Since there seemed little to be gained by giving much attention to the region, Clay simply notified U.S. representatives that "all expressions of contempt for their habits, civil or religious, all intimations of incompetency on the part of their population, for self Government, should be sedulously avoided,"[36] and with that he closed the first chapter in the history of United States policy toward Latin America.

Chapter 2 ～

Acquiring Northern Mexico

To incorporate such a disjointed and degraded mass into even a limited participation with our social and political rights, would be fatally destructive to the institutions of our country. There is a moral pestilence attached to such a people which is contagious—a leprosy that will destory.

～ *Senator John Clarke, 1848*

The initial encounter between the United States and its only contiguous Latin American neighbor occurred in the early 1820s, when the United States was enjoying a period of economic and political stability. At that moment Mexico's inexperienced Creole elites had barely reached an agreement on independence, and, unable to choose between a monarchy and a republic, they tried both. The Constitution of 1824 settled the issue in favor of republicanism, but this event provided only a brief respite, and a series of regional, economic, and ideological disputes soon plunged Mexico into nearly continuous political turmoil. To compound these difficulties, the Mexican political stage included an ominous backdrop of foreign interference and threatened recolonization. Until 1825 Spanish troops held San Juan de Ulloa, the fortress controlling Veracruz harbor, and in 1829 they invaded Tampico in an ill-conceived attempt to regain their rebellious colony. Spain agreed to negotiate recognition only after the death of Ferdinand VII in 1833, and then it took six years before the first Spanish minister arrived in Mexico. Meanwhile, foreign interests quietly assumed control of Mexico's mines, the nation's only significant source of exports; and an ever-shifting combination of complex tariffs, nuisance taxes, forced loans, and severely discounted credits from European bankers provided an insecure anchor for the nation's finances. In stark contrast to its northern neighbor, Mexico was soon completely destitute.

This political and economic instability served as the leitmotiv of reports from the initial U.S. envoys in Mexico. As Chargé Anthony Butler wrote near the end of his six-year assignment in 1835, revolutions were constantly "agitating the country to its remotest limits from the period of my arrival to the present moment—tranquility never continuing for six months, together."[1] One of his successors made the inevitable comparison with the United States: "During my residence in Mexico, constantly as the contrast between everything there and in my own country was presented to me, the feelings which were excited were not so much of pride and exultation in our own happier destiny, and superiority in everything, as the more generous one of a profound sympathy for the wretched condition of a country upon which a bountiful Providence has showered its blessings with a more profuse hand than upon any other upon the face of the earth."[2]

These commentaries about political instability were matched by invidious comparisons between the wealth of the United States and Mexico's impoverished economy. When in 1827 the Mexican congress appropriated $15,000 to survey the nation's boundary with the United States, Joel Poinsett reported sarcastically that "the commission has not set out on this expedition for want of funds, Congress having appropriated what the Treasury does not at this moment contain." In his 1846 evaluation, U.S. Minister Waddy Thompson noted that "whilst in our cities and towns you hear the busy hum of incessant industry, and the shrill whistle of the steam-engine, there you hear nothing but the drum and fife; whilst we have been making railroads, they have been making revolutions."[3]

The initial conflict between the United States and Mexico occurred at the border. In the 1803 treaty ceding Louisiana to the United States, Napoleon had transferred the territory that Spain had ceded to France in the 1800 Treaty of San Idelfonso. But in that 1800 agreement, Spain had simply ceded back to France the province of Louisiana that France had given Spain in 1762: it consisted of "all the country known under the name of Louisiana," with no boundaries specified, perhaps because there was no record of Louisiana's pre-1762 boundaries. Thus, as Louisiana was transferred from France to Spain (1762), back to France (1800), and then to the United States (1803), its boundaries were never defined.

As a result, officials in Washington were unclear about the extent of their new territory; an 1804 law dividing the Louisiana Purchase into two territories referred simply to an undefined "western boundary" of the territory purchased from France. By 1811, however, when Congress passed a law authorizing citizens of the territory to form a state government, it explicitly indicated the Sabine River (the current boundary between Louisiana and Texas) as the western border. So did the 1812 law admitting Louisiana to the Union.

For its part, Spain asserted ownership of all the territory west of the Mississippi, including today's Louisiana, Arkansas, and at least part of Missouri.[4] This difference of opinion was resolved by the 1819 Adams–de Onís Treaty, in which the Sabine was established as the border between the United States and the Spanish viceroyalty of New Spain.[5] In his negotiations with Spanish Minister de Onís, John Quincy Adams's two principal objectives were to obtain clear possession of east Florida and to gain Spain's recognition of U.S. territorial claims across the continent above the forty-second parallel (today's Oregon-California border). Spain's objective, in turn, was to establish a firm limit to U.S. expansion into the southwest, and it did so at the expense of conceding Louisiana to the United States.

U.S. expansion was accelerating rapidly at the same time that these negotiations were occurring, and so in 1820, when it appeared that the Spanish government would refuse to ratify the agreement, Jefferson wrote President Monroe that "I am not sorry for the non-ratification of the Spanish treaty," reasoning that "to us the province of Techas will be the richest State of our Union, without any exception."[6] A trickle of U.S. citizens had begun to move into the Mexican state of Texas even before Spain's 1821 ratification of the Adams–de Onís Treaty. Then, in that year the Spanish commandant of the Eastern Interior Provinces of the viceroyalty of New Spain granted a colonization concession to Moses Austin. Having been bankrupted by the panic of 1819, Austin planned to rebuild his finances by charging a fee to each of the three hundred families whom he was authorized to settle in Texas. When he died six months later, the concession passed to his son, Stephen, who in January 1822 established the first legal Anglo settlement in Mexican Texas.

Anxious to populate its territory, in 1825 the Coahuila and Texas legislature of a now-independent Mexico enacted a colonization law of exceptional generosity: each married male settler could purchase up to a league of land (4,428 acres) for less than $200—about $.05 an acre—on easy credit and exempt from taxation for seven years. When combined with the severe tightening of credit in the United States following the panic of 1819, this open invitation led to a surge in immigration controlled by Austin and similarly licensed *empresarios*. What began in 1822 as the settlement of

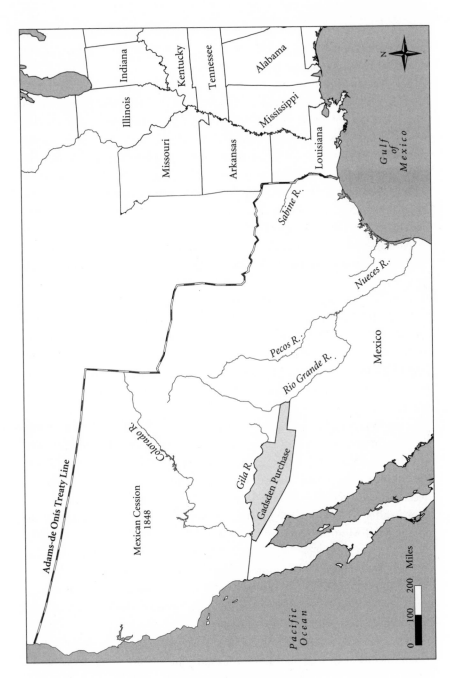

Map 1. Mexico and Southwestern United States

three hundred frontier families near the Gulf coast of eastern Texas soon became a significant flow of U.S. citizens moving ever deeper into Mexico's sparsely populated northern territory.

The Mexican government was frankly ambivalent about this immigration. The initial Mexican minister to the United States was instructed to report on the intentions of Anglo immigrants and to encourage settlers who seemed "honorable and virtuous."[7] At the same time, Mexico sought to reduce the risks that it was taking by mandating the "Mexicanization" of the colonists; all were required to be Catholics, none were allowed to settle within sixty miles of the border, all official transactions were to be in Spanish, and a settler who married a Mexican was qualified for additional land. The new settlers simply ignored all but the last of these measures.

Thus when John Quincy Adams began his presidency in 1825, two fundamental changes had occurred since his treaty with the Spanish minister in Washington: Spain had been ousted from Mexico, and U.S. citizens were pushing steadily westward into Texas. Newly independent Mexico immediately confirmed the Sabine boundary,[8] but the United States was having second thoughts. "The line of the Sabine approaches our great Western mart nearer than could be wished," wrote Secretary of State Clay in 1825, and so he instructed U.S. Minister Joel Poinsett to negotiate a boundary farther west. If necessary, however, the United States was willing to accept the Sabine, at least for the moment. Poinsett approached the Mexican government, found it unwilling to alter the 1819 line, and so he and his successor negotiated a treaty of limits based on the Adams–de Onís boundary.[9] In one decade, then, the United States ratified two treaties designating the Sabine as the nation's southwestern boundary. But during this same decade the United States became committed to expansion into Mexico. Shortly after recognizing the independence of the first five Latin American nations, the Monroe administration considered the acquisition of both Texas and Cuba. On November 7, 1823, the cabinet selected a policy of careful observation, as the notes of Secretary of State Adams indicate: "Without entering now into the enquiry of the expediency of our annexing Texas or Cuba to our Union, we should at least keep ourselves free to act as emergencies may arise."[10]

The Mexicans saw what was coming. Although initially pleased by his reception in the United States, the Mexican minister in Washington soon found the Yankees offensive: "the arrogance of these republicans does not permit them to see us as equals, but as inferiors," he informed his foreign office in December 1822. "Their vanity goes so far, in my judgment, as to believe that their capital will be that of all the Americas. They have a profound love for our money, not for us, and they are not able to enter into a treaty of alliance or commerce except as it suits them, without any thought of reciprocity."[11]

The first formal move by the United States to acquire Mexican territory had come in 1825 when Secretary Clay instructed Poinsett to seek a river boundary farther to the west of the Sabine, but the effort began in earnest only in mid-1829 when the new administration of Andrew Jackson launched an eight-year acquisition effort. Secretary of State Martin Van Buren issued Poinsett a direct order: "you should, without delay, open a negotiation with the Mexican Government for the purchase of so much of the province of Texas as hereinafter described, or for such a part thereof as they can be induced to cede to us." If Mexico indicated a reluctance to sell, Van Buren continued, Poinsett should seek to gain the Mexican government's agreement to move the Sabine westward: "Of the two streams which empty into the Sabine bay through the same channel," he wrote, "the one farthest west is the most considerable, and may, with reason be claimed to be the one referred to in the [Adams–de Onís] treaty."[12] This statement was untrue. From the day that they were first given names by Europeans, the Sabine was the Sabine, whereas the stream to the west was the Neches. Four miles apart when they enter the Sabine Bay, the two rivers drain a substantial portion of east Texas, creating between them a widening triangle of territory to the northwest.

It is not certain that any diplomat could have implemented Van Buren's instructions, but by the late 1820s Poinsett had become more of a hindrance than a help to U.S. diplomacy. The first in a long line of U.S. proconsuls to Latin America, Poinsett composed despatches that dripped with disdain for the people with whom he was forced to associate. He referred to Mexicans as "an ignorant and immoral race" and to the clergy as "the very dregs of the people, . . . disgustingly debauched and ignorant." He criticized the tendency of Creole Mexicans to engage in "constant intercourse with the aborigines, who were and still are degraded to the very lowest class of human beings"; this miscegenation, he said, "contributed to render the Mexicans a more ignorant and debauched people than their ancestors had been." Making no attempt to conceal contempt for his hosts, Poinsett focused his attention upon providing the nation with new leadership. He wrote Clay that "the state of society here is scarcely to be credited.

I hardly know a man however high his rank or office whose word can be relied on and many of the leading members in both houses will receive a bribe to advocate a private claim with as little scruple as you would have received a fee to argue a cause before the Supreme Court."[13]

The Mexican government soon requested Poinsett's recall. President Jackson replaced him with Colonel Anthony Butler, a trusted acquaintance who had fought alongside him at the Battle of New Orleans and had subsequently become a land speculator with a personal financial stake in Texan independence. The President instructed Butler to "let a listening ear, a silent tongue and a stedfast [*sic*] heart, the three jewels of wisdom, guard every advance which you make on the subject of Texas. The acquisition of that territory is become every day an object of more importance to us." In a postscript he informed Butler that he would be provided with two sets of instructions, one real and one false, the latter omitting any mention of Texas. Butler was to tell the Mexicans that the United States had no interest whatsoever in acquiring Texas and then, as an act of candor to gain their confidence, to offer to let the Mexican authorities take a peek at the false instructions as proof of his innocent intentions. Do this coyly, Jackson said, "in such a manner as to induce a belief that it [the showing of his instructions] must be kept a profound secret from you[r] own government, as on that event, it would destroy you."[14] Presumably the Mexicans would then trust Butler and allow him to raise anew the issue of Texas.

The deceit proved unsuccessful, and so Butler turned to another tactic proposed by the President: bribery. "I scarcely ever knew a Spaniard who was not the slave of averice [*sic*]," Jackson wrote, "and it is not improbable that this weakness may be worth a great deal to us, in this case." Taking the President's suggestion seriously, Butler was so open in his efforts to bribe Mexico's leaders that Jackson had to warn him to be more circumspect. The envoy responded with his view of Mexican civics: "What you advise of being cautious of 'these shrewd fellows' who may draw me into imputations of attempting to bribe them proves how little you know of mexican character. I can assure you Sir that bribery is not only common and familiar in all ranks and classes, but familiarly and freely spoken of." Indeed, Butler saw no other way to implement his instructions: "let this negotiation be concluded when it may, if it is done in Mexico resort must be had to bribery."[15]

After this tactic had also failed, Butler advised President Jackson to seize the triangle of territory between the Sabine and Neches Rivers: "I am convinced that they would cede all the very moment they ascertained that we had made good our claim to the west branch of the Sabine, but which they call the Naches [*sic*]." Butler couched his suggestion in the language of a sycophant: "Why do I recommend this course? It is because I am anxious for your glory." The President, though, declined to lunge at the bait, penning his opinion at the bottom of his envoy's letter: "A. Butler: What a scamp." [16]

It was not diplomacy but demography that spelled the end to Mexico's sovereignty over Texas. By 1830 the policy of obligatory "Mexicanization" had failed and Mexico had prohibited further colonization, but by then the government in faraway Mexico City had lost control of the Anglo population in Texas. Perhaps because they now outnumbered their hosts, the new Texans saw no need to assimilate into Mexican society. They maintained their Anglo culture, including not only their language and religion but also their slave economy. Their financial ties naturally linked Texas to the U.S. South, particularly New Orleans, which became a center for Texan venture capital and land speculation. The long-standing linkages between Texas and central Mexico were hardly counterbalancing; indeed, most were prejudicial to the maintenance of Mexican sovereignty. Texas's representatives in the Saltillo-based legislature were hopelessly outnumbered, for example, and even that meager provincial representation was vitiated by the growing centralism of the Mexican state. Just before the outbreak of war in 1846, Waddy Thompson wrote that "the northern departments of Mexico . . . all hang very loosely to the confederacy;—they receive no earthly benefit from the central government, which in truth they only know in its exactions." [17]

These push-and-pull factors combined to encourage a separatist subculture, and in January 1836 a convention of Anglo Texans met and seceded from Mexico. In April the rebels effectively claimed their independence (and avenged their earlier defeat at the Alamo) by routing the Mexican army in a battle along the banks of the San Jacinto River. Texas became a republic de facto.

Unwilling to rush into premature recognition, Secretary of State John Forsyth sent a special agent to assess the new nation's viability, who reported that "without foreign aid, her future security must depend more upon the weakness and imbecility of her enemy, than upon her own strength." [18] Paralyzed by bitter internal disputes, Mexico found it impossible to muster the resources to recover its rebellious territory, while at the same time Anglo Texans obtained substantial private support from the United States, often by giving away land that had belonged to Mexico. They were able to maintain their independence for nearly a year, and that was enough to convince Andrew Jackson. On the last day of his presidency he recognized the Lone Star republic's independence.

The new Van Buren administration was presented almost immediately with Texas's formal application to enter the Union. Former envoy Waddy Thompson, now serving South Carolina in the House of Representatives, sponsored a resolution encouraging a favorable response, but he was opposed by antislavery Whigs led by John Quincy Adams, who refused to consider annexation on the grounds that slavery had been spread to a territory that had been free. Congress adjourned without taking action, and then the Panic of 1837 led to the onset of a grave depression; after that, the Van Buren administration could expend little of its precious political capital on Texas.

Van Buren's successor, the Whig William Henry Harrison, died within a month of his 1841 inauguration, and that event left the nation's affairs in the hands of Vice President John Tyler, a Southerner of vacillating party loyalties who had been placed on the Whig ticket for regional balance. A leader without a following, Tyler took the fateful step of naming Duff Green, a prominent Democratic power broker, to a position where he could define the debate over Texas.

Green was originally recruited to serve as Tyler's confidential agent in Europe, in part because Southern Democrats distrusted the U.S. minister in Great Britain, Edward Everett (a Harrison Whig), and in part because Tyler wanted a special envoy to negotiate a loan from European bankers. This latter task required exceptional diplomatic skill, for a number of U.S. states had defaulted on European debts after the Panic of 1837; and when Green arrived in Europe, he discovered that Baron James Rothschild was impatient for repayment: "You may tell your government, that you have seen the man who is at the head of the finances of Europe, and that he has told you—that they cannot borrow a dollar, not a dollar."[19] Rather than accept on face value this simple statement that the United States needed to assure payment on its existing debt before it could contract more, Green concluded—and this was crucial to the future of Texas—that the wily British had managed to turn off the financial spigots in Europe as part of a larger British strategy to render U.S. products uncompetitive on world markets. The success of this strategy rested upon the destruction of slavery.

If Texas were left independent, Green reasoned, the impoverished republic would quickly fall under the influence of Great Britain. In return for an infusion of British capital, the Foreign Office would force Texas to abolish slavery, which, in turn, would leave the South hemmed in by free-soil Texas to the west and free U.S. territories to the north. Expansion would be impossible. Meanwhile, the North could move westward, adding free state after free state above the line established by the Missouri Compromise.* Sapped of its strength in the U.S. Senate just as Northern population growth had already destroyed slavery's power in the House of Representatives, the South would watch helplessly as the U.S. Congress abolished slavery. Abolition, in turn, would ensure British commercial superiority, for without slave labor, the South's production costs would rise above those of British planters in both the East and the West Indies. Piles of high-cost cotton would soon sit rotting on the docks of Charleston and Savannah. The South would be ruined.[20]

Secretary of State Abel Upshur accepted this logic. "No man who knows any thing of his own nature can suppose it to be possible, that two races of men, distinguished by external and ineffaceable marks, obvious to every eye; who have held towards each other from time immemorial the relation of master and slave, could ever live together as equals, in the same country and under the same Government." Because "these slaves perform nearly the whole agricultural labor of the South," he continued, "it is impossible to calculate the amount of ruin and suffering which would follow the sudden emancipation of the slaves of the United States." Great Britain would be the beneficiary of this disaster: "Here is indeed a promising field for the policy of England. What better encouragement would the industry of her colonies require than the simple rise of price in the articles of sugar and cotton, which would be caused by diminished production? What rival need she fear when the agriculture, the commerce, the manufactures, and the navigation of the United States shall be thus withdrawn from competition with her?"[21]

Once Green had convinced President Tyler and his two Southern secretaries of state, Abel Upshur of Virginia and John Calhoun of South Carolina, of the accuracy of his thesis, the annexation of Texas became essential

---

*The 1820 Missouri Compromise drew a line across the Louisiana Territory from east to west at 36°30' north latitude (today's Missouri-Arkansas border), to the north of which slavery was prohibited, Missouri excepted.

for the survival of the South. The Tyler administration proceeded to negotiate a treaty of annexation, with Calhoun and the Texans signing Upshur's annexation treaty on April 12, 1844.[22] Ratification was more difficult, however, for the issue immediately became entangled in the presidential campaign that was just beginning, and in June the Senate rejected the treaty by a vote of 35 to 16.

Slavery was the underlying issue once again. As this dispute rose from a simmer to a rolling boil in the middle decades of the nineteenth century, it focused upon the acquisition and organization of new territory. At a rudimentary level, the dispute seemed simple enough: Southerners were witnessing the slow erosion of their political equality with Northerners. In 1790 there were 57 representatives from free states and 49 from slave states; by 1819, when Alabama was admitted as the twenty-second state, the North had a 105 to 81 numerical advantage in the House of Representatives. Thereafter, as one South Carolina Representative noted in 1845, "every census has added to the power of the non-slaveholding States, and diminished that of the South. We are growing weaker, and they stronger, every day."[23] By 1830 the gap had widened to 42 seats, and by 1860 the difference was 71. Since this demographic trend was caused by accelerating differences between the industrializing economy of the North and the export-based agrarian economy of the South, an even more significant shift in power in the lower chamber of Congress appeared inevitable in the years ahead.

At the same time, the admission of new states threatened to destroy the South's power in the Senate. Of the 22 states that formed the Union before the Missouri Compromise, half were slave and half were free. Two decades later, in 1840, the balance had been maintained, but only four additional states had been added (Maine and Michigan in the North, Missouri and Arkansas in the South), and expansion to the northwest was accelerating. Without Texas (and, implicitly, the territory beyond it, for the joint resolution approving annexation envisioned "new states, of convenient size, not exceeding four in number, in addition to said state of Texas")[24] the South had only Florida to balance Iowa, Wisconsin, Minnesota, and whatever states might be carved out of the rest of the Louisiana Purchase and the Oregon Territory. The resulting dilution of southern strength in the Senate would spell the end to slavery, for the Senate, with its peculiar rules of procedure, was the only national institution that the South could hope to control.

The issue of Texas's annexation was not a simple sectional battle, however, for the nationwide tide of public opinion was favorable to the South. This tide had two distinct but complementary currents.

One was territorial expansion. Already a powerful independent political force in early Jacksonian America, by the late 1830s expansion had become a dominant ideology; in the 1840s it would have its own name, Manifest Destiny. Since public opinion favored expansion, that inclination meant that opinion favored the Democrats—as the Texas envoys in Washington wrote home in mid-1844, "the question of the annexation of Texas to this Government has . . . become strictly a party question between the democrats and whigs in the pending contest for the next Presidency."[25] The initial Democratic frontrunner, Martin Van Buren, was denied his party's nomination after publishing a letter voicing mild opposition to annexation. The Whig platform, in contrast, failed to mention either Texas or expansion, and in early 1844 the Whig candidate, Henry Clay, like Van Buren, published a letter opposing the Tyler-Upshur annexation treaty. Clay later issued a retraction, but by then the damage was done. His cautious Whig position contrasted dramatically with that of the Democratic candidate, James K. Polk, who wrote that "in my judgment, the country west of the Sabine, and now called Texas, was most unwisely ceded away" by a Whig (John Quincy Adams) in the treaty of 1819 with Spain.[26] The Democrats pledged to take it back; their platform called for "reannexation."

Polk's November 1844 victory was widely interpreted as the public's endorsement of this position, and in the annual message in December, the lame-duck Tyler administration again asked Congress to act on the issue. In early 1845 a joint resolution offering Texas statehood passed the House. Opposition in the Senate required the intervention of President-elect Polk, who assured key senators that his administration would negotiate with Mexico over an appropriate boundary. Accepting Polk's assurances, a bare majority of the Senate agreed to the joint resolution, and President Tyler submitted it to Texas on his last day in office. Three months later, Texas accepted the offer, and in December it entered the Union.

Beyond the general appeal of Manifest Destiny, the annexation of Texas was augmented by a second current in U.S. public opinion, a national unease over the presence of millions of African Americans in the United States. For decades many Northerners had feared that if slavery were abolished, a substantial proportion of over three million freed blacks would flood into northern cities. This fear increased in the mid-1840s, when proslavery activists led by Mississippi Senator Robert Walker launched a propaganda campaign to convince Northerners that liberated slaves would become a major public nuisance. Walker and others used data from the defective 1840 census to buttress their claim that free blacks in the North were significantly more likely to suffer from mental and physical disorders than their enslaved cousins in the South. If, as Northerners feared, emancipated blacks were to move to their cities en masse, then "the poor-house and the jail, the asylums of the deaf and dumb, the blind, the idiot and insane, would be filled to overflowing, if, indeed, any asylum could be afforded to the millions of the negro race whom wretchedness and crime would drive to despair and madness."[27]

Texas was a godsend to worried Northerners who may not have been enthusiastic about expansion, per se, but who were unwilling to concede a place for blacks in their society. Walker was probably correct when he noted that white Northerners had exhibited no desire to live with African Americans: "They are nowhere found in the colleges or universities, upon the bench or at the bar, in the muster, or the jury-box, in legislative or executive stations; nor does marriage, the great bond of society, unite the white with the negro, except a rare occurrence of such unnatural alliance, to call forth the scorn or disgust of the whole community."

The acquisition of Texas would open a land route to the tropical lands that blacks were believed to find most congenial. Walker argued that "as the number of free blacks augmented in the slaveholding states, they would be diffused gradually through Texas into Mexico, and Central and Southern America, where nine-tenths of their present population are already of the colored races, and where, from their vast preponderance in number, they are not a degraded caste, but upon a footing, not merely of legal, but what is far more important, of actual equality with the rest of the population." In this way, expansion into Texas offered a much-needed answer to the question of race in mid-nineteenth-century America, and it was this wedding of Manifest Destiny expansionism with racial anxieties—the two strong currents of U.S. public opinion at the time, neither of them sectional—that facilitated the annexation of Texas.

After the election of 1844, these two domestic political questions were merged into a single foreign policy issue: how to convince Mexico to accept the annexation of Texas. In mid-1843 the Mexican foreign minister had informed Tyler's envoy that annexation would mean war, and several months later the Mexican minister in Washington repeated this warning.[28] Two days after Polk's inauguration Mexico closed its legation in Washington, and three weeks later it formally severed relations.

Almost immediately Polk sent William Parrott as a confidential agent with instructions to ask the Mexican government if it would receive a U.S. negotiator to begin the process of reconciliation. In October Mexico agreed to discuss the renewal of relations, and Polk named Mississippi's John Slidell as a new minister. Fluent in Spanish and gracious in manner, Slidell may have been an excellent choice, but it will never be known whether his diplomatic talents would have been sufficient to avoid war, for the Polk administration provided the new envoy with instructions that ensured his failure: Slidell was ordered not simply to defuse Mexican opposition to the annexation of Texas, but also to obtain even more territory. The minimum acceptable agreement would fix the Texas boundary at the Rio Grande, which would include more than half of present-day New Mexico and Colorado, or about three times the size of Texas as a Mexican state. For this Slidell was authorized to offer Mexico $5 million plus the assumption of U.S. citizens' claims against the Mexican government. Slidell was to offer an additional $15 million if Mexico would cede its territories of New Mexico (the rest of today's New Mexico, Arizona, Nevada, southern Utah, and southwestern Colorado) and Upper California, including San Francisco Bay. The envoy was also told that "the larger the territory south of this bay, the better," and to add $5 million or "any reasonable additional sum" if Mexico would cede California as far south as Monterey.[29]

Aware of Slidell's instructions, the Mexican government refused to receive him. Polk later asserted that Slidell had been turned away "by the most frivolous pretexts," but that was not so. The United States had sent Slidell as a minister, whereas Mexico was willing to receive only "an envoy" to discuss the renewal of relations. Mexico's position was that the act of receiving a minister would have automatically restored diplomatic relations, thereby acknowledging that the reason for breaking relations (the annexation of Texas) was no longer an issue in dispute. This was precisely the issue that Mexico wanted to discuss, as the Mexican minister of foreign relations explicitly informed Slidell.[30]

Polk now had to reassess his options. Virtually everything that he and Secretary of State James Buchanan knew about Mexico came from U.S. envoys, who painted a picture of a disorganized, incompetent government and a debauched people—a military pushover. Confidential agent Parrott had reported that "the people know not what they want, nor is there, a man in the country, of sufficient moral courage and prestige to establish any stable form of Government, out of the chaos that now exists." Pushing for war, Parrott told Buchanan that he hoped "to see this people well flogged by Uncle Sam's boys." Slidell reported that "the country, torn by conflicting factions, is in a state of perfect anarchy." Fortunately, no harm was likely to come from this perverse situation, since "there is such an entire absence of energy and decision among them that they dare not take any step which involves the least responsibility." The common citizens of Mexico were also reported to have debilitating shortcomings. "As for a people, in the proper sense of the term, it does not exist in Mexico, the masses are totally indifferent to all the revolutions that are going on and submit with the most stupid indifference to any matters that may be imposed upon them."[31] A war with Mexico would be brief.

On January 13, 1846, immediately after receiving word that Slidell would not be received, President Polk ordered General Zachary Taylor to occupy the contested territory between the Nueces and the Rio Grande. On April 25, Mexican troops attacked what they considered to be an invading detachment of U.S. soldiers, killing eleven, wounding five, and capturing the rest. Word of the attack reached Washington on May 9, a Saturday; and on the following Monday, Polk submitted his war message to Congress, declaring that "after reiterated menaces, Mexico has passed the boundary of the United States, has invaded our territory and shed American blood upon the American soil. She has proclaimed that hostilities have commenced, and that the two nations are now at war. As war exists, and, notwithstanding all our efforts to avoid it, exists by the act of Mexico herself,[32] we are called upon by every consideration of duty and patriotism to vindicate with decision the honor, the rights, and the interests of our country."[33]

The Congressional vote on Polk's war resolution indicated how hopelessly outnumbered the antiexpansionists had become. In the House, only 14 of the 188 votes were cast against the declaration of war, all by abolitionist Whigs; the vote in the Senate was equally lopsided: 40 to 2, with 3 abstentions. But one ominous abstention was the nation's most prominent champion of slavery, John C. Calhoun. Two years earlier, while serving as Tyler's secretary of state, he had written that "it is our policy to increase by growing and spreading out into unoccupied regions, assimilating all we incorporate. In a word, to increase by accretion, and not through conquest by the addition of masses [?] held together by the cohesion of force." To this principle Calhoun added a more important sectional consideration: his understanding that a plantation slave economy could not be established in Mexico. He therefore would support the annexation of Texas, but not a war of conquest with Mexico.[34]

The vote to declare war identifies the very peak of expansionist sentiment. At about this time the abolitionists rediscovered their political savvy, dropped their opposition to expansion (which they had adopted only as an adjunct to their opposition to slavery), and began to rebuild their political base into what would become the core of the Republican party. It is here, soon after the declaration of war, that the twin currents of expansionism and racial anxiety were rediverted into separate streams, and the nation then moved quickly to a defining moment in its history.

The Polk administration needed money to pursue the war, and Congress did not hesitate to appropriate it. But then after the initial military victories, President Polk requested $2 million to *end* the war—ostensibly to pay Mexico for territory that it would be forced to cede. Since Texas was already a state in the Union, implicit in this request was Polk's intention to annex additional territory, or at least to pay for Mexico's agreement to an expansive definition of the western boundary of Texas, much of it below the line of the Missouri Compromise. Congressional abolitionists reacted to the possibility of the further expansion of slavery by offering an amendment to Polk's "Two Million Bill." It authorized the expenditure, but only "provided, that, as an express and fundamental condition to the acquisition of any territory from the Republic of Mexico by the United States . . . neither slavery nor involuntary servitude shall ever exist in any part of said territory." Named the Wilmot Proviso after the Pennsylvania Democrat who introduced it, this amendment passed the House by a vote of 83 to 64, but the Two Million Bill died with adjournment of the first session of the 29th Congress. In the second session (1846–47), the administration's request was increased to $3 million. Once again the House succeeded in attaching the Wilmot Proviso, but only by a narrow margin, and the Senate deleted it. The Three Million Bill was then returned to the House without the Proviso, where it was approved.[35]

Although it failed to receive Congressional approval, the Wilmot Proviso had an immense effect on the war. With Texas already admitted as a slave state and the road to the tropics therefore open for freed blacks, Northerners' fears had been assuaged. No tide of free blacks would inundate their cities. Thus the race-expansion coalition was ripe for destruction as Wilmot rose to offer his amendment, and when he sat down ten minutes later, expansion beyond Texas had become a straight sectional issue. His Proviso nearly destroyed the Union more than a decade before secession actually occurred.

The moment of truth came on February 9, 1847, when John Calhoun, the very soul of the Southern slaveocracy, rose in the Senate to oppose further expansion. He told his colleagues that "we are involved in a domestic question of the most irritating and dangerous character." He spoke of a "terrible difficulty to be met" by acquiring large portions of Mexico: "How should these lands be acquired?" he asked. "To whose benefit should they enure? Should they enure to the exclusive benefit of one portion of the Union?" To avoid this fight over slavery in new territory, a fight he knew the South would lose, Calhoun declared, "Mexico is to us the forbidden fruit; the penalty of eating it would be to subject our institutions [i.e., slavery] to political death."[36]

But Calhoun's Southern colleague, Senator John Berrien, a Georgia Whig, had already referred to the acquisition of land beyond Texas as a "demon of discord," and had reminded his fellow Southerners that "on the question of the admission of the territory as a State, the numerical superiority of the free States would hold us in chains." Calhoun's fear was not simply that the South would be outvoted on this issue. The Wilmot Proviso would undermine what segregationists a century later would call "states' rights"—the state-federal division of political authority that permitted the South to maintain racial discrimination. To support Wilmot would be tacitly to agree that the federal government had the right to legislate on the issue of slavery, something no Southerner would countenance. Acutely aware of the South's declining political power in the national legislature, Calhoun's speech was primarily a warning to the many Southerners who wished to replace Wilmot's initiative with a proslavery amendment. Calhoun argued instead that Southerners should deny the legitimacy of *any* federal legislation on the topic of slavery.[37] The proper position for a Southerner, then, was to oppose all acquisition of territory.

Joining the Calhoun Democrats and Southern Whigs were virtually all antiexpansionists and abolitionists, now emboldened by the possibility of revenge. They had been defeated in the election of 1844, outvoted in their opposition to annexation in 1845, railroaded into declaring the existence of a state of war in 1846, and now in 1847 they were being asked to finance the acquisition of additional land, probably for the expansion of the South. They would have none of it. A recent Whig arrival in the House, Abraham Lincoln, provided the most colorful criticism, asserting that Polk's justifications for the war resembled "the half insane mumbling of a fever dream . . . He is a bewildered, confounded, and miserably perplexed man."[38] Enough was enough, said Columbus Delano, an Ohio Whig, shouting his accusation that the Polk administration had unconscionably decided to "make war upon Mexico, cut the throats of her people, rob her of her territory, and then, I suppose, carry slavery upon a soil now free." Not if Delano could stop it: "Never, never shall you extend your institution of slavery one inch beyond its present limits . . . If you will drive on this bloody war of conquest to annexation, we will establish a cordon of free States that shall surround you; and then we will light up the fires of liberty on every side, until they melt your present chains, and render all your people *free*."[39]

Having incensed the Whigs and lost the Calhoun Democrats, the Polk administration found it impossible to marshall an effective reply.[40] Any hope for slavery's expansion beyond Texas was dead.

The discussion then moved from the subject of slavery in the new territories to the desirability of annexing part of Mexico as *either* slave or free. Calhoun had raised this issue on February 9, when he noted that he was not opposed to annexing "the country from the pass [El Paso] of the Del Norte to the upper end of the Gulf of California," because that part of Mexico's territory "is occupied only by a savage population . . ., an unpeopled country, or a country peopled only with savages; and it was this which rendered it really valuable." But the rest of Mexico was already occupied by Mexicans, and so Calhoun asked, "After you have forced Mexico into a compliance with your terms, what are you to do with what you have thus gained? Can you incorporate Mexico into your Union? Can you bring her seven millions of people—all differing from you in their religion, in their habits, in their character, in their feelings—can you bring them into connecxion [*sic*] with your citizens? Can you incorporate them into this Union, and make them a part of the people of the United States? No, sir, you cannot."[41]

Senator John Berrien again spoke for the worried Southern Whigs. "Consider it as already yours, and then tell me, what will you do with it? Will you *expel the present inhabitants*, and settle the vacant territory, by emigrants from this, or foreign countries? . . . Will you govern them as *subject provinces*? . . . Will you govern them as territories, whose inhabitants will of course instantly become citizens of the United States, and entitled when they have attained to the requisite number, to the privilege of being admitted as States of this Union? Are you willing to put your birthright into the keeping of the mongrel races who inhabit these territories, by incorporating them into this Union?" Berrien answered his own questions by proposing an amendment to the Wilmot Proviso: "the war with Mexico ought not to be prosecuted by this Government with any view to the dismemberment of that republic, or to the acquisition, by conquest, of any portion of her territory."[42]

Responding for the administration and Northern Democrats in general, Michigan's Lewis Cass told his colleagues that "all we want is a portion of territory, which they nominally hold, generally uninhabited, or, where inhabited at all, sparsely so, and with a population, which would soon recede, or identify itself with ours."[43]

Sensing that it had the opposition on the run, Northern Whigs were not willing to concede that these were uninhabited territories. In an apparent reference to California, Abraham Lincoln asserted that "half is already inhabited, as I understand it, tolerably densely for the nature of the country; and all it's [sic] lands, or all that are valuable, already appropriated as private property. How then are we to make any thing out of these lands with this incumbrance on them? or how, remove the incumbrance? I suppose no one will say we should kill the people, or drive them out, or make slaves of them, or even confiscate their property."[44] "If we acquire New Mexico and California," asserted New York's Washington Hunt, "think of the character of the population which must come with them into our Confederacy. We must prepare to receive an incongruous mass of Spaniards, Indians, and mongrel Mexicans—a medley of mixed races, who are fitted neither to enjoy nor to administer our free institutions: men of different blood and language, who cannot dwell and mingle with our people on a footing of social or political equality. They must be governed as a colonial dependency, under provincial laws, or else be incorporated into our federal system, to become an eternal source of strife, anarchy, and civil commotion." Thus Hunt would draw any new boundary line far, far to the north, or else "a hundred thousand people and negroes in the State of Chihuahua [would] neutralize the voice of New York, with her three million freemen, in the Senate of the United States."[45]

So there it was, the rarest bird in the Washington political aviary: a perfect consensus. Abolitionists and slave owners, Southern Democrats and Southern Whigs, Northern Democrats and Northern Whigs, all agreed on one thing: whatever the outcome of the war might be, the land to be taken from Mexico should be as devoid of Mexicans as possible.

As the debate over expansion was occurring in Washington, a war was being fought in Mexico. It involved much pain and suffering, and its long-term effect was to poison relations between the people of Mexico and the United States. Its short-term effect was the defeat of the Mexican army, with General Winfield Scott occupying the Mexican capital in September 1847. President Polk had begun to explore the possibility of peace more than a year before the Marines seized the halls of Montezuma. In mid-1846 he ordered Commodore Connor to take a peace message to Veracruz under a flag of truce, and the President's diary indicates that he considered sending Secretary of State Buchanan to negotiate an end to the war as early as January 1847.[46] Two months earlier, Polk had taken advantage of the business trip of Moses Yale Beach, the archexpansionist editor of the New York *Sun*, to commission him as a confidential agent. Traveling to Mexico in the hope that he might obtain rights to a transit route across the Isthmus of Tehuantepec, Beach discovered that the route had already been awarded to a Mexican citizen. He then began to dabble in Mexican politics, but soon reported "finding it expedient to leave instantly for the coast" and return to the United States.[47]

Serious efforts to negotiate did not begin until April 1847, when Secretary of State Buchanan notified the Mexican minister of foreign affairs that he had named "Nicholas P. Trist, esq., the officer next in rank to the undersigned in our department of foreign affairs, as a commissioner, invested with full powers to conclude a definite treaty of peace with the United Mexican States. This gentleman possesses the entire confidence of the President, and is eminently worthy of that of the Mexican government." Technically, Trist was the second-ranking administrative official in the Department of State, but his title was that of chief clerk. Since Trist was to be backed by a victorious army that soon would be in possession of the enemy's capital, Polk could well have reasoned that the task required no more than a clerk's attention to the details of Mexico's capitulation.[48] Trist's instructions included a carefully worded draft of a proposed treaty of peace, with vast territorial expansion assumed: "The extension of our boundaries over New Mexico and Upper California, for a sum not exceeding twenty millions of dollars, is to be considered a *sine qua non* of any treaty. You may modify, change, or omit the other terms of the projét if needful, but not so as to interfere with this ultimatum."[49]

Trist quickly revealed his amateur status when he began the negotiations by offering the Mexicans the largest sum that Polk had authorized, and he compounded this error by forwarding to Washington Mexico's counter-proposal to create a buffer state between the Nueces and the Rio Grande. Polk received the proposal with disbelief, since he considered the territory in question to have become part of the United States when Texas entered the Union two years earlier. How could Mexico, after being defeated at war, even suggest the notion of a buffer state, and why did Trist lack the common sense to dismiss it out of hand? The question that Washington wished to have Trist answer was simple: how much of Mexico *beyond Texas* could be obtained for how little money? Since Trist obviously did not understand the central point of his mission, Polk recalled him.

The envoy responded with a sixty-page report explaining that a delay in negotiating peace would favor the efforts of those U.S. citizens who had begun to push for the seizure of all Mexico. The President recognized that Trist's fear was not unfounded.[50] A wide-open presidential election was now less than a year away (Polk had promised to serve only one term), and few of the potential candidates had forgotten the lesson voters had taught Van Buren and Clay in 1844: timid expansionists lose elections. The "All Mexico" movement had grown slowly during the initial year of the war, declined after the debates over the Wilmot Proviso, but then quickly began to develop new adherents after U.S. troops seized Mexico City in September 1847. By early winter the movement had become a major force, and by late winter it had reached its greatest strength. Trist argued that if he accepted his recall, domestic political considerations might require different instructions for his replacement, perhaps ordering the annexation of all Mexico. This possibility would damage the United States: "Whilst among the nations of the earth we are the one above all others . . . Mexico occupies the very lowest point on the same scale, a point beneath even the one proper to the Indian tribes within our borders." Why, he asked, would anyone want to incorporate these people into the United States?

Since no one could provide him with an acceptable answer, Trist refused to accept a direct order from the President and assumed responsibility for negotiating a settlement that would frustrate the rapidly growing annexationist sentiment in the United States. On February 2, 1848, four months after being recalled, he signed the Treaty of Guadalupe Hidalgo.

While Trist was negotiating with the Mexicans, antiannexationists in Congress were holding off the All Mexico partisans. As in the debate over the Wilmot Proviso a year earlier, the core opposition to the absorption of any part of inhabited Mexico consisted of an odd-bedfellow coalition of antiexpansionist Northern and Southern Whigs and the proslavery Democrats led by John C. Calhoun. The Northern Whig position was best expressed by Rhode Island Senator John Clarke: "With no fixed principles of government—a degraded population, far inferior to the Aztec race in civility and personage, accustomed only to obey—their condition cannot, perhaps, but be improved. But to incorporate such a disjointed and degraded mass into even a limited participation with our social and political rights, would be fatally destructive to the institutions of our country. There is a moral pestilence attached to such a people which is contagious—a leprosy that will destroy."[51]

Calhoun and his fellow Southern Democrats reached the same conclusion, but they used a new logic. Many of them had been dubious from the beginning about the economic viability of slavery in Texas, and by 1848 they were convinced that it could not survive in the other sections of Mexico. Slavery required a special type of social organization—a handful of white masters directing the forced agricultural labor of a mass of African laborers. Where plantation agriculture was possible, a relatively empty territory could be adapted to slavery, but beyond eastern Texas to the southwest the land was suitable only for livestock grazing, not for slavery. Isolated on vast expanses of open rangeland, slave cowboys would ride off into the Mexican sunset and probably take the herd with them.

That state of affairs led Calhoun to ask a slightly different question: does the United States want to take the desert in order to gain access to central Mexico, which might be adaptable to slave-based agriculture? The problem here, of course, was that central Mexico was already full of Mexicans. Former envoy Waddy Thompson had seen the problem, as he warned his fellow South Carolinians in a 1847 speech: "It is not the country of a savage people whose lands are held in common, but a country in which grants have been made for three hundred and twenty-five years . . . It is all private property." This statement led proslavery Southern Democrats to precisely the same conclusion as antislavery Northern Whigs. "We shall get no land," Thompson concluded, "but will add a large population, aliens to us in feeling, education, race, and religion—a people unaccustomed to work, and accustomed to insubordination and resistance to law, the expense of governing whom will be ten times as great as the revenues derived from them." President Polk agreed.[52]

Taking to the Senate floor once again, John C. Calhoun offered a formal resolution opposing the annexation of Mexico. After some debate, the resolution was tabled, but Calhoun made his point before letting his proposal die quietly: "How can you make a free government in Mexico?" he asked. "Where is the intelligence in Mexico adequate to the construction of such a government? That is what she has been aiming at for twenty-odd years; but so utterly incompetent are her people for the work, that it has been a complete failure from the beginning to end." Warming to his subject, Calhoun then spoke directly to the prejudices of Southern Democrats: "We have never dreamt of incorporating into our Union any but the Caucasian race—the free white race. To incorporate Mexico, would be the very first instance of the kind of incorporating an Indian race; for more than half the Mexicans are Indians, and the other is composed chiefly of mixed tribes. I protest against such a union as that! Ours, sir, is the Government of a white race. The greatest misfortunes of Spanish America are to be traced to the fatal error of placing these colored races on an equality with the white race."[53]

This agreement between Northern Whigs and Southern Democrats came as a great relief to Southern Whigs, who could now be true to both their party and their section, and so they lined up by the speaker's podium to tell their colleagues that they, too, were opposed to incorporating Mexicans into the Union. Referring to Mexicans as "miserable, bigoted creatures," Florida's Edward Cabell asked, "shall we by an act of Congress, convert the black, white, red, mongrel, miserable population of Mexico— the Mexicans, Indians, Mulattoes, Mestizas [sic], Chinos, Zambos, Quinteros—into free and enlightened American citizens, entitled to all the privileges we enjoy?"

North Carolina Senator Willie Mangum warned his colleagues that the absorption of Mexico would lead the United States "to surrender its free institutions" and, although everyone knew the meaning of Mangum's euphemism, Delaware's John Clayton took a few minutes to spell out its significance: "There are in Mexico not less than eight millions of human beings, (men, women and children,) of a race totally different from ourselves—a colored population, having no feelings in common with us, no prejudices like ours; but, on the contrary, with prejudices directly the antipodes of all of ours, and especially bigoted on this very subject of slavery. Do you suppose that if you annex to the American Union these eight millions of people, backed by the millions of colored men in this country, they will remain idle spectators of the proceedings of this Government, stimulated as they will be by Abolitionists of the most fanatical cast? What, then, must become of that peculiar institution of ours, which has existed for so many years in this country?"[54]

Tennessee Whig John Bell provided the numerical calculations: "The several States or provinces of Mexico, twenty-one in number, now enjoy a separate political organization, with sufficient population in each to form a State under our system, except two. These may be well merged into one; which would still leave twenty new States to be admitted to the Union . . . We shall have forty new Senators." Looking to foreclose the alternative of annexation without statehood—the creation of an empire—Bell conjured a nightmare for the U.S. army of occupation: "do you consider the race with which you have to deal? . . . They are Spaniards, who walk the streets and highway, carrying the stiletto under their sleeve, the dagger under the folds of their cloaks, and bide their time. The race [has] deteriorated; but still blood will show itself, at the distance of centuries, when the cup of bitterness overflows, and when the oppressor least expects it."[55]

The supporters of All Mexico were hopelessly outnumbered, and only a few made feeble attempts to overcome the argument against expansion. Senator Ambrose Sevier extrapolated from the experience of Arkansas where, he alleged to senators who knew better, Indians "had become an orderly, prosperous, and easily-governed people"; he, for one, "did not see any greater difficulty in civilizing and governing the mass of Mexicans."[56] Only one All Mexico senator, Illinois Democrat Sidney Breese, offered anything close to a vigorous rebuttal to the torrent of opposition, but, he admitted, "I do not suppose, sir, the Mexicans are at this time fitted for an equal union with us; and much is to be done before they will be. By the infusion of our own population among them . . . together with emigrants from Europe, who will not be slow to avail themselves of the unsurpassed advantages such a country enjoys, a gradual change in their manner, customs, and language, will ensue." This dream of an "improved" Mexico in the distant future was the best answer that the All Mexico enthusiasts could develop to the question posed by South Carolina's Andrew Butler: "Why infuse the lifeless blood of a ruined Republic into the healthy veins of this Confederacy?"[57]

In the midst of this debate (nominally over the administration's request for funds to support ten new army regiments), in February 1848 the Treaty of Guadalupe Hidalgo arrived in Washington. Polk was still furious with Trist, yet he had to agree that the envoy had fulfilled his instructions. The treaty provided for the United States to assume U.S. citizens' claims against Mexico in an amount up to $3.25 million and to pay Mexico $15 million, in return for which Mexico was to accept the Rio Grande as the border with Texas and to cede to the United States a huge tract of land—essentially everything west of Texas to the Pacific Ocean.

The alternative to accepting Trist's treaty was to send a new negotiating team to Mexico. In that case no one was certain what might happen. The U.S. position would become hopelessly tangled in the upcoming electoral campaign, and Polk knew that the public had tired of the war; moreover, as Calhoun told a friend, Mexico's unstable political situation probably made renegotiation out of the question.[58] The Senate promptly consented to the treaty's ratification. Of the fourteen senators who opposed the treaty, seven were Whigs, most of whom wanted less territory, and seven were Democrats, all of whom wanted more.

Coming on the heels of the 1846 agreement with Great Britain to split the Oregon Territory at the forty-ninth parallel, Trist's treaty established the boundaries of the contiguous United States. Although its members did not know it at the time, the work of a generation had been completed. The debates over the Wilmot Proviso and All Mexico had the singular effect of increasing the salience of slavery in the debate over expansion. Soon antislavery Northern Democrats had formed a loose coalition with Conscience Whigs, leading to the creation of the Free Soil Party and the defeat of the fragmented Democrats in 1848. The following year Democrat James Buchanan lamented to Francis Blair that Texas was "the Grecian horse that entered our camp."[59] Beyond party politics, the conflict with Mexico accelerated the disintegration of the Union. Years later, one of the young officers who fought in Mexico and later rose to become President would write in his memoirs that "the Southern rebellion was largely the outgrowth of the Mexican war. Nations, like individuals, are punished for their transgressions."[60] Finally, the war with Mexico revealed the general tone that the United States would adopt in dealing with its Latin American neighbors. Borrowed in part from the thinking of John Quincy Adams's generation and now supplemented by the imperatives of Manifest Destiny, this tone would be a prominent part of the upcoming debates over further expansion into the Yucatán, Cuba, and Central America.

Chapter 3

Struggling over Slavery in the Caribbean

It is our mission to instill new life into the feeble and misgoverned people grown on the *débris* of Spanish power in America, and of the colonies still subjected to the withering influence of her rule; but we must not expect to fulfill it in our age, or in a century. We must not be tempted to absorb faster than we can assimilate.

⌒ *Representative Milton Latham, 1854*

The creation of a consensus against further expansion into the Caribbean went hand in hand with the struggle over slavery and disintegration of the Jacksonian party system. At mid-century the Whigs were nearly dead. A party of old-fashioned elitism and bourgeois values, of social deference and noblesse oblige, the Whigs had never been able to match the populist Jacksonian Democrats in a national contest refereed by the voting public. Only twice between John Quincy Adams's minority election in 1824 and the party's demise in the 1850s were Whigs able to win the presidency, and these two victories were the result either of economic distress (1840) or of a split among the Democrats (1848). And, in an eerie preview of the party's fate, both Whig victors promptly died.

The Whigs favored cautious expansion. Like the party's elders, in the late 1840s the young Whig representative Abraham Lincoln had condemned the Mexican war as unnecessary and unconstitutional,[1] and after the territorial gains of 1848, few Whigs wished for more. They could not even develop an internal consensus on what to do with the nation's newly acquired territories. When a recently elected Whig senator, William Seward, gave a speech supporting New Mexico statehood, the Whig old guard led by Henry Clay rose to advise him that New Mexicans were too "mixed" to permit equal footing with the citizens of Ohio, Michigan, Indiana, Illinois, Iowa, or Florida, all of which, Seward had noted, possessed smaller populations at the time of their admission to the Union. The difference, Clay replied, was not the size but the quality of the population: New Mexicans were a jumble of "Americans, Spaniards, and Mexicans; and about eighty thousand or ninety thousand Indians, civilized, uncivilized, half civilized, and barbarous people."[2] Statehood would have to wait until the territory's population had been bleached by Anglo settlers. And until the party could reach a consensus on what to do with the people whom it had just annexed, the Whigs certainly were not going to unite behind any effort to add additional territory.

The rival Democrats were severely divided over regional differences in economic development, differences that eventually focused upon slavery. On expansion, the primary questions that Democrats continued to address were how far and how fast to expand, not whether expansion was desirable. Some urged caution. In 1854 Representative Milton Latham from the sparsely populated state of California agreed that "it is our mission to instill new life into the feeble and misgoverned people grown on the *débris* of Spanish power in America, and of the colonies still subjected to the withering influence of her rule; but," he continued, "we must not expect to fulfill it in our age, or in a century. We must not be tempted to absorb faster than we can assimilate."[3]

On the other side of this internal party debate were the radical expansionists, loosely linked in the Young America movement. In the early 1850s they had seized control of the Democratic party from the "Old Fogies," and in both 1852 and 1856 the Democrats' platforms contained exceptionally ambitious territorial agendas. Within a few years a leading Young American, Stephen Douglas, would be the party's presidential candidate; in the meantime Young Americans pushed the Democratic party to focus upon territorial expansion. In his 1853 inaugural address, Franklin Pierce openly committed his administration to territorial expansion, and at the 1856 convention, delegates voted 229 to 33 to include in the platform a statement that "the Democratic party will expect of the next Administration that every proper effort be made to insure our ascendancy in the Gulf of Mexico."

Because the logical focus of expansion was to the south, this new wave of expansionist sentiment soon began to divide Democrats by section. Every potential acquisition required a discussion of whether slavery was to be permitted in the territory to be acquired, and by 1860 the party was so splintered that it was unable to choose a presidential nominee. The disintegration of the Democratic party was symptomatic of the divisions that developed among the general public. As the politics of expansion became alloyed with the politics of slavery, expansion evolved from a party to a sectional issue. The focus was on Mexico and Cuba.

Mexico had been devastated by the war. "There is something indeed almost painful in witnessing the degree of self abasement to which this people have been brought down from their former inordinate pride of place," reported U.S. Chargé Robert Walsh from Mexico City in late 1848. "The most open confessions are every where made that the fate of the country is sealed—that there is no possibility of ever resuscitating it to efficient existence." Defeat in war and the loss of half the national territory would seem to be an adequate reason for this despairing attitude, but Walsh had a different explanation: it was the product of the nation's racial makeup and the deficient leadership skills of the Hispanic elite, all of which could be "summed up in a few words—ignorance in the lower classes, corruption in the higher, impotency and despair in both." The political situation was especially unsettled, with Walsh noting that "rumors of revolution are constantly rife, and . . . the inhabitants seem to stand upon a volcano which may belch forth its flames whenever least they are expected."[4]

It was within this context that a civil war erupted in the Yucatán. Often called the Caste War because it pitted the Indian majority against the Creole elite, the dispute provided the All Mexico movement with a final opportunity to acquire even more Mexican territory. The initiative came from Yucatán's ruling autonomists, who had earlier sent a delegate to Washington both to proclaim the region's neutrality in the war between the United States and Mexico and to determine whether the Polk administration would be interested in annexing the peninsula. Secretary of State Buchanan had turned down the offer, but now, having discovered that Mexico's central government could offer no assistance in repressing the Indian rebellion, the desperate state governor offered sovereignty to any power that would offer assistance.

President Polk submitted the offer to the Senate in April 1848, telling Senators that the Yucatán "is situate in the Gulf of Mexico, on the North American continent; and from its vicinity to Cuba, to the capes of Florida, to New Orleans, and indeed to our whole southwestern coast, it would be dangerous to our peace and security if it should become a colony of any European nation."[5] Responsibility for shepherding the proposal through the full Senate fell to Edward Hannegan, the Indiana expansionist whose ringing oratory had been responsible for popularizing the Oregon battle cry, "54°40' or Fight." He began the floor debate by placing the question in a humanitarian framework, telling his colleagues that "Yucatan applies to the United States for assistance to protect her people against the barbarous savages who are pursuing them, their wives and families, to the ocean." Unable to match Hannegan's vivid image of Hispanics fleeing into the surf, another Democratic expansionist, Michigan's Lewis Cass, instead invoked God's will: "Providence has placed us, in some measure, at the head of the republics of this continent, and there never has been a better opportunity offered to any nation to fulfill the high duty confided to it, than the present affords to us."[6]

Not everyone was sympathetic to the Creoles' cause. Opposition Whigs noted that the natives seemed surprisingly barbarous after three hundred years of Spanish tutelage, and one U.S. official wrote Secretary of State Buchanan that the Creoles were besieged only because of "their want of energy, union, and courage to resist the ravages and incurtions [sic] of the Indians." Regardless of whether these Creoles deserved to be rescued, the opposition was concerned about the precedent-setting act of humanitarian intervention in a region noted for its instability. John Calhoun asked, "Are we to declare now, by our acts, that in all those cases we are to interpose by force of arms, if need be, and thereby become involved in the fate of all these countries? Ought we to set such a precedent? No."[7]

Sensing that his plea for humanitarian intervention was not working, Senator Hannegan adjusted his appeal to focus, as Polk had, on national security. "Sir," he responded to Calhoun, "there is a most formidable Power in Europe menacing American interests in that country, and let me add, American institutions [slavery], too. That power is hastening with race-horse speed to seize upon the entire Isthmus." Hannegan argued that "the possession of Yucatan by England would soon be followed by the possession of Cuba."[8] Hannegan and Polk's use of the Monroe Doctrine for further territorial expansion annoyed Calhoun, who had served in Monroe's cabinet and, as his reply to Hannegan demonstrated, had not forgotten a single detail of the discussions held a quarter-century earlier. His May 15 speech made hash out of the argument that the Yucatecan Creoles' predicament was even remotely related to the Monroe Doctrine.

Apparently the fear that Britain would acquire the Yucatán was unfounded. Having recently extended their position southward along the Mosquito Coast to incorporate San Juan del Norte, the British seemed content to let the United States have its way in Mexico. When the U.S. Army had captured Veracruz in 1847, Foreign Secretary Palmerston wrote his ambassador in Paris: "What dashing fellows our Cousins Transatlantic are . . . The Yankees will end by becoming masters of the great part of Mexico." That did not bother him, he continued, because "if the Union becomes very large it will either split, or else the multitude of conflicting interests which will belong to its various component parts will be an obstacle to any unnecessary war with a great maritime power and wealthy customer like England. Moreover a great extent of fine land to the south will render the Americans less anxious to think as[?] of Canada."[9]

Then, in the midst of the Senate debate, news reached Washington that the Caste War had ended, and Senator Hannegan moved to table his own bill. The one opportunity of the United States to annex the Yucatán peninsula quietly slipped away.

The other principal issue of postwar U.S.–Mexican relations would not be settled as easily, for it involved a subject of enormous interest to U.S. citizens: the construction of a transcontinental railroad. Rail transportation was quickly coming of age in the United States, and in 1850 Congress accelerated the process by expanding federal land grants to spur construction. The nation's railroad lines expanded from 8,800 miles in 1850 to 21,300 miles in 1854; by the outbreak of the Civil War, the nation had 30,000 miles of track, almost as much as the rest of the world combined. None of this growth was part of a grand project to construct a transcontinental railroad, however. Technical opinion held that a line across the Rockies to the Pacific would be extremely difficult to build, even more difficult to operate during the winter months, and, since public opinion was divided along sectional lines as to the appropriate route, almost impossible to encourage with federal legislation. Only in mid-1862 did an all-Northern Congress pass the law creating a mechanism for funding a northern transcontinental railroad, and it was no accident that it carried the name Union Pacific.

The pre–Civil War stalemate in the United States created considerable interest in two rail lines across Mexico—one along the Gila River and the other across the Isthmus of Tehuantepec. Years earlier, in 1842, President Santa Anna had awarded the right to operate a route across Tehuantepec to José de Garay. De Garay had then sailed for Europe in search of capital, and while abroad he decided instead to sell his concession to British merchants, who quickly resold it to two New Yorkers, Peter and Louis Hargous, owners of a shipping line between the U.S. east coast and Veracruz.

The de Garay grant provided for the construction and operation of a road, not for its defense, which Washington considered equally important; and so, in mid-1850, U.S. Minister Robert Letcher completed negotiations on a complementary treaty "for the protection of a transit way across the Isthmus of Tehuantepec." Letcher's treaty gave the United States the right to send troops to protect the roadway if requested by Mexico, or to intervene unilaterally in the case of interrupted relations. After several points were clarified, the Senate consented to ratification, but opposition quickly arose in Mexico to both the treaty and the concession, and in mid-1851 the Mexican congress nullified the de Garay grant and refused to ratify the Letcher treaty. Although Mexico cited a technicality as the reason for revoking the grant,[10] the primary but unspoken reason was that a grant to a Mexican citizen had become the possession of U.S. citizens.

The succeeding Pierce administration (1853–1857) was initially indifferent to the Tehuantepec line, with Secretary of State William Marcy instructing U.S. Minister James Gadsden not to pursue the matter. Marcy's indifference almost certainly reflected the fact that Pierce's senior advisors were partisans of the northern route along the Gila River—a route that would be of substantial benefit to the South. At the very end of his administration, however, Pierce responded to pressure from other Southern Democrats and instructed Minister John Forsyth to seek Mexico's approval of a U.S.-operated Tehuantepec line.[11]

Many of the details surrounding the line's financial transactions remain obscure,[12] and at the time they clearly confused U.S. Minister Forsyth, who had not only to fend off meddling by U.S. citizens (including a visit by Senator Judah Benjamin, who was simultaneously serving as the attorney for the Louisiana Tehuantepec Co.) but also to negotiate with the understandably suspicious government of Mexico. Forsyth soon came to loathe everyone involved, especially Mexican officials, writing that "the present government of Mexico is as useless for any good to the country and as vicious and tyrannical as it is possible to conceive." Forsyth was appalled by the "depth of duplicity and falsehood in the atmosphere of the Mexican Palace which cannot be conceived of in countries where fair dealing and honor are held to be as essential in politics and diplomacy as in the intercourse of private life." At a particularly difficult moment in mid-1858, Forsyth reported that "evil and only evil fills the land," and so he locked the U.S. legation and returned to the United States.[13]

Later that year Special Agent William Churchwell was sent to reopen relations with the Juárez government. He, too, characterized the Mexicans as "eight millions of people, degenerate and degenerateing." On the eve of the French intervention, Churchwell reported that "Mexico, assuredly, is in a most pitiable condition. Incessant intestine commotion since the achievement of her independence has at length involved her in difficulties so complicated and of such magnitude that her redemption from anarchy is scarcely within the range of possibility." Like Forsyth, he concluded that "no course can be adopted, but one, that will give the U.S. an effective but indirect Protectorate"; on another occasion he reported that the only hope was "efficient moral aid from an external source"—a premonition, perhaps, of the French occupation from 1862 to 1867. On the brink of its own civil war, the United States could offer no such assistance, but that circumstance did not change Churchwell's prognosis: "Of herself, you may depend upon it, she is incapable of accomplishing, either now or hereafter, any salutary improvement in her present demoralized condition."[14]

Just before the outbreak of the U.S. Civil War, negotiations were finally completed for a transit treaty by yet another envoy, Robert McLane. For a payment of $4 million, the McLane-Ocampo Treaty gave the United States the right to construct and protect three new routes across Mexico (Tehuantepec, Nogales to Guaymas, and the lower Rio Grande to Mazatlán via Monterrey), but the rising sectional dispute made ratification by the U.S. Senate impossible.[15] In the meantime, the Louisiana Tehuantepec Company obtained a new concession to construct first a stagecoach road and then a railroad across the isthmus, and with lobbying assistance from Louisiana's John Slidell, now a U.S. senator, the company obtained a Post Office subsidy to carry the mail between New Orleans and San Francisco. The railroad was never constructed, and the unprofitable stagecoach route was abandoned in 1859. Devastated by the Civil War, Southern entrepreneurs never rekindled their interest in the Tehuantepec route.[16]

The second part of U.S. railroad interest focused upon the northern Mexican territory immediately south of the Gila River. Through no fault of his own, Trist had drawn the border at the wrong spot, as Secretary of State Marcy noted in 1853: "A better knowledge of the country in the vicinity of the Gila has demonstrated the great difficulty,—not to say, impossibility— of constructing a rail-road along its banks or within the space on either side mentioned in the Treaty [of Guadalupe Hidalgo]." And so the Pierce administration's new minister to Mexico, James Gadsden, was instructed to seek Mexico's cession of a strip of land south of the Mexico–New Mexico boundary.[17]

A railroad entrepreneur from Charleston, South Carolina, Gadsden had been selected for his diplomatic post by President Pierce and Secretary of War Jefferson Davis because he was an ardent champion of a southern transcontinental route. As the new envoy set about his diplomatic task, he too noted that postwar Mexico was a demoralized society characterized by acute political instability. Gadsden observed serious behavioral shortcomings ("Mexicans are very slow in all their business transactions"), and he was not surprised to discover that a significant number of Mexicans wished to be annexed to the United States, with "protection as a Territory untill [sic] they are tutored and prepared for a final consummation of a Union of all the States of North America under one *Continental Federation.*"[18]

Receiving no encouragement for annexation from Washington, Gadsden turned to focus on the negotiation of territorial cessions. The precise nature of the negotiations remains murky, but at one point in late 1853, Gadsden informed Secretary of State Marcy that a bribe would be necessary: "*money:* & *money* alone would be the sole inducement on the part of Santa Anna to relinquish Territory & dismember further the Mexican Republic." [19] At first Marcy balked, but only at the amount requested, not at the idea of bribery. "The secret service fund at the control of the President is small," he replied, and an attempt to obtain a larger amount from Congress would trigger a prolonged partisan debate. But Marcy apparently agreed with Gadsden's argument that "immediate pecuniary means" were needed to convince Mexico to part with more territory, and he soon notified Gadsden that a special messenger had departed for Mexico with the cash that he had been able to scrape together.[20] The Gadsden Purchase was the outcome of this effort. In addition to bribes of an untold amount, the Treaty provided Mexico with $10 million in exchange for nearly 30,000 square miles to be used as a route for a southern railroad, a line that was completed only in 1883, long after the hopes of the South had been crushed.[21]

The final years of the Buchanan administration were spent in a fruitless attempt to expand into Mexico through the purchase of Lower California, most of Sonora, and the northern quarter of Chihuahua above the thirtieth parallel, all for $15 million. Mexico balked at any further sales, and then the U.S. Senate defeated the McLane-Ocampo Treaty,[22] signaling the end of the pre–Civil War drive for further expansion into Mexico. It had been blocked in part by the domestic dispute over slavery and in part by the general belief that there was not much more of Mexico worth acquiring, especially

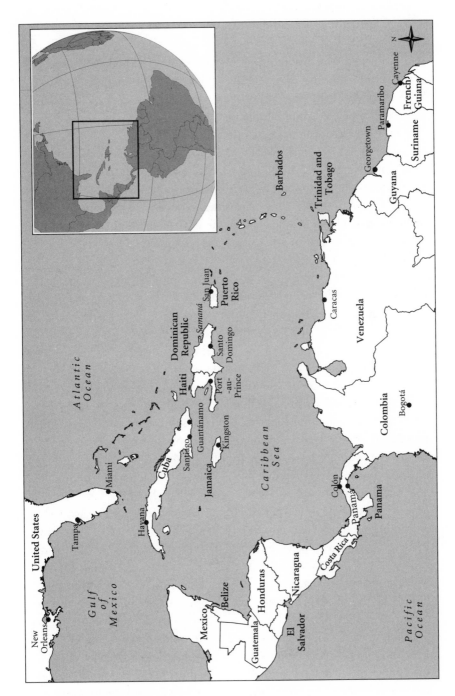

Map 2. Caribbean Region

if it involved the incorporation of Mexicans into the Union. This was the sort of conclusion that U.S. officials would reach elsewhere in the Caribbean region, for the Pierce and Buchanan administrations were simultaneously attempting to acquire Cuba.

Cuba's strategic geography had long attracted the interest of officials in Washington. Like Spanish Florida, the island was located alongside shipping lanes of rapidly growing importance, and it was sufficiently close to the thirteen colonies to serve as a base for armed aggression by a European enemy. Moreover, the fragility of existing colonial arrangements had been demonstrated in the second half of the eighteenth century, when Great Britain seized Havana briefly during the Seven Years' War, and then returned it to Spain in exchange for the Floridas in 1763. Acutely aware of this unique combination of geographic proximity and geostrategic instability, Thomas Jefferson was the first President to consider acquisition of the island. In 1807 Jefferson wrote to Secretary of State Madison that if there was to be a war with England, he preferred to fight Britain's ally Spain as well, for that would permit the United States to seize the Floridas and Mexico, and "probably Cuba would add itself to our confederation."[23]

As the nineteenth century unfolded, U.S. leaders remained vigilant lest a European adversary take advantage of instability in the region to seize Cuba. Like Jefferson and Monroe, John Quincy Adams considered Cuba and Puerto Rico "natural appendages to the North American continent." In 1823 he wrote to the new U.S. minister in Madrid that "the annexation of Cuba to our federal republic will be indispensable to the continuance and integrity of the Union itself." This is what the aging Jefferson told Monroe at the same time: "her addition to our confederacy is exactly what is wanting to round our power as a nation to the point of its utmost interest." A few months later he again wrote President Monroe: "I candidly confess, that I have ever looked on Cuba as the most interesting addition which could ever be made to our system of States. The control which, with Florida Point, this island would give us over the Gulf of Mexico, and the countries and isthmus bordering on it, as well as all those whose waters flow into it, would fill up the measure of our political well-being."[24]

Adams and his generation were willing to continue Jefferson and Madison's policy of leaving well enough alone, and neither he nor his immediate successors would move to acquire Cuba so long as the island remained a possession of Spain, an impotent European power.[25] But as Adams and Clay slowly faded out of the political picture, a new generation of leaders, emboldened by the successful war against Mexico, decided that the time was right to acquire Cuba. The issue arose during the 1848 debate over the proposed military occupation of the Yucatán, a debate that focused upon British expansionism. "We have seen Great Britain year after year extending her naval stations, until . . . she almost surrounds the Gulf of Mexico," asserted Mississippi's Jefferson Davis. "Yucatán and Cuba are the salient points commanding the Gulf of Mexico, which I hold to be a basin of water belonging to the United States. Whenever the question arises whether the United States shall seize these gates of entrance from the south and east, or allow them to pass into the possession of any maritime Power, I am ready, for one, to declare that my step will be forward, and that the cape of Yucatán and the island of Cuba must be ours." Although a reluctant expansionist, John Calhoun agreed: "it is indispensable to the safety of the United States that this island should not be in certain hands. If it were, our coasting trade between the Gulf and the Atlantic would, in case of war, be cut in twain, to be followed by convulsive effects."[26] Neither Davis nor Calhoun mentioned that Cuba was a slave society.

The 1848 debate over the Yucatán, which seemed to expand almost effortlessly to include Cuba, was dominated by Southerners eager to annex slaveholding societies. This was probably not President Polk's motivation, but the discussion in Congress clearly sparked his sympathy, and he confided to his diary that he, too, was now "decidedly in favour of purchasing Cuba & making it one of the States of [the] Union." And so on May 30, 1848, just weeks after the ratification of the Treaty of Guadalupe Hidalgo, he instructed his minister in Madrid, Romulus Saunders, to purchase Cuba for $100 million.[27]

But Polk resisted the urging of Young Americans to go beyond diplomacy.[28] His reluctance to become involved in Creole rebellions possibly reflected his interpretation of the reports that the Department of State was receiving from the U.S. consul in Havana, who noted "the listless, timid character of the population, great distrust of each other, and fear of loss of property, and risque of life"—all, the consul admitted, were characteristics "unworthy of those who are capable of a love of liberty." Unfortunately, he continued, "the Cubans are not animated by those high impulses of Patriotism which prompt to great, daring, and generous undertakings"; on the contrary, "the Creoles have an abiding conviction of their utter incapacity for self government, a conviction which must be felt by any one who has had opportunities of studying or even observing their character."[29] The consul clearly wished to make a case for an easy U.S. takeover, but lame-duck President Polk was hardly in a position to gain Congressional approval for a second war of expansion.

Having rejected armed intervention, Polk had no alternative strategy to pursue when Minister Saunders reported that the Spanish authorities "regard Cuba as their most precious gem and nothing short of extreme necessity will ever induce them to part with it."[30] Some in Washington suspected progress could be made if the U.S. minister would learn to communicate in either Spanish or French, but Saunders, whose despatches indicate only a modest mastery of English, was not about to try the impossible. Secretary of State Buchanan would later write that "a more skilful agent might have been selected to conduct the negotiations in Spain"; moreover, in a subsequent Senate debate, Whig John Thompson called Saunders "a rough, coarse, North Carolina man—a gentleman, though, but I reckon, from his manner and his walk and his look, (for he was ugly although he was clever,) the last man in the world to send upon such an errand."[31] Regardless of his diplomatic skills, Saunders was probably correct to assert, as he did in his final despatch, that the Spanish minister of foreign relations "believed such to be the feeling of the country, that sooner than see the Island transferred to *any power,* they would prefer seeing it sunk in the Ocean." That declaration sounded pretty definite to Saunders, who closed his mission and returned home.[32]

In keeping with the Whig philosophy of cautious growth, the succeeding administrations of Zachary Taylor (1849–50) and Millard Fillmore (1850–53) explicitly reversed Polk's policy. Taylor's new secretary of state, John Clayton, instructed the U.S. minister to Spain not to seek the island's purchase, but, he warned, the United States "is resolutely determined that the Island of Cuba shall never be ceded by Spain to any other power than the United States," and that "we shall be ready, when the time comes, to act. The news of the cession of Cuba to any foreign power would, in the United States, be the instant signal for war."[33]

Congress had already begun its bitter debate over slavery in the territory acquired from Mexico when Zachary Taylor's death thrust Fillmore into the presidency in mid-1850. The debate ended in September with the Compromise of 1850, a series of five separate bills that gave two clear victories to the abolitionists (the admission of California as a free state and the prohibition of the slave trade in Washington, D.C.); one to the slave states (a tightened fugitive slave law); left one issue for the future (Utah and

New Mexico were organized as territories without preconditions as to the status of slavery); and compromised on New Mexico's eastern border, placing it further to the east than Texans desired, in exchange for the federal government's assumption of Texas's state debt. The prize was California, and the compromise was therefore not an even draw. The Democratic senator from Illinois, Stephen Douglas, noted that perhaps as many as seventeen new states were to be formed in the Oregon Territory and the lands acquired from Mexico in the West. Given the decision regarding California, he asked his Southern colleagues, "where are you to find the slave territory with which to balance these seventeen free territories, or even any one of them?"[34]

The answer was Cuba. Mississippi's Albert Brown told his House colleagues that "if I go for the acquisition of Cuba, or for any other territory in the South, let it be distinctly understood now, and through all time, that I go for it because I want an outlet for slavery." Were Cuba to be acquired as a free state, he frankly admitted that "a vast amount of my zeal and enthusiasm would ooze out very suddenly." Some Southerners wanted Cuba because it would add new slave senators; Brown's idea, however, was to use Cuba to jettison the South's black population "when they have become profitless and troublesome." Just as Northern border states had sent blacks south when they abolished slavery, he said, "we, too, want a South to which we can send them."[35]

The Whig administration held firm against expansion. In his 1852 message to Congress, President Fillmore emphasized not simply that the United States had "no designs against Cuba," but that "I should regard its incorporation into the Union at the present time as fraught with serious peril." His reasoning captured perfectly the Whig approach to expansion: "Were this island comparatively destitute of inhabitants or occupied by a kindred race, I should regard it, if voluntarily ceded by Spain, as a most desirable acquisition. But under existing circumstances I should look upon its incorporation into our Union as a very hazardous measure. It would bring into the Confederacy a population of a different national stock, speaking a different language, and not likely to harmonize with the other members." In a direct reference to the Compromise of 1850, Fillmore also argued that the acquisition of Cuba "might revive those conflicts of opinion between the different sections of the country which lately shook the Union to its center."[36]

In response to the Taylor-Fillmore antipathy toward expansion, a series of privately organized armed invasions of Cuba were launched from bases in the Southern United States, but the principal leader of these expeditions, Narciso López, was captured and executed by the Spanish in mid-1851. Then, when the Democrats returned to the White House in 1853, they again made the annexation of Cuba a national policy. Franklin Pierce set the tone in his inaugural address, asserting that "the policy of my administration will not be controlled by any timid forebodings of evil from expansion." With Cuba the obvious but unspoken target, Pierce used national security to justify his policy: "it is not to be disguised that our attitude as a nation and our position on the globe render the acquisition of certain possessions not within our jurisdiction eminently important for our protection."[37]

Young America expansionists had been instrumental in according Pierce the Democratic nomination, and they were rewarded with a prominent role in the cabinet; "Old Fogy" William Marcy was named Secretary of State, but expansionist Jefferson Davis filled a key position as Secretary of War, while expansionists claimed most of the administration's European diplomatic appointments, including James Buchanan to Great Britain, John O'Sullivan (who coined the term "Manifest Destiny") to Portugal, August Belmont to The Hague, and Pierre Soulé to Spain. Soulé's appointment came as a surprise to many, for the Louisianan's well-publicized Senate position supporting both the López filibuster and the annexation of Cuba was almost certain to make him unwelcome in Madrid. Marcy's instructions to Soulé included a flat prohibition on acquiring Cuba,[38] but the Pierce administration soon fell under the influence of the Southern wing of the Democratic party, especially Jefferson Davis, and Marcy was forced to relent. The immediate cause of the policy shift was a series of reform decrees issued in late 1853 by the Spanish governor of Cuba, which provided stricter penalties for importing slaves, granted citizenship to freed slaves, and provided for the importation of apprentices from China, India, and Africa. These reforms started Cuba on the path toward abolition, and the Southerners were worried; soon even Secretary Marcy was voicing his concern that "the Africanization of Cuba is in contemplation by Spain." To preclude this calamity, the Secretary of State gave Soulé permission to broach the question of cession, instructing him to offer Spain up to $100 million, but not to let that stand as the final offer "if an additional amount of 20 or 30 millions were required."[39]

At this point the domestic debate over slavery fell like a lead weight on

U.S. policy toward Cuba and Spain. On May 26, 1854, Congress passed the Kansas-Nebraska Act, which effectively repealed the 1820 Missouri Compromise prohibiting slavery in the Louisiana Territory above 36°30′. It seems ironic today that such a grave step would be taken to gain a simple economic advantage, a northern railroad route to the Pacific, but at that time the location of railroad lines was crucial, and in this particular case it appeared that a major advantage was about to be awarded to the South. At precisely the moment that Congress was considering the Kansas-Nebraska Act, the Senate was also agreeing to the Gadsden Purchase, which acquired the territory needed for a southern rail line to the Pacific. Spurred to action by Northern economic interests, Senator Stephen Douglas sought Congressional permission to run a rival northern line from Illinois across federal land to California or Oregon.

But Congress had not yet taken the necessary step of "organizing" the Nebraska Territory west of Iowa and Missouri and east of Utah, and since members of Congress from the South correctly perceived the organization of Nebraska as the first step toward the creation of a new state (or states) above the line of the Missouri Compromise, *and* since organization of this free territory was coupled with the added menace of Northern railroad competition, they had not the slightest intention of supporting Douglas's initiative. But then he made them an offer that they could not refuse: a slave state. His organizing legislation divided Nebraska into two parts, giving settlers in the southern part of the Nebraska Territory, now known as Kansas, the right to determine for themselves whether to be slave or free. Kansas was above 36°30′, but immediately west of Missouri, a slave state. Since the history of U.S. expansion had been a flow from east to west, Southerners concluded that the new territory would be dominated by settlers sympathetic to slavery.

A complex man whose motivations are still debated, Douglas had made the decision that it was preferable to risk alienating abolitionists in order to obtain the handful of Southern votes needed for the organization of Nebraska. His mistake was to underestimate the depth of the abolitionists' hostility. At the moment Douglas was pushing his measure through Congress, a group of abolitionists—Free Soilers, Whigs, and Democrats—were meeting to form the Republican party, and abolitionists in Massachusetts were forming the Emigrant Aid Society to finance antislavery settlement of Kansas. Within a year, proslavery "border ruffians" from western Missouri were responding with violent attacks to intimidate abolitionist settlers; and the actions of these "hirelings, picked from the drunken spew and vomit of an uneasy civilization"—to use Senator Charles Sumner's classic characterization[40]—soon led to Bleeding Kansas, dual governance in the Kansas Territory, a series of political crises (including John Brown's rebellion), and the destruction of Franklin Pierce's administration.

On the day that the Kansas-Nebraska Act passed Congress, an oblivious Secretary of State Marcy wrote the U.S. minister in London, James Buchanan, that "the Nebraska question now disposed of, the next important matter to come up will be Cuba. It is under advisement, but the course to be taken, unsettled."[41] It did not take long for Marcy to realize that the administration's Cuba policy had been imperiled by the Kansas-Nebraska Act. Two months later he wrote John Mason in Paris "to tell you an unwelcome truth, the Nebraska question has sadly shattered our party in all the free states and deprived it of that strength which was needed and could have been much more profitably used for the acquisition of Cuba."[42]

Pushed by Southerners to acquire Cuba but having no idea how that goal might be achieved, in August 1854 President Pierce took the highly unusual step of ordering Soulé and the U.S. ministers to Britain and France "to meet, as early as may be, at some convenient central point, (say Paris), to consult together, to compare opinions as to what may be advisable, and to adopt measures for perfect concert of action in aid of your negotiations at Madrid."[43] Buchanan and Mason (and even Secretary Marcy) were unenthusiastic about the idea, but the two envoys arranged to meet with Soulé at Ostend and then Aix-la-Chapelle in mid-October.[44]

The resulting document, a diplomatic despatch known to history as the Ostend Manifesto, is a quintessential statement of the ardent expansionism of Young America. It begins with an assertion that "Cuba is as necessary to the North American republic as any of its present members," and therefore "an immediate and earnest effort ought to be made by the government of the United States to purchase Cuba from Spain." This was what Soulé had been trying without success to accomplish, of course, and since all three envoys knew that Spain was not interested in selling, they carried their argument one step further by asking, "after we shall have offered Spain a price for Cuba far beyond its present value, and this shall have been refused, it will then be time to consider the question, does Cuba, in the possession of Spain, seriously endanger our internal peace and the existence of our cherished Union?" Their response served as the Manifesto's conclusion: "Should this question be answered in the affirmative, then, by every law, human and divine, we shall be justified in wresting it from Spain if we possess the power."[45]

The Ostend Manifesto arrived in Washington on November 4, 1854, the same day that voters in an off-year election virtually annihilated the Democratic party in the North. The response of abolitionist Democrats to the Kansas-Nebraska Act had been to desert *en masse* to the Whigs, Republicans, and Know-Nothings, who swept every Northern state but two. Across the North, only 7 of 42 Democrats who had voted for the Kansas-Nebraska Act were reelected. The Democratic party lost 76 seats from their 159-member majority, while the Republicans, in their first national contest, swept to a 108-seat majority. It was an absolute catastrophe for the Democrats.

The voters had spoken with uncommon clarity, and the chastened administration's first response was to halt efforts to secure Cuba, which by then had been identified as the next "Southern" project after Kansas-Nebraska. A week after the election, Marcy instructed Soulé to confine himself to "free and friendly intercourse among official and influential men . . . to determine the proper course to be pursued in regard to opening a negotiation for the acquisition of Cuba." If, in this process, Soulé should discover that Spain was "averse to entertaining such a proposition . . . then it will be but too evident that the time for opening, or attempting to open, such a negotiation, has not arrived." Soulé read these instructions exactly as they were intended, and replied from Madrid that he had no desire "to linger here in languid impotence"; he hoped the President would accept his resignation.[46]

Having tucked Soulé back in the closet, Marcy then did his best to distance the Pierce administration from the Ostend Manifesto. He wrote to L. B. Shepard that Cuba "would be a very desirable possession, if it came to us in the right way, but we cannot afford to get it by robbery or theft . . . I am for getting the Island, if it can be acquired fairly & honestly, not otherwise."[47]

With the opposition vote split between Republicans and Whig-American (Know Nothing) parties, Democrat James Buchanan entered the White House in early 1857 and proceeded to lead the United States to the edge of civil war. It is not at all clear that Buchanan had a firm grip on prevailing political opinion, particularly on the issue of Cuba. His commitment to the island's annexation had its origin in an earlier era; in 1849, when he left his position as Polk's secretary of state, he wrote his successor: "Cuba is already ours. I feel it in my finger ends."[48] But much had happened since 1849, and even allowing for the fact that Buchanan had spent the preceding three years as minister to Great Britain, it is difficult to believe that the new President could be so out of touch as not to see the depth of political feeling aroused by any discussion of southward expansion. Nonetheless, the annexation of Cuba soon became Buchanan's favorite project.

At the same time, Congress was preparing to admit two new free states (Minnesota in 1858 and Oregon in 1859), and Southern leaders were growing every day more concerned that slavery was imperiled. "I want Cuba, and I know that sooner or later we must have it," said Mississippi's Albert Brown, now a Senator. "I want Tamaulipas, Potosi, and one or two other Mexican States; and I want them all for the same reason—for the planting or spreading of slavery." Brown continued: "It may seem strange to you that I thus talk of taking possession of Central America, or any part of it, seeing, as you suppose you do, that it belongs to some one else. Yet, it belonged to some one else, just as this country once belonged to the Choctaws. When we wanted this country we came and took it. If we want Central America, or any part of it, I would go and take that."[49]

Of all of the Caribbean Basin locales, Southerners made it clear that Cuba, the only slave society among the acquisitions being considered, was the most important. At this late date Southern leaders still thought there was a possibility of convincing Congress to finance the island's purchase. In 1859 Senators Jefferson Davis and John Slidell championed a bill to provide the President with a $30 million down payment should he manage to strike a bargain with Madrid. "The fruit is now ripe," Davis told his colleagues, "shall we gather it, or shall we permit it to remain on the stem until it decays, under the delusive hope that it may fall into our lap without a struggle? No; I propose we shall take it now." Davis made it clear that Cuba was to be only the first acquisition: "The North, enervated by the vices of luxury and love of wealth, may hang upon us like an incubus for awhile; but we will break from her thralldom ere long, and by the vigorous spirit of our pioneer people, yet uncorrupted by cities and towns, we will advance our eagles until the tread of our columns shall be heard upon this whole continent, and the shadow of their wings shall be seen in all its parts." Davis was convinced that the citizens of neighboring nations would be pleased by this invasion: "With swelling hearts and suppressed impatience they await our coming, and with joyous shouts of 'Welcome! welcome!' will they receive us."[50]

The $30 million proposal ignited a firestorm of opposition. Having watched the nation teeter toward the edge of civil war, John Thompson, a Kentucky Whig, argued that "at this time we ought to compact and bind together and build up and strengthen what we have. We are young. Let the gristle grow into the bone; let us get our muscles developed." Agreeing that there was "a great deal to be done in the interior of our country," John Crittenden, Kentucky's other Whig senator, was more adamant: "Tell me that Cuba is necessary, absolutely necessary to the preservation of this Government! Why, sir, my national pride as an American revolts at the idea . . . I do not want to see our Anglo-Saxon race; I do not want to see our American tribe, mingled up with that sort of evil communication." Mixing references to Cuba and Mexico, John Bell, a Tennessee Whig, warned that "when you shall have extended your dominion over the states of Mexico and Central America, you will have added twelve million of a population, for the most part perfectly imbecile." Next came Anthony Kennedy of Maryland, who wanted to assure his colleagues that "I do not stand here to denounce the institution of slavery. Unlike other gentlemen who do not understand that institution as well as I do, I am free to declare that, for the African, it is the best condition in which he can, by possibility, be placed. The slaves of our own country [are] the happiest race of laboring people in the world." But, he continued, "I do not desire to see here a wholesale naturalization of five or six hundred thousand Cubans, utterly ignorant of the institutions of this country, utterly unfit to exercise the rights of a republican government."[51]

And so it went. With each speech by a Southern slave owner, Cuba became equally important to abolitionists, and equally worrisome to Calhoun Democrats and the few remaining Southern Whigs. The nation's legislature was deadlocked as never before in its history.

Buchanan slowly became better acquainted with the odds against him. In 1858 the Democrats again lost the House, and in early 1859 the news came from Europe that the Spanish legislature had voted unanimously against the sale of Cuba. The new U.S. minister reported that the continual importuning of his predecessor had been "a grave offense to Spain"; he had been told that any further effort to discuss Cuba "would result in the immediate cessation of all intercourse communication [sic] between the two countries," at least on that issue.[52] Given these reports and his own revised judgment of the Washington political environment, Buchanan conceded. Knowing full well that neither the House nor the Senate could muster a majority on any controversial issue, in late 1859 he told Congress that it should decide whether to negotiate a transfer with Spain.[53] At long last Buchanan and the Southerners had discovered what Marcy and Pierce had learned years earlier—that the domestic conflict over slavery had effectively ended any hope of acquiring Cuba. But while a domestic political dispute may have frustrated this generation's hope, it did not destroy the general belief, best voiced by John Quincy Adams, that the annexation of Cuba was "indispensable to the continuance and integrity of the Union itself." Thirty years after the end of the Civil War, a new generation of U.S. leaders would fix its sights on Spain's Caribbean colony, and by the end of the century Cuba would fall under the control of the United States.

Chapter 4

Ending an Era: Regional Hegemony over a Defective People

I witnessed little else than ignorance, indolence, wretchedness, dishonesty, and misery, on the part of the great mass of the people, and selfishness, low-cunning, sordid ambition, avarice, and blood-thirsty revenge on that of those who either lead or force the unconscious, unthinking multitude.

⌒ *Special Agent Delazon Smith, 1845*

On July 13, 1854, a small U.S. Navy sloop, the *Cyane*, dropped anchor off San Juan del Norte, a village the British called Greytown, situated on a sleepy tropical lagoon at the Caribbean outlet of Nicaragua's San Juan River. What happened next, according to President Franklin Pierce, is that the ship's captain gave the residents "seasonable notice" that the U.S. government "required them to repair the injuries they had done to our citizens." Then, since "neither the populace nor those assuming to have authority over them manifested any disposition to make the required reparation," the *Cyane* began to destroy the village with its cannon. After a six-hour bombardment, the *Cyane's* captain determined that the residents remained unrepentant. "By their obstinate silence," President Pierce continued, "they seemed rather desirous to provoke chastisement than to escape it," and so the ship's crew was sent ashore to burn everything that was left. They did their job quickly, reembarked, and sailed away.

President Pierce justified the attack as retaliation for molestations by "a heterogeneous assemblage gathered from various countries, and composed for the most part of blacks and persons of mixed blood," who "had previously given other indications of mischievous and dangerous propensities."[1] This version is not even remotely close to the story offered by eyewitnesses. The immediate cause of the clash is clear: as the Vanderbilt riverboat *Routh* was descending the San Juan River toward Greytown in May 1854, it collided with a small Nicaraguan boat. Thus provoked, Captain T. T. Smith engaged in a sharp verbal dispute with the Nicaraguan boat's sailor, Antonio Paladino, whose lack of contrition led Smith to conclude that it was inappropriate for Paladino to continue living. After shooting him dead, Captain Smith proceeded downriver to Greytown, where he was surprised to discover that local authorities wished to charge him with murder. They were stopped by the vigorous protests of the U.S. minister to Nicaragua, Solon Borland, who happened to be on board the *Routh*. Later that day, when Borland paid a visit to the U.S. agent in Greytown, a group of demonstrators hurled refuse at the Americans, and a broken bottle grazed the cheek of Minister Borland. The *Cyane* was sent to avenge this injury to a U.S. diplomat.

Although precipitated by the murder of Paladino, the hostility of the local residents was related to a nagging labor dispute between Cornelius Vanderbilt's transit company and local laborers, who felt they had been treated unfairly when the company erected a private port at Punta Arenas across the river from Greytown. As a British naval officer reported, the economic threat to Greytown posed by this rival dock developed into "the most bitter hatred between the townspeople and the employés connected with the Transit company."[2]

In any event, it was President Pierce's view that the U.S. conduct was not so bad as the administration's rivals had claimed. "If comparisons were to be instituted, it would not be difficult to present repeated instances in the history of states standing at the very front of modern civilization where communities far less offending and more defenseless than Greytown have been chastised with much greater severity." Nor should it be forgotten, Pierce continued, that "most of the buildings of the place [were] of little value generally," and "owing to the considerate precautions taken by our naval commander, there was no destruction of life."

It is frequently the case that villages in small nations become enmeshed in disputes between great powers, and this was in fact the fate of San Juan del Norte. Although the *Cyane* destroyed a hapless Nicaraguan village, its true target was Great Britain. Since 1824 the British had claimed a vague authority over San Juan del Norte as part of their protectorate of the Mosquito Indians who inhabited the coastal region, but they arrived permanently only in 1848 when they formally changed the town's name to Greytown, after Sir Charles Grey, governor of Jamaica. This action extended Britain's control southward from Belize, and, as Pierce noted in his message to Congress, the residents' "conduct of wanton defiance on their part is imputable chiefly to the delusive idea that the American Government would be deterred from punishing them through fear of displeasing a formidable foreign power, which they presumed to think looked with complacency upon their aggressive and insulting deportment toward the United States."

President Pierce's concern about Great Britain's presence along the Mosquito Coast of Central America was understandable, for the United States now consisted of two parts, one on the Atlantic and the other on the Pacific; and "at the present time the most practicable and only commodious routes for communication between them are by way of the isthmus of Central America. It is the duty of the Government to secure these avenues against all danger of interruption." The initial expression of U.S. interest in the area had come in the 1820s, when the representative of the Central American Republic in Washington spoke with Secretary of State Henry Clay about the region's obvious selling point, its narrow girth; Clay and Adams were sufficiently interested in the prospects of improved transportation to appoint U.S. representatives to the region. Unlike the colony-minded British, however, Washington's interest was limited to the negotiation of a pro forma commercial treaty in 1825; and it was not until 1835, and then only in response to a request from the Senate, that the Jackson administration sent Charles Biddle on a mission to make "inquiries into the present state of the projects for uniting the Atlantic and Pacific Oceans through the Isthmus of Darien." In early 1837 President Jackson reported back to the Senate that neither a railroad nor a canal was likely to be constructed in the near future.[3]

Then, the issue of Atlantic-Pacific communication skyrocketed to the top of the U.S. foreign policy agenda when the acquisition of Oregon in 1846 and California in 1848 was followed almost immediately by the gold rush. At the time, it took six months for the mail to go from New York around South America to the Pacific Coast, and the transcontinental land route would remain long and hazardous until completion of the Union Pacific railroad in 1869. Until then, a bridge across the Central American isthmus—at Tehuantepec (130 miles), Nicaragua (188 miles), or Panama (47 miles)—was the quickest, easiest, and most secure route between the Atlantic and Pacific coasts of the United States. For this reason Central America became the principal focus of U.S. foreign policy in the years immediately prior to the outbreak of the Civil War.

Washington's early initiatives were in support of U.S. entrepreneurs. The

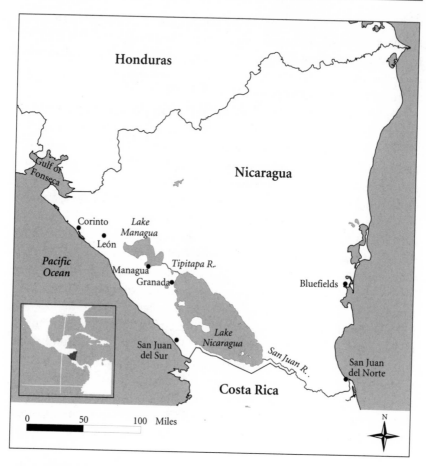

Map 3. Nicaragua

most significant of such aid came from the U.S. chargé in Bogotá, Benjamin Bidlack, who negotiated a treaty in 1846 that gave the United States the right to establish a transportation route across the isthmus of Panama in exchange for a U.S. guarantee of "the rights of sovereignty and property which New Granada has and possesses over the said territory."[4] Almost immediately William Aspinwall's Pacific Mail Steamship Company secured permission from New Granada (today's Colombia) to construct a transit route across Panama; in addition, a river barge–mule line opened in 1848, cutting the travel time between New York and San Francisco to 32 to 35 days. After the railroad was completed in 1855, the time dropped to 23 to 26 days.

Farther to the north in Nicaragua, in March 1849, the first U.S. citizens crossed Nicaragua on their way to California, and events moved quickly after that. By August, Cornelius Vanderbilt's representative had obtained a concession to build a Nicaraguan canal. When Vanderbilt was unable to raise the necessary capital—he claimed that the failure was due to the fact that Lake Nicaragua was too shallow to accommodate ocean liners—in May 1851, the agreement was renegotiated, creating the Accessory Transit Company to handle noncanal travel. Vanderbilt's Nicaraguan route ran 120 miles up the San Juan River to Lake Nicaragua, 56 miles across the lake in a steamer, and then a short 12-mile land crossing to ships at the Pacific port of San Juan del Sur. Opening in mid-1851, Vanderbilt's line operated profitably until its charter was revoked in February 1856, although Panama won the competition for customers during the period when both lines were functioning, moving more than twice as many people and four times as much gold as Nicaragua was moving.

These commercial ventures were complicated enormously as the 1850s unfolded, for Central America became the focus of a special type of entrepreneur, the filibuster.* Reared in the Manifest Destiny ambience that encouraged expansion, these adventurers claimed a variety of motivations, ranging from the expansion of slavery to financial gain to personal glory and political power. All were born a bit too late to participate in the expansion westward, and so their eyes fell upon Latin America as a target for future territorial aggrandizement.

The most persistent filibustering campaign centered on northern Mexico, but the most prominent filibuster occurred in Nicaragua. It was led by William Walker, who began his career with an ill-advised takeover of Baja California. Leading a fifty-man army, Walker first captured La Paz in November 1853 and declared the entire peninsula an independent republic. Moving northward, he then seized Ensenada, and in early 1854 he declared adjacent Sonora independent—just before being obliged to flee across the

---

*"Filibuster" is derived from the Dutch *vrijbuiter*—"freebooter," or pirate—which linguistically evolved into the Spanish *filibustero*. Gradually its meaning expanded to identify any type of private warfare (such as obstructing trade through privateering), and then in the late nineteenth century to characterize the obstruction of a legislature.

border to California ahead of pursuing Mexican troops. Then, in late 1854, Nicaragua's Liberals, locked in a civil war, invited North American mercenaries to assist their cause. Walker responded, and in mid-1855 led fifty-eight soldiers of fortune in a daring invasion that quickly moved beyond aid to the Liberal cause. Characterizing Nicaragua as "a country for which nature has done much and man little; and the effect of even what little man had done was marred by the constant signs of revolutionary violence,"[5] Walker sought to seize the country, and he did. Within months he had established sufficient control to have himself elected president, but his hold on power was always tenuous, and in mid-1857 he was forced to abandon the country. After four additional attempts to reestablish his authority, in 1860 Walker was captured by the British and handed over to the Hondurans, who shot him. Among those relieved by this outcome was Cornelius Vanderbilt, whose shipping business had been ruined.

Although ostensibly acting first on behalf of Nicaraguan Liberals and then for his own reasons, Walker also received substantial support from U.S. entrepreneurs, including two rivals of Cornelius Vanderbilt; the ubiquitous Caribbean deal maker William Cazneau (who contracted with Walker to provide Nicaragua with U.S. settlers); a number of New Orleans business leaders; and the Atlantic and Pacific Guano Company, an enterprise launched with President Walker's blessing by Joseph Fabens, Duff Green, and Charles Stearns. A related interest was that of the slaveholding South, which saw Nicaragua as another opportunity to add balance to the growing influence of free states in the Congress. Mississippi Senator Albert Brown was a spokesman for this interest, and in 1858 he complained that the U.S. government's opposition to Walker's expeditions showed favoritism toward Northerners working through Vanderbilt's "American [Accessory?] Transit Company. That company has its headquarters in Wall street and State street [in Boston]. If Central America is ever colonized through its agency, it will, at the same time, be Abolitionized."[6]

On the other side of the ledger, Walker's adversaries included U.S. foreign policy officials, who actively opposed all filibustering in the Caribbean Basin. In mid-1849, when the Taylor administration obtained evidence that eight hundred men were about to embark for Cuba on the first Narciso López expedition, the President responded by issuing a proclamation warning "all citizens of the United States who shall connect themselves with an enterprise so grossly in violation of our laws and our treaty obligations that they will thereby subject themselves to the heavy penalties denounced against them by our acts of Congress and will forfeit their claim to the protection of their country. No such persons must expect the interference of this Government in any form on their behalf, no matter to what extremities they may be reduced in consequence of their conduct."[7] This was more than a verbal warning: the U.S. attorney in New Orleans was instructed to prosecute violators of the Neutrality Act, and the Navy was ordered to patrol the Gulf coast to prevent López's departure from Round Island. The blockade was effective, and in September the Round Island filibusters surrendered and were taken on Navy ships to the mainland and then released. President Fillmore continued his predecessor's policy, declaring in his second annual message that "no individuals have a right to hazard the peace of the country or to violate its laws upon vague notions of altering or reforming governments of other states."[8]

All this activity was hardly surprising, coming from Whigs who opposed expansion, but the strong opposition to filibustering continued through the Democratic Pierce and Buchanan administrations. In his first annual message in 1853, President Pierce warned that should an expedition be organized on U.S. soil, "all the means at my command will be vigorously exerted to repress it," and a month later he issued a formal proclamation against filibusters who were preparing to invade Mexico. The day after signing the Kansas-Nebraska Act in May 1854, Pierce issued yet another proclamation, this one aimed at John Quitman's expedition to Cuba; in December 1855 he signed a final proclamation against Walker's activities in Nicaragua, and although the 1856 Democratic platform endorsed Walker's Nicaraguan adventure, Buchanan's first annual message to Congress in 1857 condemned "the lawless expeditions" that had been launched against Latin American republics: "Nothing is better calculated to retard our steady material progress or impair our character as a nation than the toleration of such enterprises in violation of the law of nations." Buchanan indicated the outrage that he would feel "if such expeditions were fitted out from abroad against any portion of our own country, to burn down our cities, murder and plunder our people, and usurp our government."[9]

Filibusters aside, the State Department recognized the need for a secure transit route, reporting to Congress that "it would be difficult to suggest a single object of interest, external or internal, more important to the United States than the maintenance of the communication, by land and sea, between the Atlantic and Pacific States and Territories of the Union. It is a material element of the national integrity and sovereignty."[10] The problem of continued access to this international highway had two dimensions. First, the report continued, was the unsettled political condition of much of Latin America: "in the midst of the violent revolutions and the wars by which they are continually agitated, their public authorities are unable to afford due protection to foreigners and to foreign interests within their territory, or even to defend their own soil against individual aggressors." In his final message in 1856, President Pierce notified Congress that because "local authorities cannot be relied on to maintain the public peace in Panama," he had decided "to station a part of our naval force in the harbors of Panama and Aspinwall [today's Colón], in order to protect the persons and property of the citizens of the United States in those ports and to insure to them safe passage across the Isthmus." The immediate precipitant of Pierce's action was the one-day Watermelon War, a riot that erupted on April 15, 1856, when a U.S. traveler quarreled with a Panama city fruit vendor over the cost of a slice of watermelon. A group gathered, general mayhem ensued, and when the dust settled, fourteen U.S. citizens had been killed and twenty-eight injured (versus three Panamanians killed and twelve injured).[11]

A modest naval force might have been able to handle these problems of indigenous instability, but it would not have been sufficient to address the second dimension of the problem, the challenge posed by Great Britain, a powerful rival that seemed to be everywhere the United States turned in Latin America. Much of Britain's ubiquity was interpreted as the result of Latin Americans' incompetence. As Secretary of State Buchanan asked U.S. Minister Elijah Hise, "What can the United States do to resist such European interference whilst the Spanish American Republics continue to weaken themselves by division and civil war and deprive themselves of the ability of doing any thing for their own protection?" Buchanan hoped that Central Americans would learn from the U.S. example ("in your intercourse with the authorities in Guatemala and the other States of Central America, you will not fail to impress upon them our example, where all political controversies are decided at the ballot box"),[12] but he recognized that Great Britain's prominence was not owing simply to Latin America's weakness: British merchants had high-quality goods to sell, its bankers had money to loan and invest, and they were backed by the world's largest navy.

The United States, in contrast, had an insignificant navy and was a net importer of capital. British trade with Latin America was perhaps four times that of the United States, and England's presence was particularly obvious in Central America, where English merchants had taken advantage of the Spanish decision to place their settlements in the highlands and to leave the Caribbean coastline to the native inhabitants. British traders had moved into Belize nearly two centuries before the independence movement of the nineteenth century, and by mid-century, when the United States developed an interest in the region, British influence extended down the Caribbean coastline from Yucatán to Panama. When news arrived in Washington of Britain's formal seizure of San Juan del Norte, Secretary of State Buchanan concluded that "her object in this acquisition is evident from the policy which she has uniformly pursued throughout her past history, of seizing upon every valuable commercial point throughout the world, whenever circumstances have placed this in her power. Her purpose probably is to obtain the control of the route for a railroad and a canal between the Atlantic and Pacific oceans through the lake Nicaragua."[13]

So it was that the British were entrenched in an area that the United States now needed to traverse, and it was for this reason, and not the expansion of slavery (or any other reason) that Central America became the site of U.S.-British conflict in the 1850s. The focal issue—control over the interoceanic transit routes—was addressed in 1846 by the Bidlack Treaty with Colombia and then in 1849 by two U.S. envoys, Elijah Hise and Ephraim Squier, who negotiated separate treaties with Nicaragua that would guarantee favorable treatment to U.S. capital and commerce. The Hise-Selvas Treaty of June provided the United States with control of a future route in exchange for a U.S. guarantee of Nicaraguan sovereignty over the Mosquito Coast and San Juan del Norte. Two months later, Squier signed a commercial treaty with Nicaragua that contained a provision confirming the Vanderbilt concession. Reluctant to become a guarantor of territorial sovereignty, the Taylor administration submitted neither treaty to the Senate; instead, Secretary of State Clayton negotiated with the British minister in Washington, Lord Bulwer, and in April 1850 they signed a treaty calling for joint control and neutral operation of any canal that might be built. The treaty pleased both Washington and London—Washington because it limited British activity in a region where it had long been dominant, and London because, as Palmerston later noted, it constructed "a barrier to North American advance . . . It fetters them and makes them halt."[14]

But not for long. Whig President Fillmore had done little more than grumble in 1852 when the British seized the Bay Islands off the Honduran coast, but the Pierce administration refused to be passive. Surrounded by expansionist Democrats and especially influenced by Jefferson Davis, his expansion-minded Secretary of War, President Pierce sought to preempt European competition by repeating the Monroe Doctrine in his 1853 inaugural address. Then, sensing an opportunity when the British became distracted by the Crimean War, in 1854 the administration began to press Britain to withdraw from Central America. This was when the *Cyane* destroyed Greytown. At the same time, Secretary of State Marcy instructed the U.S. minister to Great Britain to express opposition to England's continued hold on Belize, arguing that "her persistence in claiming a right to it would indicate on her part a policy of retaining for her hands the means of annoying this country, and of interrupting its intercourse with its possessions on the Pacific."[15] The pressure then increased: in his 1855 message to Congress, the first issue President Pierce raised was the presence of Great Britain in Central America; and in his special message on Central America six months later, the President expressed "surprise and regret" over Britain's recent reoccupation of San Juan del Norte, "the necessary terminus of any canal or railway across the Isthmus within the territories of Nicaragua." He continued: "It did not diminish the unwelcomeness to us of this act on the part of Great Britain to find that she assumed to justify it on the ground of an alleged protectorship of a small and obscure band of uncivilized Indians, whose proper name had even become lost to history."[16]

As the pre–Civil War decade continued, Southern expansionists in Washington became increasingly insistent that Britain leave Central America. In 1858, Mississippi Senator Albert Brown again spoke for many Southerners when he argued that "if we want Central America, the cheapest, easiest, and quickest way to get it is to go and take it, and if France and England interfere, read the Monroe doctrine to them."[17] Other Southerners urged caution, however, for Britain purchased over three-quarters of the cotton fiber and two-thirds of the raw cotton exported by the United States—and cotton, it is important to recall, provided the lion's share of all U.S. export earnings in the 1850s. Because England was by far the best customer of what was by far the nation's most important export, not everyone in Mississippi agreed that the United States should jeopardize that market for the sake of Central America.

The British, in turn, were offended by the attitude of the Pierce administration. Foreign Secretary Clarendon characterized the United States as a "nation of pirates," and Prime Minister Palmerston agreed that "these

Yankees are most disagreeable fellows."[18] In 1854, when rumors spread in Europe that the Pierce administration was considering the purchase of a Mediterranean naval base from the destitute prince of Monaco, Clarendon worried that the United States "would be robbing & quarrelling with every body within 6 months. The annexation of Piedmont would be their first object & it would be argued & advocated in all the American newspapers until we should have filibustering steamers fitted out to avenge some imaginary Sardinian insult."[19]

Palmerston and Clarendon were initially inclined to confront the United States in Central America. Complaining about the *Cyane*'s destruction of Greytown ("destroying on an unjust pretense a town known to all the world to be under the protection of Great Britain"), Palmerston asserted that "in dealing with Vulgar minded Bullies, and such unfortunately the people of the United States are, nothing is gained by submission to Insult & wrong; on the contrary the submission to an Outrage only encourages the commission of another and a greater one—such People are always trying how far they can venture to go." Clarendon agreed that "there is no country which will not in its turn be exposed to American insolence & encroachment unless the commercial & dollarmaking classes there are made to feel that their Government will end by turning all mankind against them & that there will be a universal league to compel them to observe the usages of civilized nations." But Palmerston also recognized that Britain had its hands full in the Crimea, and "a quarrel with the United States is at all times undesirable, & is especially so when we are engaged in war with another power."[20]

And so officials in London slowly concluded that the need to be attentive to British interests elsewhere, combined with the growing U.S. interest in Central America, made control over the Mosquito Coast not simply difficult but undesirable. When they had seized San Juan del Norte in 1848, the British thought it would become a major transportation hub; by 1855 the Panama railroad had reduced transit time across the narrowest part of the isthmus to less than half a day; in contrast, Vanderbilt's Nicaragua concession was about to be revoked, and Walker's highly publicized adventures had convinced merchants and the traveling public to use the Panama route. Clarendon blamed the Nicaraguans, writing in mid-1857 that "those wretched mongrels in Central America are absolutely inviting aggression. Their utter inability to do any thing but cut each other's throats & the proofs they have recently afforded that neither common danger nor common interest can induce them to unite offer temptations to filibusters which cannot be resisted." In 1847 Palmerston had noted that going to war to support "such a set of people as the Mexicans would not go down with the H[ouse] of C[ommons] in the best of times"; a decade later there was even less support for fighting on behalf of the Central Americans.[21]

At the same time, Clarendon believed U.S. expansion was almost certain to continue, now aided by filibusters who were "of course acting under secret instru[ction] from the U.S. Govt." Clarendon's fears had been exacerbated by the British minister in Washington, who "has sent me a catalogue of infamous but very hostile proceedings toward us on the part of the U.S. Govt."[22] Concluding that U.S. dominance of Central America was inevitable, in 1857 Clarendon wrote Cowley in Washington that unless the French and British were willing to station troops in the region, "sooner or later those countries will be overrun and occupied just as have been Louisiana, Texas, and California added to the Union." Palmerston agreed: "I have long felt inwardly convinced that the Anglo-Saxon Race will in Process of Time become Masters of the whole American Continent North and South, by Reason of their superior Qualities as compared with the degenerate Spanish and Portuguese Americans."[23]

In this way British officials slowly convinced one another that Britain would benefit if the United States controlled Central America. As early as 1854, Aberdeen admitted that Great Britain's claim to the Mosquito Coast and Greytown was "very questionable" and that its title to the Bay Islands was "little better than manifest usurpation," but he had worried that withdrawal would be interpreted as a symbol of weakness during the Crimean War.[24] By 1856 that war was over, and an *Economist* editorial probably captured British elite opinion: "You cannot for ever uphold the semi-civilised, semi-Spanish, degenerate Mexicans or Nicaraguans—with their incurable indolence and their eternal petty squabbles—with their effeminate habits and their enfeebled powers—against the hasting, rushing, unresting, inexhaustible energies of the Anglo-Saxon Americans. Criminal, coarse, violent as they often are, it cannot be denied that they rule and conquer by virtue of superior manhood . . . Central America peopled and *exploité* by Anglo-Saxons will be worth to us tenfold its present value." This was also the view of many U.S. officials, including Representative Thomas Anderson of Missouri, who told his House colleagues in 1859 that if the United States were to assume control over Central America, "wave upon wave of immigration will roll in upon that country, until, ere long, its internal wars, ignorance, superstition, and anarchy, will be supplanted by peace, knowledge, Christianity, and our own Heaven-born institutions."[25]

And so Palmerston, who never quite mastered the rules of capitalization, wrote Clarendon that the Yankees "are on the Spot, strong, deeply interested in the matter, totally unscrupulous and dishonest and determined somehow or other to carry their Point; we are far away, weak from Distance, controlled by the Indifference of the Nation as to the Question being discussed, and by its Strong commercial Interest in maintaining peace with the United States."[26] With only limited rights to defend, the English ceded a dominant role in Central America to the United States. They signed one treaty with Honduras in November 1859 that provided for the reversion of the Bay Islands, and another with Nicaragua in August 1860 relinquishing their protectorate over the Mosquito Coast. With this nagging problem resolved, in late 1860 President Buchanan could report in his final annual message to Congress that "our relations with Great Britain are of the most friendly character."[27]

True to the 1856 Democratic party platform, the Buchanan administration had been careful to "hold as sacred the principles involved in the Monroe Doctrine." In Central America, the United States had demonstrated that the physical expansion of the Manifest Destiny era was matched by a corresponding growth in the mental horizons of U.S. officials, a new conception of the nation's sphere of influence. The fledgling republics of Central America were an ideal site for this demonstration: they were themselves impotent, they were close to home, and they had become a major transit route between the two coasts of the continent-wide republic, ensuring an ever-increasing U.S. presence in the Isthmus. But even though this generation of U.S. officials could make Central America safe from European encroachment, the question of what the United States wanted to do with this new freedom of action would have to await another era. Within a few months the South would fire on Fort Sumter, and the United States would be sucked into the maelstrom of its own civil war.

The second generation of U.S. envoys to Latin America had completed its work. It had expanded the nation's borders significantly but had not reached a firm decision on further expansion southward. It had checked British power in the Caribbean region but had not replaced their economic influence. Most significantly, it had helped to cement a mental picture of Latin America in the U.S. political consciousness that, like the view of John

Quincy Adams's first generation, highlighted the cultural gulf separating the United States from Latin America. But in contrast to the opinion of Adams and his generation, which was based upon an ethnocentrism uninformed by firsthand knowledge of Latin America, this second generation of U.S. envoys actually lived and worked in the region. The interesting thing about this generation is the extent to which its predispositions solidified during its residence in the region.

Life was not easy for the pre–Civil War generation of U.S. representatives in Latin America, as the experience of Commodore Oliver Hazard Perry testifies. In 1819 the hero of the Battle of Lake Erie was instructed to travel to Venezuela and Buenos Aires in order to protest the depredations of privateers flying South American flags.[28] The first stop was Bolívar's headquarters at Angostura, 300 miles up the Orinoco in a shallow-draught sloop. Perry's notebooks contain some of the most vivid passages ever written about the frustrations of living in the tropics. Here is one day's entry:

> Confined on board a small vessel. Rise in the morning after being exhausted by the heat. The sun, as soon as it shows itself, striking almost through one; moschetoes, sandflies and gnats covering you. As the sun gets up, it becomes entirely calm, and its rays pour down a heat that is insufferable. The fever it creates, together with the irritation caused by the insects, produce a thirst which is insatiable; to quench which, we drink water at eighty-two degrees. About four o'clock, a rain squall, accompanied by a little wind, generally takes place. It might be supposed that this would cool the air; but not so. The steam which rises as soon as the sun comes out, makes the heat more intolerable. At length night approaches; the wind leaves us. We go close inshore and anchor; myriads of moschetoes and gnats come off to the vessel, and compel us to sit over strong smokes created by burning oakum and tar, rather than endure their terrible stings. Wearied and exhausted, we go to bed to endure new torments. Shut up in the berth of a small cabin, if there is any air stirring, not a breath of it can reach us. The moschetoes, more persevering, follow us, and annoy us the whole night by their noise and bites, until, almost mad with the heat and pain, we rise to go through the same troubles the next day.

While in Angostura, Perry contracted yellow fever and died aboard the sloop as it carried him downriver. Left with the task of deciphering the

Commodore's log, his purser reported that among "the various impressions made upon the mind of the Commodore" was that "ignorance of the grossest kind is a prevailing feature in the character of the people."[29]

Commodore Perry's fate was far from unique, and his trials were anything but uncommon. Only rarely could early U.S. envoys fully accomplish their instructions, and all placed the blame on Latin Americans, as the mid-nineteenth-century despatch from the U.S. chargé at Caracas illustrates: "Mr. Pedro Carlos Gellineau has been appointed Secretary of the Treasury and of Foreign Affairs. He is the fourth individual who has filled these offices during the four months now elapsed of the year 1851. The Department will readily perceive the difficulties which these incessant changes of Ministry oppose, to the transaction of any business with this Government." At about the same time the first U.S. diplomatic representative in La Paz explained that "I have now been more than two months in Bolivia, without being able to find any Government with whom it was possible to transact business, or to whom I could properly present myself as a Minister of the United States. Since the sixth of October last, the Republic has been in a state of complete anarchy, its Congress dispersed, its capital deserted by every national officer, its business wholly suspended, the lives and property of its citizens without any adequate protection, and all its resources exhausted in the support of two opposing armies."[30]

Once the envoys had established themselves, they began to describe their environment. Their despatches almost always focused first on the region's economic underdevelopment. "When I see how much nature has done for this part of the globe I cannot but exclaim to myself what a pity it is that the people cannot appreciate their advantages and improve them," wrote U.S. Chargé Richard Pollard after surveying the entire West Coast of South America in 1838. The first U.S. envoy to Ecuador, Special Agent Delazon Smith, was appalled by the backwardness he encountered, and eight years later Smith's successor reported that "there [still] is not a carriage nor a wagon and not more than a dozen carts in the whole Republic," that "crooked sticks instead of ploughs are used in cultivating the Earth," and that "all vessels under the Ecuatorian flag united are not equal in tonnage to one of our first class Clipper ships."[31]

The envoys especially wanted to educate officials in Washington to Latin America's political instability, as an early U.S. chargé in Argentina, Francis Baylies, instructed Secretary of State Livingston: "Such, Sir, is the happy condition of society in this *Sister Republic* of ours, whose free *and* liberal principles and hatred of despostism [*sic*] have so often been themes for the panegyrics of our mistaken, romantic and imaginative politicians. I think one weeks [*sic*] residence here would cure them of this hallucination."[32] Several reports from Peru described "a tissue of violence, oppression, rapine, and persecution," and sought to clear up any misconceptions in Washington: "the Republics or rather Military Despotisms of South America are not well known by the people of the United States. Instead of being governed by a legal or constitutional authority, submitting to, and acting upon the broad principles of international law, the Supreme power is generally in the hands of some military chief, who, looking only to his personal aggrandisement, tramples upon the rights of all, countrymen, and foreigners who are unable or unwilling to defend themselves."[33] The next U.S. chargé in Lima continued this educational effort, but obviously felt frustrated by his inability to describe the depths to which Peruvian politics had sunk in the mid-1840s: "it is difficult, without residing in this country and being an eye-witness, to form an idea of the abject and miserable condition to which it is reduced and of the disorder, anarchy and profligacy that prevail."[34]

These reports of Latin America's political instability were often linked to charges of official corruption. In Argentina, reported Chargé Baylies, "the business of Government is a job and its offices are considered as a kind of employment to gain money—a sort of a license to take bribes," and this dishonesty spilled over into international relations. Argentines "consider the violation of a treaty no greater offence than a lie told by a schoolboy," and "if a temporary advantage could be gained they would violate a treaty on the day of its ratification." "You cannot conceive the extent of their Stupid insolence and meanness," he wrote on another occasion. "I pray God to deliver me from the hands of these Philistines."[35]

The interesting thing about these despatches is not how well they meshed with the predispositions of officials in Washington, but what led U.S. envoys to write them. The easy answer is that they reported what they saw, but in many cases these were snap judgments. Baylies, for example, closed the U.S. legation in Buenos Aires (which remained shut for twelve years), and justified his action by depicting Argentines as incorrigible liars. But Baylies had no prior experience in Latin America, nor a command of Spanish, and he had spent fewer than four months at his post. Despite these handicaps, six weeks after he arrived in Buenos Aires, he reported that Argentines are "proud, bigotted, narrow-minded and oppressive."

Delazon Smith also prematurely terminated his mission to Ecuador.

Twenty-nine years old, homesick, and eager to return to the United States and make his mark (which would include a brief tenure as Oregon's first U.S. senator), in 1845 Smith wrote from Quito that "I shall best answer to the letter and spirit of my instructions from the Department of State . . . by returning immediately to the United States, than by remaining here for an indefinite number of months in waiting upon an ignorant, a selfish, a pennyless, and a rebellious people for the formation of a Government which I can properly address;—a people whose presumption displays a constant burlesque upon the very name of republican." Like Baylies, Smith wrote with a confident pen, seeming to know his subject. He reported that "in travelling nearly five hundred miles on the territory of this republic, I witnessed little else than ignorance, indolence, wretchedness, dishonesty, and misery, on the part of the great mass of the people, and selfishness, low-cunning, sordid ambition, avarice, and blood-thirsty revenge on that of those who either lead or force the unconscious, unthinking multitude."[36] Yet Smith spent less than a month in Quito. His five hundred miles were straight in (arriving from Lima on July 16) and straight out (leaving for Bogotá on August 12). Like Baylies, he may have seen what he reported, but he could not possibly have seen it in sufficient depth to generalize about the character of Ecuadorans.

The rush to judgment does not fully explain the content of these despatches, however, for most of Baylies's successors reached much the same conclusions. Two decades later, one successor wrote that Argentine politicians were characterized by "treason, and venality, to an extent not to have been expected in even the most demoralized and corrupt communities," and seven years after that another U.S. minister reported on the general disorder that existed throughout the country.[37] Similar despatches about political instability and corruption flowed northward from every corner of Latin America, many of them written by knowledgeable envoys. They indicated that Venezuela's "Ministers of State are inferior men," that the government of Nicaragua had been "left to incompetent men," that Brazilians were a "degraded & corrupt people, who are ignorant of the first rudiments of either administrative or judicial justice," and, generally, that "in these new countries all is intrigue, treachery and bribery in conducting war measures, as in most other matters. Open and magnanimous war is unknown among them."[38]

Some envoys attempted to explain rather than simply describe Latin America's underdevelopment, instability, and corruption. Their over-

whelming consensus was that Latin Americans, products of Hispanic culture intermingled with native blood, were an inferior branch of the human
species. Even where indigenous blood had not been mixed with the European, as in Argentina, the nation's leaders were considered "*fac-similes* of
the old Spaniards[:] proud, bigotted, narrow minded and oppressive: hat-
ing all foreigners, especially Protestants."[39] This Hispanic heritage presumably predisposed Latin Americans to irrational behavior. "The Spanish
Americans are incapable of calmly examining a subject of public interest or
dispassionately discussing the acts of a Government," was a typical comment from Peru, as was that of the U.S. chargé in Caracas, who reported
that since Venezuelans were incapable of "acting upon any settled principle,
expedients and speculations rise continually in their excited imaginations,
until the mere shadow of events produce to them, substantial reality."[40] In
1847 the U.S. chargé in Buenos Aires, William Harris, wrote that "the
actions of these people often seem prompted by motives as extraordinary
and unaccountable as their general character is contradictory and irrecon-
cileable [sic] to that of the great mass of mankind." He depicted Argentines
as edgy adolescents whose "estimate of their own prowess and resources, is
extravagant and ridiculous." These were people "who spend their whole
lives in trifling with great subjects, and in exhausting their utmost powers
in disputing about small ones."[41]

The darker side of this irrational behavior was a disturbingly high level
of violence, often bordering on savagery. Some of this was common street
crime,[42] but the envoys' reports tended to focus upon *political* violence,
which was almost always described as unnecessary or capricious. Advising
Washington of the approach of war between Peru and Bolivia, an 1840
despatch from Lima observed that "there is really no cause for war; but the
military adventurers who rule these countries, being ever ready to shed
blood, it is not material, whether there is cause or not." An envoy to
Colombia wrote that "again, Venezuela, seems almost determined to pick a
quarrel and Get up a war between the two Republics" despite the fact that it
had only "pretended Grievances, no one of which would justify a school
boy fight." In a despatch about Uruguay, William Harris referred to "the
restless spirit of a people, whose appetite for rapine, blood, and revolution,
can never be satiated"; and from Chile came the summary evaluation that
"all these new countries appear to be dissatisfied in Peace and prosperity.
They must fight within themselves or against one another. They cannot be
content in tranquility and settled order."[43]

The composite picture sent to Washington by the second generation of U.S. envoys, then, was of an economically underdeveloped and politically unstable region. And the explanation offered for these unfortunate conditions was that Latin Americans, heirs to Hispanic civilization, were irrational and often uncontrollably violent. This vision of Latin Americans was sitting on the State Department shelf when, after recovering from its own Civil War, the next generation of U.S. foreign policy officials began to develop an interest in the region.

Chapter 5

Beginning a New Era:
The Imperial Mentality

The great nations are rapidly absorbing for their future expansion and their present defense all the waste places of the earth. It is a movement which makes for civilization and the advancement of the race. As one of the great nations of the world, the United States must not fall out of the line of march.

⌢ *Senator Henry Cabot Lodge, 1895*

By 1865 the citizens of the United States were exhausted. Four years of bloodshed had left more than 600,000 soldiers killed, untold numbers maimed for life, and almost every citizen grieving a relative. But slavery had been abolished, the Union preserved, and the vicious political battles of the 1850s would no longer need to be fought. Now it was time to recover—to till new lands and develop new resources, to build rather than destroy. The United States turned inward, and in a single generation the nation was transformed.

It was during these final three decades of the nineteenth century that U.S. citizens slowly developed the desire to acquire an overseas empire. This was different from the growth prior to the Civil War, when the United States had expanded by absorbing sparsely populated lands to the West, always arguing, as Teddy Roosevelt did about Texas, that the people already living in the area benefited as their nationality was extinguished by the beneficent embrace of the United States: "It was out of the question that the Texans should long continue under Mexican rule; and it would have been a great misfortune if they had. It was out of the question to expect them to submit to the mastery of the weaker race."[1]

With this logic, the United States had acquired all the territory to the Pacific Ocean. Expansionists then directed their energies southward, but growth had stopped when it became intertwined with the domestic issue of slavery. Once the Civil War had resolved this conflict, the momentum of expansion could never be regenerated. In part, this was the case because there was no longer any need for slave senators from Cuba, the Yucatán, or Nicaragua, but it was also because Southerners did not want to add Latins to their confederacy. As William Yancey told his fellow delegates to the Alabama secession convention even before the war, Mexican annexation would involve the absorption of "a mass of ignorant and superstitious and demoralized population."[2] When the war ended, the North considered sending emancipated slaves to settle in Central America under U.S. protection, while the South's defeat prompted thousands of Confederate troops to flee southward, most to Mexico (because it was nearby) and Brazil (where slavery had not yet been abolished). Disillusioned by what they found, nearly all soon returned home. Reinforcing the Southerners' disillusionment with Latin American migration were the 1862 Homestead Act, which opened vast new federal lands to the West, and the transcontinental railroad, which nearly eliminated the significance of the Central American isthmus to this generation. By the late 1860s, the South's enthusiasm for expansion had completely disappeared.

At this point, the banner of southward expansion was passed to a small group of Northerners led by William H. Seward and Ulysses S. Grant, both intellectual holdovers from the earlier era of Manifest Destiny. As secretary of state during both the Lincoln and Johnson administrations, Seward was the last of the great expansionists of his generation.[3] Best remembered for his purchase of Alaska, Seward also sought to acquire Panama, Hawaii, Midway, and especially the Virgin Islands. Although he concluded an agreement to pay Denmark $7.5 million for two of the Virgin Islands in October 1867, the Senate Committee on Foreign Relations refused to release the treaty until after Seward left office, when it was reported unfavorably and tabled. The Senate's foot-dragging was a product of domestic political divisions over Reconstruction and general frugality. At almost the exact moment that news of the Virgin Islands treaty became public, the House both impeached Seward's President, Andrew Johnson, and placed his administration on notice that "in the present financial condition of the country any further purchases of territory are inexpedient."[4]

The second indication that the political mood was unfavorable to expansion came early in the Grant administration (1869–77) when Cuban Creoles, having launched a major bid for independence from Spain, sought support in the United States. A month after Grant's inauguration, the House passed a resolution of sympathy for the rebels, and in May the insurgents named Confederate General Thomas Jordan as their military chief of staff. Soon several filibustering expeditions had been launched from the United States, but unlike the pre–Civil War era, however, there was little discussion of annexation; instead, Secretary of State Hamilton Fish pushed through the cabinet a plan to negotiate with Spain for the independence of Cuba, with the U.S. role limited to guaranteeing bonds that the Cubans would issue to buy out the Spanish. When Fish discovered only weak cabinet support for a plan that Madrid would never accept anyway, the United States quietly decided not to intervene.

By far the best indicator that the era of expansion had come to a halt was the fate of a proposed treaty to annex the Dominican Republic. The issue was straightforward: Dominican officials offered their country to the United States as a gift. Did officials in Washington want to accept it?

Not so long as the country shared an island with black people. When the Dominican Republic declared its independence from Spain in 1821, the United States had refused to recognize that nation's existence because it was considered either a mulatto republic or a dependency of Haiti. Within weeks of its independence, the Dominican Republic had in fact been incorporated into Haiti, and although independence was reestablished in the mid 1840s, it was not until 1849 that Zachary Taylor sent Benjamin Green to determine whether the nation qualified for recognition. One criterion that Secretary of State Clayton told him to employ was "whether or not the Spanish race has the ascendancy in that government, is likely to maintain it, and whether in point of numbers that race bears as fair a proportion to the others as it does in the other Spanish American States."[5] Although Green and subsequent informal agents recommended recognition, the slavery issue made any decision impossible, and so in 1861 President Santana instead proclaimed the Dominican Republic's reannexation to Spain. The U.S. Civil War was over when independence was restored in 1865, and in September 1866 Washington recognized the country.

Haiti remained in diplomatic limbo until June 1862. The issue of recognition had been decided in 1826 during the debate over U.S. participation in the Panama Congress, when Southerners such as Georgia Senator John Berrien insisted that recognition of Haiti "would introduce a moral contagion, compared with which, physical pestilence, in the utmost imaginable degree of its horrors, would be light and insignificant." Berrien asked, "is the emancipated slave, his hands yet reeking in the blood of his murdered master, to be admitted into [Southern] ports, to spread the doctrines of insurrection, and to strengthen and invigorate them, by exhibiting in his own person an example of successful revolt?" Missouri Senator Thomas Hart Benton favored only commercial relations: "The peace of eleven states in this Union will not permit the fruits of a successful negro insurrection to be exhibited among them. It will not permit black Consuls and Ambassadors to establish themselves in our cities, and to parade through our country, and give their fellow blacks in the United States, proof in hand of the honors which await them, for a like successful effort on their part. It will not permit the fact to be seen, and told, that for the murder of their masters and mistresses, they are to find *friends* among the white People of these United States."[6]

On the other hand, U.S. officials had long believed that the United States needed a Caribbean naval base to protect commerce flowing out of the Mississippi Valley and Gulf ports. In the 1850s the Pierce administration was so eager to obtain such a base (and perhaps a slave state) that it appointed an unofficial special agent to visit the Dominican Republic in late 1853. After his initial reports appeared favorable, William Cazneau was instructed to negotiate a treaty permitting the United States to establish a naval base at Samaná Bay. Both the British and the French opposed a U.S. military presence, and their envoys in Santo Domingo convinced the Dominican government to insert into Cazneau's October 1854 agreement a stipulation that Dominican citizens be treated as white people when in the United States. That was the end of the treaty because, as Secretary of State Marcy noted, any treaty that "proposed to place Dominicans in this country, of all complexions, on the same footing as citizens of the United States . . . would certainly be contrary to the feelings of a large proportion of our citizens, which the government, in such a proceeding, is bound to respect."[7]

There the matter rested until 1866, when Cazneau convinced William Seward to visit the Dominican Republic to discuss the offer of annexation—the first foreign trip by a sitting secretary of state. As early as 1848 Seward had argued that the absorption of Mexico's territory would pose no problem, since "all exotic elements are rapidly absorbed and completely assimilated." The Dominicans would be no more difficult than the Mexicans, whom Seward characterized as "the effeminate descendant of the Castilian."[8] Thus after meeting with Dominican President Buenaventura Baez, Seward agreed not simply to recognize the nation's independence, but also to begin the process of absorption. No formal agreement had been signed before Seward left office in early 1869, but in September a treaty of annexation was signed by Baez and President Grant's special envoy, General Orville E. Babcock.

Sent as a special agent to the Dominican Republic in July 1869, Babcock had not been authorized to sign any diplomatic document, and the President had not even discussed annexation with his cabinet. When he finally got around to raising the issue, Grant discovered that Secretary of State Fish and other cabinet members were opposed to Babcock's treaty. Thinking that his advisors objected primarily to his unconventional method, Grant sent Babcock back to the Dominican Republic in November to renegotiate a proper annexation treaty and a second treaty providing the United States with a lease on Samaná Bay. This time the documents were signed by an accredited official. Then, for reasons that have never been adequately explained (most focus on a combination of lobbying by interested speculators and Grant's legendary stubbornness), annexation became the President's foreign policy passion. While President Baez held a plebiscite to demonstrate popular support for annexation—15,169 for annexation, 11 opposed—Grant sent the proposed treaty to the Senate.[9]

In March 1870 the Committee on Foreign Relations recommended that the treaty be rejected. In two subsequent speeches, committee chair Charles Sumner cited nearly every conceivable reason to explain his committee's opposition, but the central thrust of his argument was that "the island of San Domingo, situated in tropical waters, and occupied by another race, of another color, never can become a permanent possession of the United States. You may seize it by force of arms or by diplomacy," he continued, "but the enforced jurisdiction cannot endure. Already by a higher statute is that island set apart to the colored race. It is theirs by right of possession, by their sweat and blood mingling with the soil, by tropical position, by its burning sun, and by unalterable laws of climate."[10] On the last day of June the Senate voted 28 to 28 to reject the treaty.

Arguing that "the subject has only to be investigated to be approved," the unyielding President demanded authority to send a fact-finding commission to the Dominican Republic. Congress reluctantly acquiesced, and, following a two-month visit, the commission issued a positive report.[11] By this time Congress had already adjourned, and the new 42nd Congress was, if anything, less favorably inclined to annexation. The new Senate's discussion of the commission's report gave Senator Carl Schurz the opportunity to hammer a final set of nails into the treaty's coffin. He reminded his colleagues that "if you incorporate those tropical countries with the Republic of the United States, you will have to incorporate their people too." There was a time, not many years earlier, when members of Congress would argue that the United States should forsake "the barren forests of Canada or the black fogs of Newfoundland" for "the orange gardens of Cuba, and the palmy fields of Mexico."[12] That was before the Civil War, however, when the advocates of annexation had a plan (slavery) for handling the population. The tide had now turned, Schurz argued, and in the tropics "the very sun hatches out the serpent's eggs of danger to our republican institutions." He warned his colleagues, "do not touch a scheme like this; do not trifle with that which may poison the future of this great nation, beware of the tropics."[13]

With that said, an immensely significant moment in the history of U.S.–Latin American relations occurred: buried with the Dominican annexation treaty was the process of expansion through absorption. Since that moment in 1870, a consensus has existed in the United States that it is inadvisable to expand the nation's boundaries if it entails the addition of Latin Americans to the Union. The single exception, Puerto Rico, was just that—an exception—and one that virtually everyone in Washington still hopes will never be repeated.

With annexation rejected and reconstruction coming to an end, Washington was not a stimulating capital. Aside from the general health of the economy, the domestic political stew consisted of fairly unattractive ingredients, with plenty to nourish those whose interests were directly affected, but no meaty national problems to stimulate the nation's political appetites as had slavery or antebellum expansion. International issues were particularly unimportant to most citizens in the early postwar period. Not one word about Latin America was included in either the Republican or the Democratic platforms of 1868, 1872, 1876, and 1880, and even though both parties broke their twenty-year silence in 1884, it was simply to voice support for trade with the region.

Only the domestic economy emerged as a political issue capable of generating intense and sustained public opinion, and this, more than any other factor, determined the contours of Washington's policy toward Latin America in the final decades of the nineteenth century. Taken as a whole, the post–Civil War years constituted an era of dramatic economic growth. As the nation's population doubled from 35 to 70 million, its GNP (in constant dollars) trebled. Corn production (in constant kernels) also doubled, wheat nearly tripled, and the nation's 35,000 miles of railroad track, already the envy of the world in 1865, increased sevenfold to 242,000. Industrial production expanded even more: from 2.3 million installed horsepower in 1869, most of it water powered, to 10.1 million horsepower in 1899, most of it steam power generated by coal, the production of which rose 800 percent. Petroleum production shot up from 3 million to 55 million barrels between 1865 and 1898.

The nation's foreign trade also grew, but not quite as remarkably. Exports in 1860 (the last year before the South's cotton exports were decimated) totaled $316 million, rising to the $1 billion level in 1897. But U.S. exports to Latin America hardly grew at all, remaining fairly steady at less than $100 million per year for the period from 1865 to 1896. The value of imports from Latin America more than doubled, spurred by surging U.S. demand for the products of tropical agriculture, overwhelmingly sugar and coffee—the latter product, noted an 1886 trade commission, "has become to us almost a necessary of life."[14] With the consumption of coffee and sugar rising sixfold during the years from 1865 to 1897, Cuba and Brazil remained the largest U.S. trading partners in Latin America, generally followed at a considerable distance by Mexico. U.S. exports to Latin America were diverse, ranging from snuff and cuspidors to popcorn and toothpicks. Aside from a few eyebrow-raising items,[15] the most notable feature of the list of traded goods was the trivial quantities. During the late nineteenth century, Europe was still taking about 80 percent of U.S. exports, with Great Britain the single largest customer.

Although overall growth was impressive, the post–Civil War boom years were punctuated by severe recessions. The economy was thrown into a tailspin almost immediately after the Civil War, when Jay Cooke's financial empire collapsed; then followed the depressions of 1873 to 1878, 1882 to 1885, and 1893 to 1897. Because each of these downturns ruined the careers of more than a few politicians, virtually every public figure developed a favorite explanation and a proposed cure. Some focused upon the "underconsumption" of U.S. workers, whose low wages did not provide them with sufficient purchasing power to justify high levels of production, while others turned the coin over and identified "overproduction" as the culprit—when the nation's ever-more-efficient farms and factories had produced more than could be sold, production stopped until the surplus was absorbed by the market. Although in either case, goods sat on a shelf unsold while workers sat at home unemployed, waiting to voice their discontent on election day, the different hypotheses about the causes of recession suggested two radically different solutions. The "underconsumers" focused upon the need to raise wages, while the "overproducers" naturally tended to focus upon the development of new markets.

But overseas markets were not simply waiting for ships full of U.S. products to sail into their harbors. Then as now, new markets had to be pried open by the mutual reduction of tariffs, and many worried that this tactic could expose domestic producers to low-cost foreign competition. Unless the process was handled with great care, reciprocal reductions in tariffs would unleash a flood of cheap foreign goods, driving down wages and exacerbating underconsumption.

This logic turned everyone's attention to Latin America, since it primarily produced goods that the United States could not produce (coffee) or could not produce in sufficient quantity (sugar)—commodities that U.S. consumers would purchase anyway. As California Republican John Miller told his Senate colleagues, "new markets are necessary to be found in order to keep our factories running. Here lies to the south of us our India, and if we have the nerve, and the foresight, and the sagacity to utilize it by proper methods we shall have new markets for our products and for our manufactures which will keep every loom, and every anvil, and every manufactory of this country in motion." Then, to illustrate once again how U.S. self-interest "would have also a beneficial influence upon the political conditions of the republics of this continent," Secretary of State William Evarts noted that Latin Americans would have to work in order to pay for these U.S. goods, and that "the popular energy, now wasted upon schemes of revolution or military aggrandizement, shall have been turned toward more peaceful and profitable enterprises."[16]

Great Britain was the principal European competitor for Latin American markets. Her merchants handled over a third of the world's trade in manufactures, while the United States had a nearly invisible 4 percent. Britain was especially dominant in Latin America—in the mid-1880s about half the region's trade was with Britain, which ran a huge surplus, compared with less than 20 percent with the United States, which operated at a deficit. The British maintained a merchant marine that was about four times larger and increasingly more modern than that of the United States; and just as England's ships dominated Latin America's ports, its financial services industry completely controlled the credit and banking relationships that were essential to world trade.

By the early 1880s, virtually everyone in Washington had concluded that if the problem of cyclical recessions was to be addressed by expanding exports, the United States would have to steal Britain's customers. This would not be an easy task, for the renewed U.S. interest in foreign trade coincided with the second great wave of European imperial expansion. Beginning about 1870, Great Britain expanded from Cairo to the Cape in Africa and farther into India, Afghanistan, and Burma. France made a similar move, adding Indochina and various parts of Africa, while Germany, a latecomer, claimed South West Africa. Even Belgium and Italy participated in the scramble, primarily in the Congo and Abyssinia, respectively. Russia expanded into Central Asia, Japan focused on the Far East, and nearly everybody tried to grab a piece of China.

By 1890, U.S. officials looking at a map of the world were struck by the extent to which national wealth covaried with the acquisition of an empire. Senator Henry Cabot Lodge observed that "the modern movement is all toward the concentration of people and territory into great nations and large dominions. The great nations are rapidly absorbing for their future expansion and their present defense all the waste places of the earth. It is a movement which makes for civilization and the advancement of the race. As one of the great nations of the world, the United States must not fall out of the line of march."[17] Alfred Thayer Mahan, the principal intellectual mentor of late-nineteenth-century naval expansion, argued that the United States should try to make up for its late start by seizing key maritime straits and canal routes. "By the very characteristics which make [imperial powers] what they are, they are led perforce to desire, and to aim at, control of these decisive regions; for their tenure, like the key of a military position, exerts a vital effect upon the course of trade, and so upon the struggle not only for bare existence, but for that increase of wealth, of prosperity, and of general consideration which affect both the happiness and dignity of nations."[18]

For this the United States would need a navy. Occasionally this very pragmatic economic necessity was masked by the muscle-flexing of Social Darwinists as, for example, when Tennessee's Washington Whitthorne told his House colleagues that "the seeming lesson in the history of those nations which have attained the highest rank in dominion, power and civilization is that they have flourished most in wealth and prosperity when they had powerful navies and commercial marine"; or, similarly, when the Navy's senior admiral noted in 1887, "an absence of warlike appliances, are among the things which denote the decadence of a country."[19]

Behind this puffery was the reason that the United States embarked on an ambitious program of naval construction in the late nineteenth century: to expand trade. What the United States discovered when it began looking for overseas customers was a neomercantilist world where navies controlled access to markets—a world where U.S. producers would have to fight for their markets. "Our merchant marine and our Navy are joint apostles," wrote Commodore Robert Shufeldt, a precursor of Mahan. "We are urged imperatively to the re-creation of our commerce through the absolute necessity of procuring a market for our surplus products. At least one-third of our mechanical and agricultural products are now in excess of our own wants, and we must *export* these products or *deport* the people who are creating them. *It is a question of starving millions.*" A strong navy was essential: "the man-of-war precedes the merchantman and impresses rude people with the sense of the power of the flag." Two years later, Secretary of State Evarts used Shufeldt's logic to order the navy to make frequent port visits in Latin America, Africa, and Asia—"the National flag must be carried to such coasts before the merchant flag can be safely or profitably exhibited." [20]

Before long, the mere existence of this new navy began to exert an influence upon U.S. colonial thinking. The new generation of steam-powered ships needed strategically placed fuel depots, for example; therefore, as early as 1880 a resolution was submitted in the House "instructing the Secretary of the Navy to take necessary steps to secure adequate coaling stations and harbors for the use of the naval forces of the United States at proper points on the Atlantic and Pacific coasts of Central America and of the American Isthmus." Although it was still too early for everyone to agree on this expenditure,[21] the die was cast once a naval advisory board recommended the complete shift from sail to steam power. If that was going to occur, then "the question of providing coaling stations abroad . . . becomes year by year more important and pressing," the secretary of the navy asserted in 1884. Soon the United States was searching in earnest for Latin American bases—the secretary proposed retaining an existing base in Baja California and adding facilities at Samaná Bay or Haiti, Curaçao, Brazil, the Straits of Magellan, and the Pacific coast of Central America—and a few years later the Harrison administration (1889–93) sought to purchase or lease harbors in the Danish West Indies and Samaná Bay in the Dominican Republic, and it reopened negotiations for Haiti's Môle Saint Nicholas.[22] By the end of the century, the drive to secure overseas bases had become a significant (and at times a dominant) influence upon U.S. policy, particularly in the Caribbean.

The construction of a large navy also increased the temptation to resort to force as an instrument of foreign policy. Just as President Eisenhower would warn of the military-industrial complex seven decades later, in the 1890s former Senator Carl Schurz cautioned his readers about the growing power of "the navy interest—officers of the navy and others taking especial pride in the development of our naval force, many of whom advocate a large increase in our war-fleet to support a vigorous foreign policy, and a vigorous foreign policy to give congenial occupation and to secure further increase to our war-fleet. These forces we find bent upon exciting the ambition of the American people whenever a chance for the acquisition of foreign territory heaves in sight."[23]

It is not always easy to excite the imperial ambition of a people. Late-nineteenth-century European imperialism was a landgrab, pure and simple. There were no *Mayflowers* packed with persecuted Pilgrims, no Conestoga wagons ferrying families across the plains to settle the Oregon Territory. Since the new imperialism was not part of their historical experience, U.S. citizens at first seemed uncertain about the wisdom of participating in the rush to dominate new territories. Meanwhile, the British, Mahan wrote, were perfectly willing to take "possession of and rule over barbarous, or semi-civilized, or inert tropical communities"; unlike the United States, the British found that "no feeble scrupulosity impeded the nation's advance to power."[24]

The problem was this: the nation's leaders had convinced the public that prosperity depended upon trade; now, using the British as their example, they began to convince voters that expanded trade required dominance. This meant changing the nation's commitment to self-determination, a principle deeply embedded in the self-perception of the American people: their geographic isolation, their role as a refuge for the oppressed, their oft-stated desire to break from European *realpolitik,* their ideology of self-abnegation—their belief, in short, that the northern Europeans who had come to the New World were "special" largely because they had renounced the European pattern of conquest and pillage as a way of life. Reinforcing this ideological commitment was the nation's reluctance to absorb nearby but alien cultures.

It is difficult for a nation ideologically committed to self-determination (and opposed to the incorporation of alien cultures) to justify the acquisition of an empire. Previous generations had never needed to agonize over this contradiction, for the sparse population of the West had permitted expansion *and* self-determination: "absorbed" people were either shunted onto reservations or overwhelmed by northern European immigrants and then granted self-determination through statehood. Neither reservations nor absorption was an option in heavily populated Latin America, however, and it was here that officials in Washington were confronted for the first time with a tension between the nation's long-standing commitment to self-determination, on the one hand, and the widespread desire to use the nation's new power for commercial expansion, on the other. The management of this tension became a central issue of public discussion in the 1890s and 1900s, and *the* central issue of U.S.–Latin American relations.

The tension was resolved by a new paternalism, as President McKinley explained his 1899 decision to acquire a colony to a group of clergymen:

I walked the floor of the White House night after night until midnight; and I am not ashamed to tell you, gentlemen, that I went down on my knees and prayed Almighty God for light and guidance more than one night. And one night late it came to me this way—I don't know how it was, but it came: (1) that we could not give them back to Spain—that would be cowardly and dishonorable; (2) that we could not turn them over to France or Germany—our commercial rivals in the Orient—that would be bad business and discreditable; (3) that we could not leave them to themselves—they were unfit for self-government—and they would soon have anarchy and misrule over there worse than Spain's was; and (4) that there was nothing left for us to do but to take them all, and to educate the Filipinos, and uplift and civilize and Christianize them, and by God's grace do the very best we could by them, as our fellow-men for whom Christ also died. And then I went to bed, and went to sleep, and slept soundly, and the next morning I sent for the chief engineer of the War Department (our map-maker), and I told him to put the Philippines on the map of the United States.[25]

Not a scintilla of evidence suggests that McKinley (or any other senior U.S. foreign-policy-maker at the time) believed a word of this. But it was a perfect justification, exactly what was needed to induce public support for imperialism. U.S. political leaders obtained the public's acquiescence by arguing in each specific case—never as a general principle—that the alternatives to U.S. domination, whatever they might be, would be worse. The United States had a moral responsibility to act, not in self-interest, but in the best interests of the inferior people whom they aimed to dominate.

No one ever captured this generation's understanding of its calling better than Senator Albert Beveridge:

> God has not been preparing the English-speaking and Teutonic peoples for a thousand years for nothing but vain and idle self-contemplation and self-admiration. No! He has made us the master organizers of the world to establish system where chaos reigns. He has given us the spirit of progress to overwhelm the forces of reaction throughout the earth. He has made us adepts in government that we may administer government among savage and senile people. Were it not for such a force as this the world would relapse into barbarism and night. And of all our race He has marked the American people as His chosen nation to finally lead in the regeneration of the world. This is the divine mission of America, and it holds for us all the profit, all the glory, all the happiness possible to man. We are the trustees of the world's progress, guardians of the righteous peace.[26]

The era of self-serving paternalism had begun.

Chapter 6

Testing the Imperial Waters:
Confronting Chile

The only effectual way for the United States to control the commerce of Peru, and to preserve a commanding or even a material influence, along this coast, is, either actively to intervene in compelling a settlement of peace upon reasonable terms, or to control Peru by a protectorate or by annexation.

⌇ *Minister Isaac Christiancy, 1881*

The first test of the new paternalism occurred in a remote region of Latin America, where the United States attempted to mediate the War of the Pacific between Chile and Peru. The war had begun in early 1879, when Chile seized the Bolivian province of Antofogasta. Aware of Bolivia's alliance with Peru, Chile immediately demanded that the Peruvians declare their neutrality. When Peru refused, Chile declared war on that country as well.[1] By October Peru's only significant naval vessel had been captured, and by November the Bolivian army had disintegrated. Peru soon abandoned its southernmost province of Tarapacá, then its next-southernmost provinces of Tacna and Arica. Pressing northward, the Chileans first blockaded Callao and then occupied Lima in January 1881, when the fighting stopped and the political wrangling began.

At the moment when the War of the Pacific began, the attention of the United States had just been drawn to Latin America by Colombia's grant of a concession to a French naval officer, Lucien Napoléon Bonaparte Wyse, to build a canal across Panama. The plot thickened when Wyse sold his concession to Ferdinand de Lesseps's interoceanic canal company, and then President Rutherford Hayes, fearful that the engineer who had completed the Suez Canal might replicate his feat in Panama, responded with the assertion that "the policy of this country is a canal under American control." Colombia suggested instead that the major European powers collectively guarantee the neutrality of the proposed canal, but the new Garfield administration's secretary of state, James G. Blaine, informed both Europeans and Colombians "that the existing guarantees, under the [Bidlack] treaty of 1846 between the United States and Colombia, are complete and sufficient, and need no supplemental reinforcement from any other source."[2] The next day Blaine also expressed his dismay that Colombia and Costa Rica had agreed to ask European monarchs to mediate their boundary dispute. Although the United States was "far from making any pretension to be the only or necessary arbiter to whom the republics of South and Central America should appeal," Blaine felt there was no reason to involve others since the United States stood ready to serve as arbitrator.[3]

Europe's presence was especially obvious along the west coast of South America. In 1885 the U.S. minister to Chile reported that "foreign commerce is represented in Valparaiso by England first and then by France and Germany . . . The people of the United States are greatly deceived as to the influence which they command in this section of the world."[4] Given Chile's long-standing relationships with British merchants, it was a short logical leap to the presumption of British complicity in the War of the Pacific. "The British Lion dominates this coast and to a great extent forges Chile's thunder bolts," reported the U.S. consul at Callao. As Chile's military piled success upon success, Consul Moore observed that "on this coast every Englishman is strutting about" and, he continued, "it is needless to say that all this is extremely mortifying to an American citizen." Similarly, former Secretary of State Blaine (his first term lasted only nine months) told members of the House that "it is a perfect mistake to speak of this as a Chilian war on Peru. It is an English war on Peru, with Chili as the instrument."[5]

Because Blaine and other Anglophobes in Washington were predisposed to accept the assertion of British complicity, it was all the more important that senior officials receive accurate reports from U.S. diplomats on the spot. Unfortunately, not one of these envoys seems to have been capable of reasoned analysis. They became partisans of the governments to which they were accredited, and the confusion that flowed from this bias was compounded by extreme geographic isolation. Because there was as yet no direct telegraph line to the United States, cable communication from Chile and Peru had to go first to Argentina, then across the South Atlantic to France, and finally back across the North Atlantic to the United States. Instructions from Washington were cabled to the end of the line in Panama, then sent by boat. Other peculiar problems complicated U.S. diplo-

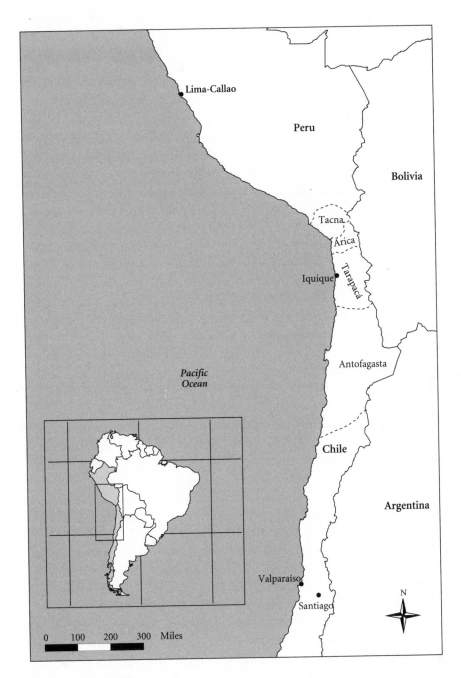

Map 4. Chile and Peru

macy. Two envoys died in office, and a third, abused by "the vile slanders of a woman," required a leave of absence in order to prepare his defense "against the most unjust and extravagant charges which have ever been wrongfully brought against any man since the days of Adam."[6]

Washington's initial reaction to the War of the Pacific was to declare U.S. neutrality, to insist that its neutral right to trade be respected, and especially to refuse to participate with European powers in a mediation effort.[7] It was not until a year after the outbreak of hostilities that U.S. officials, prodded by Congress (which had been prodded by U.S. investors), began to demonstrate an active interest in resolving the conflict. Secretary of State William Evarts instructed U.S. envoys to press for peace, and their efforts led to three days of meetings on the U.S.S. *Lackawanna* anchored at Arica. The discussions were doomed from the beginning, however, for the U.S. minister to Chile, Thomas Osborn, had neglected to tell the U.S. minister to Peru, Isaac Christiancy, that Chile would insist on a territorial cession; similarly, Christiancy had failed to tell Osborn that Peru would attend only if the negotiations were based on the status quo antebellum. The outcome was predictable: "Conference closed without result."[8]

The height of U.S. interest in the War occurred in 1881 during the brief first tenure of Secretary of State James Blaine, who believed that Latin Americans "are of hot temper, quick to take affront, ready to avenge a wrong whether real or fancied." Outbreaks of violence in the region "are not only frequent but are sanguinary and sometimes cruel," he wrote, and since Latin Americans "require external pressure to keep them from war; when at war they require external pressure to bring them to peace," Blaine proposed a U.S.-sponsored inter-American conference. Observing how the United States behaved in an international setting would have had a positive "moral influence upon the Spanish-American people," he continued, and "it would have raised the standard of their civilization."[9]

In addition to his general view of Latin Americans' culture and their innate bellicosity, in this particular dispute Blaine was convinced that Chile was in the wrong. It is not certain how he reached this conclusion, but his long-standing anti-British prejudice almost certainly made at least a modest contribution. More important, however, were the reports Blaine received from his envoys in Peru and Chile. Christiancy sent especially frequent messages from Lima, all of which painted the offensive picture of Chile's bullying a prostrate nation. Peru's humiliation, he noted, had its origin in the nature of the Peruvian people. Far from home and deprived of Castilian affection, the original European conquerors had let their libidos get the better of them: "Nearly all the Spanish adventurers either took Indian wives, or, which was more common, kept a harem of Indian girls, as many as he chose; but as a general rule they did not treat their children as slaves, but recognized them as their children. In this way it has happened that almost all the people of Peru, are of this mixed race, and the mixture with the negro."

Spanish Catholicism compounded the problem of licentious interaction with the natives. "If there is any one thing for which you and I and the great mass of the American people ought to be more thankful for than any other, it is that we were not born and raised under the dominion of the Catholic church, which, wherever it prevails, makes all permanent or settled popular government impossible." With this sentence Christiancy began a lengthy discussion of the evil influence of the Church upon Peru, a discussion so inflammatory that it was censored when the despatch appeared in both the annual *Foreign Relations of the United States* and the President's communications to Congress. "This letter must be treated as perfectly confidencial [sic]," the envoy warned Blaine. "My own life, even, would not be safe here for one day, if it were made public."

Returning to the immediate problem posed by the Chilean invasion, Christiancy reported that he had been "unable to discover any sufficient elements here for establishing an independent, or even any kind of regular or permanent government of Peru, certainly no form of popular government by the Peruvians themselves." Clearly, then, the Peruvians needed some help. One way to assist would be to annex the country. Christiancy argued that "fifty thousand enterprising citizens of the United States would control the whole population and make Peru wholly North American." The United States would benefit from expanded trade; with "Peru under the control of our country, we should control all the other Republics of South America, and the 'Monroe doctrine' would become a verity. Large markets would be opened to our productions and manufactures, and a wide field opened for the enterprize [sic] of our people."

However, since Peru was populated by mixed-blood Catholics, Christiancy also told Blaine that "I must declare my utter repugnance to the idea of its incorporation as a part of our Union, until American ideas first get control of its population." At one point, he suggested that "Peru should, for at least ten years, be subject to a territorial government on the general plan of our territorial governments . . . In that ten years Peru would, under such a system, become wholly North American in its ideas." But then Christiancy ended his despatch by offering Secretary Blaine a choice: "Upon the whole, my conclusion is, that the only effectual way for the United States to control the commerce of Peru, and to preserve a commanding or even a material influence, along this coast, is, either actively to intervene in compelling a settlement of peace upon reasonable terms, or to control Peru by a protectorate or by annexation."[10] Given what he had just read about the people of Peru, Blaine logically selected the former option.

If the United States was to assist Peru, then Blaine would need his own envoys in the region, and so he sent Stephen Hurlbut to Peru and Judson Kilpatrick to Chile; both were former Civil War generals. As with all diplomatic appointments, the new envoys needed instructions, and this necessity provided Blaine with the opportunity to state the Garfield administration's policy: "The United States cannot refuse to recognize the rights which the Chilian Government has acquired by the successes of the war, and it may be that a cession of territory will be the necessary price to be paid for peace," he told Hurlbut. "But as the Chilian Government has distinctly repudiated the idea that this was a war of conquest, the Government of Peru may fairly claim the opportunity to make propositions of indemnity and guarantee before submitting to a cession of territory." Kilpatrick was instructed to encourage the Chileans to moderate their demands.[11]

Of the many poor choices that Blaine made in his lifetime, the appointment of Hurlbut was among the worst, with Kilpatrick, for different reasons, not much better. An early advocate of the imperial control of Latin America, Hurlbut had served as U.S. minister to Colombia from 1869 to 1872. He shared none of Christiancy's interest in improving the region's people by incorporating them into the United States, but, he wrote, "I myself, am a profound believer in the right and duty of the United States to control the political questions of this continent, to the exclusion of any and all European dictation."[12] In executing this vision, Hurlbut did virtually everything wrong. Acting under the influence of U.S. and European speculators, in October 1881 he completed negotiations for a U.S. Navy coaling station at Chimbote. Included in the deal was a railroad concession from the port to a nearby coal mine, which would be turned over to the United States to operate; Hurlbut would serve as the trustee of the company. Blaine quickly distanced himself from the transaction,[13] which was a fortunate step, for no sooner had he done so than the Chimbote concession and other shady financial activities in Peru hit the press. Blaine's adversaries in Congress immediately requested copies of all State Department correspondence during the War of the Pacific, and an investigative committee was appointed in the House.

The subsequent House report concluded that "there has not been the slightest intimation or even hinted suspicion that any officer in the Department of State has at any time had any personal or pecuniary interest, real or contingent, attained or sought, in any of these transactions."[14] As part of his struggle to retain his credibility in the midst of this scandal, Blaine placed U.S. mediation efforts in the hands of William Henry Trescot, a special envoy.[15] By this time President Garfield was dead, however, and no sooner had Trescot sailed for Peru than President Chester Arthur decided to replace Blaine with Frederick Frelinghuysen.

Cautious by nature, the new secretary of state quickly concluded that U.S. policy had become the handmaiden of financial speculators and, in the words of his assistant, "that we were on the highway to war for the benefit of about as nasty a set of people as ever gathered about a Washington Dept." The assistant recommended "an instant halt and about face," and Frelinghuysen accepted his advice.[16] The gist of the new policy was that the United States would no longer voice an opinion about how the conflict should be concluded. The new minister to Chile was instructed to encourage moderation but to assume that Peru would lose territory; the minister to Peru was told to inform the Peruvians that the United States would not support their efforts to avoid ceding territory.[17]

Peru was able to delay the inevitable until October 1883, when it ceded Tarapacá outright and agreed to Chilean occupation of the provinces of Tacna and Arica for at least ten years. So it was that by 1883, after four years of bungled diplomacy, the United States had managed to alienate both sides of the conflict. The Peruvians, who had been led to believe that they enjoyed the support of the United States, were understandably upset by Frelinghuysen's policy reversal, since it ended any hope that Peru could retain its southern provinces. The Chileans, in turn, had been angered by what they perceived as Blaine's unfriendly meddling in a dispute that was none of Washington's business.

It was in this context that the Arthur administration sent a trade commission sailing down the west coast of South America, looking for customers. The commission was composed of three undistinguished and unqualified individuals who, while provided with access to the leaders of each country that they visited, did not know what questions to ask. In Buenos Aires they opened their discussion with the hemisphere's most distinguished living statesman, former President Domingo Sarmiento, with "Please tell me when you were president, and what other offices in the Republic you have filled"; they then asked him to "give the history of primary and higher education in the Argentine Republic."[18]

Although Frelinghuysen had specifically instructed the commission *not* to recommend that the United States become involved in local politics, the commission concluded that "the first step for our country [is to] give to our diplomatic representatives to these Republics such instructions beyond those embraced in the ordinary powers of such agents as will enable them to become friendly advisers in any emergency." These special instructions would convert U.S. envoys to proconsuls: "Without offense or irritation, since their action would be the prompting of amity alone, they could avert many a revolution, suppress incipient wars, and foster the enactment and enforcement of wise legislation." Moreover, "the fact that our Government is taking a more particular interest in the domestic policy and progress of the Republics than is manifested by other foreign powers, would tend to tranquillity and inspire confidence in the stability of the constituted authority. In other words, we advise that our representatives to these Republics be charged to respond to that feeling that is so often expressed by them as that of a child to a mother."[19]

So it was that two related motivations came to underlie United States policy in the mid-1880s—motivations that would influence Washington's thinking about Latin America well into the twentieth century. One was an aspiration to supplant European commercial influence in the region; emerging directly alongside this desire was a complementary effort to help Latin Americans with their problems. These two features had been a part of U.S. relations with Chile and Peru since the days of Joel Poinsett, but paternalistic meddling was not officially approved in those early nineteenth-century years; indeed, it was discouraged. In 1846 Secretary of State Buchanan instructed the U.S. chargé in Lima to desist: "It is impossible that you can reform either the morals or the politics of Peru, and as this is no part of your mission, prudence requires that you should not condemn them in public conversations. You ought to take its institutions and its people just as you find them and endeavor to make the best of them for the benefit of your own country."[20] Buchanan's policy was reversed during the early 1880s, as the task of U.S. ministers was enlarged to include advice on internal political and economic politics; by the end of the century, few in Washington would think it either unusual or undesirable for the United States to meddle in Latin America's internal politics.

This paternalistic hegemony—the acceptance of responsibility for "improving" Latin Americans—was obviously related to the desire to exclude European influence, and in practice the two motivations reinforced one another. Nowhere is this reinforcing relationship between exclusion and hegemony better illustrated than in Chile, where a simmering internal political dispute boiled over into a civil war during the first week of January 1891. When the fighting began, U.S. Minister Patrick Egan asked that warships be sent to protect U.S. interests, and the worried consul at Talcahuano also cabled Washington: "We have no guarantee of any kind and I should feel as safe amongst the Hotentotts, as here. We need at once American vessels for our protection, as that is the only kind of argument that can reach the comprehension of those in power at present."[21] With that, President Benjamin Harrison ordered additional U.S. warships into the area, including the U.S.S. *Baltimore.*

Although Secretary of the Navy Benjamin Tracy instructed his forces simply to protect U.S. interests and avoid involvement in Chile's political dispute, in the short span of eight months the United States infuriated the side that would eventually emerge victorious. As a U.S. Navy captain would observe in a September postmortem, "the cause of the [new government's] hostility is stated to be the *Itata* case, the cutting of the telegraph cable, the *San Francisco* going to Quinteros when the insurgents landed, and false telegraph reports from Lieut. E. W. Sturdy to New York."[22] Each of these incidents was infinitely more important to Chileans than anyone in Washington ever realized.

The *Itata* incident was especially annoying. Soon after the civil war erupted, the rebel Congressionalists purchased five thousand rifles and two million rounds of ammunition in New York and arranged for them to be shipped to California. When the arms arrived in Oakland in April, they were transferred to a small coastal schooner, the *Robert & Minnie*, which was exempt from customs inspection because it did not engage in international trade. The schooner steamed out of San Francisco Bay for a secret rendezvous with a Chilean vessel, the *Itata*, that was to carry the weapons to Iquique. Secrecy was important, for President Balmaceda's minister in Washington had hired a well-connected lobbyist, John W. Foster—the next secretary of state—to stop the arms transaction. Exploiting the fear of a repetition of the *Alabama* claims dispute, in which Great Britain violated the obligations of a neutral state by selling warships to the Confederacy, Foster intimidated both the Harrison administration's attorney general and the unsophisticated California judiciary. Yielding to his pressure, the *Itata* was impounded when it steamed into San Diego.

The ship's captain waited in port for three days, then dashed out of the harbor and headed for the Channel Islands, where it met the *Robert & Minnie,* transferred the arms, and turned south for Chile. The Secretary of the Navy responded by sending warships in pursuit, for however legal the arms sale may or may not have been, the flight from San Diego was not, and officials in Washington considered the flight a challenge to the sovereign rights of the United States. The *Itata* was never intercepted, but the Congressionalists agreed, for the sake of good relations, to hand the ship and its cargo over to U.S. authorities when it arrived in Iquique. So it was that the U.S. Navy escorted the *Itata* and its much-needed cargo of arms back to San Diego at the height of the Chilean civil war. The indignant Chileans were even more upset when the arms transaction was declared lawful.[23] Admiral McCann noted that "surrender of the steamer Itata and arms had deeply wounded the feelings of the Insurgent leaders, and had excited an unfriendly if not hostile spirit towards Americans, who they conceived were sympathizing with the Balmaceda government." The insurgents "regarded that act as humiliating."[24]

The second incident to offend the Congressionalists occurred when the U.S.-based Central and South American Telegraph Company cut the insurgents' international telegraph line. Prior to the outbreak of hostilities, the company had been laying a submarine cable down the west coast of South America from Chorillos in Peru to Valparaiso, with a transfer station near Iquique. The line was completed in February, but by then the Congressionalists had seized Iquique, and they refused to grant the company access to the transfer station so that it could open the link to the south. Alarmed by the prospect of seeing its investment sit idle, the company tried to convince the insurgents to permit the cable to be connected, offering censorship rights over the Balmaceda government's traffic. When this offer was rejected, a more drastic step was taken: protected by the *Baltimore* in international waters off Iquique, a company ship cut the line from Chorillos (severing the Congressionalists' international communication) and spliced it to the line from Valparaiso, connecting the Balmaceda government in Santiago.

The third incident occurred a week before the end of the civil war, when the commander of the U.S. Pacific Squadron sailed from Valparaiso in the U.S.S. *San Francisco* to investigate a report that the Congressionalists were landing troops about 20 miles north at Quinteros Bay. Finding that eight thousand troops had landed, Admiral Brown returned to Valparaiso and sent a ship's officer ashore to telegraph the news to Washington. Apparently an unauthorized person in the telegraph office obtained a copy of the contents of the message, for the following day a pro-Balmaceda newspaper ran the story, citing as its source "trustworthy news brought us by the war-ship *San Francisco*." Once again the Congressionalists were handed evidence that the United States was supporting the government, this time by spying.[25]

The fourth incident occurred once the Congressionalists had defeated the government's forces and about eighty Chileans were obliged to take asylum in the U.S. legation. As the new government posted guards outside to prevent the escape of pro-Balmaceda politicians, on September 14 another inflammatory cable was intercepted. This one had been sent by one of the *Baltimore*'s officers, who was supplementing his Navy salary by serving as a stringer for a New York newspaper. His cable, which contained the erroneous news that deposed President Balmaceda was among the refugees who had been spirited out of Chile by the U.S. Navy, went from Valparaiso to New York and right back to Chile. As the *Baltimore*'s captain reported, it "caused much excitement and strong feeling against American citizens."[26]

Prepared to expect the worst by U.S. diplomacy during the War of the Pacific, the Congressionalists interpreted each of these four incidents as part of a U.S. policy of hostility. Each can be explained as an isolated incident, but underlying each of them was the open support of the Balmaceda government by local U.S. officials. U.S. Minister Patrick Egan was responsible for much of this bias, motivated by the belief that the Congressionalists had "the undivided sympathy, and in many cases the active support, of the English residents in Chili."[27] An ardent Irish nationalist, Egan had fled his homeland to the United States in 1883, where he become both a Blaine supporter (hence his diplomatic appointment) and a leader of the Irish National League of America, whose aim was Irish independence from Great Britain. Egan hated the English.

But he was not alone in linking the British to the Congressionalists. Another eyewitness wrote that the Chileans opposing Balmaceda "are the exponents of plutocracy, of British Capital and French Customs, they are the enemies of commercial relations with us." A few weeks later a second eyewitness, a businessman of long experience in Latin America, reported that "the revolt against the Government is everywhere regarded as an English movement." His judgment was open to question, however, for he also reported that "Balmaceda will surely win" since "the revolutionists have made no progress for the past three or four months, and since the Itata incident have been rapidly losing ground and confidence."[28]

In late August, Balmaceda's forces were defeated in major fighting north of Valparaiso, and the deposed President committed suicide soon after taking refuge in the Argentine embassy. As the Congressionalists consolidated their power, Egan observed that "on account of *Itata* and other questions bitter feeling is being fomented by Government supporters against Americans."[29] It was in this atmosphere that the captain of the *Baltimore* granted shore leave in Valparaiso to 117 enlisted men on October 16, 1891. Before the day was over, violent confrontations occurred between angry Chileans and members of the ship's crew. One crew member was killed, another mortally wounded, 17 suffered wounds of varying severity, 36 were under arrest in Valparaiso's jail, and the United States and Chile had become embroiled in a major international incident.

The subsequent reports on the incident tell us much about the amusements favored by late-nineteenth-century sailors,[30] but they do not indicate who started the fracas. Chilean authorities concluded that the incident was a brawl among sailors in a seedy part of a port city. The Harrison administration took the position that the melee was an affront to the nation's honor.[31] Although questions can be raised about the points made by both sides in the dispute, the one that seems most open to challenge is Captain Schley's assertion that his crew had been comporting themselves like choirboys. Even "Fighting Bob" Evans, the captain of the accompanying U.S.S. *Yorktown,* could not believe the *Baltimore's* captain. Having delivered a load of refugees to Peru, Evans arrived back in Valparaiso just as Schley was telling local officials "that his men were all perfectly sober when they were assaulted on shore. I did not agree with him in this, for in the first place I doubted the fact, and in the second it was not an issue worth discussing. His men were probably drunk on shore, properly drunk; they went ashore, many of them, for the purpose of getting drunk, which they did on Chilean rum paid for with good United States money."[32]

For three months the United States and Chile engaged in an exceptionally heated diplomatic dispute. The Harrison administration demanded "prompt and full reparation proportionate to the gravity of the injury inflicted." Chile's foreign minister, Manuel Antonio Matta, whose dislike of the United States dated from the War of the Pacific, responded by denouncing the United States for formulating unreasonable demands and making threats.[33] Then President Harrison brought the issue to a head by giving it a prominent place in his annual message in December, telling Congress that the attacks were unprovoked, "savage and brutal," and that he would soon take punitive measures if Chile did not provide "some adequate and satisfactory response." He specifically mentioned the need for "full and prompt reparation."[34]

Customary international law concerning reparations was unclear at the time of the *Baltimore* incident. Traditionally, U.S. officials had held that a government was under no obligation to indemnify foreigners for damages. Thus when an angry New Orleans mob protested the fate of the Narciso López expedition to Cuba by looting the Spanish consulate in August 1851, Secretary of State Daniel Webster informed Spain that the United States would indemnify the consul because he was "a public officer residing here under the protection of the United States' Government," but the United States was not bound to indemnify other Spanish citizens who had been injured. The first Cleveland administration retained this distinction between accredited foreign government officials and sojourning aliens; consequently, in 1885, when twenty-eight Chinese citizens were massacred as the police watched with approval at Rock Springs, Wyoming, Secretary of State Bayard expressed his regret to the Chinese minister, but denied any obligation to make reparations. U.S. policy became less clear immediately before the *Baltimore* incident, however, for when another New Orleans mob removed eleven men of Italian ancestry from jail and murdered them, Secretary of State Blaine recognized the obligation to provide reparations to the families of those who were Italian citizens—but only because the United States and Italy had signed a treaty in 1871 guaranteeing protection to each other's citizens. Blaine was careful to underscore the special nature of this case. He told President Harrison, "I do not think we want to have a document in the hands of the Government of Italy saying that we have recognized *the principle of indemnity in this case.* Such a paper would embarrass us in many cases yet to arise."[35]

Regardless of U.S. policy on reparations, President Harrison clearly believed that the Chileans were required to provide compensation for the

Baltimore incident. His December message to Congress and a similarly hostile attack on Chilean behavior by Navy Secretary Tracy prompted Foreign Minister Matta to respond by delivering his own inflammatory message to the Chilean congress, charging that President Harrison's message and the Navy secretary's report were "erroneous or deliberately incorrect," that their words about the *Baltimore* clash lacked "accuracy and sincerity" ["tampoco hay exactitud ni lealtad"], and that "the statement that the North American seamen were attacked in various localities at the same time is deliberately incorrect."[36]

Although Matta ordered Chilean envoys to distribute his speech abroad, Chile's minister in Washington, Pedro Montt, had the good sense not to deliver it as a formal note to the State Department. Instead, he gave Blaine a highly edited version that avoided any direct mention of President Harrison and referred only to "official documents" that were "open to the charge of inaccuracy in some essential particulars."[37] Montt also informed his brother, President Jorge Montt, of Washington's reaction to Matta's message; and on January 1 Matta was replaced by a new foreign minister, Luis Pereira, who immediately set out to calm the troubled waters in both countries. On January 4 Montt showed Blaine his new instructions: "Inform the United States government that a summary of the attorney-general's report relative to the occurrences of October 16, which Chili has lamented and does so sincerely lament, will be sent on Monday, the 4th instant."

Four days later, Montt informed Blaine that the judicial official charged with prosecuting the case had issued a 180-page report indicating that the clash had originated in a personal dispute among drunken sailors, had escalated in the midst of a neighborhood "inhabited by people of disreputable habits," and that the government would seek prison terms ranging from five years to twenty days for three Chileans and one U.S. sailor. Montt ended his note with an exceptionally conciliatory statement: "I have also received special instructions to state to the Government of the United States that the Government of Chile has felt very sincere regret for the unfortunate events which occurred in Valparaiso on the 16 of October . . . and the frank desires for American cordiality which my Government entertains have led it to cordially deplore the aforesaid disturbance and to do everything in its power toward the trial and punishment of the guilty parties."[38]

At this point it became obvious that President Harrison was spoiling for a fight. Rather than respond to Montt in kind, he demanded a public withdrawal of ex–Foreign Minister Matta's offending message. Notified of the President's demand, Minister Egan immediately replied from Chile that Foreign Minister Pereira "will not have any objection to withdrawing all that may be considered disagreeable to that of the United States in the telegram sent . . . by the former minister of foreign affairs." Nonetheless, on January 21 Blaine cabled Egan that he had been "directed by the President to say that if the offensive parts of the dispatch of the 11th December are not at once withdrawn, and a suitable apology offered, with the same publicity that was given to the offensive expressions, he will have no other course open to him except to terminate diplomatic relations with the Government of Chile."[39]

Chile then capitulated. On January 25 Foreign Minister Pereira handed Egan a lengthy note withdrawing the Matta circular, expressing regret for the *Baltimore* incident, and offering to halt the judicial proceedings in Chile and submit the question of reparation to arbitration by the Supreme Court of the United States.[40] Egan immediately telegraphed Pereira's note to Washington, but by then President Harrison had sent a highly bellicose message to Congress demanding "a suitable apology," "some adequate reparation," and the withdrawal of the Matta message along with "an apology as public as the offense." If Chile were to refuse, he concluded, "I am of the opinion that the demands made of Chile by this Government should be adhered to and enforced."

Since these demands had already been met, President Harrison waited briefly and then notified Congress that the dispute had ended.[41] The next day Blaine sent Harrison a draft of a note to Chile accepting the apology. He warned the President that his wording "may seem to you too cordial," but Harrison responded immediately with a few suggestions, adding that "what I have said I think you will agree, has rather enlarged than diminished the expressions of cordiality."[42] Chile then gave Egan $75,000 to distribute among the families of the two dead sailors and to those injured, and in his final annual message President Harrison noted his "great gratification" at the receipt of the indemnity.[43]

In hindsight, both the U.S. policy toward the War of the Pacific and the conflict with Chile were signals that the United States was recovering its self-confidence. But even though a new post–Civil War generation was beginning to make itself heard in Washington, its voice was not yet dominant, and the nation's leaders were still unsure about the direction of U.S.

foreign policy. And so, a few months after the *Baltimore* crisis had passed, the two principal political parties placed the debate over a hegemonic policy toward Latin America before the electorate. The Democrats condemned Harrison's assertiveness: "we view with alarm the tendency to a policy of irritation and bluster which is liable at any time to confront us with the alternative of humiliation or war." The Republican platform offered the electorate a hegemonic vision: "We reaffirm our approval of the Monroe doctrine and believe in the achievement of the manifest destiny of the Republic in its broadest sense." The stage was set for one of the interesting ironies of inter-American relations, as the Democratic victor, Grover Cleveland, proceeded to implement the Republican policy.

Chapter 7

Excluding Great Britain:
The Venezuela Boundary Dispute

What a suggestion it is that the issues of peace or war between the two Trustees of Civilization—the U.S. and Great Britain—should in any degree be made to depend upon the decision or conduct of such a menagerie as a *Venezuelan* Government.

～ *Ambassador Thomas Bayard, 1896*

Grover Cleveland was anything but an imperialist. "I do not favor a policy of acquisition of new and distant territory or the incorporation of remote interests with our own," he wrote early in his first term; and three years after the completion of his second term, he called the annexation of Hawaii "a perversion of our national mission. The mission of our nation is to build up and make a greater country out of what we have, instead of annexing islands."[1] Yet during his second term (1893–97) Cleveland was obliged to confront domestic economic and political pressures that seemed to call for a more aggressive foreign policy. The economic pressures were nothing new, but the political pressures were novel for this generation, and few understood their full significance until the late 1890s. Grover Cleveland's special role was to manage them in their rambunctious adolescence, when they erupted in the context of a boundary dispute between Great Britain and Venezuela.

The dispute had its origin in the failure of European powers to identify precisely their colonial limits in the New World. The British came into possession of their part of the Guianas because the Dutch, having backed the losing side in the Napoleonic wars, were obliged in 1814 to transfer ownership of "the Settlements of Demerara, Essequibo, and Berbice" to Great Britain. No boundaries were mentioned in the treaty. The 1845 Spanish agreement to recognize the independence of Venezuela was similarly vague: it simply stipulated that Venezuela's boundaries were the same as "the American territory, known formerly by the name of the Captaincy-General of Venezuela."[2]

In between these two treaties, the British consolidated the three former Dutch settlements into a single colony, renamed it British Guiana, and commissioned a surveyor, Robert Schomburgk, to mark the colony's western border. In early 1841 Venezuela protested this unilateral delimitation, sending London a formal diplomatic note proposing the negotiation of a boundary treaty. Receiving no response, in October the Caracas government sent a second note expressing its dismay over Schomburgk's placement of his surveyor's markers. Venezuela's insistence and a handful of border incidents led to the "Agreement of 1850" that neither country would occupy certain parts of the sparsely populated territory, and there the matter rested for more than two decades. Then in November 1876 Venezuela reopened the issue by sending the British a lengthy memorandum asserting a claim to all territory west of the Essequibo River (including about two-thirds of present-day Guyana) and suggesting that the two countries negotiate a boundary treaty. Shocked by the extent of Venezuela's ambitions, the British Foreign Office waited four months to reply, and then simply requested more time. After two years had elapsed with no further response, Venezuela sent another request. This time Prime Minister Salisbury replied with an assertion of territorial claims every bit as extravagant as those in Venezuela's 1876 note.

Recognizing that the Monroe Doctrine might work to their advantage, the Venezuelans were now sending copies of this correspondence to the United States, accompanied by pleas for help. In the first request, sent at the same time as Venezuela's November 1876 note to Great Britain, Venezuela's minister in Washington suggested to Secretary of State Hamilton Fish that since the United States was "the most powerful and the oldest of the Republics of the new continent," it naturally was "called on to lend to others its powerful moral support in disputes with European nations." Written just days after a U.S. presidential election, the Venezuelan note arrived in Washington at the end of Fish's eight-year tenure. Lost in the transition, it did not receive a reply.[3] Undeterred by Washington's silence, in late 1880 Venezuela made a second attempt, equally ill-timed, sending the lame-duck Hayes administration a long memorandum noting the ominous presence of British ships and the recent construction of an English telegraph line at the mouth of the Orinoco. This time the United States replied: Secretary of State Evarts told the Venezuelan minister in Washing-

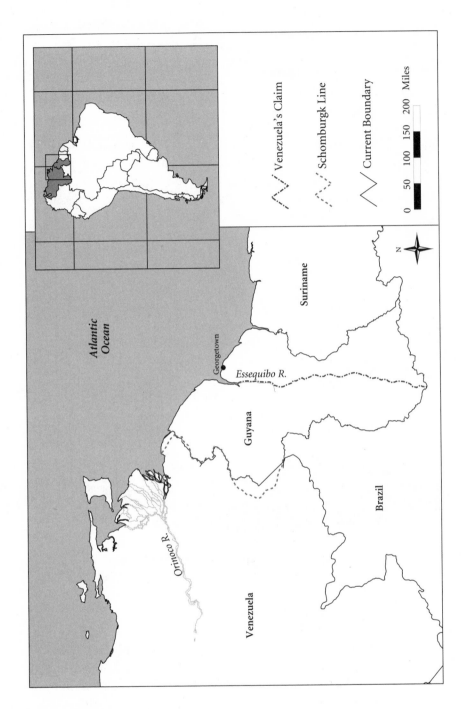

Map 5. Venezuela Boundary Dispute

ton that "this Government could not look with indifference to the forcible acquisition of such territory by England," and a month later he suggested that the Venezuelan minister contact his successor.[4]

The U.S. reaction went no further, for during his brief tenure Secretary of State Blaine was obliged to focus his attention elsewhere, and what little time he could devote to Venezuela was reserved for mediating a debt dispute with France. Thus the learning process had to begin anew in late 1881 when Blaine was replaced by Frederick Frelinghuysen. Soon Venezuelan President Antonio Guzmán Blanco asked the United States to pass along to Britain a memorandum outlining Venezuela's boundary claim, but nothing was done until mid-1884, when Guzmán Blanco, now an ex-president and a newly commissioned diplomat, visited the United States on his way to London. Pressed for assistance, Frelinghuysen yielded and instructed the U.S. minister to Great Britain to assist Guzmán Blanco where possible, but beyond that he was not willing to risk alienating the British.[5]

Venezuela's next request for assistance arrived on the desk of Secretary of State Thomas Bayard shortly after Grover Cleveland's 1885 inauguration. For the specific steps that Venezuela might take to resolve its boundary dispute, Minister Soteldo wrote that "my Government heartily desires to follow the path that may be marked out for it by the great Republic of the North." Bayard suggested arbitration to Great Britain, then pushed the issue aside for more than a year.[6] But in late 1886 an alarming despatch arrived from the U.S. minister in Caracas, Charles Scott: Venezuela was about to place a lighthouse on territory claimed by Britain, he reported, and this "may lead to a war." Prompted to reassess his passive role, in late December Bayard offered Great Britain "the good offices of the United States to promote an amicable settlement." Inexplicably, the U.S. minister in Great Britain, Edward Phelps, waited over a month before handing Bayard's offer to Lord Salisbury. Replying that Venezuela's extravagant claims precluded arbitration, the Prime Minister politely but firmly closed the door that Bayard was gently seeking to nudge open.[7]

By this time Venezuela had escalated the conflict by demanding that Great Britain evacuate a broad part of the contested area before February 20, 1887. When that day passed and Britain had not responded, Venezuela suspended diplomatic relations and turned to the United States. Citing a British newspaper article to demonstrate England's "insatiable thirst for conquest," the Venezuelan minister in Washington emphasized his country's weakness in the face of British imperialism: "The fact is that until now

England has relied upon impunity; she beholds us a weak and unfriended nation, and seeks to make the Venezuelan coast and territories the base of a conquest which, if circumstances are not altered, will have no other bounds than the dictates of her own will." Bayard immediately forwarded the note to Phelps, instructing him "to express anew to Lord Salisbury the great gratification it would afford this Government to see the Venezuelan dispute amicably and honorably settled, by arbitration or otherwise, and our readiness to do anything we properly can to assist in that end." This time Phelps failed to deliver the note at all.[8]

The Venezuelan boundary issue was once again shoved aside as the United States entered the 1888 presidential campaign season, and it seemed to disappear entirely when Cleveland lost the November election to Benjamin Harrison. But then in November 1889, just as the first inter-American conference was sitting down to business in Washington, Venezuela requested the assistance of Secretary of State Blaine (now back for a second term) in restoring diplomatic relations with Britain.[9] Absorbed by the conference, Blaine waited until adjournment, then instructed the new U.S. minister in London, Robert Todd Lincoln, to attempt to "bring about resumption of diplomatic relations between the two countries as a preliminary step toward negotiation for arbitration of the dispute." Salisbury replied that negotiations regarding the resumption of relations were already under way with the Venezuelan minister in Paris. Great Britain had made a proposal, he said, and was awaiting Venezuela's reply "before considering the expediency of having recourse to the good offices of a third party."[10]

From Hayes to Harrison, then, Venezuela had solicited the support of every secretary of state since the mid-1870s. Even though the United States had at times been responsive, it had never permitted the dispute to become a significant issue of U.S. foreign policy. There was no single reason for this reluctance to become involved; rather, it reflected several aspects of U.S. foreign policy, including a general post–Civil War focus on domestic issues. But among the important reasons for detachment was Washington's fear of becoming enmeshed in the unstable politics of Latin America, a fear best captured in 1892, when a bill was introduced to pay for the surveying of a rail route across Latin America. James Blount, a ten-term member of the House, rose to explain his opposition: "These countries are revolutionary in character; they are continually being disturbed; they are in conflict amongst themselves, and I do not wish to see any line of policy adopted which can by any possibility extend those controversies to us . . . Those people are incapable of preserving order and stability among themselves; bring them into connection with us, with all these troublesome questions, and the equipoise of our institutions, which we enjoy and preserve to-day by reason of the splendid character of our population, will be endangered." [11]

This attitude remained prominent through the mid-1890s, but it was changing, as the shift in the Cleveland administration's policy toward the Venezuelan boundary dispute clearly demonstrates. The spark that ignited Cleveland's interest remains uncertain. The President recalled in his memoirs that he became convinced that Britain's slow expansion into the disputed territory should be interpreted as the equivalent of an invasion and therefore a violation of the Monroe Doctrine. "There was nothing left for us to do consistently with national honor but to take the place of Venezuela in the controversy, so far as that was necessary, in vindication of our American doctrine." [12] It is not difficult to understand how Cleveland could make this connection between the Monroe Doctrine and the boundary dispute, for Britain was an obvious European presence throughout Latin America. Not only were her warships in the Rio harbor during the Brazilian naval revolt in 1893 to 1894, but also she continued to assert her supremacy along Central America's Mosquito Coast throughout the summer and fall of 1894. Then a grievance against Nicaragua came to a head at almost exactly the moment that Cleveland was beginning to focus on Venezuela, and in April 1895, Britain, having given Nicaragua three months to provide reparations for the mistreatment of British citizens, seized the Pacific port of Corinto. The British Navy departed two weeks later, but only after Nicaragua agreed to reparations.

The takeover of Corinto deeply offended a Republican newcomer, Theodore Roosevelt, who wrote Henry Cabot Lodge: "If we allow England to invade Venezuela nominally for reparation, as at Corinto, really for territory our supremacy in the Americas is over. I am worried and angry beyond words at what I see. England is simply playing the Administration for what she can get." Even Anglophile Thomas Bayard, a solid Cleveland Democrat who was now in London, serving as the nation's first ambassador,* was not unaware of Great Britain's tendency to seize territory belong-

---

*Until Bayard's appointment, the highest-ranking U.S. diplomats had always been ministers.

ing to others. "Political expansion in South American regions is not, in my belief, the intention or desire of Great Britain, but where a gold mine is discovered within sight of an ancient line of boundary, the greed of gold will cause that line to deflect."[13]

Despite these concerns over British challenges to the Monroe Doctrine, domestic politics provides a more convincing explanation for the Cleveland administration's shift to a more active policy in Venezuela. Cleveland had lost the 1888 election in part because of the Republicans' attacks upon his uninspiring foreign policy—using stinging phrases such as "weak and unpatriotic," the 1888 Republican platform had excoriated the Democrats for having "seen with idle complacency the extension of foreign influence in Central America and of foreign trade everywhere among our neighbors." Now, seven years later, it seemed as if this scene was being replayed when Senator Henry Cabot Lodge published an exceptionally critical assessment of Cleveland's foreign policy. Entitled "Our Blundering Foreign Policy," the article asserted that "we have done nothing to check the continued aggressions of the British upon the territory of Venezuela, although those aggressions are a violation of the Monroe doctrine." Indeed, Lodge continued, "under the present Administration our foreign policy has been everywhere a policy of retreat and surrender."[14]

The Venezuela boundary dispute reached a climax at a moment when the Cleveland administration desperately needed to recover the public's confidence. The depression that began with the Panic of 1893 hit bottom just in time for the 1894 election (a 113-seat disaster, with the Democrats going from a 218 to 127 majority to a 105 to 244 minority), and the economy had not recovered much in the intervening year. Throughout 1895 worried Democratic politicians were urging a more forceful foreign policy.[15] An active lobbying effort supplemented the push for vigorous action by worried Democrats. William L. Scruggs, who had served until 1893 as U.S. minister to Venezuela and then immediately accepted employment as Venezuela's "special agent and legal adviser," was hard at work, prowling the corridors of power in Washington. Scruggs's first public effort was a pamphlet, published in October 1894, with a title that captured perfectly Venezuela's preferred view of the dispute: "British Aggressions in Venezuela, or the Monroe Doctrine on Trial." Two months later, after Cleveland's annual message had indicated an interest in arbitration, Scruggs concluded that "the next move was to get Congress to take up the question in a tangible form of a joint resolution . . . supporting the President's recommendation." To this end, he continued, "Colonel Leonidas F. Livingston, the Representative in Congress from my home district in Georgia, very kindly agreed to introduce such a resolution," which was written by Scruggs. By late February both the House and the Senate had passed it unanimously.[16]

Then Secretary of State Walter Gresham died on May 28, 1895. His death could not have come at a worse time. Cleveland was already depressed, writing to Bayard in mid-February that "I have been dreadfully forlorn these many months, and sorely perplexed and tried." In addition to the nation's economic malaise, the President was saddened by the public disapproval of his handling of the nation's debt (a controversial bond sale that had enriched a number of New York bankers) and dismayed by a prominent minister's accusation that Cleveland had consumed alcoholic beverages. Just two months before Gresham's death, the President had written a friend that "you don't know what a comfort Gresham is to me, with his hard sense, his patriotism and loyalty. It is but little for me to say that I would trust my life or honor in his keeping at all times." Two weeks after the secretary's death, Cleveland wrote another close friend that Gresham's "companionship and constant loyalty largely constituted all the comfort that came to my official life."[17]

With the economy in shambles and his administration in disarray, Cleveland took the fateful step of selecting Attorney General Richard Olney as Gresham's replacement. A lawyer for railroad interests at a time when the term "railroad interests" was synonymous with rapacious disregard for the public's welfare, Richard Olney had recently finished writing his name into the history books as the man who broke the Pullman strike: when the strike halted the nation's passenger rail service, Olney ordered U.S. district attorneys to "see that the passage of regular trains, carrying United States mails . . . is not obstructed. Procure warrants . . . against any and all persons engaged in such obstructions." The ensuing confrontations between strikers and federal troops constitute one of the darker moments in U.S. history. As the violence escalated, on July 8 President Cleveland issued a proclamation ordering the strikers "to disperse and retire peaceably," warning those who refused that they "cannot be regarded otherwise than as public enemies." Two days later, Eugene Debs and other leaders of the American Railway Union were jailed, and the strike was broken.

Now, as secretary of state, it was Olney's responsibility to implement the President's earlier decision "to take the place of Venezuela in the controversy." The new secretary of state soon demonstrated that he intended to handle the nation's foreign relations with the same sledgehammer subtlety that had characterized his leadership of the Department of Justice. After quickly familiarizing himself with the case, Olney drafted a note to the British and took it to the President. Cleveland replied: "I read your deliverance on Venezuelan affairs the day you left it with me. Its [sic] the best thing of the kind I have ever read."[18] On July 20 Olney's note was sent to London, setting U.S. policy on a path toward confrontation.

The essence of Olney's lengthy note, known to history as the Olney Doctrine, is an assertion of two rights: the right of the United States to exclude extrahemispheric powers and the right to hemispheric hegemony. Basing the first right upon the Monroe Doctrine, Olney specifically accused Great Britain of violating the Doctrine by expanding its boundaries at Venezuela's expense. The basis of the second right was physical strength. Olney asserted that the United States had the right to exercise its hegemonic power because "its infinite resources combined with its isolated position render it master of the situation and practically invulnerable as against any or all powers." Because of this power, "today the United States is practically sovereign on this continent, and its fiat is law upon the subjects to which it confines its interposition."[19]

After delivering the note as instructed, Ambassador Bayard reported that Salisbury "expressed regret, and surprise that it has been considered necessary to present so far reaching and important a principle and such wide and profound policies of international action in relation to a subject so comparatively small."[20] Nonetheless, Salisbury added fuel to the fire. After indicating that he would have to consult carefully within his government before offering a response, Salisbury made Cleveland and Olney wait over four months for a reply. There were undoubtedly many reasons for Salisbury's delay, but perhaps the most important one was that the British colonial secretary told him to be careful lest he give away a gold mine: "It appears that there is a very rich territory close to and probably over the Schomburgk boundary . . . If it answers the description given me by the gold officer of the Colony—now in London—it may turn out to be another Transvaal or West Australia."[21]

When it finally arrived, Salisbury's response was nearly as hostile as Olney's note. "The Government of the United States is not entitled to affirm as a universal proposition, with reference to a number of independent States for whose conduct it assumes no responsibility, that its interests are necessarily concerned in whatever may befall those States simply because they are situated in the Western Hemisphere."[22] Salisbury also rejected Washington's demand that Britain submit the boundary dispute to arbitration, and, rather than do so politely, he simply told the United States to mind its own business: "the British Empire and the Republic of Venezuela are neighbors, and they have differed for some time past, and continue to differ, as to the line by which their dominions are separated. It is a controversy with which the United States have no apparent practical concern." Britain, Salisbury continued, had no intention of arbitrating "claims based on the extravagant pretensions of Spanish officials in the last century, and involving the transfer of large numbers of British subjects, who have for many years enjoyed the settled rule of a British colony, to a nation of different race and language, whose political system is subject to frequent disturbance, and whose institutions as yet too often afford very inadequate protection to life and property."[23]

Of all the offenses that Great Britain could have given, none could have been more grave than Salisbury's summary dismissal of the legitimacy of the Monroe Doctrine. Britain in effect had flicked the chip off the Cleveland administration's shoulder, so now there could be no backing down. The President went directly to Congress, charged that Great Britain had expanded its boundaries by seizing "the territory of one of our neighboring republics," and indicated that push had come to shove. Then, just as Olney had invented a clever ruse (the need to deliver the mail) to cover his attack on the railroad unions, so he devised an ingenious tactic with which to confront the British: Cleveland announced to Congress that "the dispute has reached such a stage as to make it now incumbent upon the United States to take measures to determine . . . what is the true divisional line between the Republic of Venezuela and British Guiana." He asked for congressional authorization and an appropriation for a commission to determine the boundary. Congress promptly gave its unanimous approval.[24]

Since Cleveland's words to Congress were fully as aggressive as anything his Republican adversaries would have written, Theodore Roosevelt praised his belligerency, and the President responded with a note of thanks.[25] A few months later, the Republican party wrote a campaign platform that could have been taken from Cleveland's text, reaffirming "the rights of the United States to give the [Monroe] Doctrine effect by responding to the appeal of any American State for friendly intervention in case of European encroachment."

The United States was free to appoint a commission to study anything it wished, of course; the question was what would happen when the commission had rendered its report and Britain, now locked into a game of diplomatic chicken, refused to accept it? As Cleveland wrote to Bayard, "instead of threatening war for not arbitrating, we simply say—inasmuch as Great Britain will not aid us in fixing the facts, we will not go to war—but do the best we can to discover the true state of facts for ourselves, with all the facilities at our command. When with all this, we become as certain as we can be, in default of Great Britain's co-operation, that she has seized the territory and superseded the jurisdiction of Venezuela—that is a different matter." [26]

At this point, influential citizens on both sides of the Atlantic began to worry about the escalating hostilities. Perhaps the most important opposition came from John Bassett Moore, a loyal Cleveland supporter who was rapidly establishing his reputation as the nation's most distinguished student of international law. After the substance of Olney's note had become known, Moore wrote a twelve-page letter to a Cleveland confidant, Postmaster General William L. Wilson, which was obviously intended for the President. The United States, he argued, had permitted itself to become the victim of Venezuela's manipulative behavior: "For twenty years, Venezuela, instead of settling her boundary dispute, has in various ways, some of them obviously dishonest, been trying to drag the United States into the dispute, and the United States has progressed good-naturedly step by step, without examining the merits of the case, till at length with a sudden impulse it leaps over the precipice blindly." Moore specifically challenged the widespread belief that Britain's refusal to arbitrate was evidence of ill intent. "The statement [in Cleveland's message to Congress] that the question can be reasonably settled only by arbitration as Venezuela proposes, certainly was not based on any examination of the merits of the subject," he wrote. The author of a five-volume treatise on arbitration, Moore acknowledged that "we have arbitrated boundary disputes and so has Great Britain, but never, so far as I am informed, where a line had not previously been agreed upon by direct negotiation. Governments are not in the habit of resigning their functions so completely into the hands of arbitrators as to say, 'We have no boundaries; make some for us.'" [27]

Cleveland was also having trouble convincing his own ambassador to Great Britain of the wisdom of his policy. Indeed, the President was caught squarely between his current secretary of state, Olney, who seemed to relish the confrontation, and Bayard, his first-term secretary of state, who thought the British were beyond reproach and had earlier written Gresham that Latin America represented a "lower civilization."[28] In late December 1895, at the height of the controversy, Cleveland requested Bayard's support. "It seems as if all the troubles and perplexities that can gather about the office I hold were just at this time, making a combined assault," he wrote, implicitly asking Bayard not to add to his burden by dissent. Then he gently reminded his ambassador that only one person was the President. "I am positive that I can never be made to see why the extension of European systems, territory, and jurisdiction, on our continent, may not be effected as surely and as unwarrantably under the guise of boundary claims as by invasion or any other means."[29]

Bayard believed it was lunacy for the United States to become allied with the Venezuelans: "For the U.S. to place in the control of such a set of men the virtual control of peace and war with European Powers would be simple madness." Nor was Bayard one to believe that Anglos could remake Latin culture. In late 1893 he had written Gresham that "we cannot give to the heterogeneous populations of Mexico, Central America, and South America—the racial qualities traditions and education that are the prime bases of a republican state"; a year later he continued this line of reasoning in a discussion with Lord Kimberly about the British dispute with Nicaragua: "Of course, I disclaimed the slightest intention of interfering with the right of G.B. to any *just* reclamation, but I *did* advert to the well known condition of that region and its very imperfect civilization."[30]

Given these beliefs, Ambassador Bayard continued to paint the British in the most favorable light. As soon as he had seen Salisbury's response to Olney's note, he wrote Cleveland that it was "in good temper and moderate in tone," which, of course, it was not. The problem, Bayard insisted, was Venezuela: "*Our* difficulty lies in the wholly unreliable character of the Venezuelan Rulers and people—and results in an almost undefinable, and therefore dangerous responsibility for the conduct by them of their own affairs." Then, immediately after the President's request to Congress for authority to appoint a commission, Bayard wrote Cleveland that "as the Venezuelan transactions and history are unfolded I am not able to shake off a grave sense of apprehension in allowing the interests and welfare of our Country to be imperilled or complicated by such a government and people as those of Venezuela." A month later Bayard wrote in a personal note to William Putnam that "the present imbroglio with the mongrel state of Venezuela, sickens me."[31]

This opposition among prominent Democrats led Cleveland to soften Olney's hostile edge. Immediately after delivering his menacing message to Congress, he sent Olney a half-humorous note that had the effect of informing him that issues other than Venezuela's boundary (in this case, a hunting trip) were also important.[32] At the same time, it was Cleveland's good fortune that the overextended British had problems elsewhere in their empire, especially in southern Africa, where it appeared possible that Germany might become involved on the side of the Boers. Salisbury's recommendation of a continued hard line was rejected by his cabinet on January 11, and the following day the Prime Minister sent Bayard's close friend, Lord Playfair, to the U.S. embassy with a proposal. Playfair explained to Bayard (and Bayard immediately cabled Olney) that he had come to express Britain's "earnest desire" that the boundary dispute "be promptly settled by friendly cooperation."[33] The informal emissary proposed that this begin with an effort to resolve any misunderstanding that might exist over the interpretation that Olney had given the Monroe Doctrine. Britain suggested a conference among the United States and the various European powers holding colonies in the Western Hemisphere. In addition, Playfair continued, Britain was willing in principle to submit the boundary dispute to an arbitral commission, but only under some guarantee that long-term British settlers were not to be evicted from their holdings or forcibly incorporated into Venezuela.

Olney immediately rejected Britain's proposal for a conference on the Monroe Doctrine, and Britain dropped the idea—a concession of enormous significance. Prior to this point, the United States (in Olney's note) had asserted the applicability of the Monroe Doctrine to the boundary dispute. Britain first (in Salisbury's response) had flatly rejected this assertion and then (in Playfair's message) offered to discuss its rejection at a conference. When Olney responded with a refusal to discuss the Monroe Doctrine and Great Britain let the matter drop without further comment, Britain accepted Washington's position that the dispute was, in fact, the business of the United States. Moreover, Salisbury's concession was a tacit announcement that Britain was willing to accept U.S. hegemony in Latin America—two powers could not be "practically sovereign in this hemisphere," and if the U.S. fiat is law, then Britain's is not. In the 1850 Clayton-

Bulwer Treaty the two powers had ostensibly agreed to share influence and control over any Central American canal. Now, half a century later, Britain was willing to stand aside. Just as it had recently left Rio's harbor during the Brazilian naval revolt, leaving the U.S. Navy as arbitrator, and just as it would soon agree to abrogate the Clayton-Bulwer Treaty, so in early 1896 Britain agreed to let the United States dictate the method for resolving the Venezuelan boundary dispute.

Satisfied that its basic interests were no longer threatened, the United States could now begin negotiations over the boundary dispute. To the British proposal of an arbitral commission, Olney cabled the following counterproposal:

> Let there be new Commission—two appointed by United States, probably from present American Commission,* two appointed by Great Britain, and if the four divide equally upon results, a fifth to be mutually agreed upon or nominated by ———. This Commission shall report not a line but the facts to the two Governments, which shall thereupon endeavor to fix a line satisfactory to all parties, Venezuela included. The endeavor failing, the facts reported shall be submitted to an arbitral tribunal, consisting of the Chief Justice of England, the Chief Justice of the United States, and a third arbitrator to be mutually agreed upon or nominated by ———, which tribunal shall ascertain and declare such a divisional line as the facts submitted warrant, and which line so ascertained and declared, shall be accepted by and binding upon all parties in interest, Venezuela included.[34]

Britain was willing to proceed along these general lines, especially since Olney offered to let London fill in the blanks with a friendly tie-breaking arbiter, but continued to insist that the rights of British citizens living in "settled districts" within the disputed territory be protected. Salisbury wanted these districts identified in advance and removed from the arbitration; Olney responded that it was impossible to agree on the settlements before arbitration because "the inevitable delays would be interminable."[35]

Great Britain had now made two major concessions: it had acquiesced to the U.S. position on the Monroe Doctrine, and it had agreed to arbitrate. Now Lord Salisbury asked Henry White to communicate the need for a

---

*A reference to another commission called for by a general arbitration treaty then being negotiated by the United States and Great Britain.

modicum of understanding from Washington. White reported to Olney that Lord Salisbury

> considers compulsory arbitration in matters affecting territory, without any power of appeal, a dangerous precedent to establish, and from the point of view of the British Empire, his reasons are forcible; viz— that claims to territory might—and probably would—constantly be made by countries having nothing to lose and hopeful of gaining some accession of territory through the submission of such claims to arbitration, that it would be very easy and inexpensive to make such claims, but not at all easy to find an impartial arbitrator, and the result might be that important Powers might find themselves deprived through arbitration, of portions of their territory, arbitrators being usually inclined to favor a weak power.[36]

The problem was much more serious than that of identifying unbiased arbitrators; rather, it was a question of agreeing upon the *principle* to guide arbitration. The British, relative latecomers, had a clear position: "while admitting that the American Continent was first discovered, and partly occupied, by the Spaniards," the British argued "that fact could have no necessary bearing upon the matter under discussion."[37] Venezuela based its claim to the disputed territory upon *historical evidence* of who got there first, and had denied the legitimacy of *current occupation of territory* ("adverse holding") as a basis for assigning ownership.

Olney understood this crucial difference, but he had been vague about it in his original note to Salisbury, indicating simply a willingness to permit "long-continued occupation of territory" to be "given all the weight belonging to it in reason and justice, or by the principles of international law."[38] No one knew exactly what that statement meant. Before proceeding further, Great Britain had to know whether the United States intended to permit the use of Venezuela's historical evidence (and, by implication, that of every other state bordering on the British Empire, from Guatemala to the Indian principalities) as the principle for determining ownership, or would occupation be the criterion?

Olney made the necessary concession. On July 13 he suggested to Salisbury that any British settlement established for sixty or more years be excluded from the arbitration.[39] With that, the ice was broken. Sailing home from England a few days later, John Hay, the exceptionally partisan Republican, wrote Democrat Olney that "everybody wants the matter settled if it can be done without damage to the pride and prestige of England."[40] With this type of evidence of possible cooperation among leaders on either side of the Atlantic, everyone relaxed a bit. In September, Colonial Secretary Joseph Chamberlain took the opportunity provided by a visit to his wife's family in Massachusetts (she was the daughter of Cleveland's former secretary of war, William Endicott) to negotiate informally with Olney. At that time the secretary of state rejected Britain's counterproposal that thirty years' adverse holding be definitive. Not knowing that Olney and Cleveland were ready to accept forty years, the British ambassador in Washington, Julian Pauncefote, then proposed forty-five; Olney countered with fifty, and Britain accepted. No one ever said a word to Venezuela.

Two agreements quickly emerged from Washington. The first was signed by Olney and Pauncefote on November 12, 1896—a "Proposed Treaty between Venezuela and Great Britain for Settlement of Venezuela Boundary Question, as agreed upon between Great Britain and the United States." It established an arbitral commission of five members, two named by Great Britain, two by the United States, and a fifth by common consent or, if they proved unable to agree, by the king of Sweden and Norway. Under this treaty, the tribunal "shall determine the boundary line between the colony of British Guiana and the Republic of Venezuela." Cleveland was elated, and in his annual message in early December he announced that "the provisions of the treaty are so eminently just and fair that the assent of Venezuela thereto may confidently be anticipated."[41]

It was Olney's task to inform the Venezuelan minister in Washington of the agreement, which he did on the same day as the President's message to Congress. Because it precluded the use of historical evidence to determine ownership of the settled districts, Minister José Andrade refused to accept it, and so Olney suggested that Andrade and his U.S. legal counsel, James Storrow, take the document to Caracas, which they did. There it was also received with dismay. After attempting without success every conceivable response, including a direct approach to Salisbury, the Venezuelan government suggested that one of Venezuela's citizens would be an ideal participant on the tribunal. That would not be possible, Olney replied, but a slight adjustment was not out of the question; he accepted Storrow's proposal "that Venezuela would appoint either a U.S. lawyer or judge, or an international jurist of reputation, not a Venezuelan."[42]

Thus the second agreement, signed in Washington by Pauncefote and

Minister Andrade on February 2, 1897, stipulated that the President of Venezuela could nominate the Chief Justice of the U.S. Supreme Court as a Venezuelan commissioner. In all other respects the treaty that Great Britain signed with Venezuela was identical to the British-U.S. agreement.

Once the opposing sides had prepared their cases, the tribunal began its work in Paris in January 1899, and had no trouble reaching a unanimous decision, which it announced on October 3. Venezuela fared poorly. With the exception of the important southern edge of the Orinoco delta, which was awarded to Venezuela, the commissioners gave nearly all the contested territory to Great Britain.

Venezuela had been excluded from the negotiations that determined the principle upon which the arbitral decision was to be based and had no members on the arbitration commission. As an 1897 law review article indicated, the four arbitrators "represent an English-speaking constituency." Given their grounding in English common law, the article continued, "King Oscar [of Sweden and Norway] is likely to discover that, as to the equitable principles which underlie and govern the controversy, his colleagues, though strangers to him and to each other, though coming to him, as it were, from the ends of the earth, keep step as if, all their lives, they had actually touched elbows; he will perceive that, while they may not have sat at the feet of the same Gamaliel, they have all drunk at the same fountain." [43]

It is possible to argue that the Venezuelans had only themselves to blame, for since 1876 they had been encouraging the Yankee camel to stick its nose under their tent. Venezuelans would respond by pointing out that every one of their requests for assistance was a request that the United States use its good offices to encourage arbitration, not that it replace Venezuela at the bargaining table. As Cleveland later explained, once the United States had concluded that the dispute involved an issue more important than a boundary line, then "sympathy with Venezuela and solicitude for her distressed condition could no longer constitute the motive power of our conduct, but these were to give way to the duty and obligation of protecting our own national rights." [44] This statement explains not only why Venezuela was not consulted but also why once the challenge to the Monroe Doctrine had been resolved, British and U.S. diplomats treated the rest of the dispute as a minor spat, and why the United States accepted Great Britain's view of which principle should govern the decision. Ambassador Bayard never questioned which side the United States should support.

"What a suggestion it is that the issues of peace or war between the two Trustees of Civilization—the U.S. and Great Britain—should in any degree be made to depend upon the decision or conduct of such a menagerie as a *Venezuelan* Government—'the *Sister Republic*' forsooth!"[45]

A century after the fact, it is easy for U.S. citizens to agree with Lord Salisbury that the Venezuelan boundary dispute was, in itself, of modest significance. But to U.S. officials in the late nineteenth century, the dispute over ownership of the southeastern corner of Venezuela was about something other than tropical acreage. It was an announcement that the United States intended to move upward on the hierarchy of nations, even if European powers thought the idea presumptuous. Olney would later admit that the words of his note to the British "were undoubtedly of the bumptious order," but "the excuse for them was that in English eyes the United States was then so completely a negligible quantity that it was believed only words the equivalent of blows would be really effective."[46] Venezuela was but the beginning, for the world was about to discover in Cuba and Panama what the Olney Doctrine meant when it declared that the United States was practically sovereign on this continent.

Chapter 8

Establishing an Empire:
Cuba and the War with Spain

Acceptance of a practical protectorate over Cuba seems to me very like the assumption of the responsible care of a madhouse.

~ *Minister Stewart Woodford, 1898*

Cuba's war for independence was spilling over into the United States just as William McKinley was putting together his cabinet, yet no one was certain what the new President thought about the Caribbean island that John Quincy Adams had once declared "of transcendent importance to the commercial and political interests of our Union." And so, a few weeks after the 1896 election, Senator Henry Cabot Lodge asked him. Cuba "is very much on his mind," Lodge reported to Theodore Roosevelt. "He would like the crisis to come this winter and be settled one way or another before he takes up the reins."[1]

McKinley must have known that this hope was unrealistic, for the island had been in turmoil his entire adult life. If Hamilton Fish were to have been asked to identify the most nagging problem that he faced during his eight years as secretary of state from 1869 to 1877, he almost certainly would have said Cuba, where a ten-year war for independence broke out prior to Grant's election in 1868, just as a young McKinley was setting up his law practice in Ohio. Even at that early date, the normal problems of revolutionary instability—incidental damage to the property of U.S. citizens and the disruption of U.S. shipping—were exacerbated by Cuba's proximity to the United States. Fish had hardly managed to warm the secretary of state's chair before he began receiving formal notes from Spain complaining of "the departure of various filibustering expeditions in broad day-light, and unmolested, from New York and other federal ports."[2] The rebels' most brazen exploit was to purchase a U.S. steamship, the *Virginius*, which with its U.S. crew dodged around the Caribbean for two years, carrying contraband to the rebels. When finally captured by the Spanish in October 1873, the ship's captain and thirty-six crew members were summarily executed along with sixteen revolutionaries, triggering a reaction as old as the republic: with tears in one eye and fire in the other, the dead seamen's friends and families descended upon their representatives in Congress, demanding revenge and restitution. Encouraged by this constituent pressure, members of Congress suggested everything from a declaration of war to a full investigation. In the *Virginius* case, as in others, it fell to the State Department to conduct the customary investigation and prepare two special messages on Cuba that the President used to mollify Congress. Not surprisingly, Secretary Fish concluded by the end of his tenure that close ties with Cuba would be an "unmitigated calamity."[3]

Since this was a ten-year war and Fish's tenure was but eight years, he left the problem to his successor, William Evarts. Like Fish, Evarts never did convince Madrid that the Hayes administration was doing what it could to curb filibustering, but Cuba moved out of the Washington political limelight when the rebellion entered a period of quiescence in 1878. Sporadic outbreaks of violence continued, however, and every succeeding administration was confronted with the need to press the claims of U.S. citizens whose interests were harmed by the drawn-out conflict.

In the course of this diplomatic activity, officials in Washington regularly received information from U.S. consuls in Cuba, nearly all of whom disliked and distrusted both the Cubans and the Spaniards. In 1883, for example, when the Arthur administration began to negotiate a commercial agreement with Spain for trade with Cuba and Puerto Rico, U.S. Consul Adam Badeau urged the exercise of great care. He described the island's "subjection to a financial and commercial tyranny unequalled to day in the world for rapacity, iniquity, and severity, and hardly rivalled in all the long annals of colonial despotism." This tyranny led, in turn, to "the misery and anxiety of all, condemned alike to poverty and ruin," and insurgency was the consequence—"the yoke that is laid upon every neck . . . has aroused anew the rebellious sentiment." Badeau was nonetheless enthusiastic about Cuba's "enticing opportunities" for U.S. traders, although he warned that Spanish colonial authorities, "actuated by jealous malevolence and selfish cupidity combined, persistently do every thing in their power to outrage and injure American citizens, American ships, American seamen, and American trade." Because the native residents were hardly better than their Spanish oppressors, Badeau advised against the annexation, suggesting instead that trade might remedy Cuba's backwardness: it would "extend to the country and its inhabitants the advantages of contact with the higher civilization, the greater energy, the purer morality of America."[4]

Badeau's description of Spanish Cuba was typical of many others received in Washington during the decades after the U.S. Civil War, and they almost certainly contributed to the official view of Spanish Cuba, a view that first Cleveland and then McKinley would employ to interpret a major new revolt that erupted in early 1895. The news this time came not from Cuba but from New York, the headquarters of the Cuban Revolutionary party, which issued the call for revolution. By April, Antonio Maceo, José Martí, and Máximo Gómez had returned to lead the fighting against Spanish authorities, and this time the rebels seemed to capture the support of large numbers of Cubans, many of whom had been affected by a severe recession brought on by a drop in the price of sugar.[5] Beginning in the eastern end of the island, the insurgency soon spread into the central Cuban provinces of Camagüey and Las Villas, the heart of Cuba's sugar economy. By year-end the rebellion had spread across the island.

In late 1895 the attention of President Cleveland and Secretary of State Olney was focused upon the Venezuelan boundary dispute, and their initial U.S. reaction to the Cuban rebellion was simply to issue two pro forma warnings to filibusters. But in September Olney had been approached by "one of the largest landed proprietors of Cuba, a man of great wealth, an employer on his estates of some eight hundred people, an American citizen," and the secretary of state had written President Cleveland a lengthy memo indicating a sympathy for the insurgents. Olney argued that the rebels "have a right to ask, I think, that we inform ourselves upon the point, whether they are merely gangs of roving banditti, or are a substantial portion of the community revolting against intolerable conditions and earnestly and in good faith seeking the establishment of a better form of government."[6]

Then in early 1896, when the British expressed a willingness to negotiate an end to the Venezuelan boundary dispute, Olney was free to turn his full attention to Cuba. In April he presented the Spanish with a lengthy note describing the disruptive effect of the conflict on U.S. economic interests and the dangers faced by U.S. citizens living in Cuba. Warning that "the United States can not contemplate with complacency another ten years of Cuban insurrection," Olney politely suggested that the Spanish permit limited home rule. The Spanish reply was conciliatory, expressing Madrid's willingness "to adopt such reforms as may be useful or necessary," but only "as soon as the submission of the insurgents be an accomplished fact." Spain's envoy noted tactfully that this would occur more quickly if "all the people of the United States . . . will completely cease to extend unlawful aid to the insurgents."[7]

At this point neither Cleveland nor Olney knew how to proceed. In July 1896, three days after the Democratic convention had rejected Cleveland's leadership by nominating William Jennings Bryan as its presidential candidate, the now very lame-duck President wrote Olney in reaction to a proposal that the United States purchase the island: "It would seem absurd for us to buy the island and present it to the people now inhabiting it, and put its government and management in their hands." Cleveland did not indicate why he found this absurd, but one reason may have been his evaluation of the Cuban insurgents. Two years later, just as war erupted, he remarked to Olney that they are "the most inhuman and barbarous cutthroats in the world."[8]

The President waited until his final message to Congress to raise the issue again. After presenting a lengthy overview of the conflict, Cleveland proposed a solution ("a measure of home rule . . . while preserving the sovereignty of Spain") and cautioned that "it can not be reasonably assumed that the hitherto expectant attitude of the United States will be indefinitely maintained." He gave two reasons for concern—the magnitude of U.S. investments in Cuba and humanitarianism: "When the inability of Spain to deal successfully with the insurrection has become manifest and it is demonstrated that her sovereignty is extinct . . ., and when a hopeless struggle for its reestablishment has degenerated into strife which means nothing more than the useless sacrifice of human life and the utter destruction of the very subject-matter of the conflict, a situation will be presented in which our obligations to the sovereignty of Spain will be superseded by higher obligations, which we can hardly hesitate to recognize and discharge."[9]

The McKinley administration thus inherited what had become (and has remained) a chronic problem of U.S.–Latin American relations: Caribbean instability was spilling over into the United States, damaging U.S. economic interests and arousing U.S. humanitarian concern. Then, as now, this was a volatile mixture, and it is indicative of President McKinley's temperament that he was not immediately swept up by the clamor for action. Quite the contrary, for in choosing the aging John Sherman as his secretary of state (to free up an Ohio Senate seat for Marcus Hanna), McKinley signaled that foreign policy was not going to be his highest priority. Were it not for the ringing endorsement of activism that had been written into the Republican platform, a well-informed gambler on inauguration day would have wagered that the foreign policy team of McKinley and Sherman, assisted by McKinley confidant William Day—three Ohioans with extremely limited foreign policy experience—would be far less active than that of Cleveland and Olney.

But the new President accepted his party's 1896 declaration that "the government of the United States should actively use its influence and good offices to restore peace" in Cuba. Pressured by U.S. Minister Stewart Woodford, in late 1897 the Spanish government announced a series of reforms, and McKinley responded with guarded optimism, telling Congress in his first annual message that Spain "should be given a reasonable chance . . . to prove the asserted efficacy of the new order of things to which she stands irrevocably committed."[10] If the reforms failed, McKinley warned, "other action by the United States will remain to be taken." However, even at this late date—a few months before the sinking of the *Maine*—the President was clear about his opposition to expansion: "I speak not of forcible annexation, for that cannot be thought of. That, by our code of morality, would be criminal aggression."[11] Referring to the clamor for war, McKinley told former Secretary of State John Foster that "these people will have a different view of the question when their sons are dying in Cuba of yellow fever."[12]

There are two complementary explanations for the war that was soon to come, despite McKinley's sentiments. One was the public mood, which favored a more aggressive foreign policy, a mood created by three separate but related groups. The first group was McKinley's own Republicans, for as one newspaper noted just before the inauguration, "a party that has been for four years raging like a lion for a foreign war may not find it so easy to reform and lead the sweet, submissive life of a lamb, even in the green pastures of power and patronage."[13]

The attention of aggressive Republicans was focused on Cuba by a new political force, the Cuban expatriate community, led by a New York–based junta, a force at once sophisticated and crude. The crudeness showed in its direct lobbying, much of which was counterproductive, while the sophistication was evident when it focused its energies upon the media, virtually writing the news for a number of major newspapers. One of the most important of these stories exploded in the headlines at a critical moment in early 1898, when the junta destroyed the credibility of the Spanish minister in Washington, Enrique Dupuy de Lôme. The envoy had sent a private letter to a Spanish publisher in which he characterized President McKinley as "weak and a bidder for the admiration of the crowd, besides being a pandering politician [*politicastro*] who tries to leave a door open behind himself while keeping on good terms with the jingoes of his party." There are various explanations of how the letter found its way into the hands of the junta's legal counsel, Horatio Rubens, but there is no doubt that Rubens gave it to the New York *Journal,* which published a facsimile on February 9. Understandably offended by Dupuy de Lôme's words, McKinley demanded the envoy's recall, and Dupuy de Lôme immediately tendered his resignation. As a result, Spain had only a chargé in Washington a week later when the *Maine* disaster occurred.

The second group helping to create the public mood for a more aggressive U.S. foreign policy was composed of the nation's newspaper editors and publishers. By 1896 the major parties were already supportive of Cuban independence, and so the role of the press was to build upon this existing sentiment, intensifying public opinion into a war fever during an era when journalism was dominated by sensationalism. The mecca of the new journalism was New York; it was there in 1895 that a young Californian, fresh from converting his father's respectable San Francisco newspaper into a sleazy but highly profitable tabloid, purchased the ailing New York *Journal* and promptly entered into a circulation war with Joseph Pulitzer's New York *World.* Like that of Pulitzer, who needed no instruction in sensationalism, William Randolph Hearst's strategy was to capture the mass market of unsophisticated readers, many of them immigrants who were learning English through the newspapers. He halved the price of an issue to a penny, bought the best talent available,[14] and sensationalized the news with little regard to the accuracy of the stories he printed. Years later, progressive Senator George Norris would assert that Hearst's newspapers, "spreading like a venomous web to all parts of our country, constitutes the sewer system of American journalism."[15]

That, however, was years later. Now in the late 1890s Hearst was only beginning to develop his talent for weaving in and out of the gray area between truth and fantasy, only beginning to demonstrate that there was no journalistic low to which he would not stoop; to protect his market, Pulitzer (who had been Hearst's model when he sensationalized the San Francisco *Examiner*) also became agile at weaving and stooping. Searching for copy to excite their readers, reporters from both dailies soon locked their sights on the colonial war in Cuba. From the beginning they were aided immeasurably by the New York junta. In his memoirs, the junta's legal counsel, Horatio Rubens, describes how reporters would come to his office each afternoon in search of news; in time, the gathering came to be known as the "peanut club," with Rubens providing both the goobers and whatever information about Cuba, truthful or otherwise, that the junta wished to see appear in the papers.[16]

So it was that yellow journalism came to earn its reputation for exaggeration and sensationalism through stories about the abuse of liberty-loving Cubans by cruel Spaniards. It took only a few months for Pulitzer, Hearst, and a raft of competitors to convert the Cuban rebellion into a modern-day morality play, with detailed reports of pitched battles, fictional and real, often supplemented by first-person accounts of questionable authenticity, all focusing upon particularly dastardly acts by the Spanish. Every article carried an implicit or explicit call for officials in Washington to protect the nation's honor in the face of Spanish indignities. Typical was the coverage given to an episode in which Spanish authorities boarded a ship flying the U.S. flag, the *Olivette*, as it prepared to steam out of Havana in early 1897. Suspecting that some of the passengers were carrying messages to the rebels, the Spaniards ordered that they be searched. Outraged by this interference with U.S. shipping, the *Journal* erupted with a characteristically inflammatory headline—"Does Our Flag Protect Women? Indignities Practiced by Spanish Officials on Board American Vessels. Refined Young Women Stripped and Searched by Brutal Spaniards While Under Our Flag on the Olivette"—and presented its readers with a drawing by Frederic Remington of leering Spanish officials searching a naked young Cuban woman. Urging a declaration of war, reporter Richard Harding Davis wrote that "war is a dreadful thing, but there are things more dreadful, and one of them is dishonor."[17] The rival *World* subsequently produced one of the women, who reported that they had been searched in private by a matron, but by that time New York Representative Amos Cummings had submitted a "Resolution of Inquiry in House Relative to Alleged Stripping of Lady Passengers on Steamer Olivette."[18]

Then came the Cisneros affair. It featured a young Cuban woman, Evangelina Cosio y Cisneros—"only eighteen years old, cultured, talented and beautiful"—who was being held in Havana's notorious Recojidas prison, "persecuted for resisting the insulting advances of a savage in Spanish uniform," reported a Hearst publication.[19] Ms. Cisneros was also the daughter of a rebel leader. The *Journal* reported that her incarceration was under the most oppressive conditions imaginable, and that she was slowly sinking into "the last stages of despair." Accusing the McKinley administration of refusing to act, in 1897 Hearst launched his own campaign to save Ms. Cisneros. The widow of Jefferson Davis was recruited to send a petition to María Cristina, the Queen Regent of Spain. At the same time, the *Journal* found that Julia Ward Howe was willing to be of assistance, and the newspaper facilitated (and publicized) her appeal to Pope Leo, eventually sending him a petition signed by twenty thousand women, including President McKinley's mother and the wife of the secretary of state.

When this strategy did not yield quick results, Hearst had his star reporter in Havana arrange a jailbreak, and on October 10 the *Journal* erupted with this headline: "Evangelina Cisneros Rescued by the Journal. An American Newspaper Accomplishes at a Single Stroke What the Red Tape of Diplomacy Failed Utterly to Bring About in Many Months." The journalist, who told his story of the escape in the preface to Ms. Cisneros's quickly published autobiography, reported: "I have broken the bars of Recojidas and have set free the beautiful captive of monster Weyler . . . It is an illustration of the methods of new journalism."[20] Exactly what happened will probably never be revealed, but it is difficult to believe that the escape could have been successful without the liberal distribution of Hearst's money among the prison authorities. However it was accomplished, the young woman was freed, then quickly spirited out of the country to a hero's welcome in New York—a ticker-tape parade up Broadway, a mass rally, lunch at Delmonico's with New York's most prominent politicians, and then on to Washington for a meeting with the President. In the next few days the *Journal* gave the Cisneros story 375 full columns of newsprint.[21]

Did all this activity affect public opinion? Certainly that is how a New York ticker-tape parade would be interpreted today, as would readership data that indicated the public's interest. As he published more about Spanish atrocities in Cuba, Hearst sold more, and his stories (along with those of Pulitzer) were picked up by dozens and dozens of U.S. newspapers across the country, many of them combined into the nation's first media conglomerates, owned by men like Pulitzer and Hearst. In New York, the *Journal*'s circulation rose from 30,000 in 1895 to 400,000 in 1897; and after the U.S.S. *Maine* sank in Havana's harbor, when the *Journal* devoted a daily average of eight *pages* to the tragedy every day for a week, Hearst's newspaper became the first to sell a million copies in a single day. Public officials undoubtedly recognized that the Cisneros affair, like so many others, had been fabricated almost entirely by the press, but that was not the point. The point, as Senator Orville Platt observed as early as 1895, was that all this was affecting public opinion: "the newspaper rot about what is going on there, though published one day and contradicted the next, seems to stir up all the aggressive spirit in the minds of the people."[22] That assertion was sufficient to encourage action in Washington. President McKinley strongly disliked the Yellow Press, most of it owned by Democrats, but the Senate almost chanted for war in the aftermath of the *Olivette* affair.

The third group creating the public mood for a more aggressive foreign policy was composed of politicians known collectively as "jingoes,"* who represented this generation's advocates of Manifest Destiny, dressed up in the modern language of Social Darwinism. Led by Theodore Roosevelt, McKinley's assistant secretary of the navy, and Senator Henry Cabot Lodge, these leaders exerted constant pressure for a more aggressive, belligerent foreign policy.

Restless, unreflective, and possessed of an unquenchable desire to guard the nation' masculinity, Roosevelt fought tooth and nail against any proposal that might make people soft, going so far as to conceive of the tariff as an issue of manly character: "In this country pernicious indulgence in the doctrine of free trade seems inevitably to produce fatty degeneration of the moral fibre." To Roosevelt, war was how superior civilizations demonstrated their superiority, by "crowding out" their inferiors, thereby improving the human race. This Social Darwinism may be sufficient explanation for Roosevelt's bellicosity, but it is difficult to read his correspondence and not conclude that some additional motivation came from the perception that warfare offered an opportunity for personal advancement. In 1886, when trouble broke out along the Mexican border while the recently widowed Roosevelt was recovering at his ranch in the Dakota Territory, he quickly wrote Lodge to ask a favor: "I have written on to Secretary [of War] Endicott offering to try to raise some companies of horse riflemen out here

---

*The term "jingo" was originally a euphemism for "Jesus," coined by supporters of British belligerency toward Russia in 1878, who said "by jingo" instead of the blasphemous "by Jesus" in a chauvinistic song of the era. In time, "jingo" came to describe anyone who favored expansion or imperialism.

in the event of trouble with Mexico. Will you telegraph me at once if war becomes inevitable? . . . I haven't the least idea there will be any trouble; but as my chance of doing anything in the future worth doing seems to grow continually smaller I intend to grasp at every opportunity that turns up."[23] Instead of making him a college dean, as usually happens with this type of person, fate made Roosevelt a politician.

Leaders such as Roosevelt could hardly announce publicly that war would constitute a boon to their careers, but they could and did argue that war was the measure of a nation's character. In 1895 Roosevelt published an article lambasting the "solemn prattlers" who urged a peaceful solution to the Venezuelan boundary dispute: "They are utterly incapable of feeling one thrill of generous emotion, or the slightest throb of that pulse which gives the world statesmen, patriots, warriors, and poets, and which makes a nation other than a cumberer of the world's surface." To Roosevelt, "all the great masterful races have been fighting races, and the minute that a race loses the hard fighting virtues, then, no matter what else it may retain, no matter how skilled in commerce and finance, in science or art, it has lost its proud right to stand as the equal of the best. Cowardice in a race, as in an individual, is the unpardonable sin."[24] That this was not simply the bluster of a politician is corroborated by Roosevelt's associates, who joked with one another about his commitment to war. Responding to Roosevelt's 1911 suggestion that the United States declare war on Mexico, President William Howard Taft warned Secretary of State Knox, "the truth is he believes in war and wishes to be a Napoleon and die on the battlefield. He has the spirit of the old Berserkers."[25]

A Freudian would argue that Roosevelt supported war because he was stimulated by the manly act of shooting guns—big guns with long, firm barrels that jerked with savage abandon when triggered. He took aim at any legal prey (including humans during their open season, wartime); indeed, it is entirely possible that he killed more animals than any other U.S. city dweller in history.[26] In 1902 he briefly reconsidered the implications of his pastime, telling Congress that "the senseless slaughter of game, which can by judicious protection be permanently preserved on our national reserves for the people as a whole, should be stopped at once." Roosevelt soon fell off the wagon, however, and from 1909 to 1910 went on a year-long binge in Africa to celebrate the end of his Presidency. At one point he wrote his son that "I have killed four good Lions in addition to two cubs; it was exciting, and you would have loved it. I also killed two Rhinos both of which charged, a Hippo and two Bull Giraffes, and various Antelopes Zebras and so forth."[27]

Roosevelt's war fever was fanned by his close friend Henry Cabot Lodge, who held a Massachusetts Senate seat from 1893 until his death 31 years later. Lodge's principal contribution to late-nineteenth-century U.S. politics was to legitimize the discussion of Manifest Destiny. He reminded U.S. citizens of their proud heritage "of conquest, colonization, and territorial expansion unequalled by any people in the nineteenth century," then added: "We are not to be curbed now . . . In the interests of our commerce and of our fullest development we should build the Nicaragua canal, and for the protection of that canal and for the sake of our commercial supremacy in the Pacific we should control the Hawaiian Islands and maintain our influence in Samoa. England has studded the West Indies with strong places which are a standing menace to our Atlantic seaboard. We should have among those islands at least one strong naval station, and when the Nicaragua canal is built, the island of Cuba, still sparsely settled and of almost unbounded fertility, will become to us a necessity."[28]

For years it was common to assert that all of this pressure (a triple combination of Cuban lobbying, yellow journalism, and jingoism) inflamed public opinion and thereby dragged a reluctant but ultimately powerless McKinley into war. No one was more convinced of this explanation than former President Cleveland: "It seems to me to be the old story of good intentions and motives sacrificed to false considerations of complaisance and party harmony. McKinley is not a victim of ignorance, but of amiable weakness not unmixed with political ambition."[29]

As Louis Pérez has demonstrated, however, the public mood is probably an incorrect or at least an incomplete explanation for the war. Pérez's alternative is the second major explanation; it emphasizes the McKinley administration's concern for the fate of U.S. strategic and economic interests under an independent Cuban government.[30] As we have seen, U.S. merchants had developed a substantial trade with Spanish Cuba in the eighteenth century, and in the nineteenth century these merchants were joined by a significant number of investors, so that President Cleveland was not exaggerating when he told Congress in his 1896 valedictory that "our actual pecuniary interest in [Cuba] is second only to that of the people and government of Spain."[31] Then Cleveland went back to Princeton, and left the McKinley administration to worry about the safety of U.S. financial interests in Cuba.

Had they looked in the files, the new administration's officials would have seen that the Department of State had for years been receiving unflattering information about the Cubans; in 1886, for example, Consul Adam Badeau had characterized the island's residents as "a heterogeneous and foreign people, unused to republicanism and many of them either to civilization or Christianity."[32] The flow of these diplomatic despatches and communications from private investors increased significantly once the rebellion broke out in 1895, and most of them asserted or implied that the Cuban rebels were unstable radicals. Sugar magnate Edwin Atkins described "the insurgent side" to Secretary Olney as "the Negro element, together with adventurers from abroad (of whom there are many) who are seeking power or gain."[33] Cleveland did not need to be convinced, for he had seen this radicalism firsthand in his dealings with Cuban expatriates; he complained of being "time and again threatened by frenzied men and women with dire calamities to be visited upon myself and children because of what they saw fit to assert was my enmity to the Cuban cause." McKinley, in turn, was warned by his minister to Spain that the Cubans' lack of education, the island's substantial nonwhite population, its bitter divisions between *Peninsulares* and Creoles, and its history of official corruption all pointed to the need for U.S. control: "Acceptance of a practical protectorate over Cuba seems to me very like the assumption of the responsible care of a madhouse."[34]

The solution was to be found in the division within Cuban Creole society. As Consul-General Fitzhugh Lee reported, "the Cubans bearing arms want an Independent Republic and the intelligent and educated Cuban citizens desire Annexation to our Republic."[35] So it was that when the revolution got out of hand (both the hand of Spain and of the Creole elite) and McKinley sat down to write his war message, his focus was on evicting the Spanish *and* controlling the revolutionaries. This, Pérez argues, is what the President meant when he wrote of acting on behalf of "endangered American interests" and of the need "to secure in the island the establishment of a stable government, capable of maintaining order and observing its international obligations."[36]

That message, however, was still some months in the future. In late 1897 and early 1898, there was intense diplomatic maneuvering, much of it focused upon pressuring Spain to sell Cuba to the United States. At this time the administration also took the precaution of exploring how European powers might react if the United States were to declare war. McKinley's new envoy to Spain reported "that most Englishmen, Frenchmen and Germans regard Cuba as within the legitimate zone of American influence and would not be disposed to resent any action by the United States that would be just, humane and in line with the progressive purposes of modern civilization." Later, Lord Balfour told Ambassador John Hay that "neither here nor in Washington did the British Government propose to take any steps which would not be acceptable to the Government of the United States." [37]

As the U.S.-Spanish diplomatic dialogue continued, in early 1898 the Spanish inaugurated a new reformist colonial government that included substantial home rule. Havana's Tories protested, and Consul-General Fitzhugh Lee reported their protest in inflammatory language: "Mobs, led by Spanish officers, attacked to-day the offices of the four newspapers here advocating autonomy." [38] After Lee sent several similar cables, including one suggesting that "ships must be sent" because "excitement and uncertainty predominates everywhere," McKinley decided to move the battleship *Maine* from Key West to Havana's harbor. It arrived on January 25 and sat quietly at anchor until the night of February 15, when an explosion tore open the ship's hull, sending it to the bottom of the harbor and extinguishing the lives of 260 U.S. seamen. In addition to the human tragedy, the sinking of the *Maine* proved to be a diplomatic disaster of the highest magnitude. It broke the will of those who had resisted the pressures of Cuban filibusters and lobbyists, of Hearst and Pulitzer, of Roosevelt and Lodge.

President McKinley immediately appointed a Navy board to investigate the cause of the blast. While it looked into the disaster, the press fanned the smoldering public opinion into a flame. "The Whole Country Thrills with War Fever," trumpeted the *Journal,* while Pulitzer's paper headlined, "War Fever Rising from *World*'s Evidence." [39] Senator Orville Platt complained in a letter to a friend that "those who have been clamoring for liberty and freedom and war, have worked up a spirit in the country that something must be done and done quickly to stop the condition of things in Cuba, and I think Congress believes that sentiment to be stronger and more general than it really is." [40] Thrown into an absolute fury, Assistant Secretary Roosevelt contributed to the hysteria. "Personally I cannot understand how the bulk of our people can tolerate the hideous infamy that has attended the last two years of Spanish rule in Cuba; and still more how they can tolerate the treacherous destruction of the *Maine* and the murder of our men! I feel so deeply that it is with very great difficulty I can restrain myself." [41]

It was into this highly charged atmosphere that President McKinley sent the Navy's report to Congress. It asserted that the blast "could have been produced only by the explosion of a mine situated under the bottom of the ship." The President told Congress "that the ship was destroyed by the explosion of a submarine mine."[42] Only years later did it become clear that the damage was so severe and the muck on the harbor floor so dense that no one could be certain what had happened. One diver reported to the Board of Inquiry that he sank into the mud "near the armpits." When questioned about his eyesight, another diver responded, "I can see well, when the water is anyway clear, but this water is not clear. We can't see any more than about a foot or eighteen inches out from you." At length the principal hole was located, but then the divers could not easily inspect it: "They report that the mud is so deep that it will be impossible for them to walk on the bottom."[43]

Perhaps because these details of the Navy's inquiry were not made public at the time, or perhaps because the President's message sounded so definite, no one suggested that the United States pause to be certain of what had happened. The suspicion of a cover-up became a prominent partisan issue after the war, however, and Democrats demanded a second look at the wreck; they were supported by veterans' groups that wanted to give the dead a proper burial and by Havana port engineers who wanted to get the shattered hulk out of their harbor. The Navy initially refused to discuss revisiting a closed case, but in 1912 to 1913, just before the Democrats reclaimed the White House, the Maine was raised and reinspected. At the time no report was issued to contradict the Navy's 1898 opinion, and to make sure that the incoming Democrats had access to no further evidence, in March 1913 the Navy towed what was left of the ship into deep water four miles off the Cuban coast and sank it. Years later, the Navy's legendary maverick, Admiral Hyman Rickover, prepared an elaborate study using the detailed photographs and other data obtained in 1912 and 1913. He concluded that "in all probability, the Maine was destroyed by an accident which occurred inside the ship . . . What did happen? Probably a fire in bunker A-16." "There is no evidence that a mine destroyed the Maine."[44]

Rickover's study was published in 1976, however; in 1898 no one contradicted McKinley and the Navy, which firmly pinned responsibility on a submarine mine. With that the die was cast. "I have no doubt at all that the war would have been averted had not the *Maine* been destroyed in Havana harbor," wrote Senator Shelby Cullom in his memoirs. "The country forced us into it after that appalling catastrophe." Senator Platt agreed: "when, by accident or design, the good ship *Maine*, with its American sailors on board, was blown into the air, and its sailors found a grave in the harbor of Habana, there was no power on earth that could prevent the war." Even the Democrats were ready to fight, with McKinley's 1896 opponent, William Jennings Bryan, asserting that "the time for intervention has arrived. Humanity demands that we shall act."[45]

Declaring that "the present condition of affairs in Cuba is a constant menace to our peace," on April 11 McKinley sent his war message to Congress, insisting "in the name of humanity, in the name of civilization, in behalf of endangered American interests which give us the right and the duty to speak and to act, the war in Cuba must stop." He asked Congress to empower him to use military force "to secure a full and final termination of hostilities."[46] Congress debated for eight days before completing work on a brief but complex joint resolution that authorized the President to evict the Spanish. The resolution asserted, in the Teller amendment, that "the United States hereby disclaims any disposition or intention to exercise sovereignty, jurisdiction, or control over said island except for pacification thereof, and asserts its determination, when that is accomplished, to leave the government and control of the island to its people."

There is little question that Colorado Senator Henry Teller proposed his antiannexation resolution primarily to ensure that Western beet sugar interests would never have to face "domestic" Cuban competition. Four years earlier, in 1894, he had been an archexpansionist, telling his Senate colleagues that he favored the annexation of Hawaii, Canada, and Cuba. But this was on the eve of the beet sugar boom in the West, and soon Teller was adamantly opposed to the annexation of lands suitable for growing sugar. In late 1903 he led the fight against Roosevelt's proposal to grant tariff preferences to Cuba.[47] McKinley's war resolution came exactly between these two dates, and Teller was by then almost certainly interested in protecting his constituents. Yet he was also both a political loose cannon, switching parties at least three times during his long career, and a champion of the underdog: he supported women's suffrage years before most other politicians; he opposed Roosevelt's 1903 takeover of Panama; and he was especially offended by the U.S. struggle against Aguinaldo's nationalists in the Philippines. Thus, while protectionism almost certainly played a role in Teller's motivation (as perhaps did lobbying by the New York Junta),[48] it is equally possible that he and other anti-imperialists had heard enough from the jingoes to fear that they would seize any opportunity to annex the island.

Since the Republicans were themselves divided on the wording of the proposed war resolution, it was deliberately confusing—almost but not quite amounting to a recognition of independence. This wording represented an attempt to finesse the difference of opinion between those who, like Senators Foraker and Lodge, argued for recognition, and those who, like Assistant Secretary of State Alvey Adee, argued that humanitarian intervention was preferable to outright recognition, because then "we would be free, if successful, to dictate the terms of peace and control the organization of an independent government in Cuba."[49] This division gave Teller and his probeet, antiannexationist colleagues the opportunity to insert their amendment into the war resolution. By doing so, they guaranteed that the United States would pass over an opportunity to acquire Cuba.

On April 21, the day after President McKinley signed the joint resolution, the Spanish informed U.S. Minister Woodford that it considered McKinley's signature a declaration of war. On April 22 McKinley declared a blockade of Cuba, and on April 25 he asked for and immediately received from Congress a formal declaration of war retroactive to April 21.

It was, as John Hay would remark, "a splendid little war."[50] Admiral Dewey's Pacific squadron sailed unobserved into Manila's harbor on the night of April 30, and as dawn broke, he told Gridley, the skipper of his flagship, to fire when ready. After several hours of shelling, the battle broke off for a three-hour breakfast, then resumed for another hour. By lunchtime Dewey had destroyed Spain's control over the Philippines. It took two months longer for U.S. troops to mass in southeastern Cuba, but once they had arrived, the victory came almost as quickly. On July 1 and 2 about 15,000 U.S. soldiers, including Roosevelt in his custom-made Brooks Brothers uniform, defeated about 2,000 Spanish troops at San Juan Hill and the village of El Caney a few miles east of Santiago; and on July 3 Admiral Pascual Cevera's rickety flotilla was destroyed as it attempted to escape from Santiago. These three days of fighting ended Spanish resistance, and Santiago capitulated on July 17. U.S. casualties were light (about 300 dead and fewer than 1,500 wounded), citizens at home were elated, and Theodore Roosevelt was on the fast track toward the White House.

The armistice that was signed in Washington on August 12 required

Spain to relinquish its sovereignty over Cuba (without specifying to whom), cede Puerto Rico and Guam to the United States, and permit the U.S. occupation of Manila pending negotiation of a treaty of peace, which would determine control of the Philippines. A peace conference began in Paris on October 1, and a treaty was signed on December 10. It declared that Cuba "is, upon evacuation by Spain, to be occupied by the United States," confirmed the cession of the other islands mentioned in the armistice, and transferred sovereignty over the Philippines to the United States in exchange for $20 million.[51]

Excluded from all the negotiations, Cubans now had a hazy status. Until this time, Henry Cabot Lodge had favored permitting the Cubans to take over from the Spanish, noting in 1896 that "the officers of the provisional government are Cubans, white men, and of good family and position. Among the principal military officers there are only three of negro blood."[52] In general, Cubans had received wide praise in the United States for their tenacious three-year struggle against the Spanish, yet once the U.S. forces landed, there was only one early attempt at military cooperation, when the U.S. Army sent Lieutenant Andrew Rowan to meet with General Calixto García in Bayamo. García agreed to provide covering fire if needed during the U.S. landing east of Santiago, but beyond that there was no joint activity. The U.S. participants never reported that their victory was made immeasurably less difficult because the rebels had pinned down nearly all of the 200,000 Spanish troops on the island.

With the fighting over, the Army commander in Santiago, William Shafter, reported that the Cuban rebels now wanted to assume control of the country. "The trouble with General Garcia was that he expected to be placed in command at this place; in other words, that we would turn the city over to him. I explained to him fully that we were at war with Spain and that the question of Cuban independence could not be considered by me."[53] General Shafter then issued an order excluding insurgents from Santiago, and only on September 23 was General García allowed to enter with his troops, this time as a guest of the U.S. Army, which escorted the Cubans in their symbolic victory parade, then marched them back out of the city.

Even before the fighting, Secretary of State Day (the aging Sherman had been forced into retirement) had written the President of his hope that Cubans "may prove more orderly and less likely to plunge into civil war and brigandage than has been expected," and in his December 1898 message to Congress President McKinley reassured anti-imperialists by agreeing that "Spanish rule must be replaced by a just, benevolent, and humane government, created by the people of Cuba." But U.S. officials were obviously skeptical of the Cuban capacity for self-government, and so McKinley added that "until there is complete tranquillity in the island and a stable government inaugurated military occupation will be continued."[54] This took until mid-1902, and in the intervening years Cuba was administered by the U.S. Department of War.

One reason for the four-year delay is that much of the Democrats' early anti-imperialist sentiment seemed to disappear as party leaders jumped on the jingo bandwagon, and this led some Republicans to believe that it might be possible to repeal the Teller Amendment. After all, the Democratic ranks contained a fair share of imperialists, and as early as 1884 the party's platform had bragged about the "grand acquisitions of Democratic statesmanship" and criticized the Republicans for limiting their vision to Alaska.[55] Now, in 1898, if one were looking to assign the title of "The War's Most Active Imperialist" to a U.S. political leader, the runner-up to Theodore Roosevelt might be William Jennings Bryan, who rushed into uniform and complained bitterly when his "Silver Battalion" of Nebraska volunteers was kept out of the fighting. On the other side of the Democratic party, former President Cleveland also made Cuba an exception to his traditional anti-imperialism; he opposed the war in 1898, but in 1900 assumed a period of tutelage leading to annexation: "I am afraid Cuba ought to be submerged for awhile before it will make an American state or territory of which we will be particularly proud."[56]

To the extent that a Democratic opposition to imperialism existed, it seemed to be based upon the desire not to incorporate the unruly peoples of the captured islands into the Union.[57] The 1900 Democratic platform formally asserted that "the Filipinos cannot be citizens without endangering our civilization; they cannot be subjects without imperiling our form of government; and as we are not willing to surrender our civilization nor to convert the Republic into an empire, we favor an immediate declaration of the nation's purpose to give the Filipinos, first, a stable form of government; second, independence; and third, protection from outside interference, such as has been given for nearly a century to the republics of Central and South America." The Silver Republican platform agreed: "It is clear and certain that the inhabitants of the Philippine archipelago cannot be made citizens of the United States without endangering our civilization."

There was another broadly nonpartisan side to anti-imperialism, and it also focused upon the Philippines, not Cuba, for it was there that the people refused to accept the U.S. occupation. At home this opposition was best articulated by Mark Twain, who spent nearly all of the 1890s abroad, returning home in 1900 as both the nation's most popular author and something of an authority on international relations. In a shipboard interview he told reporters that "I have tried hard, and yet I cannot for the life of me comprehend how we got into that mess [in the Philippines]. I thought we should act as their protector—not try to get them under our heel." The following year Twain wrote that "we have invited our clean young men to shoulder a discredited musket and do bandit's work under a flag which bandits have been accustomed to fear, not to follow; we have debauched America's honor and blackened her face before the world."[58]

Theodore Roosevelt later responded for the nation's jingoes by asserting that "history may safely be challenged to show a single instance in which a masterful race such as ours, having been forced by the exigencies of war to take possession of an alien land, has behaved to its inhabitants with the disinterested zeal for their progress that our people have shown in the Philippines. To leave the islands at this time would mean that they would fall into a welter of murderous anarchy. Such a desertion of duty on our part would be a crime against humanity."[59]

But that was later; now, in 1899, the McKinley administration was worried about the political backlash from a growing Philippine insurgency, and this concern directly affected the administration's policy toward Cuba. In his annual message to Congress in December, the President reported that U.S. ground forces in the Philippines now numbered some 65,000, despite the fact that none had been needed to oust the Spanish, while the Army's strength in Cuba had been reduced to 11,000. The last thing that McKinley wanted was to launch his bid for reelection with a second anticolonial rebellion in Cuba dominating the headlines, and with his Democratic opponent (probably Bryan) hurling charges of disobeying the Teller amendment—God only knows what the man who had taken an obscure issue like the free coinage of silver and crucified Republicans on a cross of gold could do with an issue like imperialism.[60] Balancing this electoral threat from public opinion was pressure from those who were fearful of a U.S. withdrawal, including the powerful sugar grower Edwin Atkins, who wrote the President in mid-1899 that "the insurgent independent party (wishing to be rid of American control) represents no property interest as a class, and their control of affairs is equally feared by the Cuban property-holders, Spaniards, and foreigners."[61]

Thus McKinley walked right down the middle of the road, warning against "a hasty experiment bearing within itself the elements of failure," but also telling Congress in late 1899 that the nation's pledge of Cuban independence "is the highest honorable obligation and must be sacredly kept." A census was under way in Cuba, he reported, and when it was completed, municipal government elections could be held. After that, there would be "the formation of a representative convention of the people to draft a constitution and establish a general system of independent government for the island."[62]

In the meantime, Governor-General Leonard Wood had his own policy: he was seeking to convince the Cubans to take the initiative and demand annexation. In mid-1899 Roosevelt told Lodge, "Wood believes that we should not promise or give the Cubans independence; that we should govern them justly and equitably, giving them all possible opportunities for civic and military advancement, and that in two or three years they will insist on being part of us." Two months later Wood, a Rough Rider, wrote Roosevelt that "clean government, quick decisive action and absolute control in the hands of trustworthy men, establishment of needed legal and education reforms and I do not believe you could shake Cuba loose if you wanted to."[63]

Thus Cuba became a laboratory for progressive social reforms, especially in public health and public works. Some like Wood may have pursued these reforms for ulterior motives, but they were nonetheless of substantial benefit to Cubans. They stand as a tribute to the positive aspects of the U.S. occupation. In politics the military governors were less competent. Among their less successful reforms was the development of a police force, a move prompted originally by the fear of disorder among the Cuban soldiers who no longer had the Spanish army to fight. About a month after the fall of Santiago, General Shafter wrote Washington that "the whole trouble here is that there is nothing for men to do in the country. It has absolutely returned to its wild state and has got to be settled and made anew."[64] The progressive response was to enlist these former rebel fighters on the side of law and order. While serving as military governor of the eastern part of Cuba, General Wood had created the Rural Guard, and soon after his promotion to Governor-General, he and Secretary of War Elihu Root developed plans for the creation of an army led by U.S. officers. Wood argued that "these native regiments would embody the restless and wild spirits which have been engaged in the recent war." Root agreed, writing President McKinley that such a force "would dispose of a lot of men most likely to make trouble in Cuba, turn them from possible bandits, and educate them into Americans."[65] Wood and Root had no idea of the consequences of their actions.

Only limited political reforms had been implemented by the end of 1899 when McKinley announced his transition plan to Congress, and so General Wood tried to convince the President to extend the transition period, writing that "the people here, Mr. President, know that they are not ready for self government and those who are honest make no attempt to disguise the fact. We are going ahead as fast as we can, but we are dealing with a race that has steadily been going down for a hundred years into which we have got to infuse new life, new principles and new methods of doing things. This is not the work of a day or of a year, but of a longer period."[66] Resisting delay, McKinley insisted on concrete results before the autumn U.S. election campaign.

And so Wood got to work. His first task was to disenfranchise that part of the Cuban population that had gone furthest downhill. Suffrage was restricted to Cuban-born males over the age of twenty who could meet one of three requirements: the ability to read and write, the possession of real or personal property valued at $250 or more, or military service in the insurgent forces before the fall of Santiago. These restrictions eliminated two-thirds of Cuba's males over the age of twenty, and Root was especially pleased to learn that the Cuban-born outnumbered the Spanish-born (a reflection of the lingering fear that Cuban tories would seek reannexation to Spain) and that "whites so greatly outnumber the blacks" in the truncated electorate.[67] The remaining citizens were those whom Wood regularly called "the decent element" in Cuba, and Root could congratulate him on the progress he had made: "when the history of the new Cuba comes to be written the establishment of popular self-government, based on a limited suffrage, excluding so great a proportion of the elements which have brought ruin to Hayti and San Domingo, will be regarded as an event of first importance."[68]

Governor-General Wood was unwilling to permit even this limited number of Cubans to determine who should fill public offices or what public policy should be. In his memoir, Edwin Atkins described one effort to thwart the electorate: "In preparing for the first election, General Wood sent for me and asked me to use my influence in support of a very respectable man whom he wished to elect as alcalde of Cienfuegos. I sent for one of the alcaldes de barrio and told him my wishes. He told me to have no anxiety; the man I suggested would be elected. I asked him how he proposed to do it. He said it was a simple matter; they would take possession of the ballot boxes and destroy the ballots of the opposition candidates. I told him that was a magnificent idea and worthy of Tammany Hall. Needless to say, this candidate was elected." In a sense, this meddling was unnecessary, for as Wood informed McKinley, the municipal governments were "subject always to the veto of the Military Governor. This will be necessary for some time, as many of the municipalities are as ignorant as children of the value of the rights which they would give away [to private entrepreneurs] for little or nothing."[69]

The wisdom of McKinley's decision to push toward Cuban independence became apparent as the U.S. presidential campaign began. In stark contrast to the progress in Cuba, the situation continued to deteriorate in the Philippines, and as a result the 1900 election was the only one ever to focus upon imperialism—"the paramount issue of the campaign," read the Democratic platform. "We assert that no nation can long endure half republic and half empire, and we warn the American people that imperialism abroad will lead quickly and inevitably to despotism at home." The Democrats told voters that "we are not opposed to territorial expansion when it takes in desirable territory which can be erected into States in the Union, and whose people are willing and fit to become American citizens," but in the case of the Philippines "we are unalterably opposed to seizing or purchasing distant islands to be governed outside the Constitution, and whose people can never become citizens." As for Cuba, "we demand the prompt and honest fulfillment of our pledge to the Cuban people and the world."

Focusing upon the Philippines, the People's party was even more vehement in its anti-imperialism, accusing the McKinley administration of violating "the plain precepts of humanity. Murder and arson have been our response to the appeals of the people who asked only to establish a free government in their own land." The Prohibition party charged that "while our exportation of liquors to Cuba never reached $30,000 a year previous to American occupation of that island, our exports of such liquors to Cuba during the fiscal year of 1899 reached the sum of $629,855." The nation had been "humiliated, exasperated and grieved, by the evidence painfully abundant, that this Administration's policy of expansion is bearing so rapidly its first fruits of drunkenness, insanity and crime under the hot sun of the tropics."[70]

The Republicans responded that they were doing nothing more in the Philippines than attempting "to put down armed insurrection and to confer the blessings of liberty and civilization upon all the rescued peoples." In Cuba, "independence and self-government were assured in the same voice by which war was declared, and . . . this pledge shall be performed." In an electoral contest that slowly moved away from the discussion of imperialism to a number of unrelated issues, including the old bugaboo of free silver, the Democrats lost more heavily than in 1896. Accepting the Democratic platform's assertion that the election was a referendum on imperialism, the victorious Republicans immediately claimed a mandate for the long-term occupation of the Philippines, and for the very special arrangement that they were about to impose upon Cuba.

When General Wood brought Cuba's constituent assembly to order on November 5, 1900, one day before the U.S. presidential election, he informed its members that "it will be your duty, first, to frame and adopt a constitution for Cuba, and when that has been done to formulate what in your opinion ought to be the relations between Cuba and the United States." Even before the war, President McKinley had hinted at the need for a special U.S.-Cuban relationship—"The new Cuba yet to arise from the ashes of the past must needs be bound to us by ties of singular intimacy"—but exactly what that entailed, he continued, "is for the future to determine in the ripeness of events."[71] General Wood believed that the newly installed constituent assembly could not be relied upon to design an appropriate relationship, for despite his best efforts, the Cuban electorate had not managed to select many representatives from among "the decent element." He wrote Secretary of War Elihu Root that "I hoped they would send their very best men. They have done so in many instances, but they have also sent some of the worst agitators and political rascals in Cuba." More pessimistic was Wood's report to Senator Orville Platt, chair of the Senate Committee on Relations with Cuba: "the dominant party in the Convention to-day contains probably the worst political element in the Island."[72]

Given the nature of the constituent assembly, Wood again pressed for a halt in the transition process, telling Secretary of War Root that the Cubans themselves "realize that many of the officials recently elected are wholly incompetent . . . It is my opinion that at the next municipal elections we shall get hold of a better class of people. If we do not, we must chose [sic] between establishing a Central American Republic or retaining some sort of control for the time necessary to establish a stable government."[73] Wood worried about the welfare of the Spaniards—since they owned "practically [all] the commerce of the island it is very important they be assured that they are not to be left to the caprices of an untried government." He also was concerned about the fate of wealthy Cubans: "the commercial element, the property owning element whatever their patriotic sentiments may be, are very reluctant to see a change of government, unless it be annexation to the United States." Senator Platt found that Wood's description of the Cubans' political immaturity fit closely with his own thinking: "In many respects they are like children."[74]

With continued U.S. occupation out of the question, the task facing Platt, Wood, Root, and like-minded U.S. officials was to devise a mechanism whereby the United States could grant formal independence but maintain control over people whom they considered unfit for self-government. To this end, they fashioned a unique document, the Platt Amendment.* Its preamble authorized the President "to leave the government and control of the island of Cuba to its people as soon as a government shall have been established under a constitution which, either as a part thereof or in an ordinance appended thereto, shall define the future relations of the United States with Cuba, substantially as follows: . . ." The heart of the "as follows" was Article 3, which restricted the independence of the Cuban government by granting the United States "the right to intervene for . . . the maintenance of a government adequate for the protection of life, property, and individual liberty."

The Amendment's other seven articles severely curtailed the new nation's autonomy. As a reflection of this generation's fear of European intervention to collect on defaulted debts, Article 2 provided that "the Government shall not assume any public debt to pay the interest on which the ordinary revenues of the Island shall be inadequate." As Root wrote, "the preservation of that independence by a country so small as Cuba, so inca-

---

*The document is called an amendment because Senator Platt and his colleagues did not complete work on it until mid-February 1901. Since there was not time for the proposal to be submitted as a separate bill before the 56th Congress adjourned on March 3, it was attached as an amendment to the Army appropriations bill for fiscal year 1902.

pable, as she must always be, to contend by force against the great powers of the world, must depend upon her strict performance of international obligations . . . and upon her never contracting any public debt which in the hands of the citizens of foreign powers shall constitute an obligation she is unable to meet."[75]

Article 7 provided that "the Government of Cuba will sell or lease to the United States lands necessary for coaling or naval stations at certain specified points." In subsequent years these bases would be justified by the need to protect the approaches to the Panama Canal—but that was later. At the time that the Platt Amendment was being drafted, Secretary of War Root indicated that Article 7 was designed to control the Cubans:

> I think it is very important that the United States should become the actual owner of the water front for naval stations, not only at Guantanamo but at Havana, and, probably, at some other points in the Island. When we turn the government of Cuba over to Cuban hands, some one will have to decide what means the United States shall retain to require that government to fulfill all the obligations for protection of life and property for which we will continue to stand as practically a guarantor to the other civilized powers. When that situation arises it will be much more difficult for any Cuban to object to the United States continuing to occupy its own property of Cuba, even though the occupation in both cases would be one involving political as well as property rights. For this reason I am very desirous that the Guantanamo purchase should be made.[76]

Originally there were to be four military bases, but that was soon reduced to two (Bahía Honda west of Havana and Guantánamo Bay east of Santiago), and in 1912 the Navy gave up its right to Bahía Honda in exchange for more land at Guantánamo.

The brief Senate floor debate on the Platt Amendment occurred on February 27, with the general sentiment among anti-imperialists captured by Mississippi Democrat Hernando Desoto Money, who told his colleagues: "I would rather have this amendment passed . . . than to see the United States continue to be the possessor of Cuba, holding her people in a state under which they are already chafing."[77] Money was probably not being altruistic; he had been a longtime champion of Cuba's earliest possible independence, and it was broadly rumored (but never proved) that he was one of the senators who had accepted as a gift some bonds that were issued by the

New York junta; however, until Cuba was independent and the junta had its hands on Cuba's treasury, the bonds were worthless. Whatever the motivation, neither Senator Money nor any of his colleagues vigorously opposed the Platt Amendment. Alabama Democrat Edmund Pettus took only a few minutes to complain that "we promised to make them free and independent; that is the amount of it, and we are not doing it." Most anti-imperialists either remained moot or took the opportunity provided by the debate to criticize the administration's continued hold on the Philippines. Even Senator Hoar, the backbone of Republican anti-imperialism, called the Platt Amendment "eminently wise and satisfactory." The most substantial opposition came from Alabama Democrat John Morgan, who called the amendment "a piece of arrant hypocrisy."[78] Morgan convinced only a few of his colleagues, however, and after about an hour of back-and-forth discussion, the Platt Amendment was approved by a vote of 43 to 20; it then zipped through to a House-Senate conference and was promptly signed into law by President McKinley.[79]

Then the task was to convince the Cuban constitutional assembly to accept the Platt Amendment. Governor-General Wood had written Root that "in my opinion the demands are liberal, equitable and just and should be insisted upon throughout." But the Cubans objected, and when their opposition became known in Washington, Root wrote Wood that there would never be independence "if they continue to exhibit ingratitude and entire lack of appreciation of the expenditure of blood and treasure of the United States to secure their freedom from Spain."[80] Despite this admonition, in April the Cuban assembly rejected the Platt Amendment by a vote of 24 to 2, opting instead to send a delegation to Washington to negotiate a less intrusive document.

The delegates were received politely and told that the Amendment did not mean what absolutely everyone knew it meant. At Root's request, Senator Platt assured the Cubans that "the amendment was carefully drafted with a view to avoid any possible claim that its acceptance by the Cuban Constitutional Convention would result in the establishment of a protectorate or suzerainty, or in any way interfere with the independence or sovereignty of Cuba." Root believed that the Cuban delegation had left Washington with "a feeling of kindliness towards the United States, arising from the nature of their reception and treatment here, both the social attention paid to them and the careful consideration given to their questions and arguments."[81]

The Cuban delegates returned to Havana with the news that the constituent assembly would have to accept the Platt Amendment if it wanted independence, and so on May 28 the assembly voted, 15 to 14, to incorporate a slightly modified version of the Amendment into the Cuban constitution. The United States insisted on no modifications whatever, and so the assembly was obliged to cast yet another ballot: by a vote of 16 to 11, with four abstentions, on June 12 the unmodified Platt Amendment was added to the same spot in the Cuban constitution where the framers of the U.S. constitution had placed a Bill of Rights. "Happily now they have at last concluded to trust the United States," wrote Senator Platt.[82]

And so it was that the United States ended its initial occupation of Cuba by obliging Cubans to accept continued supervision, largely because leaders in Washington believed that the island's pacification was incomplete. The Platt Amendment was an insurance policy, issued on behalf of U.S. strategic and economic interests in the island. Several months before General Wood sailed out of Havana harbor for the last time on May 20, 1902, Cuba's independence day, he had written that "there is, of course, little or no independence left Cuba under the Platt Amendment." That was by design, as Senator Platt noted: "The United States will always, under the so-called Platt Amendment, be in a position to straighten out things if they get seriously bad."[83] Hegemony had been formalized.

Chapter 9 ⌣

Creating a Country, Building a Canal

We shall have a treaty in the main very satisfactory, vastly advantageous to the United States, and we must confess, with what face we can muster, not so advantageous to Panama.

⌣ *Secretary of State John Hay, 1904*

Thomas Jefferson once voiced the opinion that a canal across Central America would be "a work much less difficult than some even of the inferior canals of France." Although it did not take long for U.S. officials to be disabused of that notion, from the beginning they assumed that a Central American canal would be constructed fairly soon, and they naturally wanted to ensure U.S. access. In 1826 Henry Clay instructed his envoys to Bolívar's Panama Congress to ensure that any route across the isthmus be internationalized, for "what is to redound to the advantage of all America should be effected by common means and united exertions, and should not be left to the separate and unassisted efforts of any one power." [1] This policy was restated from time to time through the middle decades of the nineteenth century, most notably in 1849 when President Zachary Taylor informed Congress that a private contract had been concluded with Nicaragua for the construction of a canal. Despite the fact that the contractors were U.S. citizens, Taylor reasserted Henry Clay's policy that "such a work should be constructed under the common protection of all nations, for equal benefits to all." [2]

Travelers in the 1850s had been content with a transisthmian railway in Panama and a river-lake transit route in southern Nicaragua, but expanding post–Civil War trade required a route for ships. That said, it is not certain why the construction of a canal became so important to the Grant administration (1869–77), but it did. Perhaps it was because the President had learned firsthand of the potential advantages of a canal, having been obliged to cross the isthmus on his way to California as a young army captain in 1852. "I wondered how any person could live many months in Aspinwall [now Colón], and wondered still more why any one tried," he wrote. Mired in mud and attacked by tropical fevers, "we were delayed six weeks. About one-seventh of those who left New York harbor with the 4th infantry on the 5th of July, now lie buried on the Isthmus of Panama."[3]

Whatever his motivation, President Grant created an Interoceanic Canal Commission that sent seven separate expeditions to identify the most appropriate canal route in Central America. As the teams of surveyors and engineers fanned out across the isthmus to conduct their fieldwork, the Grant administration signed a treaty with Colombia giving the United States the right to build a canal; then after the Commission recommended a route through Nicaragua in its 1876 final report, the United States prepared another treaty with that country. Both agreements died after arousing substantial opposition in the host countries, and in the end the Grant administration did little more than identify Nicaragua as the most suitable route.

The United States was not the only maritime nation interested in a canal. As part of his successful effort to popularize the concept of "Latin" America, in 1846 Louis Napoléon (Napoléon III) published a book, *Canal de Nicaragua,* designed to generate public interest. A decade later, immediately after the filibustering era of William Walker, a French venture capitalist, Félix Belly, obtained an exclusive concession from Nicaragua and Costa Rica to build a canal along the San Juan River. This led Secretary of State Lewis Cass to instruct the U.S. minister to tell the governments of Nicaragua and Costa Rica that neither nation "would be permitted in a spirit of eastern isolation to close these gates of intercourse on the great highways of the world [or] to encumber them with such unjust regulations [a reference to the French concession], as would prevent their general use. The United States do not seek either the control or the exclusive use of these routes. They desire that the advantages should be equally common to all nations."[4] Severely hampered by political instability in Central America and unable to obtain adequate financing in Europe, Belly's project died by late 1859.

This was but a prelude to the events of 1878 and 1879, when a French navy officer, Lucien Wyse, was sent to the Colombian province of Panama to identify an appropriate canal route. He did that and more, obtaining a concession from the Colombian government to build and operate a canal across the isthmus of Panama. Ferdinand de Lesseps, the French engineer-entrepreneur acclaimed for the construction of the Suez Canal, was soon brought into the project, and he kicked it off with a splash by inviting nearly 150 canal specialists to an international conference in Paris in May 1879. The purpose was to select the specific canal route, to make technical recommendations regarding its construction, and—primarily—to generate the publicity needed to sell construction bonds. The United States was represented by two participants from the Grant administration's Interoceanic Canal Commission, and they championed a route through Nicaragua. The balance of opinion was overwhelmingly in favor of a sea-level canal through Panama, however, with the conference estimating that the twelve-year construction project would cost $240 million.[5] De Lesseps and his associates then created the *Compagnie Universelle du Canal Interoceanique de Panama*, paid Wyse $10 million for his concession from Colombia, and set out to build the Panama Canal.

All this came as something of a shock to officials in Washington, who had assumed that any Central American canal would be built by private U.S. capital, aided perhaps by a formal understanding between the U.S. government and the Central American state of Washington's choice. True, the efforts to date had been unsuccessful, but U.S. officials believed that it was just a matter of time until acceptable arrangements could be made and U.S. entrepreneurs could set to work, probably in Nicaragua. Now, however, the administration of Rutherford Hayes was chagrined to discover that a smooth-talking Frenchman had invited Washington's backup date to the prom and, even worse, that Colombia had accepted.

And so, in one of the most ill-conceived initiatives in U.S. diplomatic history, President Hayes set out to convince Colombia to stay home from the dance. His Secretary of State, William Evarts, lodged a formal protest against the Wyse concession, alleging that the 1846 Bidlack Treaty gave the United States special rights to control access to the Panamanian isthmus.[6] This was almost certainly not true, but that was hardly the issue being discussed in Bogotá. For several years Colombians had watched with growing unease as the United States repeatedly announced its intention to destroy Panama's economy by building a canal in nearby Nicaragua. If the United States wanted to build elsewhere, that was its privilege, but officials in Bogotá were unwilling to sit at home while the United States and Nicaragua held hands in the tropical moonlight. Since the United States was not interested in a commitment to Panama, then the French would do fine.

After visiting Panama to inaugurate construction, de Lesseps traveled to the United States to raise money and to assuage the fears of U.S. officials. He met with President Hayes, testified before a Congressional committee, and did his best to dampen the hostility of many U.S. journalists. Playing shamelessly to the nation's vanity, he wrote that "civilization lives again on the American Continent in our day; at its head marches the intelligent people of the United States." He repeatedly invited U.S. citizens to invest in the project, which he saw as an especially appropriate opportunity for those "who strive after the works of peace and of progress, in which the United States are especially preeminent." As for the imagined threat of French intervention, de Lesseps emphasized that "the maritime canal is to be the private property of all nationalities." He also began the process of convincing his North American audience that the Nicaraguan route was inferior to that of Panama, citing in particular the delays that would be required for passage through the large number of locks envisioned in Nicaragua, as well as the extensive excavation that would be needed to straighten the sinuous San Juan River to accommodate large ocean liners.[7]

U.S. citizens were not eager to invest in the French company or, for that matter, in *any* project to construct a Central American canal. In a direct challenge to the French, in late 1879 a U.S. syndicate led by Admiral Daniel Ammen had formed the Provisional Interoceanic Canal Society, obtained a concession from Nicaragua, and then reorganized into the Maritime Canal Company of Nicaragua. With former President Grant and his Wall Street associates helping to raise funds, the Company announced that it would build a twelve-lock, fifty-mile canal across southern Nicaragua using Lake Nicaragua and part of the San Juan River. But the U.S. economy was entering another cyclical decline, Grant's firm was unable to raise the necessary money (indeed, it soon collapsed, impoverishing the former President), and the Nicaraguan concession lapsed in September 1884. The Maritime Canal Company of Nicaragua was subsequently reincorporated by a different group of investors. Ground was broken in October 1889, and work on ancillary facilities continued for three years, but funding evaporated in the wake of the Panic of 1893, and the company again fell into bankruptcy.

Meanwhile, it fell to the Hayes administration to develop the official U.S. response to the French challenge. He ordered the Secretary of the Navy to send U.S. warships to both the Atlantic and the Pacific sides of Panama, near the Costa Rican border at Chiriqui, where there was some question about the validity of an earlier Colombian land grant to a U.S. citizen, Ambrose Thompson. The warships were "to establish naval stations in these important harbors," he said, and "if it shall be deemed best by Congress to take possession of this interest [Thompson's Chiriqui grant], the presence of our ships and the establishing of our coaling stations will give us a foothold which will be of vast service in controlling the passage from ocean to ocean either at Panama or Nicaragua lake." Then President Hayes considered negotiating a multilateral treaty guaranteeing the canal's neutrality, but this approach was quickly discarded in favor of one that would give the United States full control. With his cabinet's approval, in March 1880 Hayes informed Congress of a major policy shift: "the policy of this country is a canal under American control," he said. "The United States can not consent to the surrender of this control to any European power."[8] Although President Hayes promised to give "due regard to the rights and wishes of our sister republics in the Isthmus," in the same sentence he simply dismissed them: "the United States will insist that this passageway shall always remain under American control." Hayes was even more candid in his diary, noting that "the true policy of the United States as to a canal across any part of the Isthmus is either a canal under American control, or no canal."[9] Only one couple would be going to this dance: the United States and whomever it decided to invite.

President Garfield's 1881 inaugural address quoted with approval the policy announced a year earlier by President Hayes, and during his brief first term as secretary of state, James G. Blaine unsuccessfully sought to abrogate the 1850 Clayton-Bulwer Treaty that prevented either the United States or Great Britain from exercising exclusive control over any future canal. Then in late 1881, just after Garfield's assassination, word reached Washington that Colombian diplomats in Europe were seeking a multinational guarantee of the neutrality of the de Lesseps canal. President Chester Arthur responded by reiterating the Hayes-Garfield policy that any such guarantee "would be in direct contravention of our obligation as the sole guarantor of the integrity of Colombian territory" through the Bidlack Treaty.[10]

The new secretary of state, Frederick Frelinghuysen, continued Blaine's efforts to modify the Clayton-Bulwer Treaty.[11] Rebuffed by the British, Frelinghuysen turned to Nicaragua and negotiated a treaty providing the United States with exclusive rights to build and operate a canal in return for a permanent U.S.-Nicaraguan alliance to "protect the integrity of the territory" of Nicaragua. Signed on December 1, 1884, immediately after the voters had ousted the Republicans from the White House for the first time since 1860, the Frelinghuysen-Zavala Treaty was greeted with marked ambivalence in Washington, for although it granted the United States access to the isthmus, it also converted Nicaragua into a formal U.S. protectorate, and, of course, it obviously violated the Clayton-Bulwer Treaty with Great Britain. The Senate refused to consider the lame-duck administration's initiative.[12]

Neither Grover Cleveland nor Secretary of State Bayard wished to irritate Great Britain, nor did either relish the idea of becoming responsible for the territorial integrity of Nicaragua, and so Cleveland promptly withdrew the Frelinghuysen-Zavala Treaty from Senate consideration. Noting his distaste for "the incorporation of remote interests with our own," Cleveland also rejected the broader Grant-Hayes policy of unilateral control of an isthmian canal. Instead, he reestablished Henry Clay's policy: "Whatever highway may be constructed across the barrier dividing the two greatest maritime areas of the world must be for the world's benefit—a trust for mankind, to be removed from the chance of domination by any single power, nor become a point of invitation for hostilities or a prize for warlike ambition."[13] There the matter rested in Washington during the mid-1880s, while in Panama the de Lesseps company pushed ahead with construction.

This gave the Republican party an issue, and in its 1888 platform it accused the Cleveland administration of watching "with idle complacency the extension of foreign influence in Central America." The victorious Republicans immediately changed U.S. policy, with Benjamin Harrison announcing in his 1889 inaugural address that he expected all European powers to refrain from dominating any canal route.[14] The issue was especially sensitive at this moment, for the de Lesseps company had just declared bankruptcy. The partially dug canal had drained $260 million from the pockets of the thrifty French bourgeoisie, and the question that preoccupied Washington was whether the French government might succumb to political pressures and rescue the failing project. Harrison's inaugural admonition may have helped the French decide, and construction was suspended in May. About 40 percent of the canal had been completed.

With the French competitors bankrupt, the United States could adopt a more leisurely approach to canal construction. Until the mid-1890s nearly all of the interest in a canal had been generated by the lure of increased trade or lower shipping costs, but these economic benefits, although substantial, were not sufficient to generate action. Then steam replaced sail during the final three decades of the nineteenth century, and it spurred sea transport in much the same way that the transition from propeller to jet aircraft later spurred the airline industry. The technological transition dictated a different cost structure for the shipping industry (unlike wind, coal had to be purchased) and this circumstance led to increased interest in cost-cutting devices such as canals. Then the Spanish-American War added a national security dimension to the calculus, and it soon became the driving force behind canal construction. Just before war was declared, the Navy ordered its Pacific-based pride and joy, the U.S.S. *Oregon*, to join the North Atlantic squadron in the Caribbean—the first battleship ever to be ordered around the tip of South America. Leaving San Francisco on March 19, the voyage received front-page coverage in the nation's newspapers as it made a record dash around South America, arriving in Florida on May 24. The two-month, 14,000-mile trip underscored as nothing ever had the need for a canal.

The canal was originally to be built by private capital, perhaps subsidized by government-guaranteed bonds. In his second inaugural address in 1893, Cleveland endorsed the concept of ownership by U.S. investors, but he noted that "the canal company has unfortunately become financially seriously embarrassed" (an understatement—it was bankrupt); moreover, although he did not promise a government subsidy, he did assert that "the United States are especially interested in the successful achievement of the vast undertaking this company has in charge."[15] A few weeks later the Panic of 1893 threw the country into a deep depression, however, and private venture capital all but disappeared, while the U.S. Treasury was hardly in a position to support overseas construction projects. The revived Maritime Canal Company ceased operations, and in his final three annual messages President Cleveland never mentioned a canal, nor did his Democratic party include the topic in its 1896 platform. Thus the Republicans found no opposition when its 1896 platform eliminated the private sector, and by 1900 both major parties had endorsed a government-constructed canal.

Once it had become their full responsibility, officials in Washington began to focus on site selection. At first this issue was restricted to the choice among several routes through Nicaragua, primarily because the principal Congressional proponent of a canal, Senator John Tyler Morgan, preferred Nicaragua. A former Confederate cavalry officer, the Alabama Democrat was keenly aware of the boost that any canal would give to Southern commerce, and the closer that canal was to Mobile Bay, the better. Since the late

1880s Morgan had sought government guarantees for the bonds of the Maritime Canal Company, and it was chiefly his initiative that led to the creation of the 1895 Senate Select Committee on Construction of the Nicaragua Canal and the 1899 Senate Committee on an Interoceanic Canal, both of which he chaired. It was also through Morgan's effort that Congress agreed in 1895 to create the United States–Nicaraguan Canal Board (the Ludlow Commission), whose purpose was to examine the Grant administration's studies of the Nicaraguan canal routes and select the one that seemed most appropriate. Concluding that the earlier studies were inadequate, the Ludlow Commission instead recommended that the government undertake a thorough new study. In 1897, while everyone else in a special session of Congress was debating what was supposed to be its sole topic—the new Republican administration's tariff proposal—Senator Morgan slipped the Ludlow Commission's recommendation through both houses. It authorized the creation of the *Nicaragua* Canal Commission.[16]

Chaired by Admiral John G. Walker (hence its common name, the Walker Commission and, later, the "First" Walker Commission), the Commission sent a hundred-member expedition of surveyors, engineers, and geologists to San Juan del Norte at the very end of 1897. There they began more than a year of exhaustive field exploration, and in mid-1899 the Commission issued a report recommending construction of a canal from San Juan del Norte on the Caribbean coast to Brito on the Pacific. But even before the Walker Commission had issued its final report, Congress had decided to create another commission, this one called the *Isthmian* Canal Commission, with a mandate "to determine the most feasible and practicable route" in Central America.[17] This second Walker Commission was a lobbying triumph by the French owners of the Panama route.

What happened was simple. When the de Lesseps company fell into bankruptcy in 1889, its assets consisted of a partially dug canal, the Panama railway, some rusting machinery, and, most important, a concession from the Colombian government. Bulky and indivisible, these assets could not be distributed among the disappointed investors, nor was there a market where they could be sold. Unable to obtain even a partial distribution of what little remained of their investment, the frustrated shareholders turned with a vengeance on the company's officers, many of whom had managed to grow wealthy as the company went broke.

Following years of litigation, the company's court-appointed receiver struck upon an exceptionally clever plan. In October 1894 he created a *New*

Panama Canal Company *(La Compagnie Nouvelle du Canal de Panama)*, with a total capital of 65 million francs. Of that amount, 5 million was assigned to Colombia in return for an extension of the Wyse concession, which was about to expire. Two-thirds of the remaining 60 million francs was to come from a forced purchase by people identified as "penalty share-holders," or *pénalitaires*—the insiders whom the courts had found to have profited improperly during the de Lesseps effort. In return for their 41 million francs (plus additional highly speculative subscriptions to bring the total up to 60 million francs, all of which was distributed to the original investors), the new company received ownership of the fixed assets of the original company, with the understanding that 60 percent of any future distributions would go to the old shareholders.

Recognizing that a once-failed enterprise would have difficulty raising sufficient additional capital in Europe, in 1896 the New Panama Canal Company took the fateful step of hiring a New York attorney to sell its interests in the United States. The man whom they selected was William Nelson Cromwell, lawyer for the Panama Railway, cofounder of the now-venerable Wall Street firm of Sullivan and Cromwell and, as a reporter would later observe, "the man whose masterful mind, whetted on the grindstone of corporation cunning, conceived and carried out the rape of the Isthmus." Representative Henry Rainey called him "the most danger-ous man this country has produced since the days of Aaron Burr."[18]

The year 1896 was also the one in which the victorious Republican plat-form advocated U.S.-government construction, so that Cromwell's task, simply stated, was to convince officials in Washington to purchase the assets of the New Panama Canal Company. This was among the most dif-ficult lobbying tasks imaginable, for the United States had been committed to Nicaragua for two decades, ever since President Grant's commission had reported in favor of that route. Senator Morgan's parochial interests not-withstanding, Nicaragua had a healthier climate, it was substantially closer to the United States (579 miles shorter on a 6,000-mile trip from New Orleans to San Francisco), and it had a large lake and a river that could be made passable—about 120 miles of lake-river travel and sixty miles of canal, which largely compensated for the fact that Nicaragua was three times wider than Panama. When, in the end, the United States opted for Panama, credit for the shift had to be awarded to Cromwell and his some-time-colleague, Philippe Bunau-Varilla, who had served briefly as chief engineer of the de Lesseps company and whose brother had been a prime subcontractor specializing in excavation. Bunau-Varilla was a *pénalitaire.*

The two lobbyists' first step was to encourage Congress to authorize the second Walker Commission, an achievement for which both Cromwell and Bunau-Varilla would later take credit.[19] Then they convinced the Commission to visit Europe and inspect the canals at Manchester and Kiel and the records of the French project in Paris. Bunau-Varilla virtually met the Commissioners' ship when it arrived in Europe—"our conferences were long and frequent," he reported in his memoirs, and "when the Commission left Paris I was certain that the scales had fallen from the eyes of at least three of its members."[20]

In addition to its European excursion, the second Walker Commission's thirty-one working parties examined various routes from Tehuantepec in Mexico to northwestern Colombia. In this process the Commission inquired about the purchase of the New Panama Canal Company's assets and especially the Wyse concession, without which no canal could be built in Panama. The Company responded that it would be pleased to sell everything for $109,141,500. Admiral Walker and his colleagues determined that $40 million would be a fair price, and since "the price fixed by the Panama Canal Company for a sale of its property and franchises is so unreasonable," in late 1901 the Commission recommended once again that the canal be built in Nicaragua.[21]

The Commission's report signaled the beginning of a two-month flurry of activity in both Washington and Paris. Two days after it was issued, Secretary of State John Hay and British Ambassador Julian Pauncefote concluded completely independent negotiations by signing a treaty abrogating the Clayton-Bulwer Treaty, clearing the way for U.S. control over the canal.[22] Coming on the heels of Britain's capitulation in the Venezuelan boundary dispute and its acquiescence to the U.S. takeover of Spain's possessions in the Caribbean, the Hay-Pauncefote treaty was an unequivocal signal that Great Britain had decided to yield control of the Caribbean region to the United States. The agreement zipped through the Senate in less than a month, just days after Theodore Roosevelt delivered his first annual message to Congress, in which he referred to a Central American canal as the "single great material work which remains to be undertaken on this continent."[23]

The business of government then paused for the year-end holidays, while behind the scenes Cromwell and Bunau-Varilla redoubled their efforts. They were particularly effective in communicating to their French colleagues the U.S. distaste for haggling over prices. On January 4, 1902, the Company announced that the sale price would be $40 million, and President Roosevelt promptly asked Admiral Walker to reconvene his Commission. Two days later it issued an amended report "that 'the most practicable and feasible route' for an isthmian canal . . . is that known as the Panama route." [24]

This was only the President's recommendation; now Congress had to select the site through authorizing legislation. It could have permitted the President to decide by simply authorizing a canal somewhere in Central America, but that was never a genuine possibility, since the legislation had to originate in the Republican House with Representative William Hepburn's Committee on Interstate and Foreign Commerce and in the Democratic Senate with John Morgan's Committee on an Interoceanic Canal. Both legislators were strong partisans of the Nicaragua route. During the brief period between the French announcement of its reduced sale price and the Walker Commission's reconsideration, Hepburn secured House approval of a Nicaragua site by an overwhelming majority of 308 to 2. It took longer for the Senate to decide: in March Senator Morgan's committee issued both a majority (Nicaragua) and minority (Panama) report, with Morgan, a Democrat, facing a Republican minority led by Marcus Hanna and John Spooner.

The elaborate minority report was written by Bunau-Varilla and Cromwell. It and numerous other documents demonstrating the close relationship between Hanna and the two lobbyists have always had the effect of clouding the Senator's reputation, perhaps undeservedly. What is certain is that Senator Hanna was crucial to the site decision; Senator Shelby Cullom wrote that Hanna "changed the whole attitude of the Senate concerning the route for an interoceanic canal. We all generally favored the Nicaraguan route. Senator Hanna became convinced that the Panama route was best, and he soon carried everything before him." [25] What has always remained unclear is *why* Hanna changed his mind. One unsubstantiated allegation is that Hanna's support was purchased by Cromwell with a $60,000 donation to the Republican party's 1900 campaign fund. It is plausible that he was bribed, but it is at least as plausible that Cromwell and Bunau-Varilla convinced Hanna of the superiority of the Panama route. Perhaps it was both.

Whatever the case, Senator Spooner's minority proposal authorized the President to acquire the assets of the New Panama Canal Company for $40 million and to acquire from Colombia a strip of land across Panama upon which to build a canal. If either of these acquisitions could not be arranged "within a reasonable time and upon reasonable terms," then the President was instructed to build the canal in Nicaragua.

The Senate debate over the two reports had all the trappings of a championship bout featuring two of the era's aging political heavyweights, Morgan versus Hanna. Now in rapidly failing health, Hanna began his speech on June 5, stopped after about two hours, and finished the next day, all the time using notes provided by Cromwell and Bunau-Varilla. The Hepburn-Morgan side made a vigorous presentation on behalf of Nicaragua. As the debate continued, so did the lobbying, with Bunau-Varilla going so far as to distribute Nicaraguan postage stamps showing belching volcanos—"an official witness of the volcanic activity of Nicaragua," he wrote on the card given to each senator. It is not certain whether the senators were fearful that a Nicaragua canal might be buried in volcanic ash or were convinced that, other things being equal, a shorter canal would be a better investment than a longer one, but on June 19 Spooner and Hanna prevailed. The House-Senate conference began the following day, and after several days of resistance, Morgan and Hepburn finally capitulated. After having voted 308 to 2 in favor of Nicaragua six months earlier, the House accepted the conference report endorsing Panama by a vote of 260 to 8—a turnaround unequaled in the history of the House of Representatives. President Roosevelt signed the Spooner Act two days later.[26]

Now the Roosevelt administration turned to Colombia. In 1846 the United States had guaranteed Colombia's sovereignty over its province of Panama in order to gain permission to build a road across the isthmus, but not every resident of the isthmus was pleased with the sovereignty guarantee of the 1846 Bidlack agreement. Panama's political status had always been that of an isolated outlying territory, separated from the center of the country by jungle so dense that to this day no road has ever been constructed. In time this isolation produced both a separatist political subculture and an autonomous economy, and Panamanians attempted separation in 1831, gained independence briefly in 1840 to 1841, and were granted substantial autonomy from 1855 to 1886. But Colombia had held on, often with the help of U.S. Marines, who landed periodically to restore order and keep the railroad open.

With this history of disintegration serving as a backdrop, Secretary of State John Hay sat down with Colombia's minister to the United States, Tomás Herrán, to negotiate a treaty permitting the United States to construct and operate a canal across Panama. The two diplomats reached an agreement in January 1903, and two months later the Hay-Herrán Treaty was ratified by the U.S. Senate.

The treaty's experience in Colombia was different. The nation was at the end of its principal civil war—the War of a Thousand Days—and the country's domestic politics were as chaotic as they had been in the U.S. South in the mid-1860s. Political disagreements, both petty and profound, influenced Colombia's reception of the Hay-Herrán Treaty; so did financial considerations. The duration of the Wyse concession was open to debate, and some Colombians wondered whether it might be better to delay ratification until the concession expired so that Colombia could claim the $40 million authorized by the Spooner Act—since the Hay-Herrán Treaty provided for a payment to Colombia of $10 million followed by annual payments of $250,000, it would take 120 years for Colombia to make what the French shareholders of the New Panama Canal Company would receive immediately in a lump-sum settlement. Another important issue was sovereignty: the Hay-Herrán Treaty stipulated that Colombia had to give the United States a 100-year lease on a six-mile-wide strip of territory bisecting Panama. The U.S. minister in Bogotá warned that "if the proposed convention were to be submitted to the free opinion of the people it would not pass," and in August 1903 the Colombian Senate unanimously rejected the treaty.[27]

President Roosevelt was outraged by the decision, firing off three letters referring to Colombians as "contemptible little creatures," "jack rabbits," and "foolish and homicidal corruptionists." To Charles Lummis he wrote: "To the worst characteristics of 17th Century Spain, and of Spain at its worst under Philip II, Colombia has added a squalid savagery of its own, and it has combined with exquisite nicety the worst forms of despotism and of anarchy, of violence and of fatuous weakness, of dismal ignorance, cruelty, treachery, greed, and utter vanity. I cannot feel much respect for such a country." Once out of office, Roosevelt could drop the diplomatic circumlocutions and be frank: "To talk of Colombia as a responsible Power to be dealt with as we would deal with Holland or Belgium or Switzerland or Denmark is a mere absurdity. The analogy is with a group of Sicilian or Calabrian bandits; with Villa and Carranza at this moment. You could no more make an agreement with the Colombian rulers than you could nail currant jelly to a wall."[28]

President Roosevelt's attitudes were nothing new; this is how U.S. officials had thought of Colombia since the first envoy arrived in Bogotá in the 1820s. In the early 1830s Minister Thomas Moore reported that "although the people are singularly good and pacific; with a few exceptions, the chiefs are in the daily profession of every virtue & the hourly practice of every vice." In the mid-1830s U.S. Chargé Robert McAfee reported that Colombia was "a bigotted Catholic country controlled by the Priests," while in 1850 Chargé Thomas Foote wrote that "their quarrels and revolutions are like family quarrels—as frivolous, often, in their inception, and as fierce and unforgiving in their prosecution." Noting that Colombia was inhabited by "miserable wretches," in the mid-1850s Minister James Bowlin concluded that "even in contrast with Nations of her own kind, formed of the same revolution, from the same people, she occupies the lowest round on the ladder."[29] This was hardly the type of people one wanted living near one's canal.

"Great though our patience has been, it can be exhausted," Roosevelt wrote to Senator Hanna. The Colombian Senate's decision "does not mean that we must necessarily go to Nicaragua. I feel we are certainly justified in morals, and . . . justified in law, under the treaty of 1846, in interfering summarily and saying that the canal is to be built and that they shall not stop it."[30] Physically, this undertaking was possible, of course, but politically it was out of the question, since both the Spooner Act and Senator Morgan's opposition would prohibit a simple armed takeover of Panama. The point did not need to be contested, however, for it was at about this time, in late 1903, that Roosevelt became aware of Cromwell and Bunau-Varilla's efforts to engineer Panama's independence.

Fearful that the Colombian Senate's decision would permit the canal to slip out of their hands, Panamanians had already begun to plan the isthmus's secession from Colombia. Since a successful revolution would require arms and, if possible, external support, in late August 1903 the rebels sent Manuel Amador Guerrero, the physician of the Panama Railroad, to New York. There he consulted with Cromwell, the railroad's U.S. attorney, who placed Amador in the hands of Bunau-Varilla. After meeting with Amador on September 23, Bunau-Varilla traveled to Washington and spoke with Assistant Secretary of State Francis Loomis, who arranged for him to meet with President Roosevelt on October 9 and with Secretary of State Hay on October 16. No minutes of these meetings were taken, but it is beyond belief that Bunau-Varilla discussed anything other than Amador's visit.

Amador sailed for home on October 20, carrying with him a declaration of Panamanian independence, penned by Bunau-Varilla; a constitution, copied by Bunau-Varilla from the recent work of the Cuban constituent assembly; a flag for the proposed new republic, designed and sewn by Madame Bunau-Varilla; and, most important, a promise from Bunau-Varilla that the United States would prevent Colombians from recovering their rebellious territory once the revolutionists declared Panama's independence. Arriving in Panama on October 27, Amador met immediately with his fellow conspirators. They did not like the flag. It was a U.S. flag, modestly altered by Madame Bunau-Varilla, and so the conspirators commissioned Amador's son to design a new one. They also expressed disappointment over Amador's failure to obtain a formal commitment from the U.S. government or to purchase arms; instead, Amador had returned with a Frenchman's promise of U.S. military protection. Unwilling to put their necks in a noose with such flimsy assurances, the group ordered Amador to telegraph Bunau-Varilla that they wanted visible protection.

Amador's cable arrived in New York on October 29, and the following day Bunau-Varilla once again boarded the train to Washington. There he informed Secretary of State Hay of Amador's telegram (he later was unable to recall whether he also met with President Roosevelt), and in the early evening headed back to New York. When the train made its scheduled stop in Baltimore, Bunau-Varilla got off and sent a cable to Amador: "Thirty-six hours Atlantic, forty-eight Pacific." The reference was to the time that U.S. Navy ships would arrive in Panama. Bunau-Varilla had almost certainly been told this by Hay and perhaps by Roosevelt, for on this same day (October 30) the Acting Secretary of the Navy sent the following cable to the captain of the U.S.S. *Nashville* in Kingston, Jamaica: "Hold vessel in readiness to return to Guantanamo," was the first sentence in normal English. The rest was in code that translated as "Secret and confidential. Proceed at once to Colon."[31]

The rest is history: the *Nashville* steamed into the harbor at Colón early in the evening on November 2. That same day the Navy cabled the captain of the *Nashville* and three other ships nearby with instructions to "prevent landing of any armed force, either Government or insurgent, with hostile intent." With the evidence of U.S. support now visible, the conspirators declared Panama's independence on November 3. Later that day a Colombian gunboat lying off the Pacific coast lobbed five or six shells into Panama City, and, according to a report by the U.S. House of Representatives, "finally withdrew after killing a Chinaman in Salsipuedes Street and mortally wounding an ass in the slaughterhouse." Just before midnight the skipper of the *Nashville* received instructions from Washington to "make every effort to prevent [Colombian] Government troops at Colon from proceeding to Panama," and with that the issue was decided. The following morning, November 4, the Panamanian junta cabled Secretary of State Hay to inform him that "on yesterday afternoon, in consequence of a popular and spontaneous movement of the people of this city, the independence of the Isthmus was proclaimed." On November 6 Hay instructed the U.S. consul in Panama to establish diplomatic relations the moment that order had been restored.[32] Since order had already been restored, recognition took place immediately.

The Panamanians understood that Washington's willingness to keep the Colombians at bay was dependent upon the negotiation of an acceptable canal treaty, and even prior to the revolt, they had agreed to name Philippe Bunau-Varilla as the new nation's first Envoy Extraordinary and Minister Plenipotentiary in Washington. The new minister had lunch with Hay on November 9, and the two men immediately began to negotiate a treaty.

A document prepared by Senator John Morgan served as the treaty's initial working draft. Created during a last-ditch effort to save the Nicaragua route, Morgan focused upon amending the Hay-Herrán Treaty to make it even more unacceptable to Colombia. After filling a hundred pages of the *Congressional Record* with the most virulent possible attacks upon the Colombians ("degraded, dissatisfied, turbulent, mixed, and filthy"), Morgan proposed that the Hay-Herrán Treaty be modified to ensure that the Colombians would be kept out of sight and under control.[33] This, he said, was the reason he was proposing sixty amendments to the treaty, but in fact each one was designed to make the treaty so insulting that Colombia would reject it. It never came to that, for the U.S. Senate rejected Morgan's proposed changes before it ratified the Hay-Herrán Treaty. His proposals were not placed in the wastebasket, however; instead, the Morgan-modified Hay-Herrán Treaty became the first draft of the Hay–Bunau-Varilla Treaty. John Hay would later write the president of the Massachusetts Institute of Technology that Senator Morgan "is as much the author of the present canal treaty as I am."[34]

On November 10 Hay presented Bunau-Varilla with the first treaty draft based upon Morgan's rejected amendments. The treaty *projet* quickly went through seven versions, with Hay writing his daughter of the haste with which the process was pursued:

> As for your poor old dad, they are working him nights and Sundays. I have never, I think, been so constantly and actively employed as during the last fortnight. Yesterday morning the negotiations with Panama were far from complete. But by putting on all steam, getting [Secretary of War Elihu] Root, [Attorney General Philander] Knox, and [Secretary of the Treasury Leslie] Shaw together at lunch, I went over my project line by line, and fought out every section of it; adopted a few good suggestions: hurried back to the Department, set everybody at work drawing up final drafts—sent for Varilla, went over the whole treaty with him, explained all the changes, got his consent, and at seven o'clock signed the momentous document in the little blue drawing-room, out of Abraham Lincoln's inkstand.[35]

The haste was prompted by news that the Panamanian junta had sent Manuel Amador and two colleagues to replace Bunau-Varilla, and both Hay and Bunau-Varilla wanted to complete the canal treaty before the Panamanians arrived. On November 17 their ship landed in New York, where they were met by another of Cromwell's associates, Roger Farnham, who took them to a hotel. The next afternoon they left by train for Washington, arriving at 11 P.M. Having signed the canal treaty only four hours earlier, Bunau-Varilla met them at the station platform, told them what had occurred, and watched with delight as Amador "nearly swooned on the platform."[36]

Bunau-Varilla had signed away a 10-mile-wide strip of the isthmus, giving "the United States all the rights, power and authority within the zone . . . which the United States would possess and exercise if it were the sovereign of the territory within which said lands and waters are located to the entire exclusion of the exercise by the Republic of Panama of any such sovereign rights, power or authority." Additional provisions of the treaty gave the United States broad rights to interfere in virtually every aspect of Panamanian national life in order to protect the canal "at all times and in its discretion" and to expropriate, again in perpetuity, "any other lands and waters outside of the zone." In return, Panama received a $10 million one-time payment, annual rent of $250,000, and a promise, in Article I, that "the United States guarantees and will maintain the independence of the Republic of Panama." This last stipulation was a bit of diplomatic bigamy, since in the 1846 Bidlack Treaty, still in force, the United States had guaranteed Colombia's sovereignty over the isthmus.

On December 7 President Roosevelt sent the treaty to the Senate for ratification. The same anti-imperialists who opposed the continuing U.S. hold over the Philippines were dismayed by the extent to which the Hay–Bunau-Varilla Treaty created yet another quasi-colony. They were joined in their opposition by senators favoring a Nicaragua route, led again by John Morgan, who this time did not face Marcus Hanna, who was on his deathbed. Senator Edward Carmack spoke for many opponents when he expressed his distaste for the manipulative policy that had led to the treaty. "There never was any real insurrection in Panama," he said. "To all intents and purposes there was but one man in that insurrection, and that man was the President of the United States."[37]

Roosevelt could not even convince his fellow Republicans that he had acted honorably. Massachusetts Senator George Hoar was among the most suspicious of this group, and so the President sought to win him over by showing him a document purporting to demonstrate his innocence of high-handed behavior. Senator Shelby Cullom was also present, and sketched the proceedings: "The President was sitting on the table, first at one side of Senator Hoar, and then on the other, talking in his usual vigorous fashion, trying to get the Senator's attention to the message. Senator Hoar seemed adverse to reading it, but finally sat down, and without seeming to pay any particular attention to what he was perusing, he remained for a minute or two, then arose and said: 'I hope I may never live to see the day when the interests of my country are placed above its honor.'"[38]

The Senate was clearly reluctant to consent to ratification of a document tainted by acts of questionable integrity, especially since Nicaragua sat waiting as a patient wallflower for the dance long promised her. But then, in early January, President Roosevelt went on the offensive, using two different tactics. First he wrapped himself in the flag, telling Congress that U.S. involvement began only when a Colombian army officer made a threat against U.S. citizens. He had been obliged to react. "It was only the coolness and gallantry with which this little band of men wearing the American uniform faced ten times their number of armed foes, bent on carrying out the atrocious threat of the Colombian commander, that prevented a murderous catastrophe." The President flatly denied his administration's involvement in the Panamanian revolution: "no one connected with this Government had any part in preparing, inciting, or encouraging the late revolution on the Isthmus of Panama, and that save from the reports of our military and naval officers, given above, no one connected with this Government had any previous knowledge of the revolution except such as was accessible to any person of ordinary intelligence who read the newspapers and kept up a current acquaintance with public affairs." Given what we know about Bunau-Varilla's itinerary, it is not possible for this sentence to be true.

The President introduced his second explanation in his annual message to Congress in December 1903, when he asserted that "the experience of over half a century has shown Colombia to be utterly incapable of keeping order on the Isthmus." Roosevelt told Congress that "we, in effect, policed the Isthmus in the interest of its inhabitants and of our own national needs, and for the good of the entire civilized world." The President argued that "if ever a government could be said to have received a mandate from civilization to effect an object the accomplishment of which was demanded in the interest of mankind, the United States hold that position with regard to the interoceanic canal."[39] During the ratification debate, he wrote Cecil Spring-Rice, then Secretary in the British embassy, "it was a good thing for Egypt and the Sudan, and for the world, when England took Egypt and the Sudan. It is a good thing for India that England should control it. And so it is a good thing, a very good thing, for Cuba and for Panama and for the world that the United States has acted as it has actually done during the last six years. The people of the United States and the people of the Isthmus and the rest of mankind will all be the better because we dig the Panama Canal and keep order in its neighborhood."[40]

This argument carried the day. On February 23, 1904, the Senate overwhelmingly (66 to 14) consented to ratification, and since Panama had already ratified,[41] the U.S. Treasury was then free to purchase for $40 million the assets of the New Panama Canal Company. Cromwell submitted his bill to the Company for $800,000 (eventually a French arbitrator awarded the attorney $200,000), and Bunau-Varilla received his *pénalitaire*'s share of the $40 million, although he professed to be satisfied with a nonmonetary reward. "I had fulfilled my mission, the mission I had taken on myself; I had safeguarded the work of French genius; I had avenged its honour; I had served France."[42]

Now it was time to build the canal. After U.S. military and public health officials set to work wiping out yellow fever, the scourge of the French, and after U.S. engineers resolved a series of difficult technical questions, construction went as smoothly as could be expected; not only that, it attracted so much public attention that Roosevelt could not resist visiting the site—the first time a sitting president had traveled outside the country. On his way home in late 1906 he wrote his son that "with intense energy men and machines do their task, the white men supervising matters and handling the machines, while the tens of thousands of black men do the rough manual labor where it is not worth while to have machines do it."[43] Earlier in the year Secretary of State Elihu Root (who had succeeded John Hay in mid-1905) had also visited the site, and in a speech to local citizens he made a somewhat similar analysis of the division of labor: "The achievement of this work is to be accomplished by us jointly. You furnish the country, the place, the soil, the atmosphere, the surrounding population among which the people who do the work are to live and where the work is to be maintained. We furnish the capital and trained constructive ability which has been grown up in the course of centuries of development of the northern continent."[44]

Since a thousand and one details governing the U.S.-Panamanian relationship had not been specified in the Hay–Bunau-Varilla Treaty, the initial relations with Panamanian authorities were characterized by continuous negotiation over everything from tariffs to postage rates. U.S. officials soon concluded that it would be best if the Panamanians bargained from a position of complete impotence, prompting them to pressure President Amador to disband the nation's 250-member army. "It would be far better for Panama if the army could be disbanded and four or five good brass bands established in this city so that there might be plenty of music every day. This would amuse, interest and occupy the minds of the people and also save much money."[45] With that goal accomplished, Minister John Barrett wrote Secretary of State Hay that he did not expect "further trouble in Panama or any efforts at insurrection." He worried about the future, however, for "it must be remembered that the masses of people are schooled and experienced in all kinds of uprisings, agitations, and popular excitements, and great harm might be done on some occasion if there were not a force, like a company of marines, convenient at Ancon, the effect of whose moral presence, even if they did not participate in preserving order, would maintain quiet or protect property."[46] The overall thrust of U.S. policy was to get the Panamanians out of the way so that the canal could be built by U.S. personnel and laborers imported from the Caribbean islands.

About two years after the separation of Panama, the United States began to seek reconciliation with Colombia, although at first President Roosevelt made rapprochement impossible by continuing to characterize Colombians as frustrated thieves, writing Cecil Spring-Rice that "the politicians and revolutionists at Bogota are entitled to precisely the amount of sympathy we extend to other inefficient bandits."[47] Thus Secretary of State Root knew that if he wanted to improve relations, he would have to overcome the resistance of his President; nevertheless, he apparently thought it was important to make an effort, in part because he wished to alter overall U.S. policy toward Latin America and in part because U.S. envoys were so dismayed by the antipathy that they found in Bogotá. In mid-1906 the minister in Colombia wrote Root that "you could not realize how strong still was the feeling, amounting almost to intense hatred, among the people of Colombia against the United States."[48] Root was sufficiently concerned to make an unplanned stop in Cartagena at the very end of his 1906 South American tour, where he was convinced that an apology needed to be made.

Since Roosevelt would never permit a straightforward statement of regret, Root devised a complex trilateral treaty that would permit Panama to launder a U.S. apology to Colombia. One of the final acts of Root's tenure as secretary of state came in early January 1909, when Panama signed a treaty agreeing to pay Colombia $2.5 million, characterized as its share of the Colombian national debt prior to separation, in return for which Colombia would recognize the independence of its former province. On the same day the United States signed a treaty with Panama agreeing to pay half the $2.5 million by beginning to pay its $250,000 annual rent to Panama in 1908 instead of 1913 as provided by the Hay–Bunau-Varilla Treaty. And, third, the United States signed a treaty with Colombia granting its citizens shipping preferences through the Canal and additional commercial concessions in the Canal Zone, all justified by Colombia's "peculiar historical and geographical relationship" to Panama. The United States and Panama ratified both their treaties, but the Colombians, not yet inclined to forgive, responded by overthrowing the government that had signed the accords. By then, both Root and Roosevelt had left office, and the Taft administration was uninterested in initiating new negotiations.

There the matter would have rested had not Roosevelt reopened it in 1911. Rather than do what he did to nearly every other animal that he encountered and shoot it dead, Roosevelt instead let the cat out of the bag. Departing from his prepared remarks at the University of California's

Charter Day ceremonies, the former President was understood to have said, "I took the Isthmus."[49] Since this version contradicted the President's lengthy explanation to Congress in January 1904, the California statement set off yet another storm of partisan protest in Congress, this time led by Democratic Representative Henry Rainey, who engineered passage of a resolution calling for a full inquiry into the circumstances of Panama's declaration of independence. After much preparation and nine days of sworn testimony (including page after page of William Nelson Cromwell declining to answer questions on the basis of attorney-client privilege), the Rainey committee produced one of the most fascinating documents every published on United States–Latin American relations, a seven-hundred-page chronicle entitled *The Story of Panama.*[50]

Roosevelt had started the process years earlier, in mid-December 1908 when, exasperated by the continual stream of accusations of impropriety by Joseph Pulitzer's *World,* the lame-duck President lost all sense of proportion and sent a special message to Congress, arguing that "it should not be left to a private citizen to sue Mr. Pulitzer for libel. He should be prosecuted for libel by the governmental authorities." Two weeks before the end of Roosevelt's term, the Attorney General was able to convince a District of Columbia grand jury to indict the owners of the *World* and its associated Indianapolis *News.* To prepare his legal defense, Pulitzer set reporters to gathering every scrap of information available on the circumstances surrounding Panama's independence, and he soon amassed the single largest collection of source material on the subject. All this appeared to have been for naught, because in early 1911 the Supreme Court ruled unanimously that the government's suit was flawed on the technical ground that it should have been brought in state rather than federal courts. Already embarrassed by a use of government power for Roosevelt's personal vendetta, the Taft administration was completely uninterested in pursuing the matter.

But then, two months later, Roosevelt made his Berkeley speech, and the former President soon came to rue the day that he had attacked Pulitzer. Representative Rainey, who otherwise would have been at a distinct disadvantage in the days before professional committee staffs and special prosecutors, simply asked Pulitzer to loan him the *World*'s materials, which he used as the basis for his hearings. In fact, much of the testimony is given by the *World* reporter, Henry Hall, who had coordinated the newspaper's libel defense.

While all this was occurring in Washington, the reports from Colombia continued to indicate great hostility. In 1912 U.S. Minister James Du Bois wrote Secretary of State Philander Knox that "by refusing to allow Colombia to uphold her sovereign rights over a territory where she had held dominion for eighty years, the friendship of nearly a century disappeared, the indignation of every Colombian, and millions of other Latin-Americans, was aroused and is still most intensely active. The confidence and trust in the justice and fairness of the United States, so long manifested, has completely vanished, and the maleficent influence of this condition is permeating public opinion in all Latin-American countries."[51]

A Democrat finally reached the White House in 1913, and in April 1914, Secretary of State William Jennings Bryan signed a treaty expressing "sincere regret that anything should have occurred to interrupt or mar the relations of cordial friendship that had so long subsisted between the two governments," and he agreed to pay Colombia a $25 million indemnity. An indignant Roosevelt called the treaty "an attack upon the honor of the United States," and the Senate refused to consider ratification.[52] It was only seven years later, after Roosevelt was dead, that a new treaty was negotiated, this time without an expression of "sincere regrets," and the United States paid Colombia $25 million to end the dispute.

James Bryce once called the Panama Canal "the greatest liberty Man has ever taken with Nature."[53] It is still one of the wonders of the world and, given the obstacles that had to be overcome in its construction, little short of a miracle. Today visitors can sit in bleachers alongside the Pedro Miguel Locks and be unaware that they are surrounded by some of the globe's most inhospitable terrain. But then a ship appears around a curve in the distance, and even the most blasé sightseers pay attention. The mammoth doors of the twin locks swing open, small locomotives gently pull two ships in, one from each direction, the gates close, and one ship slowly rises while the other falls. After a few minutes the gates reopen, and the ships glide out and continue on their way—two more sets of locks, about 20 miles of lake and a few more miles of narrow trench replacing a hazardous 10,000-mile voyage around the tip of South America. Say what you will about Theodore Roosevelt and his generation, they built a fine canal.

From the beginning, this generation recognized that its engineering achievement had been diminished by the government's unethical behavior.

Senator Money noted that even he, a staunch supporter of the rival Nicaragua route, could not possibly vote against a Panama treaty that gave the United States "more than anybody in this Chamber ever dreamed of having." He wondered how it came to be so one-sided. "We have never had a concession so extraordinary in its character as this. In fact, it sounds very much as if we wrote it ourselves." At the same time Secretary of State Hay was urging the treaty's floor manager to hurry with ratification, for "as soon as the Senate votes we shall have a treaty in the main very satisfactory, vastly advantageous to the United States, and we must confess, with what face we can muster, not so advantageous to Panama."[54]

Convinced that Colombians and Panamanians could not be relied upon to act responsibly, the United States had seized control over the single most valuable piece of Latin America's territory. In doing so, the Roosevelt administration exceeded the limits of U.S. public opinion, but no political force arose to challenge the jingoes, in large measure because nearly everyone wanted a canal, and nearly everyone agreed that the United States needed to control it. As this desirable end was allowed to justify distasteful means, the United States took a step beyond the Platt Amendment, setting up a formal colony in Latin America without ever intending to incorporate it into the Union. For the next seven decades the Panama Canal Zone would stand as the most obvious legacy of the age of imperialism in United States policy toward Latin America.

Chapter 10 ∽

Chastising Chronic Wrongdoing

I am seeking the very minimum of interference necessary to make them good.
∼ *President Theodore Roosevelt, 1908*

From the initial instructions to U.S. envoys in the 1820s to the Cuban Liberty and Democratic Solidarity (Helms-Burton) Act in 1996, the United States has always placed a heavy emphasis upon protecting its citizens' property in Latin America. Compensation has been sought for acts allegedly committed by Latin American governments (illegal arrests and imprisonments, abrogation of concessions, unlawful confiscation of goods), and for the failure of local authorities to protect U.S. citizens' lives and property. This protection became an especially salient issue in the early twentieth century, when several Latin American governments regularly demonstrated an inability or unwillingness to pay their debts to foreign bondholders.

This was a time when governments with sufficient strength were willing not simply to pursue the claims of their citizens but also to adjudicate them, and, if necessary, to enforce their decisions with gunboats. In this the United States has never been unique, although it has been unusual in one way: its claims policy has always reflected the habit of aggrieved investors to hire members of Congress to help them, formerly by retainers, today by campaign contributions. This tactic is almost guaranteed to generate some government assistance, for the Department of State has usually found it politic to send a cable, as in late 1903, notifying the U.S. chargé in Caracas that "the President, at the request of Senator Hiscock, counsel for the Warner and Quinlan Asphalt Company, directs me to send you the statement enclosed herewith . . .," followed by instructions on what would be needed to mollify the Senator.[1]

The significance of this lobbying should never be underemphasized, but in the early twentieth century, two additional factors made such claims the dominant issue of U.S.–Latin American relations. One was the prevailing ideology of jingoism, which held that one responsibility of the United States was, as President Roosevelt wrote in 1904, to "show those Dagos* that they will have to behave decently."[2] The other was the perception that European powers, particularly Germany, were using the claims of their citizens as a subterfuge to probe the limits of the Monroe Doctrine. These two distinct factors combined twice in the early twentieth century—once in Venezuela (in two distinct episodes), the other in the Dominican Republic—spurring U.S. officials to develop a new policy toward Latin American debtors, a policy known as the Roosevelt Corollary to the Monroe Doctrine.

Had State Department officials in the early twentieth century looked into their archives, they would have discovered that foreigners had been pursuing claims against Venezuela since the establishment of independence. President Zachary Taylor mentioned the problem in his 1849 annual message to Congress, as did President Fillmore in 1852; and as early as 1864 several European nations threatened military action if Venezuela refused to sign treaties providing for payment based on a percentage of customs duties, which at the time was the principal form of government revenue almost everywhere. The French actually followed through with their threat, and, with their gunboats lying just over the horizon, they secured their claims with 10 percent of the duties of four Venezuelan ports.

In theory, this tap on the government's principal source of revenue provided an ideal payment mechanism, but in practice, disputes often arose over how much had been collected, over delays in disbursements, and occasionally over the commitment of customs receipts to more than one claimant. No one wanted to rely upon Venezuelan officials, wrote one U.S. minister in 1867, three weeks after his arrival in the country. "Its President, its Cabinet, and Chief Officers, if one half of what I hear may be relied upon, worse than robbers, appropriating the revenues of the Government to their own use without authority of law, in fact without any, save that which might, and a rabble soldierly give them." The preceding U.S. minister had reported a few months earlier that Venezuelan judges were "subject

---

*"Dago," a corruption of the Spanish "Diego," was originally used in the mid-19th century as a derogatory reference to Mexican men in the U.S. Southwest.

to the suspicion of bribery and often easily controlled in their action by dislike to foreigners," and that "the honesty of almost every public man in this country is doubted."³

To avoid the need to rely upon corrupt Venezuelans, Minister Thomas Stilwell proposed annexation to the United States. At this moment President Grant was having difficulty convincing Congress to annex the Dominican Republic, and so he decided that a better approach would be not simply to impose a lien but also to take actual control of Venezuela's customs collections. His proposal to this effect became moot before the new U.S. minister could deliver it, however, because Venezuela began to pay its creditors.⁴ For a few years the government in Caracas was able to service just enough of its debt to forestall intervention, but never enough to provide full satisfaction.

This delicate balance between default and compliance was upset in mid-1881 when the French government lost patience and threatened to intervene on behalf of its citizens who held defaulted Venezuelan bonds. At this point Secretary of State James Blaine dusted off the Grant administration's proposal and suggested to the French a process that would become standard practice in the first three decades of the twentieth century:

> the President suggests that the U.S. will place an agent in Caracas authorized to receive such amount each month from the Venezuelan Government as may be agreed to be paid—not less than the aggregate now paid—and to distribute said amount *pro rata* to the several creditor nations. Should the Venezuelan Government default for more than three months in the regular instalments, then the agent placed there by the U.S. and acting as a Trustee for the creditor nations shall be authorized to take charge of the Custom Houses at Laguayra and Puerto Cabello and reserve from the monthly receipts a sufficient sum to pay the stipulated amounts.⁵

Negotiations to implement this proposal were under way when Blaine was replaced by the more cautious Frederick Frelinghuysen, who did not agree that the United States should accept responsibility for satisfying European creditors.

The claims of U.S. citizens expanded significantly during the final years of the nineteenth century, a time when the cobblestone streets of many U.S. cities were being paved with asphalt from eastern Venezuela. To connect this supply to demand, the Venezuelan government granted several concessions to U.S. entrepreneurs, who made handsome profits by scooping out the asphalt and transporting it northward. Noting these profits, rival investors sought by various means, not all of them ethical, to convince the Venezuelan government to transfer the concessions, and this created a mare's nest of claims and counter-claims that the aggrieved investors regularly dropped in the lap of the Department of State.[6]

U.S. officials were aware that many of these claims were inflated and that some were patently illegitimate. In 1903, for example, a U.S.-Venezuelan mixed claims commission examined fifty-five claims totaling 81.4 million bolivares, discarded half as unfounded, and awarded the remainder about one-half of one percent of the original claims. Investors who would make such outlandish demands apparently did not balk at other types of fraud, and at one point the U.S. minister in Caracas complained to the secretary of state: "It is now time for our American Companies in Venezuela and in all the other republics of South, and Central, America to change their policy. I have never known one of them to conduct its relations with this Government in an honest way." The envoy immediately added, however, that "the fault is not wholly theirs. It is only after they have invested their capital here that our Companies learn that the general policy of the Venezuelan authorities towards all froeigners [sic] is one of deception, intimidation, and spoliation." President Roosevelt eventually sent a special agent to Venezuela to study "how far these interests have by their own misdeeds forfeited the right to protection."[7]

Against this historical backdrop of steadily increasing foreign investment punctuated by sporadic threats of intervention, Venezuela passed through a particularly stormy period of political unrest at the turn of the century. Through it all, the nation was led by General Cipriano Castro, who seized power in 1899 and held it uneasily until 1908. U.S. officials commonly characterized President Castro as a capricious dictator—"an unspeakably villainous little monkey" was Theodore Roosevelt's view.[8]

Much of the animosity toward Castro was motivated by his insistence that foreigners seek redress for grievances through the Venezuelan judicial system, not diplomatic channels. This position was supported by the doctrine associated with Carlos Calvo, an Argentine jurist. Basing his argument on the principle of sovereign immunity, Calvo insisted that investors and creditors were entitled to no special rights simply because they were foreigners. In late 1902 Calvo's doctrine was supplemented by a formal diplomatic note to the United States from Argentine Foreign Minister Luis

Drago. Written during yet another Venezuelan claims crisis, Drago's long memorandum began by noting that "the recovery of loans by military methods supposes a territorial occupation." This, he continued, was contrary to the principle of sovereign equality, long supported by the United States, *and* it violated the Monroe Doctrine.[9] Officials in Washington were clearly uncomfortable with Drago's suggestion that a conflict might exist between accepted behavior (intervention to enforce claims) and their most cherished foreign policy principle, the Monroe Doctrine. Secretary of State Hay did not know how to respond, and so he delayed for six weeks while he sought advice. Noting that Drago's argument would preclude U.S. as well as European intervention, the Department's solicitor warned against being taken in by Drago's argument. Hay accepted this advice and that of Assistant Secretary Alvey Adee, who urged the secretary to respond by quoting Roosevelt's 1901 annual message to Congress: "We do not guarantee any state against punishment if it misconducts itself."[10]

Although slow to germinate, the seed of nonintervention had been planted in the fertile soil of the Monroe Doctrine, and in 1914 former President Roosevelt would himself write that "I am inclined to think we shall ultimately come to the doctrine of the distinguished Argentine international jurist, Senor Drago." During his presidency, however, Roosevelt would not consider permitting the Monroe Doctrine to serve as protection for "small bandit nests of a wicked and inefficient type" such as he saw in Venezuela.[11] Instead, he continued the policy announced by McKinley's first secretary of state, who admonished the U.S. minister to Haiti in 1897 for suggesting U.S. protection from European intervention to enforce claims: "The Monroe Doctrine to which you refer is wholly inapplicable to the case." Advocating this position when he was vice president, Roosevelt wrote a German diplomat that "if any South American State misbehaves towards any European country, let the European country spank it."[12]

Thus the Roosevelt administration did not object in late 1902 when Germany and Great Britain notified the United States that they were preparing to enforce the claims of their citizens in Venezuela. Both European powers were careful to avoid arousing any concern over European expansion; the German ambassador emphasized that "under no circumstances [do] we consider in our proceedings the acquisition or the permanent occupation of Venezuelan territory." Secretary of State Hay replied to the British and Germans by quoting the President's recent annual message: "We do not guarantee any state against punishment if it misconducts itself, provided that punishment does not take the form of the acquisition of territory by any non-American power."[13]

Given a green light by the United States, in early December, Germany and Great Britain (now joined by the Italians) issued Venezuela ultimata to pay or suffer the consequences. Receiving no response, all three countries withdrew their diplomats from Caracas, seized most of the tiny Venezuelan navy, declared a formal blockade of Venezuela's ports, and bombarded Puerto Cabello.

At this point U.S. officials began to reconsider their acquiescent policy. Their initial reaction was to send a Navy officer to survey Venezuela's coastal defenses and to interview Venezuelan military officials about the condition of the nation's armed forces. To this day it is unclear what, exactly, the United States planned to do with this information, but someone in Washington was obviously engaged in contingency planning for a possible U.S. defense of Venezuela. At the same time, Minister Herbert Bowen convinced Venezuela to arbitrate, and President Castro, in turn, took the unprecedented step of appointing him as Venezuela's counsel.

Bowen's task was daunting, for citizens of Belgium, France, Mexico, the Netherlands, Spain, Sweden and Norway, and the United States also had claims against Venezuela; with Germany, Great Britain, and Italy, that made ten countries in all. In early 1903 Bowen proposed to create ten mixed claims commissions, and then to pay the claims these commissions judged legitimate with 30 percent of the customs receipts of La Guaira and Puerto Cabello. Adept at identifying free riders, the British Foreign Secretary immediately responded that Britain "can not accept a settlement which would force them to place their claims on the same footing as those of the non-blockading powers." After two weeks of negotiations in Washington proved fruitless, on February 13 Venezuela and the blockading powers agreed to submit the question of preferential payment to judges from The Hague Permanent Court of Arbitration.[14] In the meantime, the ten mixed claims commissions met in Caracas. This was the process noted earlier in which the U.S.-Venezuela commission disallowed 99.5 percent of the U.S. claims. All nine of the other claimants fared somewhat better; Belgium came out best with 73 percent of its claims.

During the same summer, Francis P. Loomis, a Republican loyalist from Ohio who had recently spent nearly four years as William McKinley's minister to Venezuela, landed in the number two position in the Department of State. Having a mirror-perfect reflection of the thinking of Theodore Roosevelt, Loomis had watched from Caracas as the Spanish-American War unfolded. When U.S. troops were landing in Cuba, he wrote his fellow Ohioan, Secretary of State William Day, that "I think it our destiny to control more or less directly most all of the Latin American countries." Part of this control could come "by lending them money and administering their revenues," but Loomis also supported the outright annexation of new lands. "I am glad it is to fall to the lot of this administration to strengthen our country by adding to its domain the islands that we may need to sustain ourselves as one of the foremost nations of the earth and the-soon-to-be leading one in every good sense of the term."[15] Loomis felt that Puerto Rico would be an ideal first acquisition because "the people are not restless and warlike as are those of Cuba." The rest of Latin America would be more difficult: "Those who have control [that is, Secretary Day] must learn one thing that I have learned . . . and that is to place no belief in the word of a man of Latin race if he may have anything to gain by lying. This may be laid down as a rule."[16]

Loomis was therefore not surprised when new claims against Venezuela developed within a year of the judgment of the mixed claims commissions. Minister Bowen reported that "there is absolutely no hope for Venezuela as she now is. If she does not reform, or is not reformed, she will sink to the lowest depths of political degradation. As she has no desire to reform herself, the sooner she is reformed by the United States the better."[17] A month later the Castro government seized an asphalt deposit operated by a U.S. concessionaire, and Bowen cabled for immediate help: "Pressure should be brought to bear by our warships at La Guaira, and Customhouse should be seized if necessary." Two days later Bowen wrote Secretary of State Hay that "whatever [President Castro's] plans and purposes are, I feel sure they are iniquitous, and that he should receive a lesson right now that neither he nor any other international disturber of the peace on this side of the water will ever forget." By early August Bowen had completely lost patience with Venezuela's President. "President Castro has now reached a point where he will only yield to force . . . He passes his time in the country drinking brandy and consorting with low women, and his head has been turned to such an extent by flattery and the apparent success of his nefarious schemes that he has become a very dangerous ruler."[18]

While Bowen and Loomis grew agitated over Venezuela's offenses, the focus of the claims issue shifted to the Dominican Republic. For years the Department of State had been receiving despatches similar to that of

Chargé William Powell, who reported in late 1902 that "the future of the country is dark, and for this reason those who are not aspirants for political office or honors, will hail the day when the Republic knows no other flag than ours."[19] The situation appeared especially unstable in early 1904, when President Roosevelt wrote his son that "San Domingo is drifting into chaos, for after a hundred years of freedom it shows itself utterly incompetent for governmental work . . . Sooner or later it seems to me inevitable that the United States should assume an attitude of protection and regulation in regard to all these little states in the neighborhood of the Caribbean."

Roosevelt's reaction to the turmoil was to dispatch three commissioners (one of them Assistant Secretary Loomis) to investigate conditions.[20] The commissioners returned with a bleak report: "The Dominican Republic is approaching—indeed, if it has not already reached—a state of anarchy." Foreigners' claims exceeded the nation's ability to pay, and Dominican authorities were fighting among themselves for the very resources that would be needed to satisfy the claimants. Reporting that "the country is largely in the grasp of desperately selfish, irresponsible political brigands . . . little better than savages," the commissioners recommended that the United States establish a receivership, a suggestion seconded by Commander Albert Dillingham of the Navy's Caribbean Squadron: "as the great civilizing power of the world, we will be obliged . . . to control the finances of the country until every cent of the debt, both internal and external, had been paid."[21]

This was the hothouse environment that incubated the Roosevelt Corollary to the Monroe Doctrine. It had nothing to do with expansion, for Roosevelt had lost his appetite for annexation after seven years of nearly continuous involvement in Caribbean adventures.[22] But he was coming to believe that U.S. intervention was the only way to solve the claims problem. In early 1904 the President wrote: "the attitude of men like myself toward the weak and chaotic governments and people south of us is conditioned not in the least upon the desire for aggrandizement on the part of this Nation, but solely on the theory that it is our duty, when it becomes absolutely inevitable, to police these countries in the interest of order and civilization."[23]

It was in this context that the U.S. minister in Venezuela once again raised the specter of European intervention in the Caribbean. This time—mid-1904—Washington's concern focused on the Germans, long one of

Roosevelt's worries. On the eve of the Spanish-American War, he had written "that of all the nations of Europe it seems to me Germany is by far the most hostile to us." The Navy's Caribbean squadron fed this suspicion with alarming reports about the growing German naval presence in the Caribbean. We know today that these assertions of Germany's expansionist intentions were wildly inaccurate, but Roosevelt did not know that in 1903 and 1904, when the on-site reporting by U.S. diplomats and military personnel appeared to confirm his preexisting fear of German adventurism.[24]

This fear was exacerbated in late February 1904 when The Hague tribunal dropped a bombshell—a unanimous decision that the blockading powers had a right to preferential payment from Venezuela.[25] The tribunal argued that Germany, Great Britain, and Italy, unlike the other claimants, had made a significant investment to secure justice, and they therefore deserved special consideration in any compensation resulting from the blockade. By the standards of the time, the court's decision was defensible, but its principal implication was to reward the use of force in international relations—in this case, the blockading powers were paid in full by 1907, whereas investors from the nonblockading powers had to wait until 1912.

Now fearing a European stampede to join in any future blockade to enforce claims, on May 20, 1904, Roosevelt had Elihu Root read his response at a New York banquet celebrating the second anniversary of Cuban independence. The President was characteristically blunt: "If a nation shows that it knows how to act with decency in industrial and political matters, if it keeps order and pays its obligations, then it need fear no interference from the United States. Brutal wrongdoing, or an impotence which results in a general loosening of the ties of civilized society, may finally require intervention by some civilized nation, and in the Western Hemisphere the United States cannot ignore this duty."[26]

Roosevelt's message was enthusiastically endorsed by jingoes, but it was delivered on the eve of the 1904 presidential campaign, and an insecure candidate Roosevelt (he had only inherited the Presidency upon McKinley's assassination) was preoccupied by the need to deflect charges of imperialism in the Philippines and allegations of having stripped Colombia of Panama. In their 1904 platform the Republicans answered this criticism by pointing to their ability to avoid intervention in Venezuela, and Roosevelt wrote Secretary Hay that "we do not want to act in the closing weeks of the campaign, but I think we should make up our minds ourselves to take the initiative and give Castro a sharp lesson."[27] With the election behind him, in December Roosevelt restated his position in his annual message to Congress (substituting "chronic" for "brutal" as the adjective describing wrongdoing), and with that the Roosevelt Corollary to the Monroe Doctrine became a formal part of United States foreign policy.

That same day, Commander Dillingham wrote Assistant Secretary Loomis that "the people of Sanot [sic] Domingo are ready to be taught . . . Govern the country, control its finances, use native police force well organized, employ the unemployed in building roads, etc., revise the tariff, and we will give the world and in no very long time, another prosperous and orderly Republic."[28] So it was that the first application of the Corollary came in the Dominican Republic. The background of U.S. investors' claims in that country was extremely complex, but the simple outcome in July 1904 was an arbitration award that gave the U.S.-based San [sic] Domingo Improvement Company the right to receive revenues from the Puerto Plata customs house until a debt of $4.5 million had been paid. When the Dominican government defaulted in its payments almost immediately, the Company exercised its right under the arbitration award and took over the customs house, and that action triggered an outcry from several European investors who claimed a prior right to the Puerto Plata revenues.[29] Coming on the heels of The Hague tribunal's decision granting preference to nations exercising force, these protests convinced U.S. officials that European creditors would soon seize the Dominican Republic's remaining customs houses.

Given this prospect, in late 1904 U.S. Minister Thomas Dawson was instructed to suggest that the Dominican government ask the United States to take charge of the collection and disbursement of its revenues. He immediately sought out President Morales, and, he reported, "I did not disguise from him my conviction that the European creditors would wait no longer for their money."[30] In case the Dominicans needed to be impressed with the seriousness of the U.S. suggestion, President Roosevelt named Commander Dillingham as a special commissioner to assist with the negotiations. Since late 1903 Dillingham, captain of the U.S.S. *Detroit*, had been a familiar figure in Caribbean waters, and, as he later bragged, "I am entirely responsible for the placing of Morales in power."[31]

As one of the first professional Latin Americanists in the Department of State, Dawson probably did not need Dillingham's support. An Iowa attorney and a classmate of McKinley confidant Charles Dawes, the young Dawson had been rewarded in 1897 for his work on behalf of the Republican party with an appointment as secretary of the U.S. legation in Rio de Janeiro, where he married a Brazilian woman and wrote one of the first English-language political histories of Latin America. Published on the eve of his appointment to the Dominican Republic, Dawson's two-volume survey was a primer for U.S. citizens, with the tone set in the Preface: "The question most frequently asked me since I began my stay in South America has been: 'Why do they have so many revolutions there?'" His answer was that "constitutional traditions, inherited from Spain and Portugal, implanted a tendency toward disintegration; Spanish and Portuguese tyranny bred in the people a distrust of all rulers and governments; the war of independence brought to the front military adventurers; civil disorders were inevitable, and the search for forms of government that should be final and stable has been very painful."[32]

Dawson's negotiations for a customs receivership took only two weeks. The terms were fairly simple: the United States would collect the nation's customs revenues, give 45 percent to the Dominican government, and disburse the rest to foreign creditors. "Agreement signed," began Dawson's terse cable announcing the accord. "Presence of force advisable for moral effect upon malcontents."[33]

The accord contained ancillary stipulations that worried some Washington officials—a U.S. guarantee of Dominican territorial integrity and a commitment to renegotiate the private debt of the Dominican government—but its critical flaw was the failure to call for Senate approval; since it was scheduled to go into effect eleven days after being signed, apparently Dawson assumed that Senate consideration was unnecessary. With President Roosevelt already deeply at odds with Congress over a series of pending arbitration treaties (none of which was approved), this assumption proved to be a grave tactical mistake, and Dawson was promptly instructed to negotiate a new agreement explicitly providing for Senate consent to ratification. Signed on February 7, the new Dawson-Sánchez agreement eliminated the U.S. guarantee of Dominican territorial integrity and stipulated that the United States would only "attempt" to adjust the Dominican debt. Since these now-deleted stipulations were eagerly sought by the Dominican government, the second agreement was not an easy one to negotiate, and Dawson therefore thanked Secretary Hay for sending additional warships, which "has had a powerful moral effect on the rash and ignorant elements, who unhappily are in the majority and who do not yet understand the real benefits the country will derive from the arrangement."[34]

President Roosevelt sent the revised treaty to the U.S. Senate with a vigorous appeal for immediate ratification, emphasizing that "if the United States Government declines to take action and other foreign governments resort to action to secure payment of their claims, the latter would be entitled, according to the decision of The Hague tribunal in the Venezuelan cases, to the preferential payment of their claims; and this would absorb all the Dominican revenues and would be a virtual sacrifice of American claims and interests in the island."[35] The Committee on Foreign Relations recommended approval, but because the entire Senate failed to act before adjournment, Roosevelt called a special session immediately after his election. A coalition of rival Democrats and anti-imperialists had sufficient votes to defeat the treaty, however, and so the special session was also allowed to adjourn; formal action would have to await the convening of the new Congress in December.

The Roosevelt administration feared European intervention would occur in the meantime. Within a week of the signing of the first protocol, the Italian embassy in Washington had informed Secretary Hay that its citizens held a prior claim to those of U.S. citizens, and four days before the U.S. Senate's special session ended, an Italian warship steamed into the harbor at Santo Domingo to inquire about payment.[36] The ship soon left for Jamaica, but then after the special session adjourned, it returned to make a further inquiry. At almost the same time, the Belgian chargé in Santo Domingo made a formal demand for payment of its citizens' claims.

To preempt a European blockade or even a takeover of the Dominican government, Minister Dawson suggested implementing the unratified Dawson-Sánchez agreement without Senate approval.[37] This seemed reasonable to President Roosevelt, who promptly converted Dawson's suggestion into U.S. policy via an exchange of notes with the Dominican government. He also instructed the Secretary of the Navy to "tell Admiral Bradford to stop any revolution. I intend to keep the island in statu quo until the Senate has had time to act on the treaty, and I shall treat any revolutionary movement as an effort to upset the modus vivendi. That this is ethically right I am dead sure, even though there may be some technical or red tape difficulty."[38]

Opposition Senators were quick to point out that this was hardly a technical issue. Roosevelt's action threatened to transform the treaty-making provisions of the Constitution, for if the President could provisionally execute a treaty pending Senate approval, then in the future a simple majority of the Senate could indefinitely prevent a vote on any treaty that an administration supported but that a two-thirds majority might not approve. That is, a simple majority (or less, given the Senate's peculiar rules of procedure) could vote not to vote on a treaty, and the Senate's constitutional responsibility to consent to ratification of treaties by a two-thirds majority would become meaningless.

The ensuing constitutional debate consumed much of the Senate's time in the early months of 1906. Roosevelt justified his provisional execution by arguing that there was imminent danger of foreign intervention, but the unconvinced Democratic minority continued to block Senate consideration of the 1905 agreement, and an entirely new treaty had to be negotiated and signed in 1907. It removed any reference to the Monroe Doctrine and committed the United States to nothing more than the collection and disbursement of the Dominican customs receipts. With their point made, Senators approved the new treaty seventeen days after it had been signed. In the intervening two years, the U.S. customs receivership was conducted by executive agreement.[39]

It was not an easy receivership to administer. The claims of foreign investors and bondholders were so complex that President Roosevelt commissioned a professor of political economy as a special envoy to sort out the creditors. To this day Professor Jacob Hollander's report is an astounding document, with page after page of sneaky deals and sneakier counter-deals, dirty crosses and dirtier double crosses, and nearly all involving the active complicity of the investors who were now benefiting from the first application of the Roosevelt Corollary.[40] And then there were the local residents. Of President Morales, Minister Dawson wrote "that like most Latin-Americans he is subject to being diverted from his serious purposes by considerations of personal dignity," and this immature behavior was characteristic of Dominican leaders in general: "In times of stress they practically revert to more primitive ways of thinking and acting. In a word they are like children."[41]

So it was that the Roosevelt administration claimed the right to control small Caribbean nations, setting the stage for his successor's Dollar Diplomacy and creating the expectation, common in our own time, that U.S. financial guidance—today's "Washington Consensus"—is the only alternative to economic chaos. In Roosevelt's time, this chaos was believed to encourage European intervention. At first (in 1901 to 1902 in Venezuela), the United States did not object to Europeans' providing the guidance, but then, after The Hague ruling and the growing fear of German adventurism, the Roosevelt administration decided that the only way to preserve the integrity of the Monroe Doctrine was for the United States to step in and straighten out the financial chaos. This action required more than a simple financial receivership; it required the control over immature local politicians, the source of the problem. "Poor Santo Domingo!" Secretary of State Elihu Root told a group of U.S. business leaders in 1907. "The island had been the scene of almost continued revolution and bloodshed. Her politics are purely personal, and have been a continual struggle of this and that and the other man to secure ascendancy and power. She has come to us for help." [42] Modified in 1924, the 1907 Dawson receivership remained in force until 1947.[43]

In April 1905, just as U.S. officials were taking over the Dominican customs houses, the New York *Herald* trumpeted the headline "Scandals Cloud Our Diplomacy in Venezuela." After inspecting the books at his legation, U.S. Minister Herbert Bowen had concluded that his predecessor, Assistant Secretary Francis Loomis, had accepted bribes. Secretary of War Taft had already conducted a private investigation of the charges and reported to Roosevelt that Loomis was blameless; it was then that Bowen leaked the story to a *Herald* reporter in Caracas. By this time the envoy had refused reassignment and a promotion in return for silence (a bribe not to protect Loomis, but to avoid a public airing of the dispute); and an exasperated Roosevelt, seeking to kill two birds with one stone, wrote that "I am tempted to wish that Castro would execute Bowen and thereby give us good reason for smashing him."[44] Bowen was dismissed. Loomis was sent first to France to retrieve the bones of John Paul Jones, and in late 1905 was quietly retired at the age of forty-four.

In the interval between the 1902 to 1903 European blockade and his 1905 dismissal, Bowen had regularly reported on the Castro government's financial misbehavior.[45] Increasingly alarmed by his envoy's despatches, in mid-1904 Roosevelt wrote Cecil Spring-Rice that "we may possibly have to chastise Venezuela, though I hope not," and he sent attorney William J. Calhoun to Venezuela to assess the behavior of U.S. investors and the influence of foreign powers. Calhoun downplayed the European threat, but he reported that it was "a thankless task to attempt to analyze or decide [claims] questions, in a country where there is no continuous and orderly administration of public affairs, where constitutions are so frequently changed or amended and so often suspended or abrogated."[46] By this time Roosevelt had already instructed Elihu Root (who had become Secretary of State in mid-1905 when John Hay died) to prepare an ultimatum to President Castro. At the last minute Root decided not to send it, fearing that further U.S. pressure would irritate Latin American opinion on the eve of his departure for a trip around South America. Instead, he instructed the Department to prepare a straightforward statement of U.S. claims and a request for compensation, which he sent to Caracas in late February 1907.[47]

After a year of diplomatic sparring, in early 1908 the Castro government indicated that the claims cases were a matter for the Venezuelan courts to decide, and refused to discuss the matter further.[48] Roosevelt responded, "I think it would be well to have several ships at once sent there . . . We can at least seize the customs houses."[49] Root worked for three months to calm his President, and by June 1908 he had convinced Roosevelt simply to sever diplomatic relations. President Castro soon ended his turbulent tenure by sailing to Europe, ostensibly to seek medical treatment, and Root immediately sent a special representative (accompanied by several naval vessels) to negotiate a settlement with the new government of Juan Vicente Gómez.[50] "You will perhaps have seen in this morning's newspapers an announcement of the fact that we are in a fair way of settling our differences with Venezuela by arbitration," Root wrote to Andrew Carnegie. "I am very much gratified by this because one of the most difficult things I have had to do in the State Department has been to stand up against the pressure to bulldoze Venezuela . . . To have a success gained in the way of a peaceable settlement without any bulldozing in this most difficult case is extremely gratifying."[51] Elihu Root had begun the transition to a good neighbor policy.

This transition reflected a change within Latin America. In late 1905, exactly a year after announcing his Corollary to the Monroe Doctrine, President Roosevelt told Congress that "there are certain republics to the south of us which have already reached such a point of stability, order, and prosperity that they themselves, though as yet hardly consciously, are among the guarantors of [the Monroe] doctrine. These republics we now meet not only on a basis of entire equality, but in a spirit of frank and respectful friendship, which we hope is mutual." These two sentences revealed the imprint of Secretary Root; by himself, Roosevelt almost certainly would never have written them. Until Root returned to Washington in mid-1905, Roosevelt's response to almost any problem of U.S.–Latin American relations had been to flail about with a Big Stick until everyone did things his way. Root took a different approach. A few days after Roosevelt's message to Congress, Root wrote Senator Benjamin Tillman that "the South Americans now hate us, largely because they think we despise them and try to bully them. I really like them and intend to show it. I think their friendship is really important to the United States, and that the best way to secure it is by treating them like gentlemen. If you want to make a man your friend, it does not pay to treat him like a yellow dog."[52]

Blessed by the inestimable good fortune of being reared by a professor, Elihu Root was a successful corporate lawyer and a major Republican powerbroker when his party reclaimed the White House in 1897. Citing his ignorance of Spanish, Root had declined McKinley's offer of the U.S. legation in Spain, but in mid-1899 when he tried to back away from an appointment as secretary of war by claiming ignorance of warfare, McKinley responded that he was not seeking military expertise, but rather "a lawyer to direct the government of these Spanish islands"—the War Department's Bureau of Insular Affairs administered the territories seized from Spain in 1898.[53] And so Root went to Washington, where he served under both McKinley and Roosevelt before returning to private practice in early 1904. When Hay died a year later, Roosevelt insisted that Root return to Washington. "Welcome back," began the note that Root found waiting on his State Department desk. "I shall now cheerfully unload Venezuela and Santo Domingo on you."[54] From that day forward Elihu Root took charge of United States policy toward Latin America.

Although Root was every bit as patronizing as his fellow jingoes, he seemed to have a strong moral compass,[55] and, above all else, he lived in perfect pitch with his time. Now secretary of state, Root could hardly help but notice that the public's enthusiasm for conquest had deteriorated into frustration over expensive, time-consuming efforts at colonial consolidation, particularly in the Philippines. From his comfortable retirement Admiral Dewey could write, almost as an afterthought, that "the delegates to the Peace Conference scarcely comprehended that a rebellion was included with the purchase" of the Philippines; Root, however, had to deal with this oversight, and when he entered the State Department, no one knew how many Filipinos would have to be killed before those who survived would lay down their arms. The disheartened jingoes who once joked about splendid little wars now had only brute force as an answer to the nagging Philippine question, and in Latin America they found that each major initiative—Panama, Venezuela, the Dominican Republic—left them tainted by allegations of impropriety and outright corruption.

For nearly two decades, U.S. policy toward Latin America had been impelled by the public's lusty surge of imperial ambition. The electorate had embraced leaders committed to acquiring an empire—and then, about halfway through the first decade of the century, the fickle public disappeared over a different political horizon, and these same leaders were left alone to raise the children of their adolescent indiscretion. Theodore Roosevelt's presidency was now tied down with the tedious and often messy details of colonial administration—not just the Philippine rebellion, but also yellow fever, labor unrest, financial scandals and bankruptcy, all unanticipated and uncomfortable bumps on the knotty log of imperial ambition. Many of the most prominent citizens of Root's generation were quietly coming to wonder about the wisdom of an expansionist foreign policy. The taste of empire was no longer in the mouths of the people. In 1908 Root explained that he had not intervened in Venezuela because "my sober judgment always has been that the circumstances were not such that the people of the country would sustain the Administration in making war or in asking for authority to make war."[56]

Elihu Root's specific contribution to inter-American relations was to disaggregate the nations of the region into two different classes—one the turbulent Caribbean region, the other the stable, progressive countries of southern South America and Mexico. For several decades much of Latin America had been experiencing profound structural changes. In the north, Mexico under Porfirio Díaz had completed a quarter-century of breathtaking economic growth, achieving a relatively high level of economic development and political stability. Similar progress was occurring in the distant south, where Argentina had become one of the world's wealthiest nations and where her Southern Cone neighbors were making substantial, if less spectacular, progress; and, as in Mexico, economic growth was occurring alongside an equally impressive emergence of political stability.

All this change meant that there was money to be made in Latin America. Much of the potential profits were in direct foreign investment, a new area of U.S. entrepreneurial interest. From 1897 to 1908 U.S. investments had mushroomed in Latin America, particularly in Mexico ($200 million to $672 million) and Cuba ($49 million to $225 million), part of a fourfold expansion of U.S. investments worldwide—a remarkable achievement in little more than a decade. There was also money to be made from simple trade. U.S. imports from Latin America doubled between 1890 and 1910, while U.S. exports tripled from $93 million to $263 million.[57]

These rapidly growing economic ties almost certainly explain why Root, a corporate lawyer, began to perceive Latin America in two distinct parts, but some of the credit for his changed thinking must also go to Joaquim Nabuco, the urbane Brazilian ambassador who had arrived in Washington at about the same time that Root returned as secretary of state. The two men apparently enjoyed each other's company, and within months they were working together to corral Washington's attention. In early 1906 Root wrote Henry Cabot Lodge that "the dinner to which the Brazilian Ambassador will invite you and Mrs. Lodge on January 23rd has considerable significance with reference to the good understanding between the United States and South America, and I hope very much that you and Mrs. Lodge will be able to accept." When he discovered that Admiral Dewey had continued the tradition among senior Washington officials of declining social invitations from Latin Americans, Root wrote: "Is there any chance of your reconsidering the Brazilian Ambassador's invitation for dinner on the 23rd of January? The dinner has an important bearing upon the new *rapprochement* we are endeavoring to bring about between the United States and Brazil and the United States and South America generally (with a few exceptions)."[58]

In mid-1906 Root became the first sitting secretary of state to visit South America, traveling to the Third International Conference of American States at Rio de Janiero, then circumnavigating the continent. He obviously had the time of his life. Each stop was a diplomatic success, but none was greater than Root's reception in Buenos Aires: "It is impossible to picture the enthusiasm of the audience as it listened to and grasped the full meaning of Mr. Root's words," reported the U.S. minister. "Repeatedly interrupted by the most spontaneous applause, he became, at the close of his speech, the object of the most unrestrained ovation that, I am assured, was ever offered to any person in this city."[59] It must have been a spectacular evening—a dinner for six hundred guests at the Teatro Colón, still today the hemisphere's grandest opera house—and completely different from anything that Root had experienced when he visited Cuba in 1900 as secretary of war.

What could Root possibly have said to merit such an enthusiastic response from South Americans? Predictably, he spoke "of doing away with the misconceptions, the misunderstandings, and the resultant prejudices that are such fruitful sources of controversy," but this diplomatic cliché would never have led *porteñas* to shower Root with corsages ripped from their bosoms; a better explanation for the secretary of state's response from South Americans is that he acknowledged their stature. The leaders of "developed" Latin America were proud of their achievements but acutely aware of their exclusion from the main currents of international relations (Mexico and Brazil had been the only Latin American nations invited to the first Hague Conference in 1899, for example), and by traveling to Rio Root did as much as any U.S. secretary of state could do to end this marginalization. His hosts reciprocated by naming him honorary president of the Rio conference and by renaming the conference building Palacio Monroe. Then in his keynote speech Root took the next step by endorsing Latin America's sovereign equality: "We deem the independence and equal rights of the smallest and weakest member of the family of nations entitled to as much respect as those of the greatest empire; and we deem the observance of that respect the chief guaranty of the weak against the oppression of the strong. We neither claim nor desire any rights or privileges or powers that we do not freely concede to every American republic."[60]

This was a symbolic step forward, but South Americans wanted to know how the endorsement of sovereign equality would be translated into policy on the specific issue of intervention to satisfy claims. Root waited until he was in Buenos Aires and sharing the dais with Luis Drago to make his principal statement on this topic: "The United States of America has never deemed it to be suitable that she should use her army and navy for the collection of ordinary contract debts of foreign governments to her citizens . . . We deem it to be inconsistent with that respect for the sovereignty of weaker powers which is essential to their protection against the aggression of the strong."[61]

This was pure diplomatic legerdemain. Careful diction could hardly obscure the fact that U.S. armed forces were at that very moment protecting U.S. customs collectors in the Dominican Republic. But there is some evidence that South Americans were themselves willing to disaggregate Latin America and let the United States dominate the Caribbean region. Writing to Root's successor after a 1910 meeting in Buenos Aires, diplomat Henry White reported that "I ascertained from talks with their representative men, that they have a contempt for the Central American countries, which they consider a disgrace to the very name of America, and anything which we can do, whether by occupation, protection or otherwise, to improve existing conditions in those countries will meet with their sympathy and approval. I may add that from what I could discover, they don't think much of Mexico either."[62]

This willingness of "developed" South Americans to accept U.S. hegemony in the Caribbean was encouraged by Root's proposal that the Drago Doctrine—a Latin American initiative—be placed on the agenda of the upcoming second Hague Conference; moreover, he not only ensured that all Latin American states received invitations to the 1907 conference, but also instructed U.S. delegates to support the efforts of Latin American states to attain equality with the other participants, turning over to them part of the U.S. quota of committee chairs and vice-chairs. With Root as their sponsor, the elite leaders of the "developed" nations of Latin America were admitted to the club. This was the secret of his success.

A new relationship is never entirely free of misunderstandings, however, and one occurred when Root prepared a modified version of the Drago Doctrine for The Hague conference. It renounced the use of force to collect debts, but only if the debtor agreed to arbitration and then complied with the arbitral decision. This, the Porter Convention (named after General Horace Porter, a U.S. delegate), was the U.S. way of leaving the door open for action against the likes of Cipriano Castro, but it was unacceptable to Root's new friends in South America. He criticized these friends for their slavish adherence to principle: "A peculiarity of the Latin races is that they pursue every line of thought to a strict, logical conclusion and are unwilling to stop and achieve a practical benefit as the Anglo Saxons do."[63] Root's compromise position reflected the fact that his South American speeches had moved ahead of official opinion, including the opinion of President Roosevelt, who was not prepared for an unequivocal prohibition on the use of force.

Upon his return from South America, Root's challenge was to convert what he had said during his trip into policy. He began with an address to a group of business leaders in Kansas City. Although he titled his speech for audience appeal—"How to Develop South American Commerce"—it was really a lecture on cultural understanding. "In many respects the people of the two continents are complementary to each other; the South American is polite, refined, cultivated, fond of literature and of expression and of the graces and charms of life, while the North American is strenuous, intense, utilitarian. Where we accumulate, they spend. While we have less of the cheerful philosophy which finds sources of happiness in the existing conditions of life, they have less of the inventive faculty which strives continually to increase the productive power of man and lower the cost of manufacture." Root's words may seem hopelessly condescending by today's standards, but in 1906 they were the very antithesis of the jingoes' uncamouflaged disdain for their Hispanic neighbors. Until Root spoke these words, no senior U.S. official had ever publicly characterized Latin Americans as refined or cultivated.

Root also told his Kansas City audience that they might have something to learn from their neighbors, a view that came perilously close to heresy. "There is nothing that we resent so quickly as an assumption of superiority or evidence of condescension in foreigners; there is nothing that the South Americans resent so quickly. The South Americans are our superiors in some respects; we are their superiors in other respects. We should show to them what is best in us and see what is best in them."[64] This message was heard by the U.S. business community. In 1907 the president of the National Association of Manufacturers gave a speech that could have been written by the secretary of state. "As a people we Americans have inherited from England some good qualities and a few bad ones. One of the bad traits is a feeling of superiority over the rest of the world." U.S. business could no longer afford such a luxury, he continued, for "while airs of superiority over the rest of the world may not harm us when we want to buy, they must be dropped when we want to sell."[65]

As for the "underdeveloped" part of Latin America, Root noted that "some of them have had a pretty hard time. The conditions of their lives have been such that it has been difficult for them to maintain stable and orderly governments. They have been cursed, some of them, by frequent revolution."[66] His words about the Caribbean were every bit as friendly as those about South America, but there was no mention of sovereign equality. Instead, Root substituted a cordial concern laced with offers of assistance, and to this concern Root added a national security dimension that did not apply to nations farther south. "The inevitable effect of our building the Canal must be to require us to police the surrounding premises. In the nature of things, trade and control, and the obligation to keep order which go with them, must come our way."[67]

Thus when Root opened the 1907 Central American Peace Conference in Washington, he spoke to the delegates as if he were their parent, lecturing them about playground squabbles: "It can be nothing but the ambition of individuals who care more for their selfish purposes than for the good of their country, that can prevent the people of the Central American states from living together in peace and unity." Although he did not say this directly to the delegates, to a U.S. audience at about the same time Root explained that he wanted to help the nations of the region "along the road that Brazil and the Argentine and Chile and Peru and a number of other South American countries have travelled—up out of the discord and turmoil of continual revolution into a general public sense of justice and determination to maintain order."[68]

If citizens from the Caribbean region had been in that audience and wondered how these words applied to them, they had only to look at the experience of Cuba. The Republican party's 1904 platform had gloated over its success: "We fought a quick and victorious war with Spain. We set Cuba free, governed the island for three years, and then gave it to the Cuban people with order restored, with ample revenues, with education and public health established, free from debt, and connected with the United States by wise provisions for our mutual interests." Later that year, in his annual message to Congress, President Roosevelt had wished for more Cubas. "If every country washed by the Caribbean Sea would show the progress in stable and just civilization which with the aid of the Platt amendment Cuba has shown since our troops left the island," he said, "all question of interference by this Nation with their affairs would be at an end." [69]

Certainly there had been occasional problems, such as in mid-1905, when the United States sent a note to the Cuban foreign minister to "call to your attention the besmearing with excrement of the escutcheon and door of the American consulate at Cienfuegos last night." Minister Juan O'Farrill responded "that the person culpable of so execrable an act shall be discovered and punished at once," but the perpetrators of this outrage were never brought to justice.[70] Some tension also continued over the Cubans' alleged inability to maintain the U.S. Army's public health standards, and when an epidemic of yellow fever broke out in 1904, Secretary of State Hay warned that the United States would quarantine ships coming from Cuba if the Estrada Palma government did not enforce the sanitary provisions of the Platt Amendment. A year later, Secretary Root sent a second warning on the same topic. On the positive side of the ledger, in mid-1903 the two governments reached an agreement on the lease of Cuban land for U.S. naval bases, and after much debate the U.S. Senate approved the 1902 Reciprocity Treaty, a document that proved decisive in the two nations' economic integration. Two years later the Hay–de Quesada Treaty removed another potential problem by recognizing Cuban sovereignty over the Isle of Pines, although it took the Senate twenty-one years to grant its consent to ratification.

All in all, U.S.-Cuban relations were positive until 1906, when the fraudulent reelection of President Tomás Estrada Palma, a Moderate, provoked a rebellion by the Liberal opposition, and in early September the experienced U.S. consul-general in Havana dropped a bombshell on Washington: "*Absolutely confidential.* Secretary of state, Cuba, has requested me, in name of President Palma, to ask President Roosevelt send immediately two vessels; one to Habana, other to Cienfuegos; they must come at once. Government forces are unable to quell rebellion. The Government is unable to protect life and property." Consul-general Frank Steinhart emphasized the need for confidentiality: "It must be kept secret and confidential that Palma asked for vessels. No one here except President, Secretary of State, and myself know about it. Very anxiously awaiting reply."[71]

At that moment the secretary of state was sailing between Chile and Peru, and President Roosevelt's first reaction was to ask Root to "stop in Havana and make a serious address to the people."[72] But Root's visits to Peru and Panama were also important, and even more consequential was a hastily scheduled meeting at Cartagena with the foreign minister of Colombia, which Root considered a significant step toward normalization of relations—the initial gesture in a process that would lead to his trio of reconciliation treaties in 1909.

Left to his own devices, Roosevelt's response was firmly noninterventionist. The day after Steinhart's cable, he wrote that "on the one hand we cannot permanently see Cuba a prey to misrule and anarchy; on the other hand I loathe the thought of assuming any control over the island such as we have over Porto Rico and the Philippines. We emphatically do not want it." Assistant Secretary of State Bacon warned Steinhart against intervention: "The President directs me to state that perhaps you do not yourself appreciate the reluctance with which this country would intervene."[73]

But Roosevelt never had much patience, and a few days later he wrote this to Henry White:

> I am so angry with that infernal little Cuban republic that I would like to wipe its people off the face of the earth. All we have wanted from them was that they would behave themselves and be prosperous and

happy so that we would not have to interfere. And now, lo and behold, they have started an utterly unjustifiable and pointless revolution and may get things into such a snarl that we have no alternative save to intervene—which will at once convince the suspicious idiots in South America [a reference to Root's new friends] that we do wish to interfere after all, and perhaps have some land-hunger!

For the moment Roosevelt managed to restrain himself, telling Cuban Minister Gonzalo de Quesada that "our intervention in Cuban affairs will only come if Cuba herself shows that she had fallen into the insurrectionary habit, that she lacks the self-restraint necessary to secure peaceful self-government, and that her contending factions have plunged the country into anarchy."[74]

With the Liberal rebellion gaining strength and his options either to capitulate or obtain protective U.S. intervention under the Platt Amendment, Estrada Palma decided to force Roosevelt's hand. A week after Steinhart's first bombshell, the consul-general cabled with another: "President Palma has resolved not to continue at the head of the Government." The vice president would refuse to accept the office, he continued, and the cabinet would resign. "Under these conditions it is impossible that Congress will meet, for the lack of a proper person to convoke same to designate a new president. The consequences will be absence of legal power, and therefore the prevailing state of anarchy will continue unless the United States Government will adopt the measures necessary to avoid this danger."[75] In response, Roosevelt ordered Secretary of War William Howard Taft to go to Cuba and restore stability, a move that was warmly supported by congressional Republicans. Henry Cabot Lodge wrote that "disgust with the Cubans is very general. Nobody wants to annex them, but the general feeling is that they ought to be taken by the neck and shaken until they behave themselves . . . I should think that this Cuban performance would make the anti-imperialists think that some peoples were less capable of self government than others."[76]

Taft reached Havana on September 19, and within hours he cabled that "the situation is most serious. The Government controls only coast towns and provincial capitals. Anarchy elsewhere." For safety's sake Taft soon had nine U.S. warships anchored in Havana's harbor.[77]

Two years earlier Taft had written that "the Spanish American, or one educated in the Spanish political school, has no idea of impartiality, and if he is an election officer, regards it as a duty to cheat for his party."[78] This situation is exactly what he discovered in Cuba: "The Govt. seems to have abused its powers outrageously in the election," Taft wrote his wife. "No such formidable force could have been organized, had there not been some real feeling of injustice and outrage on the part of the less educated and poorer classes, who seemed more or less dimly to understand that the victory of the Moderates at the polls was the beginning of the end of power which they might exercise in the government." The secretary of war never mentioned this class conflict in his official report, however; instead he argued that "the cause for the insurrection is to be found primarily in the election and the methods which were pursued in carrying it for the Moderate party." A somewhat deeper problem lay with the nation's politicians. Taft wrote one of his brothers that "the men with whom I have had to deal were, most of them, broken reeds; no manhood, no patriotism, no nothing to attract." But the most profound problem was embedded in the Cuban culture, as Taft asserted in his final report. The insurrection "could not have occurred in a country in which the common and ignorant people are not as easily aroused by personal appeals of local leaders as they are in Cuba." The conclusion, he told his wife, was that "Cuba is no more fitted for self government than the Philippines and the proper solution of the present difficulties would be annexation if we consulted the interest of the Cuban people alone but the circumstances are such that the U.S. can not take this course now, though in the future it may have to do so."[79]

Taft's immediate problem was to find someone to run the country after the Cuban President made good on his threat and resigned.[80] The Moderate-dominated Cuban Congress received Estrada Palma's resignation and promptly asked him to withdraw it. When the President went into seclusion and refused to reply, Congress declined to reconvene, and Cuba had no chief executive and no constitutional way of getting one. At that point Estrada Palma resurfaced long enough to inquire what the U.S. secretary of war would recommend be done with the $13,625,539.65 that had been left unattended in the Treasury, and Taft decided to take action. On September 29 he issued a proclamation establishing a provisional government "in the name and by the authority of the President of the United States."[81]

During all this time, President Roosevelt had resisted a U.S. takeover, and as late as September 25 he had instructed Taft to deliver a message pleading for Estrada Palma's cooperation. At least part of Roosevelt's reluctance reflected his reading of U.S. public opinion; two years later he would write that public opposition, working through uninformed legislators, was what made it difficult to control "thickly peopled tropical regions by self-governing northern democracies." And so he warned Taft to "remember that we have to do not only what is best for the island but what we can get public sentiment in this country to support, and there will be very grave dissatisfaction here with our intervention unless we can show clearly that we have exhausted every method by which it is possible to obtain peace." On the eve of the 1906 mid-term elections, Roosevelt twice cautioned Taft to "avoid, so long as it is possible, the use of the word 'intervention.'"[82]

The jingoes blamed everything on the Cubans. Senator Lodge wrote that "after all we did for them and the way in which we started them without debt and the Island all in perfect order, to find them fighting and brawling at the end of four years furnishes a miserable picture of folly and incompetency." Returning to the United States, Elihu Root forgot that it was he who, as secretary of war, had disenfranchised the majority of the Cuban people. "The trouble was that the Cuban Congress seems never to have passed the laws necessary for really giving the Constitution a fair trial. They had absolutely no idea of a fair election."[83] Roosevelt believed that "Palma's utter weakness . . . made it absolutely imperative that I should take some step unless I wished to see chaos come in the Island." He instructed Taft that if Estrada Palma were to resign without a replacement, "it seems to me that we must simply put ourselves for the time being in Palma's place." Two days later Taft asked for six thousand U.S. troops, Roosevelt replied that they were on their way, and a few weeks later he issued an executive order establishing the "temporary administration of the Government of the Republic of Cuba" under the supervision of the U.S. secretary of war. Roosevelt permitted Taft to return to Washington in mid-October, leaving the U.S. Army and Charles Magoon in charge, and his disgust was nearly palpable as he wrote to his son: "Mr. Taft and Mr. Bacon came home from Cuba in good health and having done a great work, but really tired out with the nervous strain. They said they never could tell when those ridiculous dagos would flare up over some totally unexpected trouble and start to cutting one another's throats."[84]

It was never intended that the U.S. occupation would last for long. Roosevelt's orders to the War Department were characteristically blunt: "Our business is to establish peace and order on a satisfactory basis, start the new government, and then leave the island." A month later he told a Harvard audience: "I am doing my best to persuade the Cubans that if only they will be good they will be happy; I am seeking the very minimum of interference necessary to make them good."[85]

Elections were scheduled almost immediately, but they were first postponed so as not to disrupt the sugar harvest, and then in April 1907 Governor Magoon announced that the voter registration lists were so unreliable that an election could not be held until a census had been taken. In the meantime, Magoon would administer the government. A modestly successful Nebraska attorney who had come to Washington in 1899 as a lawyer in the Bureau of Insular Affairs, in 1904 Magoon was sent to Panama as counsel of the Isthmian Canal Commission. Described by one associate as possessed of "the gentle nature which so often accompanies vast bulk," Magoon quickly advanced to become a member of the Commission itself, and in mid-1905 Roosevelt named him both minister to Panama and governor of the Canal Zone.[86]

Now transferred to Cuba, Magoon recognized that the Platt Amendment had contributed to the problem that he was to solve, for it had given those Cubans "fully capable of good judgment" (a group he often identified as "the business class") the freedom to ignore politics. "The real reason for their inactivity is their unwillingness to make the exertion, their willingness to allow others to assume the responsibility and trouble, and the belief that the United States should and will attend to the matter." But although the Platt Amendment may have contributed to Cuba's turmoil, the fundamental cause lay in the fact that the Island's occupants were largely of the Hispanic race. "Like all other people of Spanish origin they are hot blooded, high strung, nervous, excitable and pessimistic. They are suspicious of every one." Improvement would be slow, for "we cannot change these racial characteristics by administering their Government for two years or twenty years, nor would they be changed by a military occupation."[87]

Magoon viewed his primary task as creating the "guarantees of stability which before were lacking." To supply these guarantees, Magoon appointed an Advisory Law Commission to revise the nation's legal code. Composed of nine Cubans and three U.S. citizens and chaired by Colonel Enoch Crowder, the Army's leading legal expert, the Commission worked day and night to prepare an impressive array of administrative laws, which Magoon's provisional government enacted by decree. Cuba's armed forces received the Commission's special attention. Years earlier, Leonard Wood had requested a permanent U.S. military presence to serve as "the moral force to hold these people up to their work until the decent element assumes its normal position in the government of this island"; furthermore, in 1906 Taft had voiced his hope that "the next government will have sense enough to lay the foundation of an army that will suppress future resorts to violence." Crowder's Advisory Law Commission created a new Permanent Army to complement the Rural Guard that Leonard Wood had established a few years earlier. It was initially quite small, consisting of only an infantry brigade and complemented by the five-thousand-member Rural Guard, which Taft considered "really a fine body of men." Magoon left the Guard distributed in small units around the island for police duty, while the Permanent Army's concentration at Camp Columbia, just to the west of Havana, gave it a political role that the Rural Guard would never possess.[88]

Among the other laws created by the Advisory Law Commission was a thoroughly revised electoral code, which expanded suffrage to nearly all male adult citizens and established a complex method of proportional representation to encourage the participation and loyalty of minority parties. Magoon also recommended that several military and legal officers remain in Cuba as advisors, and he called for the establishment of a "high joint commission" of prominent U.S. and Cuban citizens "to hear and determine contested elections or other controversies involving the relations of an administration and any large portion of the population."[89]

These proposals for a permanent U.S. presence in Cuba were firmly rejected by the Roosevelt administration, and in mid-1908, when the census had been completed, Magoon called for municipal and provincial elections, followed by elections for a new president and members of congress. On January 28, 1909, the anniversary of José Martí's birth, Governor Magoon turned the Cuban government over to President-elect José Miguel Gómez, a Liberal. U.S. troops remained in Camp Columbia for a few months to ensure a smooth transition, but it was the Platt Amendment that endured as the principal indicator of U.S. power over the island. In its 1908 platform the Republican Party had argued obliquely that "the present conditions in Cuba vindicate the wisdom of maintaining, between that Republic and this, imperishable bonds of mutual interest"; and in his final annual message, President Roosevelt could not resist a blunt admonition: "I would solemnly warn them to remember the great truth that the only way a people can permanently avoid being governed from without is to show that they both can and will govern themselves from within."[90]

Out of office, Roosevelt adopted Root's practice of praising the stable, economically vibrant part of the region and condemning the nations of the Caribbean and Central America. In 1914 he wrote his son that "it would be mere folly, the silliest kind of silliness, to ask Mexico [fallen now into revolution], Venezuela, Honduras, Nicaragua, to guarantee the Monroe doctrine with us. It is eminently proper to ask Brazil, the Argentine and Chile to do it . . .; but to ask the other countries I have named to guarantee it would be about like asking the Apaches and Utes to guarantee it."[91]

Looking back over his own term of public service, Elihu Root concluded that "two-thirds of the suspicion, the dislike, the distrust with which our country was regarded by the people of South America, was the result of the arrogant and contemptuous bearing of Americans, of the people of the United States, for those gentle, polite, sensitive, imaginative, delightful people."[92] His words and deeds in the Caribbean region indicate fairly clearly that here Root was referring to "developed" Latin America, and so he could be accused of exaggerating his accomplishments. But on balance Elihu Root's ideas constituted a significant step forward, and two decades later a new generation of U.S. diplomats would use them as the foundation for the Good Neighbor Policy. Before that outcome could occur, however, citizens of the United States and their leaders had to become not merely uninterested but completely fed up with Roosevelt's Big Stick. This was the coming contribution of William Howard Taft's dollar diplomacy and Woodrow Wilson's quixotic crusade.

Chapter 11 ⌒

Providing Benevolent Supervision:
Dollar Diplomacy

Nature, in its rough method of uplift, gives sick nations strong neighbors.

⌒ *Assistant Secretary of State Huntington Wilson, 1916*

"Incidentally, Taft is a cabinet officer," began a magazine profile of Theodore Roosevelt's secretary of war. "Primarily, he is the proconsul of American good faith to fractious islands; an ambassador to stubborn tasks at far corners of the earth."[1] Taft's proconsular assignments had begun in 1900 when McKinley named him to the U.S. Philippine Commission, and a year later to be the islands' first civilian governor. Then in 1904 President Roosevelt tapped him to succeed Elihu Root as secretary of war, and Taft's exposure to tropical countries expanded to include what he called the "dirty so-called republics of South America."[2]

Now William Howard Taft was President. Like Roosevelt and Root, he recognized "the seed of development and improvement" in southern South America, and he reasoned that his administration could ignore the region's stable countries and concentrate on the Caribbean and Central America. Unlike Roosevelt, however, Taft's Caribbean policy was not motivated primarily by the fear of European meddling. When Roosevelt had invoked the Monroe Doctrine during the Venezuelan claims crisis, Taft wrote that "the reason why I find [Roosevelt's corollary] a doctrine so hard to subscribe to is not that I would not be willing to have the United States sacrifice much to secure the elevation and benefit of the people of South America, but the character of the Governments of that continent is so miserable and the absolute hopelessness of any improvement under present conditions so appalling that it would seem as if we were protecting nothing but chaos, anarchy and chronic revolution." Thus Taft shared Roosevelt's view of Latin Americans as people in need of supervision, and in 1909, the year he entered the White House, he claimed "the right to knock their heads together until they should maintain peace."[3]

For his secretary of state, President Taft selected Philander Chase Knox, a man who had come to wealth by marrying the daughter of steel magnate Andrew D. Smith and then by serving as an attorney for Henry Frick and other Pittsburgh industrialists. A striking peculiarity of his official papers is that so many of them are written on Palm Beach hotel stationery, where he liked to spend the winter playing golf. His semiofficial travel also frequently took him away from Washington; in 1912, for example, he left Washington on August 16 to attend the funeral of Japan's Emperor Mutsuhito, and did not return until mid-October. When in Washington, he arrived at the Executive Office Building just before noon. Three days a week he left almost immediately to lunch with his assistant secretary, always with cocktails and wine. He then went home, took a nap to sleep off his stupor and, weather permitting, played a round of golf before dinner and enjoyed an active social life in the evening. As Knox's assistant secretary once observed, "I have frequently been in charge of the Department for months at a time."[4]

Since Knox had almost no knowledge of foreign affairs, he decided to continue the policy of the Roosevelt-Root administration, modified to give the southern portion of the region almost no attention whatever. The most prominent comment about Knox's Latin American policy is Elihu Root's accusation that his successor was "absolutely antipathetic to all Spanish-American modes of thought and feeling and action."[5] Knox reciprocated by criticizing Root's "delicate entente with the Latins which has been nourished and maintained largely in the past upon champagne and other alcoholic preservatives," but his own two-month tour of the Caribbean in 1912 promised more of the same. Knox loaded his U.S. Navy cruiser with 864 bottles of wine (most of it champagne), 1,500 Cuban cigars, 5,000 cigarettes, 6 pounds of caviar, 24 tins of foie gras, and box after box of light desserts, including 5 pounds of Turkish mints to kill the taste of the cigars.[6] He set the trip's tone at the first stop, telling Panamanians that "our policies have been without a trace of sinister motive or design, craving neither sovereignty nor territory." Oblivious to the irony of making such a statement while standing just steps from the Canal Zone, Knox asserted that the problems of U.S.–Latin American relations could be traced to ineffective public relations: "our motives toward you have not always been fortunately interpreted either at home or faithfully represented by some of our nation-als who have resided in your midst."[7]

Knox's thinking about Latin America was based upon principles taken directly from Roosevelt and Root. In contrast to Taft's early position, he believed that the Monroe Doctrine required U.S. hegemony—a "meas-ure of benevolent supervision over Latin American countries" is the way that he phrased it in a 1911 letter to the President. This, he later argued, "will reflect credit upon the hegemony of our race and further advance the influence of Anglo-Saxon civilization."[8] He also believed "prosperity means contentment and contentment means repose." These two beliefs were linked in Knox's mind: "The most effective way to escape the logi-cal consequences of the Monroe doctrine is to help them to help them-selves . . . We diminish our responsibilities in proportion as we bring about improved conditions."[9] This was the mental calculus behind Dollar Diplo-macy.

It was upon the shoulders of Assistant Secretary Francis Mairs Hunt-ington Wilson that responsibility for U.S.–Latin American relations rested during the Taft administration. "He was a fellow of the most dangerous character for diplomatic service," Elihu Root confided to his biographer. "He was suspicious and egotistical and sensitive and took offense readily, full of suspicion of everybody and he did a very great deal of wild work. I think you will find that most of the things in Knox's administration of the State Dept. which were objectionable came from him." "Tactless and insin-cere," was the characterization made by the German ambassador.[10]

Huntington Wilson[11] championed "a diplomacy seeking the political and economic advantage of the American taxpayer, the American nation." To this he coupled a strong Social Darwinism, writing that "the march of civilization brooks no violation of the law of the survival of the fittest." Huntington Wilson saw the Caribbean region as an arena for playing out a fixed pattern of human advancement: "nature, in its rough method of uplift, gives sick nations strong neighbors and takes its inexorable course with private enterprise and diplomacy as its instruments. And this course is the best in the long run, for all concerned and for the world."[12]

It is hardly surprising that Huntington Wilson was not impressed by his first contact with Hispanic culture, which occurred in Panama, after he retired: "What can you expect from the formula for this mixture: the crude brutality of the African; the stolidity, shiftlessness and craftiness of the

Indian; the cruelty and greed of the Spaniard. Here and there in the towns a dash of the subtlety of Chinese blood. With these potentialities in an environment of intrigue and graft, the cheap vanity and the false pride characteristic of the political leaders, you will not expect much and you will not be disappointed."[13] He was impressed by the U.S. Canal personnel, however—"What nation in the world could show such fine types of intelligent, well-behaved, pleasant people as these, class for class."

Ecuador was the next stop. "The people here were much whiter than in Peru and Bolivia, the trouble being that they were crazy white people. Close intermarriage, it seems, has been very common." They were constantly fighting, but without doing much damage, since "the Ecuadoreans, unless inflamed with drink, are not fighters, with the exception of the tough negro element of Esmeraldas, so they always drink hard when they are to fight, and their revolutionary activities, either of government troops or revolutionists, commonly degenerate into drunken rioting, indiscriminate shooting, especially at windows, the looting of shops and the violation of women." From there it was on to Peru, Bolivia (at this point his wife returned to the United States and filed for divorce), Chile, and Venezuela, where he found little to please him. "Here is a beautiful country with considerable possibilities being wasted and nine-tenths of its population being oppressed by a wretched little minority that ought to be spanked, and where guilty conscience and craven fear of the United States as the probable spanker make them heartily hate us."

This was the thinking of the leadership of the Taft State Department, which, to an extent unrivaled by any era before or after, was dominated by an inbred group of exceptionally provincial Eastern men led by Philander Knox and Huntington Wilson.[14] These people took the policy that Roosevelt and Root had created in the Dominican Republic and applied it elsewhere. They called their approach Dollar Diplomacy.

The term "Dollar Diplomacy" does not convey a clear sense of who is doing what for whom. Is it dollars helping diplomacy, or diplomacy helping dollars? Assistant Secretary Huntington Wilson believed that the dollars were helping diplomacy, "using the capital of the country in the foreign field in a manner calculated to enhance fixed national policies. It means the substitution of dollars for bullets."[15] But Taft, in his valedictory message, asserted that his policy had been "directed to the increase of American trade upon the axiomatic principle that the Government of the United States shall extend all proper support to every legitimate and beneficial

American enterprise abroad."[16] To Taft, Dollar Diplomacy meant diplomacy helping dollars.

In practice, administration officials saw no contradiction because they saw no conflict: capital helped diplomacy, and diplomacy helped capital. Huntington Wilson combined the two in an explanation for President-elect Woodrow Wilson:

> Rotten little countries down there run heavily into debt to Europe. They wont [sic] pay. Europe comes along and demands payment. The United States must either let Europe land marines and hold custom houses for security, and so open the way for further penetration and for flagrant violation of the Monroe Doctrine, or else the United States must compel the little republics to be decent and to pay up . . . If the United States lends a helping hand and helps Central America get on its feet and keeps the peace long enough for it to begin to develop, we shall soon have immediately at the doors of our southern states a great and valuable commerce. "Dollar diplomacy" simply means intelligent team work.[17]

Thus the Taft administration blurred the public-private distinction to the point of irrelevance. But—and this is crucial for understanding Dollar Diplomacy—every case began with U.S. government intervention, after which government officials brokered a financial arrangement between the intervened Latin American government and the U.S. private sector. That bankers lunged at the bait cannot be denied, but the causal question is not who devoured the assets of small Caribbean nations, but who was holding the fishing pole. The answer is the Department of State. An understanding of Dollar Diplomacy begins, then, with the motivation of U.S. government officials.

Like its predecessors, the Taft administration saw foreign trade and investment as promoting the general health of the U.S. economy, and only coincidentally as boosting corporate profits. This view was linked to a changing perception of national security and, specifically, to the manner in which the Panama Canal was transforming the Caribbean from a dead end to a major thoroughfare. But the principal motivation for Dollar Diplomacy came from a belief that was distilled from a blend of these economic and security considerations, a belief that the Roosevelt Corollary conferred upon the United States an obligation to ensure that Latin Americans paid their debts.

Nowhere is the confluence of these beliefs more evident than in the Taft administration's quixotic effort to create a protectorate in Nicaragua. Although for many years Nicaraguan president José Santos Zelaya had been one of Washington's best friends, the cordial relationship slowly deteriorated after 1903, and in 1909 it reached the breaking point when Secretary of State Knox handed Managua's envoy in Washington his passport along with a note calling the Zelaya administration "a blot upon the history of Nicaragua." [18] Although this was the strongest note that had ever been sent by the United States to any Latin American country, the official condemnation was mild when compared with the State Department's private correspondence. Huntington Wilson, the author of Knox's note, wrote privately that Zelaya "was an unspeakable carrion." [19]

Whereas it is probably true that Zelaya was not the type of person one would want one's sister to marry, the deterioration of U.S.-Nicaraguan relations was not the result of his personal misbehavior. Until late 1903 the United States was pleasant to Zelaya because it wanted permission to build a canal through the country that he governed, and Zelaya was pleasant to the United States because he understood the value of a canal. The selection of Panama as the canal site removed the necessity for cordial relations. After a full decade of courting, the United States had abandoned Nicaragua. This time the breakup was definitive, for Washington had not simply invited someone else to the prom: the Spooner Act was the marriage license, the Hay–Bunau-Varilla Treaty was the ceremony, and on the wedding night Nicaragua's heartbroken leaders could do nothing but watch with dismay as the Yankee steam shovels plunged into the fertile Panamanian earth.

Then, as canal construction got under way, U.S. officials began to place a much stronger emphasis upon regional stability. Zelaya also favored stability, but he defined it as Nicaraguan hegemony over neighboring countries so as to check what both he and Mexico's Porfirio Díaz perceived as the expansive intentions of his principal regional rival, Guatemala's Manuel Estrada Cabrera. U.S. officials viewed Zelaya's efforts to establish control as destabilizing, and Zelaya cooperated with this interpretation by contributing his full share to the disorder, but he was no more responsible for Central America's instability than the Kaiser was responsible for World War I. Whatever instability existed was a product of a variety of social forces, including not only Zelaya's rivalry with Estrada Cabrera for regional influence but also the machinations of the region's foreign concessionaires.

But hell hath no fury like the spurned owner of a canal site, and when Roosevelt's new minister to Nicaragua, John Gardner Coolidge, arrived in Managua in August 1908, Zelaya made no attempt to be friendly. In early November the Managua police broke up a small demonstration by Zelaya's opponents who were ostensibly celebrating Taft's electoral victory, and in the process they confiscated a U.S. flag. Outraged by this affront to his nation's honor, Coolidge demanded an apology. The lame-duck State Department officials tried to calm their envoy down, but this treatment only annoyed him further, and he resigned in a huff. The new Taft administration not only refused to replace Coolidge but also immediately recalled the U.S. chargé, leaving only a Nicaraguan citizen, Vice-consul José de Olivares, as Washington's representative in Managua.[20] At the same time, Washington beefed up the U.S. naval presence, and in April, when the administration learned that Zelaya was preparing to invade El Salvador, Taft sent the Navy into action: "acting upon the moral right and duty which the United States shares with Mexico under the Washington Conventions [a reference to the joint sponsorship of the 1907 Peace Conference], you will stop any expedition across Fonseca Bay."[21]

Despite this initial focus on protecting El Salvador, the Taft administration recognized that Honduras was the centerpiece of the regional struggle. The 1907 Central American Peace Conference had sought without success to neutralize this nation sandwiched between Zelaya's Nicaragua and Estrada Cabrera's Guatemala. Once it was clear that this effort had failed, in 1908 to 1909 the State Department conceived of a second conference, cosponsored by Mexico and the United States, to guarantee Honduras's neutrality. At the same time, the Taft administration sought to provide Honduras with a Dominican-style customs collectorship.[22]

The more Taft administration officials thought about it, however, the less they liked the idea of Mexico's participation. Huntington Wilson's deputy believed that "Mexico probably wants her own hand in Nicaragua to counterbalance Estrada Cabrera," Mexico's annoying southern neighbor, and the assistant secretary suggested that the Porfirio Díaz government "is actuated now, it seems obvious, by the most contemptible motives."[23] Seeking both to isolate Zelaya and to diminish Mexico's influence, the Taft administration told Porfirio Díaz that the United States did not intend to invite Mexico's principal Central American ally to the proposed conference. Rather than fight for Zelaya's inclusion, the Díaz government opted out of the process, notifying Washington that Mexico had no interest in any issue south of Guatemala.[24] This reaction sealed the Nicaraguan leader's fate, for with Mexico out of the picture, the United States had a free hand to act.

This activity did not go unobserved by Zelaya's domestic opponents, and in October 1909 a rebellion led by General-Governor Juan Estrada broke out in Bluefields on the Atlantic coast. Many residents of that town were U.S. citizens—merchants whom a U.S. Marine officer, Smedley Butler, described as "*renegade swine* from the slums of our race." In his view, "the whole game of these degenerate Americans down here is to force the United States to intervene and by so doing make their investments good." Admiral William Kimball agreed.[25]

The U.S. role in the Estrada rebellion has been interpreted as a case of diplomacy helping dollars, with U.S. investors (specifically, the Pittsburgh owners of the United States and Nicaragua Company, a mining concession) influencing U.S. policy through their association with Secretary of State Knox. No evidence exists that Knox's association with these entrepreneurs influenced U.S. policy, however; quite the contrary, one letter to Knox from the firm's secretary-treasurer begins with a telling introductory statement ("You have no doubt heard of the United States and Nicaragua Co. . . .") that precludes familiarity.[26] It is true that the principal U.S. official in the area, the U.S. consul in Bluefields, Thomas Moffat, was strongly supportive of Estrada's rebellion, but this support cost Moffat his job. Admiral Kimball complained that "his partisan and unneutral attitude throughout the late troubles in Nicaragua and the stupid or false reports as to military conditions that he furnished officers under my command and the public, tended to make our government ridiculous." A rubber stamp on this page of Kimball's report indicates "Noted for Efficiency Records," and the director of State Department personnel added that the consul "ought to find useful employment in some quiet, unimportant place." Rather than accept a position in Singapore, Moffat left the Department of State.[27]

As Zelaya's forces moved to quell the rebellion, on November 12 they captured two U.S. citizens, Lee Roy Cannon and Leonard Groce, employees of the United States and Nicaragua Company who had been drafted to serve as demolition experts with Estrada's rebels. The two prisoners were given a perfunctory military trial and promptly shot. That execution provided Knox and Huntington Wilson with the grievance that they had been seeking, and thereafter nothing Zelaya could have done would have placated the Taft administration.[28] On December 1, after the execution of

Cannon and Groce, the United States broke relations with the Zelaya government; then, on December 10, Maryland Senator Isidor Rayner introduced a resolution authorizing the President "to take all necessary steps for the apprehension of Zelaya, the alleged perpetrator of the crime," using "whatever methods and process may be necessary to accomplish this purpose." Zelaya resigned a week later, seeking asylum in Mexico and leaving the government in the hands of José Madriz.[29]

After some debate over whether Madriz was an improvement over Zelaya, Huntington Wilson convinced Knox and Taft to oppose Madriz, who continued Zelaya's attempt to put down the Estrada rebellion.[30] Madriz appeared poised to capture Bluefields in May 1910, when Captain William Gilmer of the U.S.S. *Paducah* landed 100 Marines to stop the fighting, allegedly to protect U.S. lives and property. This action had the effect of protecting the rebels, and when Madriz countered by capturing the all-important customs house just outside the city at El Bluff, Huntington Wilson intervened to neutralize that advantage: "Naturally the Government of the United States would not permit a double levy of duty and when the de facto authorities of Bluefields [Estrada] removed their customs house to another place where duties could be paid, Commander Gilmer would not permit the forces occupying Bluff also to collect duties."[31] Obliged by the U.S. military to abandon its offensive against the rebels, the Madriz government slowly disintegrated, and in late August Estrada's forces entered Managua and set up a new government.

For nearly a year Smedley Butler and his fellow Marines had been in Nicaraguan waters, "waiting for the 'Spigs' to stop scrapping."* In that time, he had become convinced that Nicaraguans "are the most worthless, useless lot of vermine I have struck yet, even worse than our 'Little brown brothers' the Filipinos." The Estrada rebellion represented "simply a sordid desire on the part of one dog to take from another cur a good picking bone and I really don't see why we don't either thrash both of them or go away and let them eat each other up."[32] The Taft administration's officials independently decided to pursue a somewhat different option: they began to supervise the day-to-day activities of the Nicaraguan leaders whom they had helped to install in office.

The Dominican Republic was used as a model. A U.S. financial expert

---

*"Spig" is a now-obsolete variant of "Spic," both thought to be derived from a mocking of the way Mexican-Americans pronounced "No speak English."

sent to advise the new Estrada government reported that "five years ago, Santo Domingo was one of our turbulent neighbors, almost continually disturbed and disturbing," but since the establishment of the U.S. financial receivership the nation's commerce and tax revenues had doubled.[33] Unlike the Dominican Republic, however, Nicaragua was not overburdened by foreign debt, and although the revolution had disrupted economic activity, the nation's finances fell into disarray only at the very end of the Zelaya administration. Nonetheless, U.S. officials simply assumed that Nicaragua's economic problems could not be resolved without foreign assistance, and so the Taft administration took over the country's finances.

As the Zelaya-Madriz government was coming to an end, the Taft administration was simultaneously negotiating a Dominican-style takeover of neighboring Honduras, a highlight of which was the first chase scene in U.S.–Latin American relations since the *Itata* affair. After sending Honduras's U.S. agent a message inquiring, "At what time may the Department expect to see you and General Parades [*sic*] tomorrow," Huntington Wilson was startled to receive Finance Minister Juan Paredes's reply indicating his departure for New York—apparently the Honduran official had decided to leave town rather than sign a document he considered treasonous. Wilson immediately ordered that the envoy be tracked down, and if he refused to return, "the United States will be inclined to leave the whole matter to Great Britain and to interpose not the slightest objection even to the forcible occupation of Honduranian custom houses on behalf of the British debt."[34] That threat convinced the envoy to sign, but the Honduran senate promptly voted 33 to 5 to reject the treaty, and most members of the Honduran congress endorsed a lengthy statement that the treaty would convert Honduras "from a free country into an administrative dependency of the United States."[35]

No sooner had Paredes been coerced into signing than the chief of the State Department's Division of Latin American Affairs sent Huntington Wilson his draft of a treaty for Nicaragua, "following the Honduranean convention but substituting the name of Nicaragua and making it conform otherwise. The preamble I think can also largely follow the Honduranean convention, containing somewhat more pointed allusion, perhaps, to the Nicaraguan request for assistance."[36]

This request for assistance had not come from a Nicaraguan but from Huntington Wilson, who almost a year earlier had instructed his deputy, Thomas Dawson, to "please draft a letter from Mr. Castrillo, as representative of the Provisional [Estrada] Government, to the Secretary of State containing some expression of appreciation of the impartial attitude of the United States." In the letter Dawson was to "put in trade-mark [Dominican] Convention, and about exploitation of the country and the need of placing its finances upon a better basis and a declaration of their intention to enter upon negotiations with a view to making with American bankers a satisfactory financial arrangement; also a paragraph guaranteeing fair and equitable treatment of American commerce and business; also a paragraph undertaking to reestablish a constitutional regime and hold free elections. [Also] draft a letter announcing the occupation of Managua by the Provisional forces and formally requesting recognition." Huntington Wilson concluded by indicating, "my idea would be to have Castrillo bring around both letters the moment Managua is taken."[37]

When Estrada's forces seized Managua on August 28, 1910, all that was missing was a Nicaraguan's signature on the request for intervention. The Dawson-Huntington Wilson document was cabled to Estrada in Bluefields by Salvador Castrillo, the rebel envoy in Washington:

> I [Castrillo] must have an immediate telegram in this form: Juan Estrada having taken possession of the Presidency and inaugurated an administration asks recognition as Provisional President until elections take place in six months. In order to refund the national debt, to stimulate development, and to rehabilitate national finances he asks the aid of the Government of the United States in order to negotiate a loan in the United States secured by part of the customs receipts the collection of which shall be conducted in such manner as may be agreed upon between Nicaragua and the United States as will certainly secure the loan and assure its object. He undertakes to take adequate measures to prosecute those responsible for the death of Cannon and Groce with the end of punishing them and to pay a reasonable indemnity to their relatives. For the purpose of facilitating the fulfillment of this and other arrangement he asks the Government of the United States to send a Commissioner to Nicaragua to act as to any of these matters which require the formality of a Convention. Castrillo. End Quote.[38]

Estrada signed immediately.

Then Thomas Dawson, now U.S. minister to Panama, traveled to Managua to negotiate the details of Nicaragua's debt consolidation and customs receivership. During one week in October 1910 Dawson negotiated four separate agreements with leaders of the Conservative party. The first provided for the creation of a constituent assembly to adopt a democratic constitution and elect Juan Estrada president and Adolfo Díaz vice president for a two-year transitional term. The second provided for the establishment of a claims commission, for Nicaragua's payment of all justified claims, and for reparation to the families of Cannon and Groce. The third provided for the negotiation of a private loan and the initiation of a customs receivership, and the fourth for a popular election of Estrada's successor from among candidates selected by the Conservative leaders who negotiated the accord with Dawson. This document specified that "the one chosen must represent the revolution and the Conservative party."[39]

Juan Estrada was a Liberal appointed by another Liberal, Zelaya, to his previous position in Bluefields. Converted into the lamest of lame ducks by the Dawson accords, in early May 1911 he resigned, acting, according to the U.S. minister, "in a fit of drunken insanity."[40] The resignation catapulted Vice President Adolfo Díaz into the presidency. An accounting clerk in the La Luz & Los Angeles Mining Company, a firm created to develop the concession granted to the Pittsburgh-based United States and Nicaragua Company, Díaz was also a figurehead assistant secretary-treasurer of the latter company, since, as U.S. Consul Moffat later explained, "one of the officials had to be a Nicaraguan."[41]

Before he resigned, Estrada had instructed his minister in Washington to negotiate a treaty to implement the third of the Dawson agreements. The Knox-Castrillo Treaty committed the new Díaz administration to negotiate a loan with "some competent and reliable American banking group," with repayment assured by Nicaraguan customs, whose activities were to be supervised by an official selected by Nicaragua, but from a list of individuals submitted by the U.S. bankers and approved by the U.S. President.[42]

Signed in Washington on June 6, 1911, the Knox-Castrillo Treaty was ratified eight days later by the Nicaraguan congress. But in Washington the agreement never moved beyond a tie vote (in May 1912) of the Senate Committee on Foreign Relations, some of whose members were averse to assuming further responsibilities in the Caribbean region, and some of whose members were motivated by partisan politics during an election year. While the Senate debate was occurring, the bankers decided to go ahead with two loans. The first in September 1911 (the Treasury Bill Agreement) and the second in March 1912 (the Supplemental Loan Agreement) provided the Díaz government with cash in exchange for the bankers' control of the newly created National Bank of Nicaragua and an option to purchase majority control of the nation's railroad, the government's only significant capital asset.

The bank and railroad arrangement were major innovations. Organized as a Connecticut corporation, the *Banco Nacional de Nicaragua* had a seven-member board of directors, six named by the U.S. banks and one appointed by the U.S. Secretary of State. Although Nicaragua soon obtained the right to appoint two directors, there was never any question about who was in charge. As the bankers wrote to Nicaragua's fiscal agent, "the Bank is under our management and control."[43] Similarly, Nicaragua's *Ferrocarril del Pacífico* was reorganized as a Maine corporation. In the beginning all the shares belonged to the Nicaraguan government, but in return for the Supplemental Loan, the bankers obtained 51 percent of the stock for $1 million. Seven years later the bankers loaned Nicaragua $1.75 million to repurchase the stock.

The fairness of these transactions has never been established. In its defense the Taft administration could note that it commissioned U.S. law firms to inspect the loan agreements in order to ensure fairness to Nicaragua, but critics have always charged that the bankers made excessive profits. In 1933 Roscoe Hill, a member of the soon-to-be-created Nicaraguan High Commission, set the banks' profits in Nicaragua at just less than $2 million, which represented an annual return of 15 percent on the investment in the National Bank and 20 percent on the railroad.[44] Although this is not an outrageously high return, neither is it insignificant. U.S. government bonds were then yielding between 3 and 4 percent, and the bankers' money was guaranteed by U.S. Marines and a U.S. customs collector. Moreover, these earnings represented only the profits from government transactions, not the profits from private merchant banking activities that came along with the official contracts. Perhaps the overall profit potential of these activities is best gauged by evidence that the banks were eager to participate, and one firm complained bitterly when it was not included in the business.[45]

More important is that the loans and the customs receivership tied Nicaragua to the U.S. economy, and, as Secretary Knox noted in a personal letter to the chair of the Senate Committee on Foreign Relations, these ties were "of vast commercial advantage, especially to the Southern States." Before the receivership, in 1911, the United States received 31 percent of Nicaragua's exports; aided by wartime dislocations, by 1917 that proportion had risen to 85 percent, and Nicaragua's European trading partners have never again challenged U.S. economic dominance.[46]

With the Treasury Bill agreement successfully negotiated, Adolfo Díaz began to think about his political future, and it did not take him long to recognize that he, like Estrada, lacked a political following in Nicaragua. To compensate, he proposed that the United States establish a protectorate. "The grave evils affecting us can only be destroyed by working with a more efficient and direct assistance of the great American nation, like the assistance which it has with such good results given to the people of Cuba." Díaz wanted Washington's approval of a treaty "permitting the United States to intervene in our internal affairs to maintain peace and the existence of a lawful Government." Since Congress would not even consent to the Knox-Castrillo treaty, Secretary Knox replied that the proposal would have to put off pending "deep and careful consideration."[47]

With the country led by a president lacking a constituency and with the Liberals angry at having been disenfranchised by the Dawson accords, in late July the Conservative minister of war, Luis Mena, launched an armed rebellion and was soon joined by substantial Liberal forces. President Díaz asked the United States for help, and 100 U.S. Marines were immediately sent to Managua. Within a few days 360 more were stationed along the Corinto-Managua railroad line, and for safety's sake, Knox obtained permission to deploy additional U.S. forces stationed in Panama.[48] He then departed on his three-month trip to Japan, leaving Huntington Wilson in charge of U.S. foreign policy. As Mena's revolt gained momentum, the assistant secretary sent Taft a blizzard of memos requesting additional troops. The President acquiesced, and the United States landed more and more Marines until the U.S. force reached 2,700 in September. Only after Huntington Wilson began requesting the deployment of regular Army troops (as opposed to the Marines), and only after it became obvious that those additional troops were unnecessary—only then did Taft signal an end to the buildup.[49]

Now quite ill, in late September Mena was obliged to surrender and was taken as a prisoner to the Canal Zone. Continuing to fight from their hillside encampment between Managua and Granada, the rebels led by Liberal General Benjamín Zeladón were dislodged on October 4 in hand-to-hand combat with the Marines, and the revolt ended two days later after Marines seized the Liberal stronghold of León.[50] The full U.S. force remained for a few weeks to supervise Adolfo Díaz's presidential election on November 2, and then all but about 130 Marines left the country. This force, which subsequent administrations would refer to as a "legation guard," was kept in Managua because "withdrawal of all marines would be construed as the tacit consent of the United States to renew hostilities."[51]

When Philander Knox had visited Nicaragua just prior to the Mena revolt, he had gone out of his way to convince a Managua audience of his government's good intentions. "I beg to assure you . . . that my Government does not covet an inch of territory south of the Rio Grande." Knox was being absolutely candid. But what he did not say was what his actions in Nicaragua demonstrated: that while the United States was perfectly willing to renounce territorial conquest, it was at the same time absolutely determined to exercise hegemony over the Caribbean region. This control boosted U.S. commerce and ensured stability around the new Canal, but President Taft preferred to emphasize the good that he was doing for Latin Americans: "The United States has contributed much to the cause of peace by assisting countries weak in respect to their internal government so as to strengthen in them the cause of law and order. This relationship of guardian and ward as between nations and countries, in my judgment, helps along the cause of international peace and indicates progress in civilization."[52]

Chapter 12 〜

Continuing to Help in the
Most Practical Way Possible

These wretched politicians do not intend to fall in with our American plans and ideas for their betterment.

〜 *General Smedley Butler, 1917*

"Mere commercial exploitation and the selfish interests of a narrow circle of financiers extending their enterprises to the ends of the earth"—that is the way Woodrow Wilson characterized Dollar Diplomacy in his final campaign speech in 1912.[1] If that was not a sufficient harbinger of a change in U.S. policy, then Wilson's selection of William Jennings Bryan as his secretary of state certainly was. "A repudiation of the fundamental principles of morality" is the way Bryan had described Dollar Diplomacy—"a phrase coined to describe a policy of government under which the state department has been used to coerce smaller nations into recognizing claims of American citizens which did not rest upon a legitimate basis." This is exactly what one would expect from a Democrat who called the Platt Amendment "a scheme of injustice," who criticized Roosevelt's use of the Navy to prevent Colombia from retaking Panama, and who insisted that every Democratic platform from 1900 until the day he died contain a plank endorsing Philippine independence. Bryan had sometimes startled his supporters with expansionist postures—especially shocking was his 1910 endorsement of Taft's policy in Nicaragua—but in 1913, when he strode into his office, the new secretary of state could justifiably claim the mantle of anti-imperialism.[2]

Bryan's long-standing opposition and Wilson's campaign criticism led officials of the outgoing administration to anticipate instability in the Caribbean during the lame-duck period. To acquaint the incoming administration with the perils of a radical policy shift, Assistant Secretary Huntington Wilson warned the President-elect that "prominent persons of revolutionary habit, have in some instances promulgated the belief that . . .

after March fourth the United States would not only be indifferent to revolution, but would positively sympathize with revolution by those now out of power. The result is that all the professional revolutionists, grafters, would-be dictators and cutthroats, many of them with long records of crime, have become conspicuously active."[3] To preclude this activity, the outgoing Taft administration ordered U.S. warships to make additional Central American port visits during the lame-duck period, and in February the Navy increased its strength along Mexico's two coasts following the Huerta coup. Secretary of State Knox argued that "not only will the local population be left with a wholesome regard for the might of the United States government but the central government in Mexico City will be kept in a state of watchful regard."[4]

Nicaragua was a particular problem, for the government there continued to teeter on the edge of political and economic chaos—or so it seemed to U.S. officials in Managua and Washington. Huntington Wilson provided the incoming President with an analysis of the problem: The U.S.-backed government of Adolfo Díaz had been assisted by "respectable American bankers" who "have established a bank at Managua, which does the Government's business and is beginning to flourish. Nicaragua has an American financial adviser, two Americans on their claims commission and an American collector of customs and the efforts of the bankers and these Americans have already increased their customs receipts, outlined for them complete currency reform and better system of internal taxation, besides relieving them of an onerous debt, at high interest, to Jewish bankers in Europe."[5]

Since the New York financial community could hardly have missed the incoming administration's menacing comments about Dollar Diplomacy, they threatened to withdraw from Nicaragua after Taft's electoral defeat. A few days before Woodrow Wilson's inauguration, the chief of the Division of Latin American Affairs warned that "the bankers had gone as far as they thought they could in the matter, in the absence of any knowledge of what the attitude of the incoming administration might be."[6] Not wanting to appear uncooperative, at 9:45 P.M. on inauguration day, the bankers cabled the State Department that they would make a small loan, but they wanted the new authorities in Washington to understand that they were not nearly as bad as had been suggested during the campaign: the new loan "adds one more to the many disinterested and uncompensated services which we have rendered Nicaragua."[7]

The bankers need not have worried. On his first full day in office, Bryan prepared his initial instruction to U.S. officials in Managua, which began with a telling clause straight from the Dollar Diplomacy handbook: "Brown Brothers now telegraph Department as follows"—and what followed were the details to be negotiated by the minister, every word written by the bankers themselves.[8] Then, at Wilson's first cabinet meeting a few days later, Navy Secretary Josephus Daniels asked permission to recall the warships that Taft had sent to Mexico. Daniels recorded that "it was the opinion of the President that, inasmuch as the ships were sent because of troubles, if withdrawn now, it would be construed as proof that the Government was satisfied because of present conditions. It is not satisfied."[9]

Bryan's cable and Wilson's decision were signs of things to come, and seven years later, as the Wilson administration was coming to an end, a State Department commercial advisor would write that the Taft-to-Wilson transition had been "one of the few instances in which no break is shown, and no national administration overturns the policies of its predecessor."[10] Nothing changed. In 1920, Woodrow Wilson's final full year as President, the acting secretary of state commented that the best way for the United States to resolve a Central American border dispute was "to bang them over the head," a statement indistinguishable from Taft's 1909 assertion of "the right to knock their heads together."[11] The torch of Dollar Diplomacy was passed without a flicker.

The imperial spurt from the 1890s through the era of Dollar Diplomacy had generated a new set of powerful political interests that relied upon the U.S. government to maintain stability in the Caribbean region. These interests were the usual suspects—the bankers, who may have been looking for ways to get out of Nicaragua, but were poised to expand dramatically throughout the rest of Latin America; the concessionaires in the Caribbean region, all of them well versed in the tactic of applying pressure through their representatives in Congress; and the State Department's bureaucrats, who seemed perfectly comfortable with Dollar Diplomacy. And they were, in a negative sense, both public opinion, which ignored the region and so exerted no constraining influence on policy-makers, and members of Congress—a Democratic majority that repudiated Dollar Diplomacy in their speeches but refused to challenge their President.

Perhaps most important, they were the forces of ignorance. For all his brilliance, Woodrow Wilson knew little about international relations when he entered the White House, and, although obliged to learn quickly, he made the crucial mistake of selecting tutors who were themselves extraordinarily uninformed. As a result, Wilson agonized interminably over U.S. relations with its neighbors. He, like the Dollar Diplomats, prized stability in Latin America, but, unlike the Dollar Diplomats, his progressive instincts told him that it was wrong simply to take over unstable countries. Lacking a clear alternative vision of how to achieve stability, his administration tried a little bit of everything in Latin America.

Presidential ignorance of foreign affairs is not unknown, of course, but most Presidents who plan to focus on domestic politics, as Wilson did, select knowledgeable secretaries of state, as Wilson did not. "His mind is wholly undisciplined and unregulated," wrote John Bassett Moore after a long meeting with William Jennings Bryan. "The difficulty with the Secretary was not more his inattention by reason of absence [a swipe at former Secretary Knox's long vacations] than his apparent inability when present to give consecutive thought or really intelligent consideration to anything brought before him. He never seems to have a reasoned judgment on anything or any real appreciation of what he was doing."[12]

If the Great Commoner was ignorant of foreign affairs, it was not for want of exposure. Bryan was surprisingly well traveled, so that when he entered office, he already had seen more of Latin America than any other secretary of state, including a three-month tour of the entire region in 1910, something no other presidential candidate or future secretary of state has ever done. The problem of William Jennings Bryan was not that he failed to see the facts of international relations, but that he never developed an intellectual framework that would make sense of the information he had accumulated. Like Wilson, he knew there was instability in the Caribbean region, but he did not know why, and so he accepted the explanations offered by the Dollar Diplomats.

In fact, not one member of Wilson's Caribbean policy team, diplomat or informal agent, had a fresh idea of how to deal with the central issue of instability in Latin America. Edward House, the President's closest advisor, thought that the long-term solution lay in German immigration—"the German population would be in every way preferable to the population now in the majority of South American countries." Moreover, Bryan's successor, Robert Lansing, conceived of the problem of Caribbean instability exactly as Knox and Huntington Wilson had done: "within this area lie the small republics of America which have been and to an extent still are the prey of revolutionists, of corrupt governments, and of predatory foreigners. Because of this state of affairs our national safety, in my opinion, requires that the United States should intervene and aid in the establishment and maintenance of a stable and honest government, if no other way seems possible to attain that end."[13]

Immediately below Wilson's political appointees was the accumulation of sixteen years of Republican control of the Department of State. Wilson was wary of these lower-level officials, and his caution did not disappear when Bryan filled the ranks with deserving Democrats; his response was to use informal advisors, the first of whom was William Bayard Hale, whom he asked "to undertake a tour of the Central and South American states [so that] we might find out just what is going on down there."[14] In the meantime, the President and his secretary of state no longer enjoyed the luxury of criticizing Republicans from the outside. Their watch had begun, and so they divided up responsibility for the region—or at least that is how it appears—with Bryan taking Central America and the Caribbean, while Wilson handled revolutionary Mexico.

Nicaragua was Bryan's first problem. Adolfo Díaz's government was destitute, and other powers were nosing about in the tangled Central American underbrush. Earlier, while serving as chief of the Division of Latin American Affairs, the U.S. minister to Nicaragua, George Weitzel, had suggested that the State Department kill two birds with one stone by purchasing a canal option from the Díaz government. The Panama Canal was not yet open, and the last thing the United States wanted to do was build another, but an exclusive option would both give Díaz some cash and "forever dispose of the bogy of a German or Japanese canal anywhere on the American continent."[15] When he was transferred to Managua a year later, Weitzel negotiated a treaty with foreign minister Emiliano Chamorro that would have given Nicaragua $3 million in exchange for an exclusive canal option, a naval base in the Gulf of Fonseca, and other privileges. Signed in February 1913 and submitted to the Senate barely a week before Woodrow Wilson's inauguration, Weitzel's treaty never saw the light of day.

That outcome left Bryan with the problem of a penniless Nicaragua. Worried by their existing exposure, the New York bankers were not inclined to offer much help. If the Wilson administration wanted Wall Street financiers to invest additional funds in order to pull Nicaragua back from the financial abyss (and, implicitly, political turmoil), then Bryan would have to convince them to do so. The actual task was assumed by the State Department's Division of Latin American Affairs, which sent Bryan a lengthy memorandum outlining Nicaragua's destitution, praising the achievements of Dollar Diplomacy, and warning that if the United States did not provide assistance, then "Nicaragua will probably look to Europe for a new loan." Two days after its receipt, Bryan wrote President Wilson that he favored reviving Weitzel's treaty: "I am inclined to think that the purchase of the Canal option might give sufficient encouragement to the bankers to loan."[16]

Standing in the wings prompting Bryan was his friend Charles Douglas, a lawyer-lobbyist hired by Adolfo Díaz to represent Nicaragua's interests in Washington. In mid-June 1913 he handed Bryan a revised draft of the Weitzel treaty that added, at Díaz's insistence, a Platt amendment giving the United States the right to intervene. President Wilson's response was the only thing more surprising than Bryan's decision to forward the proposal to the White House: "the proposed Nicaraguan treaty has my entire approval."[17]

The secretary of state then consulted with the Senate Committee on Foreign Relations, which was dominated by Democrats who had spent the previous four years criticizing Dollar Diplomacy. On August 2 the Committee voted informally to advise Bryan that it would not consider a treaty that included a Platt-style protectorate. With this option eliminated, Bryan next proposed that the U.S. Treasury sell bonds on the open market at 3 percent interest, then loan the proceeds to Nicaragua and other Latin American countries at $4\frac{1}{2}$ percent, a much lower rate than they could expect to negotiate with private bankers. Interest and principal on the 3 percent bonds would be paid by the $1\frac{1}{2}$ percent spread, with repayment guaranteed in the Nicaraguan case by the customs collector. The President delayed responding, and so Bryan wrote once more:

> I beg pardon for bringing this subject to your attention again, but it is pathetic to see Nicaragua struggling in the grip of an oppressive financial agreement. As I think I have stated in a former letter, we see in these transactions a perfect picture of dollar diplomacy. The financiers charge excessive rates on the ground that they must be paid for the *risk* that they take and as soon as they collect their pay for the risk they then proceed to demand of the respective governments that the *risk* shall be *eliminated* by governmental coercion. No wonder the people of these little republics are roused to revolution by what they regard as a sacrifice of their interests.

Wilson incorporated Bryan's indignant words in his first speech on Latin American policy—adding "I rejoice in nothing so much as in the prospect that they will now be emancipated from these conditions"—but he refused to approve the secretary's "novel and radical proposal."[18] The U.S. government was not going to get into the business of bankrolling Latin America.

As these discussions were occurring in Washington, the U.S. legation in Managua was warning of the dire consequences of inaction. Convinced that Nicaragua would collapse into anarchy without U.S. aid, Bryan turned to the bankers, requesting the terms that they would require for a new loan. President Díaz added urgency to the process by sending his finance minister racing to Washington with a memorandum indicating that "public tranquility may be placed in danger." After some delay, the bankers agreed to help if Nicaragua would hand over more of its railroad and national bank as security.

This step might forestall immediate disaster, but it would not be sufficient to address Nicaragua's medium-term financial difficulties. As State Department personnel continued to cover Bryan's desk with memos predicting a foreign policy disaster, the secretary of state was pushed to negotiate yet another version of the moot Weitzel treaty. No one has ever been able to explain what led Bryan to accept, for a second time, Adolfo Díaz's suggestion that the treaty include a Platt-type protectorate, but since the secretary of state realized that the Senate was wary of the idea, Bryan instructed Adolfo Díaz to send Wilson a personal request for a protectorate, which the State Department drafted. Handed to President Wilson after making a quick round-trip to Managua, the Díaz-Bryan message asserted that "the effect of the Platt Amendment on Cuba has been so satisfactory that, since your Government is considering a canal convention with Nicaragua, I respectfully request that said convention be made to embody the substance of the Platt Amendment."[19]

President Wilson was almost certainly in on this charade to convince the Senate. Writing with the telltale prose of someone seeking to cover himself, he replied to Díaz: "Having the assurance that the provisions of the proposed treaty embodying the substance of what is known as the Platt amendment have been written at your request, and that, in your judgment, they will prove helpful to your country, it will afford me great pleasure to give to the treaty my cordial approval."[20] Unconvinced, in July the chair of the Senate Committee on Foreign Relations informed Bryan that the committee would stick to its earlier decision and refuse to consider a treaty providing for a protectorate. With that, the secretary of state finally dropped the idea. Instead, he signed a new treaty with Emiliano Chamorro, now Nicaragua's minister in Washington, that was essentially a duplicate of the

Weitzel treaty, giving Nicaragua $3 million in exchange for a canal route, but without a Platt amendment.

The new treaty greatly alarmed Costa Rica and El Salvador, both of which immediately asked the newly created Central American Court of Justice to block its implementation. Costa Rica had already lodged a formal protest against the Weitzel agreement, arguing that its provisions for use of the San Juan River violated not simply the 1858 Cañas-Jerez boundary treaty, but also the 1888 Cleveland arbitration award and the 1907 Central American Treaty of Peace and Friendship. Costa Rica used these same arguments to urge the Central American Court to invalidate the Bryan-Chamorro treaty. For its part, El Salvador claimed that any treaty granting the United States a naval base in the Gulf of Fonseca violated its rights of coownership of the Gulf. The United States and Nicaragua responded that the Court lacked jurisdiction over any of these issues and refused to participate in the proceedings. Sitting in the handsome judicial building in Cartago (constructed at Elihu Root's request with Andrew Carnegie's money), in September 1916 and March 1917 the Court ruled in favor of Costa Rica and El Salvador, respectively. Nicaragua promptly withdrew from membership in the Court, and in March 1918 the tribunal that Philander Knox had called "the first perfect type of international court of arbitral justice" was disbanded.[21]

In the meantime, the U.S. Senate consented to ratification of the Bryan-Chamorro Treaty. Despite the fact that they had blocked the nearly identical Weitzel treaty in early 1913, Democrats voted 40 to 5 to accommodate their President. Not to be outdone in flexibility, the Republicans moved from pro to con, focusing their criticism on the puppet status of the Díaz government that they themselves had created. Typical was the comment by Minnesota's William Smith, who argued that "the present administration of Nicaragua, headed by Adolfo Diaz as president, has been maintained for upwards of two years by the active presence of American marines in the capital at Managua, under the guise of a legation guard, and in defiance of the wishes of the people of that Republic."[22]

Ratification of Bryan's treaty cemented U.S. control over Nicaragua. Majority ownership of Nicaragua's national bank and railway was in the hands of U.S. bankers, and Washington now had an exclusive canal option that kept Nicaragua from pursuing any other offer. Washington also had the right to surround the country with naval bases; to operate a customs receivership; and, in order to ensure that nothing changed without their approval, to keep the Marines in Managua. In return, Nicaragua received $3 million from the United States, 70 percent of which it never saw. Under a plan approved by the two governments in 1917, $800,000 was given to British bondholders, $768,000 went to the New York bankers, and $485,000 was used to pay off the long-standing Emery claim. The remaining $836,000 was sent to Nicaragua.[23]

The threat of instability never disappeared. As the Senate was considering ratification of the Bryan-Chamorro treaty, Nicaragua was preparing for its 1916 presidential election. From the U.S. perspective, the problem was that the hostile Liberals were united behind the candidacy of Julián Irías, while the Conservatives were split into three factions. Seeking to ensure that the Conservatives settled on a single candidate, U.S. Minister Benjamin Jefferson and Admiral William Caperton met with Díaz and reported: "Have just had a most satisfactory conference with President Diaz [who] will gladly accept the name of any candidate for the presidency of Nicaragua that the secretary might indicate."[24] But when it became obvious that Emiliano Chamorro would be the choice of Secretary of State Lansing (Bryan had resigned in mid-1915), Díaz decided to seek reelection. The U.S. response was to send a warning message and military reinforcements. Shortly after two additional warships dropped anchor in Corinto, Admiral Caperton reported that "with the advent of a squadron of American ships, political leaders are again giving the usual weight to the Minister's words . . . The Commander-in-Chief [Caperton] and American Minister then had a conference with President Diaz who agreed to use his utmost to reunite the three factions of the Conservative party in favor of General Chamorro."[25]

The State Department next turned its attention to the Liberals, whose constituency was "the ignorant masses of the people who either do not appreciate the intentions or policies of this Government or who are readily susceptible to political oratory." To solve this sticky problem of voters' lacking sufficient wisdom to make an appropriate decision, Caperton and Jefferson notified the Liberals that anyone who had been associated with the Zelaya administration (Julián Irías, for one) would not be allowed to run for office.[26] The Liberals then abstained, assuring Chamorro of an uncontested victory.

The day President Chamorro entered office—January 1, 1917—was the same day that the U.S. customs collector began retaining all of Nicaragua's customs receipts in accordance with the default provisions of the bankers' contracts. Adolfo Díaz had looted the treasury, and in order to obtain any revenue with which to operate its government, the incoming Chamorro administration was obliged to enter into yet another round of negotiations with the U.S. government. This time the product was a complex agreement known as the Lansing Plan, which provided for another bank loan in return for the creation of a three-member High Commission to supervise Nicaragua's finances. Composed of one member appointed by the U.S. secretary of state and one by the President of Nicaragua, with a third selected by the United States in the event that the two disagreed, the High Commission represented a compromise after President Chamorro refused to accept a U.S. fiscal advisor. Once Chamorro agreed to the plan, Nicaragua began receiving its share of the customs revenues; thereafter, burgeoning wartime demand for coffee and timber enabled the nation to make it through the remaining years of the Wilson administration with a budget surplus.

The situation Bryan inherited in the Dominican Republic was similar. In 1914, the year after Woodrow Wilson entered office, the economist-consultant Jacob Hollander published an evaluation of the Dominican customs receivership that he had helped the Roosevelt administration establish a decade earlier. Under U.S. supervision, "little short of a revolution, social, political and economic, has been wrought in the country. Not a revolution of the old type, involving waste and ruin, but a revolution in the arts of peace, industry and civilization. The people of the island, protected from rapine and bloodshed, free to devote themselves to earning a livelihood, are fairly on the way to becoming a decent peasantry, as industrious and stable as sub-tropical conditions are likely to evolve."[27]

Hollander's analysis contained no mention of the Dominican Republic's renewed political instability, but Bryan knew about it. Soon after taking office, he had been obliged to instruct the U.S. chargé in Santo Domingo to "take the earliest favorable opportunity to communicate . . . the profound displeasure that is felt by this Government at this pernicious revolutionary activity."[28] When a new insurgency broke out in early 1914, the secretary of state began to consider additional U.S. supervision. By now virtually everyone in Washington had accepted the opinion that the turmoil represented a simple contest for control over the treasury—"the minute we take charge of the Customs House all illegitimate expenses cease, and the business of politicians and revolutionists is at an end," promised Captain Dillingham in 1904—and so Bryan proposed to supplement the existing U.S. customs receivership by taking charge of all the Dominican Republic's finances.[29] Hoping to avoid such a blatant takeover, Wilson would approve only the appointment of a "Commercial Attaché to the Legation," but in mid-1914 renewed instability prompted instead the dispatch of a commission to restore peace. Clearly Hollander had spoken too soon.

The U.S. invasion of Mexico in April and the assassination of Austria's Archduke Francis Ferdinand in June reinforced the Wilson administration's determination to brook no nonsense in the Dominican Republic. Accompanied by several hundred Marines, the three U.S. commissioners arrived in Santo Domingo with a proposal that came to be known as the Wilson Plan, perhaps the least-subtle document in the history of U.S.–Latin American relations. It began, "The Government of the United States very solemnly advises all concerned with the public affairs of the republic to adopt the following plan." First, the nation's leaders were ordered to select a provisional president, and "if they cannot agree, the Government of the United States will itself name a provisional President." Second, the provisional president would hold an election, and "let it be understood that the Government of the United States will send representatives of its own choosing to observe the election throughout the republic and that it will expect those observers . . . to be accorded a courteous welcome." Third, "let it be understood that if the United States Government is satisfied that these elections have been free and fair . . . it will recognize the President and Congress . . . If it should not be satisfied that elections of the right kind have been held, let it be understood that another election will be held at which the mistakes observed will be corrected." Finally, once a new government had been installed in office, the Wilson Plan stipulated that "the Government of the United States would feel at liberty thereafter to insist that revolutionary movements cease."[30]

Looking down the barrel of a Marine Corps rifle, the Dominicans more or less agreed to these terms, but only briefly. In 1915 Bryan felt obliged to warn that "this government meant what it said when it declared that it would tolerate no more insurrections in Santo Domingo," and when repeated admonitions failed to produce the desired calm, Bryan's replacement convinced President Wilson to order a full-scale military occupation. In late 1915 Captain Harry Knapp sailed his battleship into Santo Domingo and issued the following proclamation: "I, H. S. Knapp, Captain, United States Navy . . . acting under the authority and by the direction of the Government of the United States, declare and announce to all concerned that the Republic of Santo Domingo is hereby placed in a state of Military Occupation by the forces under my command."[31]

The occupation would continue for eight years. From the beginning it was anything but pleasant, according to Admiral Caperton. "I really believe these people are worse than the Haitiens, if such a thing be possible, and I am more convinced each day that the only way to handle them is by force and the big stick. Their rascality, grafting and total unreliability, are beyond all conception." Unlike Nicaragua, where men like Adolfo Díaz could be found who were willing to cooperate with the United States, Caperton reported that in the Dominican Republic "I have never seen such hatred displayed by one people for another as I notice and feel here. We positively have not a friend in the land."[32]

The Wilson administration's experience was similar in neighboring Haiti, where U.S. attention was attracted by continual reports of political and economic instability. Like the Dominican Republic, Haiti had a strong European presence that had worried U.S. officials for decades. Also like the Dominican Republic, Haiti stood guard over the approach to the Panama Canal, and just as Washington's envoys had regularly sought to acquire Samaná Bay for a Navy base, since the late 1880s the United States had been asking Haiti to lease or sell the Môle Saint-Nicolas, a port on the country's northwest coast, just across the Windward Passage from Cuba. The Navy's interest declined after the acquisition of Guantánamo, but Bryan believed that the Môle "would be of great value to us and even if it were not valuable to us it is worth while to take it out of the market so that no other nation will attempt to secure a foothold there." And so he sent Assistant Secretary of State John Osborn to Haiti with instructions to purchase not simply the harbor but a 20-mile-wide strip of land as a buffer, allowing the Haitians living on the property to choose whether to become U.S. citizens or to sell their property to the United States and leave. Given U.S. racial attitudes, it is difficult to imagine that such an agreement would have received Congressional approval, but Bryan's proposal never became an issue in Washington because the government of Haiti was not interested in selling.[33]

No sooner had this matter been put to rest than the French and German governments, not yet at war with one another, inquired about Bryan's interest in a joint financial receivership for Haiti. Since 1823, when the United States rejected collaboration with Great Britain and instead issued the unilateral Monroe Doctrine, the United States had avoided this type of cooperation with European powers in Latin America; instead, since 1904 the Roosevelt Corollary had required the United States to act on behalf of European interests. Continuing both policies, in July 1914 Bryan proposed a treaty for Haiti modeled after Roosevelt's convention establishing the Dominican receivership. The Haitian government was considering the proposal when war broke out in Europe and another change of government occurred in Haiti, and Bryan took the opportunity to insist upon a customs receivership and favorable treatment of U.S. capital as conditions for recognition. When his proposal was rejected and instability continued into 1915, Bryan prepared for firmer action, warning President Wilson that "it may be necessary for us to use as much force as may be necessary to compel a supervision." [34]

It was not until July 28, 1915, that U.S. troops finally landed in Haiti, sent by Secretary Lansing, who told Haiti's minister in Washington "that in case we had not taken the step, in all probability some other nation would have felt called upon to do so." Lansing believed "that the intelligent Haitians should feel gratified that it was the United States rather than some other power whose motives might not be as unselfish as ours." [35] To Lansing as to Wilson, the end justified the means. Military occupation was "the only thing to do if we intend to cure the anarchy and disorder which prevails in that Republic. I believe it will be welcomed by the better element of the haytien people." For two weeks Wilson remained uncomfortable with his decision, finally writing Edith Bolling Galt, whom he would marry in December, with an explanation that probably comes closest to reflecting the President's view of the situation: "our object, of course, is not to subordinate them, but to help them in the most practical and most feasible way possible." [36]

While Wilson sought to rationalize his policy, Caperton proceeded with the U.S. takeover. His first major task was to supervise an election. On the eve of that contest, Lansing cabled, "in order that no misunderstanding can possibly occur after election, it should be made perfectly clear to candidates as soon as possible and in advance of their election, that the United States expects to be entrusted with the practical control of the customs, and such financial control over the affairs of the Republic of Haiti as the United States may deem necessary for an efficient administration." When the new legislature balked at ratification, in late 1915 Caperton was instructed to tell the Haitians that "my government has the intention to retain control in Haiti until the desired end is accomplished." [37] The treaty was ratified the next day.

In addition to general Platt-type language permitting the United States to intervene, the agreement obliged the President of Haiti to name a General Receiver of revenues and a Financial Advisor, both nominated by the U.S. President, and to create a constabulary "organized and officered by Americans." On February 1, 1916, Admiral Caperton issued a decree abolishing all local government, and Smedley Butler's Marines "assumed all responsibility for the safety and proper policing of the Republic of Haiti."[38] Along with his successors, Butler ran the country for the next nineteen years, helping the Navy's assistant secretary, Franklin Delano Roosevelt, prepare a new constitution. When the hand-picked Haitian legislature discovered that FDR's constitution contained a novel provision permitting the foreign ownership of land, Butler wrote, "the Haitian National Legislature became so impudent that the Gendarmerie had to dissolve them, which dissolution was effected by genuinely Marine Corps methods"—methods that he would not mention in a letter "for fear the Department of State might get hold of the letter by means of the censors." After physically evicting the legislators from their hall, Butler and his colleagues then decided to conduct instead a plebiscite, in which the new constitution was accepted by a vote of 98,225 to 768.[39]

As for Butler, his heroism in killing two hundred Haitians at Fort Rivière without a single U.S. casualty earned him his second Congressional Medal of Honor, but to his chagrin he never received the title of governor, because Lansing believed that Haitian nationals should exercise titular sovereignty. Butler wrote home that "I am reduced to a very humiliating position, am simply the very subservient chief of a nigger police force." After quiet returned and the United States entered World War I, Butler sought a transfer to Europe, arguing that "these wretched politicians do not intend to fall in with our American plans and ideas for their betterment."[40]

And so it went throughout the Caribbean region during the administration of Woodrow Wilson. U.S. Marines were landed in Cuba during a period of civil unrest in 1917, where they stayed until mid-1919, when most were withdrawn. Two companies of about five hundred soldiers remained in Camagüey until 1922, but by then Enoch Crowder had returned to serve as proconsul, beginning a separate chapter of U.S.-Cuban relations that ended only in 1959.

In Honduras, Bryan had barely warmed the secretary of state's chair when he sent the first U.S. warship to that nation's waters in April 1913; significant additional deployments occurred in August 1913, September 1915, October 1916, and April 1919. A variety of problems prompted these deployments, but underlying all of them was the Wilson administration's belief that Honduras could not manage without U.S. help. Boaz Long—a stockbroker friend of National City Bank's Roger Farnham and completely inexperienced in Latin American affairs, but nonetheless now serving as chief of the Division of Latin American Affairs—wrote that "the condition of the people is pitiable. The population is approximately 500,000, showing little or no increase for many years. Of these about 80% are bitterly poor and illiterate. About 18% can read and write and compare with our average laboring class and about 2% can be compared with our better elements. Chronic revolutions have removed all incentive to application and industry and most of the people are given over to shiftlessness and drunkenness. About 20% of the people are habitual drunkards." To Long, "there is no hope of improvement and every prospect of worse conditions unless the country is afforded decided help from without."[41]

With this type of thinking as its justification, the Wilson administration supervised the most active period of military intervention in the history of U.S.–Latin American relations: in Nicaragua, the Dominican Republic, Haiti, Cuba, Honduras—even Panama was twice obliged to cede domestic police powers to U.S. armed forces. And, of course, we have yet to consider Woodrow Wilson's policy toward the Mexican revolution.

This policy completely confused the British ambassador in Washington, Cecil Spring-Rice. He had grown accustomed to the thinking of William Howard Taft, who felt nothing but contempt for those who proposed that the United States "uplift the downtrodden citizens" of Mexico, and so he was surprised to discover that Woodrow Wilson had accepted a calling: "the foremost duty of the United States is declared to be,—the internal reform of this unhappy neighbor. Since the days of the Holy Alliance it is doubtful if any government has thus declared its mission to reform the moral shortcomings of foreign nations."[42]

The introduction to Mexico for Woodrow Wilson's generation focused on the neighbor's inability or unwillingness to curb cross-border raids by groups generally identified as "desperados" or "bandits"—generic terms that usually meant destitute Native Americans. By the 1850s these desperados had recognized that both Anglos and Hispanics had vested an unguarded shallow river with a special significance: it was something called an "international border," and law enforcement officials on one side were not supposed to cross to the other. Taking advantage of this quaint European convention, for many years U.S. bandits plundered Mexico, and Mexico's desperados pillaged the U.S. borderlands. In time the United States was more efficient in pacifying its Indians, however, and by 1877 the Army general commanding the U.S. side of the border reported that "all those Indians who then made raids into Mexico from the United States are now living in Mexico, and have made peace with the citizens on that side, and now raid back on the United States. They are wild, savage Indians, living in mountains that are inaccessible, in a country which is reported on the Mexican maps as unknown."[43]

Throughout Woodrow Wilson's childhood (he was born in 1856) the vulnerable residents along the Texas side of the border regularly demanded protection. In 1869 these demands prompted Secretary of State Hamilton Fish to request Mexico's cooperation, and when the response was perceived as halfhearted, in early 1873 he told Mexico that the United States would pursue raiders across the border. Then in May a group of Kickapoo Indians (a tribe of Algonquian stock that had been deprived of their lands in Wisconsin) made a highly publicized incursion into southern Texas, and the United States responded by sending troops into northern Mexico. The Mexican government reacted by complaining about raids into Sonora by Arizona-based Apaches.

Neither side wanted to escalate this conflict, and neither thought it advisable for the armed forces of one nation to be invading the territory of the other; therefore, in early 1875 the two governments negotiated an agreement for military cooperation without border crossings. When this proved ineffective, in May 1875 Fish asked the Mexican government either to permit U.S. military occupation of part of northern Mexico or to authorize hot pursuit across the border. After Mexico refused both requests, the Grant administration made oblique but ominous threats of further incursions.

President Grant's participation in the Mexican-American War left him reluctant to badger Mexico further, but his successor, Rutherford Hayes, felt no such compunction, and he insisted on the doctrine of hot pursuit. Less than three months after Hayes took office, the commander of U.S. forces in Texas was told "that in case the lawless incursions continue he will be at liberty, in the use of his own discretion, when in pursuit of a band of the marauders, and when his troops are either in sight of them or upon a fresh trail, to follow them across the Rio Grande, and to overtake and punish them, as well as retake stolen property taken from our citizens and found in their hands on the Mexican side of the line."[44] Mexico responded by sending additional troops to the border with orders both to repel U.S. forces and to capture the bandits. Although U.S. troops entered Mexico about a dozen times over the next two years, somehow they managed to avoid any armed clash with Mexican forces. After three years in office, President Hayes revoked the hot-pursuit order.[45]

It also fell to the Hayes administration to address the question of recognizing the new government of Porfirio Díaz, which consolidated its power just as the 1876 U.S. presidential election was occurring. Lame-duck Secretary Fish encouraged prompt recognition, "as we cannot receive from a government which we do not acknowledge, the instalment of indemnity payable by Mexico,"[46] but he deferred to the incoming administration, which postponed recognition for more than a year while insisting that Mexico exercise greater control over border raids *and* that it respond to a broad variety of additional U.S. concerns, including issues of internal Mexican political organization. Specifically, the U.S. minister in Mexico was informed that the United States "waits before recognizing General Diaz as the President of Mexico, until it shall be assured that his election is approved by the Mexican people."[47]

Until this moment the United States had followed the policy established by Thomas Jefferson of recognizing new governments whenever they assumed de facto power and indicated an ability to fulfill their international obligations. It was unprecedented for Washington to insist that a Latin American government hold a legitimizing election as a condition for recognition. Since this would necessarily involve the United States in Mexico's internal affairs and, by precedent, prepare the ground for similar involvements elsewhere, both houses of Congress scheduled hearings, with the House of Representatives conducting a major study that included testimony by Secretary Evarts and U.S. Minister John Foster, who took advantage of this recall to Washington to convince the secretary of state to recognize the Díaz government.[48]

By this time the issue was moot, for Porfirio Díaz had not only held an election but also indicated a desire to cooperate with the United States. On the subject of hot pursuit, for example, the United States and Mexico signed a treaty stipulating that "regular federal troops of the two Republics may reciprocally cross the boundary line of the two countries, when they are in close pursuit of a band of savage Indians."[49] Díaz's cooperative spirit was even more evident in his effort to attract U.S. investors, and a vast number of U.S. citizens soon tied their fortunes to Mexico. These were not simply the trader of John Quincy Adams's day nor the railroad entrepreneur or mining engineer of the immediate post–Civil War era, but a dense network of enterprising citizens, some of them with names like Rockefeller, Doheny, and Guggenheim—citizens with direct access to the levers of political power in both countries. Only a minority focused primarily on trade; the lion's share of U.S. entrepreneurial interest was investment capital in mining, railroads, and petroleum. These politically vulnerable investments (two extractive industries and one transportation utility) soon accounted for 85 percent of total U.S. capital in Mexico and nearly a quarter of all U.S. investment abroad.[50] Petroleum became a special focus after the turn of the century, a time when the world's thirst for oil was growing by leaps and bounds, and when wildcatters found it nearly oozing out of the ground along Mexico's east coast. They quickly transformed Mexico into one of the world's most important producers—second to the United States during Woodrow Wilson's presidency.

From the beginning, these investments worried some U.S. officials. As early as 1882 Louisiana Representative John Ellis warned his colleagues that "Mexico is now undergoing a physical conquest by our people. Our railroads and other enterprises are permeating her territory. Before long Mexico will wake up to the fact that she is gradually being subjugated by the United States; and then will come the recoil and the revolt, and the United States may be called upon to conserve the interests and property of her citizens there."[51] This was the fate waiting for Woodrow Wilson, who would remark in 1916 that his administration's policy toward Mexico had been complicated immeasurably by the fact that Mexico "is exceedingly to be desired by those who wish to amass fortunes . . . No enterprising capitalist can look upon her without coveting her."[52]

As U.S. investments increased, stability became increasingly important to officials in Washington, and by the time Secretary of State Elihu Root traveled to Mexico in 1907, no one was surprised when stability emerged as the dominant theme of his speeches. Unfortunately, he linked it to the increasingly unpopular government of Porfirio Díaz, emphasizing in one speech that Díaz was "one of the great men to be held up for the hero worship of mankind." This was a bipartisan appraisal, as William Jennings Bryan wrote after a Mexican vacation in 1903: "Certainly no people have made greater relative progress than the Mexican people have made under the administration of Porfirio Diaz." William Howard Taft also agreed, writing his brother that "Diaz has done more for the people of Mexico than any other Latin-American has done for any of his people; . . . the truth is they need a firm hand in Mexico and everybody realizes it."[53]

Aware of minor rumblings of discontent, President Taft sought to bolster Díaz's stature by meeting with him in El Paso/Ciudad Juárez in October 1909—the first sitting President to visit Mexico. He wrote his wife that Díaz "is very anxious to strengthen himself with his own people by a picturesque performance in which we show our friendship for him and his government, and I am glad to aid him in the matter for the reason that we have two billions American capital in Mexico that will be greatly endangered if Diaz were to die and his government go to pieces." Recognizing that Díaz was no longer a spring chicken, Taft admitted that his visit was intended to buy time: "I can only hope and pray that his demise does not come until I am out of office."[54]

It was not to be. The rebellion against the *porfiriato* that began in 1910 climaxed with Díaz's ouster in May 1911, and the Taft administration now had to construct a working relationship with a man who called himself a revolutionary, Francisco Madero.

Much of the naivete in Washington's reaction to Díaz's ouster reflected a history of incompetent diplomatic representation. Not every U.S. envoy deserves to be tarred with this generalization—Minister John Foster (1873 to 1880) stands out as a particularly effective envoy, but no other Díaz-era U.S. diplomat possessed Foster's abilities. Minister Henry Jackson spent most of his sixteen-month tenure in 1885–86 criticizing everything he observed, prompting Secretary of State Bayard to complain that Jackson "has inculcated the greatest distrust in that Country and its government. He has pictured in the darkest colors the senility and corruption of the officials, and the hopelessness of dealing with them on a basis of justice and honesty."[55] Jackson's replacement, Thomas Manning, had serious problems with alcohol, and at one point the legation secretary cabled Bayard: "Minister Manning wildly drunk again yesterday and thoroughly unfit for business to-day and possibly for days. Send instructions."[56]

The Taft administration continued this tradition of incompetence by naming Henry Lane Wilson as ambassador a year before Díaz's ouster. Wilson was both a political appointee (his brother was a U.S. senator from Washington until 1899 and a prominent Seattle newspaper publisher thereafter) and an experienced diplomat, having served as minister to Chile and Belgium. He shared the common turn-of-the-century U.S. view of Mexico, believing that "practically all of the material development of Mexico is due to American enterprise, initiative, and capital," and he explained Mexico's backwardness by the fact that it had too many Indians: "The grading of Latin-American States is very different. Chile and the Argentines are very high types of the evolution of Latin-American popular government. This may also be said of Brazil, of Costa Rica, and very largely of Salvador. Wherever the Indian element predominates, as it does in nearly all of the Latin-American States, the tendency to anarchy and revolution is very marked." From this came Ambassador Wilson's attachment to strong authoritarian governors such as Porfirio Díaz, who maintained the order needed to attract U.S. investors, who in turn developed the nation. Only such a government could create internal peace, and only with peace would Mexico benefit from "the immediate proximity of a great civilized power to a nation of anarchistic tendencies." One of the reasons why Ambassador Wilson opposed Díaz's successor was his conviction that Francisco Madero was a weak leader. Madero, he reported, "believed that the Mexican people should be governed by kindness and love, which, in my judgment, showed a deficient mental grasp of the situation."[57]

The U.S. envoy's criticism went substantially beyond Francisco Madero's leadership skills, however; he thought the new Mexican president was mentally ill. "The responsibilities of office and the disappointments growing out of rivalries and intrigues shattered his reason completely, and in the last days of his government, during the bombardment of the capital, his mental qualities, always abnormal, developed into a homicidal, dangerous form of lunacy . . .; clothed with the chief power of the nation, dormant evil qualities in the blood or in the race came to the surface and wrought ruin to him and to thousands of the Mexican people." Ambassador Wilson was also upset that Madero failed to appreciate "the material benefits which American intelligence and energy and American capital had bestowed upon Mexico." In contrast, Porfirio Díaz "was profoundly impressed with the immense benefits of American capital and energy," and "he never failed to listen to me with patience, intelligence and comprehension."[58]

Ambassador Wilson sent a torrent of messages to Washington describing the horrors of post-Díaz instability. He reported that "entire villages have been burned, their inhabitants, men, women, and children, slaughtered and mutilated indiscriminately, plantations have been ravaged and burned, trains have been blown up and derailed and passengers slaughtered like cattle, women have been ravished and men mutilated with accompaniments of horror and barbarity which find no place in the chronicles of Christian warfare." This may or may not have been accurate, but what seems most interesting about Wilson's many despatches is his failure to recognize that he was living through a defining moment in the history of Mexico—a genuine social revolution. The problem, as he perceived it, was much simpler: the unfortunate overthrow of a strong leader and the absence of a strong successor.[59]

Eventually Henry Lane Wilson overstepped even the most generous boundaries of diplomatic propriety, as the new administration of Woodrow Wilson discovered when it sent William Bayard Hale as a special agent to Mexico in mid-1913. Hale reported that Ambassador Wilson had been sending despatches "which are so exactly opposed to the truth as to be beyond all understanding," and, if that were not bad enough, Wilson also had been involved in Madero's murder. Victoriano Huerta's plot to overthrow Madero's government had been hatched and matured in the ambassador's presence, and "President Madero was not betrayed and arrested by his officers until it had been ascertained that the American Ambassador had no objection to the performance." Moreover, "Madero would never have been assassinated had the American Ambassador made it thoroughly understood that the plot must stop short of murder." President Wilson's special agent accused Taft's envoy of "treason, perfidy and assassination in an assault on constitutional government. And it is particularly unfortunate that this should have taken place in a leading country of Latin America, where, if we have any moral work to do, it is to discourage violence and uphold law."[60] Henry Lane Wilson was promptly recalled.

But Mexico was not high on Woodrow Wilson's initial agenda. The new President had chosen to focus his administration on domestic economic reform, and on April 8, 1913, he became the first president since John Adams to go in person before Congress, which the Democrats controlled for the first time in twenty years. The purpose of his ice-breaking speech was to urge tariff reform. Then two months later he returned to Capitol Hill, this time to prod action on legislation creating the Federal Reserve system. Nothing could have better underscored Wilson's priorities than these two appearances, and neither he nor anyone in his administration thought that a revolution in Mexico could remotely compare in significance to either the Federal Reserve Act, which transformed the nation's banking system, or the Underwood Tariff, which reduced the average rate from 41 to 27 percent and replaced the lost revenue with the first income tax under the Sixteenth Amendment.

It was not possible to ignore a major social revolution just across the nation's border, however, and early cabinet discussions indicate that Woodrow Wilson accepted his generation's assumption that the United States had both a right and a responsibility to control its immediate neighbors. Underlying this hegemonic presumption was the belief that Latin Americans were inferior people, although Woodrow Wilson was infinitely more circumspect than Theodore Roosevelt, who often seemed to go out of his way to call someone a dago or a spic. Wilson never said any such thing in public, but the hint of traditional thinking was there. In 1915, for example, the President sought to console Edith Bolling Galt after she had discovered that her niece had somehow managed to fall in love with a Panamanian, Jorge Boyd: "it would be bad enough at best to have anyone we love marry into any Central American family, because there is the presumption that the blood is not unmixed; but *proof* of that seems to be lacking in this case."[61]

What made Woodrow Wilson stand apart from his predecessors and in perfect tune with the Progressive era was his desire to instill democracy in Latin America. The administration's first policy statement on Latin America asserted that "cooperation is possible only when supported at every turn by the orderly processes of just government based upon law, not upon arbitrary or irregular force" and, with the Mexican usurper Victoriano Huerta almost certainly on his mind, Wilson added that "we can have no sympathy with those who seek to seize the power of government to advance their own personal interests and ambition." These dictators constituted Woodrow Wilson's Latin American adversary, and in his first annual message he told Congress that "we are the friends of constitutional government in America; we are more than its friends, we are its champions."[62]

Prior generations of U.S. officials had shared Wilson's view of Latin American political history, but no prior administration had sought to change Latin American political values. Until the Wilson administration, all U.S. Presidents had inserted some term other than "constitutional government" (usually it was "stability") in Wilson's sentence about Haiti: "We consider it our duty to insist on constitutional government there."[63] The Hayes administration may have mentioned the absence of an election as one reason for delaying recognition of Porfirio Díaz in 1877 to 1878; but until Woodrow Wilson entered the White House, no U.S. President had ever said that "so long as the power of recognition rests with me the Government of the United States will refuse to extend the hand of welcome to anyone who obtains power in a sister republic by treachery and violence."[64]

This change in U.S. policy did not go unchallenged. John Bassett Moore, the now-venerable international lawyer who had returned to Washington as State Department counselor, was never one to balk at intervention, but he thought the idea of intervening on behalf of democracy was so inappropriate that he dared to lecture the President: "The Government of the United States having originally set itself up by revolution has always acted upon the de facto principle. We regard governments as existing or as not existing. We do not require them to be chosen by popular vote." Moore's position was that "we cannot become the censors of the morals or conduct of other nations."[65]

President Wilson rejected this advice. All he knew, however, was that Mexico did not have a democracy; instead, it had a dictatorship led by General Victoriano Huerta, who was still washing Francisco Madero's blood off his hands. Wilson's initial policy was to refuse recognition,[66] but he was clearly baffled by the situation that lay before him, and so he commissioned a trusted associate, William Bayard Hale, to visit Mexico and report on what he saw. Hale's on-site evaluation was instrumental in forming Wilson's policy. To complement his condemnation of Ambassador Henry Lane Wilson, Hale reported that "General Huerta is an ape-like old man, of almost pure Indian blood. He may almost be said to subsist on alcohol. Drunk or only half-drunk (he is never sober), he never loses a certain shrewdness. He has been life-long a soldier, and one of the best in Mexico, and he knows no methods but those of force."[67] This report confirmed all the President's worst suspicions, and probably those of Secretary of State Bryan, who was so opposed to alcohol that his only condition upon entering the cabinet was that he would not serve spirituous beverages at official functions.

With Hale's report as their primary source of information, in late July, Wilson and Bryan hammered out the administration's initial policy toward the Mexican revolution. Henry Lane Wilson had been recalled and the administration did not want to recognize Huerta by sending a new ambassador, and so President Wilson commissioned a Democratic stalwart from Minnesota, John Lind, as a second special envoy to take the new policy statement to Huerta. Meeting with Foreign Minister Federico Gamboa in mid-August, Lind delivered a letter that began with a patronizing disclaimer that spoke volumes about Wilson's view of the U.S.-Mexican relationship: "we are seeking to counsel Mexico for her own good." The gist of the message was that the United States would not recognize any Mexican government until four conditions were met: an immediate internal armistice, an early free election, a promise by Huerta not to be a candidate, and an agreement that all parties would abide by the election results. The Mexican government responded that the four conditions were of a "humiliating and unusual character, hardly admissible even in a treaty of peace after a victory."[68]

Lind retreated to Veracruz, where he stayed for seven months rather than spend another Minnesota winter with the type of people who would select a rodent as their state university's mascot. His primary activity was to comment on the Mexican panorama from the perspective of a Swedish-born, one-handed (sawmill accident), non-Spanish-speaking, ex-governor of Minnesota. "Politically, at least, the Mexicans have no standards," he reported. "They seem more like children than men. The only motives that I can discern in their political action is *appetite* and *vanity*." Although he admitted that he had seen little of the country, Lind reported that "the Indians especially of the southern states give great promise of both moral and economic efficiency. Their potential capacity of development does not seem to be limited as is the case with the American Negro. In the valley of Mexico the race is inferior, debauched by pulque and vice and oppression." Given Mexico's equally poor leadership, Lind concluded that the United States had no choice but "to guide and compel decent administration and a government that will at least in a measure approach the constitutional form. From this necessity there is in my judgment no escape unless revolution and anarchy are to continue the order of the day in Mexico."[69]

The only positive news from Mexico came when Huerta acquiesced to Wilson's demand that he give up the presidency, but then Huerta's military forces, having never consolidated power in Zapata's south or the Constitutionalists' north, suffered a series of minor military reverses, capped by a major defeat at Torreón. Emboldened by these victories, Venustiano Carranza announced that his Constitutionalist forces would not participate in the election scheduled for October 26; they would settle for nothing less than total victory over Huerta, followed by major economic and political reforms. When the reform-oriented Congress that was elected along with Madero indicated that it might abandon Huerta and reconvene somewhere in territory controlled by the Constitutionalists, Huerta responded by arresting more than a hundred of the legislators and establishing an open dictatorship.

Officials in Washington were infuriated by the coup, but they focused their attention on indirect evidence of meddling by British petroleum concessionaires. President Wilson had been concerned from the beginning that the British government was acting as the handmaiden of private investors. "What to do with Mexico is the great problem and was discussed at length," wrote Navy Secretary Josephus Daniels in his diary after a cabinet meeting six months earlier. "The general opinion in the Cabinet was that the chief cause of this whole situation in Mexico was a contest between English and American Oil Companies to see which would control; that these people were ready to foment trouble and it was largely due to the English Company that England was willing to recognize Mexico before we did."[70]

These fears were confirmed when the new British minister ostentatiously presented his credentials to Huerta the day after his coup; and in his initial speech on Latin America in October 1913 at Mobile, President Wilson referred indirectly to Britain when he warned that the dominant influence of foreigners in Latin America is "a condition of affairs always dangerous and apt to become intolerable."[71] With access to Mexican petroleum an absolutely central concern of the British navy on the eve of World War I, and with Ambassador Spring-Rice recuperating from an illness, British Foreign Secretary Edward Grey dispatched Sir William Tyrrell to meet with the President in Washington. At their interview in mid-November 1913, Wilson said something quite different from what he had said publicly two months earlier at Mobile. He asserted that his quarrel was not with foreign investors but with Latin America's unprincipled leaders. Tyrrell's report to Foreign Secretary Grey paraphrases Wilson as asserting that "with the opening of the Panama Canal it is becoming increasingly important that the Governments of the Central American Republics should improve, as they will become more and more a field for European and American enterprize: bad government may lead to friction and to such incidents as [the] Venezuela affair under Castro. The President is very anxious to provide against such contingencies by insisting that those Republics should have fairly decent rulers and that men like Castro and Huerta should be barred."[72] It was during this conversation that Wilson was alleged to have uttered his famous comment that the goal of U.S. policy was "to teach the South American Republics to elect good men."[73]

With the British now reassured and willing to follow the U.S. lead, the Wilson administration could turn to the problem of dictatorship in Mexico. After Huerta closed Congress, Colonel House wrote that "the President has in mind to declare war against Mexico even though actual armed entrance into Mexico is not made." House indicated that the administration would establish a blockade, including "throwing a line across the southern part of Mexico, and perhaps another line just south of the Northern States." Bryan confirmed this possibility, telling the U.S. ambassador to Great Britain that "the President feels it his duty to force Huerta's retirement, peaceably if possible but forcibly if necessary."[74]

President Wilson simultaneously commissioned William Bayard Hale to initiate discussions with Huerta's principal opposition, the Constitutionalist forces led by Venustiano Carranza. The envoy's reports from Nogales emphasized the Constitutionalists' uncompromising stance: "Carranza and his Cabinet strongly insist that they will go into no negotiations with Huerta or any remnant of his Government. They require its total extinction." Another of Hale's reports indicated that "there is no limit to their detestation of the whole predatory aggregation at Mexico City." Huerta's Constitutionalist opposition was pictured as pure as puritans: "With few exceptions the leaders are plain men, their speech is remarkable for Quaker-like conscientiousness and precision." Foreshadowing today's tendency to favor U.S.-educated Mexicans, Hale noted that one of Carranza's advisors "acts like the best type of an old-fashioned Philadelphia Quaker. He is a Massachusetts Technology graduate with an American wife."[75]

In early 1914 the administration lifted Taft's arms embargo in order to permit Carranza and his generals to prepare for the denouement. At the same time the United States warned European governments to stay away from the scene, and soon a dozen U.S. warships were lying off Mexico's east coast.[76]

With this much smoke pouring out of the foreign policy crater, it was just a matter of time until the volcano erupted. The inevitable provocative incident occurred at Tampico on April 9, 1914, when U.S. Navy personnel who had come ashore for supplies were briefly detained by Mexican authorities. Admiral Henry Mayo immediately informed the Mexican official commanding the port that "I must require that you send me [by] suitable members of your staff, formal disavowal of and apology for the act together with your assurance that the officer responsible for it will receive severe punishment. Also that you publicly hoist the American Flag in a prominent position on shore and salute it with 21 guns which salute will be duly returned by this ship." Bryan and Wilson fully endorsed Mayo's position.[77]

The Huerta government first rejected the demands as "equivalent to accepting the sovereignty of a Foreign State to the derogation of the national dignity and decorum."[78] Then, when it became evident that the United States was determined to press the issue, Huerta suggested a simultaneous salute, which the United States rejected. Mexico then proposed a reciprocal salute, and when the United States insisted on nothing less than the precise fulfillment of Mayo's demand, the Mexican foreign minister replied that "the Government of Mexico is not disposed to accede to the unconditional demands of the American Government."[79]

After learning of this refusal, President Wilson decided to use the Tampico incident as an opportunity to overthrow Huerta. Telling Congress "that the representatives of Gen. Huerta were willing to go out of their way to show disregard for the dignity and rights of this Government," he requested permission to use force "to obtain from Gen. Huerta and his adherents the fullest recognition of the rights and dignity of the United States."[80] Within hours the House authorized the use of force by a lopsided margin, 337 to 37, while the Senate delayed a vote for two days until Henry Cabot Lodge was convinced that he could not obtain even stronger wording authorizing the U.S. occupation of Mexico.

Making haste in order to block the arrival of an arms shipment for Huerta's forces, the U.S. Navy began the seizure of Veracruz a day before Senate approval. The initial invasion party encountered unexpected resistance (the occupation was denounced by Mexican nationalists generally, including most of Huerta's opponents) and had to be reinforced the next day by five battleships; when the dust settled, U.S. forces had killed about two hundred Mexicans and wounded perhaps three hundred more, losing in the process the lives of nineteen U.S. servicemen. Although he was offered one of the fifty-five Congressional Medals of Honor awarded during the brief conflict, even Smedley Butler was appalled by what had occurred. Referring to an incident in Veracruz, he wrote his father that "I was an ear and eye witness to the first and only official report made by Minnesota's mail orderly relative to his supposed arrest in Vera Cruz, he considered it a joke and yet we lost 112 killed and wounded avenging his wounded dignity and the boat business at Tampico is not much better."[81]

Chastened by the death toll and aware of growing dismay among core Democratic constituents, President Wilson quickly accepted the offer of Argentina, Brazil, and Chile to mediate the dispute. Mexico also accepted, and from May 20 to July 2 Wilson's and Huerta's representatives faced one another across a negotiating table at Niagara Falls, Canada. Since the U.S. commissioners were instructed to hold out for complete capitulation,[82] the meetings came to nothing, but they served the purpose of buying time. Now provided with access to U.S. arms, the Constitutionalists continued to increase their military pressure, and in mid-1914 Huerta was obliged to cede power. In November the United States withdrew from Veracruz, effectively handing the city over to Carranza, but by then the always-fragile anti-Huerta coalition had fractured completely, with Pancho Villa and Emiliano Zapata now allied against Carranza, Obregón, and the remaining Constitutionalists. Although they briefly seized Mexico City, Villa and Zapata soon returned to their separate struggles and to their roots in rural Mexico, where they waged a war that frustrated Carranza's effort to consolidate political power.

Despite this continuing instability, Huerta's ouster provided President Wilson with the opportunity to take a deep breath. In early 1915 he gave a remarkable speech to Indiana Democrats:

> I hold it as a fundamental principle, and so do you, that every people has the right to determine its own form of government; and, until this recent revolution in Mexico, until the end of the Díaz reign, 80 per cent of the people of Mexico never had a "look-in" in determining who should be their governors or what their government should be. Now, I am for the 80 per cent. It is none of my business, and it is none of your business, how long they take in determining it. It is none of my business, and it is none of yours, how they go about the business. The country is theirs. The government is theirs. The liberty, if they can get it, and Godspeed them in getting it, is theirs. And, so far as my influence goes while I am President, nobody shall interfere with them.[83]

Then in mid-1915 President Wilson told his new secretary of state that "the first and most essential step in settling affairs of Mexico is not to call general elections. It seems to me necessary that a provisional government essentially revolutionary in character should take action to institute reforms by decree before the full forms of the constitution are resumed."[84]

So much was occurring at this time that it is impossible to determine the precise combination of factors that influenced Wilson to alter his policy. Certainly he was encouraged to place Mexico in a broader strategic context when in June 1914, only a few weeks before Huerta's ouster, Archduke

Francis Ferdinand was assassinated in the streets of Sarajevo, triggering the troop mobilization that would push Europe into war two months later. Then, just as the European cannon erupted, the President's wife, Ellen, died of Bright's Disease, and Wilson sank into a profound depression. As the President struggled to recover his mental health in 1914 and 1915, he had no choice but to focus upon the European conflict, especially after May 1915 when German torpedoes sank the *Lusitania*, killing more than a hundred U.S. citizens. Then in July the United States invaded Haiti, and it was not difficult to predict the takeover of the Dominican Republic ten months later.

The time had clearly come to defuse Washington's conflict with Mexico. In October 1915 the United States joined a half-dozen Latin American countries in granting de facto recognition to Carranza, and two months later Wilson told the Democratic National Committee that "if the Mexicans want to raise hell, let them raise hell. We have got nothing to do with it. It is their government, it is their hell."[85]

But then in January 1916 Pancho Villa interrupted the slowly developing calm when his forces murdered sixteen U.S. mining engineers at Santa Ysabel, Chihuahua. Two months later his raid on the New Mexico railroad town of Columbus left nineteen U.S. citizens dead and Wilson's policy under renewed criticism. These attacks occurred at an exceptionally delicate political moment, with the success of the Democratic party hanging in the balance. The Republicans were not about to repeat the debacle of 1912 by presenting two candidates to the electorate, and, with a battle royal in the offing, Villa's raid injected Mexico into the campaign. Former Assistant Secretary Huntington Wilson was typical of Republican loyalists in urging drastic action. Taking time off from his never-completed volume on how to write incomprehensible English, Huntington Wilson recommended that Mexico be handled with a dose of Dollar Diplomacy: "The seizing and holding of revenues amply to cover all actual damages at once suggests itself as a practical measure and one readily assimilable with the chastisement and chastening due from us if we do not repudiate the duties imposed upon us in the nature of things by laws as real as those of biology."[86]

The administration was particularly concerned about the demonstration effect that Villa's raids might have on the rest of the Caribbean region. As Wilson's secretary of the interior noted, "my judgment is that to fail in getting Villa would ruin us in the eyes of all Latin-Americans. I do not say that they respect only force, but like children they pile insult upon insult if they are not stopped when the first insult is given."[87] The United States had only recently taken control of Haiti, and preparations were under way for the occupation of the Dominican Republic, which would occur before the November election. In Nicaragua, Liberal Julián Irías was threatening to participate in the nation's October presidential election, and in Cuba it was anyone's guess what would happen during the months before its November 1 presidential contest. Not one Democrat could campaign effectively if U.S. citizens were being mowed down by Villa-inspired rebels in the Dominican Republic, Haiti, Cuba, Panama, and Nicaragua. Not to react strongly to Villa's raids would be to court an electoral disaster.

President Wilson emerged from a Cabinet meeting the day after the Columbus attack to announce that "an adequate force will be sent at once in pursuit of Villa with the single object of capturing him and putting a stop to his forays." The Carranza government responded with a confusing warning that it would fight to protect Mexican soil from an invasion but that it would consider negotiating a renewal of the long-defunct 1882 hot-pursuit agreement. Before that could be accomplished, Wilson ordered General John J. Pershing's six-thousand-man Punitive Expedition to move south in search of Pancho Villa. Probing several hundred miles into north-central Mexico, the inevitable clash with the Mexican army finally came on June 21, 1916, at Carrizal, about 100 miles southeast of Columbus. Once again the dust settled on U.S. soldiers in Mexico, and this time fourteen of them were dead and twenty-five had been taken prisoner by Carranza's army.

If domestic U.S. politics had mandated the Pershing expedition in the first place, they clearly prohibited anything but a forceful response to the Carrizal encounter. On June 26 President Wilson sat down to compose a message asking Congress for authority to use additional U.S. forces "in any way that may be necessary to guard our frontier effectively, if necessary to enter on Mexican soil."

But he never sent the message. After the sentence asking Congress for authority to call up additional forces, he wrote that "I cannot bring myself to recommend that the United States make war upon Mexico." Then he began to write out his thoughts about the Mexican Revolution, repeating what he had said at Indianapolis eighteen months earlier—that "it does not lie with the American people to dictate to another people what their government shall be." When he showed the draft to his secretary of state, Lansing questioned the commitment to nonintervention, adding his famous "? Haiti S Domingo Nicaragua Panama" in the margin next to the preceding sentence.[88] Lansing was correct, of course, for the Wilson administration had sent more U.S. gunboats into more Caribbean harbors than any other administration in history. But even though this single sentence of Wilson's draft was written as if it were about the general topic of intervention, it was embedded in a document about Mexico. The President was not writing a speech about his Caribbean policy; he was conceding that he had no right to teach Mexico, at least, how to elect good men.

The day after Wilson drafted his never-sent message, President Carranza agreed to release the prisoners taken at Carrizal. Wilson responded with a conciliatory speech to the New York press in which he asked the rhetorical questions, "Do you think the glory of America would be enhanced by a war of conquest in Mexico? Do you think that any act of violence by a powerful nation like this against a weak and distracted neighbor would reflect distinction upon the annals of the United States?"[89] Wilson promptly accepted the alternative suggested by President Carranza—direct negotiations—and the two nations created a Joint High Commission, which met in various locations in the northeastern United States from September 6, 1916, to January 15, 1917.

Then in his nomination acceptance speech, which occurred just before the commission began meeting, Wilson blamed Mexico's problems upon the least-popular group that might logically be responsible: "Outsiders, men out of other nations and with interests too often alien to their own, have dictated what their privileges and opportunities should be and who should control their land, their lives, and their resources—some of them Americans, pressing for things they could never have got in their own country." Sounding more and more like a revolutionary, Wilson asserted that "the people of Mexico are striving for the rights that are fundamental to life and happiness,—15,000,000 oppressed men, overburdened women, and pitiful children in virtual bondage in their own home of fertile lands and inexhaustible treasure! Some of the leaders of the revolution may often have been mistaken and violent and selfish, but the revolution itself was inevitable and is right."[90]

The Joint High Commission effectively helped Wilson through the very close presidential race. After the election, he recalled the futile Punitive Expedition, and the final U.S. troops left Mexico on February 5, 1917.

By now, however, it was the eve of the nation's entry into World War I, and Germany was looking for allies. The Kaiser's foreign secretary, Arthur

Zimmermann, instructed his minister in Mexico to approach the Carranza government with the following proposition: "We propose Mexico an alliance upon the following terms: Joint conduct of war. Joint conclusion of peace. Ample financial support and an agreement on our part that Mexico shall gain back by conquest the territory lost by her at a prior period in Texas, New Mexico, and Arizona."[91] Germany had already recommenced unrestricted submarine warfare, and the Zimmermann telegram provided the final nudge toward war.

Intent upon pursuing the claims of U.S. investors in Mexico, the State Department's Boaz Long, chief of the Division of Latin American Affairs, was upset when President Wilson granted the Carranza government de jure recognition a month before the United States declared war. Long had no choice but to accept this diplomatic triage, but he did so with the understanding that "the logical and natural thing for us to contemplate is a settlement of the Mexican situation immediately after the conclusion of European peace," perhaps by seizing Mexico's oilfields. In the meantime, U.S. investors formed the National Association for the Protection of American Rights in Mexico, and, with the State Department's active assistance, the Association lobbied for U.S. government protection from Mexico's new Constitution, especially its dreaded Article 27 providing public ownership of the subsoil—a provision Boaz Long believed "was inserted at the last moment upon the suggestion of a German lobbyist, and was paid for by German money."[92] Working together, the investors and their State Department allies were able to delay the full normalization of U.S.-Mexican relations until the mid-1920s, but they were never able to rekindle Washington's prewar obsession with Mexico.

Woodrow Wilson left office in 1921, entering the history books as the leader who saw the nation through its first European war and who made the first serious attempt to encourage an internationalist mentality among the U.S. public. That this attempt was unsuccessful is no longer held against him; a prophet before his time, Wilson's League of Nations would become the United Nations of the next generation. In domestic politics, Wilson's progressive reforms have had an enduring impact on the lives of twentieth-century citizens; indeed, it is difficult to imagine a time without a Federal Reserve system to control the economy and an income tax to fund the government. In his administration's relations with Latin America, however, Woodrow Wilson made only one substantial contribution. Ignoring most of Latin America while focusing upon the Caribbean region and

Mexico, Wilson implemented a policy that was largely indistinguishable from Dollar Diplomacy, adding only the high-minded rhetoric of democracy, which at the time prompted greater intervention and encouraged a paternalistic attitude that has led, in our time, to the creation of the National Endowment for Democracy and an Agency for International Development, whose mandates include teaching the Latin Americans how to elect good leaders.

Chapter 13

Removing the Marines,
Installing the Puppets

The Haitians, as you no doubt know, are a very hysterical people. Hundreds of rumors are circulated among them daily that are simply ridiculous, but like children they believe them and completely lose their heads. It is very hard, in consequence, to quiet them.

◌ *Colonel John Russell, 1919*

The end of World War I provided the United States with an opportunity to reassess its relations with Latin America. Change would not be obvious for nearly a decade, but in 1920 even a casual observer could see that officials in Washington were rethinking the nature of U.S. commitments, spurred by an awareness that the war-weary public had grown disenchanted with its Caribbean protectorates. In their 1920 campaign platforms, neither of the two major parties said a word about Latin America other than to praise or criticize (as party lines dictated) the Wilson administration's policy toward Mexico. The Democratic platform did not mention the U.S. military occupation of either Haiti or the Dominican Republic, or the Marine guard propping up the government in Nicaragua or protecting U.S. sugar mills in Cuba—a sure sign that party leaders doubted the public's approval of these initiatives.

An ever surer sign was the furor created over U.S. human rights abuses in Haiti. The controversy began on an early autumn day in 1919, when the commandant of the Marine Corps sat down to conduct the always unpleasant review of recent court martial proceedings. When he reached the records on Haiti, Major General George Barnett was so shocked by what he found that he drafted a confidential message to the commander of U.S. forces in Port-au-Prince, Colonel John Russell, ordering an immediate halt to the murder of Haitians in the custody of U.S. Marines and the U.S.-supervised Haitian gendarmerie. After several days, General Barnett decided that this order had not been strong enough, and so he sent another. The court martial reports from Haiti had "showed me that practically indiscriminate killing of natives has gone on for some time," he wrote. "I look to you to see that this is corrected, and corrected at once."[1]

Colonel Russell responded with a vigorous defense of his troops. "The Haitians, as you no doubt know, are a very hysterical people. Hundreds of rumors are circulated among them daily that are simply ridiculous, but like children they believe them and completely lose their heads. It is very hard, in consequence, to quiet them."[2]

Sensing that Russell might not be a disinterested source of information, General Barnett went up the chain of command to Navy Secretary Josephus Daniels, who appointed Marine Generals John Lejeune and Smedley Butler to conduct an on-site investigation. Their October 1920 report was a whitewash, coauthored by a man who had himself joked in a letter to his father about terrorizing the citizens of Haiti, and then lied when he told a Congressional committee that "we never tolerated abuse of prisoners or the public."[3]

Although Secretary Daniels used the Lejeune-Butler assessment to defuse General Barnett's charges of generalized brutality,[4] he also requested a second opinion from Admiral Harry Knapp, the former military representative of the United States in Haiti. Knapp had simultaneously been governor of the Dominican Republic and been living in Santo Domingo, and for his knowledge of events on the other side of Hispaniola he had relied upon the commanders of the U.S. Marine brigade in Haiti. Typical was the 1917 report of General Eli Cole: "No matter how much veneer and polish a Haitian may have, he is absolutely savage under the skin and under strain reverts to type." Cole told Knapp that "I have seen European Haitians (part Haitian) of highest standing, European education, and long years of residence in Europe revert in a few minutes to the mental state of a savage in the heart of Africa," and he added that "the Negroes of mixed type, who constitute the majority of educated people and politicians, have the general characteristics of such people the world over—vain, loving praise, excitable, changeable, beyond belief illogical, and double-faced." This was also the view of Colonel Littleton Waller, Smedley Butler's immediate commander, who wrote General Lejeune, "you know how the nigger is. It takes very little to sway him either way." Colonel Waller was especially opposed to the creation of the *Garde d'Haiti*, arguing that "you can never trust a nigger with a gun. These people are niggers in spite of the thin varnish of education and refinement. Down in their hearts they are just the same happy, idle irresponsible people we know of."[5]

Given this advice, Admiral Knapp concluded in his report to Secretary Daniels that there was no alternative to military occupation: "I personally believe that it will take at least a generation to have in Haiti sufficient men of a high enough standard of ethics to provide personnel for an honest administration."[6]

To suggest that a military occupation begun in 1915 would have to continue for several more decades was the wrong answer in 1920, an election year. At first, the Republican candidate Warren Harding said almost nothing about Latin America, Mexico excluded, but then the Democratic vice presidential candidate stuck his foot in his mouth. Responding to charges that Great Britain would have more than one vote in the League of Nations because certain of its colonies had been granted membership, Franklin Delano Roosevelt told a Montana campaign audience that the United States had a few extra votes of its own, including those of "Cuba, Haiti, San Domingo, Panama, Nicaragua, and of the other Central American States." FDR reminded listeners that he had been active in the Caribbean while serving as Woodrow Wilson's assistant secretary of the Navy: "You know, I have had something to do with the running of a couple of little republics. The facts are that I wrote Haiti's constitution myself, and if I do say it I think it is a very good constitution."[7]

Harding unloaded with both barrels: "If I should be, as I fully expect to be, elected President of this just and honorable Republic, I will not empower an Assistant Secretary of the Navy to draft a constitution for helpless neighbors in the West Indies and jam it down their throats at the point of bayonets borne by United States Marines. We have a higher service for our gallant marines than that. Nor will I misuse the power of the Executive to cover with a veil of secrecy repeated acts of unwarranted interference in domestic affairs of the little republics of the Western Hemisphere."[8]

Coming fast on the heels of General Barnett's charges of indiscriminate killing of Haitians, FDR's gaffe provided a feeding frenzy for the nation's muckraking press. Although Roosevelt attempted to dismiss the Republicans' charges as "the merest dribble," Harding realized that he had grabbed the Democrats by the most sensitive part of their foreign policy anatomy, and so he squeezed: "To the best of my information, this is the first official admission of the rape of Haiti and Santo Domingo by the present Administration . . . Practically all we know now is that thousands of native Haitians have been killed by American marines, and that many of our own gallant men have sacrificed their lives at the behest of an Executive Department in order to establish laws drafted by an Assistant Secretary of the Navy, to secure a vote in the League and to continue at the point of a bayonet a military domination."[9]

Once in office Warren Harding made an attempt at change. Within three weeks of his inauguration, he asked Secretary of State Charles Evans Hughes for "your recommendations effecting a modification of the present order which will be a reflecx [reflection?] of the high purpose we wish to pursue in exercising our peculiar relationship to the Haitian Republic."[10] Hughes first gave the President a noncommittal response, and it was not until four months later that he sent Harding a full report recommending cosmetic administrative changes, but firmly asserting that "we cannot leave Haiti at the present time."[11]

This position was challenged by a handful of Progressive senators from the Midwest and Far West. Now wearing the anti-imperialist mantle passed along by Carl Schurz and George Hoar, these largely Republican rebels demanded that the Senate Committee on Foreign Relations create a special committee to study U.S. policy toward Haiti and Santo Domingo. Composed of mainstream senators selected on the basis of their unusual first names (Medill McCormick as chair, with Tasker Oddie, Atlee Pomerene, and Andrieus Jones, who was later replaced by Philander Knox), plus one Progressive, William King, the committee held hearings in Washington and then took the unprecedented step of conducting additional hearings in both Haiti and the Dominican Republic. Like Secretary Hughes, the committee recommended that the United States do a better job of administration. President Harding obediently reshuffled the bureaucracy and "civilized" the U.S. military governor by changing the title of Brigadier General John Russell to High Commissioner. Everything else remained unchanged because everyone except the Senate's few Progressives believed, as the McCormick committee asserted, that withdrawal would mean "the abandonment of the Haitian people to chronic revolution, anarchy, barbarism, and ruin."[12]

This fear was based on a belief in the savage immaturity of the Haitians. Smedley Butler told the McCormick committee that "ninety-nine per cent of the people of Haiti are the most kindly, generous, hospitable, pleasure-loving people I have ever known. They would not hurt anybody. They are most gentle when in their natural state. When the other 1 per cent that wears vici [?] kid shoes with long pointed toes and celluloid collars, stirs them up and incites them with liquor and voodoo stuff, they are capable of the most horrible atrocities; they are cannibals." In 1925 the U.S. High Commissioner reported that "the peasants, who form the mass (85 per cent) of the population and who have so long been held by their literate brothers in a backward state, have the mentality of a child of not more than seven years of age reared under advantageous conditions."[13]

Senator William Borah was one of only a few prominent political leaders to challenge this argument. "We ought to get out of Haiti and out of every place where we have no right. It may be true that they are not capable of self-government as we understand it, but it is their government." Senator King agreed, and he refused to sign the McCormick committee's final report; instead, he introduced an amendment cutting off Navy funds for the occupation of Haiti, Santo Domingo, or Nicaragua. It was defeated by an overwhelming margin, 9 to 43,[14] which is a much better indicator of majority sentiment than the campaign remarks of candidates such as Warren Harding, who criticized U.S. bullying of "the little helpless republics of our own hemisphere." Like the flap over FDR's misstatement on Haiti, this was only a jab, not a sustained attack, and Harding contradicted himself when he professed to be one of the "Americans who believe in the good old Monroe Doctrine of America dominating the affairs of the New World."[15]

Harding was an undistinguished President—perhaps worse, according to the best-selling autobiography of his mistress[16]—but during his brief term, cut short by a fatal stroke in 1923, he did some good for U.S.–Latin American relations by making peace with Colombia. Acting at the urging of oil interests eager to gain concessions, just days after his inauguration President Harding made ratification of the Thomson-Urrutia treaty the subject of his first message to Congress. Signed early in the Wilson administration to make amends for despoiling Colombia of Panama, the treaty had languished for three years before the Foreign Relations Committee would even pass it to the Senate floor, accompanied by a dissenting report from Henry Cabot Lodge's Republicans, who objected on behalf of Theodore Roosevelt to any expression of regret. But now Roosevelt was dead, and the accord had been renegotiated to delete the apology, and within a month of Harding's inauguration it received Senate approval. The United States then paid Colombia $25 million in five annual installments.[17]

Aside from this brief moment of attention to inter-American relations, President Harding appeared uninterested in Latin America. Secretary of

State Charles Evans Hughes was only somewhat less distant, but he made up for his lack of warmth with a formidable intellect. He vigorously supported ratification of the Thomson-Urrutia treaty and the even-more-neglected 1904 Hay–de Quesada treaty recognizing Cuban sovereignty over the Isle of Pines; he pushed Panama to accept an arbitration award of disputed territory to Costa Rica; he promoted a three-nation Central American summit aboard a U.S. warship in the Gulf of Fonseca and the subsequent Central American peace conference in Washington in 1922 to 1923; and he did what he could to resolve a series of Latin American border disputes, most notably the long-festering Tacna-Arica conflict between Chile and Peru. These initiatives were important, but Hughes's principal contribution to inter-American relations was his modification of the U.S. policy toward intervention, and in this he set the tone for the next generation. With no visible European threat on the horizon, in 1923 Hughes told an audience that the Monroe Doctrine "gives no justification for . . . intervention on our part." More broadly, he renounced the right of the strong to control the behavior of the weak: "I utterly disclaim, as unwarranted, . . . a claim on our part to superintend the affairs of our sister republics, to assert an overlordship, to consider the spread of our authority beyond our own domain as the aim of our policy, and to make our power the test of right in this hemisphere."[18]

The logical extension of this thinking was that the United States would have to dismantle its Caribbean and Central American protectorates. But what would replace them? To the extent that these countries resembled Haiti, independence would be impossible, so something in between a protectorate and autonomy would have to be worked out. It would take Hughes and his State Department colleagues four years to settle on their answer—an alliance with local military chieftains—but it was one that lasted for decades. This was the moment when the United States invented the Trujillos and Somozas, the military strongmen who would dominate Caribbean Basin politics for a generation.

It began in the Dominican Republic, where Woodrow Wilson ordered the U.S. Marines home in order to accommodate the wishes of his third secretary of state, Bainbridge Colby, who wanted to make an appropriate gesture on the eve of his December goodwill visit to Brazil, Argentina, and Uruguay. Just before President Wilson's withdrawal decision, the military governor of the Dominican Republic, Rear Admiral Thomas Snowden, reported that he "found conditions in a very satisfactory state." Although this news was meant to justify continued U.S. occupation, the Wilson administration interpreted it as an indicator that it would be safe to leave, and Admiral Snowden was instructed to announce both the U.S. departure and the creation of a Dominican commission to draft the required transitional legislation.[19] Not eager to obey this order from a lame-duck President, Snowden dragged his heels by announcing a process that he knew the Dominicans would reject: his plan called for the United States to select the commission members and for their proposals to be subject to a U.S. veto. Unwilling to grant the United States this power, Dominicans rejected both the Snowden transition plan and, in mid-1921, a Harding administration plan prepared by the chief of the Division of Latin American Affairs, Sumner Welles, who had obtained part of his plan from General Enoch Crowder. Dusting off an old idea first advocated by Captain Dillingham in 1904, Crowder suggested that Welles include a Platt-type amendment in any withdrawal plan, and Welles added a U.S.-supervised constabulary. When Dominican leaders objected, Welles recommended continuing the U.S. occupation.[20]

Then in late 1921 the McCormick committee added to the controversy over Haiti by producing disquieting evidence of U.S. human rights abuses in the Dominican Republic. Testifying before the committee, one Dominican doctor reported seeing a U.S. Marine dragging an old man through the streets of Hato Mayor, tied to the tail of a horse. The doctor alleged that "the man was tortured in such a manner because he carried a prescription to a drug store in which sulphur and lard were mentioned. This was for some skin disease, [but] the doctors of the forces stated that it was for dressing wounds, and that was sufficient reason to have what I have just stated done to him. After that he was shot, and after being shot he was hung from a tree." The same witness continued with another story about a Dominican civilian who "appeared to have made some remarks that offended Capt. Merckle." Having taken offense, "Capt. Merckle took him by the left arm and took him to a corner of the house, drew his revolver, and shot him in the left ear . . . More than three or four hundred of the same kind of cases happened in that community." The doctor also asked permission "to present the commission one of the victims of the water torture committed by Capt. Merckle" and to submit for the record "a picture of the concentration camp [handing a picture in], which is similar to the Weyler camps in Cuba."[21]

Hughes could see where this evidence was heading, and he clearly did

not like it. Rejecting the Welles-Crowder approach in favor of direct negotiations in Washington, in mid-1922 he reached an agreement with Dominican leaders that allowed the nation's politicians to form a provisional
government and supervise their own transition process. The reestablishment of Dominican independence then proceeded fairly quickly. A free
election was held in March 1924, General Horacio Vásquez was inaugurated in July, and the last U.S. troops left the country in September. Within
a few years the U.S. minister recognized that "General Vasquez has been at
times too easily persuaded by politicians who place their own interests
above that of the country," but he reported that "these countries have need
of a man of his type at the head of their affairs. They are democracies more
in name than in fact. For years the people have been accustomed to permitting the political chieftains to do their thinking for them, and this condition will, for the most part, continue for much time to come."[22]

So it was that the Dominican experience came to be cited as an example
of wise U.S. policy. In the heat of a 1928 debate over the U.S. occupation of
Nicaragua, Senator William Bruce noted that "we went into San Domingo,
into that distracted country, whose finances were utterly disordered, and
with what result, pray? For the first time San Domingo soon found herself
endowed with something that might be called a real civilization." Secretary
of State Stimson agreed, writing in his diary in 1930 that he was especially
satisfied with the choice of a leader for the new Dominican constabulary:
Rafael Trujillo "is panning out to be a very good man. His work is energetic
and he has brought in an American marine, named Watson, to help him."[23]
Trujillo soon seized power and held it until he was assassinated in 1961; the
U.S. customs receivership continued until 1941.

The situation in Nicaragua was considerably more complex, but the
outcome was similar. By the early 1920s the collector of customs, the High
Commission, and the legation guard of 100 to 130 Marines appeared to
have the situation well in hand. Quickly adjusting to the dislocations of
World War I, Nicaragua's coffee-based economy had begun to produce a
substantial surplus, and by 1924 the government had repurchased its national bank and railroad, reduced its indebtedness by two-thirds, and begun to pay the awards of a claims commission.

Nicaragua's international relations appeared equally stable, with the
country's leaders willing to do almost anything that the United States
requested. In 1921 when other Central American states proposed creating a
unified federation, for example, the Nicaraguan envoy in Washington in-

formed the State Department that "Nicaragua wanted to adopt, with regard to the Central American Union, a policy consistent with the wishes of the United States Government."[24] For a time, regional rivalries led to border clashes among Honduras, El Salvador, and Nicaragua, and the United States moved to defuse the crisis by hosting a three-nation conference aboard the U.S.S. *Tacoma;* the calm following that meeting was further encouraged when a Central American peace conference began in Washington in late 1922. Since much of the regional conflict centered upon third-party support for rebel movements, Article 2 of the conference's Treaty of Peace and Amity discouraged meddling by mandating nonrecognition of any government "which may come into power in any of the five Republics through a *coup d'etat* or a revolution against a recognized Government."

With Nicaragua's economy strong and its international relations stabilized, the only obvious problem was domestic politics, in which three consecutive rigged elections had shredded the government's thin veil of popular legitimacy. The fraud was brazen, beginning with the first U.S.-supervised election in 1912. Smedley Butler, who helped that year to arrange the unopposed election of Adolfo Díaz, later bragged that by manipulating the electoral rolls, "our candidates always win."[25] These candidates were invariably Conservatives, with Conservative Emiliano Chamorro elected to succeed Conservative Adolfo Díaz in 1916; four years later another Conservative—uncle Diego Chamorro—was elected, and when he died in office, Conservative Vice President Bartolomé Martínez succeeded him.

It was after the 1920 sham that the increasingly angry voices of Nicaragua's Liberals began to be heard in Washington, and their accusations were supported by reports of fraud from U.S. observers. Reacting to these complaints, the State Department notified President-elect Diego Chamorro that it required a promise of free elections in 1924 prior to recognition of the 1920 results. Chamorro promptly made the required commitment and accepted the U.S. suggestion that he hire an expert to reform Nicaragua's electoral system.[26] The Department of State had in mind Harold Dodds, then secretary of the National Municipal League.

After several months of work in Nicaragua, Dodds prepared an allegedly fraud-proof electoral code, which the Nicaraguan Congress enacted into law in March 1923. By that time the Conservatives had split, with a portion of them joining with Liberals to offer a coalition slate in the 1924 elections: Conservative Carlos Solórzano for president and Liberal Juan Sacasa for vice president. Incumbent President Bartolomé Martínez also offered his candidacy, as did former President Emiliano Chamorro. Since the Nicaraguan constitution prohibited the President's immediate reelection, State Department officials informed Martínez that the United States "would be highly indisposed to recognize him as the constitutional President of Nicaragua after the expiration of his present term of office." Martínez quickly withdrew his candidacy, threw his support to Solórzano/Sacasa, and spent his remaining months in office undermining the Dodds reforms and harassing Emiliano Chamorro. As a result, the October 1924 election was clearly unfair.[27]

Realizing that he possessed a weak mandate, President-elect Solórzano asked the Marines to stay, but from Washington's perspective nothing more remained to be done: Nicaragua's claims had been paid, its finances put in order, its foreign relations stabilized, and Dodds had done his best to set the government upon a democratic foundation. Solórzano was inaugurated on New Year's Day 1925, and by August the Marines had left the country.

Within two months Emiliano Chamorro had launched a rebellion, had intimidated President Solórzano (who resigned) and Vice President Sacasa (who fled the country), and by early 1926 had become President. The State Department was dismayed by the backsliding. Citing the 1923 Central American treaty as his justification, on January 22 Secretary of State Frank Kellogg (Hughes had resigned in 1925) informed Chamorro that he would not be recognized.[28] Lacking what had become the imprimatur of legitimacy, Chamorro soon found his position weakened by a counterrebellion on the East coast, and in August the United States joined in by landing Marines at Bluefields and Corinto. In late October Chamorro was forced to resign, but then his banner of rebellion was seized by the long-disenfranchised Liberals led by Vice President Sacasa. By that time the Marines had reoccupied Managua and placed Washington's long-time favorite, Adolfo Díaz, back in the presidency.[29]

Díaz could not have lasted long without the continuing presence of U.S. troops, which he immediately requested. The Coolidge administration responded by dispatching additional Marines, with the public announcement coming from Assistant Secretary of State Robert Olds, who spoke to reporters on November 16, 1926, the day after receiving Díaz's request for troops. Chamorro was not the problem, Olds said; rather, Mexico was causing the trouble by backing Sacasa. To support this claim, the State Department produced a study that alleged "that the Mexican Government now hopes to set up Governments in the five Central American countries which will be not only friendly but subservient to Mexico and completely under Mexican domination. To accomplish this end the Mexican Government has undoubtedly lent its aid to the Liberal party in Nicaragua." [30]

This interpretation of Nicaragua's instability was prepared by a mid-level official, Stokely Morgan, and then quickly pushed up the State Department hierarchy to Assistant Secretary Olds, one of Kellogg's Minnesota law partners whose career gave no hint of preparation in foreign policy. Olds briefed the press, Secretary Kellogg, and President Coolidge. "The action of Mexico in the Nicaraguan crisis is a direct challenge to the United States," asserted the assistant secretary in a memo to prepare Kellogg for an appearance before the Senate Committee on Foreign Relations. Secretary Kellogg parroted Olds's memorandum to a closed session of the Senate Committee on Foreign Relations, while President Coolidge informed Congress that "I have the most conclusive evidence" of Mexican meddling. [31]

This stance set off an uncommonly vigorous foreign policy debate which, while indecisive, demonstrated that the Coolidge administration was in trouble: the President's most strident critics were fellow Republicans, and their margin in the Senate had just been reduced to three seats after the 1926 election. [32] When the Senate unanimously passed a resolution urging the arbitration of U.S. differences with Mexico, President Coolidge reacted by sending Dwight Morrow to Mexico and former Secretary of War Henry Stimson to Nicaragua. [33]

Arriving in Managua in mid-April 1927, Stimson promptly arranged to meet with Liberal military leader José María Moncada at a neutral site beside the Tipitapa River connecting Lake Managua and Lake Nicaragua. After presenting Moncada with a plan designed to permit the possibility of Liberal success at the polls, Stimson ended his negotiations with an ultimatum: "I am authorized to say that the President of the United States intends to accept the request of the Nicaraguan Government to supervise the elections of 1928; that the retention of President Diaz during the remainder of this term is regarded as essential to that plan and will be insisted upon; that a general disarmament of the country is also regarded as necessary for the proper and successful conduct of such election; and that the forces of the United States will be authorized to accept the custody of the arms of those willing to lay them down including the government and to disarm forcibly those who will not do so." The Liberals were reluctant to permit Adolfo Díaz to continue as President, but they were given no choice. As Stimson wrote in his diary, "we know no other Nicaraguan whom we could trust to so cooperate." For the future, however, Stimson had identified a promising young member of Moncada's military staff: "Somoza is a very frank, friendly, likable young Liberal and his attitude impresses me more favorably than almost any other."[34]

Within days Stimson was able to report that Moncada had accepted the Tipitapa ultimatum, and "while there will probably be resistance by small irreconcilable groups and scattered bandits, I believe that there will be no organized resistance to our action."[35] That assessment proved almost accurate. Moncada was able to convince eleven of his twelve military lieutenants to accept Stimson's plan; only Augusto Sandino refused. Retreating into Nicaragua's rugged northwestern highlands, in mid-July Sandino's forces attacked a group of 39 Marines at Ocotal. The Marines called in U.S. air support and killed somewhere between 50 and 300 Nicaraguans. News of this attack shattered the Coolidge administration's effort to defuse the controversy over Nicaragua. "Afternoon papers here carry sensational reports concerning bombing operations," cabled Secretary Kellogg to Managua. "Extremely important to have at earliest possible moment fullest details concerning Sandino's attack."[36]

While deploying additional forces—the maximum troop strength quickly rose to 5,673—the Coolidge administration launched an effort to defuse the public outrage. The earlier argument blaming Nicaragua's troubles on Mexico could no longer be used for this purpose, however, because at this very moment Dwight Morrow was on his way to Mexico to negotiate an agreement on the more pressing issue of oil, and so the administration argued instead that the United States was only helping with law enforcement. It did this by converting Sandino from a Liberal military leader into a bandit. "Sandino is reported to be an erratic Nicaraguan about thirty years of age with wild Communist ideas acquired largely in Mexico," read the first sentence of Minister Eberhardt's reply to Kellogg's urgent request for details. Rejecting the Stimson plan, Sandino "returned to Northern Nicaragua where he has since roamed at will with a few followers committing every known depredation and acts of outlawry," and where he "preached Communism, Mexican brotherly love and cooperation and death to the Americans, until the rabble of the whole North country joined him in his plan to massacre Americans there."[37]

This legend had no basis in fact, but it became the Coolidge administration's response to its critics. In his 1927 annual message to Congress, the

President asserted that after the Tipitapa agreement "the population re-turned to their peace-time pursuits, with the exception of some small roving bands of outlaws." A few weeks later an administration supporter in the Senate asserted that "this man was for some years a lieutenant of the Mexican Pancho Villa, probably one of the most murderous, atrocious cutthroats that ever headed a band of marauders anywhere in Latin Amer-ica."[38] In February, when skeptical Senators asked Admiral Latimer how Sandino was able to recruit so many fighters, he responded that "there are plenty of men up on that border that are willing to join anybody that will promise them a profitable adventure, whether looting, stealing, murdering, or anything of that sort."[39]

From time to time the administration reported that Sandino had been killed or had fled into exile, but the primary result of each erroneous report was to erode the administration's credibility and fuel the foreign policy debate in Washington. As both sides dug in their heels, it became obvious that more was at stake than U.S. policy toward a small Central American country; indeed, it was here—in the debates over the U.S. occupation of Nicaragua—that the force of public opinion made its principal contri-bution to the development of the Good Neighbor policy. This opinion emerged as part of the debate over a broader issue, isolationism, which had begun years earlier over U.S. membership in the League of Nations, but had been cut short by a weakened President and the Republican victory in 1920. Even after that election, however, U.S. participation in the League was the single issue that absorbed most of Secretary Hughes's attention during the truncated Harding years, and a consensus had still not been reached on the nation's role in global politics when the Marines returned to Nicaragua in 1926. The debate over Nicaragua would not provide the answer, but just as U.S. efforts to acquire Cuba had become the battleground over slavery in the 1850s, now Nicaragua was about to become the site of a struggle over U.S. involvement in international affairs.

The debate began to broaden beyond Washington when a handful of citizens, upset by the reinvasion of Nicaragua, did what citizens have always done: they formed interest groups to seek a change in U.S. policy. In the mid-1920s these groups were so new that they did not have a name, but they probably would have approved of the title given to similar groups in the 1980s: the solidarity network. Church-based, emotional, and super-charged with the energy of indignation, the members of these groups were adamantly opposed to U.S. intervention in Central America and the Caribbean. Moreover—and this was a major political litmus test of the 1920s—they approved of the Mexican Revolution; indeed, their original interest in U.S.–Latin American relations had been their concern over the lingering U.S. hostility toward Mexico, which they tended to attribute to the machinations of U.S. investors.

The most prominent solidarity group was the Committee on Cultural Relations with Latin America (CCRLA), founded by Hubert Herring, then working for the Congregational Church. In 1926 Herring hit upon the idea of taking groups of opinion leaders on familiarization trips to Mexico. Thirty went on the first trip in late 1926 and early 1927, where they met with Mexican citizens and public officials, including President Calles, and then returned home to describe their experiences. One immediate product of the initial trip was a Senate resolution that prohibited sending troops to Mexico while Congress was not in session. It was a nonbinding "nuisance" resolution, but it permitted hearings by the Committee on Foreign Relations, which were arranged by Herring at a time when committees lacked a professional staff.[40] Eventually the CCRLA took over two hundred U.S. opinion leaders to Mexico. Half a century later it would serve as the model for the Witness for Peace organization in Central America.

Journalists played an especially significant role in this solidarity network. Just as the Yellow Press had contributed to the Spanish-American war, so now a growing cadre of anti-imperialist writers began to nudge the United States away from Central American intervention. Perhaps the most important of these journalists was Carleton Beals, who used an interview with Sandino to challenge the administration's assertion that the rebel leader was nothing but a bandit. His articles in the *Nation* were regularly cited on the floors of Congress, and his 1932 *Banana Gold* was a masterpiece of political partisanship, a torrid attack on "the apologists who drip greasy platitudes to oil the gun-carriages of our target-practice in Latin America."[41]

These churchpeople, journalists, and left-leaning citizens further complicated the work of U.S. officials by making a public nuisance of themselves. On one day in 1928 over one hundred pro-Sandino protesters were arrested for picketing without a parade permit in front of the White House, and the *New York Times* reported that the Post Office had barred the All American Anti-Imperialist League from attaching stickers ("Protest Against Marine Rule in Nicaragua") to letters sent through the mail. Congressional speeches were sprinkled with references to opposition groups, from the Philadelphia Peace Council to the Brooklyn Society for Ethical Culture to the New York Women's Peace Union to the Jacksonville Calvary Baptist Church.[42] Today it is still difficult to identify the breadth of this public opposition, but it clearly affected officials in Washington, including Secretary Kellogg, who cabled General Frank McCoy in Nicaragua: "There is a great deal of criticism in this country about the way in which these operations are being dragged out with constant sacrifice of American lives and without any concrete results . . . People cannot understand why the job cannot be done, and frankly I do not understand myself."[43]

The State Department's permanent staff rejected all criticism out of hand. The chief of the Latin American Division, Francis White, told his colleagues that "much of the criticism [of U.S. policy] is due to propagandists, professional ones." According to Stokely Morgan, the critics were partially to blame for Central American instability: "suspicion is steadily fostered by a critical and uninformed section of public opinion both at home and abroad." When this approach did not seem appropriate, as with Samuel Guy Inman, whose credentials as a knowledgeable critic went back to his work as a Protestant missionary in Porfirio Díaz's Mexico, then the tendency was to engage in name-calling: the State Department's Franklin Mott Gunther referred to Inman as "an uplifter of note of the parlor bolshevist type, a leader of 'teachers and preachers.'"[44]

Although the Coolidge administration retained a fair number of supporters in Congress, the most capable among them were now silent. Particularly surprising was the behavior of Connecticut Senator Hiram Bingham, who a year earlier had retracted the central message of a book that he had published while a Yale professor, *The Monroe Doctrine: An Obsolete Shibboleth,* and who had subscribed to both the Doctrine and the Roosevelt Corollary; now he confined his comments to snide remarks. This silence left the administration's case in weak hands, and it showed. Senator William Bruce, a Maryland Democrat, was the most ardent supporter of the Republican administration's policy, employing the "silent majority" language that Spiro Agnew would later find useful in defending the Nixon administration's policy in Vietnam: "about the only elements in the country that do not approve of the action of our Government in relation to Nicaragua are the extreme pacifists and the radicals."[45] Although there were moments of substance, more often than not, the day's exchanges ended with something like the comment by North Dakota's Peter Norbeck: "Why not accept the situation frankly and admit that we must rely on the white population in those countries for whatever stability can be given the government and whatever protection there may be to life and property, until such a time as the native population has reached [the] test of civilization?"[46]

The administration's critics responded with an emotionalism rarely seen in Congress. To the Secretary of the Navy's assertion that "there was no bombing of civilian population and there was no destruction of any large number of civilians," Senator Norris replied that the Coolidge administration "has used the armed forces of the United States to destroy human life, to burn villages, to bomb innocent women and children from the air." Senator King immediately joined in, observing that "in the case of those poor, defenseless people in Nicaragua we send our armies down there and our airplanes, and we drop bombs upon their little villages and hamlets and destroy and kill and wound and burn."[47]

This was criticism with a personal sting, and the best reply that the administration could muster was that it simply wanted to oversee a fair election and get out, to which Senator Norris replied: "If President Coolidge wants to use the Army and the Navy and the marines and the sailors to purify elections, why does he not go into Philadelphia?" Nicaraguans "are moved by the same things that move us," he said. "They love their little children. They love their homes. We would call them hovels, but they are the best they have. We have burned them and destroyed them and killed some of their little children, killed some of their wives, killed some of their women, every one of whom was unarmed and not a single one of whom had ever raised a finger against us." Senator Dill brought to the floor a letter from a Missouri father who almost apologized for the death of his son: "We, as a Nation, have no legal or moral right to be murdering those liberty-loving people in a war of aggression." The most vociferous attacks were reserved for the "Eastern money interests" that populists regularly identified as causing most of the nation's ills. Alabama's Senator Thomas Heflin criticized the way in which "our army is now being used to collect the debts of Wall Street financiers," and Senator Dill accused the administration of "riveting upon the people of Nicaragua the control of American business men."[48]

Heated words were not votes, however, and the balance of political power weighed heavily against the critics. From the beginning, every disengagement initiative failed by a wide margin. But then in early 1929, when the Coolidge appointees were understandably distracted by the need to empty their desks, Senator Dill's amendment prohibiting the use of Navy funds in Nicaragua was accepted by a surprising eight-vote margin.[49] The Senate leadership forced reconsideration the next day after rounding up the forces needed to reverse the decision, but the balance of political power had become extremely shaky, and by this time President-elect Herbert Hoover had visited Nicaragua, and he, along with nearly everyone else, agreed on the need to leave Nicaragua as quickly as possible.

The Coolidge administration had already been preparing for an occupation-ending election. Soon after Stimson returned to the United States in May 1927, Secretary of State Kellogg dispatched Harold Dodds to prepare yet another electoral law and General Frank McCoy to supervise the subsequent election. Dodds's draft legislation was ready by the fall, but since Nicaragua already had an electoral law (the one Dodds had written in 1923), the Nicaraguan Congress had to repeal the first document before approving the second, which to avoid confusion came to be known as the McCoy Law. It provided for a three-member electoral board, with a U.S. citizen (McCoy) as chair and two Nicaraguan members, one representing each party, whose task was to supervise the election. This arrangement was contrary to Dodds's earlier law that gave the job to Nicaragua's Congress, and the legislature therefore balked at accepting the new proposal.

Now suffering through the height of Sandino's insurgency and the worst period of Congressional criticism, Secretary Kellogg was not prepared to discuss the niceties of the Nicaraguan electoral code. In an impatient cable, he instructed U.S. Chargé Dana Munro to get the McCoy Law enacted, and to do it quickly. Munro placed most of the blame on Emiliano Chamorro, who controlled a large bloc of congressional votes, but the envoy added that "I think that it may be difficult for Chamorro to hold the majority in line against our policy if we show a resolute attitude and exert pressure in proper but effective ways. It must be remembered that the Latin American shows little stability of character even in wrong doing." Brushing aside the legislature's qualms, U.S. Minister Eberhardt reported that its members simply wished to continue meeting because it would mean additional pay.[50]

In the end, an election was held, McCoy counted the votes, and on New Year's Day 1929 José María Moncada was installed as Nicaragua's President. This left one major problem. The Tipitapa agreement had disbanded Nicaragua's partisan armed forces, replacing them with the U.S. Marines. Since a Nicaraguan constabulary had to be created before the Marines could be withdrawn, the Nicaraguan foreign minister and Chargé Munro negotiated an "Agreement between the United States and Nicaragua Establishing the Guardia Nacional de Nicaragua."[51] Then over the next few years the Marines put the force together and provided it with arms and training, while at the same time continuing the fight against Sandino's rebels.

Herbert Hoover's desire to remove U.S. forces from Nicaragua only increased after the October 1929 stock market crash signaled the onset of the Great Depression, but President Moncada requested that the United States supervise Nicaragua's 1930 nonpresidential elections. Since U.S. armed forces were already in the country, Hoover agreed.[52] The administration's Congressional opponents consented, but the honeymoon (and Republican control over the House of Representatives) was over by late 1931 when President Hoover indicated that the United States would also supervise Nicaragua's 1932 presidential election. Sandino's forces had waxed and waned over the years, but his opposition never ceased completely until the United States withdrew its troops, and by that time 135 Marines had lost their lives. Eight Marines had died in a Sandinista ambush on the last day of 1930; the following April 9 more U.S. citizens had been killed by another antigovernment group, and the Congressional reaction was to prohibit the use of Navy funds to supervise Nicaragua's 1932 election. Although Hoover found sufficient money elsewhere to chair half the election boards, the fight was over. Secretary of State Henry Stimson had already announced a new policy, unique in the history of U.S.–Central American relations: "the Department recommends to all Americans who do not feel secure . . . to withdraw from the country, or at least to the coast towns whence they can be protected or evacuated in case of necessity. Those who remain do so at their own risk and must not expect American forces to be sent inland to their aid."[53]

Juan Sacasa won the 1932 election, and at almost the same time U.S. Minister Matthew Hanna tapped Anastasio Somoza to replace the Marine commander of the *Guardia Nacional*. "I look on him as the best man in the country for the position," he reported to Washington. "I know no one who will labor as intelligently or conscientiously to maintain the non-partisan character of the Guardia, or will be as efficient in all matters connected with the administration and command of the Force."[54] The United States turned the National Guard over to Somoza on the same day that Sacasa was inaugurated—January 1, 1933—and the following day the last contingent of Marines left the country.

An uneasy jockeying for political power ensued. Sandino was assassinated by the *Guardia* in early 1934, and Sacasa watched helplessly as So-moza stripped him of his authority. By mid-1936 there was nothing for Sacasa to do but resign, and after a rigged election, Anastasio Somoza assumed the presidency. As he observed this process unfolding, a new U.S. ambassador wrote that "the people who created the G[uardia] N[acional] had no adequate understanding of the psychology of the people here. Otherwise, they would not have bequeathed Nicaragua with an instrument to blast constitutional procedure off the map. Did it ever occur to the eminent statesmen who created the G.N. that personal ambition lurks in the human breast, *even* in Nicaragua? In my opinion it has been one of the sorriest examples on our part of our inability to understand that we should not meddle in other peoples' affairs."[55]

This was an observation from hindsight, however. As the pre-Depression era was coming to an end, leaders in Washington did not know what would occur in places like Nicaragua, and they therefore remained uncertain about an appropriate policy to follow. They had ended the practice of long-term military intervention and economic control, breaking the norm that had been established under the Roosevelt Corollary, but they were as yet unwilling to grant complete freedom to the people of the Caribbean region. As an alternative, they continued the process developed in Nicaragua by the Dollar Diplomats—of identifying and supporting friendly dictators. Since these chosen leaders would not be able to count on a Marine backup, the chosen leaders ceased to be complaisant civilians like Adolfo Díaz; now they were military or paramilitary leaders. Soon the Caribbean region would be dotted with long-term dictatorships under the leadership of men like Rafael Trujillo and Anastasio Somoza.

If this were the sole achievement of the pre-Depression generation of U.S. officials, the judgment of history would be unfavorable. Alongside this transfer of power to military strongmen, however, U.S. policy in the 1920s also featured a substantially different phenomenon: the development of a new spirit of accommodation that led directly to the Good Neighbor policy. The initial steps in this direction occurred in U.S. policy toward Mexico and in the development of an institutional framework for cooperation, Pan Americanism.

Chapter 14

Establishing the Foundations of Honorable Intercourse

What are we to do when government breaks down and American citizens are in danger of their lives? Are we to stand by and see them butchered in the jungle?

〜 *Charles Evans Hughes, 1928*

Although the fighting had stopped years earlier, the United States had never come to terms with the Mexican Revolution. Alvaro Obregón had replaced Venustiano Carranza as Mexico's President just before the 1920 U.S. nominating conventions, and the outgoing Wilson administration had refused to recognize the new government because, as the Democrats explained in their campaign platform, Mexico had not yet "signified its willingness to meet its international obligations, especially to foreign investors." Many Democrats, including Interior Secretary Franklin Lane, considered nonrecognition too weak a response, writing Secretary of State Lansing, "I wish somehow that you could be given a free hand in this matter. I know it would be a stiff hand, an authoritative hand, and that is what those people need. They are naughty children who are exercising all the privileges and rights of grown ups."[1]

Targeting both Mexico and the Democrats, the Republican platform asserted that the Wilson administration's policy "has earned for us the sneers and jeers of Mexican bandits, and added insult upon insult against our national honor and dignity." During the campaign, candidate Harding criticized the administration's "vacillating and un-American policy which from first to last has comprised every possible attitude, from active warfare to truculent weedling," but he was careful to add that "we never intend to tell them who shall govern there—that is Mexico's own affair."[2]

Underlying this election-year rhetoric was an issue of genuine importance to twentieth-century international relations: the rights and responsibilities of transnational capital. In their 1917 Constitution the Mexicans had undermined the European norm by granting the state inalienable ownership of "all mineral or other substances which in veins, layers, masses or beds form deposits the nature of which is different from the component elements of the soil." Private individuals could buy land, but not the subsoil. Article 27 further challenged existing norms by specifying that only Mexican citizens could own land or obtain concessions to exploit the subsoil, although for the purpose of this requirement non-Mexicans might be treated as Mexicans if they agree "to be considered as Mexicans in respect to such property and, accordingly, not to invoke the protection of their own Governments."

Something close to hysteria characterized Washington's response to Article 27, in part because it was adopted in the same year as the Bolshevik Revolution, and in part because it deprived the most powerful U.S. petroleum companies of the underground oil deposits that they had purchased during the Porfiriato. Understandably concerned, these investors demanded government help in reclaiming what a Senate committee estimated as $505 million in losses.[3] But the aggressive lobbying of those who stood to lose the most under Article 27—the U.S. petroleum industry— served only to arouse the hostility of progressive Republicans and Democratic leaders, especially President Wilson. The day after Harding's election he instructed Secretary of State Bainbridge Colby to "act upon no suggestions whatever from anybody connected with the oil interests down there. These are particularly dangerous interests and are certain to lead us astray if we follow their advice in any particular."[4]

The *principal* reason for Washington's concern over Article 27 was the burgeoning demand for oil. The United States had imported virtually no petroleum at all until Edward Doheny's first major Mexican oil well came into production in 1904, and on the eve of its revolution, Mexico was producing only 3.6 million barrels of oil, barely 1 percent of the world total. But by 1920 Mexican production had reached 157 million barrels, 24 percent of world production, 80 percent of which was exported to the United States, where—and this fact is crucial for understanding U.S. policy—there were now an astonishing 9.2 million cars on the road, up from 1.8 million in 1914. Nearly everyone either had, planned to have, or dreamed of having an automobile.

Understanding the electoral significance of millions of cars without gasoline was one job of the Harding administration's secretary of commerce, Herbert Hoover. Since the best estimates of the early 1920s predicted that

U.S. petroleum reserves would be exhausted in about a decade, Hoover approached the secretary of state, and "Mr. Hughes supported a suggestion of mine that the practical thing was to urge our oil companies to acquire oil territory in South America and elsewhere before the European companies preempted all of it. As a result, a conference of the leading oil producers was called, and such action taken that most of the available oil lands in South America were acquired by Americans."[5] Writing three decades after the fact, Hoover took perhaps too much credit, for U.S. petroleum companies were already acquiring oilfields in Venezuela and Colombia, but the government's encouragement was probably helpful in accelerating the companies' move into Latin America. Venezuela's production of oil rose from 121,000 barrels in 1917 to over a million barrels in 1921; U.S. investment in Colombian oil rose from less than $4 million in 1913 to $30 million in the early 1920s. By 1928 there were 199 U.S. oil companies in Latin America, primarily in Mexico, Colombia, and Venezuela.

Seeking to satisfy the growing demand for industrial raw materials, U.S. entrepreneurs were making similar investments in extractive industries elsewhere in Latin America. In Chile it was copper, with the family names of Braden and Guggenheim (later corporate giants Kennecott and Anaconda) operating immense facilities at El Teniente and Chuquicamata; and iron, beginning in 1913 when Bethlehem Steel bought out the French interest in Coquimbo. Overall, U.S. investment in Chile rose from $15 million in 1912 to over $100 million in the early 1920s, nearly all of it in mining. And this was just the beginning. What U.S. political leaders saw in the early 1920s was not so much the amount that had already been invested, but the staggering sums that U.S. investors were continuing to funnel into the foreign investment pipeline in order to meet rising domestic demand for petroleum and other raw materials. During the 1920s the $30 million in Colombia grew to $124 million, and the $100 million in Chile became $423 million.[6]

As U.S. industrialists were moving to acquire industrial raw materials, other U.S. entrepreneurs were seeking profitable outlets for surplus capital. This search led most frequently to Latin America's soaring demand for new technologies, primarily public utilities and especially electricity and telephone services. Mexico's Constitution particularly worried investors in these politically vulnerable sectors, because if Mexico could demand a Calvo clause, then others could follow suit, stripping U.S. investors of their protection. As U.S. Minister James Sheffield informed Secretary of State Kellogg, "this principle is at stake not alone in Mexico but in other Latin

American countries, and perhaps elsewhere, and it will become increasingly important as the surplus of capital for investment in the United States compels our citizens to seek new outlets for such investments, in short with our development as a creditor nation. Of the total of American investments abroad in 1924, 44% were made in Latin America. Any weakness in our attitude here is certain to be reflected almost immediately in other foreign countries."[7] Every year the potential for damage increased, as U.S. investment in Latin American utilities rose from $101 million to $676 million during the 1920s. To handle this capital flow the 1913 Federal Reserve Act had opened the door to branch banking overseas, and wartime dislocations immediately helped U.S. bankers to take over most of the Latin American market from European houses. The first of these branches—the National City Bank's office in Buenos Aires—opened in late 1914, and by the time Warren Harding was elected six years later, National City had fifty-six branch offices in Latin America.

The world war also provided new opportunities for U.S. manufacturers to capture Latin American consumers who had been cut off from their traditional European suppliers. As the war-induced surge in U.S. exports of consumer goods melded into the export flow created by Latin America's new need for petroleum and other capital equipment, the overall numbers became truly impressive: U.S. exports to Latin America rose from $540 million in 1916 to $1.6 billion in 1920, a threefold increase in four short years. Europe has never recovered more than a fraction of these markets.

The participants in this private-sector stampede were encouraged by the understanding that they would receive U.S. government protection against confiscation or any other form of damaging treatment. As the Republican and Democratic platforms indicate, by 1920 virtually everyone considered this service an entitlement, and even though opposition was growing to the cruder forms of dollar diplomacy, the underlying protective principle continued to receive wide support. This is why the Wilson administration refused to recognize Alvaro Obregón's new government in 1920—Mexico first had to negotiate a treaty protecting U.S. investors from the ex post facto application of Article 27. President Harding and Secretary of State Charles Evans Hughes continued Wilson's nonrecognition policy, and although Hughes regularly underscored his friendly disposition toward the Mexican people, he always added a warning: "no State is entitled to a place within the family of nations if it destroys the foundations of honorable intercourse by resort to confiscation and repudiation."[8]

Since the stakes were now too high to permit a drawn-out estrangement, it was not long before officials in both countries were taking steps to end the impasse. On the U.S. side, the initiative came from a unique public-private partnership between the Department of State and investment bankers led by J. P. Morgan partner Thomas Lamont. To an extent not previously observed in inter-American relations, Lamont became a diplomat in everything but official title. This status surprised U.S. officials in Mexico, and after observing the partnership for some time, in 1925 Chargé Arthur Schoenfeld sent to Hughes's successor, Secretary of State Frank Kellogg, a confidential cable suggesting that Lamont and his fellow bankers were perhaps gaining too great a control over both U.S. policy and Mexican finances. The reply from Washington assured Schoenfeld that "the Department has taken careful note of your observations," but it also stated that "Mr. Lamont has been informed of the substance of your telegram" and wished to make a response. This reply introduced two separate memos providing Lamont's detailed refutation of Schoenfeld's views.[9] Although the chastised envoy never again despatched an unkind word about the bankers, he soon found himself representing the United States in Bulgaria.

Lamont's initial negotiations with Mexico also revealed a conflict of interests that divided the Wall Street bankers from the U.S. petroleum industry. The petroleum concessionaires had long since burned their bridges with Democrats and progressive Republicans, and in early 1923 they destroyed their credibility with mainstream Republicans when Woodrow Wilson's nemesis, former New Mexico Senator Albert B. Fall, now serving as Harding's interior secretary, was forced to resign from the cabinet. The principal target of the Teapot Dome bribery scandal, Secretary Fall had accepted $409,000 (and a herd of cattle) from Edward Doheny and Harry Sinclair, in return for which he used his position as custodian of federal lands to grant the two men leases on the naval oil reserves in Elk Hills, California, and Teapot Dome, Wyoming. Because these reserves were intended to get the Navy through a national security crisis, Teapot Dome smelled not just of peculation, but also of treason. Thus when U.S. and Mexican negotiators were finally sitting down to discuss their differences in mid-1923, just weeks after Fall's resignation, most U.S. politicians were eager to distance themselves from the petroleum industry.

This isolation was probably never complete (Treasury Secretary Andrew W. Mellon never stopped consulting with the president of Gulf Oil, his brother William), but it took the petroleum industry out of the direct negotiations with Mexico. Acting on behalf of the Harding administration *and* his clients, who sought nothing more than the creation of a stable political environment so that Mexico could begin repaying its debts, Lamont held preliminary discussions with the Mexican government, and the two nations agreed to negotiate directly in Mexico City. Meeting in the former home of Porfirio Díaz's minister of finance on Avenida (now Calle) Bucareli, in 1922 and 1923 the two sides hammered out an agreement to create a general claims commission and a separate commission to assess specific damages from the Revolution. Then, in a classic piece of diplomatic legerdemain, the negotiators finessed their intractable differences regarding the interpretation of Article 27: the United States negotiators inserted into the record a statement objecting to the retroactive application of Article 27, and Mexico's negotiators inserted a statement that they had read the U.S. statement.[10] (Five years later, the minutes of a meeting between J. Reuben Clark and petroleum industry executives have Clark saying "that he had made a careful study of the diplomatic correspondence and of the Bucareli proceedings and that frankly they were not clear to him.")[11] The United States then recognized the Obregón government, and in early 1924 the first U.S. ambassador in more than five years arrived in Mexico City. Later that summer when the Republicans met to write their platform, they reported that "our difficulties with Mexico have happily yielded to a most friendly adjustment." The Democrats said nothing.

In addition, 1924 was an election year in Mexico, with Plutarco Calles replacing Alvaro Obregón as the nation's chief executive. The President-elect was promptly invited to visit Washington in October, where he received a cordial welcome from outgoing Secretary of State Charles Evans Hughes. As another goodwill gesture the U.S. Navy agreed to abandon its Baja California coaling station at Pichilingue Bay, just north of La Paz, a site it had used since 1861. But then in 1925 the two nations returned to diplomatic loggerheads when the inexperienced incoming secretary of state, Frank Kellogg, decided that Mexico was dragging its feet on settling claims and was harassing U.S. petroleum and mining interests with its lingering threat to exercise subsoil ownership rights. Kellogg was guided by the advice of lower-level State Department officials, none of whom had a good word to say about Mexico or Latin America in general.

By far the best indicator of this disdain is the series of lectures that senior State Department officials gave in the early days of the Foreign Service School, which had been established in 1924 to professionalize U.S. diplomacy. Presentations were made by Francis White, the Department's principal Latin Americanist, and three of his associates: Franklin Mott Gunther, Stokely W. Morgan, and Dana G. Munro.[12] Now in his mid-thirties, White had joined the Department in 1915, two years after graduating from Yale. In 1920 he received his first Latin American assignment in Havana, where he stayed for a year before moving to the embassy in Buenos Aires for another year; then in mid-1922 he was tapped to be head of the Division of Latin-America, a position that he held continuously until 1933, with only a brief interlude in Spain. Here, then, was someone who was on the Foreign Service fast track, who had exposure to Latin America, and who had a full decade of hands-on experience with U.S. foreign policy.

White's lectures began with a brief description of the type of people whom the new recruits were likely to encounter. His notes on Ecuador were limited to three sentences: "Population 2,000,000. About 5% pure white, rest mixed blood or pure Indians. Very backward country." No other lecturer mentioned Ecuador. White's principal message was that trainees should be ready for political instability if they happened to be assigned to a nonwhite country in the region: "Political stability in these countries more or less in direct proportion to percentage of pure white inhabitants. The greater the percentage of white inhabitants and the more temperate the climate the more stable the government." Then White moved to discuss the corruption that allegedly existed throughout the region, which he also explained as a product of race and climate. "With certain exceptions general characteristic of most Governments of Latin America, especially those in tropics and having very small pure white population, is that great dishonesty exists among public officials." Then White added a third explanation for Latin America's political problems—its Hispanic colonial history. "Many of the difficulties of Latin American government come from their early history. As Spanish colonies they had no self government." He concluded, however, with the observation that "Latin Americans [are] very easy people to deal with if properly managed. Force not necessary. They respond very well to patience."

Francis White set the tone for the other lecturers, who all began with a general description of the people of each region before turning to a discussion of Latin America's social problems. Stokely Morgan told the students that "life is cheap in Central America, and murder both of natives and foreigners is unfortunately quite common." Even the positive comments were backhanded slaps. When Morgan sought to balance a series of negative comments, for example, he remarked that "it should not be thought, however, that these people have no good qualities. Many of them are remarkable for their high ideals and fine feelings. That idealism and refinement, however, which is often associated with the Latin temperament is usually more Utopian than practical."

The values identified by these lecturers are found embedded throughout the State Department documents of the era—as, for example, in a 1922 briefing memo by an unknown State Department official, warning Secretary Hughes that the semiwhite leaders whom he would meet on his trip to Brazil were "self centered, lovers of power and pleasure"—"being almost wholly illiterate and of childlike ignorance the negroes are seldom interested in anything aside from their simple wants."[13] Nowhere is this type of comment so dominant as in the files on Central America and Mexico. Francis White wrote Undersecretary Grew that "the Latin American mind does not work along the same groove as the Anglo Saxon mind. While the Latins are great theorists they can throw over their theories in a very light-hearted manner when it suits their convenience to do so. Constitutional principles mean little to them." White also argued that "Latins, as many of them quite frankly admit, are bad losers and will not accept defeat with good grace and turn over the Government to their opponents should they lose the elections at the polls."[14] In this same vein, in 1923 Matthew Hanna of the Division of Mexican Affairs informed Secretary Hughes that "Mexico is and will continue to be governed by an Indian race of low civilization, and it would be a fundamental error to deal with such a government as with that of a highly civilized white race, or to expect to obtain justice by the mere force of logic when justice conflicts with national aspirations."[15]

Private papers from this era are even more candid. In 1925 the U.S. ambassador to Mexico wrote the president of Columbia University that the motivation behind Mexico's leaders "are greed, a wholly Mexican view of nationalism and an Indian, not Latin, hatred of all peoples not on the reservation. There is very little white blood in the cabinet—that is it is very thin. Calles is Armenian and Indian; León almost wholly Indian and an amateur bullfighter; Saenz, the Foreign Minister, is Jew and Indian; Morones more white blood but not the better for it; Amaro, Secretary of War, a pure blooded Indian and very cruel." All this filtered up to senior officials during the 1920s. Undersecretary of State Joseph Grew joked in his diary about "revolutions in Central America, the national sport," while Secretary of State Stimson noted in his diary that "this makes the seventh

Latin-American revolution, six of them successful, since this administration took office. When I announced it at Cabinet there was a general laugh."[16]

When combined with the desire to protect U.S. investors, this type of thinking led these lower-level officials to draft Secretary of State Kellogg's heavy-handed press release in mid-1925. Observing "that another revolution may be impending in Mexico" (a reference to heightened unrest over Church-state relations), the release stated that the Coolidge administration "will continue to support the Government in Mexico only so long as it protects American lives and American rights and complies with its international engagements and obligations. The Government of Mexico is now on trial before the world."

President Calles immediately replied that the press release was "a threat to the sovereignty of Mexico that she cannot overlook,"[17] and not long thereafter the Mexican government enacted a new petroleum law reiterating the substance of Article 27, with the stipulation that owners of oil properties who had begun exploitation before the 1917 Constitution could apply for a fifty-year concession to replace their ownership rights. The law also stipulated that the application for a concession must include a Calvo clause. Constrained by the fragility of his own governing coalition, President Calles's offer of concessions was as far as he could go on an issue that Mexicans defined in terms of their national sovereignty, especially once the State Department had used a press release to raise the issue to the public level.

On the U.S. side, the Coolidge administration was increasingly suspicious that the Calles administration had come under the influence of Bolsheviks, and if Mexican nationalism and U.S. anticommunism were not a sufficiently volatile mixture, this was the very moment that Juan Sacasa was using Mexican support to underwrite his fight for the Nicaraguan presidency. Congress and the solidarity groups deserve most of the credit for helping President Coolidge see the need for a more moderate U.S. approach. After watching Mexican and Nicaraguan relations go steadily downhill for more than a year, Progressives such as Montana's Senator Burton Wheeler complained of sending "the sons of Americans to protect the property of the oil companies,"[18] and in late January 1927 the Senate unanimously approved a resolution urging arbitration of U.S. differences with Mexico. Within weeks the Coolidge administration retreated slightly from its threatening posture. Although the President stood by his opposition to the Calvo clause, he indicated publicly that "we do not want any controversy with Mexico" and signaled his willingness to negotiate by sending Dwight Morrow to Mexico.[19]

A Coolidge supporter since their undergraduate days together at Amherst, Morrow had invested his talents in Wall Street, where he had moved steadily up the ladder of success. For the thirteen years prior to his appointment as ambassador to Mexico, he had been a partner of the most powerful financial house in the nation, J. P. Morgan, whose senior partner, Thomas Lamont, continued in his semipublic role as a financial adviser to both the U.S. and Mexican governments. Morrow was a confirmed capitalist, but a breed apart from the typical Dollar Diplomat. Five years before his appointment to Mexico, Morrow wrote Enoch Crowder, whom he had met in Cuba while on a business trip: "Of course, the Government in Cuba has been and is very bad. It is possible, yes, it is probable, that the United States might run Cuba much better. As I get older, however, I think I become more and more convinced that good government is not a substitute for self-government. The kind of mistakes that America would make in running Cuba would be different from those that the Cubans themselves make, but they would probably cause a new kind of trouble and a new kind of suffering."[20] Although these words were included in a letter approving of Crowder's heavy-handed diplomacy, they nonetheless identify Morrow as belonging to a different species of the banking genus than, for example, First National Bank's Roger Farnham, who spent his career looting Caribbean treasuries under the protection of U.S. Marines. There is no evidence that Morrow thought of his ambassadorial appointment as anything other than a challenging opportunity to decrease tension between two neighbors, and there is substantial evidence that he sacrificed the interests of the U.S. petroleum industry, some of whom were Morgan clients, to achieve improved relations.

Appointed and confirmed in mid-1927, the new ambassador spent two months studying the files in Washington and discovering that the State Department's Latin Americanists were so rigid in their opposition to compromise that he needed to hire his own private staff. Arriving in Mexico in late October, Morrow accomplished in exactly three weeks what his predecessors had been unable to do in two years—convince President Calles that it would not violate any basic principle of the Mexican Revolution to void the most offensive sections of the 1925 petroleum law. Beset by a host of political and economic problems, Calles probably did not need much convincing; what he needed was some indication of respect for Mexican sovereignty. When Morrow offered this intangible concession, Calles broke the deadlock, and the Mexican Supreme Court promptly issued a mollifying interpretation of the petroleum law: Mexico would not require a Calvo clause, but it maintained the principle of state ownership of subsoil deposits. The pre-1917 owners would now exploit their "concessions."

A host of details and ancillary issues remained to be negotiated, but from this moment forward it was primarily a process of give-and-take, smoothed by the best public relations effort in U.S. diplomatic history, including wildly popular visits to Mexico by the nation's unassuming superhero, Charles Lindbergh (who later married Morrow's daughter), and by its most *simpático* citizen, Will Rogers. In early 1928 the Coolidge administration notified the U.S. petroleum industry that Mexico's Supreme Court decision and Calles's supplementing regulations "had satisfied the U.S. government's concerns."[21]

Oil industry leaders (especially Harry Sinclair, who broke ranks and settled early) were pleased to retain their ability to pump Mexico's oil out of the ground and into their customers' gas tanks, but Morrow's settlement did not satisfy the industry's broader anxiety. The Mexican agreement still demonstrated that a Latin American government could abrogate property rights. As Gulf Oil president W. L. Mellon told Morrow on April 11, "our great concern in the matter is not so much as to our Mexican rights themselves, as [the effect that] such a settlement might have on negotiations which the different American oil companies are conducting in South America and other Latin American countries."[22] A month later petroleum industry representatives pursued this concern in a three-hour meeting with J. Reuben Clark, a member of Dwight Morrow's private staff. A stenographer's notes indicate that Clark told the oil executives to stop thinking of the Mexican settlement in symbolic terms and get on with their business: "Mr. Clark then stated that in his opinion the Mexican Government would not grant any more than it had; that the feeling in Mexico was that the Mexican Government had given a lot away; and while he could not speak for Mr. Morrow, if he were in Mr. Morrow's position, he would not ask for any more."[23] That became the view of President Coolidge, who told Congress in his final annual message that "our relations with Mexico are on a more satisfactory basis than at any time since their revolution."

The process of accommodating Mexico went hand-in-hand with the development of Pan Americanism. Although the concept was at least as old

as Bolívar's 1826 Congress of Panama, the modern era of an institutionalized Hemispheric community properly began in late 1881, when Secretary
of State James Blaine issued an invitation to the independent countries of
the Hemisphere (Haiti excluded) to meet in Washington "for the purpose
of considering and discussing the methods of preventing war between the
nations of America." The invitations were withdrawn after Garfield's assassination, but then in mid-1888 Congress authorized new invitations. This
time, however, President Cleveland announced that the conference's purpose had shifted from the prevention of war to the promotion of trade.[24]
The agenda was the best indicator of this change in emphasis: at the
opening session in October 1889, an also-resuscitated Secretary of State
Blaine announced that there would be a *six-week* recess so that the delegates could board an excursion train for a 6,000-mile trip from factory to
factory across the Northeast and Midwest.[25] The obvious idea was to convince Latin Americans that U.S. manufacturers could supply their every
need.

It was considered a bit gauche to commercialize a diplomatic conference,
and delegate Roque Sáenz Peña, a future President of Argentina, would
later complain that Blaine "wished to make Latin America a market, and
the sovereign states tributaries." He also broadened his criticism to attack
the Monroe Doctrine, which "commands one hemisphere in the name of
the other hemisphere; gives orders to Europe in the name of our America;
and ends up creating a New World chancellery without the authorization
of the rest of the States, which neither ask for nor need protection." The
"chancellery" was the product of a conference resolution creating a modest Washington-based bureaucracy to provide "such commercial statistics
and other useful information as may be contributed to it by any of the
American republics."[26] So was born the International Bureau of American
Republics, which slowly evolved into today's Organization of American
States.

In its initial years the Bureau was lodged within the U.S. Department of
State, and even though it was soon folded into the newly created Pan
American Union, a U.S. citizen always served as the director, and the U.S.
secretary of state always chaired the Governing Board, which determined
the timing and the agenda of future meetings, the second of which convened in Mexico City in 1901 to 1902 and the third in Rio de Janeiro in
1906. This latter was the meeting attended by Elihu Root, and it was such a
triumph that he asked Andrew Carnegie for funds to construct a perma-

nent building for the newly established Pan American Union. With nearly a million dollars from Carnegie and $200,000 from the U.S. government to purchase five acres of land fronting on Washington's Ellipse, the Pan American Union building became the visible evidence of the emerging inter-American institution. It was dedicated in 1910, just prior to the fourth International Conference of American States in Buenos Aires.

By this time, interest in Pan Americanism had waned, in part because the organization was the personal project of Elihu Root, who was now out of office, but primarily because the Taft administration (Philander Knox and Huntington Wilson) could think of no good reason to sustain U.S. support. World War I then intervened, and thirteen years passed before delegates assembled in Santiago to inaugurate the fifth conference in 1923.

Times had changed significantly, and with them the mood of the Hemisphere. In addition to the rapidly increasing U.S. commercial presence, there was an important noneconomic change: sensing that international institutions could serve as weapons of the weak, Latin American governments had greeted the establishment of the League of Nations with considerable enthusiasm, and the delegates who gathered in Santiago were thinking about creating a similar regional organization for the Western Hemisphere. To achieve this end, the Pan American Union would have to be transformed from a U.S.-dominated organization into a true international institution. A modest attempt in this direction had already occurred in Buenos Aires in 1910, when Latin American governments had proposed that the U.S. secretary of state remain the chair of the Governing Board, but that in his absence the senior Latin American diplomat present would preside instead of the secretary of state's assistant. Delegate Henry White wrote Knox that this change "is of no consequence, as of course when there is any business of importance the Secretary of State would naturally attend; whereas in the absence of such business it is as well that Latin-America should be flattered by the chairmanship."[27]

Now, thirteen years later in Santiago, Costa Rica proposed to go a step further and stipulate that the members of the Governing Board (one per country) be named by the member states, eliminating the requirement that the Latin Americans on the Board also be accredited to the United States government. Endorsed by fourteen of the seventeen Latin American delegations, Costa Rica's proposal was a none-too-subtle statement about who was to blame for Mexico's absence in Santiago; since the United States had refused to recognize the Obregón government, Mexico did not have a diplomat in Washington and, hence, no representative on the Governing Board, and Mexico refused to participate in a conference whose agenda was set by a Board on which it lacked representation.

The Costa Rican proposal launched the first real debate in the history of inter-American conferences, and other Latin American nations seized the opportunity to express their disapproval of U.S. dominance. The discussions were civil but pointed, with the U.S. delegation reporting that "one of the Colombian delegates intimated that the provision which made the Secretary of State of the United States ex officio chairman of the governing board might also imply a certain inequality."[28] The United States could hardly object to the Colombian intimation or the Costa Rican proposal, and the conference agreed not only that "the Governing Board will elect its President and Vice President," but also that any government unrecognized by the United States would be permitted "to appoint a Special Representative on the Governing Board."

All this was a modest preface to Uruguay's proposal to amend a treaty on claims that had been adopted at the 1910 Buenos Aires conference. The 1910 language was not strong enough, Uruguay explained; it wanted to insert a Calvo-type statement that "every individual is subject to the laws and authorities of the State in which he resides and where he enjoys the same civil rights as nationals. In no case may he pretend to obtain other rights or exercise them in any other way than that determined by the constitution and laws of the country." This proposal had "Article 27" written all over it, of course, and the U.S. delegates responded by asserting that the existing language in the 1910 Buenos Aires agreement was perfectly adequate; when that failed, they stonewalled, telling Latin Americans simply, "the subject should not be reopened."[29] That was not possible, however, in part because Uruguay had already reopened it, but primarily because Colombia, now inundated by U.S. petroleum firms, immediately proposed even stiffer language that foreigners "may not present a claim through diplomatic channels."

To avoid a confrontation, the question was referred to a meeting of the International Commission of Jurists, with the expectation that it would make a recommendation to the next inter-American conference. Charged with codifying international law for the nations of the hemisphere, the International Commission of Jurists had been established by a resolution of the 1901–02 Mexico City conference; however, it was not until 1912 that the Commission first met in Rio, where it created a number of committees to draft legal codes on topics that ranged from immigration and nationality to investments and claims. The Commission had been scheduled to reconvene in 1914 to discuss these committee reports, but the war in Europe distracted everyone, and then the committees simply faded away. At Santiago the delegates had to reconstitute the organization by directing that a meeting be scheduled. The meeting occurred in 1927, and the Commission dutifully addressed the Uruguay-Colombia claims initiative as part of its long-delayed general effort to codify international law. Its recommendation was waiting for the delegates when they arrived in Havana for the sixth International Conference of American States in January 1928.

Secretary of State Charles Evans Hughes had backed out of attending the 1923 Santiago meeting, sending in his place an extremely conservative career diplomat (and former Rough Rider), Henry Fletcher, plus seven additional members of varying levels of intellectual achievement but consistently low political visibility, including Frank Kellogg, recently defeated in his Senate bid for reelection. Now, five years later, Kellogg was Calvin Coolidge's secretary of state, and he had not forgotten his Santiago experience. He consequently took special care in selecting the U.S. delegation. It was led by former Secretary of State Charles Evans Hughes, and included Ambassador Dwight Morrow (who took a brief leave of absence from Mexico), Stanford University president Ray Lyman Wilbur and, to participate in the opening ceremonies, President Calvin Coolidge.

The United States was fearful that the conferees would attack its recent intervention in Nicaragua, since nearly every U.S. legation in the region had reported hostile public reaction after the Marines had reentered that country in 1926.[30] Dismissing this opinion as nothing more than the carping of a disaffected minority, the State Department's Stokely Morgan circulated a memorandum indicating that "the anti-American criticism which has sprung up in Latin America since recognition of the Diaz Government does not denote any change of feeling toward the United States brought about by events in Nicaragua. These events have simply brought to the surface the strong anti-American feeling which has existed all the time. Much of it is encouraged by Mexico and most of it is carried on by irresponsible elements such as student and labor organizations and professional journalists whose living depends on the sensational character of their writing." Morgan did not accompany the U.S. delegation to Havana, but his ideas were contained in Secretary Kellogg's instructions to the U.S. delegation. "The past year has seen the development of a vigorous anti-

American propaganda throughout Latin America based on charges of 'imperialism' and characterized by violent criticism of the relations existing
between the United States and Mexico and the American policy in Nicaragua." Kellogg warned that "an effort may be made by some delegates . . . to
bring up controversial matters which the United States would not consider
appropriate for a gathering of this nature."[31]

Thus alerted, the U.S. delegates were prepared to sidetrack hostile reso-
lutions on Nicaragua or any other topic, but they obviously did not have
the foresight to obtain an advance copy of President Gerardo Machado's
opening speech, for they almost certainly would have encouraged him not
to begin with a sentence that set the tone for the entire conference:

> Intense is our joy and complete our faith in the future destinies of our
> hemisphere when, gazing over this hall, adding brilliancy to this tran-
> scendental occasion, we behold the illustrious person of His Excel-
> lency Calvin Coolidge, Chief Executive of the greatest of all democra-
> cies; head of the great people whom Cuba had the honor of seeing at
> her side in her bloody struggle for independence, which she enjoys
> without limitation, as stated in the joint resolution of April 20, 1898,
> honorably applied and inspired by the same ideals set forth in the
> ever famous Declaration of Independence of North America, liberty's
> greatest monument and gospel of rights of man and countries . . .

At this point several delegates began looking for potted palms into which
they might vomit, but Machado soon ended this unfortunate spectacle
and introduced Calvin Coolidge, whose inoffensive speech was nearly four
times longer.

The next day President Coolidge departed on the battleship that had
brought him, but the tone had been established: it was the United States
and its toadies versus independent Latin America, intent on extracting
a commitment to nonintervention. Mexico promptly proposed several
measures that would have had the effect of reorganizing the Pan American
Union into an autonomous international institution: a Governing Board
composed of one member from each country and selected by whatever
method each country thought best, a Board chair that rotated annually
among member countries according to alphabetical order, and a director
who would also be appointed annually and rotate plus a stipulation that
the director should not simultaneously accept a position with the government of any country, a direct slap at a system that permitted incumbent

director Leo Rowe to serve as a member of the U.S. delegation. Mexico's proposals were referred to committees for discussion and revision, as was the report of the Rio Commission of Jurists, which included a flat ban on intervention: "no state may intervene in the internal affairs of another." It went to the Committee on Public International Law, chaired by El Salvador's foreign minister, Gustavo Guerrero, which turned it over to a subcommittee chaired by Peru's Víctor Maúrtua for discussion and a recommendation.

Subcommittee chair Maúrtua earned a warm spot in the U.S. delegation's heart by agreeing to offer as a counterproposal a "Declaration of the Rights and Duties of States." This document had been produced in Washington in 1916 by the U.S.-dominated American Institute of International Law, and it had the following to say about intervention: "Every nation has the right to independence in the sense that it has a right to the pursuit of happiness and is free to develop itself without interference or control from other states, provided that in doing so it does not interfere with or violate the rights of other states." Maúrtua took this substitute to the full committee, where chair Guerrero insisted on the language of the Rio Commission of Jurists. As it became evident that this dispute was leading to an impasse, the committee members agreed to refer it to a special subcommittee chaired by Charles Evans Hughes, whose personal goal was to pass the problem to his successor, just as the U.S. delegates at Santiago had passed it to him. The full committee's report to the plenary was a recommendation "that the subject be given further study and that its consideration be postponed until the next conference."

That is where the issue should have been laid to rest, but at the conference's closing ceremony, an Argentine delegate revived it by expressing regret that the proposed ban on intervention had been tabled. This opened the door for additional statements, including an unexplained remark by Hughes approving the Argentine statement of regret. Some of these additional statements were quite inflammatory, and they prompted Guerrero to renege on the committee's agreement. He stood up and moved a resolution that "no state has the right to intervene in the internal affairs of another." Now recognizing what was occurring and understandably upset by Guerrero's action, Hughes simmered in silence while a series of speakers fanned the embers of resentment created by decades of U.S. intervention. When Hughes had reached the boiling point, he rose, explained the process by which Guerrero's committee had reached its unanimous decision to delay consideration, and assured the delegates that "we do not wish to intervene in the affairs of any American Republic." But, he continued: "What are we to do when government breaks down and American citizens are in danger of their lives? Are we to stand by and see them butchered in the jungle because a government in circumstances which it cannot control and for which it may not be responsible can no longer afford reasonable protection?"[32] Arguing that this action was not intervention, but rather "interposition of a temporary character," Hughes asserted that "no country should forego its right to protect its citizens." Guerrero then withdrew his proposal.

On that indecisive note, the conference ended, and Latin America's effort to extract a commitment to nonintervention from the United States would have to await FDR's Good Neighbor policy. In the meantime, the Department of State backtracked to the views of Theodore Roosevelt and Elihu Root and attempted to placate "developed" South America while continuing to control the Caribbean region. As Francis White wrote to Secretary Stimson in 1930, "as soon as South America realizes that our Central American policy is not a South American one, it will cease to care what we do in Central America. True, Central America may object, but I think they simply have got to lump it."[33] This view was expressed privately, however, for President Hoover had embarked upon a different approach to Latin America.

Chapter 15 ～

Becoming a Good Neighbor

The definite policy of the United States from now on is one opposed to armed intervention.

～ *President Franklin Roosevelt, 1933*

Immediately after his 1928 election, Herbert Hoover set out on a two-month goodwill trip around Latin America. He would later write in his memoirs that "as Secretary of Commerce I had developed an increasing dissatisfaction with our policies toward Latin America. I was convinced that unless we displayed an entirely different attitude we should never dispel the suspicions and fears of the 'Colossus of the North' nor win the respect of those nations." And so, beginning with his first stop in Honduras, the President-elect talked about being a good neighbor which, at the time, meant a halt to the deployment of U.S. armed forces in Latin America. Capping nearly three decades of slowly changing policy, President Hoover cleaned house, beginning the month after his inauguration when, in a pointed reference to the long-simmering dispute with Mexico, the new President specifically repudiated intervention to protect U.S. investors.[1]

This move would not get at the heart of the issue of intervention in other Latin American countries, however, because in the 1904 Roosevelt Corollary, the United States gave itself the right to preemptive military intervention, not to enforce the claims of *its* citizens but to forestall European intervention to enforce the claims of *their* citizens. As Stokely Morgan told State Department trainees in 1926, "unless the United States Government is willing to let other nations take whatever action they may deem necessary on behalf of their nationals it must accept this responsibility by itself."[2]

But now it was obvious that European nations were uninterested in the Caribbean, and it was difficult to argue that the continued U.S. occupation of Haiti and Nicaragua was required by even the most expansive interpretation of the Monroe Doctrine. Virtually everyone in Washington continued to agree on the need to keep European powers from expanding in the Western Hemisphere—in 1923 the aging Henry Cabot Lodge called it "just as vital, just as essential now as when Monroe and Adams formulated it and gave it to the world"; but Senator William Borah best captured the emerging center of opinion when he wrote that "the invasion of territory and the setting up of military governments are not within the implications of the Monroe Doctrine."[3]

The Roosevelt Corollary had caused so much resentment among Latin Americans that it needed to be buried in the same way it was born, with a formal message. That came in 1928, just before Hoover was elected, and even though it primarily reflected the widespread view that the Corollary had become counterproductive, the timing of the recision is explained by Secretary of State Frank Kellogg's need to work with the adamantly anti-interventionist Borah, who through the miracle of seniority had inherited the chair of the Senate Committee on Foreign Relations. In 1928 Borah's committee was about to consider ratification of Kellogg's only hope for the history books, the Kellogg-Briand Pact outlawing war; and both men feared that an effort would be made to attach an undesirable reservation based on a Rooseveltian reading of the Monroe Doctrine—that the United States would reserve the right to take over a Latin American country if it believed that a European nation was about to do so.[4] Since a takeover of similarly defenseless Belgium had triggered the Great War, such a reservation would vitiate Kellogg's pact.

Accordingly, Kellogg and Borah needed to rescind the Roosevelt Corollary in order to demonstrate that Monroe's original doctrine was a statement of nothing more than the right of self-defense, which was permitted under the "release" clause of the Kellogg-Briand Pact. To this end Kellogg commissioned Undersecretary of State J. Reuben Clark to produce an appropriate study of everything that had ever been said about the Monroe Doctrine by a U.S. official. Clark gave most of the work to an aide, Anna O'Neill, but he contributed a lengthy cover letter that did just what Borah and Kellogg wanted: it interpreted the Monroe Doctrine as a statement of the right to self-defense, and it flatly repudiated the Roosevelt Corollary. "It is not believed that this corollary is justified by the terms of the Monroe Doctrine," Clark wrote. If the United States anticipated a violation of the Monroe Doctrine, any preemptive "sanction would run against the European power offending the policy, and not against the Latin American country which was the object of the European aggression, unless a conspiracy existed between the European and the American states involved. In the normal case, the Latin American state against which aggression was aimed by a European power, would be the beneficiary of the Doctrine not its victim."[5] A month after Clark's memorandum and a month before Kellogg's retirement, the Senate ratified the Kellogg-Briand Pact.

The negotiation of the Pact had greatly expanded Kellogg's global perspective, instilling in him a sense of responsibility for making the world less vulnerable to war and other forms of physical intimidation. Indeed, Kellogg's interaction with Europeans and leaders such as Senator Borah had the effect of converting the secretary of state into a peace activist, and so it was not surprising when, just days before leaving office, he sent the Clark memorandum to U.S. legations in Latin America "as an official statement of and commentary upon the Monroe Doctrine." Aware of his lame-duck status, however, he noted that the memorandum should not be delivered to any government until the incoming Hoover administration had issued an authorization.[6]

This authorization was never given, because the new administration had its own problem with the Senate: in 1929 and 1930 the President was concerned that a conciliatory policy toward Latin America might be interpreted as weakness at a time when the administration was attempting to gain Senate approval for the equally conciliatory (to Japan) London Naval Treaty. Thus Hoover told Secretary of State Henry Stimson, long an ardent interventionist, to keep Clark's memorandum confidential. Later, after ratification of the London agreement, Stimson and other State Department officers argued that it would be unwise to publicize the memorandum. No clear record explains what happened next, although there is reason to doubt Hoover's later attempt to take credit for forcing the issue.[7] All that we know for certain is that in early 1930, the 236-page memorandum was quietly published as a government document.

Formal statements aside, President Hoover was not reluctant to move U.S. policy in the direction implied by the Clark memorandum. In his first annual message to Congress in late 1929, he almost apologized for the continuing military occupation of both Nicaragua and Haiti. "We do not wish to be represented abroad in such manner," he observed, and he reported that in Nicaragua the 1,600 remaining Marines were primarily for training purposes. "We are anxious to withdraw them further as the situation warrants." President Hoover also noted that "in Haiti we have about 700 marines, but it is a much more difficult problem the solution of which is still obscure."

Haiti was a problem because its citizens were black. That circumstance meant the absence of Latin American solidarity—years earlier when the Marines first invaded Haiti, Woodrow Wilson had correctly predicted that "the effect on 'Latin America' of our course down there will not, we think, be serious, because, being negroes, they are not regarded as of the fraternity!"[8] No subsequent pressure developed from Latin America. As a U.S. chargé reported from Bogotá a week after Hoover's 1929 message to Congress, "the recent events in the Republic of Haiti and the news reports regarding the despatch of further armed forces to that Republic have aroused but little unfriendly comment here, in marked contrast to the events of Nicaragua of two and three years ago."[9] Similarly, progressive U.S. public opinion was also far less inclined to speak out in opposition to the occupation of Haiti. A decade earlier, General Barnett's leaked allegations of indiscriminate killings had caused a brief sensation and helped to generate some opposition, but the significant domestic political debates over intervention in the 1920s focused upon Nicaragua and Mexico, not Haiti. Moreover, most of the Latin America–oriented business community was uninterested one way or the other. A set of minor U.S. investors and the National City Bank had taken advantage of the 1918 Haitian constitution permitting foreign ownership of land, while others had nudged aside French capital in Haiti's public utility, banking, and transportation sectors, but U.S. investments in Haiti amounted to very little when compared with those elsewhere in Latin America. With Latin American opinion, U.S. opinion, and the most politically potent members of the business community all on the sidelines in Haiti, the policy-making arena was dominated by the State Department, whose officials made it impossible for the Hoover administration to exit Haiti.

But Hoover tried. In his 1929 annual message he asked Congress for funds to appoint a commission "to arrive at some more definite policy than at present," and when this request was followed four days later by reports that U.S. Marines had killed ten and wounded thirty-four Haitian demonstrators, Hoover immediately sent a second request. Eager to cooperate, Senator Borah told a reporter that "over twelve years ago we dissolved their Assembly by force of arms and since that time they have not been permitted in any substantial way to have anything to do with their

Government. They are completely disenfranchised. The United States Government ought to be ashamed to stand before the world at this time, with all our professions of peace and against military power, in the attitude of keeping a military heel upon a helpless people." Congress promptly provided $50,000 for a commission, and Hoover just as promptly named its members, designating W. Cameron Forbes as chair. The President's instructions were explicit: "The primary question which is to be investigated is when and how we are to withdraw from Haiti. The second question is what we shall do in the meantime."[10]

The State Department and Navy officials who were waiting at the dock for the Forbes Commission were of the opinion that withdrawal would be a mistake. The very day that President Hoover sent his original funding request to Congress, High Commissioner John Russell cabled Secretary Stimson that the "Haitian mentality only recognizes force, and appeal to reason and logic is unthinkable." The U.S. consul at Cape Haitien argued that Washington misunderstood local opinion—specifically, that a petition from Haitians asking for immediate withdrawal "seems to be an attempt to lead President Hoover to believe that the matured minds of the Haitian people are expressing themselves while in reality it is only the children acting under bolshevist influence without realization of the possible consequence of their acts."[11]

The Forbes Commission's March 1930 report reflected these views. It argued for the gradual withdrawal of the Marines over the period leading up to the expiration of the treaty of occupation in mid-1936. To begin this process, Secretary Stimson sent Dana Munro as U.S. minister to Haiti, to ensure that the exit would not be rapid. As Stimson wrote in his diary, Munro "thought it was vitally important that we should not leave Haiti." Noting that Munro's view was "in sharp contrast with the President," the secretary wrote in his diary that "I am inclined to agree with Munro."[12] Stimson's arguments were buttressed by the U.S. chargé in Port-au-Prince, who reported that "the action of the Haitian, in common with the Latin in general, is in the main directed by emotion rather than by reason, which in the main dictates the action of the Anglo-Saxon."[13]

Secretary Stimson never directly refused to do as Hoover ordered, of course, but he implemented the President's policy without enthusiasm, writing in his diary that "we are trying to give way to the Haitians gradually, but of course that is not the way to deal with Negroes, and I am afraid it is going to make trouble."[14] The specific foot-dragging tactic adopted by

Stimson and Munro was to insist that the Haitians sign an exit treaty continuing the customs receivership. This requirement was acceptable to Haitian Presidents Joseph Louis Borno and Sténio Vincent, but not to the Haitian legislature, whose members considered the receivership an infringement upon the nation's sovereignty. That response gave Stimson the opportunity he needed to inform Hoover that it was Haiti's fault the Marines could not be withdrawn. It took a new administration, sticking to the Hoover-era demands of a continued customs receivership, to end the military occupation.[15]

Through all this the Hoover administration was nursing the fatal wound inflicted by the October 1929 stock market crash. In November 1930, the day after the U.S. electorate reacted to the economic downturn by giving the House of Representatives back to the Democrats, Stimson walked over to the White House to console the President, and then wrote in his diary that "almost pathetically he expressed his appreciation." The Depression ended any thought of major foreign policy initiatives; as Stimson noted in 1932, "the President is so absorbed with the domestic situation that he told me frankly that he can't think very much now of foreign affairs."[16]

Hoover's brief moment was over, and it is easy to forget how much he had accomplished in a short time. The Good Neighbor policy has several parents, but perhaps the two most important were Herbert Hoover and Elihu Root, although Hoover made most of his contribution before he became President. While serving nearly eight years as secretary of commerce (1921 to 1928), he was responsible for redirecting U.S. policy away from what the nation has always done poorly—military occupation—and toward what it does exceptionally well—business. Like Root's Pan Americanism, Hoover's sponsorship of wide-ranging foreign trade and investment initiatives profoundly affected U.S. policy because they helped to create new, more sophisticated private-sector interests, and they thereby encouraged the evolution of U.S. policy away from the minatory excesses of the Roosevelt-Taft era. Hoover was among the first to understand the policy implications of dramatically increased economic relations with Latin America, and he knew that legation guards had become counterproductive.

Hoover's presidency was less successful. He entered the White House with his tank full of ideas about improving relations with Latin America, but the Depression-induced puncture bled it dry almost immediately. His second annual message simply noted a new recognition policy and his commitment to withdraw from Haiti; in 1931 the region received a single short sentence ("We have continued our policy of withdrawing our marines from Haiti and Nicaragua"), and in his final message the President said nothing at all about Latin America.

There was little in Franklin Roosevelt's background to indicate that his administration would continue Hoover's step toward a Good Neighbor policy. As the Democrats' vice presidential candidate in 1920, FDR's foreign policy views were much closer to those of his Uncle Theodore than to Hoover's, although by 1933 the differences were pronounced. For one thing, FDR never publicly called Latin Americans "dagos." Times had changed, and by the mid-1930s it was becoming increasingly inappropriate to use racial or ethnic slurs in professional correspondence. It was now fairly rare to run across open anti-Semitism, for example—the sneering references had stopped appearing in diplomatic despatches, and the federal government had become a guardian of ethnic correctness. In 1935, when the State Department received an advance copy of Philip Jessup's authorized biography of Elihu Root, its officers criticized Jessup's direct quotation of an 1898 letter that Secretary of State John Hay wrote complaining that the guests at his diplomatic reception "were mostly dagoes and chargés." That the State Department's review of the two-volume biography should criticize nothing except Jessup's indiscretion are the best possible indicators that the goodwill of Latin America had become important to U.S. officials.[17]

Even more significant is the Roosevelt administration's early policy toward Cuba. This was not terra incognita to the new leaders in Washington. As assistant secretary of the navy, Roosevelt had visited the island during a 1917 Caribbean inspection tour, although his notes on that trip focus on country club entertainment, a strange new alcoholic beverage called a "daiquiri," and the clothes that people wore, with not a word about the substance of policy, even after his meeting with Cuba's president.[18] Secretary of State Cordell Hull also knew the island, but his knowledge was dated; leader of a company of Tennessee volunteers during the Spanish-American War, Hull had spent five months in Santa Clara, arriving in late 1898 after the fighting was over. On the other hand, FDR's principal Latin Americanist, Assistant Secretary Sumner Welles, had been active in the Caribbean for years and had maintained close ties with General Enoch Crowder, the U.S. proconsul and ambassador in Havana during the 1920s. During that decade Welles appears to have adopted the common State Department view of Latin America. After one trip to Cuba in 1921, for example, he advised Crowder that the U.S.-born former Cuban ambassador in Washington,

Carlos Manuel de Céspedes, was the best candidate for the Cuban presidency because of his "amenability to suggestions or advice which might be made to him by the American Legation."[19]

Although Cubans never saw Welles's memo, it would not have surprised them, for they had grown accustomed to U.S. interference. The end of the Magoon intervention in 1909 had been followed by the Liberal rule of José Miguel Gómez and a period of relative autonomy, with U.S. Marines returning only briefly in mid-1912 to quash a labor dispute in Oriente. Gómez turned the government over to Conservative Mario García Menocal after the latter's 1912 electoral victory, and the complaisant Menocal quickly became one of Washington's favorites. His fraudulent reelection in 1916 prompted the 1917 February Revolution and another U.S. intervention under the Platt Amendment.

The February Revolution could not have occurred at a worse moment for U.S. foreign policy officials—immediately after Germany had resumed unrestricted submarine warfare and Britain had informed Washington about the Zimmermann telegram. War-sensitive Washington simply would not tolerate instability in Cuba, especially when it also threatened U.S. economic interests. As the instability was at its height, John Foster Dulles, a young New York attorney representing "companies which own a very large number of sugar estates in the Island of Cuba," wrote to thank his uncle, Secretary of State Lansing, for an appointment earlier in the day. He also wanted to underscore that "it would be highly desirable to have a United States vessel appear, if only for a short time, in the Manati harbor" on Cuba's northeastern coast.[20] Two companies of U.S. Marines were sent to Camagüey and Oriente provinces (including the port of Manatí), assigned to protect U.S. sugar interests and to free up the Cuban troops that Menocal needed to suppress the Liberal rebellion. One company of 350 U.S. soldiers remained in Camagüey for five years.

It was not long before the German threat to the Caribbean subsided and the Liberal revolt was extinguished, while reports of Menocal's corruption continued to reach Washington. The State Department's reaction was to instruct the U.S. ambassador in Havana to pressure Menocal to invite General Crowder to revise Cuba's tattered electoral code.[21] At the same time, the United States switched envoys, sending to Cuba one of Bryan's deserving Democrats, Boaz Long, who had only recently written Secretary of State Lansing that "extending our influences over these less favored people with the idea of educating them and regulating and improving their agricultural and commercial development, and making them good citizens of a democracy, involves a colossal task, but one not unworthy of an enlightened American policy."[22] As for Crowder, the experienced military envoy (he had been the U.S. legal advisor in Cuba during the Magoon era) concluded that Cubans needed close supervision in a number of areas; accordingly, in late 1920 the lame-duck Wilson administration again invoked the Platt amendment, naming Crowder the President's "Personal Representative on special mission" in Cuba, and telling the Cuban government that troops would also be sent unless "President Menocal assumes a receptive attitude in respect to the advice and just recommendations which the President has instructed General Crowder to convey to him."[23] Two days later Crowder sailed into Havana's harbor aboard the battleship *Minnesota,* which served as both his home and his office for the following year.

After consultations with the new Harding administration, in 1922 Crowder began to produce a stream of memoranda directing the new government of Alfredo Zayas to reform Cuban society. Memorandum 8, for example, demanded "the immediate removal from office of every official who . . ." and then listed seven separate categories of behavior identified by Crowder as indicative of "Graft, Corruption and Immorality in the Public Administration." Memorandum 10 asked for "an immediate reform of the Lottery which is the source of widespread graft," and to make it easier for the Cuban government, Crowder attached a draft decree.[24] The ultimate political technocrat, Crowder had no interest in helping U.S. business interests in Cuba, and he especially criticized sugar magnate Edwin Atkins: "To him the Atkins group of sugar mills constitutes Cuba. He cares nothing for the future of three millions of people. He is one of the most selfish business men I have ever encountered."[25] Crowder then proceeded to build his reputation, both by overstating the problem (a "very difficult task of reconstructing or, better said, building anew the institutional life of this country") and exaggerating his achievements: "I think you would be pleased with the progress made and with the new National conscience that is awakening" in Cuba, he wrote to his commanding officer.[26] For his part, President Zayas played along with Crowder's "Moralization Program," but only until he received a loan that his government needed. Then he returned to previous policies. This behavior greatly annoyed officials in Washington, including Secretary of State Hughes, who took advantage of a meeting with the Cuban foreign minister to remind him "that the loan of $50 million had been put through on the distinct understanding that there should be a moralization program."[27]

Despite this backsliding, on balance the eight-year Crowder mission was judged a success by officials in Washington. In the 1928 Senate debate over obstreperous Nicaragua, for example, Senator William Bruce asked his colleagues to "think of our intervention in Cuba. This is absolutely one of the finest things in human history."[28] One of Crowder's principal accomplishments was the 1924 election of a U.S. favorite, Gerardo Machado, as Zayas's replacement. Machado was the man who introduced President Coolidge at the 1928 Havana conference, and it was understandable why no one in the State Department wanted him to retire when his term expired. Although he recognized that Machado "cannot be a candidate in 1928 to succeed himself without violating the Constitution," Ambassador Noble Judah argued that "it would seem an unwise policy to claim the authority to interpret the Cuban Constitution," and he advised Washington that "if we do not raise these constitutional questions no one else will."[29]

After the fraudulent 1928 election, Ambassador Judah reported that "I have been getting the utmost cooperation from Machado on everything I have asked of him, and it is certainly his policy, not only expressed but acted upon, to play as close to our Government as possible." Secretary of State Stimson confided to Senator Borah that the Machado government "was not the government that we should care for in America, but that it seemed to be in full control of Cuba; that it was popular with the Army, and that was the main thing in Latin-American countries."[30] This is the Cuba policy that Franklin Roosevelt inherited.

The onset of the Great Depression had already severely weakened Machado's power, and in 1931 Ambassador Harry Guggenheim warned that "Machado will eventually have to get out." Standing on the sidelines but preparing for action, FDR's new Latin Americanists agreed. "There are indications that the Cuban situation is getting worse and that in the near future the Department may be involved," wrote a member of FDR's transition team, Laurence Duggan. Any such involvement would have to be implemented without using the U.S. military, because the thinking of FDR's principal Latin Americanist, Sumner Welles, had evolved with the times. In early 1933 he sent the President-elect three pages of draft language about Latin America for his inaugural address, and suggested a prohibition on "the dispatch of the armed forces of the United States to any foreign soil whatsoever."[31] This commitment to military nonintervention became the defining characteristic of FDR's Good Neighbor policy.

Fearing increased instability in Cuba, the newly inaugurated President postponed Sumner Welles's already-announced appointment as assistant secretary of state and instead sent him to Havana as the new ambassador. A week after his arrival in May 1933, Welles telephoned Secretary of State Hull that "the situation is very precarious, much more so than I anticipated." He immediately set to work, and by mid-July was able to report some progress, although student groups—an omnibus term for Machado's most vehement opposition—"have not expressed their approval of what we are trying to do."[32] Then in late July a bus drivers' strike escalated into violent confrontations with Machado's army, and Welles reported that "if the present condition is permitted to continue much longer, I am positive that a state of complete anarchy will result." The next day he added that "there is absolutely no hope of a return to normal conditions in Cuba as long as President Machado remains in office," and he recommended the withdrawal of recognition.[33] With Welles's encouragement, which may or may not have been needed, the Cuban army then forced Machado from power, and Welles's old friend Carlos Manuel de Céspedes was named interim chief executive.

The problem with this arrangement, as General Crowder had reported a decade earlier, was that de Céspedes, "through sheer weakness of character, is negligible in any kind of a political crisis."[34] Sensing this weakness, in early September the Army's noncommissioned officers, led by Sergeant Fulgencio Batista, ousted Welles's favorite, replacing him with a government led by Ramón Grau San Martín. The indignant ambassador immediately reported that Grau's government was "composed of the most extreme radicals in Cuba," and later that day he discarded his commitment to nonintervention, requesting "a temporary landing of possibly a thousand men until a new government can be restored." After two days he repeated his request for "a strictly limited intervention," which he said would require "the landing of a considerable force at Habana and lesser forces in certain of the most important ports of the Republic." Realizing that the literal-minded might interpret this as a proposal for military intervention, Welles argued that U.S. troops would be only "an armed force lent by the United States as a policing power" and therefore "would most decidedly be construed as well within the limits of the policy of the 'good neighbor.'" Welles promised that the political fallout in Cuba would be minimal. The next day Welles again urged Washington to send troops quickly, because military personnel "who are in close touch with Communist leaders in Habana may resort to desperate measures if they become sufficiently drunk." [35]

These reports were all sent to Secretary of State Cordell Hull, who, as the State Department's Adolph Berle once noted, "is slow in making up his mind, sometimes, it has seemed to me, in situations that call for rapid action. But his judgment is far better than Sumner's. Sumner, on the other hand, will move like a shot in all situations." True to this characterization, Hull delayed responding until he could consult with others, including the U.S. ambassador to Mexico, Josephus Daniels, whom Hull would later describe as "a little radical at times to suit me." But the two men were friends, and after serving for eight years as Woodrow Wilson's secretary of the navy, Daniels knew more about U.S.-Caribbean relations than most other administration officials. He warned Hull to be skeptical of red-baiting: "In our own country and elsewhere people attribute to Communists all the agencies that work evil. I think it is so in Cuba, and if I were you I would accept with many grains of allowance the attempt to saddle on the comparatively few Communists all that goes awry."[36]

Hull also consulted with Latin American governments, and the President himself met with the envoys of Mexico, Argentina, Brazil, and Chile. Thinking, perhaps, that he was dealing with the other President Roosevelt, Generalissimo Rafael Trujillo volunteered the Dominican Republic's airfields for a U.S. invasion. The Argentine government sent an elegantly worded counterbalancing note indicating its belief that "no state arrives at the maturity of democracy and the fullness of destiny without experiencing, as a necessary accompaniment, the travail of difficult conflicts. The capacity to maintain order and to assure the reign of law emerges by itself as a fruit of this experience within the exercise of sovereignty, which must be characterized by absolute internal autonomy and complete external independence."[37]

Trujillo could be disregarded, but to ignore Argentina was an entirely different matter. Influential throughout South America and a prime force behind the upcoming inter-American conference at Montevideo, which Hull planned to attend, Argentina was a country that the United States could ill afford to offend if it wished to develop its Good Neighbor policy. Mexico, too, was important, and Ambassador Daniels bluntly warned "that if we intervene it will destroy the Montevideo conference." Daniels followed this conversation with a cable warning that in Mexico "the feeling against intervention by the United States is deep-seated and unanimous." Several days later Mexico delivered a note to the State Department indicating the hope that the United States might soon remove its naval vessels from Cuban waters. Praising FDR's initial policy toward the region, the

Mexican government added that "we do not want to see that good feeling fade away now, especially since we are all interested in seeing something done at Montevideo next December."[38]

To complicate matters further, at this precise moment Hull was deeply concerned that Mexico would seek a debt moratorium at Montevideo. If presented as a resolution, every Depression-devastated Latin American government would support it, and the United States, home of the banks that had made most of the loans, would be obliged to stand alone in opposition—a true diplomatic fiasco coming hard on the heels of the new secretary of state's embarrassment at the London Economic Conference. Noting that Mexico's proposal "is causing me some anxiety," Hull arranged to have President Roosevelt tell a press conference that "the United States is not owed any money by any of the South American republics and it is therefore a matter between those republics and any of the bondholders." This statement has often been taken as an example of FDR's non-intervention policy, when in fact it was nothing of the kind. It was Hull's way of preempting the Mexican initiative by asserting that private debt was not an issue for governments to discuss in Montevideo. U.S. delegates were instructed that if the debt question were raised, they should "endeavor to see that no action at all be taken by the Conference . . . You should completely disassociate yourselves from any action such as proposed by Mexico looking to a general moratorium on external debt service."[39]

Although we can never be absolutely certain, fear of a diplomatic disaster at Montevideo seems to explain why Welles's plea for troops was unsuccessful. Quoting the President, Hull informed Welles that a Cuban government installed following a U.S. intervention "would be regarded by the whole world, and especially throughout Latin America, as a creation and creature of the American Government"; intervention, Hull continued, "would have disastrous effects."[40]

Unwilling to concede, Welles played upon his family friendship (he had been an attendant at FDR's wedding) to make a case for intervention directly to the President at Warm Springs. There Roosevelt held firm by refusing to intervene with U.S. troops, but Welles convinced the President to do everything short of an invasion. FDR publicly declined to recognize Grau's government, he ringed the island with warships, and he sent Welles back to Havana to undermine the Cuban government.[41] In December, Welles took up his position as assistant secretary of state, but before handing the embassy over to Jefferson Caffery, he produced a final report indicating that the alternatives were either a Batista-dominated government or "a dictatorial government composed solely of elements of the extreme Left." Grau was able to hold out until mid-January. Advised of Batista's pending coup two days in advance, Caffery warned Washington to be ready to recognize the new government immediately. "If this is not done, Batista will probably turn definitely to the left."[42]

A decade later, when FDR welcomed a rehabilitated Grau San Martín to Washington, he remarked that "the President-Elect is largely responsible for the good neighbor policy" because he forced the 1933 decision not to send U.S. troops into Cuba.[43] Because the term "nonintervention" was defined narrowly to encompass only a military invasion, the outcome in Cuba was considered a major victory for the new administration's nonintervention policy. Now aware of Roosevelt's firm limits, Welles never again recommended dispatching armed forces to Latin America, and it was not until 1965, twenty-two years after homophobic Washington forced Welles's resignation to prevent a scandal, and twenty years after FDR's death, that a U.S. military intervention occurred once again in Latin America.

The desire not to disrupt the Montevideo conference may have been the primary reason why the Roosevelt administration did not send troops to restore order in Cuba, but underlying this immediate goal were several additional reasons. One is the belief that force was not needed; continued economic and diplomatic pressure, coupled with menacing gunboats, would undermine the Grau government, forcing it to yield to friendly leadership. Another is the influence of officials such as Josephus Daniels, who understood the depth of Latin American resentment of U.S. intervention and waged an effective bureaucratic campaign to challenge the thinking of men like Sumner Welles. A third is the Depression, perhaps the most important domestic political event of the twentieth century, which contributed to an ordering of U.S. priorities that differed substantially from that of the 1920s. Specifically, virtually everyone in Washington agreed on the need to end the dramatic contraction of U.S. trade. Plummeting trade had exacerbated the economic effects of a domestic cyclical downturn, pushing a simple recession into the Great Depression, and the Roosevelt administration's response was to spur U.S. exports by negotiating reciprocal tariff reduction treaties with its trading partners.

To begin this process, in late 1933 Secretary of State Cordell Hull, the architect of the administration's trade policy, sailed for Montevideo and the Seventh International Conference of American States. This time Leo Rowe attended as the representative of the Pan American Union, and the United States took the brazen step of replacing him on its delegation with a woman, the University of Chicago's Sophonisba Breckinridge, the first of her gender to represent the United States at a high-level international conference. Fellow delegate Spruille Braden found her "completely out of her depth throughout the conference," although he had to admit that she managed to do no damage, perhaps because she "belonged to the more moderately behaved wing" of the women's movement.[44] Paraguay and Uruguay also sent female delegates, and all three nations appear to have survived unscathed.

Intervention was still the principal issue. The conference agenda included a proposal that blended the 1927 nonintervention language prepared at the Rio meeting of the International Commission of Jurists into a broader Convention on the Rights and Duties of States, which had been prepared by the American Institute of International Law. Article 8 of the revised Convention was a blanket prohibition: "No state has the right to intervene in the internal or external affairs of another." Secretary Hull's instructions to the U.S. delegates indicated that Article 8 was "unacceptable to this Government. There are a number of situations that justify a State in intervening in the affairs of another State . . . It is apparent that proper consideration has not been given to existing International Law and to the practical, as distinguished from the theoretical, relationships between States."

These instructions soon needed to be modified, for when Hull arrived in Montevideo he found "the demand for unanimous affirmative vote was very vociferous and more or less wild and unreasonable."[45] The United States was left with little choice: ruin the conference or adjust its position from "unacceptable" to "acceptable with a reservation." Selecting the latter option, Hull told the conferees that "no government need fear any intervention on the part of the United States under the Roosevelt Administration," but then added the reservation that the United States would continue to adhere to "the law of nations as generally recognized and accepted," which was understood to permit intervention to protect the lives and property of citizens.[46] This was simply a polite way of reiterating the justification for intervention that Charles Evans Hughes had given at the last inter-American conference in Havana—his now-famous "Are we to stand by and see them butchered in the jungle?" question.

The Latin American reaction was muted, in part because Hull's wording was intentionally oblique, and in part because these were hard times, and governments throughout the region were struggling for survival in the very depths of the Great Depression. Rather than start a fight with the new U.S. administration, whose trade policies would have an important impact on Latin America's recovery, the diplomats at Montevideo quietly recoiled in reaction to Hull's words. The U.S. delegates could hardly miss the frosty reception accorded this first hemisphere-wide test of the Good Neighbor policy, however, and as they left Montevideo, they recognized the need to go a bit further to accommodate Latin American opinion. In a major speech two days after the conference closed, President Roosevelt inserted a sentence designed to reassure Latin Americans—"the definite policy of the United States from now on is one opposed to armed intervention"[47]— and a month later he reiterated this assurance in his State of the Union message.

Not long thereafter, Congress passed the 1934 Reciprocal Trade Agreements Act, which granted the executive branch the power to lower tariffs up to 50 percent in return for similar concessions from the nation's trading partners. Almost immediately the United States and Cuba signed the first reciprocal trade agreement, cutting the U.S. tariff on Cuban sugar by 40 percent and providing for equally advantageous reductions in tobacco and other products of tropical agriculture; in return, Cuba substantially reduced the protection that it was offering its infant industries, and the result was to cement the fledgling Cuban economy to that of the United States. Similar agreements were negotiated with other countries in the region, and U.S. trade with Latin America picked up significantly, tripling in dollar value between 1934 and 1941, by which time the war in Europe had once again deprived Latin American consumers of competing sources of supplies. When trade reciprocity was combined with other New Deal initiatives, especially the 1934 creation of the Export-Import Bank, the net economic result of the Depression years and the ensuing European devastation was to increase further the dominant U.S. role in Latin American markets.

At the same time, the Roosevelt administration also tidied up the loose ends of interventionist policy that had been unraveling for over a decade. In 1934 the United States reached an agreement with Cuba to abrogate the Platt amendment, replacing it with a new treaty that gave the United States the right to retain indefinitely its Navy base at Guantánamo. In 1936 a new agreement was signed with Panama to remove some of the most offensive stipulations from the Hay–Bunau-Varilla Treaty, and later that year the Haiti intervention treaty lapsed. In 1937 the United States and Mexico agreed to abrogate Article 8 of the Gadsden Treaty, which had given the United States a never-exercised right to send troops across Tehuantepec.[48]

As these changes were occurring, national security concerns began to exert an ever-increasing influence upon United States policy toward Latin America. Hitler cemented his power in German elections the day after Roosevelt was inaugurated, and FDR's European envoys immediately sounded the initial warnings. The carnage would soon begin again, and just as the Great Depression had ended Herbert Hoover's efforts to improve relations with Latin America, so a war was about to transform FDR's policy. The first war scare occurred in 1938, when the Mexican government of Lázaro Cárdenas ended a prolonged labor dispute by nationalizing the holdings of several foreign petroleum companies; Bernard Baruch then wrote President Roosevelt that the takeover "has been fomented by the representatives of Japan, Italy and Germany, particularly the last named."[49] Although the timing of Mexico's move was ominous—a week after the German-Austrian *anschluss*—neither Baruch nor anyone else was able to produce evidence to buttress the claim of fascist involvement, which is probably fortunate, for no one wanted yet another confrontation with Mexico.

Thus while the United States initially retaliated for the Cárdenas nationalization by participating in the international embargo on Mexican oil, strong voices soon began to urge accommodation. Ambassador Josephus Daniels, FDR's old boss as Woodrow Wilson's secretary of the navy, was especially effective in reducing tensions. At the time of the nationalization, he and his Mexican counterpart were preparing a mechanism for settling the claims of U.S. citizens whose land had been expropriated during Mexico's agrarian reform, and an agreement was reached just before Hitler invaded Poland in September 1939. A few weeks later, FBI Director J. Edgar Hoover implicitly attacked Daniels's accommodating approach, urging the State Department to use greater caution in dealing with Mexico. Assigned by FDR to protect the United States from subversive movements in Latin America, the FBI was in the process of preparing dossiers on virtually all Latin American leaders, and Hoover was especially worried about President Lázaro Cárdenas, who "is considered to be Pro-German." Using the unsupported innuendo that would later characterize McCarthyism, Hoover warned the State Department, "it is reliably reported that

Cardenas has for years been a member of a society in Mexico that has the specific purpose in mind to recover from the United States the States of Texas, Arizona, New Mexico, and California," and he added that "President Cardenas has always been Anti-Foreign due to his Indian Antecedents. He has always favored the ignorant 'sandal-footed' Indian-Mexican to the extent that it is known that he had received delegations of that type in his Office while Diplomatic Representatives of foreign countries were awaiting an audience with him." Cárdenas's ranking cabinet official, Ignacio García Tellez, was even worse, "a sort of 'parlor' communist, yet intensely Pro-German." [50]

Then in mid-1940 France fell to the Germans, and as U.S. participation in the war grew ever more likely, the conciliatory despatches of Ambassador Daniels began to carry increased weight. Soon nearly everyone in Washington wanted to settle the petroleum dispute, including Cordell Hull, who was persuaded to drop his adamant opposition to compromise. In mid-1941 the two governments agreed that Mexico had the right to expropriate the oilfields, that the former owners had the right to compensation, and that each country would appoint an expert commissioner to determine the proper amount. Secretary Hull then met with U.S. oil executives to obtain their acquiescence, and, he wrote, "I stressed the Axis activities being conducted in Latin America and the help Mexico had already given us in preventing strategic materials from going to Japan." [51] After three meetings, the executives remained unwilling to accept what both governments considered a fair settlement, and so Hull signed the agreement without their approval. Three weeks later the Japanese attacked Pearl Harbor.

It is no small irony that one of the aggrieved petroleum companies was the foundation of Nelson Rockefeller's immense fortune. Grandson of the founder of Standard Oil, the young Rockefeller had no concern over Mexican oil; he was much more interested in art, and in the early 1930s his attention was focused entirely upon a large mural that Diego Rivera was painting for the lobby of the new Rockefeller Center in midtown Manhattan. When Rivera overstepped the boundaries of artistic license and added a portrait of Lenin to what would probably have been a masterpiece, Rockefeller requested that the offensive Russian be replaced with a figure more congruent with capitalist values. The Mexican master refused, Rockefeller held firm, and capital scored another victory over labor: Rockefeller fired Rivera, destroyed the mural, and replaced it with today's art deco banality. Then, to mend fences, he went on a buying trip to Mexico for his family's favorite cultural project, New York's Museum of Modern Art. Ironically, it was the beginning of Rockefeller's lifelong love affair with Mexican contemporary and pre-Columbian art, a commitment that expanded to include most of the hemisphere after a three-month trip around South America in 1937.

But even art was far from Rockefeller's mind when he returned from his 1937 tour. Alarmed by the growing influence of Nazi Germany throughout the region, in 1938 Rockefeller urged President Roosevelt to launch a propaganda counteroffensive. For two years Rockefeller and FDR's White House staff traded memos, as Neville Chamberlain returned from Munich with an empty promise, as Adolf Hitler's panzer divisions rolled across Poland, as France and the Low Countries fell to the blitzkrieg. Then, two months after the German army paraded down the Champs-Elysées, in mid-1940 Roosevelt issued an executive order creating the Office for the Coordination of Commercial and Cultural Relations between the American Republics, with a mandate to "strengthen the bonds between the nations of the Western Hemisphere" and to ensure proper coordination of hemispheric defense.[52] Nelson Rockefeller entered government service as the Office's director.

Secretary of State Cordell Hull later recalled that this was a time when "German businessmen, working closely with the Nazi Party, were scattered all over Latin America. They were developing their businesses and digging in socially, commercially, and politically. They were using every method possible in the line of subversive activities."[53] Rockefeller's original job was to counter this German onslaught with U.S. propaganda—the production of all types of media, from magazines to shortwave broadcasts to motion pictures—but his most important contribution was to create the initial U.S. economic aid program. Just after the attack on Pearl Harbor, Rockefeller went to the White House with a satchel of graphs, maps, and illustrations, and laid out a compelling national security logic for development assistance: the defense of the hemisphere depended upon effective communications; effective wartime communications depended upon security guards; security guards needed to be healthy; their health depended upon the eradication of tropical diseases; tropical disease control required public health programs; Latin American governments could not afford these programs—and so, for the sake of national security, the United States had to help pay for them.

FDR was convinced, instructing Rockefeller to get busy on "measures for the control and prevention of disease, sanitation, sewage disposal, housing, improvement of food and water supplies, building of roads, highways, transportation facilities and public works, nutrition, general medical treatment and the education and training deemed necessary to achieve these objectives."[54] Outside of Cuba and other occupied Caribbean dependencies, the U.S. government had never before considered becoming involved in these activities in Latin America. Now, however, the nation's security demanded a break with tradition, and this tradition has never been restored. National security considerations required the United States to continue foreign aid for the next half-century, and aid continued after the Cold War, largely because it had become the nation's new tradition.

With a substantial budget and over 1,500 employees, Rockefeller was soon stepping on bureaucratic toes, including those of the Department of State, which always viewed the upstart organization as a threat—a "superfluous and wasteful Agency" is how diplomat-businessman Spruille Braden characterized the Office. Braden was suspicious of Rockefeller's staff ("communist-fellow-travelers" and "do-gooders and one-worlders like so many in federal agencies at the time") and unimpressed by Rockefeller himself ("what he lacked in knowledge he made up in eager willingness to squander the taxpayer's money on harebrained schemes").[55] One scheme that Braden almost certainly had in mind was Rockefeller's use of public opinion surveys to inform government officials about citizens' concerns. Just before Pearl Harbor he commissioned the first poll to explore "What People in the United States Think and Know about Latin America and Latin Americans."[56] The results indicated that U.S. citizens feared Axis subversion in Latin America.

This finding was hardly surprising, for the Roosevelt administration had been fostering this belief ever since Hitler's invasion of Poland. In mid-1940 the President had warned Congress that "Tampico is only two and a quarter hours to St. Louis, Kansas City, and Omaha"; moreover, in his 1941 State of the Union address he cautioned that "the first phase of the invasion of this hemisphere would not be the landing of regular troops. The necessary strategic points would be occupied by secret agents and their dupes—and great numbers of them are already here, and in Latin America." In a fireside chat the following September, Roosevelt said that "Hitler's advance guards—not only his avowed agents but also his dupes among us—have sought to make ready for him footholds and bridgeheads in the New

World, to be used as soon as he has gained control of the oceans." The President mentioned intrigues and sabotage in Uruguay, Argentina, and Bolivia, and he noted that "within the past few weeks the discovery was made of secret air-landing fields in Colombia, within easy range of the Panama Canal."[57]

To counter this perceived German offensive, the Roosevelt administration moved to shore up relations with the Latin American militaries. Historically, these relations had barely existed outside the occupied Caribbean nations; when FDR entered office, the only military-to-military relationship was a U.S. naval mission in Brazil (the earlier naval mission in Peru had ended), but by 1939 several U.S. military advisory groups had been established in Latin America, and U.S. military schools had been opened to students from nine Latin American countries. The pace quickened as Hitler marched across Europe, and over one hundred U.S. military advisors were at work in every Latin American nation by the time Pearl Harbor was attacked in December 1941.[58] After the war, these military-to-military linkages would facilitate the transmission of anticommunist values to Latin American militaries, replacing less-subtle foreign policy instruments such as the Roosevelt Corollary and the Platt Amendment.

These prewar military ties were complemented by a diplomatic effort to develop a single hemispheric response to the European conflict, beginning with a meeting of foreign ministers in Panama immediately after Germany's invasion of Poland. There the delegates drew a security zone around the hemisphere, agreeing to exclude all belligerents and to maintain a strict neutrality, and the United States also sponsored an obliquely worded resolution recommending that each government "eradicate from the Americas the spread of doctrines that tend to place in jeopardy the common inter-American democratic ideal." Ten months later the foreign ministers met again, this time immediately after the fall of France, and the wording was more straightforward: "Any attempt on the part of a non-American State against the integrity or inviolability of the territory, the sovereignty or the political independence of an American State shall be considered as an act of aggression against the States which sign this declaration."[59] The United States and every Latin American nation signed, but consensus was achieved only by watering down the preferred U.S. position. Secretary of State Hull wrote that "I introduced a resolution embodying the idea and method of a collective trusteeship [for European colonies such as Curaçao after the Netherlands was overrun by the Germans]. And instantly Argentina . . . opposed it. As at so many previous inter-American conferences, Argentina preferred the role of opposing the United States."[60] The foreign ministers accepted the Argentine suggestion that a procedure be created to call a meeting *to consider* creating a trustee mechanism to keep Europe's Latin American colonies out of Hitler's hands.[61]

Secretary Hull's reaction to the Argentine position was emblematic of Washington's growing war-induced intolerance. In 1941 it surfaced in Panama, where the populist government of Arnulfo Arias balked at a U.S. request for 999-year leases on ten one-acre military bases for air defense. In early 1941, when Arias appeared at the point of absolute refusal, Secretary of War Henry Stimson complained in a cabinet meeting about the "unfriendly" Panamanian government, after which President Roosevelt "told me of his [own] troubles with Arias and told Hull to try some strong arm methods on him." Arias was gone by October, overthrown by the U.S.-trained military—"a great relief for us," wrote Stimson. "Arias has been very troublesome and very pro-Nazi, and to have a man like that in Panama right near the Canal was a very dangerous thing." Although Stimson initially noted that "the new government seems to be very much better," the United States had to give up property rights in Panama City and Colón—rights that Bunau-Varilla had signed away in 1903—in order to obtain the desired bases. "The Treaty is not a very satisfactory one," Stimson wrote. "We have been held up badly by Panama."[62]

A much more important example of growing U.S. intolerance appeared five months before Pearl Harbor, when the United States published a "Proclaimed List" of 1,800 Latin American individuals and business firms alleged to be sympathetic to the Axis powers, each of whom would be treated "as though he were a national of Germany or Italy," which meant prohibiting their trade and freezing their assets in the United States.[63] Since the State Department and Rockefeller's office had created the list without consultation, many Latin American governments considered it an insult. Then, to compound the injury, when the Colombian Congress proposed to consult with other Latin American countries and develop a common reaction to the Proclaimed List, Hull warned President Eduardo Santos that "submission of the report by the Colombian Government to the other American republics will give additional ammunition to the Axis because the act of submission will be made to appear as an endeavor on the part of the Colombian Government to line up against this Government's policy the other American countries."[64]

This was the atmosphere of intolerance when, two days after the Japanese attack on Pearl Harbor, the United States requested an urgent meeting with Latin America's foreign ministers at Rio de Janeiro. Although the war crisis prohibited Hull's attendance, he instructed chief delegate Sumner Welles to convince "all the Republics to sign a joint declaration to break off relations with the Axis powers." To Hull, "this was a life-and-death struggle, the result of which could only mean freedom and advancement for Latin America or domination and probably occupation by the Axis."[65]

Not everyone at Rio agreed. The Argentines in particular had good reasons not to become involved in the war. Economically, the nation had profited greatly by remaining neutral during World War I, and politically it was difficult to generate anti-Axis sentiment in a nation with an extremely large first-generation Italian population and a substantial German community. Argentina, moreover, was far distant from the fields of slaughter, and this distance contributed not simply to indifference but also to the difficulty of distinguishing the good from the evil. Every story about Nazi concentration camps was countered with stories about U.S. internment camps, and most Argentines had no way to know the difference. As had been true of U.S. citizens in the late 1930s, Argentines were divided in their loyalties, and they had no desire to become involved in a war simply because the United States had been attacked by the Japanese in the middle of the Pacific. At Rio they refused to endorse the U.S. resolution mandating the severance of relations.

U.S. leaders put the worst interpretation on this opposition (Assistant Secretary Adolf Berle wrote in his diary "that Acting President Castillo has made commitments to the Italians and probably also to the Germans")[66] and so they were surprised when the other delegations at Rio went along with Argentina's dissent and accepted once again an embarrassingly weak resolution: "The American Republics, in accordance with the procedures established by their own laws and in conformity with the position and circumstances obtaining in each country in the existing continental conflict, recommend the breaking of their diplomatic relations with Japan, Germany and Italy."

Hull was livid; indeed, at first he refused to believe what had happened. Learning of the agreement on the radio, Hull telephoned Welles in Rio, and, he reported in his memoirs, "with Mr. Roosevelt listening in, Welles confirmed the signing of the agreement and gave me the substance of the crucial Article Three. I then spoke to him more sharply than I had ever spoken to anyone in the Department. I said I considered this a change in our policy, made without consulting me, and the equivalent of a surrender to Argentina." After witnessing this conversation, Adolf Berle wrote in his diary, "now there is a breach between the Secretary and Sumner which will never be healed."[67]

Regardless of the outcome at Rio, there was a war to be fought, and Latin Americans' assistance was necessary.[68] Since the Axis was not prepared to invade Latin America, the principal problem was the security of U.S. supply routes. In mid-February 1942 the first Caribbean U-boat attack occurred, when five oil tankers were sunk near Aruba, and within two weeks another twenty ships had been destroyed. By the end of 1942 over three hundred Allied ships were at the bottom of the Caribbean. In response, the United States scrambled to acquire Latin American air and naval bases from which to patrol the supply routes, with virtually all of the Caribbean states offering their territory, beginning with the Cubans, who permitted the construction of several airfields around the island, including Batista Field. President Somoza offered the United States a naval base at Corinto and gave the U.S. military access to the country's airfields; in return, his son Anastasio Somoza Debayle was allowed to enroll in West Point, from which he graduated in 1946.

The help of Mexico and Brazil was especially valuable. Mexico agreed not only to the reciprocal use of military airfields but also to the induction of Mexicans living in the United States; by war's end, over 250,000 Mexican citizens had served in the U.S. armed forces, and over a thousand had been killed in combat. In addition, Mexico was one of only two Latin American countries to fight in the war, sending an air force squadron to the Philippines in early 1945. Brazil was the other, dispatching a 25,000-member infantry division plus air force and navy support units to fight in Italy. Perhaps Brazil's principal contribution, however, was to permit its northeastern bulge to be used as a stopover for ships and aircraft heading to northern Africa.

All of these activities required the United States to work alongside Latin Americans, and the record left behind by the U.S. personnel stationed in the region suggests a remarkably smooth cooperative effort. But this spirit was not evident at more senior levels. In 1942 the Inter-American Defense Board (IADB) was created to provide high-level military coordination, but it did almost nothing because the United States did not want Latin Americans to get in the way. This attitude upset both the participating Latin

American militaries and the Department of State, which was responsible for maintaining smooth diplomatic relations, and in a 1943 meeting Undersecretary Sumner Welles asked that the U.S. military stop ignoring Latin America's offers of assistance. Speaking for all the services, Admiral Horne replied: "They have never served a useful purpose so far as we are concerned . . . I have wracked my brain for something for them to do . . . I am willing to give them anything we can with the understanding that they simply make suggestions and that we don't have to pay any attention to them." When the discussion turned to the specific proposal to use Cuban troops to guard the new U.S. airfields in Cuba, General McNarney drew the line, remarking that "my own personal opinion, and that of those who have looked into it, is that Cuban protection will be worse than none." This attitude was not a recent creation. "If we are driven to the Extremity of War," Joel Poinsett asked John Quincy Adams in 1818, "what assistance can we expect from our allies of South America?" His answer was that "they will require Subsidies of Money and Arms, and by their incompetence will embarrass all our operations." This could have been written by the National Security Council in 1950, which concluded that during World War II "the Latin American countries, with only one major exception [Brazil], were unable to make any contribution to Western Hemisphere defense."[69]

It is true that the United States was willing to feign military partnership in order to obtain Latin America's raw materials and military bases, as well as its cooperation in the suppression of fifth-column movements—but always with the tacit understanding, as one 1940 memo noted, that "our objective does *not* comprise expectations on our part of being able to use Latin American forces as effective allies in war."[70] Secretary of War Henry Stimson even questioned Latin Americans' ability to perform minor tasks, as he noted after attending a White House ceremony creating the U.N. Relief and Rehabilitation Agreement in late 1943. Forty-four nations were supposed to cooperate, he wrote in his diary, so that the responsibility was not put "on the shoulders of the United States and Great Britain alone. But when I saw the swarthy faces of some of the representatives of countries like Honduras who sat in front of me at this table, I 'had me doubts,' so to speak, as to how much they would take of this burden."[71]

It is tempting to argue that the aging Stimson (born in 1867, he had first been appointed to federal office in 1906 by Theodore Roosevelt) was a quaint throwback to an earlier day, but in fact he was simply echoing the broadly prevailing values of his time. In the 1941 Rockefeller survey of U.S.

views about Latin Americans, respondents were handed a page containing nineteen adjectives and asked, "from this list, which words seem to you to describe best the people who live in Central and South America?" The five *least*-selected adjectives were "efficient" (5 percent), "progressive" (11 percent), "generous," "brave" (both 12 percent), and "honest" (13 percent). The most frequently selected adjective (by 77 percent of the respondents) was "dark-skinned," followed by "quick-tempered," "emotional," "backward," "religious," "lazy," "ignorant," "suspicious"—and then finally the first unequivocally positive trait: 28 percent said that Latin Americans were friendly. That was just 1 percent more than said they were dirty.

Quite clearly, the Good Neighbor policy did not reach into the minds of U.S. leaders and the public to change the way in which they thought about Latin Americans. It was a policy that demanded a new surface respect for Latin America's sensitivities: no Marines landing in Caribbean ports, frequent high-level meetings, elaborate visits by heads of state, and new bureaucracies to institutionalize the Pan American relationship. No significant change occurred below the surface, nor was there a change in U.S. interests, which focused in the 1930s on economic expansion and then on national security. Thucydides's assertion—"large nations do what they wish, while small nations accept what they must"—remained the guiding principle of inter-American relations. Perhaps because it softened this reality, the new attitude of surface respect was welcomed by many Latin Americans. But that attitude, too, was about to change, as the United States began to fashion the postwar hemisphere.

Chapter 16

Attacking Dictatorships

It seems unlikely that there could be any other region of the earth in which nature and human behavior could have combined to produce a more unhappy and hopeless background for the conduct of human life than in Latin America.

~ *Department of State Counselor George Kennan, 1950*

In 1945 the United States was at the height of its power, and it decided to use that power to encourage democracy in Latin America. Although the concept of "good government" had played a role in U.S. policy since the time of Theodore Roosevelt, this was something new. In the past, good government had generally meant stability, not democracy, and that was certainly the case during World War II, when wartime priorities had encouraged the support of regional despots. Two weeks after the German invasion of Poland, a new member of the State Department's Latin American division wrote his chief that "the United States supports, legally and financially, such men in power as are widely recognized to be dictators holding their power by force. In the present stage of cultural and political development of some of the republics this is not only inevitable but perhaps the only way toward stability which can be realistically envisaged."[1] This argument was used regularly to justify the support of dictatorships during the war. In late 1942, for example, Undersecretary of State Sumner Welles asked President Roosevelt to roll out the red carpet for Cuba's dictator: "Since the overthrow of Batista might plunge the Island during this critical period into chaos, it is essential, if he is to remain in office, that his visit to Washington not be a failure."[2]

Stability would reemerge as the principal U.S. priority during the Cold War, but for a brief interlude the policy of supporting dictators lost much of its force the day World War II ended. U.S. officials simply preferred democracy to dictatorship; for many that had been the whole purpose of the war, and it is why they often referred to the Allies as "the democracies."

The crisis past, these officials now felt free to express their preference. In October 1944 the State Department's chief Latin Americanist, Norman Armour, wrote to calm the U.S. ambassador in Guatemala, who was upset by a revolution and a subsequent election that had terminated one of the Hemisphere's less savory dictatorships. He suggested that neither the Roosevelt administration nor the American public was upset by the change: "We wish to cultivate friendly relations with every government in the world and do not feel ourselves entitled to dictate to any country what form of government best suits its national aspirations. We nevertheless must naturally feel a greater affinity, a deeper sympathy and a warmer friendship for governments which effectively represent the practical application of democratic processes."[3]

And so, with the war drawing to a close, U.S. diplomats began to encourage a transition to democracy in Latin America. Writing from Argentina, Ambassador Spruille Braden advised Secretary of State Byrnes that "it is imperative for the security of U.S.A. that other American Republics [be] in hands of friendly cooperative govts. imbued with principles—i.e. of democracy identical to ours."[4] In Brazil Ambassador Adolf Berle gave a highly publicized speech just weeks after Japan's surrender in which he expressed gratitude for Getulio Vargas's wartime support but made clear that the United States would be happy with an end to his veiled dictatorship.

Similarly, in late 1944 and early 1945 the U.S. ambassador to Rafael Trujillo's Dominican Republic sent several despatches criticizing the continuation of military aid to Latin American dictatorships. When the War Department replied that military-to-military relations encouraged democracy, Ambassador Ellis Briggs responded that "the connection between a United States military mission and the development of democratic principles in a given foreign country, would appear to be somewhat remote." Opposing Trujillo's attempt to purchase arms, Briggs argued that "Trujillo's dictatorship represents the negation of many of the principles to which the United States subscribes."[5] Secretary of State James Byrnes agreed, and the United States rejected Trujillo's requests for arms. When the Dominican dictator asked for an explanation, the State Department handed his ambassador in Washington a scathing aide-mémoire written by Spruille Braden and his new deputy, former Ambassador Briggs: "This Government has over the past years observed the situation in the Dominican Republic and has been unable to perceive that democratic principles have been observed there in theory or in practice."[6]

The Dominican Republic was an easy decision, however; Argentina proved to be much more difficult, for it was influential in Latin America and, after 1943, governed by a military dictatorship that Washington considered fascist. During the war Trujillo was no problem—indeed, he was helpful—and in his memoirs Hull's only complaint about wartime inter-American cooperation was that "we were incessantly plagued by the dangerous, devious course of the Argentine Government."[7] Although the secretary of state did not realize it, this was not a clash with fascism but rather a struggle over hemispheric leadership, and it had been developing for decades. In 1889 Argentina's delegates boycotted the opening session of the inaugural International Conference of American States; instead, they drove around Washington in an open carriage to publicize their opposition to the unilateral U.S. decision to make Secretary of State James G. Blaine the conference chair. They also refused to join the six-week trek around the country. Subsequently, Elihu Root did much to make the Argentines feel that they shared a leading role in the hemisphere, but the principal reason that the two nations sparred very little for the next decade or so was that they had almost nothing to do with one another.

Then in the 1920s and 1930s, the development of the Good Neighbor policy led to a new U.S. emphasis upon inter-American cooperation, much of it negotiated during hemisphere-wide conferences. By this time the United States and Argentina had structured their international relations so differently that a conflict was inevitable, even if hemispheric leadership had not been an issue. Argentina's economy was heavily dependent upon trading ties with Europe, for example, and as a result the country had developed an outward-looking orientation that contrasted sharply with the isolationist spirit dominating the interwar U.S. perspective on international relations. Thus, while the United States refused to join the League of Nations, Argentina became an enthusiastic participant, and Foreign Minister Carlos Saavedra Lamas had been president of the League of Nations during the period immediately before Cordell Hull (and briefly FDR) traveled to the 1936 Inter-American Conference for the Maintenance of Peace in Buenos Aires.

Heavily influenced by the traditional U.S. isolation from European politics, to which he now added a wariness of contemporary European instability (the Spanish civil war, the Italian takeover of Ethiopia, the German rearmament program), Cordell Hull asked the Buenos Aires conference to create a permanent Inter-American Consultative Committee to monitor threats to peace. Saavedra Lamas, whose prestige had just peaked by receipt of the Nobel Peace Prize, interpreted Hull's initiative as an effort to force the entire hemisphere to accept the "we-them" U.S. view of European relations, and he openly opposed it. As the conference proceeded, Hull reported that his discussions with Saavedra Lamas "became increasingly animated. Our last conference was heated, some sharp words were exchanged at least on my side, and we parted with no signs of complete agreement." As for the 1942 Rio meeting, Hull never forgave Argentina for frustrating Sumner Welles's efforts to achieve a unanimous break with the Axis, and from his hospital bed in Washington he told the U.S. delegates to the 1945 United Nations conference "that Argentina, before being admitted to the United Nations and hence to the San Francisco Conference, should make full apology for having deserted the cause of the American Republics." When this advice was ignored, Hull wrote that Argentina's admission to the United Nations was "the most colossal injury done to the Pan American movement in all its history."[8]

Although Argentina had few friends in Washington, no one had given the country much attention in the initial two years of the war, and the June 1943 military coup against a decrepit conservative government in Buenos Aires went almost unnoticed. Only after an Allied victory seemed assured did attention swing southward, triggered by a late-1943 military coup in neighboring Bolivia. From that moment forward, the diary of Assistant Secretary of State Adolf Berle began to refer regularly to Argentina's new military leaders: "The secret information we have makes it perfectly clear that [the Bolivian coup] was planned in Buenos Aires by the Buenos Aires military government in consultation with the Nazi intelligence people." A few days later Berle added that "the particular and putative Mussolini in the lot is Colonel Perón, who has been using money lavishly to foment disorder and who proposed to set up an Argentine-controlled Fascist bloc running as far North as Peru." The Argentines, he wrote, "are working hand in glove with the Germans."[9]

Pressured by the Allies, worried by rival Brazil's growing arsenal of U.S. arms, and now aware of the war's likely outcome, in early 1944 Argentina finally broke relations with the Axis powers, but within weeks a power struggle within the Argentine military led to the ouster of General Pedro Ramírez by General Edelmiro Farrell. Assuming that the coup had been prompted by Argentine fascists who were angry over the break with Germany, the Roosevelt administration refused to recognize the Farrell government. In July the United States publicly asserted that Argentina "has openly and notoriously been giving affirmative assistance to the declared enemies of the United Nations," and when Hull's poor health forced him to limit his activities (and then to resign immediately after the 1944 election), President Roosevelt told Undersecretary of State Edward Stettinius, "Ed, you make a face to the Argentineans once a week. You have to treat them like children."[10]

It was at this point that Washington's long-standing feud with Argentina, raised to the level of open animosity by the war, became confused with the U.S. policy of encouraging democracy. As the war ended, Adolf Berle wrote in his diary that "Perón means business. He is building up his army, has made an armed camp of the Chilean frontier and the salient between Rio Grande do Sul and Paraguay; is shooting for a total army of 400,000, of which he expects to get 200,000 ready as soon as possible; has completely fascised the life of the country; there is no tangible opposition in sight."[11] We know today that none of this was correct, and that the Argentines were aware that they could not prosper in the face of U.S. hostility. In late March 1945, a month after the Act of Chapultepec had made Argentina's membership in the United Nations contingent upon its acceptance of "complete solidarity and a common policy among the American States," the Farrell government accepted the inevitable and declared war on Japan and—very reluctantly—Germany, "in view of the fact that the latter is an ally of Japan."[12]

It was too late for this step to be interpreted as anything other than cynical opportunism, and Washington responded by upping the ante. Meeting with the ambassadors of twelve Latin American republics at Blair House on March 15, the United States asked the participants to stipulate that Argentina not only had to declare war but also had to root out fascists in Argentina. At first Argentina appeared to capitulate, but only until its seat had been secured in the United Nations. Then the Farrell government ended its anti-Axis campaign, and so the new Truman administration sent Ambassador Spruille Braden to reenergize the process.

After working for twenty years to enlarge the Montana and Chilean mining fortune that his father had initially accumulated, Braden had accepted an appointment as part of the U.S. delegation to the 1933 Montevideo conference, then stayed on as the U.S. delegate to the Chaco Peace conference. Bitten by the diplomatic bug and able to make generous campaign contributions, in 1938 Braden was named ambassador to Colombia; in 1941 he moved up to the embassy in Cuba. In both countries, but especially in Colombia, he distinguished himself as a proconsul, justifying his intervention with the need to ferret out fascist sympathizers.

Braden arrived in Buenos Aires in May, just as Germany was surrendering, and he soon concluded that the Farrell government never intended to alter its fascist tendencies. Using the most pejorative word in his generation's vocabulary, Braden took the position that "appeasement will be fatal and we must rigidly stand on our principles." Equating Vice President Perón's obvious popularity with the German public's displays of enthusiasm for Hitler, he argued that "if we appease now and allow situation to drift, we will either be faced for long time to come with a Fascist anti-U.S.A. Government under German tutelage and or eventually revolution." [13] And so Braden launched a public crusade to rid the country of its fascist leaders, a crusade that roughly coincided with Argentina's political campaign leading up to elections in February 1946. Since Perón was a candidate, Braden's strategy was to convince the electorate to deny Perón the presidency. Openly intervening in domestic politics, by September 1945 (when he returned to Washington to become assistant secretary of state) Braden rivaled Perón as the best-known person in Argentina. In the United States, *Time* magazine placed his face on its cover, with a background map of South America and an insect sprayer pointed at a dozen Nazi swastikas dotting Argentina.

John Moors Cabot remained behind as chargé in Buenos Aires. "If we are able to keep the local pot really boiling for some months to come," he cabled in early October, "I am fairly hopeful that there will be a break somewhere. Democratic forces are beginning to move forward, if very cautiously, on their own steam." It almost worked. In mid-October Perón was detained by his rivals within the Argentine military, igniting an absolutely furious internal struggle for power. But then, with Perón held prisoner on an island in the estuary, Argentina's blue-collar workers changed the course of their nation's history. Just after the *descamisados* poured across the Riacheulo and into the Plaza de Mayo, demanding that Perón be released, Cabot cabled: "Fascist nature of Perón regime again emphasized by yesterday's events. Manifestations showed excellent organization of hoodlums on Fascist lines like Brown Shirts and Black Shirts. Events again indicate that Perón plans a proletarian, totalitarian dictatorship with army and police support." [14]

However disappointed he may have been when the October 17 demonstration restored Perón's power, Cabot was also an experienced career diplomat, and he recognized that a policy of hostility was now doomed to fail. Since Braden would never accept accommodation, Cabot began to work on the deputy assistant secretary, Ellis Briggs, another career diplomat and a New Deal progressive. The problem with Braden's approach, Cabot wrote, was that the anti-Peronists were profoundly unpopular: "It was they who were largely responsible, by their reactionary policies, for the present mess here." Moreover, Perón's opponents were no friends of the United States: "It was they in many instances who were fractious regarding Pan-Americanism, if not downright anti-American." The opposition was also hopelessly divided into micro factions, which simply reflected "the inherently unruly nature of Argentines (I wish you could drive a few hundred yards down a Buenos Aires street and you would understand what I mean)." Given this situation, and aware that Perón would use continued U.S. opposition to generate electoral support among Argentine nationalists, Cabot suggested moderation; "we should not carry our crack-down policy to such extremes that it becomes *contraproducente*."[15]

In the back of Cabot's mind was a mid-August cable from Washington instructing the embassy to develop a "well documented factual presentation" to convince other Latin American governments of Argentina's failure to stamp out Nazi influence. Cabot tried to convince Washington that such a presentation was not necessary, arguing first that the Farrell-Perón government had made "great progress" in suppressing Argentina's fascists. When that did not work, he warned Washington that "any publication after January 1 is certain to be pounced on by Perón clique as clumsy effort to influence election." Then when Cabot learned that Braden was going ahead with the publication of an accusatory document, he warned that inaccurate charges against Perón "may unfavorably sway wide sector of Argentine public opinion which is actually or potentially opposed [to] Perón but which objects to what it considers our constant picking on Argentina."[16]

Flush with a postwar sense of omnipotence, the Nazi-hunters in the Department of State seemed immune to Cabot's argument. For years they had been identifying subversives in Latin America—when the dean of Columbia University's school of journalism took a trip to South America in 1942, he was impressed to see that "throughout Brazil and Argentine the United States has F.B.I. and other governmental intelligence officers running down Axis agents."[17] A classified history of Latin American wartime cooperation described this Nazi hunt: "in order to eliminate this internal threat, a program of rounding up, deporting and interning the chief figures in the Axis organizations was instituted by the American republics. From one country as many as 2000 Axis espionage and sabotage agents were deported to the United States for internment because of lack of facilities in the country involved. Others set up their own internment camps for key figures and removed Axis nationals from the vicinity of vital installations." [18] To this day, no one can say whether these measures were needed, just as no one can say for certain whether the Japanese-Americans interred in the United States would have committed treason against their adopted country if they had been left free. But these difficult questions were not asked; the nation was at war, and U.S. officials would rather be safe than sorry. Thus the United States continually added names to the Proclaimed List, demanded that their property be seized, and insisted that they be arrested—about 8,500 Latin Americans in sixteen nations, 3,000 of whom were deported to the United States for internment.

In several cases, these lists of alleged Axis sympathizers were incorporated into a formal document that was given to the local government for action—as Ambassador George Messersmith reminded Assistant Secretary of State Rockefeller near the end of the war, "our people collaborated very closely with the Mexican authorities in giving information concerning dangerous enemy aliens. Usually when we gave such information the man was picked up and sent to a prison or detention camp or the other appropriate measures were taken." After the 1943 Bolivian military coup, when the alleged fascists controlled the government, the State Department instead distributed its document, "Fascist Connections of the New Bolivian Regime," to all the other Latin American governments. Similarly, Adolf Berle took a document listing Argentine Nazis to the 1945 Chapultepec conference, just in case Latin American governments were to suggest that Argentina be invited to participate. [19] Berle's document served as the first draft of Spruille Braden's Blue Book (so named because of the color of its cover), which was delivered to the press and to Latin American governments on February 11, 1946, two weeks before the Argentine election. The gist of the lengthy memorandum was that "the totalitarian machine in Argentina is a partnership of German Nazi interests with a powerful coalition of active Argentine totalitarian elements, both military and civilian." [20]

No one would deny that Argentine society contained fascist elements, nor that postwar Argentina served as a clandestine refuge for Nazi war criminals, but to characterize the Farrell-Perón government in 1946 as "a partnership of German Nazi interests with a powerful coalition of active

Argentine totalitarian elements" is so wildly inaccurate as to be irresponsible. Such an accusation ignores the overwhelming evidence that Peronism was a domestic Argentine phenomenon, representing the political mobilization of Argentina's previously peripheralized urban working class. This mobilization was based, in turn, upon structural changes in Argentina's agro-exporting economy.[21] Peronism's principal relationship to European fascism was in its timing; the former appeared after the latter had been established, and officials such as Spruille Braden mistakenly identified co-variation with causality.

Latin American reaction to the Blue Book was mixed. The U.S. ambassador in Peru reported that no one wanted to challenge the United States, but "their non-committal answers and the general impression given, however, are that publication of Blue Book was a mistake, ill-timed, and if anything may have done more harm than good." Similarly, the U.S. ambassador in Chile cabled that "commercial and Govt supporting press has published editorials seriously questioning ethics of such a publication," while Washington's best South American ally, Brazil, replied diplomatically that it "does not feel at liberty to enter into an analysis of the elements which are going to comprise the new Argentine Government." On the other hand, Nicaragua's ambassador in Washington told the State Department that "President Somoza, who reads English well, had read the book with a great deal of care and was tremendously impressed with its contents. He characterized the Book as brilliant and wished to inform Mr. Braden that he and his Government were in entire accord with its conclusions and that Mr. Braden could rely on Nicaraguan support."[22]

The Blue Book's principal audience was intended to be the Argentine electorate, and here the reaction was overwhelmingly unfavorable. Perón did not need his political genius to recognize an extraordinary opportunity, and he seized upon it by publishing the "Blue and White Book" (Argentina's national colors) as a rebuttal, and by plastering the country's walls with a new campaign slogan: "Braden or Perón." Included among the undecided Argentine voters whom this interference swung to Perón was Admiral Aníbal Olivieri, who would become Minister of the Navy. Braden, he said, "damaged my sensibilities just as he would have damaged those of the North Americans, the Indonesians, or the French if a foreigner took similar liberties against the rights and respect that free people deserve. I decided to support Colonel Perón. I would have supported any Argentine who adopted the position Perón did. If the other presidential candidates also would have rejected that interference, perhaps fate would have maintained me aloof from the open struggle, but he was the only one who did." One of Perón's most prominent opponents agreed, telling former President Herbert Hoover that "he resented the Blue Book as an attack on the Argentine people." And so, in a contest that Cabot characterized as the "cleanest in Argentine history," the electorate chose Perón.[23]

It was now apparent to almost everyone that the Hull-Braden approach to Argentina had failed, and Chargé Cabot vigorously urged a reconsideration of U.S. policy. "I must reiterate what I have mentioned in my telegrams: that the atmosphere has decidedly changed since Spruille left; that most Argentines do not like our attitude, and that the more we talk about it the less they are going to like it."[24] Braden's response was to have Cabot shipped off to Yugoslavia.

But by then Braden was out of step with the thinking of nearly all his colleagues in the State Department, and President Truman was himself growing impatient with an approach that placed the United States in the untenable position of opposing the obvious will of the Argentine electorate. In June 1946 he asked former President Herbert Hoover to serve as honorary chair of the Famine Emergency Committee, which was seeking donations of food for war-devastated Europe. At a White House meeting, the former President told Truman that he wanted to seek Argentina's cooperation, prompting Agriculture Secretary Clinton Anderson to interrupt with the observation that "the State Department will protest against Mr. Hoover's going." Truman replied, "We won't give them a chance, I will announce it at once."[25] And so Hoover went to Argentina and secured Perón's cooperation. In their meeting, Perón mentioned that Argentina's gold was still frozen in the United States and that Argentine firms remained on the Proclaimed List a year after the war's end. Hoover reported this situation to Truman, who immediately ordered the removal of all wartime restraints on relations with Argentina. By mid-1947 Braden had been eased into retirement, relations with Argentina had been normalized, and the battle against fascism was finally over. Braden had seen what was looming on the horizon, however, for just after Argentina's 1946 election, he reported that "the Commies are now actively climbing on the Perón bandwagon."[26]

If Braden and his State Department colleagues could not convince the Argentines to accept their vision of democracy, perhaps they could be more successful in Nicaragua, where antigovernment demonstrations in mid-

1944 had already prompted Anastasio Somoza to announce that he would not seek reelection when his term expired in 1947. In mid-1945 Ambassador William Warren reported that Somoza had mentioned that "he wanted me and the State Department to be thinking with him regarding a proper person to receive the nomination. He emphasized that the person selected must be one who would look out for the interests of the United States and Nicaragua." Secretary of State Byrnes immediately declined Somoza's offer. At almost the same time, one of Somoza's principal opponents asked the Department of State to recommission Harold Dodds (now president of Princeton University) to revise once again Nicaragua's electoral code. The Department replied that Nicaragua was free to contract for Dodds's services, but it declined to act as an intermediary.[27]

This hands-off approach was sorely tested by Somoza's continual requests for U.S. military assistance. A master at packaging his needs to serve U.S. interests, this time Somoza misread U.S. opinion, for in a personal note to FDR in late 1944 he argued that Nicaragua's *Guardia Nacional* needed arms because it was the only force capable of holding off Mexico's imperial ambition: "This purpose of Mexico, which does not hide its repugnance for the United States, has encountered and will continue to encounter my opposition and that of Nicaragua, [which has] become a stronghold for the closest collaboration and friendship with your nation on the worthy basis of Good Neighborship. Nicaragua is likewise a stronghold and breakwater against the communism which diligently seeks to infiltrate into Central America as an aspect of Mexican policy."[28]

What Somoza failed to recognize was that U.S.-Mexican relations were more cordial than at any time since 1910, and that communism was not yet a credible threat; indeed, when Somoza wrote his note, the United States was actively involved in helping the Soviet Union to establish diplomatic ties with Latin American governments—in March 1945 Undersecretary of State Joseph Grew even lent his home to Soviet Ambassador Gromyko so that he could meet informally with Brazilian officials.[29] Since the State Department took seriously neither the anti-Mexico nor the anticommunist part of Somoza's argument, when Nicaragua's ambassador called on the State Department to warn that Somoza's decision not to be a candidate might encourage "leftist elements" to run for office, Assistant Secretary Braden told him "that we believe that the best way to practice democracy was to practice it and that sometimes the way was hard. If leftist or anti-American elements should become active, well, that was only a part of the difficult progress toward the democratic goal."[30]

On the other hand, Somoza's requests for military aid fell within the general U.S. policy of helping U.S. manufacturers. As Secretary of War Stimson commented about the disposal of surplus aircraft in late 1944, military aid "seemed wise and helpful and it would tend to cultivate good relations with the South Americans which might prove very profitable to our aviation industry in the future." Nonetheless, when the U.S. military proposed to boost arms exports in late 1946, Assistant Secretary Braden argued that the sales would "perpetuate the grip of reactionary military groups" and "impose a heavy burden for unproductive purposes on the weak economies of Latin America, thus retarding social progress." This was also the view of Undersecretary of State Dean Acheson.[31]

In the case of Nicaragua, the U.S. embassy in Managua tended to side with those favoring military aid. Ambassador Warren argued that some reward was required for Nicaragua's rock-solid support during the war; he noted that Somoza "has been upset and his feelings hurt [by] his failure to receive the few rifles and small amount of ammunition which he had been trying to get, as he said, for two years." But the envoy was aware of the use to which these weapons would be put, and as a compromise he suggested delaying delivery of any substantial military aid such as aircraft: "Nicaraguan Govt is already experimenting with mounting machine guns on BT-13's. Any planes we supply Nicaragua at this time will be considered by a good proportion of the populace (perhaps an overwhelming majority) as aid given to present govt to suppress its own people."[32]

With the understanding that Nicaragua was preparing for a democratic election, the administration provided Somoza with most of the weapons that he requested. Then in March 1947, just days after Nicaragua's voters had selected Somoza's successor, President Truman paid a brief visit to Mexico, where he went out of his way to underscore the U.S. commitment to nonintervention, continuing a twenty-year effort to dispel Mexicans' fears of U.S. imperial ambition.[33] Somoza apparently interpreted Truman's reassurance to mean that he, too, had no reason to fear intervention, for exactly twenty-seven days after the inauguration of his successor, Somoza ordered his National Guard to overthrow the new government. Disgusted, the United States joined in the effort to exclude Nicaragua from the 1947 Rio conference, and it waited nearly a year before sending a new ambassador to Managua.

This was a discouraging moment for the fledgling U.S. policy of promoting democracy in Latin America, and as State Department officials licked their wounds over Argentina and Nicaragua, they came to believe that the

United States had been trying to accomplish the impossible. This belief was captured best by the Foreign Service Officer who had helped to midwife democracy in Nicaragua from 1929 to 1933, and later served as a Cold War ambassador in Latin America: "I knew that Tacho was *mañoso;* that he was on the clever, even cunning, side. But let us be frank: in Nicaragua's society a degree of *maña* might be a requisite to survival. Nicaraguans were not Groton graduates." This analysis was equally true of Argentina, where President Truman's ambassador wrote that "the Argentinos were far from ready in their present stage of development to understand and practice true democracy with all its attendant freedoms as we have it in the United States." [34]

This explanation for the failure of democracy in Nicaragua and Argentina reflected a type of thinking that heavily influenced the foreign policy process in the 1940s. Although the use of culture to explain political behavior (in this case, the persistence of dictatorships) was nothing new to the Department of State, in the mid-1930s its officials had begun to systematize their thinking by identifying the basic "national character" of countries around the world, following the guidelines laid out in Ruth Benedict's seminal *Patterns of Culture,* published in 1934. This effort was dramatically expanded when a number of anthropologists were pressed into government service during World War II—an exciting time, wrote Margaret Mead, when academics became activists, and "attention was focused on the need to understand and predict the behavior of a nation's enemies, its allies, and its own population, and their responses to bombing, to food scarcity, to wars of nerves, to invasion, to occupation." [35] Wartime needs motivated several of the classics of cultural anthropology, including Ruth Benedict's *The Chrysanthemum and the Sword: Patterns of Japanese Culture* (1946), Richard Brickner's *Is Germany Incurable?* (1943), and Margaret Mead's *And Keep Your Powder Dry* (1943).

By the late 1940s virtually every U.S. embassy in Latin America had produced something that resembled an analysis of the host nation's national character. Two reports from Cuba are illustrative. The more rudimentary of the two, mistitled "A Study of Cuban-American Relations," was the work of the embassy's second secretary, H. Bartlett Wells. His analysis began with a description of Cuba's "state of social ferment and license." This "organized indiscipline has become, for historical reasons the force of which his not yet passed off, a fetish of Cuban public life . . . It would perhaps be safe to say that no Cuban is guided by any system of restraints in his political, social, or perhaps even commercial conduct." Wells never identified the source of this "organized indiscipline," but he believed that it was a permanent feature of Cuban life: "This is a condition which is not curable save through the development of a sound and general social character as the result of a prolonged period of internal peace, fairly well sustained prosperity, and absence of irritation. All these things seem too much to hope for."[36]

A second, more-elaborate analysis, "Component Elements of Cuban Temperament," was produced in 1948 by James Cortada, who ran an import business in Havana before joining the embassy as an economic officer in 1942 and, like Wells, stayed on to fill a succession of State Department posts in a three-decade career. Cortada agreed that social ferment and license were Cuba's collective problem (his term for it was "the Cuban spirit of indiscipline"); but unlike Wells, who focused on the problem's effects, Cortada first examined the broadly shared personality traits—the national character—that produced the problem. Vanity, he reported, was the key that unlocked the Cuban mystery: "Although vanity is a prevailing characteristic of all Latin Americans," he wrote, "in the Cubans it has a special significance. Properly understood, this trait contains to some degree the keynote to Cuban temperament. The magnified sense of honor of the Spaniards has degenerated in Cuba into excessive and ridiculous vanity. This trait contributes to the uncompromising attitudes of the Cubans in certain economic and political matters. Vanity is at the root of the Cuban spirit of indiscipline and is responsible for the ludicrous actions followed by some of their public figures merely for the purpose of attracting attention."

Then Cortada offered a catalogue of the behavioral manifestations of Cuban vanity:

"Cubans are prone to be extremely nervous, which, coupled with a tendency to stomach and liver disorders, frequently make them short-tempered and excitable."

"In contrast with their national record of poor attainment, Cubans individually give the impression of an alert people. This may be attributed to a marked Cuban tendency to bluffing."

"Cubans laugh at everything, not with mature skepticism but with the lightheartedness of escapism."

"They are extremely open-handed with money and usually live beyond their means. This spirit of prodigality overflows to public finance and administrative expenses invariably exceed income."

"Cubans are friendlier and less formal than most other Latin Americans but they have traits accentuated to a greater or lesser degree which are common to all—such as vanity, use of indirection, personal courage, music consciousness, indiscipline and nervousness."

Some groups within Cuban society received special mention. Cuban women "lavish an exaggerated amount of tenderness on their children, utterly spoiling them from early babyhood and thus providing a basis for their future lack of discipline." The typical Cuban peasant "has little ambition or drive but in spite of his wretchedness is fairly content with his lot and resists change," whereas the "intellectual habits of [the middle class], such as reading, are as trivial as those of the upper classes; reading, for example, is confined, generally, only to newspapers and magazines."[37]

Neither Wells nor Cortada was an important policy-maker, but they represented a type of thinking that appears to have been shared by many of the senior officials responsible for making United States policy toward Latin America at the end of World War II. George Kennan was the single senior official of this era to prepare a fairly elaborate character-based explanation of Latin American behavior, and he did so only because he had been deprived of the opportunity to work on policy issues. Having lost the confidence of Secretary of State Dean Acheson, in 1950 Kennan had already resigned as State Department Counselor when he received an invitation to address a gathering of U.S. ambassadors in Rio de Janeiro. He took advantage of the invitation to convert his first trip to Latin America into an extended tour of the continent.

He did not enjoy the trip. Mexico City's "nocturnal activity struck me as disturbed, sultry, and menacing," he wrote. Caracas "appalled me with its screaming, honking traffic jams, its incredibly high prices, its feverish economy debauched by oil money"; Rio "was repulsive to me with its noisy, wildly competitive traffic"; Buenos Aires had "a curious sense of mingled apprehension and melancholy"; and in Lima "I was depressed by the reflection that it had not rained in the place for twenty-nine years, and by the thought that some of the dirt had presumably been there, untouched, for all that time." Adopting the Freudian idiom popular at the time, Kennan reported that in Latin America the "subconscious recognition of the failure of group effort finds its expression in an exaggerated self-centeredness and egotism—in a pathetic urge to create the illusion of desperate courage, supreme cleverness, and a limitless virility where the more constructive virtues are so conspicuously lacking." Kennan's conclusion, like that of John Quincy Adams, was overwhelmingly pessimistic: "it seems unlikely that there could be any other region of the earth in which nature and human behavior could have combined to produce a more unhappy and hopeless background for the conduct of human life than in Latin America."[38] This conclusion explained the failure of democracy to establish roots in the region, and, ominously, it hinted at the danger that lay ahead.

Chapter 17 ～

Combatting Communism
with Friendly Dictators

You have to pat them a little bit and make them think you are fond of them.

～ *Secretary of State John Foster Dulles, 1953*

A month after FDR's death, Secretary of War Henry Stimson gave President Harry Truman a sobering warning: the war in Europe was over, the end was in sight in the Pacific, but the administration's advisors "all agree as to the probability of pestilence and famine in central Europe next winter. This is likely to be followed by political revolution and Communistic infiltration."[1] Two years later Stimson's prediction was coming true, with European recovery stalled and Soviet expansion ever more threatening, and so in March 1947 the President went to Capitol Hill to request aid to combat communist insurgencies in Greece and Turkey. Evoking the experience of Weimar Germany, Truman asserted that "the seeds of totalitarian regimes are nurtured by misery and want. They spread and grow in the evil soil of poverty and strife. They reach their full growth when the hope of a people for a better life has died. We must keep that hope alive."[2]

This message was not meant for Latin America—at least not yet. Later that same year when the United States and its Latin American neighbors met in Rio de Janeiro to sign the Inter-American Treaty of Reciprocal Assistance, President Truman underscored his interest by attending the closing ceremonies, but his speech profoundly disappointed the conference delegates. Earlier, at the 1945 Mexico City conference, the United States had rejected Latin America's requests for aid, but Truman's European recovery plan had raised hopes anew; he dashed them in Rio. Latin America would not be included in the recently announced Marshall Plan because "the problems of countries in this hemisphere are different in nature and cannot be relieved by the same means and the same approaches which are in contemplation for Europe." Whereas Europe would receive U.S. government aid, "a much greater role falls to private citizens and groups" in Latin America.[3] In 1948 Secretary of State George Marshall bluntly repeated this message in his address to the Ninth International Conference of American States in Bogotá.

> We must face reality. Allow me to talk to you frankly regarding the tremendous problems the United States is facing. After four years of supreme effort and a million casualties, we had looked forward to a state of tranquillity which would permit us to reorganize our economy, having made vast expenditures in natural resources and money. Instead, my people find themselves faced with the urgent necessity of meeting staggering and inescapable responsibilities—humanitarian, political, and financial—all over the world, in western Europe, in Germany and Austria, in Greece and Turkey, in the Middle East, in China, Japan and Korea.

Marshall said that the money for Latin America's economic development must come from private sources.[4]

Latin Americans may not have liked what they heard at Rio and Bogotá, but U.S. officials hoped that they would understand that Europe needed the Marshall Plan not simply because Europe had been destroyed by the war but also because it had become the site of the confrontation between communism and capitalism, between totalitarianism and democracy. Europe was only the first target of communism, as President Truman's National Security Council noted: "the ultimate objective of Soviet-directed world communism is the domination of the world."[5] The U.S. response to this aggressive behavior came to be known as containment, because that was what the State Department's principal Sovietologist, George Kennan, called it: "Soviet pressure against the free institutions of the western world is something that can be contained by the adroit and vigilant application of counter-force at a series of constantly shifting geographic and political points."[6]

Far from the Soviet Union's borders, Latin America was not yet threatened, and so it did not require much attention. Just before the 1948 Bogotá conference, the State Department's Policy Planning Staff concluded "that Communism in the Americas is a potential danger, but that, with a few possible exceptions, it is not seriously dangerous at the present time." This analysis was shared by the Republican secretary-in-waiting, John Foster Dulles, who agreed that the Kremlin was not yet ready to expand into Latin American countries, but cautioned that "many of their workers—industrial and agricultural—do not enjoy good standards of living. This offers opportunity for communistic propaganda." The State Department also hedged its 1948 analysis by warning that "these assessments of Communist capability may require revision if Communist domination spreads further in Europe, particularly to Italy and France. There are large colonies of Italian immigrants in several of the American Republics in which the Communists may succeed in gaining increased influence which might constitute an important accretion to Communist strength. The influence of French culture and ideas always has been strong in the American Republics, and every effort would be made through a Communist-dominated France to make full use of this advantage."[7]

So it was that the Red Scare first came to Latin America not because of obvious communist subversion, but because of what was occurring in Europe and as a product of the paramount issue of domestic U.S. politics, anticommunism. In February 1950 Senator Joseph McCarthy pulled a piece of paper out of his coat pocket and told a Republican gathering in Wheeling, West Virginia, that the Democratic State Department "is thoroughly infested with Communists. I have in my hand 57 cases of individuals who would appear to be either card carrying members or certainly loyal to the Communist Party, but who nevertheless are still helping to shape our foreign policy." The Iron Curtain had closed off Central Europe, the State Department had lost China, and the rising Red tide threatened to sweep aside all opposition. "Today," McCarthy told his listeners, "we are engaged in a final, all-out battle between communistic atheism, and Christianity. The modern champions of communism have selected this as the time. And, ladies and gentlemen, the chips are down—they are truly down."[8] Joseph McCarthy's four-year inquisition was under way.

An intimidating anticommunism had already been tightening its grip on the federal government, especially the Department of State. In March 1947, the same month that Truman requested aid for Greece and Turkey, he also created the federal government's Loyalty Program, and by the time McCarthy gave his West Virginia speech, the State Department's Security Division had a staff of 184, including 74 trained investigators working on two "channels," the Loyalty Channel (for "anyone who indicates that he places the interest of another country or another government above his own") and the Security Channel (for anyone who "associates with known subversives" or "whose behavior places him in a position wherein he might yield to blackmail").[9] The Alger Hiss prosecution was especially devastating, and it managed to reach far enough into the State Department to destroy the career of one of the Department's rising Latin Americanists, Laurence Duggan, who committed suicide in late 1948.[10] For Duggan's surviving colleagues, extreme caution and militant anticommunism became the twin lodestones of the Cold War Foreign Service.

"Bolshevism" had long been used as an epithet in discussions of United States policy toward Latin America. Years earlier, when Secretary of State Kellogg went before the Senate Foreign Relations Committee to defend the Coolidge administration's policy toward Nicaragua, he left the senators with a lengthy memo, "Bolshevik Aims and Policies in Mexico and Latin America," the principal purpose of which was to discredit the administration's U.S.-based opposition by tarring it with the label of "communist."[11] Kellogg's analysis referred only to Mexican communists and their U.S. supporters, however, not to an international ideological movement, and it largely dropped from view when the State Department's interest in Latin America receded with the onset of the Depression. After that, antifascism necessarily preempted anticommunism in United States policy toward Latin America.

This situation changed quickly after the Axis surrender in mid-1945. In February 1946 George Kennan sent his Long Telegram from Moscow, eleven days later Churchill gave his Iron Curtain speech, and from that moment forward the containment of communism became the focus of United States policy toward Latin America, not because it was a major concern of senior officials in Washington, but because U.S. envoys in Latin America began to file reports attuned to the times. "The Soviets will quite cynically exploit any advantage they can get," wrote Brazil-based Adolf Berle the day before Kennan's telegram. "Horribly, cynically, and terribly, the Soviet policy is approximating the German policy: exploit any center of thought or action which may make trouble either for Britain or for the United States." Berle's specific concern was an inoffensive Soviet trade mission to Argentina (the Soviets needed food), but that fear quickly spread, and by 1950 Assistant Secretary of State Edward Miller was telling audiences that "the basic situation in the hemisphere today is this. The 21 American states together face the challenge of Communist political aggression against the hemisphere."[12]

Thus anticommunism had indelibly colored the content of U.S.–Latin American relations before the Republicans launched their 1952 presidential campaign, but their platform set the tone for the balance of the decade. It asserted that the Democrats "work unceasingly to achieve their goal of national socialism," that they "disrupt internal tranquillity by fostering class strife," and that they "have shielded traitors to the Nation in high places"—and this was only the Preamble. In the platform's section on foreign policy, the Democrats were said to have "traded our overwhelming victory for a new enemy and for new oppressions and new wars which were quick to come." And, of course, they had lost China. The Republicans promised not simply to "sever from the public payroll the hordes of loafers, incompetents and unnecessary employees who clutter the administration of our foreign affairs," but also to end "the negative, futile and immoral policy of 'containment' which abandons countless human beings to a despotism and godless terrorism."

The only specific Republican complaint about the Democrats' handling of inter-American relations was that "the people of the other American Republics are resentful of our neglect," and their one-sentence alternative was a vague promise that "our ties with the sister Republics of the Americas will be strengthened."[13] True to this pledge, immediately after his inauguration, Dwight Eisenhower called Secretary of State Dulles to discuss sending the President's widely respected brother on a fact-finding tour of the region. The notes from that telephone conversation indicate that Dulles approved: "The Secretary said he thought that was a very good way of doing things—in South America that was the way they should be done. The Secretary said that you have to pat them a little bit and make them think you are fond of them."[14]

Milton Eisenhower's subsequent report emphasized both the explosive demand for economic development and the danger posed by communist subversion. On economic development, Eisenhower wrote, "they want greater production and higher standards of living, and they want them *now*"—and, he added, they want the United States to help, just as it had been helping Europe with the Marshall Plan. On communist subversion, Eisenhower warned that "the possible conquest of a Latin American nation today would not be, so far as anyone can foresee, by direct assault. It would come, rather, through the insidious process of infiltration, conspiracy, spreading of lies, and the undermining of free institutions, one by one. Highly disciplined groups of Communists are busy, night and day, illegally or openly, in the American republics, as they are in every nation in the world." Already, the President's brother added, "one American nation has succumbed to communist infiltration."[15] He was referring to Guatemala.

By the end of World War II, the Boston-based United Fruit Company owned 566,000 acres of land and employed 15,000 people in Guatemala, making it both the largest landowner and the largest employer in the country. Its subsidiary, International Railways of Central America, employed another 5,000 people and owned 690 of Guatemala's 719 miles of track, making it the nation's second-largest employer. Much of this property was acquired during the dictatorship of Jorge Ubico, who used intimidation to maintain himself in power. In 1935, for example, he circumvented the constitutional ban on reelection by holding a plebiscite in which voters were asked whether they wished to suspend the constitutional provision barring reelection so that Ubico could continue as President—and were told to sign their names at the bottom of their ballots. The vote was 834,168 in favor and 1,227 opposed.[16]

Although Ubico cooperated extensively with the United States during the war—his most important contribution was to permit the FBI to destroy Guatemala's German immigrant colony—he could not withstand the pressures that were building for an end to despotism, and in mid-1944 he was ousted by the Guatemalan military. The "October Revolution" followed, and Juan José Arévalo, a professor, was elected president. A decade of reform began. United Fruit's control over its employees was threatened first by the establishment of nation's first labor unions, then by the creation of a national labor confederation, and finally by a new Labor Code. The company's control over land was threatened first by agrarian reform legislation and then in early 1953, just a month after President Eisenhower's inauguration, by the Guatemalan government's expropriation of about 40 percent of United Fruit's land. United Fruit asked the U.S. government for help.

The relationship between United Fruit and the Eisenhower administration is perhaps the best example of corporate influence on U.S. foreign policy. The list of overlapping interests is so long that it is difficult to identify anyone who made or directly influenced U.S. policy toward Guatemala in the early 1950s who did not also have a direct tie to United Fruit. But while it is true that the president of United Fruit, Thomas Dudley Cabot, was the brother of Eisenhower's first assistant secretary of state for Latin America, John Moors Cabot; while it is also true that Secretary of

State John Foster Dulles had for years been intimately connected to United Fruit's management as the executive partner of the law firm of Sullivan and Cromwell; while it is true that CIA Director Allen Dulles, another Sullivan and Cromwell attorney, had been billing United Fruit since the 1930s for his visits to Guatemala; and while it is true that Ann Whitman, President Eisenhower's personal secretary, was married to Ed Whitman, United Fruit's principal lobbyist—the real problem was the perception of communism. As John Foster Dulles told a news conference in mid-1954, "if the United Fruit matter were settled, if they gave a gold piece for every banana, the problem would remain just as it is today as far as the presence of communist infiltration in Guatemala is concerned. That is the problem, not United Fruit."[17]

It is possible that Dulles was being disingenuous, just as it is possible that United Fruit had fooled him and others into believing that Guatemala's government was communist. We can never know for certain. What is certain, however, is that the specter of communism in Guatemala had been raised in the State Department long before John Foster Dulles became Secretary of State or his brother Allen became CIA Director—and probably before United Fruit began its lobbying effort, although that is not quite clear. The record indicates that the Department of State was not concerned about communism immediately after the October 1944 revolution,[18] but that view changed quickly. Attuned to the new anticommunist orthodoxy, in October 1947 (six months after the initiation of Truman's Loyalty Program) the Department of State requested a report on the Guatemalan government's political leanings. The U.S. embassy in Guatemala City responded with a 28-page memo, "Communism in Guatemala," which included an appendix listing no fewer than 135 earlier despatches "on the general subject of communism in Guatemala." This report, like others, focused on subversion, not on the problems of United Fruit: "Communist penetration made startling progress during the immediate post-revolutionary period (1944–47), as evidenced by the radical nature of social, labor and economic reforms, accompanied by strong overtones of class warfare. Infiltration of indoctrinated communists, fellow-travelers, and Marxist ideas unquestionably reached dangerous proportions." The embassy reported that "a suspiciously large portion of the reforms advanced by the present revolutionary Government seem motivated in part by a calculated effort to further class warfare," and that Arévalo "is surrounded by many known communists who occupy positions of importance within his immediate Presidential office."[19]

Thereafter, increasingly worrisome reports began to flow from the U.S. embassy in Guatemala to the Department of State, and by early 1949 the embassy's first secretary was reporting that even the nation's literacy program was an indoctrination program—"at the same time these backward Indians get their A.B.C.'s, they get a shot of communism."[20] A month before the 1952 U.S. election, Adolf Berle, now an influential private citizen, wrote in his diary about a meeting with a Central American political leader: "I told him that in my view the Communist government of Guatemala was a clear-cut intervention by a foreign power, in this case the Soviet Union." Seeking to alert both Presidential candidates to the danger, Berle added, "I am arranging to see Nelson Rockefeller, who knows the situation and can work a little with General Eisenhower on it; I will endeavor to do the same thing with Stevenson."[21]

By this time Congress had picked up the communist scent in Central America. A few months after McCarthy's West Virginia speech, Senator Alexander Wiley asked the chair of a Senate subcommittee on Latin America to hold a hearing on Guatemala as soon as possible: "Guatemala is going to be a source of Red infection throughout Central America and the sooner we help sterilze [*sic*] that source, the better." Not long thereafter, North Carolina's Monroe Redden told his House colleagues that Guatemala was "the Communist haven of the Western Hemisphere." Thus Adolf Berle found a hospitable audience when, just days after Eisenhower's inauguration, he told a House committee that "Guatemala presents a genuine penetration of Central America by Kremlin Communism." Then he outlined the possible U.S. responses, ruling out armed intervention "except as an extremely bad last resort," and arguing instead for what would become the U.S. response to leftist revolutionary governments in both Cuba in the early 1960s and Nicaragua in the 1980s: "organizing a counter-movement, capable of using force if necessary, based in a cooperative neighboring republic."[22]

The new Republican administration did not need this Democratic advice. At his confirmation hearing John Foster Dulles compared Latin America in the 1950s with China in the 1930s, and argued that "the time to deal with this rising menace in South America is now."[23] "The current political situation in Guatemala is adverse to US interests," read the first sentence of the new administration's National Intelligence Estimate in May 1953, and almost immediately the reports from the U.S. embassy in Guatemala City took on an added sense of desperation, as did the interoffice memoranda in Washington. The officer in charge of Central America wrote Assistant Secretary Cabot that "the trend toward increased communist strength is uninterrupted. A gigantic May Day celebration was used as a Commie display of strength."[24]

From the beginning, the Eisenhower administration was determined to overthrow the government of Arévalo's successor because, as the new U.S. ambassador reported after his first interview with Jacobo Arbenz, "if the President is not a Communist he will certainly do until one comes along."[25] The administration first assigned the CIA responsibility for organizing, arming, and training the Arbenz government's military opposition in Honduras. This force was nearly ready for action by the time of the March 1954 meeting of foreign ministers in Caracas, which capped the second part of the U.S. effort, a diplomatic offensive. Telling the delegates that "there is not a single country in this hemisphere which has not been penetrated by the apparatus of international communism acting under orders from Moscow," Secretary Dulles introduced a resolution calling for a "Declaration of Solidarity for the Preservation of the Political Integrity of the American States Against the Intervention of International Communism." Interpreted as a thinly veiled attack on Guatemala, Dulles's resolution was applauded by some Latin American governments and resisted by others, but in the end, only Guatemala voted against it, and only Argentina and Mexico abstained. The State Department was not deluded by the victory, however; an internal memorandum noted that "the 17 votes for our anti-Communist resolution at Caracas were granted only after the resolution had been watered down to the point of saying virtually nothing, and then grudgingly. The speeches indicated that there was more fear of U.S. interventionism than of Guatemalan communism. The pressures we brought to bear were resented."[26]

After the Caracas meeting, the Eisenhower administration seemed determined to brook no opposition. When a prominent U.S. journalist questioned the charges of communist adventurism, the National Security Council strategized about how to stop his newspaper articles, with the minutes of one NSC meeting indicating that Secretary Dulles

> expressed very great concern about the Communist line being followed by Sydney Gruson in his dispatches to the *New York Times*. Gruson, thought Secretary Dulles, was a very dangerous character, and his reporting had done a great deal of harm. The President said that he often felt that the *New York Times* was the most untrustworthy

newspaper in the United States, at least as far as the areas of the news with which he was personally familiar were concerned. Mr. Allen Dulles pointed out some very disturbing features of Sidney [*sic*] Gruson's career to date. The Attorney General asked if it would not be a good idea for someone to talk informally to the management of the *New York Times.*

The President "thought it a good idea."[27] Since the Eisenhower administration was willing to consider such tactics to quiet its domestic opposition, it certainly would not balk at misleading its Latin American neighbors. When it appeared that many delegates to the Caracas meeting knew about the CIA's Honduras-based armed forces, the Department of State issued a public denial that was an outright lie: "The United States believes that the principle of non-intervention is an absolute principle and that we should avoid anything which could be interpreted to indicate that we would compromise it under any conditions."[28]

By this time, U.S. policy toward Guatemala was being made in a number of sites, including the NSC, the CIA, and the embassy in Guatemala City, but the Department of State was responsible for producing the anticommunist intellectual framework that justified U.S. policy. Within the Department of State, the job fell to the Policy Planning Staff's Louis Halle, who had held a number of posts related to Latin America since entering the Department in 1943.

It had been Halle's 1950 *Foreign Affairs* article, "On A Certain Impatience with Latin America," that signaled an end to the policy of encouraging democracy in postwar Latin America. The impatience to which the article's title refers was really a disgust over the region's inability to become democratic. Halle's article began by contrasting the United States and Latin America at the moment of independence: "We had already achieved, by the time of our independence in 1776, a political sophistication that the others are, for the most part, still on their way to achieving." Latin Americans "were quite unready to assume the responsibility of self-government. The result was a sordid chaos out of which Latin America has still not finally emerged." Instead of democracy, Latin America had "a tradition of political behavior marked by intemperance, intransigeance [*sic*], flamboyance and the worship of strong men." The last of these four characteristics was particularly destructive of democracy: "Worship of the 'man on horseback' (through self-identification) is another manifestation of immaturity. It is characteristic of adolescence, this admiration for the ruthless hero who tramples down all opposition, makes himself superior to law, and is irresistible to passionate women who serve his pleasure in droves."[29] This was the thinking of the Policy Planning Staff member who wrote the Eisenhower administration's justification for U.S. efforts to overthrow the Guatemalan government.

In 1954 U.S. officials had little proof that communism was gaining ground in Guatemala. They correctly saw that Guatemala was experimenting with substantial reforms that clearly threatened to alter the country's fundamental structure of privilege, but these reforms were nothing more "communist" than those proposed by John Kennedy's Alliance for Progress less than a decade later. The most careful student of the era, Piero Gleijeses, has produced evidence that Arbenz was substantially more sympathetic to communism than scholars had earlier suspected, but the level of actual communist influence on his government remains open to debate.[30] Gleijeses's evidence was collected a quarter-century after the fact; Washington had no conclusive proof in 1954. Consequently, in May 1954, Secretary Dulles told the Brazilian ambassador "that it will be impossible to produce evidence clearly tying the Guatemalan government to Moscow; that the decision must be a political one and based on our deep conviction that such a tie must exist."[31]

This was the situation when Louis Halle was preparing his lengthy memorandum, "Our Guatemalan Policy." It admits that "the international Communist movement is certainly not the cause of the social revolution in Guatemala, but it has made the same efforts there that it has made everywhere else to harness the revolutionary impulses—nationalism and social reform alike—and exploit them for its own purposes."[32] The result is that international communism "has achieved a high degree of covert control over the reformist regime of President Arbenz and is dominant in the national labor movement." This control could easily spread: "the real and direct threat that Guatemala poses for her neighbors is that of political subversion through the kind of across-the-borders intrigue that is a normal feature of the Central American scene. The danger is of Communist contagion and is most immediate with respect to Guatemala's immediate neighbors. The Communist infection is not going to spread to the U.S. but if it should in the fullness of time spread over much of Latin America it would impair the military security of the Hemisphere and thus of the U.S."

Just days earlier President Eisenhower had made this same point, and in the process, fashioned his contribution to strategic thinking. When asked why anyone should care whether Indochina were to come under the control of communists, the President responded, "you have broader considerations that might follow what you would call the 'falling domino' principle. You have a row of dominoes set up, you knock over the first one, and what will happen to the last one is the certainty that it will go over very quickly."[33] This is how Latin America was conceptualized until the end of the Cold War—as a row of dominoes whose political immaturity made for an easy Communist pushover. To prevent this from occurring, the Soviets had to be denied a toehold from which to push.

In June 1954 the U.S.-backed forces commanded by Colonel Carlos Castillo Armas crossed the border into Guatemala, and after a confused interlude, Jacobo Arbenz capitulated without a fight. Secretary of State Dulles then went on prime-time radio and television to explain what had happened: "For several years international communism has been probing here and there for nesting places in the Americas. It finally chose Guatemala as a spot which it could turn into an official base from which to breed subversion which would extend to other American Republics." Fortunately, Dulles continued, "there were loyal citizens of Guatemala who, in the face of terrorism and violence and against what seemed insuperable odds, had the courage and the will to eliminate the traitorous tools of foreign despots."[34]

And so Guatemala moved off the U.S. foreign policy agenda, although Eisenhower briefly revived it in the fall congressional campaign, repeatedly pointing with pride to this Republican victory over communism. In Guatemala, meanwhile, Castillo Armas installed himself as provisional president and then arranged an Ubico-style election in October. With all political parties banned from participation, with the military staffing the polling places, and with the ballot not secret, the results were 486,000 for Castillo Armas, 400 opposed.

Now cast as a democratic leader, Castillo Armas was promptly invited to visit the United States, where he received a hero's welcome, including honorary degrees from Columbia and Fordham universities, a two-week tour of U.S. cities, and a visit with President Eisenhower in a Denver hospital, where he was recovering from a heart attack. He also made an appearance before the Subcommittee on Communist Penetration of the Western Hemisphere of the House Select Committee on Communist Aggression, where he warned that "we have merely won the first battle in a long war. Our most complicated, and most serious difficulties are still ahead." [35]

Three years after Arbenz's overthrow, the Department of State published *A Case History of Communist Penetration: Guatemala*. For the U.S. public the lesson of Guatemala was that "what was mistakenly considered in some quarters as a 'local Guatemalan Communist orientation' was in truth a coldly calculated, armed conspiracy of international communism to extend the system of the Soviets to a small and strategically located country in the hemisphere." [36] For U.S. officials, the lesson of Guatemala was that if the Good Neighbor policy was to preclude the use of U.S. armed forces in Latin America, then the United States needed friends in the region to act against communism.

This was a significant lesson. U.S. officials had been concerned since the War of 1812 that an adversary might seize territory in Latin America and use it as a base to attack the United States, but little thought had been given to the growing ability of Latin Americans to help or hinder an extrahemispheric adversary. Woodrow Wilson was the first President to confront this oversight. On the eve of the U.S. entry into World War I, he urged investors damaged by the Mexican revolution to hold off on their demands for restitution: "Have gentlemen who have rushed down to Washington to insist that we should go into Mexico reflected upon the politics of the world? Nobody seriously supposes, gentlemen, that the United States needs to fear an invasion of its own territory. What America has to fear, if she has anything to fear, are indirect, roundabout, flank movements upon her regnant position in the western hemisphere." [37] So far this message sounded as if it could have been said by Thomas Jefferson, but then President Wilson added something that Jefferson and his generation never would have considered significant: that continued U.S. hostility would encourage the Mexicans to cooperate with the enemies of the United States. Two decades later, this same logic led Cordell Hull to accept the Cárdenas oil nationalization.

Security, then, was no longer a simple military problem of keeping an adversary from seizing a deserted Caribbean harbor and using it as a base to attack the United States. All those harbors now had people living in them, and, as the experience in Guatemala suggested, under appropriate circumstances some residents might welcome a U.S. adversary. To meet this challenge, the United States had to make certain its friends held the reins of power in Latin America. This is what the Eisenhower administration did in

Guatemala, and it seemed to work out well—after a 1955 visit to Guatemala, Vice President Richard Nixon reported that President Castillo Armas had said, "Tell me what you want me to do and I will do it."[38]

For the balance of the decade, the primary goal of United States policy toward Latin America was to prevent "another Guatemala" by ensuring that friends like Castillo Armas held power. No one in Washington quite knew how to engineer this. It was one thing to overthrow an occasional radical government in a tiny Central American republic, but quite another to ensure that none was able to seize power in any of the twenty Latin American republics. Compounding this problem of control was the realization, as President Truman said of Greece and Turkey, that the odds favored communism because destitute people would seek radical solutions to their problems, and in a rigid bipolar world, any radical shift in Latin America meant a shift in the favor of communism. "Several conditions which play into the hands of the Communists exist in many of the American Republics," wrote the Policy Planning Staff in early 1948. "There is poverty that is so widespread that it means a bare subsistence level for large masses of people. There are ignorance and a high degree of illiteracy. There are strong reactionary forces which, through extreme selfishness and lack of any sense of social responsibility, impose a minority will through military or other dictatorial governments and so alienate large segments of their populations which otherwise probably would be anti-Communist."[39] The first sentences of the basic Latin American policy document of the Eisenhower years (NSC 144/1) laid out much the same problem: "there is an increasing popular demand for immediate improvement in the low living standards of the masses, with the result that most Latin American governments are under intense domestic political pressures to increase production and to diversify their economies. A realistic and constructive approach to this need which recognizes the importance of bettering conditions for the general population is essential to arrest the drift in the area toward radical and nationalistic regimes."[40] The challenge, then, was to do something about Latin American poverty.

The United States was not up to this challenge in the 1950s. A few State Department officials were beginning to argue that Washington would eventually have to confront the problem if it wished to preempt future Guatemalas; however, they knew that any serious attack on Latin American poverty would require substantial amounts of money, and that would jeopardize the public demand for frugality, a demand that swept the Republicans into control of the White House and both chambers of Congress in 1952. Two months after Eisenhower's inauguration, the minutes of the National Security Council indicate that NSC 144/1 was adopted on the specific understanding that "approval did not constitute an endorsement of any special program of military and economic assistance for Latin America, which will be subject to review in the light of (1) the priority of financing of present and proposed programs for Latin America in relation to programs for other foreign areas and to programs for domestic security, and (2) the overall objective of achieving a balanced Federal budget."[41]

A government program of assisting Latin American development would also jeopardize the traditional U.S. emphasis upon private enterprise. NSC 144/1 flatly prohibited significant economic assistance similar to the Marshall Plan; instead it required the State Department "to assist in the economic development of Latin America by encouraging Latin American governments to recognize that the bulk of the capital required for their economic development can best be supplied by private enterprise and that their own self-interest requires the creation of a climate which will attract private investment." With policy severely constrained by domestic politics and competing foreign commitments, the best that anyone could hope for is that the benefits of private investment would trickle down to the poor.

In the meantime, something had to be done to ensure against another Guatemala, which meant that Latin America's poverty-induced disaffection had to be held in check. Unable to attack the disease, the Eisenhower administration decided to focus upon suppressing the symptoms. It is at this point that U.S. officials fell back upon a central belief about Latin American character—the belief that Latin Americans, as Louis Halle wrote in *Foreign Affairs,* admire "the ruthless hero who tramples down all opposition." The Eisenhower administration decided to support anticommunist dictators who could maintain order.

Unlike the situation in the 1920s and 1930s, when the United States consciously selected men like Trujillo, Somoza, and Batista to run their countries, the decision to support dictators in the Cold War era was never made in a formal policy directive; it just flowed naturally out of the belief that Latin Americans were already undemocratic, on the one hand, and the desire for anticommunist stability, on the other. For example, the minutes of a National Security Council meeting in early 1955 indicate that Treasury Secretary George Humphrey began a discussion about Latin America by asserting that "a strong base for Communism exists in Latin America.

He said that wherever a dictator was replaced, Communists gained. In his opinion, the U.S. should back strong men in Latin American governments." The chair of the Office of Defense Mobilization then added a comment about Soviet meddling in Latin America's strategic materials markets, but Nelson Rockefeller, the President's special assistant, wanted to pursue Humphrey's assertion: "Mr. Rockefeller returned to the comments made by Secretary Humphrey concerning U.S. support of dictators in Latin America. He said that dictators in these countries are a mixed blessing. It is true, in the short run, that dictators handle Communists effectively. But in the long run, the U.S. must encourage the growth of democracies in Latin America if Communism is to be defeated in the area." Then President Eisenhower spoke up: "The discussion of dictators recalled to the President's mind a comment which Portuguese Premier Salazar had made some time ago, to the effect that free government cannot work among Latins."[42]

The discussion was inconclusive, for the President then added "his agreement with Mr. Rockefeller that in the long run the United States must back democracies." But the National Security Council does not make policy for the long run; it makes it for now, and the policy for the 1950s was to support Latin American dictators, as Adolf Berle discovered. In 1955 he tried to help his friend, Costa Rican President José Figueres, get back in the good graces of the Department of State, from which he had fallen by refusing to participate in the 1954 Caracas conference as a protest against Venezuela's dictatorship. Berle sought out the U.S. ambassador to Costa Rica, Robert Woodward, and "Woodward gave me a little of the inside situation in the Department. John Foster Dulles has a skunk against Figueres for his refusal to attend the Caribbean Conference. His instructions are flat: do nothing to offend the dictators; they are the only people we can depend on . . . I inquired whether it was certain that Foster Dulles took this view. He said it was: he himself had been at a Staff meeting where Dulles had laid down the policy with vigor."[43]

These friendly dictators helped the United States by repressing communists and by keeping a lid on the now-simmering revolution of rising expectations. Because they scratched our back, we needed to scratch theirs, as the U.S. ambassador to Peru reported after a 1952 meeting with dictator Manuel Odría: "Odría [said] that Peru was 100 percent on the side of the United States in the struggle against communism and that we could count on her whole-hearted cooperation at all times. He added, however, that in order to make this cooperation effective Peru must be strong and able to defend herself internally as well as externally." It turned out that Odría wanted a new ship for his navy, and in return for Odría's anticommunism, Ambassador Harold Tittmann advised that "permission to purchase one of our old cruisers would create a very favorable popular reaction all over the country and would help us politically no end. I don't believe the Department fully realizes the popular appeal of a cruiser."[44] In addition to armaments, in 1953 the Eisenhower administration gave General Odría the Legion of Merit.

Similarly, in Marcos Pérez Jiménez's Venezuela, the U.S. National Intelligence Estimate indicated that "the present dictatorship . . . is not generally liked by the people, but is popular with the majority of the armed forces and of the business interests and privileged classes who prefer a government friendly to them rather than greater civil liberties." And, as the U.S. ambassador reported, "the present Government is strongly anti-Communist and has outlawed the Communist Party. It has broken diplomatic relations with Soviet Russia and Czechoslovakia, and embarked upon the closest supervision of the activities of Communist front groups." As a gesture of appreciation, the United States also awarded Pérez Jímenez the Legion of Merit. Ambassador Fletcher Warren reported that "the decoration of the President has proven to be the most popular event in Venezuelan-American relations in many, many years," and the State Department concluded that "our relations with Venezuela are in the best shape they have been for many years."[45]

The transition from World War II to the Cold War had been traumatic. Alone at the pinnacle of power, U.S. officials were forced to learn in a few short years what the leaders of other nations had taken generations to absorb. The lessons were all difficult—Greece and Turkey, Berlin, Korea, Indochina—and they all involved the expenditure of vast amounts of political capital, including the debilitating inquisition known as McCarthyism. In this environment, Latin America suffered. Absorbed by events elsewhere, a large nation did what it wanted, and its small neighbors accepted what they could not avoid. Once in a while, Latin Americans had the opportunity to voice their dismay, however, and one of those occasions was about to occur, as Vice President Richard Nixon set out on a goodwill visit to South America.

Chapter 18 ⌒

Combatting Communism
with Economic Development

I don't see why we need to stand by and watch a country go Communist due to the irresponsibility of its own people.

⌒ *National Security Advisor Henry Kissinger, 1970*

"President Carlos Castillo Armas, of Guatemala, has just died of an assassin's bullet, fired by a palace guard who stood revealed as an acknowledged Communist," announced Representative Gardner Withrow to his House colleagues in mid-1957. "Just previously, President Jose A. Remón, of Panama, was murdered, followed by President Anastasio Somozo [*sic*], of Nicaragua. These three were not only devoted friends and allies of the United States, but each was bitterly anti-Communist. The pattern is too widespread to be purely localized political unrest." Claiming special knowledge by virtue of his residence in Joseph McCarthy's home state ("we in Wisconsin have long been attuned to the dangers of communism"), Withrow warned his House colleagues that they needed to extend McCarthyism to Latin America: "We owe it to Christian and anti-Communist governments to help search out and expose the Communists and their plans." [1]

In the meantime, Withrow recommended continued U.S. support for Latin American dictators—men such as the Dominican Republic's Rafael Trujillo, whom Representative Overton Brooks characterized as "the bulwark which has protected our southeastern sea frontier from atheistic communism." Combining John Quincy Adams's characterization of Latin American political culture and an early version of Jeane Kirkpatrick's argument favoring authoritarian over totalitarian governments, Withrow asserted that "Latin America has always had its strong men, who in turn were replaced by strong men, and strong men will replace those now in power, with a continuing succession for years to come. The limited self-interest of any strong man offers more liberty than communism, which makes every person the abject slave to a strange ideology. In a police state there may be security personnel who will check on citizens, but communism offers the alternative of having a break in a long working day where you don't drink coffee or siesta but spend the time denouncing yourself or having a fellow worker do it."[2]

The Eisenhower administration responded by pointing out that the President's brother was conducting a second of three fact-finding trips, this one to Mexico, at exactly the time that Representative Withrow was proposing a study of communist tactics in Latin America; a year later Milton Eisenhower would complete his travels around the continent with a tour of the Central American countries. This was much too leisurely a pace for many, especially after the Soviets launched Sputnik in October 1957. The first U.S. attempt to send up a satellite came the following December; it rose five feet off the ground at Cape Canaveral, paused for an agonizing second, then toppled over and exploded. Warming up for the 1958 Congressional elections, Senate leader Lyndon Johnson called the fiasco "one of the best publicized and most humiliating failures in our history"; and the chair of the Senate Armed Services committee, also a Democrat, interpreted the event as "a grievous blow to our already waning prestige."

Meanwhile, the U.S. press was giving ever-increasing coverage to a guerrilla insurgency in Cuba, beginning with Herbert Matthews's series of articles in the *New York Times* in late February 1957. As Fidel Castro's 26th of July movement gained momentum, Adolf Berle (the New Dealer who would prepare the first draft of President Kennedy's policy toward Latin America) wrote in his diary that "antiintervention is all right up to a point, but we are responsible for keeping order in the hemisphere quite aside from the proprieties, and a rather bolder policy in that regard seems indicated."[3] The Eisenhower administration did not seem concerned. It supplied the Batista government with arms and, at exactly the moment that the *Times* was publishing Matthews's articles on Castro, it singled out Batista's air force commander, Colonel Carlos Tabernilla, son of the army chief of staff, to receive the Legion of Merit. Later that year, Secretary Dulles assured reporters that the State Department saw no likelihood of a communist victory in Cuba or anywhere else in Latin America.[4]

But Dulles needed to appear to be doing something to assuage the Republican right wing and to silence the Democrats—hence Milton Eisenhower's continuing travels, and hence the Secretary's March 1958 letter to

Vice President Richard Nixon: "The other day you mentioned that you might be free to make a visit to South America this spring. I want to confirm that we could be very happy if you could see your way to doing so."[5] So began one of the most significant brief episodes in the history of U.S.–Latin American relations—the Cold War generation's equivalent of sending General Zachary Taylor to the Rio Grande or the *Maine* to Havana.

Nixon had been well received during his 1955 official visit to the Caribbean and Central America, where he had gone out of his way to embrace Rafael Trujillo, to eulogize Fulgencio Batista (as Cuba's Abraham Lincoln), to toast Guatemala's Carlos Castillo Armas—and to justify U.S. support for these dictators by noting that democracy was not an option in Latin America: "Spaniards had many talents," he told an NSC meeting, "but government was not among them."[6] Now, three years later, the State Department asked eight U.S. embassies in South America to develop an appropriate itinerary for Mr. Nixon, indicating that he was willing to discuss contentious issues with both everyday citizens and controversial political figures.[7]

That is more or less what happened. The first stops were uneventful enough—a spirited exchange with Uruguayan students and some bad press for arriving late to Arturo Frondizi's swearing-in ceremony in Argentina, but nothing really notable. In Lima, however, the Vice President faced an angry crowd of students, and that was but a prelude to his reception in Venezuela. The embassy in Caracas reported by telephone that "a large and unfriendly crowd met the Vice President and his party at the airport. There were hisses and boos and no friendly applause." Then on the way from the airport to a wreath-laying at Bolívar's tomb, Nixon's motorcade was stopped by a group "made up of ruffians and riffraff and it was in an ugly mood. The mob closed in on the vehicles in which the Vice President and his party were traveling, and the Venezuelan police escort ran. The windows were broken out of the cars in which the Vice President and Mrs. Nixon were riding."[8] For fourteen agonizing minutes Nixon and his wife sat trapped in their separate limousines while the press captured an occurrence unique in U.S. history—enraged demonstrators spitting on the Vice President of the United States.

Nixon's driver eventually gunned his befinned Cadillac over the highway's median and raced down the wrong side of the road to the embassy residence, where the Vice President stayed until he left for a hero's welcome at Washington's National Airport. President Eisenhower took the unusual step of going to the airport to greet Nixon, and the White House asked federal employees to take time off from their work to provide a warm greeting. A crowd of forty thousand was at the airport for Nixon's arrival, while another eighty-five thousand lined the Vice President's motorcade route to the White House. Signs held by the spectators read "Remember the Maine" and "Don't Let Those Commies Get You Down, Dick."

In its initial telephone message to Washington, the embassy at Caracas had reported that "undoubtedly the attack on the Vice President was organized by the Communists," but in his airport remarks Nixon chose to emphasize the region's underdevelopment. "They are concerned, as they should be, about poverty and misery and disease which exists in so many places. They are determined to do something about it."[9] That is not what he told the Cabinet the next day, where "the Vice President, in reporting on the South American riots during his trip, emphasized that Communist inspiration was evident from the similarity of placards, slogans and techniques." But here, too, Nixon returned to the problem of poverty. "The United States must not, he said, do anything that would support an impression that it is helping to protect the privileges of a few; instead, we must be dedicated to raising the standard of living of the masses." Secretary Dulles agreed with Nixon's analysis, "then pointed to the difficulty of dealing with it since democracy as we know it will not be instituted by the lower classes as they gain power—rather they will bring in more of a dictatorship of the masses."[10] Nixon did not respond, but he accepted Dulles's thinking; a few days later he warned the National Security Council that "the southern continent was certainly evolving toward a democratic forms [*sic*] of government. Normally we would hail such a development, but we should realize that such a development may not always be in each country the best of all possible courses, particularly in those Latin American countries which are completely lacking in maturity." Nixon noted that the younger generation of Latin American leaders such as Argentina's Arturo Frondizi were naive about the communist threat—"so much so that their attitude is frightening."[11]

This link between communist adventurism and the immaturity of Latin America's democratic leaders immediately became a regularly recurring theme of policy discussions, largely because the Secretary of State kept bringing it up. In mid-June he warned the NSC about "a tremendous surge in the direction of popular government by peoples who have practically no capacity for self-government and indeed are like children in facing this problem," and he added that "unlike ourselves, many of the Latin American states are leaping ahead to irresponsible self-government directly out of a semi-colonial status. This presents the Communists with an ideal situation to exploit."[12]

Long accustomed to oligarchical or conservative military rule, neither Dulles nor his subordinates knew how to handle the reformist populism that had been gaining momentum in Latin America since the Depression. The State Department's confusion was highlighted by Undersecretary of State Robert Murphy, who told Congress that the alternative to popularly elected, development-oriented leaders such as Argentina's Frondizi or Venezuela's Rómulo Betancourt was a shortsighted reliance upon dictators. Now Nixon's visit had demonstrated the cost of that expedient; one reason that the Vice President had encountered angry Venezuelans, he said, was that "we gave General Jimenez [sic] a medal of the Legion of Merit." It seemed no coincidence to Murphy that Nixon's hostile reception came four months after Pérez Jiménez had been forced from power, nor had it helped the U.S. image in Venezuela that both he and his notorious secret police chief, Pedro Estrada, had been admitted to the United States. But, like most of his colleagues, Undersecretary Murphy was torn between two analyses, and when he appeared before another Congressional committee, he fell back on the time-honored explanation that the anti-Nixon demonstrations "were Communist inspired and staged." Then Murphy captured the growing Washington consensus by merging the two separate causal agents. Communists were involved, but only as an intervening force, not as the root of the problem: "the trouble in Caracas was caused by the intensive exploitation by Communist and other anti-American elements of grievances against our policies."[13]

Logic therefore dictated that the United States consider changing its policies. The slow acceptance of this need for change by the Eisenhower administration was a critical intellectual shift, a sea change in the thinking of a generation. For more than a decade this early Cold War generation had been absolving U.S. policy of all responsibility for anti–United States behavior, dismissing criticism as Communist inspired.[14] Now, not everyone agreed. Undersecretary Murphy argued that the United States needed to stop shifting the blame to communism, and the President's brother was on his side: Milton Eisenhower's long-awaited report included an admission that the United States had been "supporting Latin American dictators in the face of a strong trend toward freedom and democratic government," and this practice had to stop. "We have made some honest mistakes in our dealings with dictators. For example, we decorated several of them . . . I think, in retrospect, we were wrong."[15]

The Nixon trip (and, more generally, the instability caused by upheavals in several countries following the assassination or overthrow of friendly dictators) had the result of splitting the personality of Cold War United States policy toward Latin America. This split reflected genuine intellectual uncertainty over the cause of instability. Was it because Latin America's democratic leaders were immature, unable to control their people, and vulnerable to communist tactics; or was it because impoverished Latin Americans had been caught up in a revolution of rising expectations? These two beliefs about the cause of instability were not mutually exclusive; indeed, they reinforced one another, and throughout the Cold War era, a majority of U.S. officials probably believed both. This circumstance permitted the Eisenhower administration to develop a bifurcated policy that addressed the concerns of both perspectives.

Where anticommunist dictators were able to maintain stability, U.S. support continued, particularly in the form of military assistance. Nothing captured better this half of U.S. policy than the reaction when Nicaragua's Anastasio Somoza was shot in 1956: Ambassador Thomas Whelan had him flown to Gorgas Hospital in the Canal Zone, where he was treated by a special team of Army doctors dispatched by the President from Walter Reed Hospital. Then, when the medical effort proved unavailing, the United States simply transferred its support to his sons. Like almost all U.S. officials at the time, even Spruille Braden, who had personally pushed the early postwar effort to promote democracy in Nicaragua, came to appreciate the younger Somoza's qualities: "He is a man of high intelligence and courage and does not pussyfoot when it comes to handling the Communists."[16]

But then, in addition, there was something genuinely new: to guide the revolution of rising expectations along reformist lines, the Eisenhower administration paved the way for its successors by reversing its opposition to economic development assistance. In a flurry of announcements that began just days after Vice President Nixon returned to Washington, the administration declared that it would no longer oppose the negotiation of commodity stabilization agreements, that it would no longer oppose the creation of the soft-loan International Development Association, that it would support a plan to double the World Bank's lending authority, that it would increase Eximbank loan authority from $5 to $7 billion, and that it would support the creation of a Latin American common market.

Then came the first test of this bifurcated policy: the Cuban revolution. In January 1959 Fidel Castro used one of Fulgencio Batista's U.S.-supplied tanks for his victory parade into Havana, and at first the Eisenhower administration did not know what to make of the new Cuban leader. In April he paid a visit to Washington and met with Vice President Nixon, who reached the same conclusion that he had about Arturo Frondizi a year earlier, characterizing Castro as "either incredibly naive about Communism or under Communist discipline—my guess is the former."[17] As officials in Washington debated whether to emphasize their "communist adventurism" or their "revolution of rising expectations" explanation for Cuba's monumental instability, the Castro government accelerated the transformation of Cuban society. Since much of that transformation damaged U.S. security and economic interests, U.S.-Cuban relations deteriorated rapidly, while Soviet-Cuban friendship blossomed. By mid-1960 Nikita Khrushchev was warning that "Soviet artillerymen can support with rocket fire the Cuban people if aggressive forces in the Pentagon dare to start intervention against Cuba."

Senator Karl Mundt was flabbergasted by what he saw happening: "We who in living memory rescued the island from medieval bondage; we who have given order, vitality, technical wisdom and wealth are now being damned for our civilizing and cooperative virtues!"[18] By this time, many Washington officials understood that Senator Mundt was exaggerating the beneficence of U.S. policy, but they agreed with his view that the Cuban revolution was a major policy failure—the "another Guatemala" that U.S. policy was supposed to be focused upon avoiding. Because they sensed the ghost of Joseph McCarthy rising from the grave, their immediate reaction was the time-honored Washington ritual called finger-pointing. Adolf Berle wrote in his diary that "The F.B.I. came in to see me. They are investigating Roy Rubottom and Bill Wieland for the State Department, the charge being that they turned over Cuba to Castro."[19] In the second 1960 presidential debate, the first question to Nixon was "Mr. Vice-President, Senator Kennedy said last night that the Administration must take responsibility for the loss of Cuba." Placed on the defensive, an irritated Nixon shot back, "Cuba is not lost, and I don't think this kind of defeatist talk by Senator Kennedy helps the situation one bit." The Democrats kept it up, however, and even Harry Truman jumped into the fight, arguing that had he been President, he would have offered to help Castro with economic development, but "of course, that son of a bitch Eisenhower was too damn dumb to do anything like that."[20]

The Cuban revolution sidetracked a few careers, but its principal effect on Washington was to dynamite the logjam in U.S. policy toward Latin America. By March 1960 President Eisenhower had signed off on a Guatemala-style exile invasion designed to take care of Castro, and in October John Kennedy (then an unbriefed candidate accusing the Republicans of "blunder, inaction, retreat and failure") urged that the United States arm "fighters for freedom . . . who offer eventual hope of overthrowing Castro."[21] But as Kennedy warned in the final debate of the U.S. presidential campaign: "Castro is only the beginning of our difficulties throughout Latin America. The big struggle will be to prevent the influence of Castro spreading to other countries." It was time to win the hearts and minds of Latin America's poor, he said. "We're going to have to try to provide closer ties, to associate ourselves with the great desire of these people for a better life if we're going to prevent Castro's influence from spreading throughout all of Latin America."

The expiring Republican administration had prepared the ground well. Two days after Khrushchev's mid-1960 warning, President Eisenhower had publicly embraced a development proposal from Brazilian President Juscelino Kubitschek. "We need to consider with the other American Republics practicable ways in which developing countries can make faster progress," Eisenhower told reporters. "I have in mind the opening of new areas of arable land for settlement and productive use. I have in mind better land utilization, within a system which provides opportunities for free, self-reliant men to own land, without violating the rights of others. I have in mind housing with emphasis, where appropriate, on individual ownership of small homes. And I have in mind other essential minimums for decent living." With these words the United States committed itself to the economic development of Latin America. Two weeks later, Fidel Castro offered the Cuban alternative to U.S.-sponsored economic reforms: "We promise to continue making the nation the example that can convert the Cordillera of the Andes into the Sierra Maestra of the American Continent."[22]

Eager for a toe-to-toe contest with Castro and his Soviet supporters, the Kennedy New Frontiersmen picked up the banner of Latin America's poor, convinced that the region's political instability stemmed from a contest between those who demanded rapid and widespread economic change, on the one hand, and those who were satisfied with the status quo, on the other, with the communists waiting to take advantage of the class struggle between rich and poor. Latin America's unreconstructed oligarchy was considered unconscionably selfish and intransigent, so powerful that it could block economic reform unless the United States intervened on the side of the awakened majority and its revolution of rising expectations. And intervene it must, for the stakes were high. If change did not occur quickly, Latin America's poor would turn to communism for help; as President Kennedy warned, "those who make peaceful revolution impossible will make violent revolution inevitable."[23] However hokey his words may sound today, they were a realist's bugle cry in the early 1960s, and for a few years Latin America's economic development became an obsession in Washington.

Marketed as a new generation's path-breaking contribution to improved inter-American relations, the Kennedy administration's Alliance for Progress was based upon social science modernization theory that, in turn, was a fancified version of Huntington Wilson's crude Dollar Diplomacy hypothesis: "prosperity means contentment and contentment means repose." This hypothesis has always had enormous intuitive appeal in Washington—it just seems to make sense that a prosperous people will not attempt to destabilize a system that supports their prosperity, and in particular that a prosperous capitalist people will not turn in desperation to communism. Setting aside the Alliance's social science window dressing and its high-minded rhetoric, what distinguished the Kennedy policy from that of the Dollar Diplomats was that instead of asking Wall Street bankers to bring repose to Latin America with loans, now the U.S. taxpayers would provide the money, much of it on concessional terms.

A bureaucracy was therefore required. The 1950s Mutual Security Act was immediately replaced by the 1961 Foreign Assistance Act, and the Agency for International Development was created to administer U.S. assistance programs. AID itself was soon surrounded by a host of cooperative public and public-private institutions, ranging from the Peace Corps to the AFL-CIO's American Institute for Free Labor Development. To ensure that the communists were kept at bay while these economic aid institutions could do their work, an elaborate set of security institutions was also created. In 1961 the Kennedy administration informed Congress that it had changed the focus of U.S. military aid from hemispheric defense to internal security,[24] and Robert McNamara's Pentagon immediately created the U.S. Army's Special Forces (the Green Berets) to fight Castro-type guerrilla insurgencies. U.S. Military Assistance Advisory Groups were soon stationed throughout the region, U.S. military schools in the United States and the Panama Canal Zone were expanded to accommodate a rapidly growing number of Latin American students, and civic action teams of U.S. military engineers began building roads and related infrastructure in areas thought vulnerable to Castroite guerrilla activity.

These economic and military assistance institutions constitute the enduring legacy of the Kennedy administration. What passed quickly into history was the Kennedy élan, snuffed out by an assassin in Dallas. Thereafter, when Latin America's economic progress seemed painfully slow and when the war in Vietnam sapped a generation's optimism, stability became the holy grail of the Johnson, Nixon, and Ford administrations.

Once stability replaced development as the principal focus of U.S. policy, the post-Eisenhower generation was forced to confront the problem identified in 1957 by Representative Gardner Withrow: "it is no longer possible for us to distinguish between quarreling among political groups and what we now know to be international Communism tactics."[25] This became *the* principal intellectual problem of all subsequent Cold War administrations, and not one of them could resolve it. The case of El Salvador is illustrative of this dilemma. For decades the United States administered a bifurcated policy toward that country, which included both a Food for Peace program to feed the hungry and a military assistance program to stop communist adventurism. As the years passed, one Salvadoran village after another was caught up in the revolution of rising expectations, as impoverished Salvadoran campesinos began demanding food (or, more fundamentally, access to land) in a country that eventually produced a locally grown but Cuban-inspired guerrilla group. Post-Eisenhower U.S. policy was both to eliminate the guerrillas and to assist the impoverished campesinos. What occurred in everyday practice was that the United States regularly filled two trucks, one with a Food for Peace shipment and development specialists to address the needs of hungry campesinos, and the other with U.S.-armed and trained Salvadoran soldiers to attack the communist guerrillas, and sent both trucks down the road toward whatever region of the country happened to be unstable at the moment. Eventually the trucks arrived at a designated village, the local residents were assembled in the plaza, and . . . and then what? Since it was impossible to bifurcate a campesino, someone had to decide who gets the food and who gets shot.

Cold War U.S. policy toward Latin America glossed over the difficulty of this decision by assuming that *someone* could separate the instability caused by rising expectations among the hungry poor from the instability caused by communist adventurism. It was a flawed assumption. By the time that this flaw was recognized, eighty thousand Salvadorans were dead, because at the village level the Salvadoran military government (one army officer or another was president continuously from 1931 to 1979) decided who got which. In case after case the U.S.-trained and U.S.-armed Salvadoran military decided to err on the side of safety, assumed that most villagers were sympathetic to the guerrillas, and shot them.[26]

Officials in Washington often attributed this lamentable outcome to El Salvador's blood-thirsty political culture. Jeane Kirkpatrick, the principal intellectual architect of the Reagan administration's policy toward Latin America, wrote that "El Salvador's political culture . . . emphasizes strength and *machismo* and all that implies about the nature of the world and the human traits necessary for survival and success."[27] Perhaps. Although no one would deny the brutality of the Salvadoran military, we know very little about the nation's political culture. The military might have massacred the peasantry without U.S. support (that was what they did in 1931 to 1932), but we can never be positive. All we know for certain is that the United States used its military assistance program to pass along its own Cold War national security mentality to the Salvadoran military—a bipolar mentality that left no room for noncommunist insurgents—and that the United States increased the Salvadoran military's efficiency with arms and training. In 1971, for example, a Senate committee found that the U.S. Army's School of the Americas in the Panama Canal Zone was providing training on "cordon and search operations, counterguerrilla operations, defoliation, electronic intelligence, the use of informants, insurgency intelligence, counterintelligence, subversion, countersubversion, espionage, counterespionage, interrogation of prisoners and suspects, handling mass rallies and meetings, intelligence photography, polygraphs, populace and resources control, psychological operations, raids and searches, riots, special warfare, surveillance, terror, and undercover operations." Even the School's innocuously titled course on "Automotive Maintenance Officer" contained instruction on "fallacies of the communist theory, communist front organizations in Latin America, and communism vs. democracy."[28]

U.S. economic assistance programs reinforced this military training. As early as 1964 AID Administrator David Bell wrote President Johnson that he was sending increasing numbers of AID personnel to the Army's Special Warfare School at Fort Bragg,[29] and by 1966 AID's police assistance bureau, the Office of Public Safety, was spending 38 percent of the entire economic assistance budget for Latin America to conduct urban counterinsurgency training in every country except Cuba. The Johnson administration sent 23 police advisors to Brazil after the 1964 Castelo Branco coup, for example, and their work supplemented the training of hundreds of Brazilian police officers (641 between 1963 and 1971) who studied at AID's International Police Academy in the old Georgetown trolley barn on M Street in Washington.[30]

Washington's fixation on anticommunist stability in Latin America eventually ran aground on the political shoals surrounding the Vietnam debacle, the Watergate scandal, and the destruction of Chilean democracy. The defeat came first in Congress. From the beginning, AID's support had been provided primarily by Congressional liberals and moderates, for government-sponsored economic reforms had never been popular among conservatives.[31] But because liberals and moderates were as vehemently anticommunist as their conservative colleagues, they were slow to anger over evidence that economic aid was being used to support repressive dictatorships. In the 1950s no one raised an eyebrow over U.S. aid policy in Guatemala, where the United States had never had a significant assistance program until the overthrow of the Arbenz government; then between 1954 and 1955 U.S. aid skyrocketed from $463,000 to $10,708,000.[32] However, a handful of liberals became concerned when this funding pattern was repeated in Brazil after the U.S.-encouraged military coup against the reform-oriented Goulart government: from $15 million in the 1964 fiscal year (which ended three months after the coup), AID expenditures jumped to $122 million in 1965 and did not dip below that level until the 1970s. Along with the debacle of Vietnam, that was enough for Senator Frank Church, who captured the growing mood among Congressional liberals in the title of his 1971 speech: "Farewell to Foreign Aid: A Liberal Takes His Leave."[33]

The Nixon administration attempted to mollify angry liberals with AID's "New Directions," a renewed emphasis on aiding the poor, and the repressive military government of Brazil was quickly "graduated" from U.S. economic assistance programs. But the Brazilian generals were immediately replaced by the Chilean military. This time the chosen economic aid mechanism was food. Less than a month after the 1973 coup against the government of Salvador Allende, the Nixon administration gave General Augusto Pinochet's new government a $24 million loan to purchase U.S.

wheat, which was eight times the total commodity credit offered to Chile during all three Allende years.[34] Then the next year, Chile, with 3 percent of Latin America's population, received 48 percent of all Food for Peace (PL480) food to Latin America; the following year the figure was 40 percent, and the year after that it was 28 percent.

As food and other forms of aid to Pinochet skyrocketed, the extent of U.S. covert action against Allende's Popular Unity government was becoming a well-documented subject of public discussion. Many had seen this covert action coming, simply because it was so obvious. Two months prior to Allende's 1970 electoral victory, for example, the Army general commanding U.S. military advisory groups in Latin America told Congress, "I just hope it doesn't happen. As you know, our record of recovery of countries that have gone down the drain is practically nil. We haven't gotten any of them back once they have gone. That is what we have got to stop." Allende's election could not be stopped, but as National Security Advisor Henry Kissinger remarked at a White House meeting, "I don't see why we need to stand by and watch a country go Communist due to the irresponsibility of its own people." Immediately after Allende's September electoral victory, President Nixon told CIA Director Richard Helms to "make the economy scream," a decision implemented in part by an economic aid cutoff.[35]

President Nixon was living in retirement by the time all this became public, and Gerald Ford was left to answer the questions. Coached by holdover Secretary of State Kissinger, Ford dismissed one reporter's query about covert action against the Allende government by arguing that it was not only good for the United States but also "in the best interest of the people of Chile."[36] By this time the general public's support for U.S. foreign policy had reached rock bottom. The principal problem had been Vietnam, of course, where in April 1975 the final U.S. Marines had to be pulled off the Saigon embassy roof by helicopters. But the news from Chile was in many ways more distressing; Vietnam could now be consigned to history, whereas Chile seemed to be a slow-motion mortification without end. In 1973 the Senate published its hearings on the International Telephone and Telegraph Company's effort to finance an effort to prevent Allende from assuming office. In 1974 it was the House's turn to survey the wreckage, and then the following year a Senate select committee issued two especially damaging reports. One was titled *Alleged Assassination Plots Involving Foreign Leaders*, which not only featured more than one hundred pages of repeated plots against the life of Fidel Castro, but also included a detailed discussion of the plotting that led to the 1970 assassination of the commander-in-chief of Chile's Army, General René Schneider, whose only offense had been to stand resolutely against a preemptive military coup to deny Allende the presidency. The second Senate select committee report, *Covert Action in Chile 1963–1973,* began, "Covert United States involvement in Chile in the decade between 1963 and 1973 was extensive and continuous," and then chronicled ten years of effort by the Central Intelligence Agency to subvert Chilean democracy.[37]

By the mid-1970s it did not take a nuclear engineer to understand that the morality of U.S. foreign policy would be a good campaign issue for the Democrats. In June 1976 presidential candidate Jimmy Carter, a nuclear engineer, told New York's Foreign Policy Association that his administration would "restore the moral authority of this country in its conduct of foreign policy." He hammered on the topic in speech after speech, and when President Ford asserted in an October 1976 presidential debate that his administration had not supported repression in South Korea, Carter shot back, "Mr. Ford didn't comment on the prisons in Chile," where "his administration overthrew an elected government and helped to establish a military dictatorship." By early 1977 no one was surprised to hear the new President assert on inauguration day that "our commitment to human rights must be absolute," nor to hear him tell a 1978 audience that "human rights is the soul of our foreign policy."[38]

While the U.S. electorate's dismay over the Nixon-Kissinger anticommunist excesses contributed to Jimmy Carter's election, it is incorrect to turn the public opinion coin over and conclude that domestic politics motivated the new administration's human rights policy. President Carter and his State Department human rights officers had demonstrated a personal commitment to increasing the prominence of human rights in U.S. foreign policy long before it became popular with the public, and in that, the new administration differed substantially from its Cold War–era predecessors. Richard Nixon had brushed the issue aside in a 1971 report to Congress, and in 1974, when the U.S. ambassador to Chile reported that he had raised the subject of torture with General Pinochet's minister of defense, Secretary of State Kissinger wrote instructions to an aide in the margin, "Tell Popper to cut out the political science lectures."[39] The Carter policy also differed from that of John Kennedy, who told a 1961 audience that "if the countries of Latin America are ready to do their part, and I am sure they are, then I believe the United States, for its part, should help provide resources."[40] But dictators such as Anastasio Somoza wagered that Washington's fear of communism in the early 1960s was greater than its desire for reform, and they won: throughout its thousand days, the Kennedy administration continued to provide aid to the Hemisphere's most repressive dictatorships.

Not so with the Carter administration, as its strongest critic, Jeane Kirkpatrick, once observed: "What did the Carter administration do in Nicaragua? *It brought down the Somoza regime.*" The Carter State Department "*acted* repeatedly and at critical junctures to weaken the government of Anastasio Somoza and to strengthen his opponents."[41] Kirkpatrick was right. While the Nicaraguan people were ultimately responsible for Somoza's downfall, it was Washington that had kept his family in power in Nicaragua since the mid-1930s. From Roosevelt to Ford, prior administrations had made all manner of excuses for supporting the Somozas, but then in 1978 to 1979 Jimmy Carter and his doughty band of human rights activists pulled the plug.

Where the Carter administration (and human rights activists in general) continued the policy of their predecessors was in uncritically accepting the hegemonic tradition of U.S. policy. This practice was seen most clearly in the administration's attempt to salvage the U.S.-created Nicaraguan *Guardia Nacional* without Somoza,[42] but it was also present in the attitude of human rights activists, beginning with the seminal human rights hearings by Representative Donald Fraser's House subcommittee in 1973, when former Attorney General Ramsey Clark argued that "preaching helps, but I believe it is time for meddling, too."[43] Congress apparently agreed: "We have to start being more adamant and more forceful in our relationships with those countries," argued the author of the Harkin Amendment, the centerpiece of 1970s human rights legislation. "We always hear it said, 'Well, we don't want to interfere in those countries. We don't want to go in there and mess in their internal affairs.' I don't see why not." Representative Tom Harkin believed that "we are going to influence Latin America. We will influence every country there. The question is how. Are we going to keep supporting these dictators down there who violate human rights with some sense of security? Or will we forcefully, once and for all, say 'No, we won't put up with it'?"[44]

Since all sides in Washington continued to believe, as Theodore Roosevelt had, that the United States had an obligation to act against "chronic wrongdoing" in Latin America, the only question was the identity of the wrongdoers. To the Carter administration it was repressive dictators violating the human rights of those who would lead the nonideological revolution of rising expectations. But after four years the Democrats lost the White House to Ronald Reagan, who thought the wrongdoers were the communist adventurers: "Let's not delude ourselves," he told a 1980 campaign audience, "the Soviet Union underlies all the unrest that is going on. If they weren't engaged in this game of dominoes, there wouldn't be any hot spots in the world."[45] The Cold Warriors were back for one last stand, elected by a public that quickly got over its post-Vietnam malaise and simply did not agree with President Carter's 1977 assertion that "we are now free of that inordinate fear of communism which once led us to embrace any dictator who joined us in that fear."[46]

In the late 1970s and early 1980s, at exactly the time that the human rights versus anticommunism battle lines were being drawn in Washington, Central American instability was escalating steadily, alarming both sides. As in every prior case of Latin American instability since the 1950s, the now-traditional dispute over causality continued to characterize policy debates. In 1982 former Ambassador Robert White spoke for those who attributed the instability to rising expectations, telling Congress that "the guerrilla groups, the revolutionary groups, almost without exception began as associations of teachers, associations of labor unions, campesino unions, or parish organizations which were organized for the definite purpose of getting a schoolhouse up." The Reagan administration's assistant secretary of state for Latin America attributed the instability to communist adventurism, writing that "Cuba is now trying to unite the radical left, commit it to the use of violence, train it in warfare and terrorism, and attempt to use it to destroy existing governments and replace them with Marxist-Leninist regimes on the Cuban model."[47]

Since neither side could prove its case to the satisfaction of the other, at first U.S. policy became a function of how much money a determined Reagan administration could wring out of an ambivalent Congress to prop up the anticommunist government in El Salvador and to support the U.S.-created anti-Sandinista rebels in Nicaragua. This effort required all the rhetorical skills of President Reagan, who lectured to a prime-time television audience in mid-1983: "Many of our citizens don't fully understand the seriousness of the situation, so let me put it bluntly: There is a war in Central America that is being fueled by the Soviets and the Cubans. They are arming, training, supplying, and encouraging a war to subjugate another nation to communism, and that nation is El Salvador. The Soviets and the Cubans are operating from a base called Nicaragua. And this is the first real Communist aggression on the American mainland."[48] In what many thought might be a prelude to direct military action in Central America, a few months later the Reagan administration invaded the Caribbean ministate of Grenada, and President Reagan again went before the TV cameras to explain what had happened. Grenada, he said, "was a Soviet-Cuban colony, being readied as a major military bastion to export terror and undermine democracy. We got there just in time."[49]

Although the Reagan administration never quite received the Congressional green light that it requested, for eight years it obtained enough support from a hopelessly divided Congress to continue the fight in El Salvador. President Reagan was not as successful with Congress over U.S. policy toward Nicaragua, where legislators placed a $24 million cap on CIA funding for the Nicaraguan contras in late 1983, prompting the administration to embark upon a clandestine funding operation that became known as the Iran-Contra scandal. In the end, the Washington body count was substantial: National Security Advisor Robert McFarlane pled guilty to four misdemeanor charges of withholding information from Congress and was sentenced to two years' probation; National Security Advisor John Poindexter was convicted on five felony counts of obstructing Congress and conspiracy; Secretary of Defense Caspar Weinberger was indicted on six counts of perjury and obstructing Iran-Contra investigators; National Security Council aide Oliver North was convicted of three felony counts of destroying documents, accepting an illegal gratuity, and obstructing Congress; Assistant Secretary of State Elliott Abrams pled guilty to two misdemeanor counts of withholding information from Congress; and nine other minor administration officials were either convicted or pled guilty to crimes ranging from tax evasion and document falsification to conspiracy, theft of government property, and mail fraud.

In late 1992 lame-duck President George Bush granted presidential pardons to Abrams, McFarlane, Weinberger, and three other former officials convicted in the wake of the Iran-Contra probe. By that time, the Sandinistas had been voted out of office by a war-weary electorate, the Soviet Union had disappeared, and the major wars in Central America had ended, leaving only the chronic insurgency in Guatemala and a devastated human landscape in El Salvador and Nicaragua, where an estimated 110,000 citizens had been killed during the Reagan years—twice the number lost by the United States in Vietnam. The Bush and Clinton administrations briefly attempted to help rebuild the region's ravaged economies, but the budget now needed to be balanced, and U.S. assistance was required by the former Soviet bloc nations, so aid to Central America fell from a peak of $1.2 billion in 1985 to $167 million in 1996; military aid declined to virtually nothing, and Central America once again moved quietly off the front pages and out of Washington's consciousness.

Chapter 19

Two Centuries Later

Very much opinionated, it is difficult to administer them, any salutary advice.

⌢ *Heman Allen, U.S. Minister to Chile, 1825*

For nearly two centuries, three interests have determined the content of United States policy toward Latin America: the need to protect U.S. security, the desire to accommodate the demands of U.S. domestic politics, and the drive to promote U.S. economic development. Each generation's specific policies have changed with the times and the circumstances, as one year's fear of communist adventurism yields to next year's dismay over human rights violations, as the Big Stick transmutes into Dollar Diplomacy and then Good Neighborliness, as democracy and free trade vie for attention with drug trafficking and immigration. But although the precise mix of reasons explaining United States policy changes continuously, these three interests remain ever present.

The first of these interests—security—was never more obvious than in 1980, when the acting Assistant Secretary of State for Inter-American Affairs, John Bushnell, went before a House Appropriations Subcommittee to justify the administration's foreign aid budget. Aggressive questions came from liberal subcommittee chair David Obey, who asked why taxpayers' dollars should be used to fight communism in the Caribbean. "They don't have any weapons to threaten us. There are lots of small countries, as you indicated. Outside of Mexico, there are not very many people. Why should we worry about them?" Sensing the end of the Carter administration's human rights policy, of which he disapproved, and a return to a focus on anticommunism, Bushnell responded with near-sarcasm: "The thing that tends to worry most of your constituents and most of the American people is that they have learned enough geography to know that these places are pretty close to us."[1]

In that brief exchange lies the explanation for the extraordinary staying power of the Monroe Doctrine. Because they lack physical power, Latin Americans have never threatened the United States; rather, the fear in Washington has always been that powerful non-hemispheric powers might use a base in nearby Latin America to attack the United States. Prudent people keep a potential enemy at arm's length.

The precise distance meant by "arm's length" has changed with time and technology, however. Our earliest ancestors took this distance literally, just as late-night subway riders do today; but as soon as someone realized that a club could be at least as damaging as a fist (and safer to use), then the definition of "arm's length" started its slow slide from the literal to the figurative—a process immeasurably accelerated by the realization that a rock was even better than a club, since it could be thrown rather than held, further increasing an aggressor's safety from retaliation. With that Cro-Magnon innovation, the world was on its way to slingshots, catapults, muskets, mortars, and our generation's contribution, the intercontinental ballistic missile, all of which are conceptually the equivalent of a rock.

There are many important distinctions among projectiles, however, and the one that is most relevant to the U.S.–Latin American security relationship is the distance from which they can be wielded. Just before the War of 1812, when Great Britain needed nearby depots to stockpile their cannon-balls, it made sense for U.S. officials to issue the No-Transfer Resolution in order to keep Spanish Florida from falling into the hands of the English. Similarly, in 1962, when Soviet intercontinental missiles were still wildly inaccurate, it made sense for the Kremlin to place its more accurate inter-mediate-range missiles in Cuba—and for the United States to oppose that placement. But as President Kennedy concluded at the time, "it doesn't make any difference if you get blown up by an ICBM flying from the Soviet Union or one that was ninety miles away. Geography doesn't mean that much." [2] Within two decades, the Soviet threat came from such technologi-cal nightmares as Delta-class submarines firing highly accurate ICBMs with MIRVed warheads while cruising underwater 4,000 miles from their target.

These technology-driven advances in offensive military capabilities would have dramatically decreased the importance of Latin America to U.S. security were it not for a subtle shift in the definition of Latin Amer-ica's role in strategic thinking. Once the United States had asserted its hegemony in Latin America, officials in Washington quickly concluded that it was important to retain control for a *symbolic* reason: hegemony over the region became an indicator of U.S. credibility in international relations.

This transformation was well advanced by the mid-1920s, when Henry Stimson was sent to Nicaragua to put an end to Juan Sacasa's rebellion against the U.S.-supported government of Adolfo Díaz. Because Sacasa was supported by Mexico, wrote the State Department official responsible for Central America, the United States had no choice but to maintain Díaz in office; should he be ousted, it "will be looked upon throughout Latin America as a back-down inspired by fear of Mexico." This memo moved up to Assistant Secretary Robert Olds, who briefed Secretary Frank Kellogg. "The main thing we have at stake in this controversy is our prestige," Olds told Kellogg. "The issue is sharply defined. We must decide whether we shall tolerate the interference of any other power (i.e. Mexico) in Central American affairs, or insist upon our own dominant position. If this Mexican maneuver succeeds it will take many years to recover the ground we shall have lost. The tangible evidence of our influence will have disappeared and notice will have been conveyed to all Central America, and to the rest of the world, that recognition and support by this Government means nothing."[3]

Latin America's symbolic significance slowly increased during the ensuing decades, and by the late 1940s the entire region was seen in Washington as an essential ally in the emerging bipolar balance of power, not because Latin America could help in the fight against communism, and not because the Soviet Union might seize a nearby country and use it to menace the United States (although that, too, was a concern), but primarily because its "loss" would be interpreted around the world as a sign of U.S. weakness. That is the reason why a revised statement of U.S. policy was approved in early 1959, barely a month after Fulgencio Batista was ousted in Cuba: it asserted that Latin American defections or even neutralism "would seriously impair the ability of the United States to exercise effective leadership of the Free World, particularly in the UN, and constitute a blow to U.S. prestige." That also is why President Reagan went before a prime-time television audience in 1983 to warn that "the national security of the Americas is at stake in Central America. If we cannot defend ourselves there, we cannot expect to prevail elsewhere. Our credibility would collapse, our alliances would crumble, and the safety of our homeland would be put in jeopardy."[4]

Given the changes that have occurred in the technology of warfare, Latin America will never again have the literal "arm's distance" significance that led to the No-Transfer Resolution and the Monroe Doctrine. And, with the dissolution of the Soviet Union and the absence of any near-term replacement as a rival superpower, Latin America will not soon carry the same symbolic significance that it held during the 1980s. Concerns about credibility will remain forever at the heart of every nation's security policy, however, and Latin America's geographic proximity will continue to encourage officials in Washington to conceive of the region as a natural part of the U.S. sphere of influence.

While security concerns ebb and flow, domestic U.S. politics have been central to the explanation of nearly every important issue of U.S.–Latin American relations, beginning in the early 1820s, when John Quincy Adams and Henry Clay used the question of recognizing Latin American independence to position themselves for the Presidency. Since then, the intrusion of largely irrelevant issues of domestic politics has never stopped. Domestic politics strongly influenced (but did not entirely determine) the development of the 1823 Monroe Doctrine, and domestic politics continued to exert a strong influence on policy when Jacksonians expressed their disgust over the outcome of the 1824 election by challenging the Adams administration's request for funds to participate in the Panama Congress. Similarly, the 1895 Olney Doctrine, a defining moment in U.S.-Caribbean relations, can be attributed in part to the depression-plagued Cleveland administration's desire to save the Democrats' few remaining Congressional seats. Certainly that was the interpretation of fellow Democrat Thomas Paschal, a Representative from Texas, who wrote Secretary Olney: "just think of how angry the anarchistic, socialistic, and populistic boil appears, on our political surface, and who knows how deep its roots extend or ramify? One cannon shot across the bow of a British boat in defense of this principle will knock more pus out of it than would suffice to inoculate and corrupt our people for the next two centuries. Give the President my compliments." In addition to his desire to use the Venezuelan boundary dispute to generate domestic political support for the ailing Democrats, Representative Paschal was also concerned about "the unassimilated hetarogenious [sic] tide that has of late years poured in upon us . . . That our naturalization laws permit admission to citizenship of those most ignorant of, or inimical to, all that really makes for the true value of American citizenship, and, that existing political conditions foster a continuance of that ignorance, or hostility, is equally undeniable. A foreign war would be, in effect, from this point of view, a new and higher declaration of independence."[5] None of this had anything to do with Venezuela's boundary, but it determined U.S. policy. Using little more than thin air, the embattled Democrats manufactured the foreign policy problem of British expansion into Venezuela's territory.

This process of sucking Latin America into domestic U.S. politics happens frequently. Often it is difficult to document. It is possible to explain President Bush's 1989 invasion of Panama, for example, by reference to what was then known in Washington as the "wimp factor"—the perception that the new President's leadership qualities did not compare favorably with those of his predecessor. But it is doubtful that history will ever reveal the smoking gun of Mr. Bush telling the Pentagon, "Let's invade Panama so that the press will stop calling me a wimp," and so the evidence is often indirect and subject to challenge—in this case not much more than the chair of the Republican National Committee's calling the invasion a "political jackpot," and the Washington *Post* editorial page noting that "in political terms no one can quarrel with the polling figures showing the operation to have been an enormous success."[6]

Often the importance of domestic politics is beyond dispute, however. It is impossible to understand the pre–Civil War expansion into Texas and Mexico, or filibustering in Cuba and Central America, without reference to the domestic debate over slavery and the South's need for additional slave senators to balance the expansion that was occurring above the line of the Missouri Compromise. Similarly, the explanation for why the isthmian canal was built in Panama instead of Nicaragua is that William Nelson Cromwell convinced Marcus Hanna to revise the 1900 Republican platform, probably with a handsome campaign contribution; then, when the issue came to a conference committee showdown, the Congressional Republicans had more clout than the Democratic champion of Nicaragua, Senator John Morgan. Had the Democrats been in the majority—a domestic political decision of the U.S. electorate—the canal would have been built in Nicaragua. Perhaps the most transparent example of domestic electoral considerations determining U.S. policy came in 1992, two weeks before the November election, when the Bush administration reversed its long-standing opposition to the Cuban Democracy (Torricelli) Act at a moment when the electoral outcome in Florida was uncertain and the rival Democrats had announced their support for the measure. Four years later, in 1996, the Clinton administration was undoubtedly influenced by election-year politics when it reversed its position and signed the Cuban Liberty and Democratic Solidarity (Helms-Burton) Act. Indeed, it is impossible to explain post–Cold War U.S. policy toward Cuba without recognizing that Florida, a swing state, has twenty-five electoral votes, fourth largest in the nation, and a Cuban-American population of over 800,000.

Even though capricious and unexpected and therefore difficult to predict, these examples can be extended almost indefinitely, but they would only repeat what the previous chapters have attempted to make obvious: politics never stops at the water's edge. If there is domestic political capital to be made by doing something for or to Latin America, then the two-century history of U.S.–Latin American relations demonstrates conclusively that someone will do it.

In addition to domestic politics and security concerns, no explanation of United States policy toward Latin America is complete without including the never-ending quest for economic development. This has been obvious since early in the nineteenth century, when the Madison administration sought to keep Latin American ports open to U.S. merchants during the region's wars of independence. Today's economic relationship with Latin America is infinitely more complex, however, and economic expansion overseas often conflicts with the protection of domestic economic interests, as illustrated by the 1898 Congressional resolution permitting the McKinley administration to wage war against Spain. Cuba might now be the fifty-first state in the Union (or something akin to Puerto Rico) had the Teller amendment not been added to the war resolution, probably at the behest of domestic sugar producers who feared that Cuba's absorption would threaten their livelihood. Then, several years later, when the Roosevelt administration sought to stabilize the island's economy with a reciprocity treaty lowering the sugar tariff, Utah's Republican party chieftain sent a blunt warning to Secretary of War Elihu Root: "Now it is proposed to take the duty off from Cuban sugar through a reciprocity arrangement. If this is done, it will destroy the sugar beet industry in the State of Utah. It was through the prospect of the beet and the erection of the [refining] factories that the Republicans carried the State a year ago. It was this same prospect that carried several cities of the State for the Republican ticket, a month ago. If this duty is taken off, or materially lessened, as is proposed, you can look for a Democratic Senator and a Democratic Congressman from Utah."[7] The Roosevelt administration went ahead with the reciprocity treaty, but it set the tariff reduction at a rate (20 percent) that would primarily disadvantage other foreign producers, not the domestic U.S. sugar industry.

The behind-the-scenes nature of lobbying is such that we can never be certain whether the fear of a domestic political backlash kept Cuba's sugar tariff from being lowered by 40, 60, or 80 percent (or even eliminated entirely, as President Roosevelt and Governor-General Wood originally wanted), but the general lesson from this example is clear: specific economic interests have had a powerful impact on U.S. policy since the moment of Latin America's independence, when Secretary of State John Quincy Adams warned the European monarchies that "the situation of these Countries has thrown them open to commercial intercourse with other nations, and among the rest with these United-States. This state of things has existed several years, and cannot now be changed without materially affecting our interests."[8]

Although U.S. policy toward Latin America has regularly been used to promote specific private economic interests, a focus on these interests leads us away from the central political issue of U.S.–Latin American economic relations: the perception among politicians that their electoral fortunes are dependent upon foreign markets—a strong belief that the United States must have access to Latin America in order to maintain a strong economy, and that the condition of the economy determines the outcome of elections. In the nineteenth century these fortunes were tied to the acquisition of markets for the excess production of U.S. farms and factories; more recently they have been tied to the broader issue of U.S. competitiveness, which is believed to require access to inexpensive labor. What has remained unchanged over time has been the desire of U.S. producers to expand in order to make money, and the desire of U.S. political leaders to help them in order to win elections.

This government-assisted economic expansion is clearly leading to a merger of the hemisphere's economies. Driven by the changing technologies of production, transportation, and communication, we have come a long way since 1828, when U.S. Minister Beaufort Watts wrote that Latin America was nothing more than "twenty millions of people spread over a pathless continent." U.S. entrepreneurs would have discovered Latin America's markets and resources without government assistance, but for more than a century the process of economic integration has been accelerated by U.S. officials' consciously seeking to tie Latin America's economies to the

United States. The entire purpose of the first inter-American conference in 1889 to 1890 was to initiate the process of institutionalizing these ties, beginning with the creation of the first inter-American bureaucracy, the International Bureau of American Republics, whose purpose was to provide member states with information about commercial opportunities.

Dollar Diplomacy further institutionalized this integration by providing opportunities for the U.S. banking industry and opening the door for the financial services sector generally. Then in the 1920s the U.S. government encouraged the thrust into resource-rich South America, and by the 1930s the State Department took the goal of hemisphere-wide economic integration for granted: "Since we are engaged in the most difficult task of creating and perpetuating a complex as well as peaceful area of influence, we must be clear about our long range approaches to the attainment of the material and intangible bonds upon which this empire depends. Since trade is a permanent foundation of such influence, the whole series of inter-American economic institutions should be molded toward the simplification of the currencies and customs regulations now in force in the twenty-one republics; they should be attached inseparably to the dollar."[9]

And so it has become. What began early in the eighteenth century as a market for New England's salted cod has slowly developed into an infinitely more complex economic relationship. Latin Americans have become major consumers of U.S. goods and services, and they now provide the United States not simply with raw materials and the products of tropical agriculture, but also with millions and millions of laborers, some working at home, some in the United States. This economic integration has proceeded to the point that it now generates its own momentum, capturing the significance that national security held during the Cold War. As we enter the twenty-first century, it is difficult to imagine the U.S. economy without Latin America, something that no other generation has been able to say.

However important it may be, the sum of Washington's concerns about security, domestic politics, and economic expansion does not equal a full explanation of United States policy toward Latin America. To obtain that, we have had to add the mind-set that governs the thinking of U.S. officials as they process these concerns. Dominating this mind-set are the underlying beliefs that U.S. officials hold about Latin Americans and, specifically, their belief that Latin Americans are an inferior people.

The origin of this belief is indisputable: the dark shadow of Latin American inferiority crept across our consciousness long before the first U.S. diplomat set foot in Latin America, decades before there was such a thing as United States policy toward Latin America, years before there was an empirical foundation for any belief, one way or the other. John Quincy Adams and his generation were prejudiced in the strict sense of the word: they prejudged Catholics to be inferior to Protestants, Hispanics to Anglos, dark-skinned to light. In adopting this prejudice, early U.S. foreign-policy officials reacted much like any group encountering a different culture; indeed, their reflex prejudice, often called ethnocentrism, is so nearly universal as to be properly considered a part of human nature.

But the belief in Latin American inferiority is no longer a reflex prejudice; it has continued for nearly two centuries, and its sheer persistence has never been explained. The beginning of an explanation almost certainly lies in the initial decades of U.S. relations with independent Latin America, the decades from the early 1820s, when the first U.S. ministers took up their posts, to the late 1850s, when the Civil War interrupted U.S. diplomacy. This was the time when contradictory evidence might have overcome the uninformed prejudice of John Quincy Adams's generation, but the moment was not propitious. As the new U.S. envoys were presenting their credentials in Bogotá and Buenos Aires, the Spanish were just months away from their final defeat at Junín and Ayacucho, preparing to leave the victorious Creoles with devastated economies and a decade-long legacy of militarism, unbalanced by a tradition of self-rule. This was a recipe for instability, and this is what the initial U.S. envoys found. They attributed this instability to the inherent inferior nature of Hispanic culture.

Then in the 1840s the expansionist ideology of Manifest Destiny seized control of United States policy toward Latin America, and a justification was needed for taking land from the Hispanic Europeans who had taken it from the indigenous inhabitants. The rationale that James K. Polk's generation selected was a belief that the Latin Americans who stood in the path of expansion were only a small step above the savages who had blocked the march of civilization across the original thirteen colonies. Now saddled with the instrumental purpose of facilitating growth, Anglo prejudices were confirmed, particularly in Mexico, where the move into Texas began at the very moment of Mexican independence. The Anglos who wanted Mexico's territory took advantage of the fledgling's weakness, cloaking their acquisitive behavior in the mantle of improving upon Hispanic civilization. As Theodore Roosevelt would write years later, "it was inevitable, as well as in the highest degree desirable for the good of humanity at large, that the American people should ultimately crowd out the Mexicans from their sparsely populated Northern provinces."[10]

So it was that the mental mold of U.S. policy toward Latin America was firmly set by the time that the United States descended into its own Civil War. Then late in the nineteenth century, when the United States had recovered and was beginning to renew its interest in Latin America, this mold was once again used to fashion policy by the Young Turks of Theodore Roosevelt's generation. Identifying Latin America as a convenient site for demonstrating that their adolescent nation had matured into an international power, the United States became involved in disputes in Peru, Chile, Venezuela, Cuba, Colombia, Panama, the Dominican Republic, Haiti, and Nicaragua. In each case, U.S. policy can be explained by a mixture of security concerns, domestic politics, and economic interests, but it was the underlying belief in Latin American inferiority that guided U.S. officials to the specific policies known as the Big Stick and Dollar Diplomacy. In particular, the belief in Latin American inferiority dictated Washington's turn-of-the-century assumption of responsibility for solving Latin Americans' problems, be it their inability to end a war, draw a boundary line, achieve independence, or stabilize their economies.

The decision to help Latin Americans with their foreign debt was especially significant. Shouldering this burden was originally justified by a security argument (the need to keep European creditors out of the Caribbean), but this justification was based on the underlying belief that the region's profligate leaders were unable to manage their own money. Poised at the top of a slippery slope, U.S. officials argued that security required economic control, took one step in that direction, and immediately slid into the conclusion that economic control required political tutelage, a requirement based on the assumption that Latin America's corrupt, chaotic politics were the cause of the region's economic problems. Having learned from Europe how a powerful nation should behave, U.S. leaders seemed almost eager to accept their share of the White Man's Burden, which in Latin America manifested itself in the appointment of proconsuls, often accompanied by detachments of Marines.

As this proconsular policy gathered momentum, it quickly became the norm. By 1913, when Woodrow Wilson entered office, the new President saw nothing unusual about assuming responsibility for teaching Mexicans not simply how to handle their economy, but how to behave democratically, a task that the preceding generation—a Benjamin Harrison or a Grover Cleveland—would never have considered for a moment. Wilson instructed his new secretary of state that "we consider it our duty to insist on constitutional government there and will, if necessary . . . take charge of elections and see that a real government is erected." Secretary of State Lansing responded by upping the ante, suggesting that the entire Caribbean region receive U.S. tutelage, again blending a security rationale with an assumption of Latin American inferiority: "Within this area lie the small republics of America which have been and to an extent still are the prey of revolutionists, of corrupt governments, and of predatory foreigners. Because of this state of affairs our national safety, in my opinion, requires that the United States should intervene and aid in the establishment and maintenance of a stable and honest government."[11] In this way, Washington's early-twentieth-century leaders grafted a new belief in the need for hegemony onto the pre–Civil War belief in Latin American inferiority. It was no longer simply that Latin Americans were inferior, but that their inferiority threatened U.S. security—everything from a cutoff of vital supplies and transit routes to the establishment of military bases by powerful European rivals.

After that, the decades passed quickly—the Roaring 20s, the Great Depression, another World War, and then the Cold War, while one significant corner of the minds of U.S. officials remained frozen in time. In 1832 a U.S. envoy had written that Argentines "have all the vices of men and all the follies of children, without the virtues or the sense of either," and so he closed the U.S. legation in Buenos Aires and went home. More than a century later, as the Eisenhower administration was coming to a close, the minutes of a meeting of the National Security Council indicate that "Mr. Allen Dulles pointed out that the new Cuban officials had to be treated more or less like children. They had to be led rather than rebuffed. If they were rebuffed, like children, they were capable of doing almost anything."[12] Soon the U.S. embassy in Havana was also closed.

The generation of officials who padlocked the embassy in Argentina did not share the hegemonic vision of the generation that severed relations with Cuba, and so subsequent policies toward these two governments were quite different. But both generations compared Latin Americans to unruly children—immature, emotional, and needing supervision. To our generation this comparison seems hopelessly quaint, so politically incorrect that readers will not be surprised to discover that in 1832 Minister Francis

Baylies knew next to nothing about Argentines, and that in 1959 CIA Director Allen Dulles was uninformed about Cubans. What we have here, we tell ourselves, are two more examples of John Quincy Adams's uninformed prejudice.

But however much we might wish it were otherwise, this prejudice remains today at the core of any explanation of United States policy toward Latin America. It was especially evident during the spasm of U.S. attention to Central America in the 1980s, and can be seen most clearly in the writings of Jeane Kirkpatrick, whose articles in *Commentary* magazine served as the intellectual foundation for the Reagan administration's policy. The first of Ambassador Kirkpatrick's two articles developed the distinction between totalitarian and authoritarian regimes, and provided the rationale for continuing U.S. support of Latin America's anticommunist authoritarian governments; the second explained the region's importance to U.S. security, emphasizing the global balance of power.[13] Laced into both articles is the assertion that Latin Americans are pathologically violent. "Violence or the threat of violence is an integral part of these political systems—a fact which is obscured by our way of describing military 'interventions' in Latin political systems as if the system were normally peaceable. Coups, demonstrations, political strikes, plots, and counterplots are, in fact, the norm." To Kirkpatrick, the particularly vicious Salvadoran civil war reflected the fact that "El Salvador's political culture . . . emphasizes strength and *machismo* and all that implies about the nature of the world and the human traits necessary for survival and success. Competition, courage, honor, shrewdness, assertiveness, a capacity for risk and recklessness, and a certain 'manly' disregard for safety are valued."[14]

Since Ambassador Kirkpatrick never visited El Salvador before writing about its political culture, her views had to come from some source other than direct observation. Their precise origin is unknown, for she mentioned no sources and provided no citations, but since her ideas obviously flowed from the 1940s tradition of national character analysis, she probably relied heavily upon the work of the leading contemporary exponent of that tradition, Howard Wiarda, who at the time was her colleague at the American Enterprise Institute in Washington. Wiarda's writings contained precisely Kirkpatrick's argument, cloaked in academic regalia,[15] and like Kirkpatrick, Wiarda used his view of Latin American culture as the foundation for policy advice. "El Salvador has had a long tradition of political violence," he wrote; indeed, "*machetismo*, or the butchering of one's personal and political foes, is a way of life. Such endemic, persistent violence is very difficult for Americans to understand or come to grips with. The entire political culture—governance, challenges to it, the circulation of new and old groups in and out of power—is based on the display and use of violence."[16]

Like Kirkpatrick, Wiarda never conducted research in El Salvador. His ideas are also of second-hand provenance and, although their exact pedigree is uncertain,[17] they are remarkably similar to those of the preceding generation of scholars who pursued Ruth Benedict's national character approach to cultural analysis. They especially resemble the ideas of historian Richard Morse, who contended that "Latin America is subject to special imperatives as an offshoot of postmedieval, Catholic, Iberian Europe which never underwent the Protestant Reformation." Like Kirkpatrick and Wiarda, Morse then jumps ahead several centuries to identify the contemporary product of this background: "human laws are frequently seen as too harsh or impracticable or inequitable or simply as inapplicable to the specific case. Hence the difficulty of collecting income taxes; the prevalent obligation to pay fees or bribes to officials for special or even routine services; the apathy of metropolitan police toward theft and delinquency; the thriving contraband trade at border towns; the leniency toward those who commit crimes of passion—all the way down to the nonobservance of 'no smoking' signs on buses and in theaters."[18]

Morse never tells his readers the origin of these ideas, but every word he wrote could have been written by John Quincy Adams. Viewed in historical perspective, it seems clear that contemporary national character analysts borrow their ideas about Latin America from the early-nineteenth-century Anglo view of Hispanic culture, then adapt that view to the special circumstances of their day. Kirkpatrick's special contribution was to simplify—to discard the academic mumbo jumbo that only confuses fast-reading Washingtonians—and to highlight the cultural commitment to "*machismo* and all that implies." Then, knowing where Washington focuses its attention, she drew out the implications for U.S. policy: we may respect human rights here in the United States, she wrote, but the Carter administration should never have expected Latin Americans, heir to a violent culture, to share the same values: "Hurried efforts to force complex and unfamiliar political practices on societies lacking the requisite political culture, tradition, and social structures not only fail to produce desired outcomes; if they are undertaken at a time when the traditional regime is under attack, they actually facilitate the job of the insurgents."[19]

The history of U.S.–Latin American relations is overflowing with this type of thinking. Perhaps the best example is that of George Kennan, the intellectual father of containment, whose only exposure to Latin America was a hopscotch tour of the region's capitals in 1950. His trip report focused on Latin Americans' "exaggerated self-centeredness and egotism" and their "pathetic urge to create the illusion of desperate courage."[20] Written by a lame duck in the Truman-Acheson State Department, Kennan's report received little attention, but one cannot help but wonder how much of early Cold War policy toward Latin America was influenced by these ideas while Kennan was serving as director of State's Policy Planning Staff (1947 to 1949) and as Counselor (1949 to 1950). What we need not wonder is the origin of his beliefs about Latin Americans: just as Kirkpatrick could not possibly have uncovered the secrets of Salvadoran political culture without stepping foot in the country, Kennan could not have learned enough in his whirlwind visit to justify his analysis of Latin American personality. Instead, he modernized the thinking of John Quincy Adams, adding the Freudian argot popular at the time.

The Kennans and the Kirkpatricks are crucial to an understanding of United States policy toward Latin America, simply because every administration seems to have a quota for this type of person—like JFK's Richard Goodwin, who revealed that prior to helping formulate the Alliance for Progress, "I had never set foot south of the border (aside from one orgiastic night just beyond the Texas border during the campaign which had little to do with high policy, but which an exceptionally imaginative psychiatrist might conclude had planted the seed of my love affair with Latin America.)"[21] However shallow they and their knowledge of Latin America may be, it is important to know what this type of official believes, because their beliefs often determine policy. But for our understanding of the persistence of beliefs about Latin Americans' inferiority, it is sufficient to recognize the persistence of the thinking of John Quincy Adams.

Uninformed prejudice explains only half of the lingering belief in Latin American inferiority, however. It can explain the nineteenth-century views of Francis Baylies, but not the identical beliefs of Edward Augustus Hopkins. It can explain the twentieth-century views of Jeane Kirkpatrick, but not the similar beliefs of Lawrence Harrison.

In 1845 Hopkins was named special agent to Paraguay, a country that had declared its independence thirty-four years earlier but with which the United States had never established diplomatic relations. Traveling overland to his post, the young Yankee diplomat was delighted by what he found. "The moment you cross the Paraguayan frontier, your knives and pistols you may throw away, the most perfect security existing all over the land. The Spanish characteristics of sudden anger and swift revenge seem not to belong to them." The Paraguayans whom he met constituted "a most extraordinary people. The extent to which their manufactures are carried is far superior to *any other* people of this Continent." Hopkins did not find Paraguayans inferior; indeed, he believed that "the history of the world has never presented such a dignified and glorious aspect, as the Paraguayan nation does at the present moment"; Paraguayans "are, next to our own country, *the most united, the richest, and the strongest nation of the new world.*"[22]

Secretary of State Buchanan must have known that he was taking a risk in appointing Hopkins, for he observed in the envoy's instructions that "you are younger than most of those to whom such trusts have been confided." In nine months Hopkins fully justified Buchanan's lack of confidence by meddling in Argentine-Paraguayan relations, and the secretary of state ordered him to return to the United States immediately.[23] Hopkins decided instead to remain in Paraguay as a private businessman and, with the passage of time (and change of administrations), in 1851 he was named the first U.S. consul to the country, in which capacity he began once again to send reports to Washington. By this time Hopkins no longer held a positive view of Paraguay or anywhere else in Latin America. "It is making too much of any one of these nations of Spanish origin, to send to them a full mission," he wrote to the Secretary of State. "These unfortunate nations are unable to arrange their own affairs, for they are all weak and powerless without the means of locomotion, save Brazil. And this latter although more powerful, is far from being an emblem of progress and only uses her power to absorb the frontiers of her more feeble neighbors."[24]

This change in Edward Hopkins's evaluation directly challenges the hypothesis that beliefs about Latin American inferiority are the product of uninformed officials who rely upon hearsay and prejudice. Hopkins may have shifted his opinion for an idiosyncratic reason (he came out on the losing side of a financial conflict with Paraguayan President López), but there must be more to it than that, for his experience echoes that of dozens and dozens of additional envoys whom we have met in the preceding chapters. Like Hopkins, many experienced diplomats over a span of nearly two centuries seem not to have been prejudiced against Latin America or Hispanic Americans and, unlike Hopkins, they appear to have had successful careers. Nonetheless, a surprisingly large proportion of them turn sour on the region, and end their careers believing that Latin Americans are inferior to their northern neighbors.

A recent example is Lawrence Harrison, who spent two decades working for the U.S. government, including thirteen years in several Latin American countries. In 1964 Harrison was sent to Costa Rica as an official of the U.S. Agency for International Development, "convinced," he wrote, "that a combination of money, Yankee ingenuity, and good intentions would transform the region to one of rapidly developing, vigorous democracies in a decade or two." Twenty years later Harrison found that he had become bitterly disillusioned, and so he retired and wrote a book that explains the region's continuing underdevelopment as a product of Latin America's inferior culture: "Human development is frustrated in most Hispanic-American countries by a way of seeing the world that impedes the achievement of political pluralism, social equity, and dynamic economic progress." In Latin America, he concluded, "we see a cultural pattern, derivative of traditional Hispanic culture, that is anti-democratic, anti-social, anti-progress, anti-entrepreneurial, and, at least among the elite, anti-work."[25]

Harrison may be correct, or he may be mistaken—we have never even defined such amorphous terms as "anti-progress," yet alone conducted the research that would be needed to say whether the term characterizes Latin Americans. Perhaps some day we will have accumulated sufficient evidence to permit a generalization, but that day is in the future, and until it arrives, it seems safe only to argue, as everyone since Plato has, that culture has an effect on behavior. Everything else is a hypothesis—an educated guess. It may be possible that such a thing as "Hispanic culture" actually exists, although there is ample reason to question whether the term has much analytic utility when referring to a diverse array of peoples living in twenty or more countries marked by multiple migratory streams over several centuries. But the purported existence of this culture is only the beginning of Harrison's hypothesis; it is his independent variable. His full hypothesis, which captures perfectly the position of two centuries of U.S. foreign policy officials, is that Latin Americans, heirs to Hispanic culture, have evolved into an inferior civilization. Culture does not explain simply some undetermined portion of human behavior in an abstract sense; it explains a specific outcome: Latin American underdevelopment.

How can we be certain that nearly a half-billion human beings are "anti-progress" (or any other term describing underdevelopment) by virtue of the fact that they have inherited, in radically varying proportions, something as vague and mysterious as a Hispanic culture? The answer is that we cannot be certain; we are guessing—hypothesizing—and our guesses are biased by our own peculiar experiences. Lacking firsthand experience in Latin America, officials such as George Kennan and Jeane Kirkpatrick have no alternative other than to fall back on secondhand knowledge—they repeat the dominant Anglo view of Hispanic culture, embedded in U.S. foreign relations since the days of John Quincy Adams, but camouflaged in the post–World War II era first by national character analysis and then by social science development theory.[26] Experienced U.S. officials such as Lawrence Harrison construct the same hypothesis but by a different process: equipped with the same background, they misperceive and therefore misinterpret what they experience in Latin America.

Lawrence Harrison tells us that he went to Latin America to implement the Alliance for Progress. It was a daunting responsibility. "Many kinds of changes in attitudes and values are involved," explained President Kennedy's assistant secretary of state for inter-American affairs, Edwin Martin: "Among them is a view of the importance of precision in measurement, whether of time, or costs, or distances; a pragmatic rather than doctrinaire approach to the solution of differences and problems; an appreciation of the value of work with the hands and of scientific knowledge as compared to humanistic studies; a sense of public responsibility and public trust and through this of more respect for the contribution of good government to the public welfare; more team spirit and less individualism; an understanding of the importance of social and economic opportunity and mobility guided by performance rather than status." Assistant Secretary Martin acknowledged that "thousands of Latin Americans understand these matters and have made these changes, but it must become millions."[27] Getting from thousands to millions was Lawrence Harrison's job.

He tells us that he failed. Realizing his failure, he resigned from AID and returned to the United States, where he wrote a book blaming his failure on Latin America's cultural inferiority. But a person without Harrison's personal involvement might have written a quite different book, one that began by recognizing how the goals of the Alliance for Progress, which seemed so reasonable in the 1960s, were hopelessly naive. If we had realized then what we know today—that no power on earth can accomplish what Assistant Secretary Martin instructed AID to accomplish—then we would not be looking for an explanation of Latin America's inferiority, but of Washington's naivete. We should have expected to fail in our effort to induce millions of people to recalibrate their scientific-humanistic balance. We should have expected that AID officials would be frustrated by their inability to convince Latin Americans to accept Washington's view of progress—precision, pragmatism, science, team-spirit, and all the rest of the self- congratulatory culture that the residents of Camelot believed they had perfected. We should have expected that one product of this failure would be frustration and an occasional memoir of underdevelopment.

Seen from this perspective, the Alliance for Progress is a perfect metaphor, three words that capture the essence of the relationship between Latin America and the United States. As we have sifted through nearly two centuries of despatches from Latin America, the Alliance pattern has appeared with striking regularity: U.S. envoys undertake to help Latin Americans change their ways. Latin Americans resist. Envoys become frustrated. And, when their frustration becomes acute, either they call in the Marines (or create something like the Nicaraguan Contras), or they go home and write a memoir about Latin America's inferior culture. This pattern has been crystal clear from the beginning, when early-nineteenth-century envoys successfully negotiated commercial agreements, which both sides desired, then stubbed their toes on the issue of freedom of worship, a topic most Latin American governments did not want to discuss. Apparently they had all the freedom of religion they wanted, even if U.S. officials thought it was not quite enough.

Because of the power disparities (and trading opportunities) that exist between the United States and its neighbors, most Latin Americans have recognized the wisdom of appearing cooperative—a wisdom that the United States has continually reinforced with coercion. One way to appear cooperative is to avoid direct confrontation by humoring the powerful Yankees. If a new U.S. administration wants everyone to meet at Punta del Este and sign the Charter of the Alliance for Progress, then everyone will show up as requested, but only the most naive among us would expect the governments of Anastasio Somoza or Alberto Stroessner to implement the reforms called for in the Charter. This "obedezco pero no cumplo" [I obey but do not comply] behavioral syndrome is considered by many U.S. officials to be a pathology of Latin American culture. It is the pattern that former Assistant Secretary Huntington Wilson discovered in Ecuador— "their ingrained grace of manner and expression" masking the fact that "out of sight they amount to nothing, are not efficient, and do not make good."[28] This is the pattern that so befuddles today's envoys seeking Latin America's cooperation in stanching the northward flow of illegal drugs, leading them to conclude that the problem must be corruption, when perhaps we are witnessing nothing more complex than the invisible hand of supply and demand, with Latin American governments finding it difficult to control supply and the U.S. governments finding it difficult to control demand.

Like nearly every other frustrated envoy whom we have encountered since the second decade of the nineteenth century, Lawrence Harrison began to form his misperception when he accepted an offer of employment from the U.S. government, because that offer was based on the unrealistic premise that Latin Americans would welcome U.S. assistance in remaking their societies. That premise led the Kennedy administration to send an entire legion of AID officials southward, not simply to help Latin Americans learn to measure time more precisely, but also to assist them in creating the kind of economic system that the United States considers best for them, the kind of political system that the United States believes will improve them, the kind of international relations that the United States thinks will make them (and us) more secure—the kind of society that we believe would be best for everyone, but developed first in the United States because our progress was not retarded by a Hispanic culture. The frustration among U.S. envoys rises to the surface when Latin Americans quietly drag their feet, stubbornly resisting this well-intentioned counsel—when today's AID officials discover, as the first U.S. minister to Chile wrote 175 years ago, "very much opinionated, it is difficult to administer them, any salutary advice."[29]

If it is true that the tendency of experienced U.S. officials to denigrate Latin Americans is born of frustration over Latin Americans' unwillingness to accept well-intentioned advice, then the future is bleak indeed, for well-intentioned advice has become the principal U.S. government export to Latin America. Today AID is promoting economic growth in Nicaragua by advising "budget cuts, slower money growth, a market exchange rate, an end to state-owned foreign trade monopolies, the introduction of private banks, privatization of almost half of all state-owned companies, tariff reductions, and a 12 percent reduction in public employment." The United States is also helping to promote democracy, proudly asserting that "USAID has been the foremost donor in rule of law activities in Latin

America, enhancing the professionalism of the judiciary through merit selection of judges and establishment of judicial schools in Panama, El Salvador, Honduras and Argentina and accelerating the introduction of adversarial criminal procedures in Bolivia, Peru, El Salvador and Guatemala."[30]

Perhaps today's Latin Americans have reconsidered their traditional unwillingness to reconstruct their societies with Washington's blueprints, but history suggests otherwise. Ignoring this history, the next Lawrence Harrison is in La Paz right now, helping Bolivians to institute U.S.-style adversarial criminal procedures. His AID colleagues are in Nicaragua, dangling U.S. government checks before a destitute people in order to encourage what they call "structural adjustment," which seems to be aimed at a reconstruction of the good old days before the Sandinista revolution, minus Somoza. Anyone who has looked even briefly at the history of U.S.-Nicaraguan relations—from Cornelius Vanderbilt and William Walker in the 1850s, to Henry Stimson and Harold Dodds in the 1920s, to Oliver North and the Contras in the 1980s—would wager that it will not work out differently this time. An already-poor people ravaged by a civil war will have no alternative but to appear cooperative, but today's AID officials will almost certainly be frustrated by Nicaragua's half-hearted implementation.

Occasionally one of these officials will return home and write the next memoir about the inferiority of the people who lie beneath the United States. But most will accept their burden quietly, just as one seasoned State Department instructor advised new envoys in the mid-1920s: "If the United States has received but little gratitude, this is only to be expected in a world where gratitude is rarely accorded to the teacher, the doctor, or the policeman, and we have been all three. But it may be that in time they will come to see the United States with different eyes, and to have for her something of the respect and affection with which a man regards the instructor of his youth and a child looks upon the parent who has molded his character."[31] In the meantime, the frustrations will occasionally get the better of U.S. officials, and from time to time an exasperated President will characterize one Latin American leader or another as an unwelcome dog at a garden party, giving us a glimpse of how little has changed in the two centuries since John Quincy Adams and his generation fashioned the mold that still constrains our thinking.

Sources

Notes

Index

Sources

Documents written by U.S. officials constitute the primary source material for this volume. Most of the documents are located in Washington, D.C., at the Manuscripts Division of the Library of Congress (LC in the Notes) and at the National Archives (NA in the Notes, generally followed immediately by a letter ["M," "T," or "LM"] indicating a microform set, then a slash and a reel number as, for example, "NA M77/R44").

With the exceptions indicated in the individual notes that follow, I have read the original or a facsimile (generally on microform) of every primary document cited in this volume. It was not my original intention to do so. In Chapter 1 I relied heavily on printed collections of primary sources such as Charles Francis Adams's edition of his father's diary, but it did not take me long to discover the uneven quality of printed collections of primary sources, and so I have used the originals whenever possible. My use of these primary sources was made infinitely easier by the collections of documents produced by generations of my predecessors. When I began the research for this volume, I did not know how absolutely I could trust the work of William R. Manning, and so I simply used his work on the period up to 1860 as a guide to the originals. Manning committed the cardinal sin of penciling brackets on the original despatches to indicate parts that he intended to reprint, but that made it easier for me to determine whether he had omitted anything of significance. Perhaps a Higher Authority will forgive him in light of the fact that his compilation is virtually infallible. Anyone repeating my steps would be well advised to go no further than Manning (*Diplomatic Correspondence of the United States Concerning the Independence of Latin-America*, 3 vols., and *Diplomatic Correspondence of the United States, Inter-American Affairs, 1831–1860*, 12 vols.) and not bother squinting through a microfilm reader at the wretched handwriting in most of the originals. The same can be said for the work of Elting E. Morison (*The Letters of Theodore Roosevelt*, 8 vols.) and Arthur S. Link

(*The Papers of Woodrow Wilson*, 57 vols.). Throughout this volume I have used both Richardson's *Compilation of Messages and Papers of the Presidents* and the more recent (Herbert Hoover onwards) *Public Papers of the President of the United States* (PPP) as "primary" sources for Presidential statements. I was not so unquestioning of the government's *Papers Relating to the Foreign Relations of the United States,* published annually since 1861 and cited here as FRUS. Some volumes are so severely larded with ellipses as to be worthless, but many volumes are so comprehensive that consultation of the originals is unnecessary. The 1905 FRUS documents on the Dominican Republic (especially pp. 352, 381, and 408) and the 1928 FRUS documents on Nicaragua (especially the 20 January 1928 Munro despatch which omits a crucial comment that "the Latin American shows little stability of character") are examples of this distorting editing, whereas the 1933 FRUS coverage of Cuba contains almost everything in Record Group 59, plus additional materials from other sources. Unfortunately, there is no way to know in advance which years are comprehensive and accurate, and in the end I used the FRUS volumes as a supplement to other sources, and then only after consultation with scholars who have worked extensively with the primary materials.

Both common courtesy and sincere gratitude oblige me to acknowledge that this book rests on the scholarship of others. The work of six generations of historians has helped me to make sense out of what otherwise would have been an incomprehensible two-century blur of events and personalities, but that is not the kind of debt I mean to acknowledge here: these predecessors have served as my guides to the primary documents. In most cases their prior work meant that I did not have to read entire fileboxes or microfilm runs; indeed, I cannot recall a day when I went to the archives without a list of materials that others had already identified for me. Once I was there, I stumbled onto some things by myself, but most of my discoveries were assisted. It has been difficult for me to determine how, precisely, to recognize the contribution these predecessors have made to this work and to my thinking without ending every sentence with a note. I have limited the citations to those giving (a) the precise location of direct quotations and (b) the source of a specific idea that the reader might otherwise be led to believe had sprung from my own mind. This volume's full bibliography can be obtained electronically: http://www.unc.edu/ ~schoultz/bibliography.html.

Unless otherwise indicated, all National Archives materials are from

Record Group (RG) 59, General Records of the Department of State, which is now at Archives II in College Park, Maryland. Other record groups consulted, most of them only slightly, are as follows:

Records of United States Participation in International Conferences, Commissions, and Expositions (RG 43)
Records of the Navy (RG 45)
Records of Boundary and Claims Commissions and Arbitrations (RG 76)
Records of the Foreign Service Posts of the Department of State (RG 84)
Records of the Dominican Customs Receivership (RG 139)
Records of the Military Government of Cuba (RG 140)
Records of the War Department General and Special Staffs (RG 165)
Records of the Panama Canal (RG 185)
Records of the Provisional Government of Cuba (RG 199)
Records of the Office of Inter-American Affairs (RG 229)
Records of the House of Representatives (RG 233)
Records of the Bureau of Insular Affairs (RG 350)
Records of the Interdepartmental and the Intradepartmental Committees (RG 353)
Records of the Office of the Adjutant General (RG 407)
Records of the U.S. Foreign Assistance Agencies (RG 469)

The following papers were consulted at the Manuscripts Division of the Library of Congress, Washington, D.C.:

Chandler P. Anderson Papers
Thomas Bayard Papers
William Borah Papers
William S. Caperton Papers
Grover Cleveland Papers
William Day Papers
Hamilton Fish Papers
Walter Gresham Papers
Benjamin Harrison Papers
John Hay Papers
Charles Evans Hughes Papers

Philip Jessup Papers
Frank Kellogg Papers (LC microfilm version of Minnesota originals)
Philander Knox Papers
John Lejeune Papers
William Marcy Papers
William McKinley Papers
John Bassett Moore Papers
Richard Olney Papers
James K. Polk Papers
Theodore Roosevelt Papers
Elihu Root Papers
William Howard Taft Papers
Woodrow Wilson Papers
Leonard Wood Papers

In addition to the National Archives and the Library of Congress, I have obtained documents from the following sources, with the asterisked (*) items available in microform:

*Adams Family Papers, Massachusetts Historical Society, Boston
Bernard Baruch Papers, Princeton University, New Jersey
*Adolph Berle Papers, Franklin D. Roosevelt Library, Hyde Park, New York
James Buchanan Papers, Historical Society of Pennsylvania, Philadelphia
*Cowley Papers (Henry Wellesley, 1st Earl of Cowley), Public Records Office, London, England
Dwight David Eisenhower Papers, Eisenhower Library, Abilene, Kansas
Joseph Grew Papers, Harvard University, Cambridge, Massachusetts
Herbert Hoover Papers, Hoover Library, West Branch, Iowa
Lyndon B. Johnson Papers, Johnson Library, Austin, Texas
John F. Kennedy Papers, Kennedy Library, Boston, Massachusetts
Arthur Bliss Lane Papers, Yale University, New Haven, Connecticut
Henry Morgenthau, Jr., Papers, Franklin D. Roosevelt Library, Hyde Park, New York
Dwight Morrow Papers, Amherst College, Amherst, Massachusetts

Normanby Papers (Constantine Henry Phipps, 1st Marquis of Normanby), Mulgrave Archives, Lythe Hall, North Yorkshire, England

Palmerston Papers (Henry John Temple, 3d Viscount Palmerston), University of Southampton, England

Orville H. Platt Papers, Connecticut State Library, Hartford

Franklin Delano Roosevelt Papers, Roosevelt Library, Hyde Park, New York

Theodore Roosevelt Papers, Harvard University, Cambridge, Massachusetts

James R. Sheffield Papers, Yale University, New Haven, Connecticut

*Henry L. Stimson Papers, Yale University, New Haven, Connecticut

Harry S. Truman Papers, Truman Library, Independence, Missouri

Francis White Papers, Herbert Hoover Library, West Branch, Iowa

*Francis Mairs Huntington Wilson Papers, Ursinus College, Collegeville, Pennsylvania

Documents in these collections have occasionally been misfiled, and some have been microfilmed out of sequence or tucked away in logical but not obvious places—for example, President Polk's initial bid for peace with Mexico is filed with Ceremonial Letters, interspersed with messages of congratulations on the births and weddings of European nobility, and kept in the white-glove "treasure vault" deep beneath the National Archive's Pennsylvania Avenue facility. In these cases of incorrect or obscure filing, I have given expanded directions for locating the errant documents, but most of the notes are limited to what an experienced researcher or a reference librarian would need to replicate my steps.

I have reprinted quotations *verbatim et litteratim,* with the single exception of omitting ellipses at the beginning and the end of quotations when doing so would not in any way change the meaning of the quotation; of course, ellipses have been used to indicate words omitted in the middle of a passage.

Notes

Preface

1. News Conference, 21 February 1985, *PPP, Ronald Reagan, 1985,* vol. 1, p. 200; Address to the Nation, 16 March 1986, *PPP, Ronald Reagan, 1986,* vol. 1, p. 354.

2. News Conference, 28 October 1989, *PPP, George Bush, 1989,* vol. 2, pp. 1410, 1414.

3. Knox to Nicaraguan Chargé, 1 December 1909, Records of the Division of Current Information, Confidential Publications, Information Series A, vol. 1, no. 6, NA; Huntington Wilson to Whitelaw Reid, 1 July 1901, 817.00/1147, NA M632/R6; Elijah Hise to John Clayton, 15 September 1849, and Henry Savage to James Buchanan, 5 February 1848, both about Nicaragua but filed with Despatches from Guatemala, NA M219/R4.

4. William Hunter to John Forsyth, 12 August 1839, Despatches from Brazil, NA M121/R13.

1. Encountering Latin America

1. JQ Adams Diary, 19 September 1820, *Memoirs of John Quincy Adams, Comprising Portions of His Diary from 1795 to 1848,* Charles Francis Adams, ed., 12 vols. (Philadelphia: J.B. Lippincott, 1874–1877), vol. 5, p. 176.

2. Madison's 1811 message to Congress is reprinted in *A Compilation of the Messages and Papers of the Presidents, 1789–1902,* James D. Richardson, ed., 11 vols. (New York: Bureau of National Literature and Art, 1907), vol. 1, p. 494; the December 1811 Congressional committee resolution is in *Annals of Congress,* 12th Cong., 1st Sess., pp. 427–428; Secretary of State Monroe's notification of European powers is discussed in Monroe to Alexander Scott, 14 May 1812, in U.S. Congress, House, House Report 72, 20th Cong., 2d Sess., 10 February 1829, p. 9.

3. Beaufort T. Watts to Henry Clay, 10 March 1828, Despatches from Colombia, NA T33/R4; Bolívar to Juan José Flores, 9 November 1830, *Cartas del Libertador,* 2d ed., 8 vols. (Caracas: Banco de Venezuela, 1964), vol. 7, p. 587.

4. For an early example of this fear, see Jefferson to General John Armstrong, 17 July 1797, *The Writings of Thomas Jefferson*, Albert Ellery Bergh, ed., 20 vols. (Washington, D.C.: The Thomas Jefferson Memorial Association, 1903–1904), vol. 11, p. 284; for a prewar fear, see Madison to William Pinkney, 30 October 1810, *The Writings of James Madison*, Gaillard Hunt, ed., 9 vols. (New York: G. P. Putnam's Sons, 1900–1910), vol. 8, p. 121.

5. Smith to William Pinkney, 13 June 1810, and a second warning, 22 January 1811, Instructions to U.S. Ministers, NA M77/R2; the No-Transfer Resolution is 2 Stat. 666; for Congress's public discussion of the Resolution, see *Annals of Congress*, vol. 22, pp. 369–380, 486, 1117–1148; for the confidential record, see David Hunter Miller, *Secret Statutes of the United States: A Memorandum* (Washington, D.C.: GPO, 1918).

6. Monroe to JQ Adams, 10 December 1815, Instructions to U.S. Ministers, NA M77/R3.

7. *Journals of the Continental Congress* 20 (June 1781), p. 705.

8. JQ Adams to Albert Gallatin, 19 May 1818, Instructions to U.S. Ministers, NA M77/R3; *ASP*, vol. 4, pp. 818–819; JQ Adams to Smith Thompson, 20 May 1819, Domestic Letters, NA M40/R15; for the dominant view from Congress, see the speech by Gideon Tomlinson, *Annals of Congress*, 18th Cong., 1st Sess. (13 February 1824), esp. p. 1508.

9. Adams Diary, 9 March 1821, *Memoirs of John Quincy Adams*, vol. 5, p. 325.

10. Adams to Jefferson, 3 February 1821, *The Adams-Jefferson Letters: The Complete Correspondence between Thomas Jefferson and Abigail and John Adams*, Lester J. Cappon, ed. (Chapel Hill: University of North Carolina Press, 1988), p. 571.

11. The journey across Spain is chronicled in *Diary and Autobiography of John Adams*, L. H. Butterfield, ed., 4 vols. (Cambridge: Harvard University Press, 1961), vol. 2, pp. 417–427; vol. 4, p. 238; vol. 6, p. 240; Adams to James Lloyd, 27 and 30 March 1815, *Works of John Adams*, Charles Francis Adams, ed., 10 vols. (Boston: Little, Brown, 1850–1856), vol. 10, pp. 144–145, 150.

12. JQ Adams Diary, 24 December 1779 to 7 January 1780, *Diary of John Quincy Adams*, Robert J. Taylor and Marc Friedlaender, eds., 2 vols. (Cambridge: Harvard University Press, 1981), vol. 1, pp. 17–27.

13. JQ Adams Diary, 11 March 1785, *Diary of John Quincy Adams*, vol. 1, p. 233; for the elder Adams's view, see J. Adams to Jefferson, 22 January 1825, *Adams-Jefferson Letters*, pp. 606–607. The Adams family was living in Paris when Jefferson arrived in August 1784; they moved to London in May 1785.

14. Thomas Jefferson, *Notes on the State of Virginia* (Philadelphia: R. T. Rawle, 1801 edition of 1787 original), p. 71n. On the language claim, see the 23 November 1804 entry in Adams's diary, *Memoirs of John Quincy Adams*, vol. 1, p. 317; see also Jefferson to Peter Carr, 10 August 1787, *The Papers of Thomas Jefferson*, Julian P. Boyd, ed. (Princeton: Princeton University Press, 1950+), vol. 12, p. 14.

15. Evidence of von Humboldt's influence can be found in Jefferson's thank-you

note, 6 March 1809, *Writings of Thomas Jefferson,* vol. 12, p. 263. John Quincy Adams also had the opportunity to learn from von Humboldt when he attended one of the naturalist's seminars in Paris in early 1815. For evidence that Humboldt's positive view of Latin Americans was not lost on his North American audience, see a review of his *Political Essay,* probably written by Samuel Latham Mitchell, *New York Medical Repository* 3 (May, June, and July 1812), pp. 350–351.

16. Jefferson to Lafayette, 14 May 1817; see also Jefferson to Adams, 22 January 1821; Jefferson to von Humboldt, 6 December 1813, *Writings of Thomas Jefferson,* vol. 15, pp. 117, 170, 309; vol. 9, pp. 430–431; for Jefferson's pessimistic view of Latin Americans, see Jefferson to Thaddeus Kosciusko, 13 April 1811; Jefferson to Monsieur Dupont De Nemours, 15 April 1811; Jefferson to von Humboldt, 6 December 1813, *Writings of Thomas Jefferson,* vol. 13, pp. 40, 43; vol 14, p. 21.

17. Poinsett to JQ Adams, 4 November 1818, Communications from Special Agents, NA M37/R3.

18. Alexander Scott to James Monroe, 16 November 1812 and 1 January 1813, Consular Letters from La Guaira, NA M84/R1; for Scott's harrowing experience, see U.S. Congress, House, House Report 72, 20th Cong., 2d Sess., 10 February 1829. Scott's instructions are misfiled in Monroe to Scott, 14 May 1812, Communications from Special Agents, NA M37/R4.

19. Rodney to JQ Adams, 5 November 1818; Graham to JQ Adams, 5 November 1818; Bland to JQ Adams, 2 November 1818, *ASP,* vol. 4, pp. 219, 225, 295, 282.

20. *Memoirs of John Quincy Adams,* vol. 6, pp. 156, 159, 160; vol. 4, p. 388. A fourth report was written by the commission's secretary, Henry M. Brackenridge, and published as *Voyage to South America, Performed by Order of the American Government in the Years 1817 and 1818,* 2 vols. (Baltimore: Cushing, 1819).

21. Halsey to Monroe, 20 April 1816 and 3 July 1816, Consular Despatches from Buenos Aires, NA M70/R1; see also Forbes to JQ Adams, 24 January 1824, Consular Despatches from Buenos Aires, NA M70/R3; Forbes to Henry Clay, 18 September 1825, Despatches from Argentina, NA M69/R3.

22. Prevost to JQ Adams, 10 June 1818 and (for Peru) 27 November 1823, Communications from Special Agents, NA M37/R3; Hogan to JQ Adams, 8 July 1823 and 23 July 1823, Consular Despatches from Valparaiso, M146/R1; for an early example of the same views, see Poinsett to Monroe, 20 February 1813, Communications from Special Agents, NA M37/R3.

23. Worthington to JQ Adams, 4 July 1818, Despatches from Argentina, NA M69/R1; JQ Adams Diary, 28 March and 3 November 1818, *Memoirs of John Quincy Adams,* vol. 4, pp. 70, 158–159.

24. Lowry to JQ Adams, 22 September 1822, Consular Despatches from La Guaira, M84/R1; Hill to JQ Adams, undated May 1821, Consular Despatches from Rio de Janeiro, NA T172/R1; see also Todd to JQ Adams, 5 February 1823 and 18 November 1823, Despatches from Colombia, NA T33/R2.

25. The self-description is JQ Adams Diary, 4 June 1819, *Memoirs of John Quincy Adams,* vol. 4, p. 388.

26. JQ Adams to Rodney, 17 May 1823; for the more optimistic instructions to the first U.S. minister to Colombia, see JQ Adams to Anderson, 27 May 1823, Instructions to U.S. Ministers, NA M77/R4. On the development of these instructions, see *Writings of John Quincy Adams,* vol. 7, pp. 422–424n; Monroe to JQ Adams, circa 27 May 1823, Adams Family Papers, Massachusetts Historical Society, Boston, final (unnumbered) page of microfilm reel 460; *Writings of John Quincy Adams,* vol. 7, p. 467.

27. The new minister to Colombia, for example, was to "counteract the efforts which it cannot be doubted European negotiators will continue to make in the furtherance of their monarchical and monopolizing contemplations." JQ Adams to Anderson, 27 May 1823, Instructions to U.S. Ministers, NA M77/R4.

28. JQ Adams Diary, 19 September 1820, *Memoirs of John Quincy Adams,* vol. 5, p. 176; JQ Adams Diary, 9 March 1821, *Memoirs of John Quincy Adams,* vol. 5, p. 325; see also JQ Adams to Charles Ingersoll, 19 June 1823, *Writings of John Quincy Adams,* vol. 7, p. 488.

29. For Monroe and Adams's annoyance with Clay, see Adams Diary, 28 March 1818, 22 April and 20 June 1822, *Diary of John Quincy Adams,* vol. 4, p. 70, vol. 5, p. 496, vol. 6, p. 26.

30. Clay's motion is *Annals of Congress,* 15th Cong., 1st Sess., 24 March 1818, pp. 1468–1469, followed by the four-day speech, pp. 1474–1646. The 28 March vote is recorded on p. 1646.

31. For the Senate debate, see the *Congressional Globe,* 19th Cong., 1st Sess., 1825–26, February 15, 16, 23, 24, and March 1, 2, 13, 14 (pp. 112–132, 142–343). The House discussion began in mid-December, but the principal debates occurred on February 1, 2, 3, March 25, 27, April 4, 5, 10, 11, 12, 13, 14, 15, 17, 18, 19, 20, 21, 22 (pp. 1226–2514 *passim*). See also U.S. Congress, Senate, *The Executive Proceedings of the Senate of the United States, on the Subject of the Mission to the Congress of Panama. Together with the Messages and Documents Relating Thereto,* Senate Executive Document 68, 19th Cong., 1st Sess., 1826; *ASP,* vol. 5, pp. 834–905.

32. On the slavery issue, see *Congressional Globe,* 1 and 2 March 1826, pp. 112–132; for the envoys' instructions, see Clay to Anderson and Sergeant, 8 May 1826, Instructions to U.S. Ministers, 1801–1906, NA M77/R6; for the confirmation process, see *Senate Executive Journal,* vol. 3, pp. 457–459, 473–490, 514, 518, and, for Poinsett's later appointment in Mexico, pp. 554, 567. For the Adams-Clay speeches over recognition, see Arthur P. Whitaker, *The United States and the Independence of Latin America, 1800–1830* (Baltimore: The Johns Hopkins Press, 1941), pp. 344–369; on the general issue of domestic politics and U.S. foreign policy at this time, see Ernest R. May, *The Making of the Monroe Doctrine* (Cambridge: Harvard University Press, 1975).

33. José María Salazar to Clay, 20 November 1826, Notes from the Colombian Legation, NA M51/R2. For a first-person account of the effects of the *vómito prieto,*

see Daniel Florencio O'Leary, *Memorias de General O'Leary, publicadas por su hijo, Simón B. O'Leary,* 34 vols. (Caracas: Imprenta de la Gaceta Oficial, 1879–1888), vol. 8, p. 210.

34. Allen to JQ Adams, 9 February 1825; see also Allen to Clay, 1 September 1825, 4 February 1826, 4 April 1826, 26 August 1826, Despatches from Chile, NA M10/R1 and R2.

35. Watts to Clay, 10 March 1828, Despatches from Colombia, NA T33/R4; Tudor to Clay, 3 February 1827, Consular Despatches from Lima, NA M154/R1; Larned to Clay, 18 November 1827, Despatches from Chile, NA M10/R2.

36. Clay to John Forbes, 14 April 1825, Instructions to U.S. Ministers, NA M77/R5.

2. Acquiring Northern Mexico

1. Butler to Forsyth, 17 June 1835, Despatches from Mexico, NA M97/R7.

2. Waddy Thompson, *Recollections of Mexico* (New York: Wiley and Putnam, 1846), pp. 46, 18–19.

3. Poinsett to Clay, 6 October 1827, in U.S. Congress, House, *Boundary—United States and Mexico,* House Exec. Doc. No. 42, 25th Cong., 1st Sess., 1837, p. 25; Thompson, *Recollections of Mexico,* p. 19.

4. The statehood discussion is *Annals of Congress,* 11th Cong., 3d Sess., 1810–1811, pp. 482–486, 518–519; the laws are 2 Stat. 283 (1804), 2 Stat. 641 (1811), and 2 Stat. 701 (1812).

5. "The boundary line between the two countries west of the Mississippi shall begin on the Gulf of Mexico, at the mouth of the river Sabine, in the sea, continuing north, along the western bank of that river." 8 Stat. 252.

6. Jefferson to Monroe, 14 May 1820, in *The Writings of Thomas Jefferson,* Albert Ellery Bergh, ed., 20 vols. (Washington, D.C.: The Thomas Jefferson Memorial Association, 1903–1904), vol. 15, pp. 251–252.

7. José Manuel de Herrera to José Manuel Bermúdez Zozaya ["Zozaya" in official documents], 31 October 1822, in México, Secretaría de Relaciones Exteriores, *La diplomacia mexicana,* 3 vols. (México: Tipografía "Artística," 1910–1913), vol. 1, p. 87.

8. "Se tiene por legítimo y valedero el arreglo de límites que aparece en el Tratado de 22 de febrero de 1819." de Herrera to Zozaya, 31 October 1822, in *La diplomacia mexicana,* vol. 1, p. 85.

9. Poinsett's instructions are Clay to Poinsett, March 26, 1825, in House, *Boundary—United States and Mexico,* pp. 5–6; the new treaty (8 Stat. 372) was signed in Mexico City in January 1828 and promptly approved by the U.S. Senate, but ratifying documents were not exchanged until 1832.

10. *Memoirs of John Quincy Adams, Comprising Portions of His Diary from 1795 to 1848,* Charles Francis Adams, ed., 12 vols. (Philadelphia: J. B. Lippincott and Co., 1874–1875), vol. 6, pp. 177–178.

11. Zozaya to de Herrera, 7 December 1822, and Zozaya to de Herrera, 26 December 1822, *La diplomacia mexicana,* vol. 1, pp. 89, 103.

12. House, *Boundary—United States and Mexico,* pp. 10–14.

13. Poinsett to Clay, 12 October 1825, Despatches from Mexico, NA M97/R2; Poinsett to Van Buren, 10 March 1829, NA M97/R5.

14. Jackson to Butler, 10 October 1829, in *Correspondence of Andrew Jackson,* John Spenser Bassett, ed., 7 vols. (Washington, D.C.: Carnegie Institution, 1926–1935), vol. 4, pp. 80–81. He ended, "When you have read this P.S. and my private letter you will burn them both."

15. Ibid., p. 81; Butler to Jackson, 6 February 1834, ibid., vol. 5, pp. 244–246. Random underscoring deleted.

16. Butler to Jackson, 7 March 1834, ibid., vol. 5, pp. 251–253. Random underscoring deleted.

17. Thompson, *Recollections of Mexico,* p. 240.

18. Morfit to Forsyth, 10 September 1836, Despatches from Texas, NA T728/R1; see also Ellis to Forsyth, 19 May 1836, Despatches from Mexico, NA M97/R8.

19. Green to Calhoun, 24 January 1842, in *Annual Report of the American Historical Association for the Year 1899, volume II: Calhoun Correspondence,* J. Franklin Jameson, ed. (Washington, D.C.: GPO, 1900), pp. 842–843.

20. The clearest statement of this interpretation of British intentions is Green to Calhoun, 24 January 1842, in *Calhoun Correspondence,* p. 841.

21. Upshur to Edward Everett, 28 September 1843, Instructions to Great Britain, NA M77/R74; the argument is also in Upshur to Murphy, 8 August 1843, Instructions to Texas, NA M77/R161.

22. Upshur had completed work on the treaty when he took a day off, invited by the Navy to cruise the Potomac and witness the capabilities of the new guns aboard the USS *Princeton.* Assuming the position of precedence that befits the ranking member of the cabinet, Upshur was standing next to one of the weapons when it exploded like a grenade, blowing him to bits.

23. *Congressional Globe,* 21 January 1845, Appendix p. 146.

24. 5 Stat. 797; *Congressional Globe,* 27 February 1845, p. 363.

25. Issac Van Zandt and J. Pinckney Henderson to Anson Jones, 10 June 1844, in *Annual Report of the American Historical Association for the Year 1908, volume 2: Diplomatic Correspondence of the Republic of Texas,* George P. Garrison, ed. (Washington, D.C.: Government Printing Office, 1911), p. 285.

26. Written on 22 April 1844 to a group of Cincinnati political leaders, Polk's letter is reprinted in John S. Jenkins, *James Knox Polk and a History of His Administration* (Auburn and Buffalo, N.Y.: John E. Beardsley, 1850), pp. 120–123.

27. Robert J. Walker, "Letter of Mr. Walker, of Mississippi, Relative to the Annexation of Texas," Washington, D.C., 8 January 1844, p. 12. A facsimile of the Washington *Globe* edition of Walker's letter, from which the quotations here are taken, is repro-

duced in the appendix of Frederick Merk, *Fruits of Propaganda in the Tyler Administration* (Cambridge: Harvard University Press, 1971), pp. 221–252.

28. De Bocanegra to Thompson, 23 August 1843, enclosed with Thompson to Upshur, 25 August 1843, Despatches from Mexico, NA M97/R12; Juan Almonte to Upshur, 3 November 1843, Notes from the Mexican Legation, NA M54/R2.

29. Buchanan to Slidell, 10 November 1845. Senate Exec. Doc. No. 52, 30th Cong., 1st Sess., 1848, p. 79; Polk to Slidell, 17 December 1845, Letterbook, 1845–1846, pp. 198–201, Polk Papers, LC.

30. Manuel de la Peña y Peña to Slidell, 20 December 1845, enclosed with Slidell to Buchanan, 27 December 1845, Despatches from Mexico, NA M97/R13.

31. Parrott to Buchanan, 29 April and 11 October 1845, Despatches from Mexico, NA M97/R13; Black to Buchanan, 6 March 1847, Despatches from U.S. Consuls in Mexico City, NA M296/R5; Slidell to Buchanan, 17 and 27 December 1845, 6 February 1846, 14 January 1846, Despatches from Mexico, NA M97/R13.

32. Here President Polk was being dishonest, for the formal decision to go to war had been made the morning before news of the first shots arrived in Washington. The Polk cabinet met twice on May 9, once before arrival of the news and once after. In the morning meeting, the cabinet decided on a declaration of war; in the afternoon meeting, it simply decided the tactical questions of how the news that had just arrived would affect the content and timing of the war message.

33. *A Compilation of the Messages and Papers of the Presidents, 1789–1902,* James D. Richardson, ed., 11 vols. (New York: Bureau of National Literature and Art, 1907), vol. 4, p. 442.

34. Calhoun to King, 12 August 1844, Instructions to France, NA M77/R55.

35. For the Proviso's introduction, see *Congressional Globe,* 12 August 1846, p. 1217; for the votes, see *Journal of the House of Representatives,* 15 February 1847, pp. 346–350, and 3 March 1847, pp. 501–505, and *Journal of the Senate,* 1 March 1847, p. 252.

36. Calhoun's speech is reported in the third person in the *Congressional Globe,* 9 February 1847, pp. 356–359; an amended version is reprinted in Appendix pp. 323–327.

37. *Congressional Globe,* 5 February 1847, Appendix pp. 296–302; both quotations are on p. 301.

38. *The Collected Works of Abraham Lincoln,* Roy P. Basler, ed., 8 vols. (New Brunswick, N.J.: Rutgers University Press, 1953–1955), vol. 1, pp. 440–442; see also *Congressional Globe,* 18 June 1846, Appendix p. 952; 16 July 1846, pp. 1115–1116; 26 March 1846, Appendix p. 580, and 16 June 1847, p. 928 and Appendix p. 946.

39. *Congressional Globe,* 2 February 1847, Appendix pp. 280–281; see also the comments by New York's Washington Hunt, 13 February 1847, Appendix pp. 364–365.

40. See the attempts by Ambrose Sevier and Lewis Cass in *Congressional Globe,* 5 February 1847, Appendix p. 299; and 10 February 1847, pp. 367–368.

41. *Congressional Globe,* 9 February 1847, p. 359. Perhaps not coincidentally, Cal-

houn's fellow South Carolinian, Waddy Thompson, had written that the Northern departments "contain all the mines, and more of the wealth of the country than any others." Thompson, *Recollections of Mexico*, p. 240.

42. *Congressional Globe*, 5 February 1847, Appendix pp. 301, 297; see also 16 June 1847, Appendix p. 950, and 5 February 1847, Appendix p. 301.

43. *Congressional Globe*, 10 February 1847, pp. 368–369.

44. *Collected Works of Abraham Lincoln*, vol. 1, p. 440.

45. *Congressional Globe*, 13 February 1847, Appendix pp. 363, 365; see also 2 February 1847, pp. 280–281.

46. The peace message is Buchanan to Minister of Foreign Relations of Mexico, 27 July 1846, Diplomatic Correspondence, 1785–1906, Ceremonial Letters, Communications to Foreign Sovereigns and Heads of State, 1829–1877, vol. 2, pp. 2–3, NA; *The Diary of James K. Polk during His Presidency, 1845 to 1849*, Milo Milton Quaife, ed., 4 vols. (Chicago: A.C. McClurg, 1910), vol. 2, pp. 50, 338.

47. Buchanan to Beach, 21 November 1846, Diplomatic Instructions of the Department of State, 1801–1906, Special Missions, NA M77/R152; *Diary of James K. Polk*, vol. 2, p. 477; Beach to Buchanan, 4 June 1847, Communications from Special Agents, 1794–1906, NA M37/R7.

48. Buchanan's message to his Mexican counterpart is reprinted in Senate Exec. Doc. No. 1, 30th Cong,, 1st Sess., 1847, pp. 39–40; *Diary of James K. Polk*, vol. 3, p. 301.

49. Trist's instructions and draft treaty are reprinted in Senate Exec. Doc. No. 52, 30th Cong., 1st Sess., 1847–1848, pp. 81–89; quotation p. 83. For Polk's justification of Trist's appointment, see *Diary of James K. Polk*, vol. 2, p. 466.

50. *Diary of James K. Polk*, vol. 3, pp. 283, 286, 300–301, 345, 358. The recall notice is Buchanan to Trist, 6 October 1847, Instructions to Mexico, NA M77/R112. Buchanan's message was not received by Trist until November 16; his lengthy response is Trist to Buchanan, 6 December 1847, Despatches from Mexico, NA M97/R15.

51. *Congressional Globe*, 26 January 1848, p. 244; see also the remarks of Caleb Smith and David Fisher, pp. 296, 324.

52. Thompson's Greenville, South Carolina, speech is reprinted in *Daily National Intelligencer*, 21 October 1847, p. 2; Polk's agreement is in *Diary of James K. Polk*, vol. 2, p. 308.

53. *Congressional Globe*, 4 January 1848, pp. 96–99; see also 4 February 1848, Appendix pp. 272–278.

54. *Congressional Globe*, 4 March 1848, 14 and 17 January 1848, pp. 162, 183, 429, Appendix p. 270.

55. *Congressional Globe*, 3 February 1848, pp. 196–197.

56. *Congressional Globe*, 12 January and 4 February 1848, pp. 157, 302.

57. *Congressional Globe*, 17 January 1848, p. 188, and 14 February 1848, Appendix p. 349.

58. *Diary of James K. Polk*, vol. 3, p. 223; Calhoun to Thomas Clemson, 7 March

1848, in *Annual Report of the American Historical Association for the Year 1899, volume II: Calhoun Correspondence,* J. Franklin Jameson, ed. (Washington, D.C.: GPO, 1900), vol. 2, p. 746.

59. Buchanan to Francis P. Blair, Sr., 27 November 1849, Reel 48, Buchanan Papers, Historical Society of Pennsylvania, Philadelphia. A prominent publisher whose family home became today's presidential guest house, Blair himself soon switched to the Republican party.

60. Ulysses S. Grant, *Personal Memoirs of U.S. Grant,* 2 vols. (New York: Charles L. Webster, 1892), vol. 1, p. 56.

3. Struggling over Slavery in the Caribbean

1. The edited versions of Lincoln's two speeches in the House are in *Congressional Globe,* 22 December 1847 and 12 January 1848, p. 64, Appendix pp. 93–95. The original written speeches, which were altered during delivery, are reprinted in *The Collected Works of Abraham Lincoln,* Roy P. Basler, ed., 8 vols. (New Brunswick, N.J.: Rutgers University Press, 1953–1955), vol. 1, pp. 420–422, 431–432.

2. Clay gave two speeches on this subject, both related to the Compromise of 1850, on 21 May and 22 July 1850. They are reprinted in *The Works of Henry Clay,* Calvin Colton, ed., 10 vols. (New York: G.P. Putnam's Sons, 1904), vol. 9, pp. 458–478, 529–569. For another prominent Whig's view of the bleaching process, see the 1850 New York speech by Daniel Webster, in *The Writings and Speeches of Daniel Webster,* 18 vols. (Boston: Little, Brown, 1902), vol. 4, p. 225.

3. *Congressional Globe,* 14 June 1854, Appendix pp. 953.

4. Walsh to Buchanan, 10 November 1848, Despatches from Mexico, NA M97/R14.

5. *Congressional Globe,* 28 April 184, p. 709, and 4 May 1848, p. 591.

6. *Congressional Globe,* 4 May 1848, p. 591, and 5 May 1848, p. 596.

7. Robert Campbell to Buchanan, 17 May 1848, Consular Despatches from Havana, NA T20/R21; *Congressional Globe,* 15 May 1848, p. 633.

8. *Congressional Globe,* 5 and 15 May 1848, pp. 597, 590–591, 630–631.

9. Palmerston to Normanby, 7 May 1847, Mulgrave Archives, Lythe Hall, North Yorkshire, England.

10. México, Congreso, Senado, Comisión Especial de Tehuantepec. *Dictamen de la Comisión Especial de Tehuantepec del Senado, encargada de ecsaminar las varias resoluciones dictadas con motivo del privilegio esclusivo concedido á D. José Garay, y de proponer la que deba adoptarse, atendido el estado que guarda actualmente este negocio, presentado en la sesión del dia 24 de marzo de 1851* (México: O'Sullivan y Nolan, 1851); México, Congreso, Cámara de Diputados, Comisión Especial de Tehuantepec, *Dictamen de la mayoría de la Comisión Especial de la Cámara de Diputados del Congreso General, sobre el privilegio concedido á D. José Garay, para la apertura de una vía de comunicación interoceánica por el istmo de Tehuantepec* (México: Vicente García Torres, 1851). The

final congressional decision is on p. 37 of the latter document. The Letcher-Gómez Pedraza treaty is reprinted in *Diplomatic Correspondence of the United States, Inter-American Affairs 1831–1860,* William R. Manning, ed., 12 vols. (Washington, D.C.: Carnegie Endowment for International Peace, 1932–1939), vol. 9, pp. 364–366.

11. Marcy to Gadsden, 15 July 1853, and Marcy to Forsyth, 16 August 1856, Instructions to Mexico, NA M77/R112 and R113.

12. Particularly confusing are the relationships between the Hargous group and the interests led by Albert G. Sloo, who in early 1853 obtained a separate concession to construct a railroad across the Isthmus.

13. Forsyth to Cass, 17 June 1858; Forsyth to Cass, 31 August 1858; Forsyth to Cass, 16 April 1858; Forsyth to Cass, 1 August 1858, all Despatches from Mexico, NA M97/R22 and R23. See also Forsyth to Cass, 15 February 1858; Forsyth to Cass, 14 January 1858; Forsyth to Cass, 26 September 1857; Forsyth to Cass, 2 May 1858, all Despatches from Mexico, NA M97/R22 and R23.

14. Churchwell to Buchanan, 22 February 1859, James Buchanan Papers, Historical Society of Pennsylvania, Philadelphia; Churchwell to Cass, 8 February 1859, Despatches from Special Agents, NA M37/R10.

15. Cass to McLane, 7 March 1859, Instructions to Mexico, NA M77/R113. McLane signed two treaties—one for "transits and commerce" across the three routes, the other for U.S. intervention to maintain open transit. After the first treaty was rejected by the Senate, the second was never brought to a vote.

16. After ousting the French, the Juárez government nullified the Tehuantepec concession in October 1866. A railroad across the isthmus was not completed until 1894.

17. March to Gadsden, 15 July 1853, Instructions to Mexico, NA M77/R112.

18. Gadsden to Marcy, 16 December 1853; Gadsden to Marcy, 17 October 1853; Gadsden to Marcy, 16 December 1854; Gadsden to Marcy, 5 September 1853, all Despatches from Mexico, NA M97/R19. For similar reports from Gadsden's predecessor, see Conkling to Everett, 2 February 1853; Conkling to Everett, 8 February 1853; Conkling to Marcy, 22 April 1853, Despatches from Mexico, NA M97/R17 and R18.

19. Gadsden to Marcy, 20 November 1853, Despatches from Mexico, NA M97/R19.

20. Marcy to Gadsden, 22 December 1853; Marcy to Gadsden, 6 January 1854, both Instructions to Mexico, NA M77/R112.

21. The Gadsden Treaty is 10 Stat. 1031. A poorly worded treaty provision provided the United States with rights of transit across Tehuantepec and rights to intervene in the area: "the United States may extend its protection as it shall judge wise to it when it may feel sanctioned and warranted by the public and international law." This provision was abrogated in 1937.

22. *Journal of the Executive Proceedings of the Senate of the United States of America,* vol. 11, 31 May 1860, pp. 192–199.

23. Jefferson to Madison, 16 August 1807, *Writings of Thomas Jefferson,* vol. 11, p. 327; see also Madison to William Pinkney, 30 October 1810, *The Writings of James*

Madison, Gaillard Hunt, ed., 9 vols. (New York: G. P. Putnam's Sons, 1900–1910), vol. 8, pp. 121–122.

24. Adams to Hugh Nelson, 28 April 1823, *Writings of John Quincy Adams*, vol. 7, pp. 372–373; Jefferson to Monroe, 23 June and 24 October 1823, *Writings of Thomas Jefferson*, vol. 15, pp. 454, 478–479.

25. Clay to Anderson and Sergeant, 8 May 1826, Diplomatic Instructions of the Department of State, 1801–1906, NA M77/R6; Clay to Poinsett, 26 March 1825, Diplomatic Instructions of the Department of State, 1801–1906, NA M77/R5.

26. *Congressional Globe*, 5 and 15 May 1848, pp. 599, 632.

27. *The Diary of James K. Polk during His Presidency, 1845–1849*, Milo Milton Quaife, ed., 4 vols. (Chicago: A. C. McClurg, 1910), vol. 3, p. 446; Buchanan to Saunders, 17 June 1848, Instructions to Spain, NA M77/R142.

28. *Diary of James K. Polk*, vol. 3, pp. 476–477, 499–500.

29. Campbell to Buchanan, 18 May 1848, Consular Despatches from Havana, NA T20/R21.

30. Saunders to Buchanan, 17 November 1848, Despatches from Spain, NA M31/R35.

31. Buchanan to Clayton, 17 April 1849, *The Works of James Buchanan*, John Bassett Moore, ed., 12 vols. (Philadelphia: J. B. Lippincott, 1908–1911), vol. 8, p. 360; *Congressional Globe*, 16 February 1859, p. 1062.

32. Saunders to Buchanan, 14 December 1848, Despatches from Spain, NA M31/R35.

33. Clayton to Barringer, 2 August 1849, Instructions to Spain, NA M77/R142.

34. *Congressional Globe*, 13 March 1850, Appendix p. 371.

35. *Speeches, Messages, and Other Writings of the Hon. Albert G. Brown*, M. W. Cluskey, ed. (Philadelphia: Jas. B. Smith, 1859), pp. 324, 329.

36. *Messages and Papers of the Presidents*, vol. 5, pp. 165–166.

37. *Messages and Papers of the Presidents*, vol. 5, pp. 198–199.

38. Marcy to Soulé, 23 July 1853, Instructions to Spain, NA M77/R143.

39. Marcy to Soulé, 3 April 1854, Instructions to Spain, NA M77/R143.

40. *Congressional Globe*, 19 May 1856, Appendix p. 534.

41. Marcy to Buchanan, 26 May 1854, Marcy Papers, LC.

42. Marcy to John Y. Mason, 23 July 1854, Marcy Papers, LC.

43. U.S. Congress, House, *The Ostend Conference, &c, Message from the President of the United States*, House Exec. Doc. No. 93., 33d Cong., 2d Sess., 1855, p. 124.

44. Marcy to Peter D. Vroom, 4 November 1854, Marcy Papers, LC; Buchanan to Pierce, 1 September 1854, *Works of James Buchanan*, vol. 9, p. 251; Mason to Buchanan, 24 September 1854, Buchanan Papers, Historical Society of Pennsylvania, Philadelphia.

45. The Manifesto is reprinted in *The Ostend Conference, &c*, pp. 127–132.

46. Marcy to Soulé, 13 November 1854, Instructions to Spain, NA M77/R143; Soulé to Marcy, 17 December 1854, Despatches from Spain, NA M31/R38.

47. Marcy to L. B. Shepard, 15 April 1855, Marcy Papers, LC.

48. Buchanan to Clayton, 17 April 1849, *Works of James Buchanan,* vol. 8, p. 361.

49. *Writings of the Hon. Albert G. Brown,* pp. 594–595.

50. *Congressional Globe,* 2 February 1859, p. 705.

51. *Congressional Globe,* 16 February 1859, p. 1062; 15 February 1859, p. 160; 26 February 1859, pp. 1344–1345, 1848, 1851.

52. Preston to Cass, 9 March 1859, Despatches from Spain, NA M31/R41.

53. *Messages and Papers of the Presidents,* vol. 5, p. 561; *Congressional Globe,* 30 May 1860, p. 2456.

4. Ending an Era: Regional Hegemony over a Defective People

1. Pierce's message to Congress is reprinted in *A Compilation of the Messages and Papers of the Presidents, 1789–1902,* James D. Richardson, ed., 11 vols. (New York: Bureau of National Literature and Art, 1907), vol. 5, pp. 280–284.

2. Commander Bedford Pim, R.N., *The Gate of the Pacific* (London: Lovell Reeve, 1863), pp. 230–236.

3. Forsyth to Biddle, 1 May 1835, Diplomatic Instructions of the Department of State, 1801–1906, Special Missions, NA M77/R152; *Messages and Papers of the Presidents,* vol. 3, pp. 272–273.

4. 9 Stat. 881.

5. William Walker, *The War in Nicaragua* (Mobile: S. H. Goetzel, 1860), p. 38.

6. *Speeches, Messages and Other Writings of the Hon. Albert G. Brown,* M. W. Cluskey, ed. (Philadelphia: Jas. B. Smith, 1859), p. 594.

7. *Messages and Papers of the Presidents,* vol. 5, pp. 7–8.

8. *Ibid.,* vol. 5, pp. 78, 115–116.

9. *Ibid.,* vol. 5, pp. 208–209, 271–273, 336–337, 371, 388–389, 447–448.

10. *Ibid.,* vol. 5, pp. 368–374.

11. *Ibid.,* vol. 5, pp. 371, 416.

12. Buchanan to Hise, 3 June 1848, Instructions to Central American States, NA M77/R27.

13. *Ibid.*

14. Palmerston to Clarendon, 31 December 1857, reprinted in Richard W. Van Alstyne, "Anglo-American Relations, 1853–1857: British Statesmen on the Clayton-Bulwer Treaty and American Expansion," *American Historical Review* 42 (April 1937), pp. 491–500.

15. The inaugural address is reprinted in *Messages and Papers of the Presidents,* vol. 5, p. 200; Marcy to Buchanan, 12 June 1854, Marcy Papers, LC.

16. *Messages and Papers of the Presidents,* vol. 5, pp. 326–331, 370.

17. *Writings of the Hon. Albert G. Brown,* p. 594.

18. Clarendon to Cowley, 4 June 1856, Cowley Papers, F.O. 519/173; Palmerston to

Clarendon, 31 December 1857, reprinted in Van Alstyne, "Anglo-American Relations," p. 500.

19. Clarendon to Cowley, 23 September 1854, Cowley Papers, F.O. 519/170.

20. Palmerston, "Mem[orandum] on a Draft of Despatch from Ld. Clarendon to Mr. Crampton in Washington," 10 September 1854, Palmerston Papers, Hartley Library, University of Southampton; Clarendon to Cowley, 4 June 1856, Cowley Papers, F.O. 519/173.

21. Clarendon to Cowley, 21 May 1857, Cowley Papers, F.O. 519/175; Palmerston to Normanby, 7 May 1847, Mulgrave Archives, Lythe Hall, North Yorkshire, England.

22. Clarendon to Palmerston, 25 October 1855, Palmerston Papers, Hartley Library, University of Southampton.

23. Clarendon to Cowley, 21 May 1857, Cowley Papers, F.O. 519/175; Palmerston to Clarendon, 31 December 1857, reprinted in Van Alstyne, "Anglo-American Relations," p. 500.

24. Aberdeen to Clarendon, 5 November 1854, reprinted in Van Alstyne, "Anglo-American Relations," p. 498.

25. "Republican Morals and Monarchical Power," *The Economist* 14 (14 June 1856), pp. 641–642; *Congressional Globe,* 10 January 1859, p. 299.

26. Palmerston to Clarendon, 31 December 1857, reprinted in Van Alstyne, "Anglo-American Relations," p. 500.

27. *Messages and Papers of the Presidents,* vol. 5, pp. 639–640.

28. The instructions for Perry's mission is JQ Adams to Smith Thompson, Secretary of the Navy, 20 May 1819, Domestic Letters, NA M40/R15; the orders are Thompson to Perry, 29 May 1819, Confidential Letters Sent, February 1, 1813–March 26, 1822, Records of the U.S. Navy (RG 45), NA.

29. The purser's report is Charles O. Handy to JQ Adams, 29 September 1819, filed after accompanying letter dated 20 October 1819, Miscellaneous Letters to the Department of State, NA M179/R45.

30. Isaac Nevett Steele to Daniel Webster, 5 May 1851, Despatches from Venezuela, NA M79/R9; John Appleton to James Buchanan, 13 December 1848, Despatches from Bolivia, NA T51/R1.

31. Richard Pollard to John Forsyth, 8 August 1838, Despatches from Chile, NA M10/R5; Delazon Smith to John Calhoun, 10 August 1845, Communications from Special Agents, NA M37/R6; Courtland Cushing to William Marcy, 31 October 1853, Despatches from Ecuador, NA T50/R2.

32. Francis Baylies to Edward Livingston, 24 July 1832, Despatches from Argentina, NA M69/R5.

33. Edwin Bartlett to John Forsyth, 19 May 1839, Despatches from U.S. Consuls in Lima, NA M154/R5.

34. James Pickett to John Calhoun, 3 July 1844; John Bryan to James Buchanan, 4 July 1845, Despatches from Peru, NA T52/R6 and R7.

35. Francis Baylies to Edward Livingston, 24 July, 19 August, and 27 August 1832, Despatches from Argentina, NA M69/R5.

36. Delazon Smith to John Calhoun, 10 August 1845, Communications from Special Agents, NA M37/R6.

37. John Pendleton to William Marcy, 24 July 1853; John Cushman to Lewis Cass, 10 November 1860, Despatches from Argentina, NA M69/R9 and R14.

38. Benjamin Shields to John Clayton, 15 August 1849, Despatches from Venezuela, NA M79/R8; Ephraim George Squier to John Clayton, 23 June 1849, Despatches from Guatemala, NA M219/R5; Henry Wise to James Buchanan, 9 December 1846, Despatches from Brazil, NA M121/R18; Richard Pollard to John Forsyth, 27 December 1836, Despatches from Chile, NA M10/R4.

39. Francis Baylies to Edward Livingston, 24 July 1832, Despatches from Argentina, NA M69/R5.

40. John Randolph Clay to Daniel Webster, 8 April 1852, Despatches from Peru, NA T52/R9; John Williamson to John Forsyth, 13 February 1837, Despatches from Venezuela, NA M79/R2.

41. William Harris to James Buchanan, 17 October 1847, 14 July 1846, 15 January 1849, 16 May 1847, Despatches from Argentina, NA M69/R7.

42. See, for example, Benjamin Shields to James Buchanan, 20 May 1848, Despatches from Venezuela, NA M79/R6; see also Francis Baylies to Edward Livingston, 24 July 1832, Despatches from Argentina, NA M69/R5; Charles DeWitt to John Forsyth, 13 January 1838, Despatches from Central America, NA M219/R3; Samuel Larned to John Forsyth, 26 March 1835, Despatches from Peru, NA T52/R3.

43. James Pickett to John Forsyth, 4 January 1840, Despatches from Peru, NA T52/R5; James Bowlin to William Marcy, 3 January 1856, Despatches from Colombia, NA T33/R13; William Harris to James Buchanan, 10 October 1846, Despatches from Argentina, NA M69/R6; Richard Pollard to John Forsyth, 17 August 1836, Despatches from Chile, NA M10/R4.

5. Beginning a New Era: The Imperial Mentality

1. Theodore Roosevelt, *Life of Thomas Hart Benton* (Boston: Houghton Mifflin, 1886), pp. 175–176.

2. *The History and Debates of the Convention of the People of Alabama*, William R. Smith, ed. (Montgomery: White, Pfister and Co., 1861), p. 251. See also pp. 234–237, 253–258.

3. For Seward's 1860 proposal to absorb Canada and Latin America, see *The Works of William H. Seward*, George E. Baker, ed., 5 vols. (vols. 1–4 N.Y.: Redfield, 1852–1861, and vol. 5 Boston: Houghton Mifflin, 1884), vol. 4, p. 333.

4. *Congressional Globe*, 25 November 1867, p. 792.

5. Clayton to Benjamin Green, 13 June 1849, Diplomatic Instructions of the De-

partment of State, 1801–1906, Special Missions, NA M77/R152. For additional information on Green's mission, see Senate Exec. Doc. No. 12, 33d Cong., 1st Sess., 3 January 1854, esp. pp. 10–11.

6. *Register of Debates in Congress,* vol. 2, pt. 1 (March 1826), pp. 290, 330.

7. Marcy to Elliott, 9 October 1855, Diplomatic Instructions of the Department of State, 1801–1906, Special Missions, NA M77/R154; for the opposing opinion of the preceding Whig administration, see Everett to Rives, 17 December 1852, Instructions to France, NA M77/R55.

8. Seward's comments came in a Baltimore speech 22 December 1848; see *Works of William H. Seward,* vol. 3, p. 14.

9. For reports on the 19 February 1870 plebiscite, see the despatches of Consul Raymond H. Perry, which were loaned by the Department of State to the Senate and apparently never returned. Fortunately, they are reprinted in Senate Exec. Doc. No. 17, 41st Cong., 3rd Sess., 16 January 1871, pp. 105–107.

10. Sumner's first speech was given in executive session; his later speech is reprinted in *Congressional Globe,* 21 December 1870, pp. 226–231.

11. Sen. Exec. Doc. No. 9, 42d Cong., 1st Sess., 1871. For the proannexation report by one of the three commissioners, the husband of Julia Ward Howe, see Samuel G. Howe, *Letters on the Proposed Annexation of Santo Domingo in Answer to Certain Charges in the Newspapers* (Boston: Wright & Potter, 1871); for a Dominican critique, see José Gabriel García, *Breve refutación del informe de los comisionados de Santo Domingo dedicada al pueblo de los Estados Unidos, 2 May 1871,* pp. 605–625 of Academia Dominicana de la Historia, *Informe de la Comisión de Investigación de los E.U.A. en Santo Domingo en 1871* (Ciudad Trujillo: Editora Montalvo, 1960).

12. *Congressional Globe,* 24 July 1856, Appendix p. 1298.

13. Schurz's Senate speeches of 11 January 1871 and 28–29 March 1871 are reprinted in *Speeches, Correspondence and Political Papers of Charles Schurz,* Frederic Bancroft, ed., 6 vols. (New York: G.P. Putnam's Sons, 1913), vol. 2, pp. 71–122 and 177–252.

14. U.S. Congress, House, *Reports of the Commission Appointed under an Act of Congress Approved July 7, 1884,* House Exec. Doc. 50, 49th Cong., 1st Sess., 1886, p. 62.

15. U.S. producers were apparently satisfying the Latin American market in deviant erotica, for a three-page list of exports to the region in the late 1880s includes feather dusters, lubricating oil, twine, whips, sausages, and something called "SM parts." *Trade and Transportation between the United States and Latin America,* Senate Executive Document 54, 51st Cong., 1st Sess., 1890, pp. 15–17.

16. *Congressional Record* 28 February 1884, p. 1454; Secretary's letter, 1 May 1880, in U.S. Department of State, *Commercial Relations of the United States with Foreign Countries, 1879,* House Exec. Doc. No. 90, Pt. 1, 46th Cong., 2d Sess., 1880, p. 49. For the view of President Arthur, see his 1884 message to Congress in *Messages and Papers of the Presidents,* vol. 8, p. 251.

17. Henry Cabot Lodge, "Our Blundering Foreign Policy," *Forum* 19 (March 1895), p. 17.

18. Alfred Thayer Mahan, "The Isthmus and Sea Power," *Atlantic Monthly* 72 (October 1893), p. 461.

19. *Congressional Record,* 14 April 1880, Appendix p. 143; "Report of the Admiral of the Navy," 6 July 1887, in *Report of the Secretary of the Navy,* House Exec. Doc. 1, Pt. 3, 50th Cong., 1st Sess., 1887, p. 33.

20. Robert W. Shufeldt, *The Relation of the Navy to the Commerce of the United States: A Letter Written by Request to Hon. Leopold Morse, M.C.* (Washington, D.C.: John L. Ginck, 1878), pp. 3, 6, 8; Evarts to Thompson, 31 March 1880, Domestic Letters of the Department of State, 1784–1906, NA M40/R91.

21. The 1880 proposal is House Resolution 278, *Congressional Record,* 12 April 1880, p. 2324; the lingering opposition is seen, for example, in Frelinghuysen to Langston, 1 February 1884, Instructions to Haiti, NA M77/R96.

22. *Report of the Secretary of the Navy,* House Exec. Doc. No. 1, Pt. 3, 48th Cong., 2d Sess., 1884, pp. 40–41.

23. Schurz, "Manifest Destiny," pp. 745, 738.

24. Mahan, "The Isthmus and Sea Power," pp. 462–463.

25. McKinley quoted by General James F. Rusling, "Interview with President McKinley," *The Christian Advocate* 78 (22 January 1903), p. 137. This is almost certainly an embellished quotation, for in 1899 General Rusling had reported (*Men and Things I Saw in Civil War Days,* p. 15) that President Lincoln had told him much the same thing about the Battle of Gettysburg.

26. *Congressional Record,* 9 January 1900, p. 711.

6. Testing the Imperial Waters: Confronting Chile

1. The immediate cause of Chile's action was a move by Bolivia to impose an export tax on nitrates, which Chile considered a violation of the terms of an 1874 treaty. Chile justified its preemptive use of force upon the need to protect Chilean property, which Bolivia had threatened to seize and resell if the owners refused to pay the disputed tax.

2. Evarts to Dichman, 19 April 1880, Instructions to Colombia, NA M77/R46; Hayes's 8 March 1880 message is in *A Compilation of the Messages and Papers of the Presidents, 1789–1902,* James D. Richardson, ed., 11 vols. (New York: Bureau of National Literature and Art, 1907), vol. 6, p. 4537. For Blaine's 24 June 1881 circular to Britain, France, Spain, Germany, Italy, and Colombia, see FRUS 1881, pp. 356–357, 537–540.

3. Blaine to Lucius Fairchild, 25 June 1881, Instructions to Spain, NA M77/R146.

4. Roberts to Bayard, 24 September 1885, Despatches from Chile, NA M10/R35; see also J. Randolph Clay to Webster, 20 October 1850, Despatches from Lima, File 33A-D21.5, Records of the House of Representatives, RG 233, NA.

5. J. H. Moore to William Hunter, 20 February 1882, Consular Despatches from Callao, NA M155/R10; U.S. Congress, House, Committee on Foreign Affairs, *House Report No. 1790*, 47th Cong., 1st Sess., 1 August 1882, pp. 217–218, 229.

6. Christiancy to Blaine, 13 April 1881, Despatches, Peru, NA T52/R35. For a discussion of U.S. representation in the region, see Cornelius Logan to John Davis, Acting Secretary of State, 13 September 1883, Despatches from Chile, NA M10/R34. For examples of partisanship and backbiting, see Christiancy to Evarts, 12 August and 2 September 1879, Despatches from Peru, NA T52/R32; Osborn to Evarts, 9 August 1879, Despatches from Chile, NA M10/R30; Adams to Evarts, 14 July 1880, Despatches from Bolivia, NA T51/R8; Osborn to Evarts, 3 September 1880, Despatches from Chile, NA M10/R30; Christiancy to Blaine, 22 January 1881, Despatches from Peru, NA T52/R35.

7. Evarts to Christiancy, 9 March 1880, Instructions to Peru, NA M77/R131; Evarts to Henry Howard, 19 June 1879, Notes to the British Legation, NA M99/R47; Evarts to Andrew White, 19 June 1879, Instructions to Germany, NA M77/R67. For the Garfield administration's continuation of the Hayes-Evarts policy, see Blaine to Morton, 5 September 1881, Instructions to France, NA M77/R60.

8. *Congressional Record,* 2 February 1880, p. 650. For the minutes of the *Lackawanna* conferences, see U.S. Congress, Senate, *Papers Related to the War in South America, and Attempts to Bring about a Peace,* Senate Executive Document No. 79, 47th Cong., 1st Sess., 1882, pp. 406–418; for the cables see Christiancy to Evarts, 27 October 1880, Despatches from Peru, NA T52/R34 and Osborn to Evarts, 28 October 1880, Despatches from Chile, NA M10/R30.

9. James G. Blaine, *Political Discussions, Legislative, Diplomatic, and Popular, 1856–1886* (Norwich, Conn.: Henry Bill, 1887), p. 414.

10. Christiancy to Blaine, 4 May 1881, Despatches from Peru, NA T52/R36.

11. Blaine to Hurlbut, 15 June 1881, Instructions to Peru, NA M77/R131; Blaine to Kilpatrick, 15 June 1881, Instructions to Chile, NA M77/R36.

12. Hurlbut to Blaine, 26 October 1881, Despatches from Peru, NA T52/R36.

13. Hurlbut to Blaine, 5 October 1881, Despatches from Peru, NA T52/R36; Blaine to Hurlbut, 3 December 1881, Instructions to Peru, NA M77/R131.

14. *House Report No. 1790,* pp. iii–vii; *Congressional Record,* 13 December 1881, p. 79.

15. Blaine to Hurlbut, 30 November 1881, Instructions to Peru, NA M77/R131; Blaine to Kilpatrick, 30 November 1881, Instructions to Chile, NA M77/R36; Blaine to Trescot, 1 December 1881, Instructions to Chile, NA M77/R36.

16. J. C. Bancroft Davis to Hamilton Fish, 4 February 1882, Container 134, Hamilton Fish Papers, LC.

17. Frelinghuysen to Trescot, 9 January 1882, Instructions to Chile, NA M77/R36; Frelinghuysen to Logan, 26 June 1882 and 23 March 1883, FRUS 1883, pp. 74, 92; Frelinghuysen to Partridge, 26 June 1882, FRUS 1882, p. 707; Frelinghuysen to Phelps, 26 July 1883, FRUS 1883, p. 709.

18. U.S. Congress, House, *Reports of the Commission Appointed Under an Act of Congress Approved July 7, 1884. . .,* House Executive Document No. 50, 49th Cong., 1st Sess., 1886, p. 421; see also pp. 229, 292, 461–463.

19. U.S. House, *Reports of the Commission . . .,* pp. 23–24.

20. Buchanan to Jewett, 1 June 1846, Instructions to Peru, NA M77/R130.

21. Egan to Blaine, 17 January 1891, Despatches from Chile, NA M10/R38; J. F. Van Ingen to Blaine, 17 January 1891, Consular Despatches from Talcahuano, NA T115/R5.

22. Tracy's instructions are Tracy to Admiral McCann, 4 March 1891, in U.S. Congress, House, *Message of the President of the United States Respecting the Relations with Chile, together with the Diplomatic Correspondence,* House Exec. Doc. No. 91, 52d Cong., 1st Sess., 1892, p. 237. The *Baltimore* captain's report is Schley to Tracy, 25 September 1891, p. 290.

23. The first two of three charges were simply dismissed (47 *Federal Reporter* 84–85, 48 *Federal Reporter* 99–108); in the third case, the U.S. District Court in California ruled that the *Itata* was a transport, not a warship, and therefore the arms transfer was not a violation of U.S. neutrality laws (49 *Federal Reporter* 646–647). Three months after its return to California and shortly after the end of hostilities in Chile, the *Itata* was released and returned to Chile.

24. McCann to Tracy, 17 June 1891; McCann to Tracy, 22 June 1891, both in General Area File 1775–1910, Records of the U.S. Navy (RG 45), NA.

25. Admiral Brown later insisted that the news of a rebel landing was common knowledge in the streets of Valparaiso. See *Message of the President . . . together with the Diplomatic Correspondence,* pp. 306–309.

26. Schley to Tracy, 29 September 1891, in *Message of the President . . . together with the Diplomatic Correspondence,* pp. 290–291.

27. Egan to Blaine, 17 March 1891, Despatches from Chile, NA M10/R38.

28. Charles H. Harlow to William E. Curtis, 1 July 1891, Reel 32, Benjamin Harrison Papers, LC. Harlow's letter was typed onto Curtis's letterhead and given to President Harrison. The first eyewitness letter, from businessman W. P. Tisdel, is enclosed with William E. Curtis to Elijah W. Halford, 31 July 1891, Reel 77, Benjamin Harrison Papers, LC.

29. Egan to Blaine, 24 September 1891, FRUS 1891, p. 166.

30. The *Baltimore*'s crew had last been on leave two and a half months earlier in the tiny provincial port of Coquimbo.

31. Captain's Schley's preliminary investigation and the Navy's exhaustive Mare Island report are in U.S. Senate, *Papers Related to the War in South America,* pp. 296–298 and 341–610. Several parts of the Chilean investigation are in the same document: Montt to Blaine, with enclosures, 19 December 1891; Evans to Tracy, 4 January 1892, pp. 210–222, 334; see also Matta to Egan, 3 November 1891, FRUS 1891, p. 211.

32. Robley D. Evans, *A Sailor's Log: Recollections of Forty Years of Naval Life* (New York: Appleton, 1901), p. 259.

33. Egan to Matta, 26 October 1891; Matta to Egan, 27 October 1891, in *Message of the President . . . together with the Diplomatic Correspondence,* pp. 119–121.

34. *Messages and Papers of the Presidents, 1789–1902,* vol. 9, p. 185.

35. Webster to Calderón de la Barca, 13 November 1851, Notes to Foreign Legations, Spain, NA M99/R85; Bayard to Cheng Tsao Ju, 18 February 1886, Notes to Foreign Legations, China, NA M99/R13; Blaine to Marquis Guglielmo Imperiali de Francavilla, 1 April 1891, Notes to Foreign Legations, Italy, NA M99/R63; Blaine to Harrison, 29 March 1892, Reel 135, Benjamin Harrison Papers, LC. In the end, the United States paid the Italian victims' families 125,000 French francs, about $25,000. In five other incidents of lynchings of foreigners in the United States in the mid-1890s (two Mexicans and three Italians), President Cleveland asked Congress to appropriate $2,000 for each of the murdered men's families, but only after emphasizing that it was given "without reference to the question of liability of the Government of the United States."

36. Matta's message is printed in Spanish and English in *Message of the President . . . together with the Diplomatic Correspondence,* pp. 178–180. Tracy's attack is in U.S. Congress, House, *Report of the Secretary of the Navy,* House Exec. Doc. No. 1, Part 3, 52d Cong., 1st Sess., 1891, pp. 21–30.

37. Montt to Blaine, 11 December 1891, *Message of the President . . . together with the Diplomatic Correspondence,* pp. 208–209.

38. Montt to Blaine, 4 and 8 January 1892, *Message of the President . . . together with the Diplomatic Correspondence,* pp. 226–228.

39. Blaine to Egan, 16 January 1892; Egan to Blaine, 16 January 1892; Blaine to Egan, 21 January 1892, ibid., pp. 190–194.

40. Pereira to Egan, 25 January 1892, ibid., Part 2, pp. 7–10. Chile also agreed not to press for Egan's recall, which had been demanded on January 20.

41. *Messages and Papers of the Presidents,* vol. 9, pp. 215–227.

42. Blaine to Harrison, 29 January 1892; Harrison to Blaine, 29 January 1892; Blaine to Harrison, 30 January 1892, all Reel 34, Benjamin Harrison Papers, LC.

43. *Messages and Papers of the Presidents,* vol. 10, pp. 233, 315.

7. Excluding Great Britain: The Venezuela Boundary Dispute

1. *A Compilation of the Messages and Papers of the Presidents, 1789–1902,* James D. Richardson, ed., 11 vols. (New York: Bureau of National Literature and Art, 1907), vol. 8, p. 327; statement to the Associated Press, 24 January 1898, reprinted in *Letters of Grover Cleveland, 1850–1908,* Allan Nevins, ed. (Boston: Houghton Mifflin, 1933), pp. 491–492.

2. The British-Dutch treaty is reprinted in *British and Foreign State Papers,* vol. 2, p. 370; the Spanish-Venezuelan treaty is in *British and Foreign State Papers,* vol. 35, p. 301.

3. Eduardo Calcaño to Fish, 14 November 1876, in U.S. Congress, Senate, *Message from the President of the United States Transmitting, in Response to Senate Resolution of April 11, 1888, A Letter of the Secretary of State and Correspondence Relative to a Certain Boundary Dispute between Venezuela and Great Britain,* Senate Exec. Doc. No. 226, 50th Cong., 1st Sess., 1888, pp. 3–4.

4. Simón Camacho to Evarts, 21 December 1880; Evarts to Camacho, 31 January 1881; Evarts to Camacho, 28 February 1881, in ibid., pp. 12–15.

5. Guzmán Blanco's original request was conveyed through the former U.S. minister, George Carter, in a despatch of 30 November 1881; the response is Frelinghuysen to John Baker, 15 July 1882; the offer of assistance is Frelinghuysen to James Russell Lowell, 7 July 1884, in ibid., pp. 15–17, 47.

6. A. M. Soteldo to Bayard, 29 April 1885; Bayard to Edward Phelps, 20 July 1885, in ibid., pp. 50–52, 57–58.

7. Charles Scott to Bayard, 13 December 1886; Bayard to Phelps, 30 December 1886; Phelps to Lord Salisbury, 8 February 1887; Lord Salisbury to Phelps, 22 February 1887, in ibid., pp. 59–60, 67–68, 80–81, 84.

8. Venezuela's 1887 ultimatum is Urbenaja to St. John, 26 January 1887; J. A. Olavarría to Bayard, 15 February 1888; Bayard to Phelps, 17 February 1888, in ibid., pp. 184–185, 201–202, 204–205.

9. Scruggs to Blaine, 12 and 16 November 1889, Despatches from Venezuela, NA M79/R40; Venezuela had sought Blaine's help as soon as he had entered office: see Silva to Blaine, 11 March 1889 and 4 June 1889, Notes from the Venezuelan Legation in Washington, NA T93/R6.

10. Blaine to Robert Todd Lincoln, 1 May 1890, Instructions to Great Britain, NA M77/R88; Lincoln to Salisbury, 5 May 1890; Salisbury to Lincoln, 26 May 1890, both in *British Parliamentary Papers, volume 15: United States of America* (Shannon: Irish University Press, 1971), pp. 856–857.

11. *Congressional Record,* 26 April 1892, p. 3671.

12. Grover Cleveland, *Presidential Problems* (New York: The Century Co., 1904), pp. 247, 254, 256.

13. Roosevelt to Lodge, 23 October 1895, *Selections from the Correspondence of Theodore Roosevelt and Henry Cabot Lodge, 1884–1918,* Henry Cabot Lodge, ed., 2 vols. (New York: Charles Scribner's Sons, 1925), vol. 1, p. 193; Bayard to Robert Todd Lincoln, 9 May 1895, Letterbook Container 205, series 2, vol. 2, pp. 430–431, Bayard Papers, LC.

14. Henry Cabot Lodge, "Our Blundering Foreign Policy," *Forum* 19 (March 1895), pp. 8, 12.

15. See, for example, the letter from Texas Representative Thomas Paschal to Olney, 23 October 1895, Olney Papers, LC.

16. William L. Scruggs, *The Colombian and Venezuelan Republics, with Notes on Other Parts of Central and South America* (Boston: Little, Brown, 1900), pp. 296–298; the resolution is 28 Stat. 971.

17. Cleveland to Don Dickinson, 20 March 1895; Cleveland to E. C. Benedict, 9 June 1895, Reels 89–90, Cleveland Papers, LC.

18. Cleveland to Olney, 7 July 1895, Reel 59, Olney Papers, LC. Although Cleveland indicated that "I have some suggestions to make. I always have," Olney's draft is nearly identical to the final version sent to London.

19. Olney to Bayard, 20 July 1895, FRUS 1895, vol. 1, pp. 542–576.

20. Bayard to Olney, 9 August 1895, Despatches from Great Britain, NA M30/R170.

21. Chamberlain to Salisbury, 4 September 1895, reprinted in J. A. S. Grenville, *Lord Salisbury and Foreign Policy: The Close of the Nineteenth Century* (London: Athlone Press, 1964), p. 63.

22. Salisbury's reply came in the form of two instructions to the British minister, Sir Julian Pauncefote; both are dated 26 November 1895 and reprinted in FRUS 1895, pt. 1, pp. 563–576.

23. *British Parliamentary Papers, volume 15: United States of America* (Shannon: Irish University Press, 1971), pp. 877, 885.

24. Cleveland's message to Congress is *Messages and Papers of the Presidents*, vol. 9, pp. 655–658; the law authorizing the commission is 20 Stat. 1; the Congressional debates are *Congressional Record*, 18 December 1895, pp. 234–235 (House) and 19 December 1895, pp. 240–247, 255–265 (Senate).

25. Theodore Roosevelt, "Letter to the Editors," *Harvard Crimson*, 7 January 1896; Cleveland to Roosevelt, 26 March 1896, in *Letters of Grover Cleveland*, p. 434.

26. Cleveland to Bayard, 29 December 1895, Reel 92, Cleveland Papers, LC.

27. John Bassett Moore to William L. Wilson, 10 December 1895, Cleveland Papers, LC.

28. Bayard to Gresham, 21 March 1894, Press Copy Book, series 2, volume 1, p. 347. The ink has bled through the paper and made all but a few words in this letter illegible. For Olney's criticism of Bayard's favoritism toward Britain, see Olney to Joseph Chamberlain, 28 September 1896; Olney to Maurice Low, 20 November 1899, both Olney Papers, LC.

29. Cleveland to Bayard, 29 December 1895, Reel 92, Cleveland Papers, LC.

30. Bayard to Cleveland, 11 May 1895 and 18 July 1895, Cleveland Papers, LC; Bayard to Gresham, 28 December 1893, Gresham Papers, LC; Bayard memorandum of conversation with Lord Kimberley, 23 November 1894, Bayard Papers, LC.

31. Bayard to Cleveland, 4 and 18 December 1895, Cleveland Papers, LC; Bayard to William L. Putnam, 25 January 1896, Bayard Press Copy Book, vol. 3, Bayard Papers, LC.

32. Cleveland to Olney, 3 December 1895, Cleveland Papers, LC.

33. Bayard to Olney, 13 January 1896, Olney Papers, LC.

34. Olney to Bayard, 28 January 1896, Bayard Papers, LC.

35. Olney to Bayard, 22 January 1896, Olney Papers, LC.

36. White to Olney, 17 June 1896, Olney Papers, LC.

37. "Preliminary Statement of Great Britain, February 1896," in Great Britain, Foreign Office, *British and Foreign State Papers, 1895–1896,* vol. 88 (London: Her Majesty's Stationery Office, 1900), p. 1315.

38. In addition to Olney's original message to Britain, see Olney to Bayard, 22 January 1896, Olney Papers, LC.

39. Olney to Pauncefote, 13 July 1896, in FRUS 1896, pp. 253–254.

40. Hay to Olney, 31 July 1896, Olney Papers, LC.

41. *Messages and Papers of the Presidents,* vol. 9, p. 722.

42. Storrow to Olney, Monday [otherwise undated but probably December 1896], Reel 25, Olney Papers, LC.

43. George C. Worth and George H. Knott, "The Venezuela Boundary Arbitration," *American Law Review* 31 (July–August 1897), p. 485.

44. Cleveland, *Presidential Problems,* p. 256.

45. Bayard memorandum, undated February 1896, Bayard Papers, LC.

46. Olney to Philander C. Knox, 29 January 1912, Olney Papers, LC.

8. Establishing an Empire: Cuba and the War with Spain

1. *Writings of John Quincy Adams,* 7 vols., Worthington Chauncey Ford, ed. (New York: Macmillan, 1913–1917), vol. 7, p. 372; Lodge to Roosevelt, 2 December 1896, *Selections from the Correspondence of Theodore Roosevelt and Henry Cabot Lodge, 1884–1918,* Henry Cabot Lodge, ed., 2 vols. (New York: Charles Scribner's Sons, 1925), vol. 1, p. 240.

2. López Roberts to Fish, 18 September 1869; Fish's acknowledgment, "with regret," is Fish to López Roberts, 13 October 1869, in U.S. Congress, House, Exec. Doc. No. 160, 41st Cong., 2d Sess., 1870, pp. 133, 138.

3. Fish to Robert Schenck, 15 January 1876, Letterbook page 325, Container 216, Fish Papers, LC. While much of the handwriting in this letter is illegible, the gist of Fish's commentary is clear. The first of Fish's messages was sent to Congress on 13 June 1870; the second on 5 January 1874.

4. Adam Badeau, Confidential Memorandum, 23 October 1883, Consular Despatches from Havana, NA T20/R90, pp. 2–3, 23, 41.

5. Prices had dropped in part (but only in part) as a reaction to the boost in U.S. tariffs by the 1894 Wilson-Gorman Act. The 1890 McKinley tariff had eliminated the tariff on raw sugar; the 1894 legislation raised the tax to about one cent per pound, sufficient to spur domestic beet production, which both decreased demand for Cuban sugar and contributed to lower prices.

6. Olney to Cleveland, 25 September 1895, Cleveland Papers, LC. The warnings to filibusters are in *A Compilation of the Messages and Papers of the Presidents, 1789–1902,* James D. Richardson, ed., 11 vols. (New York: Bureau of National Literature and Art, 1907), vol. 9, pp. 591–592, 694–695.

7. Olney to Dupuy de Lôme, 4 April 1896; Dupuy de Lôme to Olney, 4 June 1896, FRUS 1897, pp. 540–548.

8. Cleveland to Olney, 13 and 16 July 1896, *Letters of Grover Cleveland, 1850–1908,* Allan Nevins, ed. (Boston: Houghton Mifflin, 1933), pp. 446, 448; Cleveland to Olney, 26 April 1898, Olney Papers, LC.

9. *Messages and Papers of the Presidents,* vol. 9, pp. 716–722.

10. *National Party Platforms, 1840–1964,* Kirk H. Porter and Donald Bruce Johnson, comps. (Urbana: University of Illinois Press, 1966), p. 108; *Messages and Papers of the Presidents,* vol. 8, p. 6262.

11. *Messages and Papers of the Presidents,* vol. 10, pp. 33–38.

12. John W. Foster, *Diplomatic Memoirs,* 2 vols. (Boston: Houghton Mifflin, 1909), vol. 2, p. 256.

13. New York *Evening Post,* January 16, 1897.

14. One such talent was illustrator Richard Outcault, creator of "At the Circus in Hogan's Alley," the nation's first continuing comic strip. Outcault's cartoon about tenement life in New York featured an elephant-eared youngster dressed in a yellow smock. When Hearst lured Outcault to the *Journal,* Pulitzer continued the cartoon in his paper as well. The promotional literature of both papers featured the Yellow Kid, and from it came the term "yellow press."

15. *Congressional Record,* 19 December 1927, p. 808.

16. Horatio S. Rubens, *Liberty: The Story of Cuba* (N.Y.: Brewer, Warren and Putnam, 1932), pp. 204–205.

17. New York *Journal,* 12 and 15 February 1897.

18. New York *World,* 17 February 1897; House Res. 541, *Congressional Record,* 13 February 1897, p. 1819.

19. Evangelina Cisneros, *The Story of Evangelina Cisneros, Told by Herself, Her Rescue by Karl Decker* (New York: Continental Publishing Company, 1897), pp. 31–32, 35.

20. Ibid.

21. Joesph E. Wisan, *The Cuban Crisis as Reflected in the New York Press* (N.Y.: Columbia University Press, 1934), p. 331n. The *World* virtually ignored it, publishing 12.5 columns, while the *Times* gave 10, the *Tribune* 3.5, and the *Sun* 1.

22. Platt to Isaac H. Bromley, 18 December 1895, reprinted in Louis A. Coolidge, *An Old-Fashioned Senator: Orville H. Platt of Connecticut,* 2 vols. (Port Washington, N.Y.: Kennikat Press, 1971 [reprint of 1910 ed.]), vol. 1, p. 266. Neither this letter nor the one cited in Note 36 is in the Platt Papers at the Connecticut State Library.

23. Roosevelt to Lodge, 27 December 1895 and 10 August 1886, *Selections from the Correspondence of Theodore Roosevelt,* vol. 1, pp. 44, 204–205.

24. "American Ideals," *Forum* 18 (February 1895), p. 749; *Address of Hon. Theodore Roosevelt Before the Naval War College, Newport, R.I., Wednesday, June 2, 1897* (Washington, D.C.: Navy Branch, GPO, 1897), pp. 5–6.

25. Taft to Philander C. Knox, 9 September 1911, Reel 508, Taft Papers, LC.

26. Roosevelt even condoned murder: "Monday we dined at the Camerons; various dago diplomats were present, all much wrought up by the lynching of the Italians in New Orleans. Personally I think it rather a good thing, and said so." Roosevelt to Anna Roosevelt Cowles, 21 March 1891, Theodore Roosevelt Papers, Harvard University.

27. *Messages and Papers of the Presidents,* vol. 10, pp. 542–543; *The Letters of Theodore Roosevelt,* Elting E. Morison, ed., 8 vols. (Cambridge: Harvard University Press, 1951–1954), vol. 7, p. 11.

28. Henry Cabot Lodge, "Our Blundering Foreign Policy," *Forum* 19 (March 1895), pp. 16–17.

29. Cleveland to Olney, 26 April 1898, Olney Papers, LC.

30. Louis A. Pérez, Jr., *Cuba Between Empires, 1878–1902* (Pittsburgh: University of Pittsburgh Press, 1983), p. 178.

31. *Messages and Papers of the Presidents,* vol. 9, pp. 716–722.

32. Adam Badeau, Confidential Memorandum, 23 October 1883, Consular Despatches from Havana, NA T20/R90.

33. Atkins to Olney, 5 May 1896, reprinted in Edwin F. Atkins, *Sixty Years in Cuba: Reminiscences of Edwin F. Atkins* (Cambridge: Riverside Press, 1926), pp. 235–236.

34. Statement to the Associated Press, 24 January 1898, *Letters of Grover Cleveland,* p. 492; Woodford to McKinley, 17 March 1898, FRUS 1898, p. 687.

35. Lee to William R. Day, 18 January 1898, Consular Despatches from Havana, NA T20/R131.

36. *Messages and Papers of the Presidents,* vol. 10, pp. 56–67.

37. Woodford to Sherman, 30 August and 10 November 1897, Despatches from Spain, NA M31/R122–123; Hay to Sherman, 6 April 1898, Despatches from London, NA M30/R180; see also White to Olney, 17 June 1896, Olney Papers, LC.

38. Lee to Judge [Day], 12 January 1898; Lee to Assistant Secretary of State [Day], 13 January 1898, Consular Despatches from Havana, NA T20/R131. A former Confederate cavalry officer and nephew of Robert E. Lee, Fitzhugh Lee's despatches indicated a strong preference for annexation. Cleveland warned his successor, then wrote Olney that "if the President stubs his toe on him, as I think he will, he cannot say he ran on it without warning." Cleveland to Olney, 16 February 1898, Olney Papers, LC.

39. New York *Journal,* February 18 and 23, 1898; New York *World,* February 20 and 21, 1898.

40. Platt to H. Wales Lines, 25 March 1898, reprinted in Coolidge, *An Old-Fashioned Senator,* vol. 1, p. 271.

41. Roosevelt to William Sheffield Cowles, 29 March 1898, *Letters of Theodore Roosevelt,* vol. 2, p. 803; see also Roosevelt to Benjamin Harrison Diblee, 16 February 1898, vol. 1, p. 775.

42. *Messages and Papers of the Presidents,* vol. 10, p. 55.

43. The U.S. Navy report of 21 March 1898 is reprinted in U.S. Congress, Senate, *Message from the President of the United States, Transmitting the Report of the Naval*

Court of Inquiry upon the Destruction of the United States Battle Ship Maine . . ., Senate Doc. No. 207, 55th Cong., 2d Sess., March 28, 1898; the quotations are on pp. 45–46, 67, 73.

44. Hyman G. Rickover, *How the Battleship Maine Was Destroyed* (Washington, D.C.: Naval History Division, Department of the Navy, 1976), pp. 91, 104. For the Navy's initial reluctance to raise the ship, see U.S. Congress, House, *Proposed Removal of Wreck of Battle Ship Maine in Harbor of Habana, Cuba,* House Doc. No. 812, 60th Cong., 1st Sess., 26 March 1908, p. 14.

45. Shelby M. Cullom, *Fifty Years of Public Service* (Chicago: A. C. McClurg, 1911), pp. 283–284; Platt's comment is in *Congressional Record,* 23 May 1900, p. 5893; Bryan's is in the *New York Times,* 1 April 1898, p. 1.

46. *Messages and Papers of the Presidents,* vol. 10, pp. 56–67.

47. *Congressional Record,* 29 July 1894, p. 1578; 8 December 1903, pp. 37–47; 9 December 1903, pp. 66–72; 12 December 1903, pp. 165–168; 14 December 1903, pp. 187–194; 15 December 1903, pp. 254–257.

48. Horatio Rubens took credit for drafting the amendment and convincing Teller to submit it. Rubens, *Liberty: The Story of Cuba,* pp. 341–342.

49. Adee to Day, 7 April 1898, Container 35, Day Papers, LC.

50. Hay to Roosevelt, 27 July 1898, Roosevelt Papers, LC.

51. 30 Stat. 1754.

52. Henry Cabot Lodge, "Our Duty to Cuba," *Forum* 21 (May 1896), pp. 282, 287.

53. William Shafter to R. A. Alger, Secretary of War, 29 July 1898, *Report of the Commission Appointed by the President to Investigate the Conduct of the War Department in the War with Spain,* Senate Doc. No. 221, 56th Cong., 1st Sess., 1900, vol. 2, p. 1052.

54. Day to McKinley, 19 April 1898, Day Papers, LC; *Messages and Papers of the Presidents,* vol. 10, p. 98.

55. *National Party Platforms,* p. 67.

56. Cleveland to E. C. Benedict, 14 April 1898, *Letters of Grover Cleveland,* p. 499; Cleveland to Olney, 26 March 1900, Cleveland Papers, LC.

57. See, for example, John Bassett Moore, "The Question of Cuban Belligerency," *Forum* 21 (May 1896), pp. 298–299.

58. New York *World,* 14 October 1900; Mark Twain, "To the Person Sitting in Darkness," *North American Review* 172 (February 1901), p. 174.

59. *Messages and Papers of the Presidents,* vol. 10, p. 437.

60. *Messages and Papers of the Presidents,* vol. 10, pp. 160–168.

61. Atkins, *Sixty Years in Cuba,* pp. 306–307.

62. *Messages and Papers of the Presidents,* vol. 10, pp. 152–153.

63. Roosevelt to Lodge, 21 July 1899, *Selections from the Correspondence of Theodore Roosevelt,* vol. 1, pp. 413–414; Wood to Roosevelt, 18 August 1899, Roosevelt Papers, LC.

64. Shafter to Adjutant-General H. C. Corbin, 16 August 1898, *Report of the Com-*

mission Appointed by the President to Investigate the Conduct of the War Department in the War with Spain, p. 1099.

65. Wood to Roosevelt, 18 August 1899, Roosevelt Papers, LC; Root to McKinley, 17 August 1899, McKinley Papers, LC.

66. Wood to McKinley, 12 April 1900, Wood Papers, LC.

67. Root to Wood, 14 April 1900, Records of the Bureau of Insular Affairs (RG 350), NA.

68. Wood to Roosevelt, 8 February 1901, Wood Papers, LC; Root to Wood, 20 June 1900, Root Papers, LC. For Root's defense of these voting requirements, see Root to Paul Dana, 16 January 1900, Personal Correspondence, Container 178, part II, Root Papers, LC.

69. Atkins, *Sixty Years in Cuba,* p. 322; Wood to McKinley, 12 April 1900, Wood Papers, LC.

70. *National Party Platforms,* pp. 113, 117, 121.

71. *Messages and Papers of the Presidents,* vol. 10, pp. 152, 224.

72. Wood to Root, 26 September 1900, Root Papers, LC; Wood to Platt, 6 December 1900, Container 28, Wood Papers, LC.

73. Wood to Root, 19 January 1901, Root Papers, LC; Wood to Root, 8 February 1901, Wood Papers, LC.

74. Wood to Root, 16 June 1901, Box 58, File 331–342, General Classified Files, 1898–1945, Records of the Bureau of Insular Affairs (RG 350), NA; Wood to Root, 30 May 1901, Wood Papers, LC; Orville H. Platt, "The Pacification of Cuba," *The Independent* 53 (27 June 1901), p. 1467.

75. Root to Wood, 9 February 1901, Wood Papers, LC.

76. Root to Wood, 20 June 1900, Container 170, Root Papers, LC.

77. *Congressional Record,* 27 February 1901, p. 3133; full debate is pp. 3132–3151.

78. Ibid., pp. 3145, 3147–3148.

79. 31 Stat. 895.

80. Wood to Root, 21 February 1901, Box 58, File 331–372, General Classified Files, 1898–1945, Records of the Bureau of Insular Affairs (RG 350), NA; Root to Wood, 2 March 1901, Root Papers, LC.

81. Root to Platt, 26 April 1901, and Platt to Root, 26 April 1901, Box 58, File 331–371, General Classified Files, 1898–1945, Records of the Bureau of Insular Affairs (RG 350), NA; Root to Platt, 9 May 1901, Root Papers, LC.

82. Platt, "The Pacification of Cuba," p. 1467.

83. Wood to Roosevelt, 28 October 1901, Wood Papers, LC; Platt to Edwin F. Atkins, 11 June 1901, Orville H. Platt Papers, Connecticut State Library, Hartford.

9. Creating a Country, Building a Canal

1. Thomas Jefferson to Monsieur Le Roy, 13 November 1786, *The Writings of Thomas Jefferson,* Albert Ellery Bergh, ed., 20 vols. (Washington, D.C.: Thomas Jeffer-

son Memorial Association, 1903–1904), vol. 5, p. 471; Clay to Anderson and Sergeant, 8 May 1826, Diplomatic Instructions of the Department of State, 1801–1906, NA M77/R6.

2. *A Compilation of the Messages and Papers of the Presidents, 1789–1902,* James D. Richardson, ed., 11 vols. (New York: Bureau of National Literature and Art, 1907), vol. 5, pp. 15–16.

3. U. S. Grant, *Personal Memoirs of U.S. Grant,* 2 vols. (N.Y.: Charles L. Webster, 1892), vol. 1, pp. 195, 198.

4. Lewis Cass to Mirabeau Lamar, 25 July 1858, Instructions to Central American States, NA M77/R27.

5. The 1879 U.S. representatives' instructions and their reports are reprinted in Senate Doc. No. 102, 58th Cong. 2d Sess., 19 April 1904. The Wyse Concession, sometimes called the Salgar-Wyse Contract, is reprinted in U.S. Congress, Senate, *Report on the Proposed Interoceanic Canal,* Senate Exec. Doc. No. 112, 46th Cong., 2d Sess., 9 March 1880.

6. Evarts to Dichman, 19 April 1880, Instructions to Colombia, NA M77/R46.

7. Ferdinand de Lesseps, "The Interoceanic Canal," *North American Review* 130 (January 1880), pp. 11, 13; for de Lesseps's appearance before Congress, see House Misc. Doc. No. 16, 46th Cong., 3d Sess., 1881.

8. Diary entries for 13 January and 7 February 1880, *Diary and Letters of Rutherford Birchard Hayes,* Charles Richard Williams, ed., 5 vols. (Columbus: Ohio State Archaeological and Historical Society, 1922–1926), vol. 5, pp. 583–589; *Messages and Papers of the Presidents,* vol. 7, pp. 585–586.

9. *Diary and Letters of Rutherford B. Hayes,* vol. 5, p. 589.

10. *Messages and Papers of the Presidents,* vol. 8, pp. 11, 41.

11. Frelinghuysen to Lowell, 8 May 1882, FRUS 1882, pp. 271–283.

12. *Journal of the Executive Proceedings of the Senate,* 29 January 1885, p. 453.

13. *Messages and Papers of the Presidents,* vol. 8, pp. 327–328.

14. Ibid., vol. 9, p. 10.

15. *Messages and Papers of the Presidents,* vol. 9, p. 438.

16. 30 Stat. 59; 28 Stat. 948–949.

17. The authorization and appropriation are contained in a single bill, 30 Stat. 1150.

18. U.S. Congress, House, Committee on Foreign Affairs, *The Story of Panama: Hearings on the Rainey Resolution,* 62d Cong., 2d Sess., 1913, pp. 61–62, 140.

19. *The Story of Panama,* pp. 224–225; Philippe Bunau-Varilla, *Panama: The Creation, Destruction, and Resurrection* (London: Constable, 1913), p. 161.

20. Bunau-Varilla, *Panama,* p. 166.

21. The Commission's 16 November 1901 report is Senate Doc. 54, 57th Cong., 1st Sess., 16 November 1901; the quotation is on page 263. The report was reprinted with appendices as Senate Doc. 222, 58th Cong., 2d Sess., 1904.

22. 32 Stat. 1903.

23. *Messages and Papers of the Presidents,* vol. 10, p. 439.

24. U.S. Congress, Senate, *Report of the Isthmian Canal Commission,* Senate Doc. No. 123, 57th Cong., 1st Sess., 1902, p. 10.

25. The 31 May 1902 report, entitled "Isthmian Canal, Views of the Minority of the Committee on Interoceanic Canals," is Senate Report 783, pt. 2, 57th Cong., 1st Sess., 1902; Shelby M. Cullom, *Fifty Years of Public Service* (Chicago: A.C. McClurg, 1911), pp. 281, 386.

26. 32 Stat. 481; the House vote on the conference report is *Congressional Record,* 26 June 1902, pp. 7441–7442.

27. Beaupré to Hay, 30 March, 15 April, and 4 May 1903, in U.S. Congress, Senate, *Diplomatic History of the Panama Canal: Correspondence Relating to the Negotiation and Application of Certain Treaties,* Senate Doc. No. 474., 63d Cong., 2d Sess., 1914, pp. 379–388.

28. Roosevelt to Hay, 14 July, 19 August, and 15 September 1903, with the first letter on Reel 331, Roosevelt Papers, LC, and the others in *Letters of Theodore Roosevelt,* vol. 3, pp. 567, 598, 625; Roosevelt to Lummis, 4 January 1904, *Letters of Theodore Roosevelt,* vol. 3, p. 688; Roosevelt to William Thayer, 2 July 1915, in William Roscoe Thayer, *The Life and Letters of John Hay,* 2 vols. (Boston: Houghton Mifflin, 1915), vol. 2, pp. 327–328.

29. Thomas Moore to Van Buren, 28 January 1831; Moore to Livingston, 10 April 1833; McAfee to Forsyth, 2 September 1834; Foote to Clayton, 5 July 1850; Bowlin to Marcy, 10 May 1855, 1 August 1856 and 20 February 1857, Despatches from Colombia, NA T33/R6, R7, R8, R12, R13; for a typical post–Civil War despatch see Burton to Seward, 3 November 1865, Despatches from Colombia, NA T33/R21.

30. Roosevelt to Marcus Hanna, 5 October 1903, *Letters of Theodore Roosevelt,* vol. 3, p. 625.

31. *The Story of Panama,* pp. 332–333.

32. Ibid., pp. 349, 351, 398, 413; the cables are reprinted verbatim on p. 335, and the logs of the *Nashville* and the U.S.S. *Dixie* are reprinted on pp. 380ff.

33. *Congressional Record,* 9 to 17 March 1903, pp. 13–120; the quotation is on p. 16.

34. Hay to H.S. Pritchett, 28 December 1903, Hay Papers, LC.

35. Hay to Helen Hay Whitney, 19 November 1903, in Thayer, *Life and Letters of John Hay,* vol. 2, p. 318.

36. Bunau-Varilla, *Panama,* p. 378.

37. *Congressional Record,* 13 January 1904, p. 706.

38. Cullom, *Fifty Years of Public Service,* pp. 212–213.

39. *Messages and Papers of the Presidents,* vol. 10, pp. 679–704; the quotations are on pp. 658–667, 695–697, 701–702.

40. Roosevelt to Spring-Rice, 18 January 1904, *The Correspondence of Theodore Roosevelt,* vol. 3, p. 699.

41. Panama's ratification occurred on 2 December 1903. Bunau-Varilla had suggested that Amador and Boyd ratify the treaty in Washington, but they insisted that they lacked the authority. The document was therefore sent to Panama for ratification. While it was in transit, Bunau-Varilla bombarded the junta with warnings of dire

consequences in the event of a failure to ratify. The junta cabled back on November 26 that it would ratify the treaty as soon as it arrived. Five days later, at 4 P.M. on December 1, the 31-page document arrived in Colón. It was ratified the next morning.

42. Bunau-Varilla, *Panama,* p. 429.

43. Roosevelt to Kermit Roosevelt, 20 November 1906, *Letters of Theodore Roosevelt,* vol. 5, p. 498.

44. *Latin America and the United States: Addresses by Elihu Root,* Robert Bacon and James Brown Scott, eds. (Cambridge: Harvard University Press, 1917), pp. 149–150.

45. Joseph Lee to Hay, 14 November 1904, Despatches from Panama, NA T726/R3.

46. Barrett to Hay, 13 December 1904, Despatches from Panama, NA T726/R3.

47. Roosevelt to Cecil Spring-Rice, 18 January 1904, and Roosevelt to George Harvey, 19 December 1903, *The Correspondence of Theodore Roosevelt,* vol. 3, pp. 699, 673; see also Roosevelt to Osborn, 19 December 1903, Reel 332, Roosevelt Papers, LC.

48. John Barrett to Root, 23 May 1906, in U.S. Senate, *Diplomatic History of the Panama Canal: Correspondence,* pp. 114–115.

49. Roosevelt's exact wording remains open to debate. His prepared text contains the innocent comment, "I took a trip to the Isthmus, started the canal and then left Congress not to debate the canal but to debate me." The University's stenographer recorded instead, "I took the Isthmus, started the canal, and then left Congress—not to debate the canal, but to debate me." The prepared text is "Charter Day Address at the University of California," Series 5, Subseries A, 23 March 1911, Reel 421, Roosevelt Papers, LC; the stenographer's report is University of California *Chronicle* 13 (April 1911), pp. 131–145.

50. U.S. Congress, House, Committee on Foreign Affairs, *The Story of Panama: Hearings on the Rainey Resolution,* 62d Cong., 2d Sess., 1913.

51. DuBois to Knox, 30 September 1912, Despatches from Colombia, 711.21/119, NA. For the envoy's further explanation, see *Ex–U.S. Minister to Colombia James T. Du bois on Colombia's Claims and Rights,* Hallstead, Pa., July 1, 1914, n.p.

52. Roosevelt to William Stone, 11 July 1914, *Correspondence of Theodore Roosevelt,* vol. 7, p. 778.

53. James Bryce, *South America: Observations and Impressions* (New York: Macmillan, 1912), p. 36.

54. *Congressional Record,* 20 February 1904, p. 2133; Roosevelt to Spooner, 20 January 1904, Reel 337, Roosevelt Papers, LC; Hay to Spooner, 20 January 1904, Letterbooks, Reel 2, Hay Papers, LC.

10. Chastising Chronic Wrongdoing

1. Loomis to Russell, 11 December 1903, Instructions of the Department of State, 1801–1906, NA M77/R175.

2. Roosevelt to Hay, 2 September 1904, *The Letters of Theodore Roosevelt,* Elting E. Morison, ed., 8 vols. (Cambridge: Harvard University Press, 1951–1954), vol. 4, p. 917.

3. James Wilson to Seward, 20 March, 21 March, and 1 June 1867; Thomas Stilwell to Seward, 26 December 1867, Despatches from Venezuela, NA M79/R16 and R17.

4. Thomas N. Stilwell to William Seward, 26 December 1867, Despatches from Venezuela, NA M79/R17; Hamilton Fish to J. R. Partridge, 25 May 1869, Instructions from the Department of State, 1801–1906, NA M77/R172; Venezuela's position on the issue is in the message of President León Colina to the Venezuelan congress, 20 February 1867, translated and enclosed with Wilson to Seward, 21 March 1867, Despatches from Venezuela, NA M79/R16.

5. Blaine to Edward Noyes, 23 July 1881, Instructions from the Department of State, 1801–1906, NA M77/R60.

6. See, for example, Bowen to Hay, undated August 1904, Despatches from Venezuela, NA M79/R58.

7. Bowen to Hay, 25 June 1904, Despatches from Venezuela, NA M79/R58; Roosevelt to William Calhoun, 24 June 1905, *Letters of Theodore Roosevelt*, vol. 4, p. 1253.

8. Roosevelt to Hay, 2 April 1905, *Letters of Theodore Roosevelt*, vol. 4, p. 1156.

9. Drago to Martín García Mérou, Minister of the Argentine Republic, transmitted to the Department of State by the Argentine Minister, 29 December 1902, Notes from the Argentine Legation, 1811–1906, NA M47/R4.

10. W. L. Penfield to Hay, memorandum dated 5 February 1903; Alvey Adee memorandum, 6 February 1903, both filed with Notes from the Argentine Legation, NA M47/R4.

11. Theodore Roosevelt, "South America and the Monroe Doctrine," *The Outlook* 106 (14 March 1914), p. 589; Roosevelt to Cecil Spring-Rice, 24 July 1905, *Letters of Theodore Roosevelt*, vol. 4, p. 1286.

12. Sherman to Powell, 22 December 1897, Instructions from the Department of State, 1801–1906, NA M77/R98; Roosevelt to Hermann Speck von Sternberg, 12 July 1901, *Letters of Theodore Roosevelt*, vol. 3, p. 116.

13. Memorandum enclosed with Von Holleben to Hay, 11 December 1901, Notes from the Legation of Germany in the United States to the Department of State, 1817–1906, NA M58/R31; Hay to Von Holleben, 16 December 1901, Notes to Foreign Legations in the United States from the Department of State, 1834–1906, NA M99/R34; for the similar view of the U.S. minister to Venezuela, see Bowen to Hay, 3 April 1902, Despatches from Venezuela, NA M79/R55.

14. A more-inclusive protocol, modeled after the February 13 agreement, was signed by all eleven nations on May 7. The relevant documents, including Castro's appointment letter, are reprinted in U.S. Congress, Senate, *Venezuelan Arbitrations of 1903*, Senate Doc. No 316, 58th Cong., 2d Sess., 1904, p. 1036, and U.S. Congress, Senate, *The Venezuelan Arbitration before the Hague Tribunal 1903*, Senate Doc. No. 119, 58th Cong., 3d Sess., 1905.

15. Loomis to Day, 20 June 1898, Day Papers, LC.

16. Loomis to Day, 27 May and 20 June 1898, Day Papers, LC; Loomis to Hay, 26 January 1901, Despatches from Venezuela, NA M79/R53.

17. Bowen to Hay, 25 June 1904, Despatches from Venezuela, NA M79/R58.

18. Bowen to Hay, 22 and 24 July 1904, 7 August 1904, Despatches from Venezuela, NA M79/R58. See also Bowen to Roosevelt, 21 August 1904, Roosevelt Papers, Reel 46, LC.

19. Powell to Hay, 4 November 1903, Despatches from the Dominican Republic, NA M93/R9.

20. Roosevelt to Theodore Roosevelt, Jr., 10 February 1904, Roosevelt Papers, LC; Roosevelt to George Dewey, 20 February 1904, *Letters of Theodore Roosevelt,* vol. 4, p. 734n.

21. Loomis, Memorandum for the Secretary of State on the Dominican Republic, 19 March 1904, Roosevelt Papers, Reel 142, LC; Dillingham to Loomis, 21 August 1904, Miscellaneous Letters to the Department of State, NA M179/R1221.

22. On this point see Hay to Loomis, 28 March 1904, attached to Sánchez to Loomis, 24 March 1904, Notes from the Dominican Legation, NA T801/R3; Roosevelt to Joseph Bishop, 23 February 1904, *Letters of Theodore Roosevelt,* vol. 4, p. 734; Loeb to Loomis, 6 February 1905, enclosed with Dawson to the Secretary of State, 6 February 1905, Despatches from the Dominican Republic, NA M93/R13.

23. Roosevelt to William Bayard Hale, 26 February 1904, *Letters of Theodore Roosevelt,* vol. 4. p. 740.

24. Bowen to Hay, 25 June 1904, in U.S. Congress, Senate, *Correspondence Relating to Wrongs Done to American Citizens by the Government of Venezuela,* Senate Doc. No. 413, 60th Cong., 1st Sess., 31 March 1908, pp. 414–415; Roosevelt to F. C. Moore, 5 February 1898, Roosevelt Papers, Reel 315, LC; Roosevelt to Lodge, 27 March 1901, *Selections from the Correspondence of Theodore Roosevelt and Henry Cabot Lodge, 1884–1918,* Henry Cabot Lodge, ed., 2 vols. (New York: Charles Scribner's Sons, 1925), vol. 1, pp. 484–485; for the reports, see Pillsbury to Admiral Henry C. Taylor, 16 January 1902, Dewey Papers, LC; Powell to Hay, 12 September 1903, 14 September 1903, 17 September 1903, 26 February 1904, Despatches from Santo Domingo, M93/R8 and R10; for debunking these alarmist views, see Nancy Mitchell, "The Height of the German Challenge: The Venezuela Blockade, 1902–3," *Diplomatic History* 20 (Spring 1996), pp. 185–209; Nancy Mitchell, "Protective Imperialism versus *Weltpolitik* in Brazil," *International History Review* 18 (May and August 1996), pp. 253–278, 546–572.

25. The tribunal's award is reprinted in *The Venezuelan Arbitration before the Hague Tribunal 1903,* pp. 106–110.

26. Roosevelt to Root, 20 May 1904, *Letters of Theodore Roosevelt,* vol. 4. p. 801.

27. Roosevelt to Hay, 2 September 1904, *Letters of Theodore Roosevelt,* vol. 4, p. 917; for an example of the jingoes' endorsement, see Bowen to Hay, 25 June 1904, Despatches from Venezuela, NA M79/R58.

28. Dillingham to Loomis, 6 December 1904, Miscellaneous Letters to the Department of State, NA M179/R1231.

29. For two formal protests from Italy, see Mayor to Hay, 3 October 1904 and 24 December 1904, Notes from the Italian Legation, NA M202/R17. For the 1904 arbitral award and the manner in which it prejudiced European claims, see U.S. Congress, Senate, *Data Relative to the Dominican Republic,* Senate Doc. No. 1, 59th Cong., Special Sess., March 8, 1905.

30. Dawson to Hay, 2 January 1905, Despatches from the Dominican Republic, NA M93/R13.

31. Dillingham to Robert Bacon, 16 January 1906, Miscellaneous Letters of the Department of State, 1784–1906, NA M179/R1278.

32. *The South American Republics,* 2 vols. (New York: G.P. Putnam's Sons, 1903–1904), vol. 1, pp. v–vi, 228, 282; vol. 2, pp. 226, 342–343.

33. Dawson to Hay, 21 January 1905, Despatches from the Dominican Republic, NA M93/R13; the agreement is reprinted in FRUS 1905, pp. 311–312.

34. Dawson to Hay, 13 February 1905, Despatches from the Dominican Republic, NA M93/R13; Dawson's instructions are Loomis to Dawson, 25 January 1905, Instructions from the Department of State, 1801–1906, NA M77/R98.

35. Roosevelt's message is reprinted in FRUS 1905, pp. 334–342.

36. Memorandum, 27 January 1905, Notes from the Italian Legation, NA M202/R17.

37. Dawson to Hay, 25 March 1905, Despatches from the Dominican Republic, NA M93/R13.

38. Roosevelt to Charles J. Bonaparte, 4 September 1905, Reel 339, Theodore Roosevelt Papers, LC.

39. For the principal opposition statements by Senator Spooner, 23 January 1906, and Senators Spooner and Bacon, 6 February 1906, see *Congressional Record,* pp. 1423–1431 and 2125–2148; for Roosevelt's justification, see *Messages and Papers of the Presidents,* vol. 9, p. 7337; for the 1905 modus vivendi see FRUS 1905, p. 366; the 1907 Tejera-Dawson treaty is 38 Stat. 1880.

40. Hollander's report is reprinted in U.S. Congress, Senate, Committee on Foreign Relations, *Debt of Santo Domingo,* Senate Exec. Doc. No. 1, 59th Cong., 1st Sess., 15 December 1905, especially page 12.

41. Dawson to Root, 23 October and 15 December 1905, Despatches from the Dominican Republic, NA M93/R14.

42. Elihu Root, *Latin America and the United States: Addresses by Elihu Root,* Robert Bacon and James Brown Scott, eds. (Cambridge: Harvard University Press, 1917), p. 274.

43. 38 Stat. 1880; 44 Stat. 2162; 55 Stat. 1104.

44. Roosevelt to Taft, 20 April 1905, *Letters of Theodore Roosevelt,* vol. 4. p. 1163.

45. Bowen to Hay, 25 June 1904 and undated August 1904, Despatches from Venezuela, NA M79/R58.

46. Roosevelt to William Calhoun, 24 June 1905; Roosevelt to Spring-Rice, 24 July

1905, both *Letters of Theodore Roosevelt,* vol. 4, pp. 1253, 1286; Calhoun to Root, 22 November 1906, Numerical File 1948/2, NA M862/R207.

47. Root to Roosevelt, 3 July 1906, Roosevelt Papers, LC; Root to Russell, 18 February 1907, U.S. Congress, Senate, *Correspondence Relating to Wrongs Done to American Citizens by the Government of Venezuela,* Senate Doc. No. 413, 60th Cong., 1st Sess, 31 March 1908, pp. 559–581.

48. J. de J. Paul to Russell, 29 February 1908, *Correspondence Relating to Wrongs Done to American Citizens by the Government of Venezuela,* p. 643.

49. Roosevelt to Root, 29 February 1908 and 29 March 1908, *Letters of Theodore Roosevelt,* vol. 4, pp. 957, 984; for earlier pressure on Root, see Roosevelt to Root, 29 July 1907, Roosevelt Papers, LC; see also Roosevelt to J. R. Roosevelt, 29 July 1907, Roosevelt Papers, Reel 1346, LC.

50. Root to William I. Buchanan, 28 December 1908, Numerical File 4832/68, NA M862/R414.

51. Root to Carnegie, 24 December 1908, Root Papers, LC.

52. *A Compilation of Messages and Papers of the Presidents, 1789–1902,* James D. Richardson, ed., 11 vols. (New York: Bureau of National Literature and Art, 1907), vol. 9, p. 7375; Root to Tillman, 13 December 1905, Root Papers, LC.

53. "Address before the New York County Lawyers Association," New York, 13 March 1915, in Elihu Root, *Addresses on Government and Citizenship,* Robert Bacon and James Brown Scott, eds. (Cambridge: Harvard University Press, 1916), p. 504.

54. Roosevelt to Root, 5 September 1905, Roosevelt Papers, LC.

55. See, for example, Root to Leonard Wood, 19 January 1901, Leonard Wood Papers, LC.

56. George Dewey, *Autobiography of George Dewey* (New York: Charles Scribner's Sons, 1916), p. 284; Root to Whitelaw Reid, 22 May 1908, Root Papers, LC.

57. Cleona Lewis, *America's Stake in International Investments* (Washington, D.C.: Brookings, 1938), Appendix D, p. 606; U.S. Department of Commerce, Bureau of the Census, *Historical Statistics of the United States,* 2 vols. (Washington, D.C.: GPO, 1975), vol. 2, pp. 861, 903–906.

58. Root to Lodge, 6 January 1906; Root to George Dewey, 6 January 1906, Root Papers, LC.

59. Arthur Beaupré to Secretary of State, 6 September 1906, FRUS 1906, pt. 1, p. 24; for Root's view of his reception, see Root to Lodge, 11 October 1906, Root Papers, LC.

60. Elihu Root, *Latin America and the United States: Addresses by Elihu Root,* Robert Bacon and James Brown Scott, eds. (Cambridge: Harvard University Press, 1917), pp. 9–10.

61. Ibid., p. 98.

62. White to Knox, 22 October 1910, 710.11/46, NA M1276/R1.

63. Root to Elbert F. Baldwin, 1 November 1907, Root Papers, LC.

64. "Address to the Trans-Mississippi Commercial Congress," Kansas City, Missouri, 20 November 1906, in *Latin America and the United States*, pp. 250, 256.

65. James W. Van Cleave, "What Americans Must Do to Make an Export Business," *Annals of the American Academy of Political and Social Science* 29 (May 1907), pp. 472–473.

66. "Address at the National Convention for the Extension of the Foreign Commerce of the United States," Washington, D.C., 14 January 1907, in *The United States and Latin America*, p. 275; see also Root to Silas McBee, 10 April 1907, Root Papers, LC.

67. Root to Henry M. Flagler, 3 January 1905, Root Papers, LC.

68. "Address Opening the Central American Peace Conference," Washington, D.C., 13 December 1907; "Address at the National Convention for the Extension of the Foreign Commerce of the United States," Washington, D.C., 14 January 1907, in *Latin America and the United States*, pp. 217, 275.

69. *National Party Platforms, 1840–1964*, Kirk H. Porter and Donald Bruce Johnson, comps. (Urbana: University of Illinois Press, 1966), p. 138; *Messages and Papers of the Presidents*, vol. 10, pp. 831–832.

70. Sleeper to O'Farrill, 20 September 1905; O'Farrill to Sleeper, 21 January 1906 in FRUS 1905, pp. 289–290.

71. Steinhart to Secretary of State, 8 September 1906, in "Appendix E: Cuban Pacification," *Annual Reports of the War Department for the Fiscal Year Ended June 30, 1906* (Washington, D.C.: GPO, 1906), pp. 444–445.

72. Roosevelt to Robert Bacon, 10 September 1906, *Letters of Theodore Roosevelt*, vol. 5, p. 402.

73. Roosevelt to George Trevelyan, 9 September 1906, *Letters of Theodore Roosevelt*, vol. 5, p. 401; Bacon to Steinhart, 10 September 1906, *Annual Reports of the War Department*, p. 445.

74. Roosevelt to Henry L. White, 13 September 1906, Roosevelt Papers, LC; Roosevelt to Gonzalo de Quesada, 14 September 1906, *Letters of Theodore Roosevelt*, vol. 5, p. 412.

75. Steinhart to Secretary of State, 14 September 1906, *Annual Reports of the War Department*, pp. 446–447.

76. Lodge to Roosevelt, 16 September 1906, *Selections from the Correspondence of Theodore Roosevelt and Henry Cabot Lodge, 1884–1918*, Henry Cabot Lodge, ed., 2 vols. (New York: Charles Scribner's Sons, 1925), vol. 2, pp. 232–233.

77. Taft to Roosevelt, 20 September 1906, *Annual Reports of the War Department*, p. 469.

78. Taft to Beekman Winthrop, 16 September 1904, Reel 465, Taft Papers, LC.

79. Taft to Helen Taft, 20 and 22 September 1906, Taft Papers, LC; Taft to Charles P. Taft, 4 October 1906, Taft Papers, LC; *Annual Reports of the War Department*, p. 456.

80. On Taft's attempt to forestall this resignation, see Taft to Roosevelt, 22 September 1906, Roosevelt Papers, LC; and Taft to Roosevelt, 24 September 1906, *Annual Reports of the War Department*, pp. 473, 476.

81. *Annual Reports of the War Department,* pp. 463, 482; Estrada Palma's query regarding the Treasury is p. 463; his letter of resignation is p. 519.

82. Roosevelt's message to Estrada Palma is in *Annual Reports of the War Department,* p. 473; Roosevelt to Taft, 26 and 28 September 1906, *Annual Reports of the War Department,* pp. 480–481; Roosevelt to Whitelaw Reid, 3 September 1908, *Letters of Theodore Roosevelt,* vol. 6, p. 1206.

83. Lodge to Roosevelt, 29 September 1906, *Selections from the Correspondence of Theodore Roosevelt and Henry Cabot Lodge,* vol. 2, p. 237; Root to General James H. Wilson, 24 October 1906, Root Papers, LC.

84. Roosevelt to Lodge, 27 September 1906, *Selections from the Correspondence of Theodore Roosevelt and Henry Cabot Lodge,* vol. 2, p. 234; Roosevelt to Taft, 26 September 1906, *Letters of Theodore Roosevelt,* vol. 5, p. 425; the cables and executive order are reprinted in *Annual Reports of the War Department,* pp. 478, 543; Roosevelt to Kermit Roosevelt, 23 October 1906, *Letters of Theodore Roosevelt,* vol. 5, p. 465.

85. Roosevelt to Taft, 22 January 1907, *Letters of Theodore Roosevelt,* vol. 5, p. 560; Theodore Roosevelt, *Presidential Addresses and State Papers,* 8 vols. (New York: Review of Reviews, 1910), vol. 6, pp. 1178–1179.

86. The description of Magoon is in diplomat William Franklin Sands's book, *Our Jungle Diplomacy* (Chapel Hill: University of North Carolina Press, 1944), p. 62.

87. Magoon to Roosevelt, 16 April 1908, Roosevelt Papers, LC.

88. Magoon to Roosevelt, 16 April 1908, Roosevelt Papers, LC; Wood to Root, 8 February 1901, Wood Papers, LC; Taft to Roosevelt, 22 September 1906, Roosevelt Papers, LC; Taft to Charles Taft, 9 October 1906, Taft Papers, LC.

89. Magoon to Roosevelt, 16 April 1908, Roosevelt Papers, LC.

90. Porter and Johnson, *National Party Platforms,* p. 161; *Messages and Papers of the Presidents,* vol. 10, p. 7614.

91. Theodore Roosevelt, "South America and the Monroe Doctrine," *The Outlook* 106 (14 March 1914), p. 585; Roosevelt to Kermit Roosevelt, 20 November 1906, and Roosevelt to Archibald Roosevelt, 2 December 1914, *Letters of Theodore Roosevelt,* vol 5, p. 497, and vol. 8, p. 852.

92. Elihu Root, "The Causes of War; An Address Delivered at the Banquet of the Peace Society of the City of New York, February 26, 1909," *International Conciliation,* No. 18 (May 1909), p. 8.

11. Providing Benevolent Supervision: Dollar Diplomacy

1. Frederick Palmer, "Taft, The Proconsul," *Collier's* 39 (13 April 1907), p. 13.

2. Taft to Horace D. Taft, 3 July 1904, Taft Papers, LC.

3. Taft to Bellamy Storer, 23 March 1903, Taft Papers, LC; Memorandum of Conversation with Enrique Creel, 21 December 1909, Num. File 6369/400, NA M862/R507.

4. Huntington Wilson to William Jennings Bryan, 16 March 1913, Huntington Wilson Papers, Ursinus College.

5. Root to Henry L. Stimson, 7 September 1927, Elihu Root Papers, Reel 72, LC.

6. The criticism is in a letter from Knox to Taft, 14 March 1911, Taft Papers, LC; the undated supply list is in Container 33 of the Knox Papers, LC.

7. U.S., Department of State, *Speeches Incident to the Visit of Philander Chase Knox, Secretary of State of the United States of America, to the Countries of the Caribbean, February 23 to April 17, 1912* (Washington, D.C.: GPO, 1913), pp. 13–14.

8. Knox to Taft, 14 March 1911, Taft Papers, LC; "Address of Hon. Philander Chase Knox at the Dedication of the Monument Erected to the Memory of Major-General Edward Braddock, Braddock Memorial Park, Fayette County, Pennsylvania, October 15th, 1913," n.d., n.p.

9. *Speeches Incident to the Visit of Philander Chase Knox*, p. 41; "The Monroe Doctrine and Some Incidental Obligations in the Zone of the Caribbean," Address before the New York State Bar Association, 19 January 1912, n.d., n.p.; for the origin of Knox's thinking, see "Address of the Honorable Huntington Wilson, Assistant Secretary of State, at the Third National Peace Congress, Baltimore, May 4, 1911," Huntington Wilson Papers, Ursinus College.

10. "Diplomatic Service: Conversation at Clinton Sept. 15, 1930," Container A243, Philip Jessup Papers, LC; Johann von Bernstorff, *Memoirs of Count Bernstorff,* trans. Eric Sutton (N.Y.: Random House, 1936), p. 111; see also T. Bentley Mott, *Twenty Years as Military Attaché* (N.Y.: Oxford University Press, 1937), p. 172.

11. "Wilson" was his last name, but he always signed his name "Huntington Wilson" and never "Francis," and this signature confused the librarians responsible for the National Union Catalogue, who have him as "Huntington-Wilson, Francis Mairs." To avoid confusion with Woodrow Wilson and Taft's ambassador to Mexico, Henry Lane Wilson, he will be referred to here as Huntington Wilson.

12. Huntington Wilson, "The Relation of Government to Foreign Investment," *Annals of the American Academy of Political and Social Science* 68 (November 1916), p. 301.

13. Huntington Wilson, untitled and undated diary notes of Latin American trip, 1914, Huntington Wilson Papers, Ursinus College.

14. Perhaps the best single example of the thinking of lower-level officials is the multiple-authored briefing book "Preparations for Secretary Knox's Central American Trip, 1912," Container 33, Knox Papers, LC.

15. "Address of the Honorable Huntington Wilson, Assistant Secretary of State, at the Third National Peace Congress, Baltimore, May 4, 1911," Huntington Wilson Papers, Ursinus College; Wilson, "The Relation of Government to Foreign Investment," p. 305.

16. FRUS 1912, p. x.

17. Huntington Wilson, undated memorandum, probably February 1913, marked "Confidential—file" and intended for President-elect Wilson, Reel 1, Huntington Wilson Papers, Ursinus College.

18. Knox to Nicaraguan Chargé, 1 December 1909, Records of the Division of Current Information, Confidential Publications, Information Series A, vol. 1, no. 6, NA.

19. Huntington Wilson to Whitelaw Reid, 1 July 1901, 817.00/1147, NA M632/R6.

20. Coolidge to Bacon, 9, 18, and 19 November 1908; Bacon to Coolidge, 17 and 19 November 1908, Num. File 6369/35–41, NA M862/R506; the envoy's formal recall is apparently lost, but Chargé J. H. Gregory, Jr., refers to it in a statement that is included with Captain Austin M. Knight to Meyer, 16 March 1909, Num. File 18432/50–52, NA M862/R1035.

21. Knox to George Meyer, 10 March 1909, Num. File 18432/10, NA M862/R1035; a copy of Taft's order is part of Huntington Wilson to U.S. Legation, San Salvador (Frazier), 24 April 1909, Num. File 18432/101A, NA M862/R1036.

22. Huntington Wilson to William Hoster, 24 June 1911, Huntington Wilson Papers, Ursinus College.

23. Huntington Wilson memorandum, 26 November 1909, Num. File 6369/334, NA M862/R507.

24. Knox to Ambassador of Mexico, 12 April 1909, Num. File 18920; Thompson to Knox, undated [received 15 April 1909], Num. file 18920/1–2, NA M862/R1051; for insight into the State Department's thinking on this issue, see Knox's 14-page memorandum on U.S.-Mexican cooperation in Central America in Knox to Taft, 28 September 1909, Taft Papers, LC.

25. Smedley Butler to Thomas S. Butler, 14 July 1910, and Butler to Maud and Thomas Butler, 1 March 1910, *General Smedley Darlington Butler: The Letters of a Leatherneck, 1898–1931*, Anne Cipriano Venzon, ed. (New York: Praeger, 1992), pp. 75–77, 87–88; Kimball to George Meyer, 25 May 1910, 817.00/985, NA M632/R5; see also Ernest H. Wands to Knox, 3 May 1911, 817.51/131, NA M632/R70; for Huntington Wilson's contrary evaluation of these merchants, see Huntington Wilson to Whitelaw Reid, 1 July 1910, 817.00/1147, NA M632/R6.

26. William M. Rees to Knox, 17 July 1911, 817.51/203, NA M632/R71.

27. Kimball to Meyer, 25 May 1910, 817.00/985, NA M632/R5; for one of the consul's partisan reports, see Moffat to Assistant Secretary of State, 28 October 1909, Num. file 6369/261, NA M862/R507.

28. Huntington Wilson interoffice memorandum, 26 November 1909, Num. File 6369/334; NA M862/R507.

29. Taft's message of 7 December 1909 is in FRUS 1909, p. xvii; Senate Jt. Res. 49, *Congressional Record*, 10 December 1909, p. 79. For Zelaya's own story (and copies of numerous documents, including the Nicaraguan government's cable traffic) see José Santos Zelaya, *La revolución de Nicaragua y los Estados Unidos* (Madrid: Bernardo Rodríguez, 1910).

30. For the decision to oppose Madriz, see Knox to de Olivares, 11 February 1910, Num. File 6369/744, NA M862/R509. For the debate over recognition, see de Olivares to Knox, 21 January 1910, Num. File 6369/683, NA M862/R508; for Kimball's accusations, see Kimball to George Meyer, 9 Feb 1910, in Meyer to Knox, 10 February 1910, Num. File 6369/744, NA M862/R509; especially Kimball to Meyer, 25 May 1910, 817.00/985, NA M632/R5; Dawson to Huntington Wilson, 17 February 1910, Num. File

6369/762, NA M862/R509; Huntington Wilson to George Meyer, 19 February 1910, Num. File 6369/762, NA M862/R509.

31. Huntington Wilson to the press, 17 June 1910, 817.00/1063, NA M632/R5.

32. Butler to Maud and Thomas Butler, 1 March 1910, *Letters of a Leatherneck,* pp. 75–77.

33. Ernest H. Wands to Knox, 3 May 1911, 817.51/131, NA M632/R70.

34. Huntington Wilson to Frederic Jennings, 19 December 1910; Juan Paredes to Knox, 23 December 1910; Huntington Wilson to Henry Dodge, 23 December 1910, all in 815.51/148A-150, NA M647/R34. Huntington Wilson had issued a similar threat several months earlier via the U.S. legation in Tegucigalpa, 18 August 1910, 815.51/112B, NA M647/R34.

35. "Manifesto of the National Congress to the Honduran People," 14 February 1911, translated and reprinted in FRUS 1912, pp. 577–580. In the U.S. Senate the Committee on Foreign Relations twice approved the treaty by such a narrow margin that it was never brought to the floor.

36. William Doyle to Huntington Wilson, 25 January 1911, 817.51/100, NA M632/R70.

37. Huntington Wilson to Dawson, 24 February 1910, 817.00/1373, NA M632/R7.

38. Huntington Wilson to U.S. Consul Managua, 1 September 1910, 817.00/1370A, NA M632/R7.

39. The Dawson agreements are reprinted in FRUS 1911, pp. 652–653.

40. Elliott Northcott to Knox, 11 May 1911, 817.00/1575, NA M632/R10.

41. U.S. Congress, Senate, Committee on Foreign Relations, *Foreign Loans,* 69th Cong., 2d Sess., 1927, p. 35; for a more positive evaluation of Díaz, see William Rees to Knox, 17 July 1911, 817.51/203, NA M632/R71.

42. The Knox-Castrillo treaty is reprinted in FRUS 1912, pp. 1074–1075.

43. Brown Brothers and Company and J. and W. Seligman and Company to the Financial Agent of Nicaragua [Ernest Wands], 2 August 1912, 817.51/487, NA M632/R73.

44. Roscoe R. Hill, *Fiscal Intervention in Nicaragua* (N.Y.: Paul Maisel, 1933), pp. 58–61; for the law firm inspection on behalf of Nicaragua, see the letter from Matthew C. Fleming enclosed with Wands to Knox, 15 August 1911, 817.51/202, NA M632/R71; for the inspection of a similar loan to Honduras, see Osborn and Fleming to Knox, 10 February 1911, 815.51/192, NA M647/R34.

45. William Doyle, Memorandum of Conversation with Hans Winterfeldt, 6 March 1911, 817.51/118, NA M632/R70.

46. Knox to Shelby M. Cullom, 17 June 1911, 817.51/154A, NA M632/R70; *Foreign Loans,* p. 89.

47. Díaz to Franklin Mott Gunther, 21 December 1911, in Gunther to Knox, 21 December 1911, 817.00/1745; Knox to Gunther, 23 December 1911, 817.00/1745, NA M632/R11.

48. Knox to Taft, 5 August 1912, 817.00/1822, NA M632/R12.

49. For the troop requests, see Huntington Wilson to Taft, 27 August 1912, 29 August 1912, 30 August 1912, and 4 September 1912, 817.00/1940A, 817.00/1919A and 1919B, NA M632/R12; Huntington Wilson to Taft, 19 September 1912, Reel 427, Taft Papers, LC. Taft's termination of the buildup is Taft to Henry L. Stimson, 2 September 1912 (microfilmed out of chronological order on Reel 514), Taft Papers, LC.

50. Smedley Butler's letters (*Letters of a Leatherneck,* pp. 112–120) provide an interesting eyewitness description of the campaign against Mena and Zeladón.

51. George Weitzel to Knox, 14 December 1912, 817.00/2175, NA M632/R14.

52. *Speeches Incident to the Visit of Philander Chase Knox . . . to the Countries of the Caribbean,* p. 57; Taft to Royal L. Melendy, 28 April 1909, Reel 469, Taft Papers, LC.

12. Continuing to Help in the Most Practical Way Possible

1. *New York Times,* 3 November 1912, p. 14.

2. *Commoner,* 2 May 1913, p. 2; 17 May 1901, p. 3; 15 March 1901, p. 6; 20 November 1903, p. 1; 7 January 1910, p. 5.

3. S. B. Bertron to Huntington Wilson, 31 January 1913, and William Bayard Hale to Huntington Wilson, 2 March 1913. The 11-page memorandum containing suggested language for Woodrow Wilson's inaugural address is undated and untitled except for the notation, "Confidential—file." All three items are in Reel 1, Huntington Wilson Papers, Ursinus College.

4. Winthrop to Knox, 13 February 1913, 812.00/6145, NA M274/R23; Knox to Meyer, 25 February 1913, 812.00/6274, NA M274/R23; Winthrop to Knox, 7 February 1913, and Knox to Secretary of the Navy, 8 February 1913, 813.00/799, NA M672/R2; Charles Hilles (Secretary to Taft) to Knox, 5 February 1913, 813.00/800, NA M672/R2.

5. Huntington Wilson, undated and untitled memorandum marked "Confidential—file" in Reel 1, Huntington Wilson Papers, Ursinus College.

6. Doyle to Huntington Wilson, 27 February 1913, 817.51/532, NA M632/R73.

7. Brown Bros. and Co., J. and W. Seligman and Co., to Secretary of State, 4 March 1913, 817.51/535, NA M632/R73.

8. Bryan to Weitzel, 5 March 1913, 817.51/535, NA M632/R73.

9. Entry for 7 March 1913 in *The Cabinet Diaries of Josephus Daniels, 1913–1921,* E. David Cronon, ed. (Lincoln: University of Nebraska Press, 1963), p. 5.

10. Charles M. Pepper, *American Foreign Trade* (New York: Century, 1919), pp. 244–245.

11. Frank Polk re. the Honduras-Guatemala border dispute, Chandler Anderson Diary, 1 March 1920, Chandler P. Anderson Papers, LC; see also Memorandum from J. Butler Wright, Acting Chief of the Division of Latin American Affairs, 28 February 1916, 817.00/2435 1/2, NA M632/R15.

12. John Bassett Moore, untitled memorandum, 21 October 1913, Container 92,

Moore Papers, LC; see also Archibald Cary Coolidge to E. V. Morgan, 3 August 1913, *Archibald Cary Coolidge: Life and Letters,* Harold Jefferson Coolidge and Robert Howard Lord, eds. (Boston: Houghton Mifflin, 1932), p. 151; George F. Kennan, "Foreward," in Lewis Einstein, *A Diplomat Looks Back* (New Haven: Yale University Press, 1968), p. x; William Phillips, *Ventures in Diplomacy* (Boston: Beacon Press, 1952), p. 63.

13. Diary of Edward House, 15 October 1915, *The Papers of Woodrow Wilson,* Arthur S. Link, ed., 57 vols. (Princeton: Princeton University Press, 1966–1987), vol. 35., p. 71; Lansing to Wilson, 24 November 1915, 710.11/188 1/2, NA M1276/R2.

14. Wilson to Hale, 19 April 1913, Wilson Papers, Reel 132, LC.

15. Cover note dated 22 December 1911 and attached to Knox to Gunther, 23 December 1911, 817.00/1745, NA M632/R11; for the envoy's warnings about Nicaragua's bankruptcy, see Weitzel to Knox, 14 September 1912 and 23 September 1912, 817.51/499 and 817.51/503, NA M632/R73.

16. "Nicaraguan Finances and the Mixed Claims Commission," Memorandum of the Division of Latin-American Affairs, 22 May 1913, 817.51/542 1/2, M632/R73; Bryan to Wilson, 24 May 1913, NA T841/R1.

17. Douglas to Bryan, 11 June 1913, 817.812/39, NA M632/R101; Bryan to Wilson, 16 June 1913, 817.812/30a, NA M632/R101; Wilson's approval is Wilson to Bryan, 19 June 1913, NA T841/R1.

18. Bryan to Wilson, 16 August 1913, Wilson Papers, Reel 284, LC; the transcript of the 27 October 1913 speech in Mobile is in Wilson Papers, Reel 477, LC; the President's rejection (in a suggestion regarding Panama) is in Wilson to Bryan, 20 March 1914, NA T841/R2.

19. Bryan to Brown Brothers and Company, 20 August 1913, 817.51/571b; Pedro Rafael Cuadra to Bryan, 30 August 1913, 817.51/571; Brown Brothers and Company and J. and W. Seligman and Company to Bryan, 2 October 1913, 817.51/577, all NA M632/R73 and R74. Díaz's request for a Platt amendment is attached to Chamorro to Bryan, 12 February 1914, 817.812/61, NA M632/R101.

20. Wilson to Díaz, 20 February 1914, 817.812/61, NA M632/R101; see also Bryan to Wilson, 12 June 1914, NA T841/R2; Wilson to Bryan, 13 June 1914, 817.812/168, NA M632/R102.

21. The original Costa Rican protest is in FRUS 1913, pp. 1022–1031, with subsequent notes in FRUS 1914, pp. 964–969, and FRUS 1916, pp. 818–822; El Salvador's complaint is in FRUS 1913, pp. 1027–1031, and FRUS 1914, pp. 954–956. For the decisions, see *Anales de la Corte de Justicia Centroamericana,* vol. 5 (1916), pp. 130–176, and vol. 6 (1917), pp. 7–9; Nicaragua's rejection is vol. 7 (also 1917), pp. 18–21; Knox's statement is in U.S. Department of State, *Speeches Incident to the Visit of Philander Chase Knox, Secretary of State of the United States of America, to the Countries of the Caribbean, February 23 to April 17, 1912* (Washington, D.C.: GPO, 1913), pp. 25–26.

22. *Congressional Record,* 6 July 1914, p. 11614 (Borah), 16 June 1914, p. 10514 (Smith); see also Root to Paul Fuller, 7 January 1915, Root Papers, Container 130, LC; the vote is 18 February 1916, p. 2770.

23. Roscoe R. Hill, *Fiscal Intervention in Nicaragua* (N.Y.: Paul Maisel, 1933), pp. 35–37; Peter Evans Brownback, "The Acquisition of the Nicaraguan Canal Route: The Bryan-Chamorro Treaty," Ph.D. dissertation, University of Pennsylvania, 1952, Appendix III, p. 216.

24. Jefferson to Lansing, 10 August 1916, 817.00/2465; Admiral William Caperton, "Review of Conditions," 16 September 1916, 817.00/2510, both NA M632/R16.

25. The warning message is Lansing to Jefferson, 25 August 1916, 817.00/2475a; and Caperton, "Review of Conditions," 16 September 1916, 817.00/2510; Report of Admiral William Caperton, Commander in Chief, U.S. Pacific Fleet, 24 September 1916, enclosed with Josephus Daniels to Lansing, 14 October 1916, 817.00/2150, all in NA M632/R16.

26. Memorandum by J. Butler Wright, Acting Chief, Division of Latin American Affairs, 28 February 1916, 817.00/2435 1/2, NA M632/R15; Jefferson to Lansing, 21 September 1916, 817.00/2493, NA M632/R16.

27. Jacob H. Hollander, "The Dominican Convention and Its Lessons," *Journal of Race Development* 4 (April 1914), pp. 398, 401.

28. Bryan to U.S. Chargé, 4 September 1913, 839.00/860, NA M626/R6.

29. Dillingham to Loomis, 21 August 1904, Miscellaneous Letters to the Department of State, NA M179/R1221; Bryan to Wilson, 27 January 1914, NA T841/R2.

30. "Plan of President Wilson, Handed to Commissioners Fort and Smith," August 1914, 839.00/1582, NA M626/R12.

31. Bryan to Sullivan, 20 April 1915, 839.00/1687, NA M626/R12; "Proclamation of Occupation and Military Government," 29 November 1916, 839.00/1965, NA M626/R14; for the President's authorization, see Wilson to Lansing, 26 November 1916, 839.00/1951a, NA M626/R14.

32. William S. Caperton to Rear Admiral William S. Benson, 15 June 1916, Caperton Papers, LC.

33. The Navy's position on the Môle is included in Lansing to Wilson, 9 August 1915, 838.00/1275d, NA M610/R6; Bryan to Wilson, dated 14 June 1913 but filed under 14 June 1914, NA T841/R2; Bryan to Wilson, 20 June 1913, NA T841/R1; Wilson to Bryan, 23 June 1913, NA T841/R1; Madison Smith to Bryan, 28 February 1914, 838.00/864, NA M610/R4.

34. Bryan to Bailly-Blanchard, 2 July 1914, 838.51/341a, NA M610/R51; Bryan to Bailly-Blanchard, 12 November 1914, 838.00/1020, NA M610/R5; Bryan to Wilson, 3 April 1915, NA T841/R3.

35. Lansing to Wilson, 7 August 1915, 838.00/1275c, NA M610/R6.

36. Wilson to Lansing, 4 August 1915, 838.00/1418, NA M610/R6; Lansing to Wilson, 13 August 1915, 711.38/24a, NA M611/R1; for Wilson's rationalization, see Wilson to Edith Bolling Galt, 15 August 1915, *The Papers of Woodrow Wilson*, vol. 34, pp. 208–209.

37. Lansing to Beale, 10 August 1915, 838.00/1246a; Daniels to Caperton, 10 November 1915, 838.00/1370, both NA M610/R6.

38. The Davis-Borno Treaty, 16 September 1915, 711.38/36, NA M611/R1; Caperton's decree is reprinted in U.S. Congress, Senate, Select Committee on Haiti and Santo Domingo, *Inquiry into Occupation and Administration of Haiti and Santo Domingo,* 2 vols., 67th Cong., 1st and 2d Sess., 1922, vol. 1, p. 513.

39. Butler to John A. McIlhenny, 23 June 1917, *General Smedley Darlington Butler: The Letters of a Leatherneck, 1898–1931,* Anne Cipriano Venzon, ed., (New York: Praeger, 1992), pp. 194–195. President of the U.S. Civil Service Commission, McIlhenny had accompanied FDR on his trip to Haiti in early 1917. A dissenting voice is Stokely Morgan to Kellogg, 5 May 1927, 838.00/2382, NA M610/R20; the election results are in Bailly-Blanchard to Lansing, 18 June 1918, 838.011/61, NA M610/R32.

40. Lansing to Wilson, 9 August 1915, 838.00/1275d, NA M610/R6; Butler to Thomas S. Butler, 1 October 1916 and 16 May 1917, *Letters of a Leatherneck, 1898–1931,* pp. 190, 193.

41. Memorandum by Boaz Long, 10 February 1914, 815.77/259, NA M647/R46.

42. Taft to Horace D. Taft, 19 January 1911, Taft Papers, Reel 125, LC; Cecil Spring-Rice to Edward Grey, 25 May 1914, Great Britain, Foreign Office, General Correspondence: Political, 1906–1953, Mexico, FO 371/2029, No. 24538, Public Records Office, London.

43. U.S. Congress, House, Committee on Foreign Affairs, *Texas Frontier Troubles,* 45th Cong., 2d Sess., 1877, p. 1.

44. McCrary to Sherman, 1 June 1877, in U.S. Congress, House, Committee on Foreign Affairs, *Relations of the United States with Mexico,* House Report No. 701, 45th Cong., 2d Sess., 1878, p. 241.

45. Evarts to Foster, 1 March 1880, Instructions to Mexico, NA M77/R116.

46. Fish to Foster, 19 January 1877, Instructions to Mexico, NA M77/R115.

47. Frederick Seward to Foster, 16 May 1877, Instructions to Mexico, NA M77/R115.

48. Evarts to Foster, 23 March 1878, Instructions to Mexico, NA M77/R115. The de facto policy was first stated in Jefferson to Charles Pinckney, U.S. minister to Great Britain, 30 December 1792, *The Writings of Thomas Jefferson,* Paul Leicester Ford, ed., 10 vols. (New York: G.P. Putnam's Sons, 1892–1899), vol. 3, p. 500.

49. 22 Stat. 934. This treaty was in effect from 1882 until late 1886, by which time the need for an agreement had disappeared.

50. On trade, see U.S. Department of Commerce, Bureau of the Census, *Historical Statistics of the United States,* 2 vols. (Washington, D.C.: GPO, 1975), vol. 2, pp. 903 (exports), 906 (imports); on investments, see Mira Wilkins, *The Maturing of Multinational Enterprise: American Business Abroad from 1914 to 1970* (Cambridge: Harvard University Press, 1974), p. 31.

51. *Congressional Record,* 5 July 1882, p. 5652.

52. Woodrow Wilson, "The Mexican Question," *Ladies' Home Journal* 33 (October 1916), p. 9.

53. Elihu Root, *Latin America and the United States: Addresses by Elihu Root,* Robert

Bacon and James Brown Scott, eds. (Cambridge: Harvard University Press, 1917), pp. 167–168, 210; *Commoner,* 20 January 1903, p. 2, and 29 March 1901, p. 1; Taft to Horace D. Taft, 19 January 1911, Taft Papers, Reel 125, LC.

54. Taft to Helen H. Taft, 17 October 1909, Taft Papers, Reel 26, LC.

55. Memorandum by Thomas Bayard, undated September 1886, filed in "General Correspondence, Undated," Bayard Papers, LC; for a typical Jackson despatch, see the 66-page discussion of official corruption in Jackson to Bayard, 31 August 1885, Despatches from Mexico, NA M97/R82.

56. J. L. Morgan to Bayard, 24 November 1886; A. W. Parsons to Bayard, report of conditions on 25 November, dated 29 November 1886; J. L. Morgan to Bayard, 26 November 1886; for Manning's defense, see Thomas Manning to Bayard, 22 November 1886, all in the Bayard Papers, LC.

57. Ambassador Wilson's comments were made in the 1920 hearings of the Fall Committee: U.S. Congress, Senate, Committee on Foreign Relations, *Investigation of Mexican Affairs,* 2 vols., Senate Doc. No. 285, 66th Cong., 2d Sess., 1920, pp. 2250, 2258, 2279, 2315.

58. Henry Lane Wilson, *Diplomatic Episodes in Mexico, Belgium and Chile* (Garden City, N.Y.: Doubleday, Page and Company, 1927), pp. 231, 287; H. L. Wilson to Knox, 28 August 1912, 812.00/4899, NA M274/R20.

59. H. L. Wilson to Knox, 28 August 1912, 812.00/4899, NA M274/R20.

60. William Bayard Hale to Wilson, 18 June 1913, 812.00/7798 1/2, NA M274/R26, filmed out of chronological order at end of reel.

61. Wilson to Edith Bolling Galt, 19 August 1915, *Papers of Woodrow Wilson,* vol. 34, p. 254.

62. Untitled statement on relations with Latin America, 12 March 1913, Wilson Papers, Reel 477, LC; "Draft of an Address to Congress," 31 October 1913, *Papers of Woodrow Wilson,* vol. 28, pp. 479–481; *Congressional Record,* 2 December 1913, p. 74.

63. Wilson to Lansing, 4 August 1915, 838.00/1418, NA M610/R6.

64. *Congressional Record,* vol. 53, Appendix p. 1896.

65. Moore to Wilson, 15 May 1913, enclosing memorandum, Moore to Bryan, 14 May 1913, Reel 49, Woodrow Wilson Papers, LC.

66. Press Conference, 26 May 1913; Charles Willis Thompson to Reuben Adiel Bull, 22 May 1913, *Papers of Woodrow Wilson,* vol. 27, pp. 465, 471.

67. William Bayard Hale, "Memoranda [sic] on Affairs in Mexico," 9 July 1913, 812.00/8203, NA M274/R27.

68. Enclosed with Bryan to American Embassy, 27 August 1913, 812.00/8614a, NA M274/R28; Gamboa to Lind, 16 August 1913, Wilson Papers, Reel 50, LC.

69. Lind to Bryan, 19 September 1913, NA T841/R1; Lind to Bryan, 5 December 1913, Wilson Papers, Reel 52, LC.

70. Daniels Diary, 18 April 1913, *Cabinet Diaries of Josephus Daniels, 1913–1921,* p. 43.

71. Speech to the Southern Commercial Congress, Mobile, Alabama, 27 October

1913, Wilson Papers, Reel 477, LC; for an approving note from Bryan, see Bryan to Wilson, 28 October 1913, Wilson Papers, Reel 51, LC.

72. William Tyrrell to Edward Grey, 14 November 1913, Great Britain, Foreign Office, General Correspondence: Political, 1906–1953, Mexico, FO 371/1678, No. 52367, Public Records Office, London.

73. These words come to us fourthhand from the biographer of Wilson's ambassador to Britain, who wrote that the ambassador told him that Tyrrell told him that Wilson said them. Burton J. Hendrick, ed., *The Life and Letters of Walter Hines Page,* 3 vols. (Garden City, N.Y.: Doubleday, Page and Company, 1923–1925), vol. 1, p. 204; for a follow-up letter expressing the same idea, see Wilson to Tyrrell, 22 November 1913, Wilson Papers, Reel 135, LC.

74. House Diary, 30 October 1913, *Papers of Woodrow Wilson,* vol. 28, p. 478; Bryan to Page, 19 November 1913, 812.00/9817a, NA M274/R31.

75. Hale to Bryan, 14 November 1913, 812.00/9735, NA M274/R31; Hale to Bryan, 15 November 1913, 812.00/9759, NA M274/R31.

76. The various versions of Bryan's warning circular, 7–10 November 1913, are filed in 812.00/9625A, NA M274/R31; Wilson also sent a "Circular Note to the Powers," 24 November 1913, *Papers of Woodrow Wilson,* vol. 28, pp. 585–586.

77. Admiral Henry T. Mayo to General Zaragoza, 9 April 1914, enclosed with Daniels to Bryan, 12 May 1914, 812.00/11988, NA M274/R37; Bryan to Wilson, 10 April 1914, 812.00/11633a, NA M274/R36; Wilson to Bryan, 10 April 1914, 812.00/11483, NA M274/R35.

78. R. A. Esteva Ruiz to Chargé Nelson O'Shaughnessy, 12 April 1914, enclosed with O'Shaughnessy to Bryan, 812.00/11486, NA M274/R35.

79. Mexican Embassy to President Wilson, 19 April 1914, 812.00/11622, NA M274/R36; Mexico's final response is enclosed with O'Shaughnessy to Bryan, 19 April 1914, 812.00/11554, NA M274/R36.

80. *Congressional Record,* 20 April 1914, pp. 6908–6909.

81. Butler to Thomas S. Butler, 20 May 1914, *General Smedley Darlington Butler,* pp. 146–147.

82. Bryan to Lamar and Lehman, 24 May 1914, 812.00/23452d; Bryan to Special Commissioners, 27 May 1914, 812.00/23445; Bryan to the Commissioners, 3 June 1914, 812.00/23455a, all NA M274/R70.

83. Samuel G. Blythe, "Mexico: The Record of a Conversation with President Wilson," *Saturday Evening Post* 186 (23 May 1914), p. 3; Jackson Day Address, Indianapolis, 8 January 1915, in *Congressional Record,* 9 January 1915, pp. 1281–1282.

84. Wilson to Lansing, 8 August 1915, 812.00/15752 1/2, NA M274/R47.

85. Speech to Democratic National Committee, 8 December 1915, *Papers of Woodrow Wilson,* vol. 35, p. 314.

86. Huntington Wilson, "The Relation of Government to Foreign Investment," *Annals of the American Academy of Political and Social Science* 68 (November 1916), p. 307.

87. Franklin Knight Lane to Wilson, 13 March 1916, Wilson Papers, Reel 78, LC.

88. "Draft of a Message to Congress," 27 [?] June 1916, Wilson Papers, Reel 479, LC.

89. Remarks to the New York Press Club, 30 June 1916, *Papers of Woodrow Wilson,* vol. 37, p. 333.

90. *Congressional Record,* 2 September 1916, Appendix p. 1986.

91. Zimmermann to von Eckhardt, 16 January 1917, in *Official German Documents Relating to the World War,* 2 vols. (New York: Oxford University Press, 1923), vol. 2, p. 1337.

92. Boaz Long, "Memorandum on the Mexican Situation," 10 August 1918, 711.12/130, NA M314/R2.

13. Removing the Marines, Installing the Puppets

1. Barnett to Russell, 27 September and 2 October 1919, U.S. Department of the Navy, *Annual Reports of the Navy Department for the Fiscal Year 1920* (Washington, D.C.: GPO, 1921), pp. 306–307.

2. Russell to Barnett, 17 October 1919, ibid., p. 309; see also "Memorandum Concerning the Replacing of the Present Occupation of Haiti by a Legation Guard," 21 March 1919, 838.105/122, NA M610/R35.

3. The report is Lejeune and Butler to Daniels, 12 October 1920, in *Annual Reports of the Navy Department for the Fiscal Year 1920,* pp. 313–315; the letter is Butler to Thomas S. Butler, 1 October 1916, *General Smedley Darlington Butler: The Letters of a Leatherneck, 1898–1931,* Anne Cipriano Venzon, ed. (New York: Praeger, 1992), p. 188; Butler's testimony before the McCormick committee, 27 October 1921, is in U. S. Congress, Senate, *Inquiry into Occupation and Administration of Haiti and Santo Domingo,* 67th Cong., 1st and 2d Sess., 1922, p. 517.

4. Daniels's report is Appendix C of *Annual Reports of the Navy Department for the Fiscal Year 1920,* pp. 222–320.

5. Cole to Knapp, 17 May 1917, in *Inquiry into Occupation and Administration of Haiti and Santo Domingo,* pp. 1780–1783; Waller to Lejeune, 1 July 1916 and 13 October 1915, John Lejeune Papers, LC.

6. *Annual Reports of the Navy Department for the Fiscal Year 1920,* pp. 318–319.

7. *New York Times,* 19 August 1920, p. 15.

8. *New York Times,* 29 August 1920, p. 12.

9. *New York Times,* 18 September 1920, p. 14.

10. Harding to Hughes, 28 March 1921, 711.38/170, NA M611/R2.

11. Hughes to Harding, 12 April 1921, 711.38/170, and 19 July 1921, 711.38/147a, both filmed out of chronological order in NA M611/R2.

12. U.S. Congress, Senate, *Inquiry into Occupation and Administration of Haiti and the Dominican Republic,* Sen. Rept. No. 794, 67th Cong., 2d Sess., 1922, p. 26.

13. Statement to the McCormick Committee, 27 October 1921, *Inquiry into Occu-*

pation and Administration of Haiti and Santo Domingo, p. 517; *Fourth Annual Report of the American High Commissioner at Port Au Prince, Haiti* (Washington, D.C.: GPO, 1926), p. 4.

14. Borah's comment was in a speech at Carnegie Hall, New York, 1 May 1922, quoted in *New York Times,* 2 May 1922, p. 2; the Senate debate and vote is *Congressional Record,* 19 June 1922, pp. 8940–8974.

15. *New York Times,* 18 September 1920, p. 14, and 15 October 1920, p. 2.

16. Nan Britton, *The President's Daughter* (New York: Elizabeth Ann Guild, 1927).

17. The majority report and the original treaty are reprinted in *Congressional Record,* 14 May 1917, pp. 72–75; the ratified treaty is 42 Stat. 2122; the vote is *Congressional Record,* 20 April 1921, p. 487.

18. Hughes, "Observations on the Monroe Doctrine," pp. 124–127.

19. Snowden to Josephus Daniels, 23 October 1920, *Annual Reports of the Navy Department for the Fiscal Year 1920,* p. 342. Wilson's withdrawal order is Wilson to Colby, 15 November 1920, 839.00/2478, NA M626/R23; its formal announcement is "Proclamation," 23 December 1920, attached to Quarterly Report of the Military Government of Santo Domingo, 839.00/2355, NA M626/R21.

20. Dillingham to Loomis, 21 August 1904, Miscellaneous Letters of the Department of State, 1784–1906, NA M179/R1236; Crowder, "Memorandum for Secretary Davis," 27 July 1920, 839.00/2223, NA M626/R20; the revised plan is Hughes to Denby (Secretary of the Navy), 7 June 1921, 839.00/2395, NA M632/R22; Welles's recommendation is Welles to Hughes, 11 October 1921, 839.00/2452 NA M626/R22.

21. *Inquiry into Occupation and Administration of Haiti and Santo Domingo,* pp. 1117–1119.

22. Evan Young to Kellogg, 26 October 1928, 839.00/3175, NA M623/R32.

23. *Congressional Record* 20 January 1928, p. 1787; Stimson Diary, 13 October 1930, Stimson Papers, Yale University.

24. Henry Fletcher, "Conversation with the Nicaraguan Minister," 7 October 1921, 813.00/1234, NA M672/R6.

25. Pittsburgh *Post Gazette,* 6 December 1929, p. 11; NY *Herald Tribune,* 7 December 1929, p. 11.

26. Colby to Jefferson, 15 December 1920, 817.00/2745, NA M632/R18. For the allegations of fraud, see the lengthy report by military attaché Jesse I. Miller, "Final Report on the 1920 Nicaraguan Elections," 11 November 1920, 817.00/2760, NA M632/R18. Chamorro's promise is in Jefferson to Colby, 22 December 1920, 817.00/2762, NA M632/R18.

27. Munro to Francis White, 19 November 1923, 817.00/2989; Hughes to Thurston, 29 May 1924, 817.00/3078a; Hughes to Thurston, 5 June 1924, 817.00/3079, all NA M632/R20; for the reports of irregularities and intimidation, see Thurston to Hughes, 29 October 1924, 817.00/3199, and especially 5 November 1924, 817.00/3222, both NA M632/R21.

28. Kellogg to Salvador Castrillo, 22 January 1926, 817.00/3416, NA M632/R25.

29. Kellogg to Secretary of the Navy, 24 August 1926, p. 15 of "Memorandum: The Nicaraguan Problem," 1 December 1926, 817.00/4169, NA M632/R29, which includes the complex details of Díaz's restoration.

30. Díaz's request for troops is Díaz to Lawrence Dennis, 8 December 1926, enclosed with Dennis to Kellogg, 8 December 1926, 817.00/4197, NA M632/R29; the State Department report is "Mexican Activities in Central America," 2 December 1926, 817.00/4170; see also "The Nicaragua Problem," 1 December 1926, 817.00/4169, both NA M632/R29.

31. "Confidential Memorandum on the Nicaraguan Situation," undated but labeled "approximate date January, 1927," 817.00/5854, NA M632/R41; "Memorandum for Use Before the Foreign Relations Committee," undated, 817.00/4852, NA M632/R33; typescript of testimony and questions, 12 January 1926, 817.00/4844, NA M632/R33; "Testimony of Honorable Frank B. Kellogg, Secretary of State, Before the Committee on Foreign Relations of the Senate, January 12, 1927," Kellogg Papers, LC. The Coolidge message is *Congressional Record,* 10 January 1927, pp. 1324–1326.

32. *Congressional Record,* 8 and 10 January 1927, pp. 1275, 1330 (Bingham) and 13 January 1927, pp. 1563, 1568 (Lenroot), 8 January 1927, p. 1272 (Wheeler) and 13 January 1927, pp. 1555–1561 (Borah), 14 January 1927, pp. 1639–1642 (LaFollette); see also U.S. Congress, Senate, Committee on Foreign Relations, *Foreign Loans,* 69th Cong., 2d Sess., 1927.

33. Stimson Diary, 1 April 1927, Stimson Papers; see also "Memorandum of a Conference with the President, the Secretary of State, Colonel Olds and Mr. Stimson, Thursday, April 7, 1927," filed in Stimson Diary, Stimson Papers, Yale University.

34. Stimson to Coolidge, 4 May 1927, 817.00/4753, NA M632/R32; Stimson Diary, 3 May 1927, Stimson Papers, Yale University.

35. Stimson to Coolidge, 4 May 1927, 817.00/4753, NA M632/R32.

36. Kellogg to Eberhardt, 18 July 1927, 817.00/4936, NA M632/R34; for a flavor of the criticism, see Peavey to Kellogg, 19 July 1927, 817.00/4939, NA M632/R34. In early 1928 the Navy asserted that the original reports of 300 fatalities were significantly inflated. U.S. Congress, Senate, Committee on Foreign Relations, *Use of the United States Navy in Nicaragua,* 70th Cong., 1st Sess., 11 and 18 February 1928, pp. 21, 48.

37. Eberhardt to Kellogg, 20 July 1927, 817.00/4940, NA M632/R34.

38. *Congressional Record,* 20 January 1928, p. 1789. The two men never met. In 1923 Sandino entered Mexico to work in the oilfields around Tampico, just after the long-retired Villa had been assassinated in northern Mexico.

39. *Use of the United States Navy in Nicaragua,* p. 26; for the Hoover administration's similar view, see U.S. Department of State, *The United States and Nicaragua: A Survey of the Relations from 1909 to 1932* (Washington, D.C.: GPO, 1932), pp. 101, 103.

40. Sen. Res. 329; U.S. Congress, Senate, Committee on Foreign Relations, *Relations with Mexico*, 69th Cong., 2d Sess., 21 February 1927.

41. Carleton Beals, *Banana Gold* (Philadelphia: J.B. Lippincott, 1932), p. 294.

42. *New York Times*, 1 February 1928, p. 5 (the stickers) and 15 April 1928, p. 21 (the White House protest); *Congressional Record*, 8 January 1927, pp. 1273–1274.

43. Kellogg to McCoy, 3 March 1928, 817.00/5444a, NA M632/R38.

44. Francis White, "Cuba, Panama, and South America," Lectures to the Foreign Service School, May 13, 14, 16, 18, 1925; Dana G. Munro, untitled lectures to the Foreign Service School, May 7, 8, 11, 1925; Stokely W. Morgan, "American Policy and Problems in Central America," Lecture to the Foreign Service School, January 29, 1926, all Entry 423, Inventory 15, RG 59, NA; Gunther to Beck, 28 April 1927, 711.12/1070, NA M314/R6.

45. *Congressional Record*, 2 April 1928, p. 1928 (Bingham) and 20 January 1928, p. 1786 (Bruce).

46. *Congressional Record*, 23 April 1928, p. 6975.

47. *Congressional Record*, 23 April 1928, pp. 6971–6974; the Navy secretary's assertion is in *Use of the United States Navy in Nicaragua*, p. 22.

48. *Congressional Record*, 23 April 1928, p. 6974 (Norris); 20 January 1928, pp. 1785, 1789–1790 (Dill); 5 January 1928, pp. 1023–1025 (Heflin).

49. The first ballot was an 8 to 44 vote in 1916 on the initiative offered by Senator Robert LaFollette, *Congressional Record*, 21 July 1916, p. 11350; later votes are 23 and 25 April 1928, pp. 6966, 7192; and 22 and 23 February 1929, pp. 4046, 4119.

50. Kellogg to Munro, 10 January 1928, 817.00/5240a; Munro to Kellogg, 20 January 1928, 817.00/5294, both NA M632/R37; Eberhardt to Department of State, 13 April 1928, 817.00/5609, NA M632/R39.

51. The agreement is reprinted in FRUS 1927, vol. 3, pp. 434–439.

52. M. Cordero Reyes to Eberhardt, 12 February 1929, enclosed with Eberhardt to Kellogg, 13 February 1929, 817.00/6218, NA M632/R43.

53. Stimson to Hanna, 16 April 1931, 817.00 Bandit Activities, 1931/31, NA M1273/R10.

54. Hanna to Francis White, 28 October 1932, 817.1051/701 1/2, NA M1273/R23.

55. Arthur Bliss Lane to Willard Beaulac, 27 July 1935, Box 61, Folder 1102, Arthur B. Lane Papers, Yale University.

14. Establishing the Foundations of Honorable Intercourse

1. Lane to Lansing, undated late 1919, 711.12/224 1/2, NA M314/R3.

2. *New York Times*, 29 August 1920, p. 12, and 15 October 1920, p. 2.

3. U.S. Congress, Senate, Committee on Foreign Relations, *Investigation of Mexican Affairs*, Sen. Doc. No. 285, 66th Cong., 2d Sess., 1920, p. 3399.

4. Wilson to Colby, 5 November 1920, 812.00/26464, NA M274/R80.

5. Herbert Hoover, *The Memoirs of Herbert Hoover*, 2 vols. (New York: Macmillan, 1951–1952), vol. 2, p. 69.

6. Mira Wilkins, *The Maturing of Multinational Enterprise: American Business Abroad from 1914 to 1970* (Cambridge: Harvard University Press, 1974), esp. pp. 55–57, 138–163.

7. Sheffield to Kellogg, 5 April 1926, 711.12/744, NA M314/R5.

8. "From Secretary Hughes' speech at Washington on May 18, 1922," 711.1211/223, NA M314/R8.

9. Schoenfeld to Kellogg, 28 August 1925, and two responses, one anonymous to Schoenfeld, 16 September 1925, and the other Kellogg to Schoenfeld, 7 October 1925, both filed immediately after Schoenfeld's original cable, 812.51/1201, NA M274/R172.

10. The September 1923 Bucareli claims treaties (43 Stat. 1722, 1730) are reprinted in FRUS 1923, vol. 2, pp. 555–564.

11. "Memorandum," 19 May 1928, 812.6363/2570 1/2, NA M274/R231.

12. Francis White, "Cuba, Panama, and South America," Lectures to the Foreign Service School, Department of State, May 13, 14, 16, 18, 1925; Dana G. Munro, untitled lectures to the Foreign Service School, Department of State, May 7, 8, 11, 1925; Stokely W. Morgan, "American Policy and Problems in Central America," Lecture to the Foreign Service School, Department of State, January 29, 1926; Franklin Mott Gunther, "Mexico," Lecture to the Foreign Service School, Department of State, May 23, 1925, all Entry 423, Inventory 15, RG 59, NA.

13. Memorandum, Division of Latin American Affairs, 22 August 1922, 832.00/255, NA M519/R5.

14. White to Grew, 7 November 1924, 711.13/65, NA M673/R1.

15. Hanna to Secretary of State, 23 March 1923, 711.12/541, NA M314/R4.

16. James Rockwell Sheffield to Nicholas Murray Butler, 17 November 1925, Sheffield Papers, Yale University; Grew Diary, 1 February 1926, Grew Papers, Harvard University; Stimson Diary, 2 January 1932, Reel 3, Stimson Papers, Yale University.

17. Kellogg to Schoenfeld, 12 June 1925, FRUS 1925, vol. 2, pp. 517–518; Calles's response is pp. 518–520.

18. *Congressional Record*, 8 January 1927, p. 1275.

19. "Address Delivered by President Coolidge to the Dinner of the United Press Association at New York," 25 April 1927, FRUS 1927, vol. 3, pp. 209–220.

20. Morrow to Crowder, 26 May 1922, Dwight Morrow Papers, Amherst College, Amherst, Mass.

21. The administration's position, announced on 17 March 1928, is reprinted in Olds to Standard Oil Company of New Jersey, et al., 24 May 1928, 812.6363/2558, NA M274/R231.

22. Mellon to Morrow, 11 April 1928, 812.6363/2545 1/2, NA M274/R231.

23. "Memorandum," 19 May 1928, 812.6363/2570 1/2, NA M274/R231.

24. *Messages and Papers of the Presidents,* vol. 8, pp. 784–785.

25. The "Excursion Appendix" of the conference report was published as a separate volume of the proceedings: U.S. Congress, Senate, *International American Conference,* Senate Exec. Doc. No. 232, pt. 3, 51st Cong., 1st Sess., 1890.

26. Roque Sáenz Peña, *Escritos y discursos,* 3 vols. (Buenos Aires: Jacobo Peuser, 1914–1935), vol. 1, pp. 163–164; *The International Conferences of American States, 1889–1928: A Collection of the Conventions,* James Brown Scott, ed. (New York: Oxford University Press, 1931), p. 32.

27. Henry White to Knox, 22 October 1910, 710.11/46, NA M1276/R1.

28. U.S. Department of State, *Report of the Delegates of the United States of America to the Fifth International Conference of American States, Held at Santiago, Chile, March 25 to May 3, 1923* (Washington, D.C.: GPO, 1923), p. 5.

29. Ibid., p. 9.

30. See, for example, Crowder to Kellogg, 29 November 1926, 817.00/4171, NA M632/R29; Caffery to Kellogg, 17 November 1926, 817.00/4165, NA M632/R29.

31. Morgan, "Situation in Nicaragua," 24 January 1927, 817.00/4868, NA M632/R33; Kellogg to the American Delegation, 5 January 1928, FRUS 1928, vol. 1, pp. 534–584; quotation p. 573.

32. There is some dispute over Hughes's exact words. The official report of the U.S. delegation quotes Hughes as saying "see them killed," while Hughes's biographer offers a convincing argument that former secretary of state said "butchered in the jungle." Compare *Report of the United States Delegates,* p. 14, and Merlo J. Pusey, *Charles Evans Hughes,* 2 vols. (New York: Macmillan, 1951–1952), vol. 2, pp. 559–560.

33. White to Stimson, 15 September 1930, Francis White Papers, Herbert Hoover Library, West Branch, Iowa.

15. Becoming a Good Neighbor

1. Herbert Hoover, *The Memoirs of Herbert Hoover,* 2 vols. (New York: Macmillan, 1951–1952), vol. 2, p. 210; Address to the Gridiron Club, Washington, D.C., 13 April 1929, *PPP, Herbert Hoover, 1929,* p. 70.

2. Stokely W. Morgan, "American Policy and Problems in Central America," Lecture to the Foreign Service School, Department of State, January 29, 1926, Entry 423, Inventory 15, RG 59, NA.

3. *Congressional Record,* 10 December 1923, p. 142; William E. Borah, "What the Monroe Doctrine Really Means," *Colliers,* 31 January 1925, p. 25.

4. Borah to Kellogg, 28 July 1928; Kellogg to Borah, 2 August 1928; Kellogg to Borah (telegram) 2 August 1928, all Box 542, Borah Papers, LC.

5. U.S. Department of State, *Memorandum on the Monroe Doctrine, Prepared by J. Reuben Clark, Undersecretary of State, December 17, 1928,* Department of State Publication No. 37 (Washington, D.C.: GPO, 1930), pp. xix–xxiv.

6. Kellogg to American Diplomatic Officers in Latin America, 28 February 1929, 710.11/1306a, NA M1276/R10.

7. Hoover to Stimson, 26 June 1929, 710.11/1450, NA M1276/R11; see also Stimson to Kellogg, 28 June 1930, 710.11/1451, NA M1276/R11, which is the reply to Kellogg's suggestion that the memorandum be delivered; Hoover, *Memoirs of Herbert Hoover*, vol. 2, p. 210.

8. Wilson to Edith Bolling Galt, 15 August 1915, in Arthur S. Link, ed., *The Papers of Woodrow Wilson*, 57 vols. (Princeton: Princeton University Press, 1966–1987), vol. 34, p. 209.

9. H. Freeman Matthews to Secretary of State, 14 December 1929, 838.00/2695, NA M1246/R1.

10. *New York Times*, 9 January 1930, p. 9; Department of State, *Report of the President's Commission for the Study and Review of Conditions in the Republic of Haiti, March 26, 1930*, Latin American Series No. 2 (Washington, D.C.: GPO, 1930), pp. 1–2.

11. Russell to Stimson, 3 December 1929, 838.42/81, NA M610/R44; Corey F. Wood, "Political Report," 5 February 1930, 838.00/2746, NA M1246/R1.

12. Stimson Diary, 1 November 1930, Stimson Papers.

13. Stuart Grummon to Stimson, 29 August 1930, 838.00/2881, NA M1246/R1.

14. Stimson Diary, 22 April 1931, Stimson Papers, Yale University.

15. Phillips to Roosevelt, 3 August 1933, *Franklin D. Roosevelt and Foreign Affairs*, Edgar B. Nixon, ed., 3 vols. (Cambridge: Harvard University Press, 1969), vol. 1, p. 344; FDR's executive agreement to maintain the customs receivership is reprinted in FRUS 1933, vol. 5, pp. 755–761.

16. Stimson Diary, 5 November 1930 and 17 May 1932, Stimson Papers, Yale University.

17. Philip C. Jessup, *Elihu Root*, 2 vols. (New York: Dodd, Mead, 1938), vol. 1, p. 468. The letter is not to be found in John Hay's papers. The State Department's criticism is Joseph F. McGurk, "Memorandum: Biography of Elihu Root," 13 November 1935, 710.11/1702 1/2, NA M1276/R13.

18. "Memorandum of Trip to Haiti and Santo Domingo," and "Trip to Haiti and Santo Domingo 1917," both undated 1917, Assistant Secretary of the Navy Files, Box 41, FDR Library, Hyde Park, N.Y.

19. Sumner Welles, Memorandum, 1 March 1921, 837.00/2216, NA M488/R14.

20. Dulles to Lansing, 14 February 1917, 337.11/162 NA.

21. For a memo acknowledging Acting Secretary of State Frank Polk's verbal instructions of 10 January 1919, see Ambassador William Gonzales to Polk, 4 February 1919, Gonzales Papers, University of South Carolina.

22. Boaz Long to Lansing, 15 February 1918, 711.13/55, NA M673/R1.

23. Crowder's appointment is Davis to Crowder, 31 December 1920, 837.00/1952b; the warning to Menocal is Davis to Boaz Long, 4 January 1921, 837.00/1949, both NA M488/R13.

24. Division of Latin-American Affairs, "Synopsis of General Crowder's 13 Memoranda," 14 November 1923, 123 C 8812/51, NA.

25. Crowder to Dwight Morrow, 10 May 1922, Dwight Morrow Papers, Amherst College, Amherst, Mass.

26. Crowder to Pershing, 30 January 1925, 210.681, General Correspondence, 1917–1925, Records of the Office of the Adjutant General (RG 407), NA.

27. Office of the Secretary, "Memorandum of Interview with the Cuban Charge d'Affaires and Dr. Torriente," 15 November 1923, Hughes Papers, LC; for the bankers' perspective, see Dwight Morrow to Edwin F. Gay, 16 June 1922, Dwight Morrow Papers, Amherst College, Amherst, Mass.; for Crowder's opinion, see Crowder, "Recent Cabinet Crisis," 21 April 1923, enclosed with Crowder to Hughes, 23 April 1923, 837.00/85, NA M488/R25.

28. *Congressional Record,* 20 January 1928, p. 1787.

29. Judah to White, 31 May 1928; White to Judah, 4 and 9 June 1928, Francis White Papers, Herbert Hoover Library, West Branch, Iowa.

30. Judah to White, 30 April 1929, Francis White Papers, Herbert Hoover Library, West Branch, Iowa; Stimson Diary, 25 November 1930, Henry Stimson Papers, Yale University.

31. "Conversation. Mr. Harry F. Guggenheim: General Discussion of Cuban Situation," 13 November 1931, 837.00/3207, NA; Duggan to Edwin Wilson, 17 January 1933, 710.11/1776 1/2, NA M1276/R13; Welles's undated memo to FDR has a filing date of inauguration day, ("3–4–33") and is in folder: "Cuba 1933–35, 42–44," Box 28, President's Secretary's File, FDR Library, Hyde Park, N.Y.

32. "Long Distance Telephone Conversation between Secretary Hull and Ambassador Welles in Cuba," 18 May 1933, 611.3731/416 1/2, NA; Welles to Roosevelt, 17 July 1933, *Franklin D. Roosevelt and Foreign Affairs,* vol. 1, p. 315.

33. Welles to Hull, 8 August 1933, 837.00/3616, NA; Welles to Hull, 9 August 1933, FRUS 1933, vol. 5, p. 344.

34. Crowder, "Recent Cabinet Crisis," 21 April 1923, enclosed with Crowder to Hughes, 23 April 1923, 837.00/85, NA M488/R25.

35. Memorandum of Telephone Conversation between Hull and Welles, 5 September 1933; Memorandum of Telephone Conversation between Caffery and Welles, 5 September 1933; Welles to Hull, 7 September 1933; Welles to Hull, 8 September 1933, 837.00/3786, all FRUS 1933, vol. 5, pp. 380–404.

36. Berle Diary, 1 February 1942, Reel 3, Berle Papers, FDR Library, Hyde Park, N.Y.; Cordell Hull, *The Memoirs of Cordell Hull,* 2 vols. (New York: Macmillan, 1948), vol. 1, p. 182; Daniels to Hull, 9 September 1933, 837.00/4033, FRUS 1933, vol. 5, pp. 413–415.

37. Trujillo's offer is in Schoenfeld to Hull, 8 September 1933; Argentine Ministry for Foreign Affairs to the Department of State, 8 September 1933, FRUS 1933, vol. 5, pp. 404–405, 409.

38. Memorandum of Telephone Conversation between Hull and Daniels, 9 September 1933; Daniels to Hull, 9 September 1933; Caffery memorandum, 13 September 1933, FRUS 1933, vol. 5., pp. 413, 428–431.

39. Hull to Daniels, 28 September 1933, FRUS 1933, vol. 4, p. 17; FDR press conference, 6 December 1933, *Franklin D. Roosevelt and Foreign Affairs*, vol. 1, p. 512; "Instructions to Delegates," 10 November 1933, FRUS 1933, vol. 4, p. 147.

40. Hull to Welles, 7 September 1933, FRUS 1933, vol. 5, p. 402.

41. Welles's draft of Roosevelt's nonrecognition statement, 23 November 1933, is reprinted in FRUS 1933, vol. 5, pp. 525–526; press conference, 24 November 1933, *Franklin D. Roosevelt and Foreign Affairs*, vol. 1, p. 503.

42. Welles to Phillips, 7 December 1933, FRUS 1933, vol. 5, pp. 533–536; Caffery to Phillips, 14 January 1934, FRUS 1934, vol. 5, p. 98.

43. Remarks at a State Luncheon, 31 August 1944, in *The Public Papers and Addresses of Franklin Delano Roosevelt*, Samuel I. Rosenman, ed., 13 vols. (New York: Harper and Brothers, 1938–1950), vol. 13, p. 253.

44. Spruille Braden, *Diplomats and Demagogues: The Memoirs of Spruille Braden* (New Rochelle, N.Y.: Arlington House, 1971), pp. 119, 121.

45. Instructions to the Delegates to the Seventh International Conference of American States, 10 November 1933; Hull to Phillips, 19 December 1933, FRUS 1933, vol. 4, pp. 67, 201.

46. In the final act approving the Convention on the Rights and Duties of States, Hull added a four-paragraph reservation that reiterated this statement, and the subsequent Senate consent included his reservation. U.S. Department of State, *Report of the Delegates of the United States of America to the Seventh International Conference of American States, Montevideo, Uruguay, December 3–26, 1933* (Washington, D.C.: GPO, 1934), pp. 19–20.

47. Speech to the Woodrow Wilson Foundation Dinner, 28 December 1933, *Franklin D. Roosevelt and Foreign Affairs*, vol. 1, p. 560.

48. The Platt abrogation is 48 Stat. 1682; the Panama revision is 53 Stat. 1807; the Gadsden revision is 52 Stat. 1457.

49. Baruch to FDR, 11 October 1938, Bernard Baruch Papers, Seeley Mudd Manuscript Library, Princeton University.

50. "Mexican Activities," 4 November 1939, enclosed with Hoover to Berle, 7 November 1939, 812.00/30886 1/2, NA M1370/R8.

51. Cordell Hull, *The Memoirs of Cordell Hull*, 2 vols. (New York: Macmillan, 1948), vol. 2, pp. 1140–1142.

52. Executive Order, 16 August 1940, *Federal Register* 5 (22 August 1940), pp. 2938–2939.

53. Hull, *Memoirs*, vol. 1, p. 813; for the State Department's thinking on this issue before Pearl Harbor, see Harley Notter, "German Inroads and Plans in the Other American Republics," 10 Sept. 1940, 862.20210/330½, NA.

54. Roosevelt to Rockefeller, 24 March 1942, in U.S. Office of Inter-American Affairs, *History of the Office of the Coordinator of Inter-American Affairs: Historical Reports on War Administration* (Washington, D.C.: GPO, 1947), p. 116.

55. Braden, *Diplomats and Demagogues,* pp. 263, 452.

56. Hadley Cantril and American Social Surveys, Inc., "What People in the United States Think and Know about Latin America and Latin Americans," 18 January 1941, enclosed with Rockefeller to Welles, 12 March 1941, 710.11/2686, NA M1276/R20.

57. The 1940 speech to Congress is *Congressional Record,* 16 May 1940, p. 6243; fireside chat, 11 September 1941, in *The Public Papers and Addresses of Franklin Delano Roosevelt,* Samuel I. Rosenman, ed., 13 vols. (New York: Harper and Brothers, 1938–1950), vol. 10, p. 387.

58. Seldin Chapin to Laurence Duggan, 13 July 1939, 710.11/2403 1/2, NA M1276/R17.

59. *The International Conferences of American States, First Supplement, 1933–1940* (Washington, D.C.: Carnegie Endowment for International Peace, 1940), pp. 333, 360.

60. Hull, *Memoirs,* vol. 1, p. 823.

61. Argentina's opposition was based on the fear of what might happen to the Falkland/Malvinas Islands if Germany were to conquer England: a mandatory inter-American trusteeship might oblige Argentina to fight Germany to preserve Britain's hold on territory claimed by Argentina.

62. Stimson Diary, 9 January and 9 October 1941, 7 July 1942, Reels 6 and 7, Stimson Papers, Yale University.

63. The Presidential proclamation creating the Proclaimed List and naming the 1,800 Latin American individuals and firms is reprinted in the *Federal Register* 6 (19 July 1941), pp. 3555–3573.

64. Hull to Braden, 12 November 1941, FRUS 1941, vol. 6, p. 304.

65. Hull, *Memoirs,* vol. 2, pp. 1143, 1145.

66. Berle Diary, 24 January 1942, Reel 3, Adolf Berle Papers, FDR Library, Hyde Park, N.Y.

67. Hull, *Memoirs,* vol. 2, pp. 1148, 1149; Berle Diary, 24 January 1942, Reel 3, Adolf Berle Papers, FDR Library, Hyde Park, N.Y.

68. By the time that the foreign ministers met in Rio, nine of the twenty Latin American nations had declared war and three others had broken off relations with the Axis powers. Five more broke relations during the meeting, and Ecuador did so the day after adjournment. That left only Chile and Argentina, which waited until January 1943 and January 1944, respectively.

69. "Minutes of the Liaison Committee, Wednesday, February 24, 1942, 2:30 P.M.," Box 2, Records of the Standing Liaison Committee, 1938–1943, in Records of the Interdepartmental and the Intradepartmental Committees (RG 353), NA; Poinsett to JQ Adams, 4 November 1818, Communications from Special Agents, NA M37/R3; NSC

56/2, "United States Policy toward Inter-American Collaboration," 18 May 1950, FRUS 1950, vol. 1, p. 628.

70. Memorandum, G-2 (Intelligence) to Chief of Staff, 8 July 1940, reprinted in Stetson Conn and Byron Fairchild, *The Framework of Hemisphere Defense* (Washington, D.C.: Office of the Chief of Military History, Department of the Army, 1960), p. 179.

71. Stimson Diary, 9 November 1943, Reel 8, Henry Stimson Papers, Yale University.

16. Attacking Dictatorships

1. Notter to Laurence Duggan, 12 September 1939, 710.11/2417 1/2, NA M1276/R17.

2. Welles to Roosevelt, 7 December 1942, 837.001/Batista, Fulgencio/80, NA.

3. Armour to Long, 3 October 1944, FRUS 1944, vol. 7, p. 1140.

4. Braden to Byrnes, 11 July 1945, FRUS 1945, vol. 9, p. 391.

5. Briggs to Stettinius, 20 December 1944, FRUS 1944, vol. 7, p. 132.

6. Briggs to Byrnes, 3 January 1945; Byrnes to McGurk, 16 November 1945; Aide-Mémoire from the Department of State to the Dominican Embassy, 28 December 1945, FRUS 1945, vol. 9, pp. 975, 987–988, 994.

7. Hull, *Memoirs*, vol. 2, p. 1377.

8. Hull, *Memoirs*, vol. 1, pp. 497–498, and vol. 2., pp. 1405, 1408. For an associate's critical view of Hull's anti-Argentine vendetta, see Sumner Welles, *Where Are We Heading?* (New York: Harper and Brothers, 1946), pp. 197ff.

9. Berle Diary, 6 and 10 January 1944, Reel 5, Adolf Berle Papers, FDR Library, Hyde Park, N.Y.

10. Department of State *Bulletin*, 30 July 1944, p. 107; see also 1 October 1944, p. 337; FDR's statement to Stettinius on 18 May 1944 is quoted by Treasury Secretary Henry Morgenthau, Jr., in a memorandum, "Re: CABINET," 18 May 1944, Morgenthau Diary, book 733, pp. 29–31, Morgenthau Papers, FDR Library, Hyde Park, N.Y.

11. Berle Diary, 12 February 1945, Reel 5, Adolf Berle Papers, FDR Library, Hyde Park, N.Y.

12. The solidarity requirement is Article 59 of the "Final Act of the Inter-American Conference on Problems of War and Peace," signed in Mexico City, 7 March 1945; the Argentine declaration of war is translated and reprinted in the Department of State *Bulletin*, 8 April 1945, pp. 611–613.

13. Braden to Byrnes, 5 July and 4 September 1945, FRUS 1945, vol. 9, pp. 389, 406, 408.

14. Cabot to Byrnes, 19 October 1945, FRUS 1945, vol. 9, pp. 422–423.

15. Cabot to Byrnes, 19 October 1945; Cabot to Briggs, 17 November 1945, FRUS 1945, vol. 9, pp. 422–423, 427–431.

16. Cabot to Briggs, 17 November 1945; Cabot to Byrnes, 4 and 13 December 1945,

FRUS 1945, vol. 9, pp. 429, 436, 493; the instructions to produce a report are Byrnes to Braden, 14 August 1945, FRUS 1945, vol. 9. p. 403.

17. Harry Ackerman, Memorandum, 10 March 1942, 740.0011 European War 1939/20564, NA M982/R108.

18. "History of Latin American Military Cooperation in the War Effort," 3 September 1944, Records of the Operations Division, War Department General and Special Staffs (RG 165), NA.

19. Messersmith to Rockefeller, 27 April 1945, 812.00/4–2745, NA LM112/R1; Division of American Republics, "Fascist Connections of the New Bolivian Regime," 1 January 1944, 844.00/1–144, NA, parts of which are included in Hull to Certain Diplomatic Representatives in the American Republics, 10 January 1944, FRUS 1944, vol. 7, pp. 430–432; Berle Diary, 21 February 1946, Reel 6, Adolf Berle Papers, FDR Library, Hyde Park, N.Y.

20. U.S. Department of State, *Consultation Among the American Republics with Respect to the Argentine Situation: Memorandum of the United States Government* (Washington, D.C.: GPO, 1946), pp. 65–66.

21. Lars Schoultz, *The Populist Challenge: Argentine Electoral Behavior in the Postwar Era* (Chapel Hill: University of North Carolina Press, 1983).

22. Pawley to Byrnes, 25 February 1946; Bowers to Byrnes, 23 February 1946; Daniels to Byrnes, 1 April 1946; Memorandum of conversation with Guillermo Sevilla-Sacasa, 1 March 1946, FRUS 1946, vol. 11, pp. 9, 219, 222, 227–228.

23. Aníbal O. Olivieri, *Dos veces rebelde* (Buenos Aires: Ediciones Sigla, 1958), pp. 26–27; Hoover Diary, "Argentina June 6, 7, 8, 9, 10, 1946," Diaries, South American Trip, Herbert Hoover Library, West Branch, Iowa; Cabot to Byrnes, 25 February 1946 and 7 March 1946, FRUS 1946, vol. 11, pp. 221–222, 230.

24. Cabot to Butler, 26 March 1946, FRUS 1946, vol. 11, p. 239.

25. Hoover Diary, "Argentina June 6, 7, 8, 9, 10, 1946," Diaries, South American Trip, Herbert Hoover Library, West Branch, Iowa.

26. Braden to Messersmith, 8 March 1946, FRUS 1946, vol. 11, p. 233.

27. Warren to Byrnes, 18 and 29 August 1945; Byrnes to Warren, 31 August and 4 September 1945, FRUS 1945, vol. 9, pp. 1216–1219.

28. Somoza to Roosevelt, 23 December 1944, FRUS 1945, vol. 9, p. 1194.

29. Duggan to Baol, 1 January 1944, FRUS 1944, vol. 7, pp. 170–171; Grew, "Memorandum of Conversation," 12 March 1945; Grew, "Memorandum of Conversation," 13 March 1945, both FRUS 1945, vol. 9, pp. 224–226.

30. Memorandum of Conversation with Sevilla-Sacasa, 17 December 1945, FRUS 1945, vol. 9, p. 1230.

31. Stimson Diary, 1 November 1944, Henry Stimson Papers, Reel 9, Yale University; Braden to Byrnes, 16 December 1946, FRUS 1946, vol. 11, pp. 109–110; Acheson to Patterson, 19 March 1947, FRUS 1947, vol. 8, pp. 105–106.

32. Warren to Byrnes, 18 July 1945 and 15 November 1945, FRUS 1945, vol. 9, pp. 1202–1204, 1210–1211.

33. *PPP, Harry S. Truman, 1947*, p. 166.

34. Willard L. Beaulac, *The Fractured Continent: Latin America Close-Up* (Stanford: Hoover Institution Press, 1980), p. 212; Stanton Griffis, *Lying in State* (New York: Doubleday, 1952), p. 264.

35. Margaret Mead, "The Study of National Character," in *The Policy Sciences,* Daniel Lerner and Harold D. Lasswell, eds. (Stanford: Stanford University Press, 1951), p. 75.

36. H. Bartlett Wells, "A Study in Cuban-American Relations," 8 September 1947, 711.37/9–847, NA.

37. James N. Cortada, "Component Elements of Cuban Temperament," 4 February 1948, 837.50/2–448, NA.

38. The report is reprinted in George F. Kennan, *Memoirs* (Boston: Little, Brown, 1967), pp. 476–483.

17. Combatting Communism with Friendly Dictators

1. Stimson to Truman, 16 May 1945, enclosed with Stimson Diary of same date, Reel 9, Stimson Papers, Yale University.

2. *PPP, Harry S. Truman, 1947*, p. 180.

3. "Speech to Rio," 2 September 1947, *PPP, Harry S. Truman, 1947*, pp. 429–431.

4. Department of State *Bulletin,* 11 April 1948, pp. 470–471.

5. National Security Council, "The Position of the United States with Respect to Soviet-Directed World Communism," NSC-7, 30 March 1948, President's Secretary's Files, Box 203, Harry S. Truman Library, Independence, Missouri.

6. "X" [pseud. George F. Kennan], "The Sources of Soviet Conduct," *Foreign Affairs* 25 (July 1947), p. 576.

7. John Foster Dulles, "Thoughts on Soviet Foreign Policy and What to Do About It," *Life,* 3 June 1946, pp. 112–126, and 10 June 1946, pp. 118–130; the quotation is from the first installment, p. 118; "Paper Prepared by the Policy Planning Staff," PPS-26, 22 March 1948, FRUS 1948, vol. 9, pp. 194–201.

8. Senator McCarthy did not use a written text in making his 9 February 1950 speech in Wheeling; these quotations are his rereading to the Senate of a tape-recorded transcript, *Congressional Record,* 20 February 1950, pp. 1952–1981, esp. p. 1956.

9. U.S. Department of State, *The State Department's Loyalty Security Program: How It Works,* Department of State Publication 4530, March 1952, p.7; U.S. Department of State, *Loyalty and Security in the Department of State,* Department of State Publication 3841, October 1950, p. 10.

10. In *This Deception,* an unsubstantiated 1951 exposé by a former Soviet spy, Hede Massing, Duggan was accused of passing information to the Kremlin.

11. Memorandum attached to "Testimony of Honorable Frank B. Kellogg, Secretary of State, Before the Committee on Foreign Relations of the Senate, January 12, 1927," Frank Kellogg Papers, Roll 24, LC microfilm version.

12. Berle Diary, 21 February 1946, Reel 6, Adolf Berle Papers, FDR Library, Hyde Park, N.Y.; Speech to the Pan American Society of New England, 26 April 1950, reprinted in Department of State *Bulletin*, 15 May 1950, p. 770.

13. *National Party Platforms, 1840–1964,* Kirk H. Porter and Donald Bruce Johnson, compilers (Urbana: University of Illinois Press, 1966), pp. 497–499.

14. Memorandum of Telephone Conversation, 26 February 1953, Dulles Papers, Seeley Mudd Library, Princeton University.

15. Milton Eisenhower, "Report to the President," Department of State *Bulletin*, 23 November 1953, pp. 695–717.

16. For an analysis of the 1935 election, see Sidney E. O'Donoghue to Secretary of State, 25 June 1935, 814.00/1229, NA M1280/R1.

17. News Conference, 8 June 1954, in Department of State, *American Foreign Policy 1950–1955, Basic Documents,* vol. 1, p. 1310.

18. See Boaz Long to Secretary of State, and Division of Caribbean and Central American Affairs to Norman Armour, both dated 13 October 1944, and both with decimal file number 814.00/10–1344, NA M1280/R13.

19. Milton Wells, "Communism in Guatemala," 6 May 1948, 814.00B/5–648; the Department's request for a report is Lovett to U.S. Embassy Guatemala, 7 October 1947, 814.00B/10–747, NA M1527/R3.

20. Milton Wells to Secretary of State, 10 March 1949, 814.00B/3–1049, NA M1527/R3.

21. Berle Diary, 17 October 1952, Reel 6, Adolf Berle Papers, FDR Library, Hyde Park, N.Y.

22. Alexander Wiley to Theodore F. Green, 22 May 1950, Richard C. Patterson, Jr., Papers, Harry S. Truman Library, Independence, Missouri, microfilmed in Carrollton Press, Declassified Documents Retrospective Collection, entry 490B; *Congressional Record,* 12 April 1951, p. 3804; "Memorandum to the Jackson Committee," 31 March 1953, Reel 6, Adolf Berle Papers, FDR Library, Hyde Park, N.Y.

23. U.S. Senate, Committee on Foreign Relations, *Nomination of John Foster Dulles, Secretary of State–Designate,* 83d Cong., 1st Sess., 1953, pp. 30–31.

24. "Probable Developments in Guatemala," National Intelligence Estimate NIE-84, 19 May 1953; Leddy to Cabot, "Memorandum: Relations with Guatemala," 21 May 1953, 611.14/5–2153, FRUS 1952–1954, vol. 4, pp. 1061, 1071.

25. John Peurifoy to Department of State, 17 December 1953, FRUS 1952–1954, vol. 4, pp. 1091–1093.

26. Louis J. Halle., Jr., "Memorandum: Our Guatemalan Policy," 28 May 1954, FRUS 1952–1954, vol. 4, p. 1148.

27. Minutes of National Security Council Meeting, 27 May 1954, FRUS 1952–1954, vol. 4, p. 1132.

28. Press Release, Caracas, 12 March 1954, reprinted in Department of State *Bulletin,* 22 March 1954, p. 425.

29. "Y" [pseud. Louis Halle, Jr.], "On A Certain Impatience with Latin America," *Foreign Affairs* 28 (July 1950), pp. 565–569.

30. Interviews with Arbenz's close associate, José Manuel Fortuny, and with Arbenz's widow, María Vilanova de Arbenz—both recalling events that occurred in the 1940s and early 1950s in interviews with Gleijeses in the late 1970s and 1980s—constitute the principal evidence Gleijeses uses in his exceptionally valuable study. Piero Gleijeses, *Shattered Hope: The Guatemalan Revolution and the United States, 1944–1954* (Princeton: Princeton University Press, 1991), esp. pp. 143–148 and, for the author's recognition of the possible bias of his respondents, pp. 5–6.

31. "Memorandum of Conversation, by the Secretary of State," 11 May 1954, FRUS 1952–1954, vol. 4, p. 1106.

32. Halle, "Our Guatemalan Policy," 28 May 1954, FRUS 1952–1954, vol. 4, pp. 1140–1147.

33. News Conference, 7 April 1954, *PPP, Dwight D. Eisenhower, 1954,* p. 383.

34. Dulles's 30 June speech is reprinted in Department of State *Bulletin,* 31 (12 July 1954), pp. 43–45; see also the President's press conference, 30 June 1954, *PPP, Dwight D. Eisenhower, 1954,* p. 605.

35. U.S. Congress, House, Select Committee on Communist Aggression, Subcommittee on Communist Penetration of the Western Hemisphere, *Communist Aggression in Latin America,* 83d Cong., 2d Sess., 1954, p. 7.

36. U.S. Department of State, *A Case History of Communist Penetration: Guatemala* (Washington, D.C.: GPO, April 1957), p. 70.

37. Speech to Railway Business Association, New York, 27 January 1916, in *The Papers of Woodrow Wilson,* 57 vols., Arthur S. Link, ed. (Princeton: Princeton University Press, 1966–1987), vol. 36, p. 11.

38. "Report of the Vice President on Latin American Trip," Memorandum of Discussion at the 240th Meeting of the NSC, Washington, March 10, 1955, FRUS 1955–1957, vol. 6, p. 618.

39. "Paper Prepared by the Policy Planning Staff," PPS-26, p. 197.

40. National Security Council, "United States Objectives and Courses of Action with Respect to Latin America," NSC 144/1, 18 March 1953, FRUS 1952–1954, vol. 4, p. 6.

41. National Security Council, "Memorandum of Discussion at the 137th Meeting of the National Security Council on Wednesday, March 18, 1953," FRUS 1952–1954, vol. 4, p. 6.

42. "Memorandum of Discussion at the 237th Meeting of the National Security Council, Washington, February 17, 1955," FRUS 1955–1957, vol. 6, pp. 4–5.

43. Berle Diary, 8 February 1955, Reel 7, Adolf Berle Papers, FDR Library, Hyde Park, N.Y.

44. Tittmann to Miller, 25 February 1952, FRUS 1952–1954, vol. 4, p. 1493.

45. Warren to Department of State, 11 May 1953; "United States Objectives and Courses of Action with Respect to Venezuela," Draft Statement of Policy Prepared in

the Department of State for the National Security Council, 22 October 1953; Warren to Atwood, 8 December 1954; Memorandum, Deputy Assistant Secretary Sparks to Under Secretary Hoover, 23 December 1954, all FRUS 1952–1954, vol. 4. pp. 1646, 1654, 1674–1676.

18. Combatting Communism with Economic Development

1. *Congressional Record,* 8 August 1957, p. 14149.

2. *Congressional Record,* 18 June 1958, p. 11658 (Brooks); 8 August 1957, p. 14149 (Withrow).

3. Berle Diary, 25 November 1957, Reel 7, Berle Papers, FDR Library, Hyde Park, N.Y.

4. Press Conference, 5 November 1957, Department of State *Bulletin,* 25 November 1957, p. 826.

5. Dulles to Nixon, 6 March 1958, FRUS 1958–1960, vol. 5, p. 222.

6. Memorandum of National Security Council Meeting, 10 March 1955, FRUS 1955–1957, vol. 6, pp. 614–618.

7. Department of State Circular, 26 March 1958, 033.1100-NI/3–2658, NA.

8. Memorandum of Telephone Conversation, Burrows (Venezuela) and Rubottom and Sanders, 13 May 1958, FRUS 1958–1960, vol. 5, pp. 226–227.

9. Department of State *Bulletin,* 9 June 1958, p. 951.

10. Minutes of Cabinet Meeting, 16 May 1958, FRUS 1958–1960, vol. 5, pp. 238–239.

11. Minutes of National Security Council Meeting, 22 May 1958, FRUS 1958–1960, vol. 5, p. 240.

12. NSC Minutes, 19 June 1958, FRUS 1958–1960, vol. 5, p. 29.

13. U.S. Congress, Senate, Committee on Foreign Relations, *Executive Sessions of the Senate Foreign Relations Committee (Historical Series),* vol. 10, 85th Cong., 2d Sess., 1958, p. 249, made public November 1980; Department of State *Bulletin,* 9 June 1958, p. 954.

14. See, for example, the official analysis of the 1948 Colombian *bogotazo* in Department of State *Bulletin,* 30 May 1948, p. 175.

15. Milton S. Eisenhower, "Report to the President: United States–Latin American Relations," Department of State *Bulletin,* 19 January 1959, pp. 3, 15. The Nixon experience affected everyone in Washington, including the President's brother, who reported that "as we boarded the plane [in Guatemala] to depart for home, my associates and I were completely worn out. Our nerves were shot from tension, anticipating Nixon-like incidents, so when we were well in the air, we all burst into hearty cheering, had a few drinks, and sat back to breathe." Milton S. Eisenhower, *The Wine Is Bitter: The United States and Latin America* (Garden City, N.Y.: Doubleday, 1963), p. 221.

16. Spruille Braden, *Diplomats and Demagogues: The Memoirs of Spruille Braden* (New Rochelle, N.Y.: Arlington House, 1971), p. 451.

17. Nixon's memorandum of his 19 April 1959 meeting with Castro is reprinted in *Diplomatic History* 4 (Fall 1980), pp. 425–431.

18. Karl E. Mundt, "How Cuban Freedom Really Was Won," *Reader's Digest* 77 (August 1960), p. 168.

19. Berle Diary, 20 September 1960, Reel 7, Adolf Berle Papers, FDR Library, Hyde Park, N.Y.

20. Merle Miller, *Plain Speaking: An Oral Biography of Harry S. Truman* (New York: G.P. Putnam's Sons, 1974), pp. 343–344.

21. *New York Times*, 21 October 1960, p. 18; in the October 21 presidential debate, Nixon, who knew about planning for the Bay of Pigs, called Kennedy's suggestion "dangerously irresponsible."

22. *PPP, Dwight D. Eisenhower, 1960–1961*, p. 570; Castro's 26 July 1960 speech is reprinted in *Obra Revolucionaria* Number 16 (July 1960), p. 13.

23. One of JFK's favorite aphorisms, this version is from his March 13, 1962, speech celebrating the first anniversary of the Alliance for Progress. *PPP, John F. Kennedy, 1961*, p. 223.

24. U.S. Congress, Senate, Committee on Foreign Relations, *Foreign Assistance Act of 1962*, 87th Cong., 2d Sess., 1962, p. 420.

25. *Congressional Record*, 8 August 1957, p. 14149.

26. For the best published illustration of this process, see Mark Danner, *The Massacre at El Mozote* (New York: Vintage, 1994).

27. Jeane J. Kirkpatrick, "U.S. Security and Latin America," in *Rift and Revolution: The Central American Imbroglio*, ed. Howard J. Wiarda (Washington, D.C.: American Enterprise Institute, 1984), p. 352. This chapter is a slightly revised version of the *Commentary* article with the same name.

28. U.S. Congress, Senate, Committee on Foreign Relations, Subcommittee on Western Hemisphere Affairs, *United States Policies and Programs in Brazil*, 92d Cong., 1st Sess., 1971, p. 89; see also Miles D. Wolpin, *Military Aid and Counterrevolution in the Third World* (Lexington, Mass.: D.C. Heath, 1972), p. 78.

29. David E. Bell, "Memorandum for the President," 27 November 1964, Confidential File, Box 25, Lyndon B. Johnson Library, Austin, Texas.

30. *United States Policies and Programs in Brazil*, pp. 3–51.

31. In 1984 Republican Senator Jesse Helms, for example, attacked the Kissinger Commission's report on Central America because its endorsement of economic reforms "makes no sense economically and usually results in a lower standard of living for the peasant." Press Release, Office of Senator Jesse Helms, 7 February 1984. The conservative Democratic chair of the powerful Appropriations subcommittee agreed: see Representative Clarence Long's comments in U.S. Congress, House, Committee on Appropriations, Subcommittee on Foreign Operations and Related Agencies, *Foreign Assistance and Related Programs Appropriations for 1983*, 97th Cong., 2d Sess., 1982, pt. 1, p. 39.

32. One of the Senate's most liberal members, Hubert Humphrey, thought that the

boost in aid was a good idea. See U.S. Congress, Senate, Committee on Foreign Relations, *Mutual Security Act of 1955,* 84th Cong., 1st Sess., 1955, pp. 316–317.

33. *Congressional Record,* 29 October 1971, pp. 38252–38258.

34. Since the Pinochet coup occurred in September and the loan was made in October 1973, it was months too late for inclusion in the FY1974 Food for Peace budget line. The selected alternative, a quick-disbursing Commodity Credit Corporation loan, was not subject to prior Congressional scrutiny.

35. General George Mather's comment is in U.S. Congress, House, Committee on Foreign Affairs, Subcommittee on Inter-American Affairs, *Cuba and the Caribbean,* 91st Cong., 2d Sess., July–August 1970, p.99; Kissinger's remark was first printed in the *New York Times,* 11 September 1974, p. 14; it was supposed to be the first sentence in Victor Marchetti and John D. Marks, *The CIA and the Cult of Intelligence* (New York: Knopf, 1974), but was censored; a photocopy of CIA Director Helms's handwritten notes is in U.S. Congress, Senate, Select Committee to Study Governmental Operations with Respect to Intelligence Activities, *Intelligence Activities,* vol. 7, 94th Cong., 2d Sess., December 4 and 5, 1975, p. 96.

36. *PPP, Gerald R. Ford, 1974,* pp. 151, 156.

37. U.S. Congress, Senate, Committee on Foreign Relations, Subcommittee on Multinational Corporations, *Multinational Corporations and United States Foreign Policy,* Hearings on the International Telephone and Telegraph Company and Chile, 1970–1971, Parts 1 and 2, 93d Cong., 1st Sess., 1973; U.S. Congress, House, Committee on Foreign Affairs, Subcommittee on Inter-American Affairs, *United States and Chile during the Allende Years, 1970–1973,* 94th Cong., 1st Sess., 1975; U.S. Congress, Senate, Select Committee to Study Governmental Operations with Respect to Intelligence Activities, *Alleged Assassination Plots Involving Foreign Leaders,* and *Covert Action in Chile, 1963–1973,* both 94th Cong, 1st Sess., 1975.

38. Department of State *Bulletin* 79 (January 1979), pp. 1–2.

39. For Nixon's statement, see *United States Policies and Programs in Brazil,* p. 290; see also U.S. President (Nixon), *U.S. Foreign Policy for the 1970's: Shaping a Durable Peace: A Report to the Congress,* 3 May 1973 (Washington, D.C.: GPO, 1973), p. 118. Kissinger's instruction was leaked to the *New York Times,* 27 September 1974, p. 18.

40. *PPP, John F. Kennedy, 1961,* p. 172.

41. Jeane Kirkpatrick, "U.S. Security and Latin America," *Commentary* 71 (January 1981), p. 36.

42. For the administration's attempts to preserve the Guard, see the statements by key participants, beginning with the transcript of a recorded 21 December 1978 conversation among Somoza, U.S. Ambassador William Bowdler, and SOUTHCOM General Dennis McAuliffe, reprinted in Anastasio Somoza, *Nicaragua Betrayed* (Boston: Western Islands, 1980), esp. p. 332; see also the first-person account by Ambassador Lawrence Pezzulo in Lawrence Pezzulo and Ralph Pezzulo, *At the Fall of Somoza* (Pitts-

burgh: University of Pittsburgh Press, 1993), pp. 172, 195, 247; also revealing is the commentary by Policy Planning staff member Anthony Lake, *Somoza Falling* (Boston: Houghton Mifflin, 1989), pp. 155, 220, 240–243, 263.

43. U.S. Congress, House, Committee on Foreign Affairs, Subcommittee on International Organizations and Movements, *International Protection of Human Rights*, 93d Cong., 1st Sess., 1973, p. 35.

44. Tom Quigley, et al., *U.S. Policy on Human Rights in Latin America (Southern Cone): A Congressional Conference on Capitol Hill* (New York: Fund for New Priorities in America, 1978), pp. 75–76.

45. *Wall Street Journal*, 3 June 1980, p. 1.

46. *Weekly Compilation of Presidential Documents* 13 (30 May 1977), pp. 774–775.

47. White's comment is in U.S. Congress, House, Committee on Foreign Affairs, Subcommittee on Inter-American Affairs, *Presidential Certification on El Salvador*, vol. 1, 97th Cong., 2d Sess., 1982, p. 228; the Reagan administration's position is by Thomas O. Enders, "The Central American Challenge," *AEI Foreign Policy and Defense Review* 4 (1982), p. 9.

48. *PPP, Ronald Reagan, 1983*, p. 1044.

49. *Weekly Compilation of Presidential Documents* 19 (31 October 1983), pp. 1, 501.

19. Two Centuries Later

1. U.S. Congress, House, Committee on Appropriations, Subcommittee on Foreign Operations and Related Agencies, *Foreign Assistance and Related Programs Appropriations for 1981*, 96th Cong., 2d Sess., 1980, pt. 2, p. 362.

2. "Cuban Missile Crisis Meetings, October 16, 1962," *Presidential Recordings Transcripts*, John F. Kennedy Library, Boston.

3. Stokely Morgan, "Re: Situation in Nicaragua," 24 January 1927, 817.00/4868, NA M632/R33; Robert E. Olds, "Confidential Memorandum on the Nicaraguan Situation," undated but noted "approximate date January, 1927," 817.00/5854, NA M632/R41.

4. National Security Council, "Statement of U.S. Policy toward Latin America," NSC 5902/1, 16 February 1959, FRUS 1958–1960, vol. 5, p. 92; *Weekly Compilation of Presidential Documents*, 2 May 1983, pp. 613–614.

5. Paschal to Olney, 23 October 1895, Olney Papers, LC.

6. *Washington Post*, 19 January 1990, p. A21.

7. James A. Miner to Root, 19 November 1901, Elihu Root File, Philip Jessup Papers, LC.

8. JQ Adams to Albert Gallatin, 19 May 1818, Instructions to U.S. Ministers, NA M77/R3.

9. Harley A. Notter to Laurence Duggan, 12 September 1939, 710.11/2417 1/2, NA M1276/R17.

10. Theodore Roosevelt, *Thomas Hart Benton* (Boston: Houghton, Mifflin, 1886), p. 175.

11. Wilson to Lansing, 4 August 1915, 838.00/1418, NA M610/R6; Lansing to Wilson, 24 November 1915, 710.11/188 1/2, NA M1276/R2.

12. Francis Baylies to Edward Livingston, 19 August 1832, Despatches from Argentina, NA M69/R5; Minutes of Discussion of the 396th Meeting of the National Security Council, 12 February 1959, Box 11, NSC Series, Whitman File, Dwight David Eisenhower Papers, Eisenhower Library, Abilene, Kansas.

13. Jeane J. Kirkpatrick, "Dictators and Double Standards," *Commentary* 68 (November 1979), pp. 34–45; "U.S. Security and Latin America," *Commentary* 71 (January 1981), pp. 29–40.

14. Kirkpatrick, "U.S. Security and Latin America," p. 34; Jeane J. Kirkpatrick, "U.S. Security and Latin America," in *Rift and Revolution: The Central American Imbroglio*, ed. Howard J. Wiarda (Washington, D.C.: American Enterprise Institute, 1984), p. 352.

15. Howard J. Wiarda, "Introduction," in *Political and Social Change in Latin America: The Distinct Tradition*, 2nd rev. ed. (Amherst: University of Massachusetts Press, 1982), pp. 14–15, 23.

16. Howard J. Wiarda, *In Search of Policy: The United States and Latin America* (Washington, D.C.: American Enterprise Institute, 1984), pp. 48–49.

17. Unlike Kirkpatrick, Wiarda provided citations, but the sources he cited do not support the statements he made. The "machetismo" assertion cited Merle Kling, "Violence and Politics in Latin America," in *Sociological Review Monographs*, No. 11, ed. Paul Halmos (Keele, England: University of Keele, 1967), pp. 119–132; and William F. Stokes, "Violence as a Power Factor in Latin American Politics," *Western Political Quarterly* 5 (September 1952), pp. 445–468. Neither source has much to say about El Salvador: Stokes mentions El Salvador only briefly (p. 459), and Kling's only discussion of the country (p. 123) indicates that the level of violence there is relatively low.

18. Richard M. Morse, "The Heritage of Latin America," in *The Founding of New Societies*, Louis Hartz, ed. (New York: Harcourt, Brace and World, 1964), pp. 137, 172–173, 175.

19. Kirkpatrick, "Dictators and Double Standards," p. 38.

20. George F. Kennan, *Memoirs, 1925–1950* (Boston: Little, Brown, 1967), pp. 476–479. Reflecting on this analysis in 1985, Mr. Kennan noted that his 1950 observations were "only those of an uninitiated and poorly qualified observer" and that they "have been overtaken by intervening events." Letter from George F. Kennan, 6 September 1985.

21. Richard N. Goodwin, *Remembering America: A Voice from the Sixties* (Boston: Little, Brown, 1988), p. 162.

22. Hopkins to Buchanan, 31 November 1845, undated February 1846, and 12 February 1846, Communications from Special Agents, 1794–1906, NA M37/R6.

23. Buchanan to Hopkins, 10 June 1845 and 30 March 1846, Diplomatic Instructions of the Department of State, Special Missions, NA M77/R152.

24. Hopkins to William Marcy, 22 August 1853 [1854?], Despatches from U.S. Consuls in Asunción, 1844–1906, NA T329/R1.

25. Lawrence E. Harrison, *Underdevelopment Is a State of Mind: The Latin American Case* (Lanham, Md.: University Press of America, 1985), pp. xv, 162, 168; for a later restatement, see Lawrence E. Harrison, *The Pan-American Dream: Do Latin America's Cultural Values Discourage True Partnership with the United States and Canada?* (New York: Basic Books, 1997); for an approving analysis by a career Foreign Service Officer, see Peter D. Whitney, "Address before the Peruvian Center for International Studies (CEPIE), Lima, Peru, November 25, 1987," Department of State *Current Policy* No. 1030, 1987, p. 2.

26. Perhaps the best introduction to the traditional social science development literature as it was translated into policy by U.S. foreign policy officials is David C. McClelland, *The Achieving Society* (New York: Free Press, 1961), and Seymour Martin Lipset, "Values, Education, and Entrepreneurship," in *Elites in Latin America,* Seymour Martin Lipset and Aldo Solari, eds. (New York: Oxford University Press, 1967), pp. 3–60.

27. Department of State *Bulletin,* 14 October 1963, p. 581.

28. Francis Mairs Huntington Wilson, untitled and undated diary notes of Latin American trip, 1914, Huntington Wilson Papers, Ursinus College.

29. Heman Allen to Henry Clay, 9 February 1825, Despatches from Chile, NA M10/R1.

30. Quotation from AID's 1997 website: http://www.info.usaid.gov

31. Stokely W. Morgan, "American Policy and Problems in Central America," Lecture to the Foreign Service School, Department of State, January 29, 1926, Entry 423, Inventory 15, RG 59, NA.

Index